Lecture Notes of the Institute for Computer Sciences, Social Informatics and Telecommunications Engineering 354

More information about this series at http://www.springer.com/series/8197

Yi-Bing Lin · Der-Jiunn Deng (Eds.)

Smart Grid and Internet of Things

4th EAI International Conference, SGIoT 2020
TaiChung, Taiwan, December 5–6, 2020
Proceedings

 Springer

Editors
Yi-Bing Lin
National Chiao Tung University
Hsinchu, Taiwan

Der-Jiunn Deng
National Changhua University of Education
Changhua, Taiwan

ISSN 1867-8211   ISSN 1867-822X (electronic)
Lecture Notes of the Institute for Computer Sciences, Social Informatics
and Telecommunications Engineering
ISBN 978-3-030-69513-2   ISBN 978-3-030-69514-9 (eBook)
https://doi.org/10.1007/978-3-030-69514-9

This Springer imprint is published by the registered company Springer Nature Switzerland AG
The registered company address is: Gewerbestrasse 11, 6330 Cham, Switzerland

Preface

We are delighted to introduce the proceedings of the 4th edition of the European Alliance for Innovation (EAI) International Conference on Smart Grid and Internet of Things (SGIoT 2020). This year, it took place at the Windsor Hotel, Taichung, during December 5–6, 2020. This conference provides an opportunity to connect with researchers, developers, and practitioners from around the world to discuss recent findings in the area of the emerging Smart Grid and Internet of Things. The technical program of SGIoT 2020 consisted of 40 full papers in oral presentation sessions at the main conference tracks.

These technical papers covered a broad range of topics in wireless sensors, vehicular ad hoc networks, security, blockchain, and deep learning. Aside from the high-quality technical paper presentations, the technical program also featured four keynote speeches. The first keynote speech was entitled "The Convergence of Sensing, Communications, Computing, Intelligentization and Storage (SCCIS): A Holistic Design Approach," by Prof. Michael Fang, from University of Florida, USA. The second keynote speech was entitled "Security Schemes for Healthcare Devices in the IoT Era," by Prof. Mohsen Guizani, from Qatar University, Qatar. The third keynote speech was entitled "IoT Talk: Let IoT talk," by Chair Professor Yi-Bing Lin from National Chiao Tung University, Taiwan. The last keynote speech was entitled "Wireless Multi-Robot Systems in Smart Factories," by Professor Kwang-Cheng Chen from University of South Florida, USA.

Coordination with the steering chair, Imrich Chlamtac, was essential for the success of the conference. We sincerely appreciate his constant support and guidance. It was also a great pleasure to work with such an excellent organizing committee team for their hard work in organizing and supporting the conference. In particular, the Technical Program Committee, led by our Chair Yi-Bing Lin and Co-Chair Der-Jiunn Deng, completed the peer-review process of technical papers and made a high-quality technical program. We are also grateful to the Conference Manager, Viltarė Platzner, for her support and to all the authors who submitted their papers to the SGIoT 2020 conference.

Yi-Bing Lin
Der-Jiunn Deng

Conference Organization

Steering Committee

Al-Sakib Khan Pathan   Southeast University, Bangladesh
Salimur Choudhury   Lakehead University, Canada
Zubair Md. Fadlullah   Lakehead University, Canada

General Chair

Yi-Bing Lin   National Chiao Tung University, Taiwan

General Co-chair

Der-Jiunn Deng   National Changhua University of Education, Taiwan

TPC Chair and Co-chair

Chun-Cheng Lin   National Chiao Tung University, Taiwan
Rung-Shiang Cheng   Overseas Chinese University, Taiwan

Sponsorship and Exhibit Chair

Hui-Hsin Chin   Overseas Chinese University, Taiwan

Local Chair

Viviane Su   Institute for Information Industry, Taiwan

Workshops Chair

Shao-Yu Lien   National Chung Cheng University, Taiwan

Publicity and Social Media Chair

Jen-En Huang   Overseas Chinese University, Taiwan

Publications Chair

Yu-Liang Liu   Overseas Chinese University, Taiwan

Web Chair

Chien-Liang Chen   Overseas Chinese University, Taiwan

Technical Program Committee

Chien-Liang Chen	Overseas Chinese University, Taiwan
Ding-Jung Chiang	Taipei Chengshih University of Science and Technology
Yu-Liang Liu	Overseas Chinese University, Taiwan
Hung-Chang Chan	Overseas Chinese University, Taiwan
Jen En Huang	Overseas Chinese University, Taiwan
Li-Wei Chang	Overseas Chinese University, Taiwan
Cl Chen	Aletheia University, Taiwan

Contents

Internet of Things, Ad Hoc, Sensor and RFID Networks

WLAN, Wireless Internet and 5G

Protocol, Algorithm, Services and Applications

Artificial Intelligence, Machine Leaning and Deep Learning

Research of Offloading Decision and Resource Scheduling in Edge Computing Based on Deep Reinforcement Learning

Zhen-Jiang Zhang[1]([⊠]), Tong Wu[2], Zhiyuan Li[2], Bo Shen[2], Naiyue Chen[3], and Jian Li[2]

[1] Department of Software Engineering, Key Laboratory of Communication and Information Systems, Beijing Municipal Commission of Education, Beijing Jiaotong University, Beijing 100044, China
zhangzhenjiang@bjtu.edu.cn

[2] Department of Electronic and Information Engineering, Key Laboratory of Communication and Information Systems, Beijing Municipal Commission of Education, Beijing Jiaotong University, Beijing 100044, China
{18125066,19120091,bshen,lijian}@bjtu.edu.cn

[3] School of Computer and Information Technology, Beijing Jiaotong University, Beijing Municipal Commission of Education, Beijing 100044, China
nychen@bjtu.edu.cn

Abstract. The increasing scale of the IOT poses challenges to the energy consumption, transmission bandwidth and processing delay of centralized cloud computing data centers. The cloud computing data centers is moving from the center of the network to edge nodes with lower latency, namely, edge computing. Meanwhile, it can meet the needs of users for real-time services. In the field of edge computing, offloading decision and resource scheduling are the hot-spot issues. As for offloading decision and resource scheduling problems of single-cell multi-user partial offloading, the system model is also firstly established from four aspects: network architecture, application type, local computing and offloading computing. Based on the system model, the optimization problem of resource scheduling is modeled, where the solution is hard to be found. Thus, the deep reinforcement learning method based on policy gradient is selected to establish the SPBDDPG algorithm that can solve the problem. Then, in order to solve the practical problems, the SPBDDPG algorithm is set up with the state and action for iteration, as well as the environment for generating new state and feedback reward value. Finally, an appropriate iteration step is written for the edge computing resource scheduling problem by combining with the original deep reinforcement learning algorithm. We also evaluate the proposed approaches by relevant experiments. The complexity and effectiveness of the results are validated.

Keywords: Edge computing · Offloading decision · Resource scheduling · Deep reinforcement learning

© ICST Institute for Computer Sciences, Social Informatics and Telecommunications Engineering 2021
Published by Springer Nature Switzerland AG 2021. All Rights Reserved
Y.-B. Lin and D.-J. Deng (Eds.): SGIoT 2020, LNICST 354, pp. 3–13, 2021.
https://doi.org/10.1007/978-3-030-69514-9_1

1 Introduction

Since the concept of edge computing was proposed, many optimization algorithms on energy consumption and delay have been proposed for edge computing offloading decision and resource scheduling. In order to improve network performance, some studies (e.g. [1–4]) focus on completing offloading strategy to minimize latency or energy consumption. Partial offloading is more suitable for applications with more stringent latency requirements than full offloading because it takes advantage of the parallelism between smart mobile devices and the cloud. In addition, since wireless networks have limited bandwidth, it makes more sense to migrate some applications rather than all.

Therefore, much work (e.g. [5–9]) has been devoted to partial offloading. Munoz et al. [5] reduced the energy consumption of intelligent mobile devices to the maximum by jointly optimizing the uplink time, downlink time and data size of intelligent mobile devices and the cloud. Huang et al. [6] proposed a dynamic offloading algorithm based on Lyapunov optimization to achieve energy saving. Lorenzo et al. [7] jointly optimized the transmission power and modulation mode to minimize the energy consumption of intelligent mobile devices under delay constraints. Yang et al. [8] jointly studied the division of computing and scheduling of offloading computing on cloud resources to achieve the minimum average completion time of all users. Cao et al. [9] proposed a framework for partitioning and executing data-flow applications to achieve maximum speed.

The combination of dynamic voltage regulation technology and computational offloading provides more flexibility for strategy design. Kilper et al. [10] considered the computing speed of intelligent mobile devices and the optimization of the transmission rate under the Gilbert-Elliott channel to make offloading decision between local execution and full offloading. In order to adapt the environment dynamics more intelligently, many researches will apply deep reinforcement learning to optimize the offloading decision. Chen et al. [11] studied a decentralized dynamic computing loading strategy based on deep reinforcement learning and established an extensible mobile edge computing system with limited feedback. Zeng et al. [12] introduced a model-free method of deep reinforcement learning to effectively manage resources on the edge of the network and followed the design principles of deep reinforcement learning, then designed and implemented a mobile aware data processing service offloading management agent. Based on the additive structure of utility functions and combined the Q function decomposition technique with double DQN, Chen et al. [13] proposed a new learning algorithm for solving the calculation of random loads.

In addition to this, there is a survey in which the computation task models considered in existing research work are divided into deterministic and stochastic [14]. By using Lyapunov optimization method, a solution considering general wireless network and optimizing energy consumption is given in [15]. In [16], a perturbed Lyapunov function is designed to maximize the network utility, balance the throughput and fairness, and solve the knapsack problem on each slot to obtain the optimal unloading plan. On the other hand, the previous research based on Markov decision process model is mainly limited to single user MEC system [17, 18]. And in [19], the paper focuses on the problem of offloading and resource allocation under deterministic task model, in which each user needs to process a fixed number of tasks locally or offloaded to the edge server.

In this paper, we mainly focus on the following works: In the next section, combining the application scenario of deep reinforcement learning and edge computing, a new architecture is proposed. Section 3 introduces an optimization scheme based on deep reinforcement learning. Then, a single-cell multi-user partial-offloading based on deep deterministic policy gradient algorithm is proposed in Sect. 4, followed by simulation and performance analysis in Sect. 5. Concluding remarks and the research prospect are illustrated at the end.

2 System Architecture

Since cellular networks can only manage the communications and not computing, a new computational control entity is required for the computational offloading architecture known as Small Cell Manager (SCM) under project TROPIC proposed on EU FP7 [20].

SCM consists of three modules: operation module, optimization module and offloading module. Based on the offloading of mobile computing architecture, the multiple user equipment (UE) through the calculation of base station, mobile edge server and SCM are linked together in a single-cell multi-user scenario. Base stations use TDMA mode to enable communication and the time is divided into several time slots. Suppose the maximum delay that users can tolerate is set to constraint L_{max}, and the set of devices that the user connects to base station k is as follows:

$$\mathcal{K} = \{1, 2, \ldots, k, \ldots, K\}$$

When UE has a compute-intensive application to process, it sends resource request to the SCM through base station (BS). Afterwards, SCM makes smart decision about whether to migrate an application, and which parts need to be migrated to the edges. Once the SCM has decided to migrate, three phases need to be performed in sequence.

a. UE sends data to BS via uplink channel.
b. MEC receives the calculated offloading data of UE from BS.
c. the results are sent back to UE through the downlink channel.

The specific system architecture is shown in Fig. 1:

The rate at which user device K uploads data to the base station is as follows:

$$R_k = Blog_2(1 + P_{t,k}h_k^2/N_0) \tag{1}$$

Where B is the bandwidth of the complex Gaussian white noise channel, N_0 is the variance of the complex Gaussian white noise channel, $P_{t,k}$ is the transmitting power of the user device K, and h_k is the channel gain of the user device K.

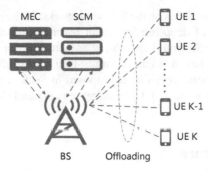

Fig. 1. Single-Cell Multi-User Complete Offloading System Architecture

3 Deep Reinforcement Learning Optimization Scheme

In a single-cell multi-user edge computation offloading scenario, suppose that all user equipment between the base station and the same channel. The application is abstract to a two-parameter profile (I_k, C_k), where I_k represents the number of input data bits that user device K computes, and C_k represents the number of CPU cycles required for each bit of input data. The ratio of the calculated offloading data of user device K to the total input data is defined as λ_k ($0 \le \lambda_k \le 1$). Therefore, the calculated offloading ratio of all user devices in the cell constitutes the decision vector:

$$\Lambda = [\lambda_1, \lambda_2, \ldots, \lambda_k, \ldots, \lambda_K]$$

The Local Model
Assuming that the local CPU computing capacity of user's device K is $F_k (bits/s)$ and the local energy consumption per CPU cycle is P_k, so user's device needs to meet:

$$(1 - \lambda_k)I_k/F_k \le L_{max} \tag{2}$$

Therefore, the energy consumption calculated locally by user device K as follows:

$$E_{l,k} = (1 - \lambda_k)I_k C_k P_k \tag{3}$$

The Offloading Model
The time of device K calculates offloading data is t_k, and the total time of all devices in the same time slot needs to less than L_{max}. And the energy consumption by the user device K offloading is as follows:

$$E_{o,k} = \frac{N_0(2^{\frac{\lambda_k I_k/t_k}{B}} - 1)}{h_k^2} t_k \tag{4}$$

Cost Model
Considering the parallelization of local and offloading computing, the total energy consumption cost is:

$$E_k(\lambda_k, t_k) = E_{l,k} + E_{o,k} = (1 - \lambda_k)I_k C_k P_k + f(\lambda_k I_k/t_k)t_k \tag{5}$$

As a result, the formulation of edge computing resource offloading scheduling problem can be deduced by changing the decision vector $\Lambda = [\lambda_1, \lambda_2, \ldots, \lambda_K]$ and $T = [t_1, t_2, \ldots, t_K]$ to minimize the total energy consumption $\sum_{k=1}^{K} E_k(\lambda_k, t_k)$. The optimization problem can be mathematically formalized as:

$$\min_{\lambda_k, t_k} \sum_{k=1}^{K} [(1 - \lambda_k) I_k C_k P_k + f\left(\frac{\lambda_k I_k}{t_k}\right) t_k] \tag{6}$$

$$s.t. C1 : \sum_{k=1}^{K} \lambda_k I_k C_k \leq F_c,$$

$$C2 : \max\{0, \left(1 - \frac{L_{max} F_k}{I_k}\right)\} \leq \lambda_k \leq 1,$$

$$C3 : \sum_{k=1}^{K} t_k \leq L_{max}.$$

3.1 Parameter Setting

Reinforcement learning is often used to make decisions. It always observes the surrounding environment state and can perform an action to reach another state according to the decision rules, then get a feedback reward.

State
After each scheduling, the total cost of energy consumption is respectively:

$$E_k(\lambda_k, t_k) = \sum_{k=1}^{K} [(1 - \lambda_k) I_k C_k P_k + \frac{t_k f\left(\frac{\lambda_k I_k}{t_k}\right)}{h_k^2}] \tag{7}$$

And the edge server computing capacity required by the actual scheduling scheme:

$$P_n = \sum_{k=1}^{K} \lambda_k I_k C_k \tag{8}$$

The state $s(s_1, s_2)$ can be calculated after each action. The system can judge whether each scheduling scheme is to minimize the energy consumption according to s_1. The size of s_2 is used to determine whether the server is fully utilized.

Action
The offloading decision vector $\Lambda = [\lambda_1, \lambda_2, \ldots, \lambda_K]$ with the base station assigning to the user equipment used to upload data time slot decision vector $T = [t_1, t_2, \ldots, t_K]$ as a deep reinforcement learning action for each turn.

Reward
In reinforcement learning, reward is the feedback of state and action, which reflects the impact of the current decision on the result. Therefore, reward is crucial to the outcome of training.

4　SPBDDPG Algorithm

Based on the deep reinforcement learning approach, this chapter further proposes a Single-cell multi-user Partial-offloading Based on Deep Deterministic Policy Gradient (SPBDDPG) algorithm superior to the traditional policy gradient REINFORCE algorithm, which is specifically designed to solve the optimization of user device partial migration in the single-cell multi-user scenario.

4.1　The Principle of Policy Gradient Algorithm

In the strategy gradient based approach, the action is finally executed according to the probability distribution. The strategy is related to the current state, that is, for each states, the strategy gives $\pi(a|s)$, the probability distribution of an action a, and because the strategy needs to be optimized, it parameterizes it by giving the parameter vector, which is denoted as $\pi(a|s, \theta)$.In order to solve the strategy gradient, the introduction of sampling Trajectory $\tau = (s_0, a_0, s_1, a_1, \ldots, s_{T-1}, a_{T-1}, s_T)$, represents the sequence of states and actions.Make $p(\tau|\theta)$ denote the probability of the whole trajectory in the case of parameter vector, and the total benefit of the whole trajectory is:

$$R(\tau) = \sum_{t=0}^{T-1} r_t \tag{9}$$

In the practical application, because the expected value cannot be calculated, a large number of samples must be collected, and the approximate expected value can be obtained by taking the mean value:

$$\nabla_\theta E_\tau[R(\tau)] = \frac{1}{N} \sum_{n=1}^{N} \sum_{t=0}^{T-1} R(\tau^n) \nabla_\theta \log \pi(a_t^n | s_t^n, \theta) \tag{10}$$

4.2　Improved SPBDDPG Algorithm

The actor-critic algorithm, as its name suggests, has two parts: Actor and Critic.

The critic network uses the deep intensive learning algorithm based on value functions, which can output the corresponding $Q^\pi(a_t^n, s_t^n)$ and $V^\pi(s_t^n)$ according to the state s_t and action a_t, while the random variable $A^\theta(a_t, s_t)$ can be expressed as:

$$Q^\pi(a_t^n, s_t^n) - V^\pi(s_t^n)$$

But it is inconvenient to construct two networks for output $Q^\pi(a_t^n, s_t^n)$ and $V^\pi(s_t^n)$, respectively, and:

$$Q^\pi(a_t^n, s_t^n) = E[r_t^n + V^\pi(s_{t+1}^n)] \tag{11}$$

Therefore, $A^\theta(a_t, s_t)$ can be approximately expressed as:

$$r_t^n + V^\pi(s_{t+1}^n) - V^\pi(s_t^n)$$

At this point, the critic network can provide actor network with $A^\theta(a_t, s_t)$ weight function for gradient rise and update.

The specific flow of the algorithm is as follows:

a. Expanding scope of action to explore the noise distribution of N and making the neural network output value into the scope of the actual scheduling problem in first initialization.;

b. Then initialize the Actor Evaluate network with the parameter of θ^π, and select the action by the strategy gradient; and the Critic Evaluate network with parameters of θ^Q to output the Q value corresponding to state actions through DQN;

c. The parameters of the two estimated networks were passed to the target network (Actor Target and Critic Target), and the two groups with same parameters constitute differential action network and evaluation network respectively;

d. Generate action a_1 according to initial state s_1 and action estimation network. Then generate the next state s_2 and value r_1 according to environmental feedback. Take $\{s_1, a_1, r_1, s_2\}$ as a set of data, and store them in memory bank R;

e. Take s_2 as the next initial state and repeat step d;

f. When the memory bank R is full, cover storage is carried out. And after each network output, a large amount of data is randomly sampled from the memory bank R to start training and update the two estimation networks;

g. Generate estimated value q_1 according to s_1, a_1 and evaluate real network; action a_2 is generated according to the next state s_2 and action real network. Then the real value q_2 is generated from s_2, a_2 and evaluation real network. $r_1 + \gamma q_2$ is taken as the comparison real value q_1', the mean square deviation of estimated value q_1 and real value q_1' is minimized by training the network parameter θ^Q:

$$TD\_error = \frac{1}{N} \sum_N \left(q_1' - q_1\right)^2 \tag{12}$$

h. The negative number of the estimated value q_1 is defined as the loss function, then update the network parameter θ^π through the gradient increase to minimize the loss function. Make the network select the highest probability of Q action;

i. Start the loop from Step c.

5 Simulation and Performance Analysis

This section is based on the Python edge structures in the network environment simulation to achieve the edge computing resource scheduling and tack-offloading system network architecture. In the simulation model, SPBDDPG algorithm is used to optimize the results. For comparison, the REINFORCE algorithm and the minimum offloading scenario are chosen as baselines. Specific simulation parameters are shown in Table 1.

5.1 Complexity

The size of simulation setup memory database is 5000. During the training process, the maximum iteration step is 1000 per round and the number of iterations is 30 rounds. And the sixth round began using memory data to train neural networks, then the new data will

Table 1. Simulation parameters

Parameters	Description	Value
L_{max}	A delay constraint that can be tolerated	100 ms
F_c	Upper limit for edge computing servers	6×10^9 cycles/slot
K	Total number of user devices	30
B	Bandwidth of a complex Gaussian white noise channel	10 MHz
N_0	Variance of complex Gaussian white noise channel	10^{-9} W
h_k	Channel gain for user device K	10^{-3}
F_k	Local CPU capacity of user device K	$\sim U[0.1, 1.0]$ GHz
P_k	Local CPU cycle power consumption of user device K	$\sim U\left[0, 20 \times 10^{-11}\right]$ J/cycles
I_k	Input data for user device K	$\sim U[100, 500]$ KB
C_k	Number of cycles required to compute data for user device K	$\sim U[500, 1500]$ cycles/bit

cover the original database. According to Fig. 2, the reward value curve began to change since the 16th round and the algorithm completed convergence when it comes to the 19th round. In a word, SPBDDPG algorithm has good training effect and convergence rate is rapid.

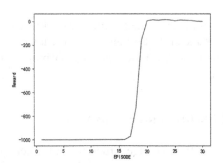

Fig. 2. The convergence of the algorithm

5.2 Effectiveness

With the increase of cell user equipment, the computing power of edge server is limited, and many tasks need to be calculated locally. According to Fig. 3(a), the total energy consumption of the scheduling scheme based on SPBDDPG algorithm is lower than the other two schemes.

As the maximum of time delay that all users can tolerate increases, many tasks can be calculated by offloading tasks to the edge server. As a result, local computing energy consumption will be reduced. According to Fig. 3(b), compared with the optimization scheme based on REINFORCE algorithm and implement minimum offloading scheme, the total energy consumption of the scheme proposed in this paper is lower.

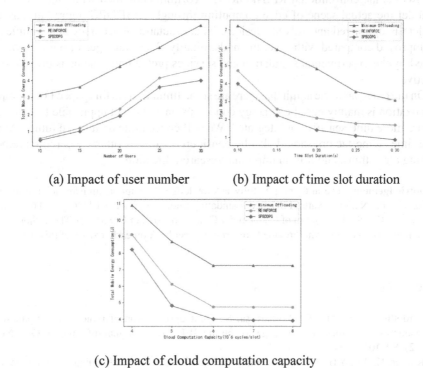

(a) Impact of user number   (b) Impact of time slot duration

(c) Impact of cloud computation capacity

Fig. 3. The comparison of 5.2 effectiveness between different algorithms

With the increase of the edge server computing capacity limit, many tasks can be offloaded to the edge server for computing, so the total energy consumption of user equipment will be reduced. According to Fig. 3(c), the total energy consumption of the scheduling scheme based on SPBDDPG algorithm is lower than the other two schemes. In addition, the total energy consumption almost stops decreasing and tends to be stable when the edge computing server's upper limit of computing capacity exceeds a certain threshold (about 6×10^9 cycles/slot). It indicates that the upper limit of edge computing server's computing capacity has a certain threshold value. If the edge server's computing capacity exceeds the threshold value, the energy consumption of user equipment will not be reduced.

6 Conclusion

In this paper, an offloading decision and resource scheduling optimization algorithm based on deep reinforcement learning is proposed, which can reduce the energy consumption in traditional edge computing problems and improve the resource utilization. Meanwhile, the conventional REINFORCE algorithm combined with DQN was used to model the actual scene of edge computing through SPBDDPG algorithm, and the problem is optimized and solved. Besides, its computational accuracy and complexity are improved compared with other methods. Finally, the advantages of our method are proved by the experimental simulation and services preloading scheme is proved to be effective.

On the other hand, we admit that there are some limitations in this paper. For example, optimization is mainly based on energy consumption and is not applicable to scenarios that are more time-sensitive or integrated. We will concentrate on it in the future. At the same time, some factors should also be considered, such as other deep reinforcement learning algorithms, and it is an important research direction.

Acknowledgement. The authors gratefully acknowledge the support and financial assistance provided by the National Natural Science Foundation under Grant No. 61772064 and 61701019, the National Key R&D Program of China under Grant No. 2018YFC0831900. The authors thank the anonymous reviewers who provided constructive feedback on earlier work of this paper.

References

1. Sardellitti, S., Scutari, G., Barbarossa, S.: Joint optimization of radio and computational resources for multicell mobile-edge computing. IEEE Trans. Signal Inf. Process. Over Netw. **1**(2), 89–103 (2014)
2. Kumar, K., Lu, Y.H.: Cloud computing for mobile users: can offloading computation save energy. Computer **43**(4), 51–56 (2010)
3. Wu, H., Wang, Q., Katinka, W.: Tradeoff between performance improvement and energy saving in mobile cloud offloading systems. In: 2013 IEEE International Conference on Communications Workshops (ICC), pp. 728–732 (2013)
4. Barbarossa, S., Sardellitti, S., Lorenzo, P.D.: Joint allocation of computation and communication resources in multiuser mobile cloud computing. In: 2013 IEEE 14th Workshop on Signal Processing Advances in Wireless Communications (SPAWC), pp. 26–30 (2013)
5. Munoz, O., Pascual-Iserte, A., Vidal, J.: Optimization of radio and computational resources for energy efficiency in latency-constrained application offloading. IEEE Trans. Veh. Technol. **64**(10), 4738–4755 (2015)
6. Huang, D., Wang, P., Niyato, D.: A dynamic offloading algorithm for mobile computing. IEEE Trans. Wirel. Commun. **11**(6), 1991–1995 (2012)
7. Di Lorenzo, P., Barbarossa, S., Sardellitti, S.: Joint Optimization of Radio Resources and Code Partitioning in Mobile Edge Computing (2013). https://arxiv.org/abs/1307.3835.
8. Yang, L., Cao, J., Cheng, H., et al.: Multi-user computation partitioning for latency sensitive mobile cloud applications. IEEE Trans. Comput. **64**(8), 2253–2266 (2015)
9. Yang, L., Cao, J., Yuan, Y., et al.: A framework for partitioning and execution of data stream applications in mobile cloud computing. ACM SIGMETRICS Perform. Eval. Rev. **40**(4), 23–32 (2013)

10. Zhang, W., Wen, Y., Guan, K., et al.: Energy-optimal mobile cloud computing under stochastic wireless channel. IEEE Trans. Wirel. Commun. **12**(9), 4569–4581 (2013)

11. Chen, Z., Wang, X.: Decentralized computation offloading for multi-user mobile edge computing: a deep reinforcement learning approach (2018)

12. Zeng, D., Gu, L., Pan, S., et al.: resource management at the network edge: a deep reinforcement learning approach. IEEE Netw. **33**(3), 26–33 (2019)

13. Chen, X., Zhang, H., Wu, C., et al.: Optimized computation offloading performance in virtual edge computing systems via deep reinforcement learning. IEEE Internet Things J. **6**, 4005–4018 (2018)

14. Mao, Y., You, C., Zhang, J., Huang, K., Letaief, K.B.: A survey on mobile edge computing: the communication perspective. IEEE Commun. Surv. Tuts. **19**(4), 2322–2358 (2017)

15. Mao, Y., Zhang, J., Song, S.H., Letaief, K.B.: Stochastic joint radio and computational resource management for multi-user mobile edge computing systems. IEEE Trans. Wirel. Commun. **16**(9), 5994–6009 (2017)

16. Lyu, X., et al.: Optimal schedule of mobile edge computing for Internet of Things using partial information. IEEE J. Sel. Areas Commun. **35**(11), 2606–2615 (2017)

17. Liu, J., Mao, Y., Zhang, J., Letaief, K.B.: Delay-optimal computation task scheduling for mobile-edge computing systems. In: Proceedings of IEEE International Symposium Information Theory (ISIT), pp. 1451–1455 (2016)

18. Hong, S.-T., Kim, H.: QoE-aware computation offloading scheduling to capture energy-latency tradeoff in mobile clouds. In: Proceedings of 13th Annual IEEE International Conference Sensing, Communication Networking (SECON), pp. 1–9 (2016)

19. Li, J., Gao, H., Lv, T., Lu, Y.: Deep reinforcement learning based computation offloading and resource allocation for MEC. In: Proceedings of IEEE Wireless Communications, Networking Conference (WCNC), pp. 1–6 (2018)

20. FP7 European Project. Distributed Computing, Storage and Radio Resource Allocation Over Cooperative Femtocells (TROPIC) [EB/OL]. https://www.ict-tropic.eu.

Using Machine Learning and Internet of Things Framework to Analyze Eggs Hatching

Shun-Chieh Chang[1], Chih-Hsiang Cheng[2], Tse-Yung Huang[3], Liou-Yuan Li[4], and Yu-Liang Liu[5(✉)]

[1] Department of Business Administration, Shih Hsin University, Taipei, Taiwan
scc@mail.shu.edu.tw
[2] Ilan Branch, Livestock Research Institute, Council of Agriculture, Executive Yuan,
Taipei, Taiwan
chcheng@mail.tlri.gov.tw
[3] Cybersecurity Technology Institute, Institute for Information Industry, Taipei, Taiwan
tseyunghuang@iii.org.tw
[4] Department of International Business Administration, Rajamangala University of Technology,
Thanyaburi, Thailand
liou_y@rmutt.ac.th
[5] Department of Multimedia and Game Design, Overseas Chinese University, Taichung, Taiwan
ylliu@ocu.edu.tw

Abstract. High-efficiency artificial incubation technology is the basis of the development of the poultry industry, and good chicks can be obtained through excellent egg breeding and good incubation technology. In Taiwan, the control of important parameters for waterfowl hatchery is still based on the inheritance of experience. The manual intervention of the cold egg operation during the hatching process will also affect the stability of the hatching environment and the risk of poultry biological safety infection.

Therefore, in addition to discussing the current factors affecting waterfowl hatching, this study will also establish a set of IoT sensing systems suitable for waterfowl hatching. We use thermal imaging cameras and air quality sensors to collect the key factors that affect the hatching of waterfowl during the hatching process, and use the machine learning analysis framework to analyze the collected big data of waterfowl hatching. Although the application of thermal imaging technology has limitations, due to the non-invasive characteristics and the cost of technology, the application of poultry science has gradually received attention.

Combining poultry science and information science, we have reintegrated a complete set of intelligent detection and application improvement solutions, which can enhance the digitalization and intelligence of the hardware and software of the waterfowl industry chain.

Keywords: Waterfowl · Thermal imager · Artificial intelligence · IoT · Sensor

1 Introduction

High-efficiency artificial incubation technology is the basis of the development of the poultry industry, and good chicks can be obtained through excellent egg breeding and good incubation technology. The manual intervention of the cold egg operation during the hatching process will also affect the stability of the hatching environment and the risk of poultry biological safety infection. In Taiwan, the control of important parameters for waterfowl hatchery is still based on the inheritance of experience. Because of the shortage of young employees in Taiwan's waterfowl breeding industry, the breeding methods have gradually moved from large-scale production to refined agriculture. The scale of operations and the age of employees are no longer comparable to the past, but the demand for waterfowl in the consumer market is increasing year by year.

We can get the number of ducks slaughtered from the annual report of agricultural statistics of the Agricultural Committee of the Executive Yuan of the Republic of China [1]. From 2010 to 2019, the number of meat ducks being raised was 28,546,000, 28,808,000, 27,253,000, 32,460,000, 36,786,000, 33,519,000, 34,748,000, 36,339,000, 35,596,000 and 37,002,000, indicating that the consumption market for meat ducks is increasing year by year. In 2014, the number of farms was 36,786,000. The reason for the decrease in the next year was the occurrence of highly pathogenic poultry influenza (avian influenza) that year. Meat ducks and breeding ducks that tested positive had to be culled, resulting in a decline in the number of farms. From 2016 to 2019, the number of breeding has gradually increased (Fig. 1).

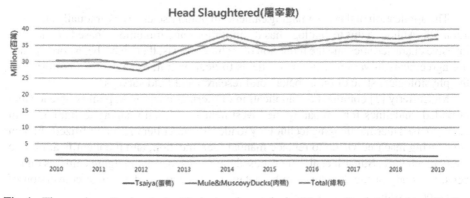

Fig. 1. The number of laying ducks (Tsaiya) and meat ducks (MuscovyDucks) slaughtered in the Republic of China.

This shows that the demand for waterfowl in the consumer market is increasing year by year. Therefore, how to increase the hatching rate in order to increase the production of waterfowl and to achieve a balance between supply and demand is what the market needs. In previous studies, many research results show that the two parameters of temperature and humidity have a decisive influence on the hatchability of breeding eggs [2–6]. However, the current domestic industry's control of temperature and humidity parameters is still mainly based on experience inheritance, and a scientific incubation model has not been established.

2 Literature Review

As far as the poultry industry is concerned, artificial incubation is the basic means to promote good poultry. Because of excellent breeding eggs and good hatching, good young birds can be obtained. The planned elimination of poorly produced poultry species and avoiding the mixing of poultry species will benefit the planned production and supply of young poultry. The operation management during the incubation process has a huge impact on the incubation performance. The eggs enter the incubator, and then move to the generator stage. There are many factors that affect hatching, as described in Table 1:

Table 1. Factors affecting hatching.

Factors of breeding poultry	Factors of breeding eggs
Genetic structure	Egg quality
Age	Storage time
Egg production	Storage temperature
Nutrition	Disinfect
management	Transport
	Altitude
	Temperature
	Operation management during the incubation period

The application of thermal imaging cameras in poultry science has gradually attracted attention. Although this technology has its limitations and limitations, based on the non-invasive characteristics and the reduction of technical costs, there have been corresponding agreements in various application fields to deal with it. Such as the monitoring of the physiological state of birds, behavioral research and field surveys, etc.

McCafferty [7] compiled the application of thermal imaging in poultry science and provided guidelines for evaluating the investment in thermal imaging technology. Lin et al. [8] used thermal imaging technology to identify and filter broken fertilized chicken eggs, using machine vision to replace manual identification, and the identification rate could reach 96%. Sunardi et al. [9] proposed the use of thermal imaging cameras on the eggs, the study of the data that can be obtained, focusing on the format conversion of image processing.

We use thermal imaging cameras and air quality sensors to build an IoT sensing environment for waterfowl hatching machines, and implement a waterfowl hatching intelligence collection system to collect data on influencing factors in the waterfowl hatching process.

3 Methodology

We installed thermal imaging cameras, gas detectors, temperature and humidity detectors in the incubation environment, and put 30 breeding eggs for system testing. The data during the incubation process will continue to be collected into the database until the

Fig. 2. IOT system architecture diagram and experimental scene.

incubation is completed. We will mark the hatching results of the hatching data and use machine learning for classification training (Fig. 2).

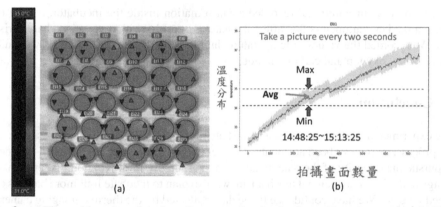

Fig. 3. (a) Thermal imaging of the breeding eggs taken by the thermal imaging camera. (b) The temperature record distribution of the hatching egg number EL1.

Figure 3(a) shows the 6*5 grid thermal image of the egg tray during shooting. We can get the highest temperature, lowest temperature and average temperature of the egg surface temperature through the temperature change of the egg surface taken by the thermal imager. Figure 3(b) is the information about the heating of the breeding egg numbered EL1 in the incubator. We recorded the temperature change in detail within 25 min. The maximum temperature difference of each breeding egg is different. When the hatching egg is completed, we will mark the hatching result of each breeding egg. After the temperature information is recorded in detail, machine learning can be used to build an incubation prediction model. After the model is calibrated and optimized, these temperature parameters can be used as a reference for the improvement of the incubator.

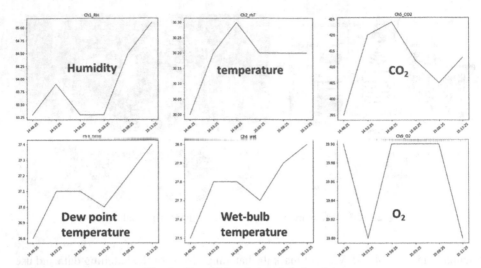

Fig. 4. Six additional recorded air values

Figure 4 is our additional recorded air information inside the incubator, hoping to find out the key parameters that affect the hatching results with diversified characteristics. We recorded the values of temperature, humidity, dew point temperature, wet bulb temperature, oxygen and carbon dioxide.

4 Conclusion

The experiment is still in progress, and the hatching time of the breeding eggs is long. In the process, there have been accidents of power failure, crash, and broken eggs. In order to pursue the integrity of the data, in addition to gradually improving our experimental design and crisis management mechanism, we also plan to incubate four more batches of breeding eggs. We have confidence in the data collected by the thermal imaging camera during the incubation process, which is completely different from the past studies of simply collecting temperature and pursuing a homogenized incubation environment. The experimental results can be used as the basis for setting the parameters of the uniform incubation environment in the past.

References

1. Council of Agriculture, Executive Yuan R.O.C., Agricultural statistics yearbook (2019)
2. Lan, W.-T.: The Development of Automatic Waterfowl Incubator with Pre-Controlled Thermal System. Master Thesis, Department of Biomechatronic Engineering, National Chiayi University (2010). https://hdl.handle.net/11296/8re84f
3. Ho, H.-Y.: Flow Field Simulation and Analysis of Automatic-Cooling Incubator. Master Thesis, Department of Biomechatronic Engineering, National Chiayi University (2010). https://hdl.han dle.net/11296/k33rzq

4. Kuo, T.-H.: Study on The Automatic Waterfowl Incubator Control Method. Master Thesis, Department of Biomechatronic Engineering, National Chiayi University (2013). https://hdl. handle.net/11296/j9mp2w

5. Yang, H.C.: Study on Automatic Waterfowl Hatching and Egg-cooling Control System Intergrated with Human-machine Interface. Master Thesis, Department of Biomechatronic Engineering, National Chiayi University, https://hdl.handle.net/11296/n29e8c

6. Shen, Y.-J.: Combining CFD software of Response Surface Methodology to Simulate the Optimal Design of the Incubate using for Waterfowl Eggs Hatching. Master Thesis, Department of Biomechatronic Engineering, National Chiayi University (2010). https://hdl.handle.net/11296/urrgsp.

7. McCafferty, D.J.: Applications of thermal imaging in avian science. Int. J. Avian Sci. **155**, 4–15 (2013)

8. Lin, C.S., Yeh, P.T., Chen, D.C., Chiou, Y.C., Lee, C.H.: The identification and filtering of fertilized eggs with a thermal imaging system. Comput. Electron. Agric. **91**, 94–105 (2013)

9. Sunardi, S., Yudhana, A., Saifullah, S.: Identity analysis of egg based on digital and thermal imaging: image processing and counting object concept. Int. J. Electr. Comput. Eng. **7**, 200–208 (2017)

An Intelligent Tea Farm Management Platform Based on AgriTalk Technology

Mei-Yu Wu[1]([✉]) and Chih-Kun Ke[2]

[1] Department of Business Management, National Taichung University of Science and Technology, Taichung 40401, Taiwan, Republic of China
`mywu@nutc.edu.tw`
[2] Department of Information Management, National Taichung University of Science and Technology, Taichung 40401, Taiwan, Republic of China
`ckk@nutc.edu.tw`

Abstract. The production of tea is a complicated. Every aspect of tea planting requires a lot of manpower and rich experience or professional fertilizer training knowledge. Applying intelligent agricultural planting technology will effectively reduce the burden of farm operations, reduce labor demand, and enable tea farmers to operate more efficiently. The research introduces the most popular artificial intelligence (AI) technology, Internet of Things (IoT) and the AgriTalk technology to a tea farm that is located in Nantou, Taiwan. Through remotely monitoring the growth of tea and various environmental data, intelligent tea farm management platform will ensure the healthy growth of tea and increase tea production. In addition, the key patterns of tea cultivation will be established through long-term data collection and analysis. The key patterns for tea cultivation include suitable temperature, humidity, sunshine, fertilization time, etc.

Keywords: Tea planting · AgriTalk · Artificial intelligence · Internet of Things

1 Introduction

Taiwan's tea is world famous. When the tea leaves from the initial tea species to the final drop in the cup, it will form different flavors due to the climate, terrain, tea species, harvest methods, baking methods, brand marketing and other processes. The production of tea is a complicated process including tea seedling cultivation, reclamation planting, field management technology (fertilization, pesticide application, weeding, pruning, irrigation, deep ploughing, etc.), harvesting, tea making technology (withering, wavering, fermentation, blanching, cloth ball), refined baking, graded packaging, quality positioning and other technologies. Besides, different types of fertilizers are required in Taiwan's diverse topography, low to high altitude, different seasons and growth periods. The demand, element types and proportions of fertilizers for tea plants need to be more precise.

Y.-B. Lin and D.-J. Deng (Eds.): SGIoT 2020, LNICST 354, pp. 20–26, 2021.
https://doi.org/10.1007/978-3-030-69514-9_3

Intelligent agriculture is already the trend of world agriculture. Intelligent agriculture emphasizes the two major issues of smart production and digital service. Through Industry 4.0 technologies such as cloud technology, big data analysis, the Internet of Things (IoT), intelligent machinery, and sensors are applied in agriculture, small farmers can reduce the impact of aging population, insufficient labor, and extreme weather on the industry. Big data database can be developed through sensors, IoT technology, collecting soil and meteorological data, recording operating methods of tea farmers and the growth trends of tea tree. Furthermore, using artificial intelligence (AI) technology to analyze related factors required for tea plant growth, such as the temperature, humidity, light, pH value, electrical conductivity (EC) value, soil fertility and carbon dioxide concentration and so on.

AgriTalk is an inexpensive IoT platform for precision farming of soil cultivation and it was proposed by W.L. Chen et al. in 2019 [1]. Related literature has adopted AgriTalk for the cultivation of turmeric, and the experimental results have improved the quality of turmeric. The curcumin concentration can be up to 5 times more than existing products. This research tries to import AgriTalk into tea farm management. As a result, assisting tea farmers can be more precise in all stages of tea production and cultivation. It is expected to effectively reduce the burden of farm operations, reduce labor demand, and enable tea farmers to operate more efficiently.

The remainder of this paper is arranged as follows. Section 2 reviews related works on intelligent agriculture, Internet of Things (IoT), and AgriTalk. Section 3 introduces the development and application of intelligent agricultural planting. Analysis and discussion for intelligent agriculture are described in Sect. 4. Finally, Sect. 5 presents conclusions and future research.

2 Related Works

Tea farm management is the main goal of this research. In this study, we must first understand the characteristics and planting methods of tea, and further propose appropriate intelligent tea farm management platform. The related works include planting and production process of tea, intelligent agriculture, Internet of Things (IoT), and AgriTalk.

2.1 Planting and Production Process of Tea

Taiwan has a variety of specialty teas from north to south. For example, there are Tiguanyin, Pouchong tea, oriental beauty tea in the north; Li-Shan Oolong Tea, Sun Moon Lake Ruby Black Tea, Dong Ding Oolong Tea in the middle and Alishan Oolong Tea, honey scent black tea, Red Oolong Tea in the south. The practical field of this research is in Lugu Township, Nantou County, Taiwan. Dong Ding Oolong Tea is the local representative tea. Dong Ding Oolong tea has a mellow taste with a hint of natural sweetness, brisk and thirst quenching. Tea farmers need to have rich experience or professional fertilizer cultivation knowledge to be able to properly and timely, appropriate fertilizer.

When planting tea, good field management is important. That includes fertilization, pesticide application, weeding, pruning, irrigation, deep ploughing, etc. In addition to good field management, tea also needs good making technology. The tea making technology includes withering, wavering, fermentation, blanching, cloth ball and so on. In the long run, Taiwan's agriculture does need to develop intelligent agriculture and turn rules of experience into system principles. In the past, the accumulated knowledge and experience existed in the heads of experts, but now it must be translated into data and stored in the computer. In order to digitize past agricultural knowledge, more data must be accumulated to be effectively used.

2.2 Intelligent Agriculture

Intelligent agriculture is an intelligent system of agricultural experts, integrated control system of agricultural products and traceability system of organic agricultural products [5]. Based on the current production model, the production and sale plans are according to the needs of the consumer market. Production management is supplemented by the development and application of labor-saving mechanical equipment, auxiliary equipment and sensor components, combined with cross-domain ICT and materials. The introduction of forward-looking technologies such as IoT, big data analysis, and block chain reduces the burden of farm operations and reduces labor demand. Internet of things (IoT) and data-driven techniques are creating greater opportunities for smart dairy farming [6].

There are many key drivers of technology in intelligent agriculture including automation, land, water, labor resource optimization, higher food crops, quality food, climate effects [7]. Intelligent agriculture mainly uses the concept and technology of the IoT, and introduces sensing components into the existing physical objects of the farm such as agricultural machinery, agricultural facilities, soil, crops, etc., and combines wireless communication technology to collect and retrieve the sensed data upload to cloud database [2, 3]. Intelligent agriculture provides farmers with a more efficient farm management model, and produces production that meets consumer needs. Safe, secure and traceable agricultural products.

2.3 Internet of Things (IoT)

The IoT integrates several existing technologies, such as wireless sensor network (WSN), radio frequency identification (RFID), cloud computing, middleware systems, and end-user applications [7]. It is expected that by the year 2021, there will be around 28 billion connected devices [9]. The IoT empowers substantial objects to see, hear, think and perform jobs by having them "talk" with each, to share information and to synchronize pronouncements. IoT is expected to be one of the main hub between various technologies by connecting smart physical objects together and allow different applications in support of smart decision making [4]. As a result, the use of Internet of Things (IoT) and data analytics (DA) are employed to enhance the operational efficiency and productivity in the agriculture sector [7, 8].

IoT is the perfect match for smart agriculture farming and dairy farming. In the research [6], the authors proposed an IoT for development of smart dairy farming. Manual milking in a dairy farm is very time consuming and slow procedure. The preserving process of milk is also not hygienic. Manual process can cause bacterial infection in milk. IoT has solved this problem more efficiently, reducing cost and manpower, by introducing automilking. IoT is usually adopted for solving most of present-day society issues such as smart cities, intelligent transportation, pollution monitoring, and connected healthcare, to name a few. Industrial IoT (IIoT), as a subset of IoT, covers the domains of machine-to-machine (M2M) and industrial communication technologies with automation applications [8].

2.4 AgriTalk

AgriTalk is an IoT platform for precision farming of soil cultivation and it was proposed by W.L. Chen et al. in 2019. The name "AgriTalk" is originated from that the nature (agriculture) always passes messages to human. However, human cannot catch the meaning of the messages through normal perception. Therefore, Chen et al. Develop AgriTalk that interprets the messages of the nature environment delivered to the farmers [1].

In AgriTalk, an intelligent agriculture platform for soil cultivation with a large number of sensors, the produced sensor data are used in several AI models to provide precise farming for soil microbiome and fertility, disease regulation, irrigation regulation, and pest regulation. The correct use of sensor data in AI modeling is very important. In the research [10], the authors proposed a solution called SensorTalk to automatically detect potential sensor failures and calibrate the aging sensors semi-automatically.

3 Development and Application of Intelligent Agricultural Planting

Ding Oolong Tea is the local representative tea in Lugu Township, Nantou County, Taiwan. The research developed and applied an intelligent agricultural planting technology based on AgriTalk to a tea farm in Lugu Township, Nantou County, Taiwan. The appearance of the original tea farm in Nantou County is illustrated in Fig. 1(1). The circle in the picture represents the automatic sprinkler equipment.

The research adopted AgriTalk platform to developing the IoT remote monitoring environment system on tea farm is illustrated in Fig. 1(2). The Position (a), (b), and (c) in Fig. 1(2) are the agricultural control module, sensors module, and IP camera.

The sensor dashboard of the IoT remote monitoring system on tea farm is illustrated as the Fig. 2(1). The sensor data include atmospheric pressure, carbon dioxide, sunlight, ultraviolet, infrared, air temperature, air humidity, soil temperature, soil humidity, pH value, electrical conductivity (EC) value, and so on. The real image from the Internet protocol camera (IPC) is illustrated in Fig. 2(2).

Because of temperature changes, whether it is raining or watering, soil fertilization or spraying pesticides, we can use historical data analysis to find the value changes shown in Fig. 3. The sensor values of CO_2, luminance, pH value, electrical conductivity (EC) value, air temperature, soil temperature, air humidity, and soil moisture are illustrated in Fig. 3(1)–(8).

This research further uses the IoT remote monitoring environment system to compare the changes of two different values. The magnitude of change of the two values pH value and EC value in the same period is shown in Fig. 4.

Fig. 1. (1) The appearance of the original tea farm in Nantou county; (2) Developing IoT remote monitoring system on tea farm based on AgriTalk

Fig. 2. (1) IoT remote monitoring environment system; (2) Real image from internet protocol camera

Through data analysis, researchers can find large changes in sensor data. The researcher further discussed possible reasons with tea farmers. Confirm whether the tea farmer has sprayed pesticides, sprayed organic weeding, manual weeding, tea tree pruning, etc. Through this learning process, it will help to establish a suitable tea planting pattern with AI technology.

4 Analysis and Discussion

In this study, an IoT remote monitoring environment system was actually installed in the tea farm in Nantou County, Taiwan. However, only six months of data have been collected so far, which is not enough to produce a complete tea planting pattern. The relevant analysis and discuss are described in the following:

- **Disadvantage:** for farmers, tea farmers are familiar with the original way of working. For the initial stage of introducing intelligent agriculture, it is necessary to meet the

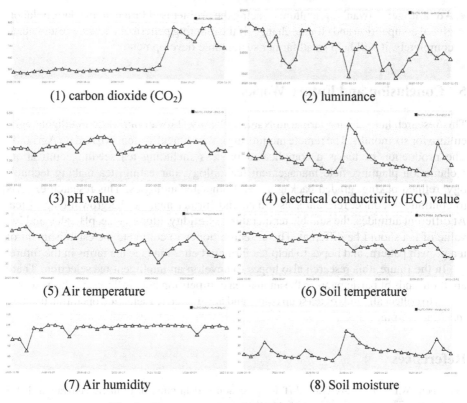

(1) carbon dioxide (CO_2)

(2) luminance

(3) pH value

(4) electrical conductivity (EC) value

(5) Air temperature

(6) Soil temperature

(7) Air humidity

(8) Soil moisture

Fig. 3. The sensor values from history data query.

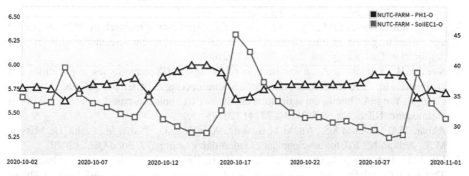

Fig. 4. Compare two sensor values from history data query.

needs of research and record related operations. This is an extra burden for tea farmers. Besides, the tea farmer ignores the physical circuit of the sensor and breaks the circuit when weeding.

- **Advantage:** Taiwan's agriculture is facing the problems of farmer aging, lack of labor, global competition and climate change. If the planting pattern of tea can be established completely, it will help small farmer sustainable development.

5 Conclusion and Future Works

This research helped a tea farmer in Nantou County, Taiwan introduce intelligent agriculture for six months. The remote monitoring environment system is based on AgriTalk. The production of tea is a complicated process including tea seedling cultivation, reclamation planting, field management technology, harvesting, tea making technology, refined baking, graded packaging, and other technologies. This research expects to continue to collect relevant sensor data and further analyze the growth data of tea. At different altitudes, the suitable temperature, humidity, illuminance, pH value and EC value of tea should be different. This research hopes to complete the establishment of tea growth pattern, and hopes to help tea farmers better manage tea farms in the future.

In the future, this research also hopes to develop an intelligent tea selection. There are thousands of participants in the annual tea competition held in Taiwan. This research hopes to collect all kinds of tea soup colors and automated tea selection operation through machine learning.

References

1. Chen, W.L., et al.: AgriTalk: IoT for precision soil farming of turmeric cultivation. IEEE Internet Things J. **6**(3), 5209–5223 (2019)
2. Gupta, N., Gupta, P.P., Pramanik, P., Saikia, A., Sengupta, L., Bhagat, R.M., Bhattacharya, N.: Integration of geoinformatics and wireless sensors for smart agriculture in Tea. In: The International Society for Optical Engineering (2014)
3. Xiong, S.M., Wang, L.M., Qu, X.Q., Zhan, Y.Z: Application research of WSN in precise agriculture irrigation. In: International Conference on Environmental Science and Information Application Technology, vol. 2, pp. 297–300 (2009)
4. Shah, S.H., Yaqoob, I.: A survey: Internet of Things (IOT) technologies, applications and challenges. In: 2016 IEEE Smart Energy Grid Engineering (SEGE), pp. 381–385 (2016)
5. Chen, J., Yang, A.: Intelligent agriculture and its key technologies based on internet of things architecture. IEEE Access **7**, 77134–77141 (2019)
6. Akbar, M.O., khan,M.S.S., Ali, M.J., Hussain, A., Qaiser,G., Pasha, M., Pasha, U., Missen, M.S., Akhtar, N.: IoT for development of smart dairy farming. J. Food Qual. (2020)
7. Elijah, O., Rahman, T.R., Orikumhi, I., Leow, C.Y., Hindia, M.N.: An overview of Internet of Things (IoT) and data analytics in agriculture: benefits and challenges. IEEE Internet Things J. **5**(5), 3758–3773 (2018)
8. Sisinni, E., Saifullah, A., Han, S., Jennehag, U., Gidlund, M.: Industrial Internet of Things: challenges, opportunities, and directions. IEEE Trans. Ind. Inf. **14**(11), 4724–4734 (2018)
9. Chen, H., Su, Z., Hui, Y., Hui, H.: Dynamic charging optimization for mobile charging stations in Internet of Things. Access IEEE **6**, 53509–53520 (2018)
10. Lin, Y.B., Lin, Y.W., Lin, J.Y., Hung, H.N.: SensorTalk: an IoT device failure detection and calibration mechanism for smart farming. Sensors **19**(21), 4788 (2019)

Deep Learning at the Edge for Operation and Maintenance of Large-Scale Solar Farms

Salsabeel Shapsough(✉) ⓘ, Imran Zualkernan ⓘ, and Rached Dhaouadi ⓘ

American University of Sharjah, Sharjah, UAE
sshapsough@aus.edu

Abstract. Real-time monitoring of large-scale solar farms is one important aspect of reliable and secure deployment of 100% renewable energy-based grids. The ability to observe sensors on solar panels using Internet of Things (IoT) technologies makes it possible to study the behavior of solar panels under various conditions and to detect anomalous behaviors in real-time. Such technologies make it possible for grid administrators to make informed decisions in reacting to anomalies such as panel damage, electrical errors, monitoring hardware decay, or malicious data injection attacks. Smart edge devices offer an opportunity to reduce the cost of continuously sending data for anomaly detection by performing analytics on local edge device within a given farm and sending only the result of the analysis back to datacenters. This paper presents the design and evaluation of a low-cost edge-based anomaly detection system for remote solar farms using Raspberry Pi and deep learning. The design was implemented and tested using real-life observations from a solar monitoring system under soiling conditions. The experiments showed that it is possible to run real-time anomaly detection algorithms on edge devices with little overhead in terms of power consumption and utilization of computational resources, making it an ideal system for large-scale implementation.

Keywords: Solar power · Neural networks · Edge analytics · Fog computing

1 Introduction

Renewable energy holds the potential to replace carbon-based fossil fuels as the main energy source for future cities. In the light of the recent rapid global urbanization, integration of clean renewable energy sources is more important than ever to reduce damage to environmental resources and ensure reliable and sustainable population growth through upcoming decades [1, 2]. As a result, the recent years have witnessed a massive increase in renewable energy installations all over the world, including solar, wind, and geothermal energy facilities. The International Renewable Energy Agency (IRENA) reported a total of over 2.35 TW of global installed capacity, with hydro, wind, and solar amounting to 50%, 24%, and 20%, accordingly [3]. The numbers showcase a growth of 7.9% from the previous year, with 55% of new capacity attributed to new solar installations alone, of which 70% is attributed to new solar installations in Asia.

Y.-B. Lin and D.-J. Deng (Eds.): SGIoT 2020, LNICST 354, pp. 27–44, 2021.
https://doi.org/10.1007/978-3-030-69514-9_4

Countries in the GCC with a desert climate such as the United Arab Emirates and Saudi Arabia are some of the biggest investors in solar energy in the region [4]. With an average daily sunshine hour of 10 h/day and a Global horizontal Irradiance index (GHI) that can go as high as 2.12 MWh/m^2/year, such countries hold the potential to generate massive amounts of solar power which can eventually replace their current dependence on carbon-based fossil fuels [5, 6]. Nonetheless, integration of solar energy sources into main grids remains relatively low. In a country with a desert climate such as the United Arab Emirates, for example, its 22.5 MW of installed solar capacity amounts to only 0.49% [4]. Despite the exponential growth in new solar installations exhibited in the GCC over the past few years, a 100% renewable energy grid remains a distant reality. This is mainly due to the challenges that solar installations face in desert climates such as overheating and soiling [7, 8]. As a result, great research efforts have been dedicated to increasing and optimizing the performance of solar modules in such environments.

One of the main challenges to solar energy integration is the intermittent stochastic nature of the source [9]. The output of a solar module is a direct product of its environment, most notably solar irradiance and temperature. The intermittent nature of weather conditions is reflected through fluctuations in power output which can propagate through main girds, causing inconveniences to power planning at best, and damage to critical assets at worst. Furthermore, solar modules are often located in remote and harsh environments where they are susceptible to damage due to environmental conditions such as overheating, surfaces scratching, and material decay. Such faults can cause serious issues such as module mismatch or open circuit, thus significantly reducing the power output of an installation. Furthermore, once a solar installation has been integrated into the grid, it is vital that the state of the installation and its output at any given moment is known to the system in order to ensure reliable power planning [10]. As a result, faults must be detected and rectified with minimal delay in order to prevent fluctuations from propagating through the grid and causing service interruptions or damage to critical assets [11]. Anomaly detection is a key component of operation and maintenance (O&M) in automated systems. It is especially critical for IoT systems where autonomous response to system failures such as hardware malfunction, software errors, or security breaches is key to ensuring reliable operation.

Anomaly detection can be performed using supervised or unsupervised methods, where the output can either be a label ("normal" or "anomaly") or a score depicting the likelihood a reading is an anomaly [12]. However, performing real-time anomaly detection requires large amounts of real-time data to be transmitted from solar farms over wireless networks back to central datacenters. For example, an edge device that measures the performance of an individual solar panel generates a message which is around 200 Bytes in size. Similarly, an edge device that monitors the environmental conditions in a facility generates a message size of 1000 Bytes [13]. In an installation where edge devices send data at a rate of 1 message/minute, two devices alone observing over a period of 12 h can generate a network load of 864 kB/12 h. Given the scale of recent solar installations such as the 2 GW Al Dhafra project in Abu Dhabi [14], the amount of data required for real-time monitoring is likely to pose a challenge in terms of data transportation. As a result, recent research in various IoT applications has shifted to edge computing and fog computing as a way to perform analytics on edge devices local to the installation [15], thus reducing the requirements of wireless communication, as well as data processing and storage at datacenters. However, this requires edge hardware that is both low in cost and capable of running sophisticated neural networks in real time.

This paper presents and evaluates an edge analytics environment that uses Raspberry Pi to detect anomalies in solar power in real time for large-scale distributed solar farms.

2 Anomaly Detection and Solar Power

2.1 Intermittency in Solar Energy

Solar energy is a product of its environment. The amount of energy generated by a solar module depends not only on the amount of irradiance absorbed by the surfaces, but also the module temperature. When solar modules are produced, the maximum power is generated at standard testing conditions where irradiance is 1000 W/m^2 and ambient temperature is 25 °C. Any decrease of irradiance or change in ambient temperature can reduce the amount of energy generated. In a real-life solar farm, numerous conditions can influence the power output. Meteorological conditions such as shading [16–18], haze, or fog [19], can significantly reduce the amount of irradiance that is absorbed by the module. In high temperature weather regions, hot temperatures can result in module overheating, which can shift the operating point of a module thus preventing it from operating at maximum power. A complex environmental phenomenon that combines several environmental elements including irradiance, temperature, humidity, and wind level is soiling. Soiling is defined as the accumulation of particles such as dust, dirt, snow, or bird droppings on the surface of a solar module, effectively reducing the amount of solar irradiance that can be absorbed [20]. Soiling represents a major hindrance to solar energy adoption in desert regions such as the GCC region. A study conducted in 2013 on solar energy generation in the smart city Masdar [21] reported a power loss of at least 40% due to regular dust storms [22].

However, while fluctuations in meteorological conditions are key to solar power generation and can significantly influence the performance of large-scale remote solar installations, they seldom require immediate intervention. Instead, navigating solar power generation through adversarial weather conditions can be done via proactive operation and maintenance. For example, overheating can be prevented using module cooling [23]. Soiling loss, on the other hand, can be avoided in a cost-effective way by optimizing cleaning methods and schedules, as shown in [24, 25]. As for factors that cannot be controlled such as shading due to clouds and fog, mathematical models as well as machine learning and deep learning methods are used to predict power fluctuation due to shading [17, 26] and plan energy reserves accordingly, which can be applied to clean modules as well as modules under soiling conditions [27].

2.2 Anomalies in Solar Energy Systems

While fluctuations in power can be severe depending on ambient conditions, in this work, such fluctuations are not considered "anomalies" due to the fact they are an inherent part of the energy source's nature. Anomalies, instead, are faults that may occur within modules or data that describes modules. Anomalies can be loosely divided into three main categories: module faults, monitoring system faults, and cyberattacks.

Array Anomalies. Array anomalies refers to faults that can occur to module bodies, module interconnection, or internal electrical connections within the farm. The first type of array anomalies is module damage and decay. Over time, PV modules can develop localized overheating or "hot spots", where a mismatch between cells within one module causes a cell or more to overheat [28]. The phenomenon can occur when parts of the module are shaded by a clouds, soiling elements, or shadows from surrounding objects such as buildings or other modules for prolonged periods of time [29]. The development of hot spots can degrade the performance of the module, damage its integrity, and cause irreversible malfunctions [30]. The same issue can occur at a higher level when a mismatch occurs between several PV modules in a string [31–33], which in the long run can accelerate module degradation. Furthermore, faults can occur within the internal connections in the farm where a configuration error, short circuit, or open circuit can bring down full strings of modules [29].

System Anomalies. The second type of anomalies is corrupted or missing readings. This type of anomaly is common in monitoring systems where values can be lost or corrupted during data collection or transmission [34]. Internet of Things systems are prone to such anomalies partially due to their inherent low-resource nature which makes it difficult and costly to deploy sophisticated hardware and software components in remote installations [35, 36]. Damage to sensors, hardware malfunctions, software exceptions, and network disconnections can generate anomalous data that, if allowed to propagate through the system, may cause disruptions or result in false decision making. Distributed solar farms represent a particularly challenging case in data reliability due to their remote nature. In addition to standard IoT challenges, solar installations often exist in harsh weather conditions [37] where sensors and processing hardware are prone to damage and decay. In such cases, early detection of system faults, or anomalies, is key to preventing false readings from propagating through grids and causing damage to assets.

Solar Power Data Security. The third type of anomalies is cyberattacks. Energy systems are some of the most critical assets in a given community. However, studies show that 54% of cyberattacks on infrastructure are directed at energy systems [38]. Isolated solar microgrids and grid-integrated solar installations are susceptible to such attacks. Cyberattacks can target solar monitoring devices, the network through which data is transmitted, or the data itself [39]. The more highly populated and further distributed a solar energy system is, the harder it is to enforce appropriate security measures end-to-end [40]. Furthermore, modern energy systems are highly heterogenous in terms of type of hardware and data allowed within the system. Protecting such systems requires sophisticated security suites to address all vulnerabilities at each point in the system. It is therefore key to implement attack detection and prevention throughout the system. While active attacks such as Denial-of-Service [40] can be immediately detected, making it easier to rectify within a short time limit, passive attacks on data may go unnoticed. "False data injection" refers to a type of attack where an intruder gains access to the systems network and proceeds to transmit false data disguised as legitimate readings [41]. In an energy system where meter readings and monitoring systems dictate the flow of power through the system [38], false information can result in damages that range from energy theft, to inconvenient minor disruptions in services, and all the way to severe damage to critical assets and drastic financial losses. Anomalies in this context refer to illegitimate readings injected by a cyber attacker in order to disrupt system operations. The ability to immediately detect and correctly classify cyberattack anomalies makes it possible to contain the attack and prevent false information from propagating throughout the system.

Anomaly Detection in Solar Power Systems. Existing anomaly detection methods for solar monitoring generally follow one of two approaches [29, 42]: model-based anomaly detection, and data-based anomaly detection. Model-based anomaly detection uses information from the healthy module to build a virtual model of the healthy module which operates in parallel with the real-life PV module. From that moment on, real-time measured values are compared to predicted healthy values to look for deviations from expected behavior. In a variation of this method, the model is built offline based on the module's characteristics and the environment. Using the virtual model, error threshold values are then set for the voltage and the current. From that point on, real-time readings are compared to the threshold, and any point beyond the minimum or maximum expected performance is marked as an anomaly. Examples of existing work are shown in Table 1.

In data-based approaches, on the other hand, machine learning (ML) and deep learning (DL) algorithms are trained and used to detect anomalies. In this approach, previous knowledge of the domain theory is not required as analysis focuses on trends and patterns in the dataset independent of domain-based assumptions. Furthermore, several works on anomaly detection extend to using ML and DL in anomaly classification. The latter is rather useful in determining the source of the anomaly, which is key for implementing cost-effective countermeasures.

While existing work on anomaly detection in solar monitoring systems covers a variety of anomalies and detection methodologies, they often assume data with a somewhat clear distinction between "valid" readings and anomalies. However, in operating conditions where environmental elements such as soiling exist and skew performance, detecting real anomalies from expected degradation becomes more complex. Furthermore, while solar panels in one location are expected to give a relatively-identical performance, contextual elements such its surface temperature [48], short-term shading [17], or aerosol particle concentration [49, 50] can vary based on its location and skew the module's "normal" behavior from identical behavior assumed at manufacturing and give it a unique profile. In such cases, treating models for individual modules with unique characteristics and behaviors makes it possible to detect slight changes in behavior that may otherwise be neglected in generalized performance modeling.

Table 1. Summary of some of key existing work on anomaly detection in solar power

Paper title	year	Input data	Method	Outputs
Hierarchical Anomaly Detection and Multimodal Classification in Large-Scale Photovoltaic Systems [42]	2019	SCADA data (current, voltage) recorded every minute	Detection: Local Context-Aware Anomaly Detection using AutoGMM Classification: SVM, Bagging, XGBoost	Anomaly detection & classification: Sensor bias/aging, building shading, hotspot/glass breakage, grass shading, surface soiling
Anomaly Detection of Solar Power Generation Systems Based on the Normalization of the Amount of Generated Electricity [43]	2015	Electric current	Offline comparison with normal distribution of historical data	Anomaly detection
Online fault detection in PV systems [44]	2015	Irradiance, module temperature,	Predict max power of healthy panel and compare	Anomaly detection
What's Wrong with my Solar Panels: a Data-Driven Approach [45]	2015		Detection: Comparison with expected output Classification: comparison with coefficient of variation, trees, SVM, KNN	Anomaly detection & classification: partial shading, full cover
Expected output calculation based on inverse distance weighting and its application in anomaly detection of distributed photovoltaic power stations [46]	2020	Station power, grid voltage, grid current	Reverse distance weighting method	Anomaly detection & classification: open circuit, short circuit
Anomaly detection and predictive maintenance for photovoltaic systems [47]	2018	Irradiance, temperature, AC power	Compares ANN predicted output with measured output	Anomaly detection for predictive maintenance
Shading prediction, fault detection, and consensus estimation for solar array control [26]	2018	Current, voltage	Clustering through Expectation Maximization	Anomaly detection & classification: arc faults, ground faults

3 Proposed Design

The design shown here is based on the study presented in [13] which evaluated the feasibility of using low-cost IoT edge devices and long-range low-power wireless networks to facilitate the real-time monitoring of large-scale and remote solar farms. As shown in Fig. 1, each solar module in a string can be equipped with a low-cost microcontroller such as ESP32 [51] which can interface with current, voltage, and surface temperature sensors in order to observe the state of the module. Module observations can be sent over a local WiFi network to a gateway which then forwards all readings to a datacenter over a long-range network such as LoRaWAN [52]. Within the farm, Message Queueing Telemetry Transport (MQTT) [53] is used by the devices to send information from module observers to the RPi gateway. A lightweight MQTT broker such as Mosquitto [54] can be hosted on the RPi, enabling it to receive observations from any module that is added to the system in real-time and with little configuration overhead.

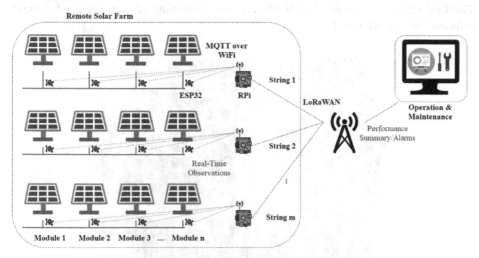

Fig. 1. Proposed edge architecture

At the datacenter, information can be processed and stored. However, as discussed earlier, sending observations from all modules in real-time generates large amounts of data which exponentially increases the network bandwidth requirements. Delegating all data processing to datacenters also significantly increases the cost of running and maintaining the datacenters and creates a single point of failure. Alternatively, utilizing an edge computer such as the Raspberry Pi (RPi) [55] as a gateway for each string makes it possible to pre-process and analyze observations from the modules locally. Not only is the RPi capable of reading and processing data from several module observers in a string, but the edge computer is able to run deep learning algorithms to predict performance based on modules' context and detect anomalies in performance. Furthermore, separate neural network models can be created for each module and trained to its own unique characteristics to be used to generate custom reports and detect anomalies that are specific to its profile.

4 Evaluation

4.1 Data Collection

Information describing the performance of two modules as well as their context was collected over the period of three months. While one of the modules was cleaned on weekly basis, the other module was left to experience soiling conditions. The two modules at the end of the testing period are shown in Fig. 2. The goal was to experiment with and compare anomaly detection in the case of clean modules as opposed to modules under soiling conditions. Hourly maximum power measurements were recorded using the IV tracing system described in [56]. Additionally, solar irradiance, and module temperature were also observed. The number of days since the beginning of the experiment was also used as a variable as it referred to the period of time for which the dusty panel has not been cleaned. This was used as a variable to roughly express the level of dust on the surface of the panel. The dataset was cleaned for invalid readings due to hardware faults. The final dataset consisted of 3308 observations containing performance and context information for each panel.

Fig. 2. The dusty and clean solar panels at the end of the testing period

4.2 Model Architecture

Observations collected over the period of the experiment were used to train a simple regression neural network that predicts the output of a remote solar panel under soiling conditions using the panel's context and a reference clean panel. This is because while real-time power can be measured in a remote solar farm, a single panel's performance is dependent on panels configuration in a string or an array. Alternatively, a better predictor of how much power a panel is able to produce in a given context is obtained through performing IV tracing [57], where voltage sweep is applied to panel starting from short-circuit to open-circuit in order to obtain short-circuit current, open-circuit voltage, as well as maximum power point and its corresponding voltage and current values. However, IV tracing requires disconnecting the panel from the rest of the array while tracing is performed. Such process is unfeasible in real-world operational conditions. Alternatively, the model built here aims to enable prediction of maximum power point using only maximum power from a reference clean model and the difference in context between the two panels. This relationship has been previously explored and a similar model was built in [58] (shown in Fig. 3). The same model can be used for anomaly detection by recognizing deviation from expected behavior using operational output power of a panel. The model can be trained to predict expected operational output of a remote solar panel based on its context and a reference panel. Since operational output of the remote panel can be measured in a real-world setting, comparing predicted output and observed output provides means to detect anomalous behaviors in real-time.

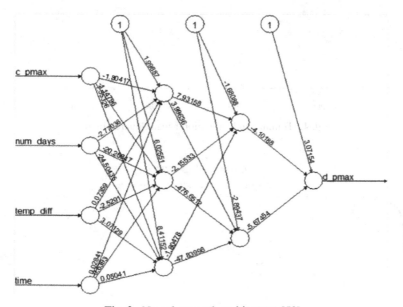

Fig. 3. Neural network architecture [58]

The model was first trained on the RPi using 80–20 training-validation split, with mean squared error (mse) and coefficient of determination (r^2) as training metrics. The formulas for mse and r^2 are shown in Eqs. 1 and 2.

$$mse = \frac{1}{n} \sum_{i=1}^{n} \left(Y_i - \hat{Y}_i \right)^2 \tag{1}$$

$$r^2 = \frac{\sum_i e_i^2}{\sum_i (y_i - \bar{y})^2} \tag{2}$$

The result of training the model for 1000 epochs is shown in Fig. 4 and Fig. 5. Once the model has been trained, an inference model was created to run on the RPi for real-time maximum power prediction. A regular Tensorflow model and a TFlite model were created to be implemented on the RPi.

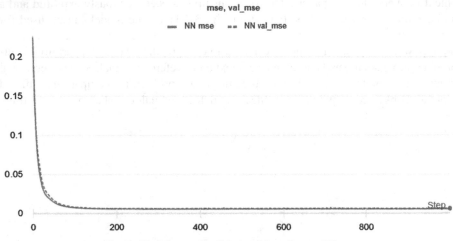

Fig. 4. Training and validation Mean Squared Error

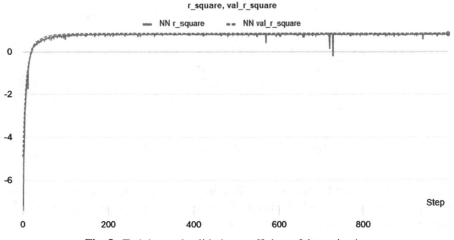

Fig. 5. Training and validation coefficient of determination

4.3 Inference Model Performance Evaluation

Experimental Setup. While the model performed well in terms of power prediction, the feasibility of running it on a RPi gateway in a solar farm depends on the amount of resources required by the RPi, as well as the number of panels that a single RPi can monitor and analyze. An experiment was designed to test the performance of the RPi and the required resources for running the algorithm as the number of panels increases. The experimental setup is shown in Fig. 6.

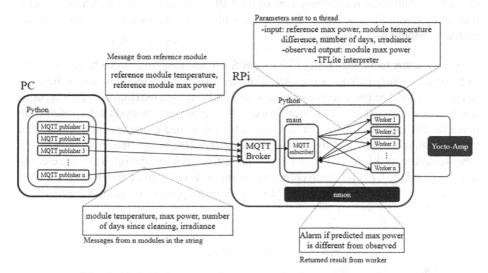

Fig. 6. Model inference performance evaluation experimental setup

As shown in Fig. 6, a python script running on a PC was used to simulate panels publishing real-time observation via MQTT over WiFi. A python script running on the RPi implements an MQTT subscriber which receives all observations from panels in its string. When an observation is received, the script uses information from the panel as well as a reference panel to combine the four inputs to the model which are the irradiance, number of days since the remote panel has been cleaned, difference in the two panels' surface temperatures, and the power output of the clean panel. The script launces a thread which uses the Tensorflow [59] model or TFLite [60] interpreter to predict the output of the remote panel and compare it with measure output. The thread then returns with an error code if deviation is detected. The error code can then be published to trigger appropriate action. A Yocto-Amp [61] is used to measure the current consumption of the RPi under a controlled voltage value of 5.0 V, while nmon [62] is used to monitor the RPi's internal resources such as CPU utilization. The number of clients, or modules in one string, was varied in power of 2 starting from 1 client, all the way to 512 clients, when possible. Each panel published at a frequency of 1 message/minute.

Experimental Results. Power consumption values and CPU% utilization while the RPi was running the inference model using TF and TFLite are shown in Fig. 7 and Fig. 8. As expected, there is a significant difference between running the inference by loading the TF model as opposed to using a TFLite version of the model. Furthermore, the TF model is only usable for up to 256 clients, at which point the system's resources including CPU and active memory get depleted, causing it to crash. A closer look into the RPI CPU utilization while serving one module as opposed to serving 16 modules is shown in Fig. 9 and Fig. 10. The cycles seen in the graph correspond to the publishing cycle of 1 batch of messages every minute. As shown in Fig. 10, almost 100% of the CPU is utilized most of the time. Furthermore, the busy state of the CPU extends for the full minute, causing it to overlap with the new batch of messages, which then causes a huge overload to the system's resources.

On the other hand, using a TFLite model for inference proves to be highly feasible as it consumes very little resources, where under 35 Wh are required to power the edge device for 12 h. The power consumption was calculated for a maximum of 12 h because that is the estimated max of sun hours in a day. As performing analysis during nighttime is not useful, the edge device can be turned off or switched to lower-power mode. The CPU utilization is also less than 40%, allowing the RPi enough free resources to run other reliability tasks. As shown in Fig. 11, the active cycles of the inference are cleanly separated and the CPU is able to complete the analysis task early enough so that it does not overlap with the following batch of messages, as opposed to the case with using a TF model.

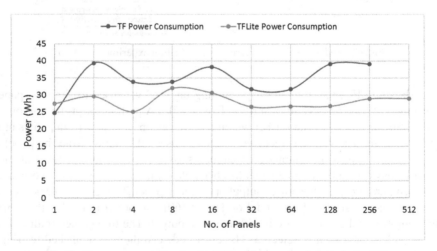

Fig. 7. Power consumption by the RPi while running inference for 12 h

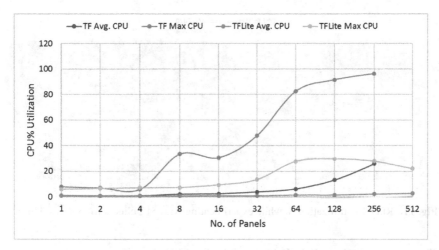

Fig. 8. CPU% utilization of the RPi while running inference

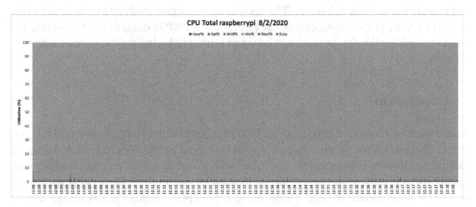

Fig. 9. RPi CPU utilization % while experimenting with 1 client for 5 min - TF

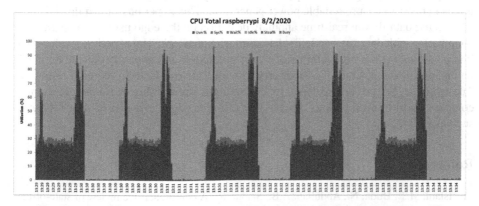

Fig. 10. RPi CPU utilization % while experimenting with 256 clients for 5 min – TF

Fig. 11. RPi CPU utilization % while experimenting with 512 clients for 5 min – TFLite

The experimental results indicate that it is possible to use a low-cost edge computing device such as the RPi to perform real-time analytics within local solar farms and detect and react to anomalous behaviors. The design can be further evolved by running TFLite models on more constrained, cheaper devices such as ESP32 devices for monitoring the modules, making the design more modular and further reducing the data communication overhead.

5   Conclusion

Real-time solar monitoring and analysis holds the key to reliable and secure grid integration. It also pushes for the possibility for solar energy to completely replace fossil-based fuels it the future. However, one key issue with solar power is its intermittency and sensitivity to volatile environment elements such as shading and heat. Solar panels are also prone to performance degradation due to natural phenomena such as soiling as well as physical withering in harsh environments. The ability to detect such anomalies using IoT and deep learning makes it possible to swiftly and appropriately react to various issues in order to ensure reliable power generation. This paper has shown that it is possible to use data-driven real-time anomaly detection on the edge using deep learning in conjunction with data from an IoT solar monitoring network. The experiments show that it is possible to run a high number of power prediction and anomaly detection models on an edge device such as the Raspberry Pi with little overhead in required resources. The work can be further developed by evaluating the possibility of running even more complex algorithms on various types of low-resource edge devices used in IoT systems such as ESP32.

References

1. Islam, M.T., Huda, N., Abdullah, A.B., Saidur, R.: A comprehensive review of state-of-the-art concentrating solar power (CSP) technologies: current status and research trends. Renew. Sustain. Energy Rev. **91**, 987–1018 (2018). https://doi.org/10.1016/j.rser.2018.04.097

2. Nuortimo, K., Härkönen, J., Karvonen, E.: Exploring the global media image of solar power. Renew. Sustain. Energy Rev. **81**, 2806–2811 (2018). https://doi.org/10.1016/j.rser. 2017.06.086
3. Renewable Capacity Statistics 2019. https://www.irena.org/publications/2019/Mar/Renewa ble-Capacity-Statistics-2019, Accessed 14 Oct 2019
4. Renewable Energy Market Analysis: GCC 2019. https://www.irena.org/publications/2019/ Jan/Renewable-Energy-Market-Analysis-GCC-2019, Accessed 25 Jan 2019
5. Treyer, K., Bauer, C.: The environmental footprint of UAE's electricity sector: combining life cycle assessment and scenario modeling. Renew. Sustain. Energy Rev. **55**, 1234–1247 (2016). https://doi.org/10.1016/j.rser.2015.04.016
6. Jamil, M., Ahmad, F., Jeon, Y.J.: Renewable energy technologies adopted by the UAE: prospects and challenges – a comprehensive overview. Renew. Sustain. Energy Rev. **55**, 1181–1194 (2016). https://doi.org/10.1016/j.rser.2015.05.087
7. Yang, L., Gao, X., Lv, F., Hui, X., Ma, L., Hou, X.: Study on the local climatic effects of large photovoltaic solar farms in desert areas. Sol. Energy **144**, 244–253 (2017). https://doi.org/10. 1016/j.solener.2017.01.015
8. Touati, F., Al-Hitmi, M., Bouchech, H.: Towards understanding the effects of climatic and environmental factors on solar PV performance in arid desert regions (Qatar) for various PV technologies. In: 2012 First International Conference on Renewable Energies and Vehicular Technology, pp. 78–83 (2012). https://doi.org/10.1109/REVET.2012.6195252.
9. Fouad, M.M., Shihata, L.A., Morgan, E.I.: An integrated review of factors influencing the perfomance of photovoltaic panels. Renew. Sustain. Energy Rev. **80**, 1499–1511 (2017). https://doi.org/10.1016/j.rser.2017.05.141
10. Pandey, A.K., Tyagi, V.V., Selvaraj, J.A., Rahim, N.A., Tyagi, S.K.: Recent advances in solar photovoltaic systems for emerging trends and advanced applications. Renew. Sustain. Energy Rev. **53**, 859–884 (2016). https://doi.org/10.1016/j.rser.2015.09.043
11. Rikos, E., Tselepis, S., Hoyer-Klick, C., Schroedter-Homscheidt, M.: Stability and power quality issues in microgrids under weather disturbances. IEEE J. Selected Top. Appl. Earth Obs. Remote Sens. **1**, 170–179 (2008). https://doi.org/10.1109/JSTARS.2008.2010557
12. Ahmed, M., Naser Mahmood, A., Hu, J.: A survey of network anomaly detection techniques. J. Netw. Comput. Appl. **60**, 19–31 (2016). https://doi.org/10.1016/j.jnca.2015.11.016
13. Shapsough, S., Zualkernan, I.: Designing an edge layer for smart management of large-scale and distributed solar farms. In: Kim, K.J., Kim, H.-Y. (eds.) Information Science and Applications. LNEE, vol. 621, pp. 651–661. Springer, Singapore (2020). https://doi.org/10. 1007/978-981-15-1465-4_64
14. Campbell, M.: World's largest solar project to provide record-low energy tar-iffs. https://www.euronews.com/living/2020/05/05/world-s-largest-solar-project-to-provide-record-low-energy-tariffs, Accessed 29 June 2020
15. Khan, W.Z., Ahmed, E., Hakak, S., Yaqoob, I., Ahmed, A.: Edge computing: a survey. Fut. Gener. Comput. Syst. **97**, 219–235 (2019). https://doi.org/10.1016/j.future.2019.02.050
16. Belhachat, F., Larbes, C.: A review of global maximum power point tracking techniques of photovoltaic system under partial shading conditions. Renew. Sustain. Energy Rev. **92**, 513–553 (2018). https://doi.org/10.1016/j.rser.2018.04.094
17. Das, S.K., Verma, D., Nema, S., Nema, R.K.: Shading mitigation techniques: state-of-the-art in photovoltaic applications. Renew. Sustain. Energy Rev. **78**, 369–390 (2017). https://doi. org/10.1016/j.rser.2017.04.093
18. Ramli, M.A.M., Twaha, S., Ishaque, K., Al-Turki, Y.A.: A review on maximum power point tracking for photovoltaic systems with and without shading conditions. Renew. Sustain. Energy Rev. **67**, 144–159 (2017). https://doi.org/10.1016/j.rser.2016.09.013

19. Said, Z., Arora, S., Bellos, E.: A review on performance and environmental effects of conventional and nanofluid-based thermal photovoltaics. Renew. Sustain. Energy Rev. **94**, 302–316 (2018). https://doi.org/10.1016/j.rser.2018.06.010

20. Andenæs, E., Jelle, B.P., Ramlo, K., Kolås, T., Selj, J., Foss, S.E.: The influence of snow and ice coverage on the energy generation from photovoltaic solar cells. Sol. Energy **159**, 318–328 (2018). https://doi.org/10.1016/j.solener.2017.10.078

21. Masdar City Solar Photovoltaic Plant. https://masdar.ae/en/MasdarCleanEnergy/Projects/MasdarCitySolarPhotovoltaicPlant, Accessed 27 May 2019

22. Crot, L.: Planning for sustainability in non-democratic polities: the case of Masdar City. Urban Stud. **50**, 2809–2825 (2013). https://doi.org/10.1177/0042098012474697

23. Nath, M., Singh, D.: A Review on Performance Improvement of Solar Photovoltaic using Various Cooling Methods (2019)

24. Al-Housani, M., Bicer, Y., Koç, M.: Experimental investigations on PV cleaning of large-scale solar power plants in desert climates: comparison of cleaning techniques for drone retrofitting. Energy Convers. Manag. **185**, 800–815 (2019). https://doi.org/10.1016/j.enconman.2019.01.058

25. Luque, E.G., Antonanzas-Torres, F., Escobar, R.: Effect of soiling in bifacial PV modules and cleaning schedule optimization. Energy Convers. Manag. **174**, 615–625 (2018). https://doi.org/10.1016/j.enconman.2018.08.065

26. Katoch, S., Muniraju, G., Rao, S., Spanias, A., Turaga, P., Tepedelenlioglu, C., Banavar, M., Srinivasan, D.: Shading prediction, fault detection, and consensus estimation for solar array control. In: 2018 IEEE Industrial Cyber-Physical Systems (ICPS), pp. 217–222 (2018). https://doi.org/10.1109/ICPHYS.2018.8387662

27. Shapsough, S., Dhaouadi, R., Zualkernan, I.: Using Linear regression and back propagation neural networks to predict performance of soiled PV modules. Procedia Comput. Sci. **155**, 463–470 (2019). https://doi.org/10.1016/j.procs.2019.08.065

28. Kim, K.A., Krein, P.T.: Reexamination of photovoltaic hot spotting to show inadequacy of the bypass diode. IEEE J. Photovoltaics **5**, 1435–1441 (2015). https://doi.org/10.1109/JPHOTOV.2015.2444091

29. Pillai, D.S., Blaabjerg, F., Rajasekar, N.: A comparative evaluation of advanced fault detection approaches for PV systems. IEEE J. Photovoltaics **9**, 513–527 (2019). https://doi.org/10.1109/JPHOTOV.2019.2892189

30. Guerriero, P., Daliento, S.: Toward a hot spot free PV module. IEEE J. Photovoltaics **9**, 796–802 (2019). https://doi.org/10.1109/JPHOTOV.2019.2894912

31. Manganiello, P., Balato, M., Vitelli, M.: A survey on mismatching and aging of PV modules: the closed loop. IEEE Trans. Ind. Electron. **62**, 7276–7286 (2015). https://doi.org/10.1109/TIE.2015.2418731

32. Niazi, K.A.K., Yang, Y., Sera, D.: Review of mismatch mitigation techniques for PV modules. IET Renew. Power Gener. **13**, 2035–2050 (2019). https://doi.org/10.1049/iet-rpg.2019.0153

33. Liu, G., Yu, W., Zhu, L.: Experiment-based supervised learning approach toward condition monitoring of PV array mismatch. Transm. Distrib. IET Gener. **13**, 1014–1024 (2019). https://doi.org/10.1049/iet-gtd.2018.5164

34. Azimi, I., Pahikkala, T., Rahmani, A.M., Niela-Vilén, H., Axelin, A., Liljeberg, P.: Missing data resilient decision-making for healthcare IoT through personalization: a case study on maternal health. Fut. Gener. Comput. Syst. **96**, 297–308 (2019). https://doi.org/10.1016/j.future.2019.02.015

35. Mukhopadhyay, S.C., Suryadevara, N.K.: Internet of Things: challenges and opportunities. In: Mukhopadhyay, S.C. (ed.) Internet of Things. SSMI, vol. 9, pp. 1–17. Springer, Cham (2014). https://doi.org/10.1007/978-3-319-04223-7_1

36. Chakraborty, T., Nambi, A.U., Chandra, R., Sharma, R., Swaminathan, M., Kapetanovic, Z.: Sensor identification and fault detection in IoT systems. In: Proceedings of the 16th ACM Conference on Embedded Networked Sensor Systems, pp. 375–376. Association for Computing Machinery, Shenzhen (2018). https://doi.org/10.1145/3274783.3275190

37. Bouaichi, A., et al.: In-situ evaluation of the early PV module degradation of various technologies under harsh climatic conditions: the case of Morocco. Renew. Energy **143**, 1500–1518 (2019). https://doi.org/10.1016/j.renene.2019.05.091

38. Kimani, K., Oduol, V., Langat, K.: Cyber security challenges for IoT-based smart grid networks. Int. J. Crit. Infrastruct. Prot. **25**, 36–49 (2019). https://doi.org/10.1016/j.ijcip.2019.01.001

39. Otuoze, A.O., Mustafa, M.W., Larik, R.M.: Smart grids security challenges: classification by sources of threats. J. Electric. Syst. Inf. Technol. **5**, 468–483 (2018). https://doi.org/10.1016/j.jesit.2018.01.001

40. Shapsough, S., Qatan, F., Aburukba, R., Aloul, F., Ali, A.R.A.: Smart grid cyber security: Challenges and solutions. In: 2015 International Conference on Smart Grid and Clean Energy Technologies (ICSGCE), pp. 170–175 (2015). https://doi.org/10.1109/ICSGCE.2015.7454291.

41. Mohammadpourfard, M., Sami, A., Weng, Y.: Identification of false data injection attacks with considering the impact of wind generation and topology reconfigurations. IEEE Trans. Sustain. Energy **9**, 1349–1364 (2018). https://doi.org/10.1109/TSTE.2017.2782090

42. Zhao, Y., Liu, Q., Li, D., Kang, D., Lv, Q., Shang, L.: Hierarchical anomaly detection and multimodal classification in large-scale photovoltaic systems. IEEE Trans. Sustain. Energy **10**, 1351–1361 (2019). https://doi.org/10.1109/TSTE.2018.2867009

43. Akiyama, Y., Kasai, Y., Iwata, M., Takahashi, E., Sato, F., Murakawa, M.: anomaly detection of solar power generation systems based on the normalization of the amount of generated electricity. In: 2015 IEEE 29th International Conference on Advanced Information Networking and Applications, pp. 294–301 (2015). https://doi.org/10.1109/AINA.2015.198.

44. Platon, R., Martel, J., Woodruff, N., Chau, T.Y.: Online fault detection in PV systems. IEEE Trans. Sustain. Energy **6**, 1200–1207 (2015). https://doi.org/10.1109/TSTE.2015.2421447

45. Gao, P.X., Golab, L., Keshav, S.: What's wrong with my solar panels: a data-driven approach. In: EDBT/ICDT Workshops (2015)

46. Shi, Y., et al.: Expected output calculation based on inverse distance weighting and its application in anomaly detection of distributed photovoltaic power stations. J. Clean. Prod. **253**, 119965 (2020). https://doi.org/10.1016/j.jclepro.2020.119965

47. De Benedetti, M., Leonardi, F., Messina, F., Santoro, C., Vasilakos, A.: Anomaly detection and predictive maintenance for photovoltaic systems. Neurocomputing **310**, 59–68 (2018). https://doi.org/10.1016/j.neucom.2018.05.017

48. Magalhães, P.M.L.P., Martins, J.F.A., Joyce, A.L.M.: Comparative analysis of overheating prevention and stagnation handling measures for photovoltaic-Thermal (PV-T) systems. Energy Procedia **91**, 346–355 (2016). https://doi.org/10.1016/j.egypro.2016.06.282

49. Caballero, J.A., Fernández, E.F., Theristis, M., Almonacid, F., Nofuentes, G.: Spectral corrections based on air mass, aerosol optical depth, and precipitable water for PV performance modeling. IEEE J. Photovoltaics. **8**, 552–558 (2018). https://doi.org/10.1109/JPHOTOV.2017.2787019

50. Balarabe, M.A., Tan, F., Abdullah, K., Nawawi, M.N.M.: Temporal-spatial variability of seasonal aerosol index and visibility—aA case study of Nigeria. In: 2015 International Conference on Space Science and Communication (IconSpace), pp. 459–464 (2015) https://doi.org/10.1109/IconSpace.2015.7283769.

51. ESP32 Overview | Espressif Systems. https://www.espressif.com/en/products/hardware/esp32/overview, Accessed 20 Oct 2018

52. What is the LoRaWAN® Specification? https://lora-alliance.org/about-lorawan
53. Banks, A., Gupta, R.: MQTT Version 3.1. 1. OASIS Standard (2014)
54. Mosquitto MQTT Server
55. Raspberry Pi - Teach, Learn, and Make with Raspberry Pi. https://www.raspberrypi.org/, Accessed 19 May 2017
56. Shapsough, S., Takrouri, M., Dhaouadi, R., Zualkernan, I.: An IoT-based remote IV tracing system for analysis of city-wide solar power facilities. Sustain. Cities Soc. **57**, 102041 (2020). https://doi.org/10.1016/j.scs.2020.102041
57. Muñoz, J., Lorenzo, E.: Capacitive load based on IGBTs for on site characterization of PV arrays. Sol. Energy **80**, 1489–1497 (2006). https://doi.org/10.1016/j.solener.2005.09.013
58. Shapsough, S., Dhaouadi, R., Zualkernan, I., Takrouri, M.: Power prediction via module temperature for solar modules under soiling conditions. In: Deng, D.-J., Pang, A.-C., Lin, C.-C. (eds.) SGIoT 2019. LNICSSITE, vol. 324, pp. 85–95. Springer, Cham (2020). https://doi.org/10.1007/978-3-030-49610-4_7
59. TensorFlow. https://www.tensorflow.org/, Accessed 20 July 2020
60. TensorFlow Lite | ML for Mobile and Edge Devices. https://www.tensorflow.org/lite, Accessed 20 July 2020
61. Yocto-Amp - Tiny isolated USB ammeter (AC/DC). https://www.yoctopuce.com/EN/products/usb-electrical-sensors/yocto-amp, Accessed 27 Mar 2017
62. nmon for Linux. https://nmon.sourceforge.net/pmwiki.php, Accessed 28 Mar 2017

Fair Resource Reusing for D2D Communication Based on Reinforcement Learning

Fang-Chang Kuo[1], Hwang-Cheng Wang[1], Jia-Hao Xu[1], and Chih-Cheng Tseng[2](✉)

[1] Department of Electronic Engineering, National Ilan University, Yilan, Taiwan
[2] Department of Electrical Engineering, National Ilan University, Yilan, Taiwan
tsengcc@niu.edu.tw

Abstract. Device-to-device (D2D) communications can improve the overall network performance, including low latency, high data rates, and system capability for the fifth generation (5G) wireless networks. The system capability can even be improved by reusing resource between D2D user equipment (DUE) and cellular user equipment (CUE) without bring harmful interference to the CUEs. A D2D resource allocation method is expected to have the characteristic that one CUE can be allocated with variable number of resource blocks (RBs), and the RBs can be reused by more than one CUE. In this study, Multi-Player Multi-Armed Bandit (MPMAB) reinforcement learning method is employed to model such problem by establishing preference matrix. A fair resource allocation method is then proposed to achieve fairness, prevent wasting resource, and alleviate starvation. This method even has better throughput if there are not too many D2D pairs.

Keywords: Device-to-Device (D2D) · Resource allocation · Reinforcement learning · Multi-Player Multi-Armed Bandit (MPMAB) · Dynamic resource allocation

1 Introduction

In order to meet mobile users' soaring demands, 5G wireless communication is projected to provide enormous data rates, extremely low power consumption and delay [2–4]. Due to the scarcity of available spectrum resources, D2D communication was proposed as a new paradigm to facilitate direct communication between two devices which are in each other's proximity. The direct communication can process without the intervention of an evolved Base Station (eNB) after the session is established, and these two devices are called a D2D pair. D2D communications can improve the overall network performance, including low latency, high data rates, and system capability [6, 7]. Several direct communication modes are defined in [8], including unicast, relay, groupcast, and broadcast. Moreover, the Third Generation Partnership Project (3GPP) is targeting the availability of D2D communication to become a competitive broadband communication technology for public safety networks used by first responders [8–10].

Y.-B. Lin and D.-J. Deng (Eds.): SGIoT 2020, LNICST 354, pp. 45–53, 2021.
https://doi.org/10.1007/978-3-030-69514-9_5

1.1 Related Work

The most charming aspect of D2D communication is that it can promote the network capacity by spectrum reusing between D2D user equipment (DUE) and cellular user equipment (CUE) [11]. The resource reusing is based on the criteria that it would not bring harmful interference to the CUEs [12].

From the prospect of system operator, in general, we may want to maximize the overall network throughput by allocating sufficient resource blocks (RBs) to some UEs with better channel conditions. On the other hand, we may expect the RBs can be scheduled fairly so that RBs would not be wasted by UEs with better channel conditions, and that UEs with poor channel conditions would not be starved.

In [5], proportional fairness (PF) algorithm is applied on D2D resource allocation. However, the authors did not consider the data rate requirements of UEs. Here, in this paper, we will take the UEs' requirements into consideration. In [5], an interference-degree-based greedy heuristic resource allocation algorithm, which is called SDF_GRA here for convenience, is explored to maximize the number of admitted D2D pairs for each CUE. SDF_GRA utilizes Conflict Graph (CG) [13] to model network interferences between devices. In Sect. 5 we will compare the performance between SDF_GRA and our proposed scheme, which is called proposed_with_AAG here in this paper.

In recent years, machine learning is very popular. Recently, some researchers tried to apply machine learning on D2D resource allocation problems [14–16]. In [17], the D2D resource allocation problem was investigated by applying a kind of Reinforcement Learning method, namely Multi-player Multi-Armed Bandit (MPMAB). This paper indicated that MPMAB algorithm is suitable for improving the capacity of D2D communication.

Here in this paper, we also apply MPMAB to deal with the D2D resource allocation problem, and propose a scheme where the eNB tries best to fairly allocate RBs to guarantee the data rate requirements of D2D pairs.

1.2 Organization of This Paper

The rest of this paper is organized as follows. Section 2 describes the system model of D2D communication underlaying 5G networks. The evaluation of SINR and capacity is also described. Section 3 describes MPMAB learning algorithm, which would be employed to learn the preference of D2D pairs for reusing resource blocks with CUEs. Section 4 explains the principle of the proposed scheme. The performance of the proposed scheme is evaluated by being compared with SDF_GRA scheme in Sect. 5. Finally, we conclude the main results in Sect. 6.

2 System Model

This section describes the model under consideration, the used symbols, the used formulas for calculating SINR and link capacity.

The system model under consideration is that an eNB serving some CUEs and D2D pairs, as illustrated in Fig. 1. Each D2D pair has a dedicated transmitter device and a receiver device. The eNB knows the locations of all CUEs and DUEs and tries to allocate multiple D2D pairs to reuse the uplink RBs of each CUE based on underlay mode. The symbols are as follows.

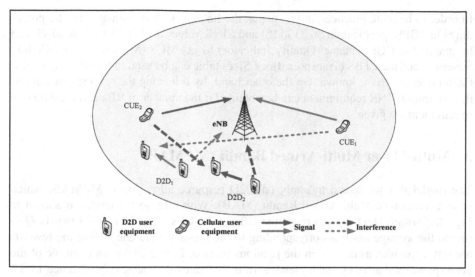

Fig. 1. System model

D_i: the i-th D2D pair with predetermined transmitting DUE and receiving DUE
$D_{i,\text{Tx}}$: the transmitting DUE of D_i
$D_{i,\text{Rx}}$: the receiving DUE of D_i
C_m: the m-th CUE
$G_{C_m,\text{B}}$: the channel gain from C_m to eNB
$G_{D_i,\text{B}}$: the channel gain from $D_{i,\text{Tx}}$ to eNB
G_{D_i,D_i}: the channel gain from $D_{i,\text{Tx}}$ to $D_{i,\text{Rx}}$ of D2D pair i
G_{D_i,D_j}: the channel gain from $D_{i,\text{Tx}}$ of pair i to $D_{j,\text{Rx}}$ of another pair j
G_{C_m,D_i}: the channel gain from C_m to $D_{i,\text{Rx}}$
P_{C_m}: the transmission power of C_m
P_{D_i}: the transmission power of the transmitting DUE of D_i

2.1 Evaluation of SINR and Capacity

To assess the performance of the system, we have to calculate two kinds of SINR. The first kind is that from a CUE C_m to the eNB and is expressed as

$$SINR_{C_m} = \frac{P_{C_m} G_{C_m,\text{B}}}{\sum\limits_{i \in U_m} \left(P_{D_i} G_{D_i,\text{B}} \right) + \sigma^2} \tag{1}$$

where σ^2 is the noise power and U_m is the set of indices of D2D pairs that reuse the RBs allocated to C_m. The second kind is that from the transmitting DUE of D_i to the receiving DUE of D_i and is expressed as

$$SINR_{D_i} = \frac{P_{D_i} G_{D_i,D_i}}{P_{C_m} G_{C_m,D_i} + \sum\limits_{j \in U_m, j \neq i} \left(P_{D_j} G_{D_j,D_i} \right) + \sigma^2} \tag{2}$$

In order to be more practical, in this paper, the link capacity is evaluated by the procedures in 3GPP specification 36.213 [18] and SINR values in [19]. Thus, link SINR can be mapped to CQI (Channel Quality Indicator) to get MCS (Modulation and Coding Scheme), and then TBS (Transport Block Size) table can be used to find the capacity if the number of RBs is known. On the other hand, by following the reverse procedures, the minimum SINR requirement can be obtained if the number of RBs and the data rate requirement are given.

3   Multi-Player Multi-Armed Bandit (MPMAB)

The model that we intend to apply on D2D resource allocation is MPMAB, which is an extension of Multi-Armed Bandit (MAB). With refer to the model as shown in Fig. 2(a) with 6 D2D pairs to reuse the RBs of 3 CUEs, there is a 6×3 matrix Q to record the average rewards corresponding to the reusing preference. Here the rewards are link capacities as defined in the previous section. Figure 2(b) is an example of the corresponding matrix Q. Each element in q_i indicates the capacity/preference to the corresponding CUE. The matrix is updated after each trial until the learning process has converged. The converged criteria is similar to that presented in [1].

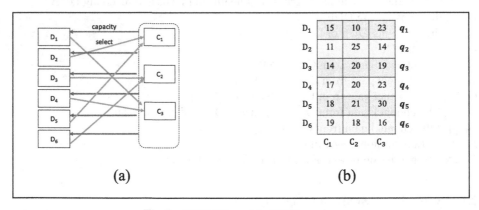

Fig. 2. MPMAB model of D2D reusing

4   Proposed Fair Resource Allocation Scheme

After the learning phase, the eNB will allocate RBs based on the final result of matrix Q. Most of the papers concerning resource allocation employs greedy strategy so as to maximize the system capacity [5]. In this paper, we propose another criteria for allocating RBs: For the D2D pairs that are admitted to be served, the eNB tries best to fairly allocate RBs independent of their SINR values.

In order to reach this goal, we propose applying Allocate As Granted (AAG) concept presented in [20], where eNB tries to fairly allocate enough RBs to all CUEs that have been granted with declared data rate requirements. For a data rate $R_{D_i}^{grant}$ in bits per second (bps), it may be converted to the number of bits $B_{D_i}^{grant}$ to be transmitted per Transmission Time Interval (TTI, 1 ms). Based on Exponentially Weighted Moving Average (EWMA) [21], we define the average allocated capacity $\overline{B}_{D_i}(t)$ corresponding to D_i at the tth TTI as

$$\overline{B}_{D_i}(t) = (1 - \lambda_{D_i}) \cdot \overline{B}_{D_i}(t - 1) + \lambda_{D_i} \cdot B_{D_i}(t), \tag{3}$$

where $B_{D_i}(t)$ is the capacity (in bits per TTI) provided by the RBs allocated to D_i at the tth TTI. The coefficient λ_{D_i} is a constant smoothing factor between 0 and 1. Our objective is that eNB tries best to fairly allocate enough RBs for D2D pairs to make $\overline{B}_{D_i}(t) \geq B_{D_i}^{grant}$. Before allocating RBs for the served D2D pairs at a general TTI, the eNB calculates the priority of each D2D pair as

$$p_i(t) = \frac{B_{D_i}^{grant} - \overline{B}_{D_i}(t - 1)}{B_{D_i}^{grant}}. \tag{4}$$

The larger the metric is, the higher the priority for the D2D pair to be allocated with RBs.

The procedure of the allocating process at the tth TTI is shown in Fig. 3 and is explained as follows.

i.   Find the D2D pair with the highest priority metric.
ii. Checks whether this D2D pair can reuse the RBs with its most favorite CUE.
iii. The constraint for the reusing is that the CUE and the D2D pairs reusing the same RBs can respectively meet their SINR requirements. If fail, then reset the preference order to zero and try the next most favorite CUE.
iv. If yes, reset the corresponding priority metric to lowest value so that the eNB can try to allocate for the D2D pair with the next highest priority metric.

5   Performance Evaluation

In this section, we are going to compare the performance of GRA_SDF with that of our proposed scheme, which is indicated as proposed_with_AAG.

5.1   Simulation Environment

The simulation environment is an eNB serving some CUEs and D2D pairs, which are randomly distributed in the coverage of radius 500 m. According to [1], the minimum distance between DUE and eNB is set to 35 m. Both the learning process and the RB allocating process are executed at the eNB. Some assumptions are listed below.

i.   The uplink resource of CUEs is allocated based on semi-persistent scheduling [18], rather than dynamic scheduling.

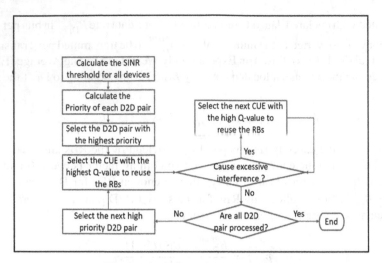

Fig. 3. Flow chart of AAG criterion

  ii. Both the CUEs and D2D pairs can declare data rate requirements to the eNB.
 iii. For simplicity, every CUE is allocated with the same number of RBs.
 iv. Each CUE can share the allocated RBs with multiple D2D pairs.
  v. Each D2D pair can reuse the RBs of only one CUE.
 vi. If a D2D pair is to reuse the RBs allocated to a specific CUE, it reuses all of the RBs.
vii. Each CUE is allocated with 2 RBs. As a result, by checking the TBS table in [18], the maximum data rate of each CUE is 1.48 Mbps, which is also set as the CUEs' data rate requirement that must be satisfied.

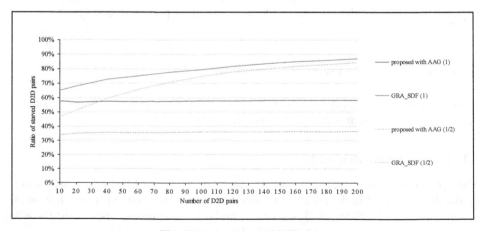

Fig. 4. Ratio of starved D2D pairs

5.2 Starved D2D Pairs

Before checking capacity, let us observe the ratio of starved D2D pairs as shown in Fig. 4. A D2D pair is regarded as starved if it gets no RBs during a simulation run.

In a whole, there are always D2D pairs that get no resource to reuse and become starved because they are located at bad positions. For a D2D pair to get higher data rate, higher SINR is required. Then, less D2D pairs can join the reusing, and more D2D pairs starve as a result. It is predictable that GRA_SDF results in higher ratios when there are more D2D pairs in the coverage. While, by introducing MPMAB to learn preference and AAG concept to fairly allocate RBs to all D2D pairs, the ratios are lower and almost constant.

It seems that it is not encouraged to have too many D2D pairs in the coverage for the GRA_SDF scheme. However, Fig. 5, which shows the numbers of non-starved D2D pairs corresponding to Fig. 4, reveals that the more the D2D pairs are in the coverage, the more are allocated to reuse RBs with CUEs. Because proposed_with_AAG tries to allocate for every D2D pair that meets SINR requirement, the numbers of allocated D2D pairs exhibit a linear increase with the numbers of D2D pairs.

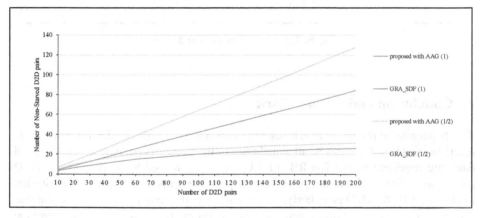

Fig. 5. Numbers of non-starved D2D pairs

5.3 Fairness of Satisfaction Degree

In the next, we are going to evaluate fairness of satisfactory based on Jain's fairness measure

$$\text{Fairness of satisfactory} = \frac{\left(\sum_{i=1}^{N} x_i\right)^2}{N \cdot \sum_{i=1}^{N} x_i^2}, \tag{5}$$

where N is the number of D2D pairs, x_i is the satisfactory degree corresponding to D2D pair i. Figure 6 shows the fairness of satisfactory. Note that all of the D2D pairs, including the starved D2D pairs, are counted in. As a result, it's not easy to reach the ideal value, one. This figure reveals that lower data rate requirements result in higher fairness. For each of the data rate requirements, fairness values of SDF_GRA decrease dramatically with the numbers of D2D pairs, while proposed_with_AAG keeps high and quite stable. From this point of view, the proposed_with_AAG also performs very well.

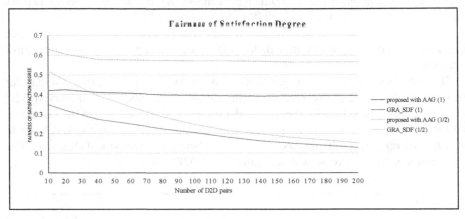

Fig. 6. Fairness of satisfaction degree

6   Conclusion and Future Work

This paper aims at proposing a D2D resource allocation method with the following characteristics: (i) One CUE can be allocated with multiple RBs depending on the declared data rate requirement. (ii) The RBs of a CUE can be reused by more than one D2D pair so as to effectively utilize the radio resource. We propose to apply AAG criterion to allocate RBs for D2D pairs fairly, rather than greedily. Simulation results reveal that this method can achieve fairness and alleviate starvation. In the future, we may combine power control to the proposed scheme.

References

1. 3GPP. TR 36.843 Study on LTE device to device proximity services; Radio aspects (2014)
2. Osseiran, A., et al.: The foundation of the mobile and wireless communications system for 2020 and beyond: Challenges, enablers and technology solutions. In: 2013 IEEE 77th Vehicular Technology Conference (VTC Spring), pp. 1–5. IEEE (2013)
3. Ericsson, L.: More than 50 billion connected devices. White Paper **14**(1), 124 (2011)
4. Agiwal, M., Roy, A., Saxena, N.: Next generation 5G wireless networks: aA comprehensive survey. IEEE Commun. Surv. Tutor. **18**(3), 1617–1655 (2016)
5. Sun, H., Sheng, M., Wang, X., Zhang, Y., Liu, J., Wang, K.: Resource allocation for maximizing the device-to-device communications underlaying LTE-Advanced networks. In: 2013 IEEE/CIC International Conference on Communications in China-Workshops (CIC/ICCC), pp. 60–64. IEEE (2013)

6. Osseiran, A., et al.: Scenarios for 5G mobile and wireless communications: the vision of the METIS project. IEEE Commun. Mag. **52**(5), 26–35 (2014)
7. Mustafa, H.A.U., Imran, M.A., Shakir, M.Z., Imran, A., Tafazolli, R.: Separation framework: an enabler for cooperative and D2D communication for future 5G networks. IEEE Commun. Surv. Tutor. **18**(1), 419–445 (2015)
8. Asadi, A., Wang, Q., Mancuso, V.: A survey on device-to-device communication in cellular networks. IEEE Commun. Surv. Tutor. **16**(4), 1801–1819 (2014)
9. Doumi, T., et al.: LTE for public safety networks. IEEE Commun. Mag. **51**(2), 106–112 (2013)
10. Lin, X., Andrews, J.G., Ghosh, A., Ratasuk, R.: An overview of 3GPP device-to-device proximity services. IEEE Commun. Mag. **52**(4), 40–48 (2014)
11. Hakola, S., Chen, T., Lehtomäki, J., Koskela, T.: Device-to-device (D2D) communication in cellular network-performance analysis of optimum and practical communication mode selection. In: 2010 IEEE Wireless Communication and Networking Conference, pp. 1–6. IEEE (2010)
12. Peng, T., Lu, Q., Wang, H., Xu, S., Wang, W.: Interference avoidance mechanisms in the hybrid cellular and device-to-device systems. In: 2009 IEEE 20th International Symposium on Personal, Indoor and Mobile Radio Communications, pp. 617–621. IEEE (2009)
13. Sutton, R.S., Barto, A.G.: Reinforcement learning: An introduction. The MIT Press, Cambridge (2011)
14. Luo, Y., Shi, Z., Zhou, X., Liu, Q., Yi, Q.: Dynamic resource allocations based on q-learning for D2D communication in cellular networks. In: 2014 11th International Computer Conference on Wavelet Actiev Media Technology and Information Processing (ICCWAMTIP), pp. 385–388. IEEE (2014)
15. Zhang, Y., Wang, C.-Y., Wei, H.-Y.: Incentive compatible overlay D2D system: a group-based framework without CQI feedback. IEEE Trans. Mob. Comput. **17**(9), 2069–2086 (2018)
16. Ren, H., Jiang, F., Wang, H.: Resource allocation based on clustering algorithm for hybrid device-to-device networks. In: 2017 9th International Conference on Wireless Communications and Signal Processing (WCSP), pp. 1–6. IEEE (2017)
17. Neogi, A., Chaporkar, P., Karandikar, A.: Multi-Player Multi-Armed Bandit Based Resource Allocation for D2D Communications. arXiv preprint arXiv:1812.11837 (2018)
18. 3GPP. TS 36.213: Evolved Universal Terrestrial Radio Access (E-UTRA); Physical layer procedures (2016)
19. Ghosh, A., Ratasuk, R.: Essentials of LTE and LTE-A. Cambridge University Press, Cambridge (2011)
20. Kuo, F.-C., Ting, K.-C., Wang, H.-C., Tseng, C.-C.: On demand resource allocation for LTE uplink transmission based on logical channel groups. Mobile Netw. Appl. **22**(5), 868–879 (2017). https://doi.org/10.1007/s11036-017-0860-7
21. Lucas, J.M., Saccucci, M.S.: Exponentially weighted moving average control schemes: properties and enhancements. Technometrics **32**(1), 1–12 (1990)
22. Jain, D.M.C.R., Hawe, W.R.: A quantitative measure of fairness and discrimination for resource allocation in shared computer systems. Digital Equipment Corporation (DEC) Research Report TR-301 (1984)

Communication Security

An Industrial-Grade API Secure Access Gateway in the Cloud-Edge Integration Scenario

Sai Liu[1]([⊠]), Zhen-Jiang Zhang[2], Yong Cui[3], and Yang Zhang[1]

[1] Department of Electronic and Information Engineering, Key Laboratory of Communication and Information Systems, Beijing Municipal Commission of Education, Beijing Jiaotong University, Beijing 100044, China
516742786@qq.com, zhang.yang@bjtu.edu.cn
[2] Department of Software Engineering, Key Laboratory of Communication and Information Systems, Municipal Commission of Education, Beijing Jiaotong University, Beijing 100044, China
zhangzhenjiang@bjtu.edu.cn
[3] Thunisoft Information Technology Co. Ltd., Beijing 100044, China
cuiyong@thunisoft.com

Abstract. In recent years, the Internet of Things technology has developed rapidly. Due to the large number of devices at the edge, the wide distribution range, and the complex environment, cloud computing and edge computing failed to fully consider security risks at the beginning of the combination, and traditional protection methods can no longer fully meet their security requirements. The establishment of a new cloud-edge integrated security system is of great significance for ensuring the data and privacy of Internet users. This article first investigates the current status of traditional network security and analyzes its inherent shortcomings, and analyzes the organizational structure and main advantages of the zero-trust network. Designed a security certification system that meets the needs of cloud-edge integrated applications. The API security access gateway part of the system is designed and implemented. According to the type of client access request, it is equipped with multiple authentication methods. It also realized the functions of reverse proxy, load balancing, flow control, log audit, analysis and monitoring of microservices, and finally developed a supporting UI management tool based on Vue. This design provides a new set of secure access solutions for clients and microservices, which has produced good industrial benefits. It is of great significance to promote the development and popularization of cloud-edge integration.

Keywords: Cloud-Edge Integration · API Gateway · Secure Access · Zero Trust · Authentication

1 Introduction

Today's world is increasingly digitized, diversified and interconnected in the context of the Internet of Everything, and almost everything has the ability to process data [1]. The

© ICST Institute for Computer Sciences, Social Informatics and Telecommunications Engineering 2021
Published by Springer Nature Switzerland AG 2021. All Rights Reserved
Y.-B. Lin and D.-J. Deng (Eds.): SGIoT 2020, LNICST 354, pp. 57–69, 2021.
https://doi.org/10.1007/978-3-030-69514-9_6

distribution and intelligence of terminal equipment are more significant. In the Internet of Things, if the massive amounts of data generated by the devices are uploaded to the cloud platform for processing, it will bring tremendous pressure to the cloud. Part of the data processing work can be performed at the edge nodes [2], but the processed data still needs to be uploaded to the central cloud for big data analysis and training and upgrading of algorithm models. The upgraded algorithm is then transferred to the front-end equipment for updating, completing the closed loop of the work [3].

In many modern scenarios, cloud computing and edge computing will form a cooperative and complementary relationship. The edge is mainly responsible for processing real-time, short-period data and performing local services, which can reduce data transmission delays and network bandwidth costs, and provide resources Services such as scheduling and distribution; cloud computing is mainly responsible for computing tasks that are difficult for edge nodes, such as optimizing business rules or models, and completing application lifecycle management. According to estimates by Uptime, by 2021, half of all workloads will be run on the cloud and network edge outside the data center. The characteristics of real-time and fast data processing and analysis, network bandwidth saving, offline operation, and high data security are fully reflected in various scenarios of cloud-edge collaboration.

Today, the scale and complexity of terminal devices and applications are growing exponentially. According to IDC estimates, the number of global Internet devices will reach 48.9 billion in 2023; according to the Cisco VNI forecasting tool and the visual network index, from 2017 to 2022, global business mobile data traffic will increase six times, and each personal computer in the network. The average weekly data usage is about 15 GB. According to Metcalfe's law, the connectivity between systems, users, applications, and devices will become more fragmented and complex as devices and users continue to join. The value and importance of network security will continue to increase, and the protection and management of the network will Becomes more important and difficult.

In summary, the highly dynamic and heterogeneous environment at the edge of the network and the numerous and complicated data on the cloud have exacerbated the difficulty of network protection. Research on cloud and edge security technologies can effectively prevent security issues in data, privacy, network, and off-site storage brought by products in services, and ensure data and privacy security for Internet users [4]. Therefore, studying the security of cloud-edge integration application is the primary prerequisite for the further development of the Internet of Everything system, which is of great significance for promoting the development of cloud-edge integration.

2 Relation Work

In this section, we will survey the related works available in the literature. In [14], the authors used blind signatures and short, randomizable signatures to provide conditional anonymous authentication. They used powerful third parties to register entities and generate a certificate for each customer, control center, and fog nodes. However, the proposed solution consumed the computational power of resource-limited edge devices to generate secret keys from public and private keys. The authors of [15] provided a secure and privacy-preserving mutual authentication solution for an Elliptic Curve Cryptography (ECC) fog-based publish-subscribe system. The proposed solution could ensure mutual authentication between subscribers and brokers, as well as between publishers and brokers. However, the proposed solution still consumed the computational power of the resource-limited edge devices. The authors of [16] introduced three Lightweight Anonymous Authentication Protocols (LAAPs). They use lightweight cryptographic primitives, such as one-way functions and EXCLUSIVE-OR operations, which led to a limited computational cost for the resource-limited edge devices. They also introduced a novel privacy protection security architecture for the D2D-supported fog computing model, which allows end-user devices to be authenticated without the intervention of a central server. However, the proposed architecture and protocols are used to validate each edge device, network access device, and centralized cloud server. They did not consider user authentication, which is responsible for managing and maintaining the system.

Edge computing has been defined by the ECC as an open platform deployed at the edge of the network near the data source and offering intelligent services for real-time processing, data optimization, security, and privacy within the mobile edge network infrastructure [18]. To cope with the above issues, a Lightweight Edge Gateway for the Internet of Things architecture [17] has been introduced, which is based on the modularity of microservices, in order to guarantee scalability and flexibility. In [19], the author presented an intelligent IoT gateway which can communicate with different networks, has a flexible protocol that converts different sensor data into a consistent format, and has a uniform external interface.

There exist several IoT platforms which provide a connection with IoT devices. Intel provides Open VINO, a deep learning toolkit that focuses on the edge, and uses visual data to gain insight into the business. Google's Edge TPU chip and Cloud IoT Edge software stack can deploy machine learning functions on edge devices to operate on data in real time. Microsoft's Azure IoT Edge product extends cloud analysis capabilities to the edge and supports offline use. Amazon launched the AWS Green grass software to extend AWS to devices, process the data generated by the terminal locally, and perform analysis, management and persistent storage. The Link IoT Edge platform launched by Alibaba can be deployed in smart devices and computing nodes of different levels, connecting devices with different protocols and data formats, and providing efficient, safe, and intelligent communication and connection capabilities. CDN Edge, launched by Tencent, sinks data center services to edge nodes, reducing user response delay and data center network load. Baidu's intelligent edge BIE can exchange data with Baidu Cloud, filter and calculate sensitive data, and provide temporary offline independent computing services. Huawei's IEF platform extends the AI capabilities of Huawei Cloud to the edge, supports heterogeneous hardware access, and provides a safe and reliable business mechanism. It is a complete edge-cloud collaborative integrated service solution.

In addition, industrial companies are actively exploring the field practice of edge computing based on rich industrial scenarios [5]. COSMO Edge, a one-stop equipment management platform developed by Haier, supports the analysis of multiple industrial protocols, provides strong equipment connection and data processing capabilities, provides digital modeling and EaaS application models, and helps industries such as steel, petrochemicals, and electronics manufacturing.

An API gateway is an entry point for forwarding requests between many microservices, which merges multiple microservice APIs into a single client and and routes the requests from one access point to the correct microservices. The API gateway uses an existing identity management and authentication service which manages accounts, such as JWT or OAuth2.0, to allow a user or client access to certain microservices. An API gateway is a service that publishes multiple APIs, updates the published API set at runtime, and is integrated with health check, load balancing, service monitoring, and security capabilities.

3   Cloud Edge Integrated Security Certification System

3.1   Related Cybersecurity Architecture

The basic idea of the traditional network security model is to protect important resources in the network by building layers of defense. The network is divided into different areas according to the degree of trust, and the areas are separated by firewalls. Since the firewall only checks whether the source address and destination address are correct when executing the security policy, the attacker can deliver remote access tools to the internal network to obtain access rights, and then move laterally in the internal network to find valuable resources [6]. Modern network design and application models greatly weaken the protection capabilities of border-based security strategies.

In a "zero trust" network, no matter where the host is, it is regarded as an Internet host and is in a dangerous network environment. Combined with distributed strategies, the network security architecture shown in Fig. 1 can be constructed.

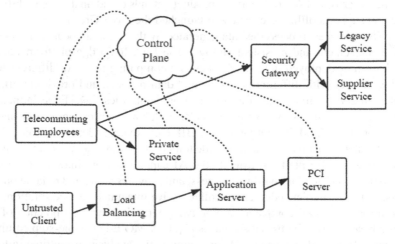

Fig. 1. "Zero Trust" Network Security Architecture Diagram

3.2 Cloud Edge Integrated Security Model

The Zero Trust model has improved the level of security to a certain extent, and even solved the contradiction between security and ease of use. Therefore, in combination with the security authentication requirements of the cloud-edge integrated computing service platform in this project, we have designed a network security architecture based on comprehensive identification and controlled by a unified identity authentication center and a trusted access gateway, [7] as shown in Fig. 2.

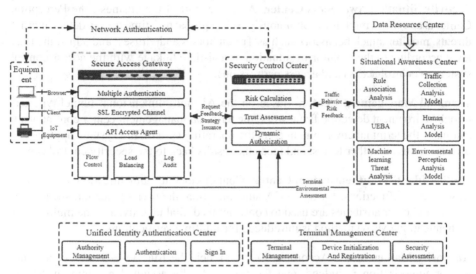

Fig. 2. Cloud Edge Integrated Security Authentication Platform Architecture Diagram

This architecture is mainly composed of the following 8 functions:

Security Control Center. According to the strategy, the authorization level is dynamically adjusted, and the "control center" conducts unified risk calculation, trust evaluation and dynamic authorization.

Risk Calculation And Trust Assessment. All access requests from the client must first go through the trust evaluation module, which conducts trust evaluation and risk calculation from the four dimensions of identity, equipment, environment, and behavior, and grants the access request corresponding trust levels based on the evaluation results.

Dynamic Authorization. Based on RBAC + ABAC, dynamic access control is established between the visiting subject and the visiting object. In terms of access subjects, this architecture will confirm the credibility of the user's identity. Basic authentication and authorization are based on user name and password authentication, while applying for higher authority requires verification with factors such as text messages, fingerprints, and faces. In addition, it is necessary to confirm whether the environment and behavior are credible, and continue to conduct behavior credibility testing based on user access behavior, because credible users also have huge security risks in dangerous environments [8]. In terms of access to objects, this architecture is based on static authorization of roles and organizational structures, combined with the trust levels of subjects and objects, to achieve dynamic access authority control.

Secure Access Gateway. The API secure access gateway, which authenticates, authorizes and encrypts all accesses, is the connection center between front-end access and back-end microservices. All access requests to the back-end microservices are proxied by the secure access gateway, which implements multiple identity authentication, load balancing, log auditing and other functions for the requester.

Security Situation Awareness Center. After the start of the business, the Perception Center uses various models to continuously collect global real-time traffic, detect internal threats, monitor attack behaviors such as Trojan horses and viruses, and adjust the trust level according to the monitoring situation in real-time linkage with the access control system to control access and access permissions.

Terminal Management Center. Based on the AI multi-dimensional funnel-type terminal environment detection framework, the terminal management center continuously evaluates the terminal environment from the operating system, file system, application, process status and other levels, and feeds the results back to the security control center.

Unified Identity Authentication Center. Contains identity authentication services and single sign-on functions. Based on CA authentication, the user's behavior, social, biological and other attributes are used to construct its digital identity, and the multi-factor authentication (MFA) method is introduced for multiple verifications.

Authority Management. According to the model, the trust level is calculated, the access authorization is judged, and the user is finally assigned a minimum access authority.

The system has many verification links, short trust validity time, more fine-grained access control, and higher data security and privacy protection capabilities. Therefore, it can be widely used in edge computing platforms, and has outstanding advantages such as high service efficiency, comprehensive identity, dynamic access control, abnormal behavior and traffic monitoring.

3.3   API Secure Access Gateway Solution

The client may need to call multiple service interfaces to complete a business requirement. The API gateway can classify, forward, and organize external requests, avoiding cross-domain requests, complicated authentication, difficulty in reconstruction, and firewall restrictions [9]. According to the function of the API gateway, the architecture diagram is designed as shown in Fig. 3:

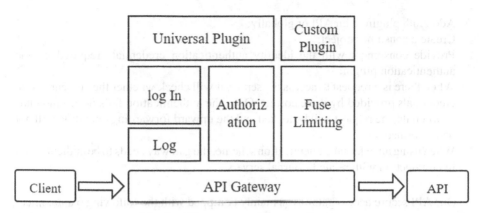

Fig. 3. API gateway architecture diagram

There are many open source API gateways, and the commonly used ones are Kong, Traefik, Ambassador, Tyk, Zuul, etc. Kong is a configurable gateway based on Nginx, mainly used for enterprise-level API management. The others are microservice gateways, providing decentralized self-service. The open source communities of Kong and Traefik are relatively active and their performance is relatively leading. In addition, compared to Traeflk and Zuul, Kong can extend functions such as identity authentication, fusing, current limiting, retry, load balancing, and health check through plug-ins. Kong has a unique architectural advantage. In terms of authentication, Kong supports Basic Auth, HMAC, JWT, Key, LDAP, OAuth 2.0 and other methods compared to other gateways. This design is implemented based on the more mature Kong gateway.

4 Implementation

By adding servers for horizontal expansion, the API secure access gateway can handle any type of request with low load. Modularization can be achieved by configuring plug-ins through Restful Admin API. The gateway can run on any infrastructure. This experiment is performed on a server with Ubuntu 18.04 system installed.

We built an Nginx development environment based on Kong Server and configured a relational database PostgreSQL. The gateway implements a reverse proxy for client requests based on Nginx. It reduces the pressure on the back-end web server and improves the response speed. In addition, we have also expanded the functions of the API gateway in terms of identity authentication, load balancing, flow control, log auditing, analysis and monitoring.

4.1 Authentication

It is usually controlled by related authentication plugins combined with configuration parameters, and requests for authentication failure or no authentication are rejected [10]. The general scheme of these plugins is as follows:

① Add Auth plugin to an API or globally;
② Create a consumer object;
③ Provide consumers with the identity authentication credentials required by the authentication plugin;
④ When there is a request to access the server, it will check whether the authentication credentials provided by it are correct. Once the authentication fails or the authentication fails, the request will be locked and the upward forwarding operation will not be performed.
⑤ When using an external authentication scheme, the gateway needs to be authenticated in conjunction with related external servers.

Our API secure access gateway is mainly equipped with the following 6 authentication methods:

Basic Auth: It is mostly used for verification of web request service. Set the user name and password on the server. When the client sends the request, enter the user name and password in the header. After receiving the request, the server will verify the request. If the verification is passed, the next step will be processed. Otherwise, "Invalid authentication credentials" will be returned.

Key-Auth: It can be used on services or routing. Before adding this plugin, all requests were proxied upstream. After setting the key for the microservice, the API can only be accessed with the correct key.

JWT-Auth: JSON Web Token as a JSON object ensures the security of information transmission between parties. The user calls the third-party interface when logging in. After logging in, a JWT token will be generated, and the returned JWT token will be put into Headers. The JWT authentication plug-in will parse out the login information before encryption at the next request, and then access the corresponding microservice. It can be used in scenarios such as authorization and information exchange.

OAuth 2.0: Used to authorize third-party applications. After the data owner agrees to the access of the third-party application, the system will generate a short-term token for the authentication of the third-party application [11].

LDAP-Auth: Add LDAP bind authentication to a route with username and password protection, and the plugin will check for valid credentials in the Proxy-Authorization and Authorization headers. All user information is stored in the LDAP server. When the user uses internal services, the LDAP server can change the original authentication strategy and must perform unified identity authentication through LDAP [12].

IP Restriction: By adding IP addresses to a whitelist or blacklist to restrict access to services or routes for some requests.

4.2 Load Balancing

The gateway uses a ring load balancer, and the addition and deletion of back-end services are handled by the gateway, without receiving updates from DNS. Ring load balancing is accomplished by configuring upstream and target entities. By default, the ring load balancer uses a weighted round-robin scheme and an IP address-based hash algorithm to implement load balancing.

When the application services deployed in multiple servers managed by load balancing are the same, two different service ports need to be opened to distinguish requests and distribute them to different ports according to the load balancing algorithm. When there are multiple back-end services, you need to use each node as a Target and set a load weight for it. The server with a higher weight is more likely to be accessed, and the server with a lower weight is less likely to be accessed.

4.3 Flow Control

There are actually two aspects of current limiting: rate limiting and request body size limiting. The more important one is the current limiting of request body size, because too large data volume can easily cause memory overflow exceptions. There are mainly three solutions:

Request-Termination: Use the specified status code and message to terminate the incoming request and fuse the specified request or service. This allows temporarily stopping the service or traffic on the route, or even blocking users.

Rate-Limiting: Control the maximum number of calls to an API interface service in a unit time. Once the limit is exceeded, the gateway will deny access and return an error message.

Request Size-Limiting: Used to limit the size of the request body. When the request body exceeds the threshold (such as 128M), the Kong gateway will reject the request.

4.4 Log Audit

We use the following 3 methods to comprehensively record the information about the service, routing and client request process on the API gateway to facilitate recording and review of user behavior:

Syslog: A standard that uses Internet protocols to transfer recorded document messages on the Internet. It is usually used for information system management or information security auditing. It can integrate log records from many different types of systems into a database.

File-Log: Write the related HTTP or HTTPS request and its response data to the log file on the disk.

Http-Log: ySend request and response logs to HTTP server. For HTTP service requests, the input and output message information of the request can be recorded in detail,.

4.5 Monitoring Alarm

It provides an open and complete monitoring solution by integrating the Prometheus system. A new model based on centralized rule calculation, unified analysis and alert notification has been formed. The core part of the program has only a single binary file, and there is no third-party dependency, so there is no risk of cascading failures. Based on its rich Client library, users can obtain the true running status of services and applications, such as CPU share. For some complex situations, it can also use Service Discovery capabilities to dynamically manage monitoring targets. In addition, intuitive information such as system operating status, resource usage, and service operating status can be directly obtained by connecting visual tools.

The server is started as a process. The data collected each time is called metrics. These data will be stored in the memory, and then periodically written to the hard disk. When the service restarts, the hard disk data is written back to the memory, so there is a certain consumption of memory.

The client uses the pull method to actively pull data. Use Node Exporter to collect the current host's system resource usage and other related data. It can process hundreds of thousands of data points per second, a single server can process millions of monitoring indicators, and has very efficient data processing capabilities. The built-in data query language PromQL of the program can realize the query and aggregation of monitoring data.

Through continuous collection and statistics of monitoring sample data, long-term trend analysis can be performed, and the time required for resource expansion can be predicted in advance. To track and compare the system, you can analyze the operating resource usage, concurrency and load changes under different capacity conditions. When a failure occurs or is about to occur, the system can respond quickly and notify the administrator through SMS, Dingding, WeChat messages, etc., to avoid affecting the business. Through the analysis of historical data, the cause of the failure can be found and the root cause can be solved.

4.6 Dashboard

Based on the VUE framework, we encapsulate the back-end API secure access gateway and other monitoring software services. Modularized the functions of the API gateway. Use Element UI framework to layout and display all pages. All modules are based on ajax technology. The front-end page sends an ajax request to call the API interface of the gateway and monitoring software. Get the response data and present the data on the page.

In all pages, we use a dynamic routing mechanism to determine whether the user has permission. If the user is not logged in, the system will force him to jump to the login page for authentication. For pages with large amounts of data, we use the paging tool of the Element UI framework to implement the paging function, and use Vuex to control the number of pages when the page jumps. Physical information, service information and log information are displayed using the dashboard directory.

We use the Element UI framework to build the layout of the login box. Use Element UI tabular tools to display data, such as host operating status, system physical information, terminal operating status, alarm information and log information.

Use the ECharts tool to build a visual chart, and then call the gateway interface to display the service information data. In the plug-in module, we use the column tool to classify various plug-ins. We can obtain the data types of all plug-in configuration items based on the pattern API interface provided by the gateway. We only need to design all possible data types in the <template> tag, and use v-if statements for conditional judgment. When you select the plug-in to be added, the page will automatically filter out the configuration items involved.

5 Performance Analysis

To test the proposed solution, different types of software and hardware components are needed. The hardware we used was a desktop computer with the Ubuntu 18.04 operating system, an AMD 64 quad core, 2 GB memory, and a 40 GB hard disk. For software, we used Docker to ease the operation of the applications, including the open-source nginx proxy server and the Edgex-Foundry edge computing framework.

To assess the practical applicability of the designed system, we analyzed the performance of gateway in reverse proxy, load balancing and security authentication. We tested the performance of the gateway on an edge computing platform with 100 back-end microservices deployed, analyzed the round-trip time of non-authentication requests and authenticated requests, the maximum data throughput of the gateway and the maximum number of concurrent connections. Table 1 shows the experimental results of sending requests to microservices with and without the authentication plugins configured. Table 2 shows the data processing capabilities of the proposed solution.

Table 1. Round trip time test results.

Test Item	Average time
Round trip time for using the microservices API without any authentication	0.004s
Round trip time for using the microservices API with Basic authentication	0.0078s
Round trip time for using the microservices API with Key authentication	0.0065s
Round trip time for using the microservices API with JWT authentication	0.0189s
Round trip time for using the microservices API with OAuth 2.0	0.0205s
Round trip time for using the microservices API with LDAP authentication	0.0223s
Round trip time for using the microservices API with IP restriction	0.0111s

Reaction time is a measure of how quickly an organism responds to a stimulus. The statistical average reaction time is 284 ms. As can be seen in Table 1, the average RTT time to complete all kinds of certifications is less than 0.023 s, which is less than the reaction time. This indicates that the proposed system is applicable within the real world and performs well. In addition, the data processing performance of the scheme shown in Table 2 fully meets the parameter requirements of load balancing.

Table 2. Data processing capabilities test results.

Test Item	Value
Data handling capacity	20 Gbps
Maximum number of concurrent connections	10 million
New connections per second	0.4 million

6 Summary and Future Work

This article mainly studies the cloud-edge integrated security authentication method under the guidance of the concept of zero trust. It analyzes and summarizes the current cloud-edge-end integration process and the research status of related authentication technologies. Designed the cloud edge integrated platform security authentication system and industrial-grade API security access gateway. At the technical level, it has completed the construction of Nginx-based API security access gateway and related functions such as identity authentication, [13] load balancing, reverse proxy, log audit, analysis and monitoring. Dashboard is designed to facilitate user management. After testing on the edge computing platform of this project, the utility and security of the proposed scheme and design have been verified, which greatly meets the complex security certification requirements in the cloud-edge integrated computing application platform.

The entire cloud-edge collaboration process also needs to be fully identified to ensure that every request and distribution process must be authenticated and authorized. Next, the author will continue to promote the improvement of the cloud-edge integrated security certification system, mainly from the following aspects:

(1) Construct a unified identity authentication center. Perform comprehensive identity management on the platform, realize basic CA authentication, and single sign-on functions, and provide multi-factor authentication services based on the above functions.
(2) Design authority management system. The design and implementation supports a dynamic access control system based on RBAC + ABAC, centralized management of permissions, and realization of different granular permissions on demand, reducing the maintenance cost of the permission system.
(3) Build a comprehensive platform that supports various algorithms such as RSA and AES, key storage, and KMS activation capabilities. Realize the function of calling API based on Python or java to achieve encryption and decryption.

Acknowledgments. The ideas in this article come from discussions and research collaborations with two people: Zhigang Xiong and Jianjun Zeng. I would also like to thank the following people who provided valuable feedback on the design of this article and helped improve it: Quancheng Zhao, Lulu Zhao and the anonymous reviewers. This work was supported by the National Key Research and Development Program of China (grant number 2018YFC0831304) and the National Natural Science Foundation (Grant number 61772064).

References

1. Shi, W., Sun, H., Cao, J., et al.: Edge computing: a new computing model in the internet of everything era. Comput. Res. Dev. **54**(5), 907–924 (2017)
2. Satyanarayanan, M.: The emergence of edge computing. Computer **50**(1), 30–39 (2017)
3. Enqing, X., Enran, D.: Exploration and practice of collaborative development of cloud computing and edge computing. Commun. World **801**(09), 48–49 (2019)
4. Lu, X.: Research on task migration and resource management of mobile edge computing (2019)
5. Yong, S., Xiaofeng, L.: Cloud-edge integrated edge computing products help enterprises' digital transformation. Shanghai Inf. Technol. **10**, 59–61 (2018)
6. Zhang, J.: Overview of cloud computing platform security technology patents. Information and Computer: Theoretical Edition 000(011), pp. 126–129 (2015)
7. Yingnan, Z.: Zero-trust architecture: a new paradigm for network security. Financ. Electron. **11**, 50–51 (2018)
8. Zhang, Q.: SAB-IABS: a design of an anonymous two-way identity authentication system for interconnected clouds based on secure active bundles (2014)
9. Zhang, J.: Research on improved trusted network connection based on behavior analysis (2017)
10. Ni, J., Lin, X., Shen, X.: Efficient and secure service-oriented authentication supporting network slicing for 5G-enabled IoT. IEEE J. Sel. Areas Commun., 1 (2018)
11. Jiang, S.: Research and implementation of cloud integrated security solutions (2015)
12. Mukherjee, M., Matam, R., Shu, L., et al.: Security and privacy in fog computing: challenges. IEEE Access **5**, 19293–19304 (2017)
13. Pang, H.H., Tan, K.-L.: Authenticating query results in edge computing. In: Proceedings. 20th International Conference on Data Engineering. IEEE (2004)
14. Zhu, L., Li, M., Zhang, Z., et al.: Privacy-preserving authentication and data aggregation for fog-based smart grid. IEEE Commun. Mag. **57**, 80–85 (2019)
15. Botta, A., Donato, W.D., Persico, V., et al.: Integration of Cloud computing and Internet of Things: A survey. Future Gener. Comput. Syst. **56**(MAR), 684–700 (2016)
16. Gope, P.: LAAP: lightweight anonymous authentication protocol for D2D-Aided fog computing paradigm. Comput. Secur. **86**, 223–237 (2019)
17. Morabito, R., Petrolo, R., Loscrì, V., et al.: LEGIoT: a lightweight edge gateway for the Internet of Things. Future Gener. Comput. Syst. **81**, 1157–1171 (2017)
18. Wang, S., Zhang, X., Zhang, Y., et al.: A survey on mobile edge networks: convergence of computing, caching and communications. IEEE Access, **PP**(99), 1 (2017)
19. Guoqiang, S., Yanming, C., Chao, Z., et al.: Design and implementation of a smart IoT gateway. Green Computing & Communications. IEEE (2013)

A Secure Edge-Cloud Computing Framework for IoT Applications

Yao Zhao, Zhenjiang Zhang, and Jian Li[✉]

School of Electronic and Information Engineering, Beijing Jiaotong University,
Beijing 100044, China
{16271208,zhjzhang1,lijian}@bjtu.edu.cn

Abstract. With the fast development of Internet of Things, more and
more applications are deployed in this "connecting everything" network.
Edge computing and cloud computing are two paradigms to implement
the Internet of Things. To utilize the advantages of both these two computing forms, edge-cloud computing was proposed. In this paper, we construct a secure edge-cloud computing (SECC) framework. Sensor nodes
and applications can interact with the framework through unified interfaces. We implement the edge server as a collection of services, including
edge device orchestration, data processing and storage, communication
management, authentication and authorization, environment sensing and
situation analysis. Through a daisy-chain approach, our framework can
be secured for heterogeneous security needs of different parts of the system. We also demonstrate the efficacy of the SECC framework through
comprehensive analysis.

Keywords: Edge computing · Internet of Things · Edge-cloud
collaboration

1 Introduction

In recent years, thanks to the characteristics of low construction and maintenance
costs, the Internet of Things (IoT) and wireless sensor network technologies have
become more and more widely used, especially in the monitoring of special environments. They have great advantages and application potential in fire alarm,
geological exploration, and safe production. However, with the development of
wireless communication technology, in general large-scale wireless sensor networks or large-scale IoT, especially in application scenarios that require extensive monitoring of the environment, the number of wireless sensor nodes and
edge sensing devices is rapidly increased, so is the amount of data generated.
Thus the backend cloud computing platforms need to undertake a large number of computing tasks and data storage tasks [1]. If all data generated by edge
sensing devices are transmitted to the cloud computing platform for processing
and analysis, it will bring great challenges to satisfy the bandwidth consumption
and response time requirements of the IoT applications.

© ICST Institute for Computer Sciences, Social Informatics and Telecommunications Engineering 2021
Published by Springer Nature Switzerland AG 2021. All Rights Reserved
Y.-B. Lin and D.-J. Deng (Eds.): SGIoT 2020, LNICST 354, pp. 70–78, 2021.
https://doi.org/10.1007/978-3-030-69514-9_7

In this situation, the cloud computing has the following disadvantages: it is difficult to shorten the system response time, to reduce the communication bandwidth and to lower the energy consumption of data centers. Therefore, edge computing, a new computing model that performs computing at the edge of the network, is introduced into the IoT technology [2]. Once the edge computing model was proposed, it has been developed rapidly and widely used in the IoT technology.

Nevertheless, edge computing technology also has certain problems. Compared with cloud computing platforms, edge computing servers usually do not have enough memory and processors to process large amounts of data, so it cannot perform complex operations such as deep learning [3]. At the same time, with the continuous development of edge computing technology, we can consider assigning different tasks to each edge computing server to improve efficiency. So the edge-cloud collaboration technology is proposed and introduced into the IoT technology [4]. In the edge-cloud collaboration model, the cloud computing platform and the edge computing platform work together to give play to their respective characteristics and provide optimized services through data analysis of the IoT.

In this paper we propose to apply edge-cloud computing in an environment dynamic perception system characterized by large-scale IoT, and build a secure edge-cloud computing (SECC) framework for edge-cloud collaboration. Our proposed framework covers all the aspects of an IoT system, including the wireless sensor nodes, the edge computing server and the cloud computing platform. In the framework we propose unified interfaces to connect wireless sensors, applications and the services provided by the framework, including edge device orchestration, data processing and storage, communication management, authentication and authorization, environment sensing and situation analysis. Through the design of the framework, we can get a trade-off between computing capability and response delay in various IoT application scenarios. We also propose a Daisy-chain approach to meet different security requirements of the system.

The rest of this paper is organized as follows: in Sect. 2 we discuss related works. In Sect. 3 the overall system architecture and details of different components of the system are elaborated. In Sect. 4 system evaluation are presented. We conclude in Sect. 5.

2   Related Works

With the introduction of the concept of the Internet of Everything (IoE), business and industrial processes that can enrich people's lives are extended to the definition of IoT [5]. IoT has become a small part of IoE, and the latter depicts a world composed of trillions of smart devices, in which all sensors are connected through a network using a specific protocol [6]. According to Cisco Systems, market of devices would touch the value of 50 billion devices by 2020 [7]. The exponential increase of access devices has put tremendous pressure on the existing IoT architecture. Cloud computing technologies have been introduced into

IoT as the canonical data processing paradigm. Since 45% of the data generated by IoT will be processed at the edge of the network [7], a new computing model that performs computing at the edge of the network is proposed [9]. With the continuous development of edge computing technology, its problems are gradually revealed: Compared with cloud computing platforms, edge computing servers usually do not have enough memory and processors to process large amounts of data. Simultaneously, the communication between edge computing server and cloud computing platform puts huge pressure on bandwidth resources.

Consequently, edge-cloud collaboration technology came into being and solve the problems mentioned above. SAT-IoT (an architectural model for a high-performance fog/edge/cloud IoT platform), which uses fog computing, edge computing, and cloud computing technology to improve the existing IoT platform and greatly improve its performance [8]. Multi-access edge computing (MEC), which can integrate telecommunications and IT services [10], and provide a cloud computing platform at the edge where radio access has been completed, involves edge-cloud collaboration technology. The collaboration between edge and cloud allows multiple access systems to have Sequence normal operation [11]. In addition, the application of deep learning in IoT edge cloud data analysis is also an application scenario of edge cloud collaboration technology [3]. For example, assigning a deep neural network (DNN) layer on an edge cloud environment can minimize the total delay of processing the DNN and solve the problem of least delay allocation (LMA). In this way, the response time of the application program can be shortened by effectively allocating deep learning tasks [12].

The rapid development of edge computing technology makes people largely ignore the security threats on the edge computing platform and the applications it supports. Distributed denial of service attacks, side channel attacks, malware injection attacks, and authentication and authorization attacks pose major challenges to edge computing security [13]. In this case, the academic community adopts a variety of methods to ensure its security. The security protection of edge computing through the perspective of classified protection of cyber security [14]. Through the popularity of containerization, many researches aim at identifying related vulnerabilities and possible security issues [15]. In this paper, we propose a secure framework that combines edge computing and cloud computing and can achieve the advantages of both the two computing paradigms.

3   Secure Edge-Cloud Computing (SECC) Framework Architecture

In this section, we will introduce the overall architecture of the proposed SECC framework and the details of all the components.

3.1   Overall Architecture

System architecture of the SECC framework is shown in Fig. 1. It is mainly composed of three components: wireless sensor nodes, edge computing server and cloud computing platform.

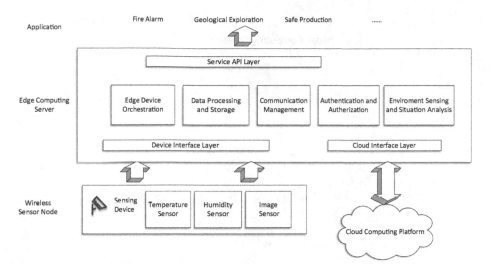

Fig. 1. System architecture of SECC framework

Sensing devices, such as temperature sensors, humidity sensors and image sensors, sense environmental changes and send these changes to the edge computing server. Then the edge computing server and the cloud computing platform collaborate and complete the tasks of the applications running on the framework. Different applications can be deployed according to application scenarios, such as fire monitoring, geological exploration, safe production, etc.

3.2 Wireless Sensor Nodes

The wireless sensor nodes are the most basic and important component of the system. As Fig. 2 shows, its role in this system is as follows: in some special environments that need to be monitored, sensing devices composed of temperature sensors, humidity sensors, and image sensors are put out randomly or according to a certain rule to form wireless sensor networks. These sensors can sense the dynamic changes of the environment in real time and collect some specific data in the environment.

As an example, in the forest monitoring system GreenOrbs deployed in Wuxi City, Jiangsu Province, wireless sensor nodes are placed on trees, including temperature sensors, humidity sensors, light intensity sensors, carbon dioxide concentration sensors, etc. These nodes can monitor and real-time detect the forest environment to prevent forest fires.

3.3 Edge Computing Server

In the SECC framework, the edge computing server belongs to the middle layer of the system. As shown in Fig. 3, the main functions of the edge computing server are as follows.

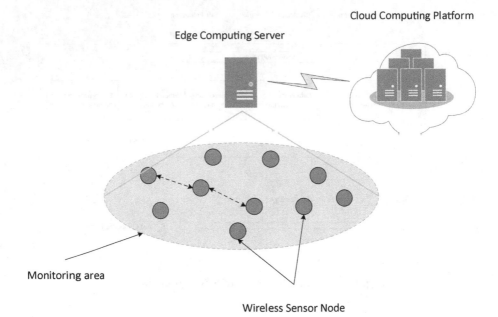

Edge Computing Server

Cloud Computing Platform

Monitoring area

Wireless Sensor Node

Fig. 2. Wireless sensor nodes

- In system initialization phase, various monitoring data in the environment collected by the wireless sensor nodes and corresponding initialization parameters are uploaded to the cloud computing platform through the relay of the edge computing server. The edge computing server is also in charge of the setting up of wireless sensor nodes on its behalf and on the behalf of the cloud computing platform.
- In the system operation stage, preliminary processing is performed on the various monitoring data collected in the environment to detect abnormal situations in time. Once an abnormality of a certain item or items of data is detected, the cloud computing platform will immediately receive an abnormal report from the edge computing server. At the same time, the controller at the bottom will be driven by the edge computing server to provide emergency solutions for the abnormal situation.
- The edge computing server also provide basic common services such as edge device orchestration, data storage and processing, communication management, authentication and authorization, environment sensing and situation evaluation and so on. Based on the common services, applications can be developed and deployed in a timely manner.

During system deployment, small base stations can be deployed on the side close to the wireless sensor nodes as a small edge computing server. It is also possible to use special equipment, such as drones, in areas where it is difficult to deploy

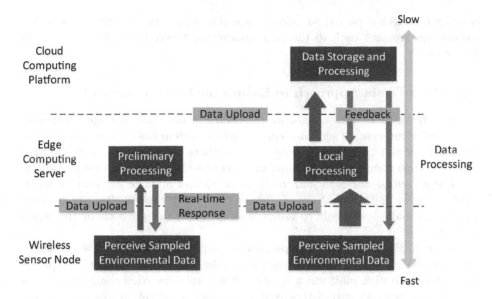

Fig. 3. The functionality of edge computing server

small base stations, as edge computing servers that can be deployed on mobile, to provide edge computing services for the system on the edge of the data.

3.4   Cloud Computing Platform

In the SECC framework, the cloud computing platform's functions are mainly as follows.

- It has the characteristics of large storage space and strong computing power. Therefore, it plays the role of remote data and control center in the system, and its role is mainly to store data and process highly complex data.
- In some application scenarios, the edge computing server and wireless sensor nodes may not be able to provide the corresponding computing power required by the system, and cannot afford the resource loss caused by complex calculations. Therefore, using cloud computing platforms for various complex tasks is also an embodiment of collaborative processing between the edge computing server and cloud computing platform.

As an example, in an IoT detection system based on edge computing that uses an autoencoder neural network to realize anomaly detection, the autoencoder has high complexity in training model parameters as an artificial neural network model for feature extraction. It is difficult for the wireless sensor nodes and edge computing server to provide corresponding computing capabilities and resource consumption caused by complex computing. Therefore, the model training process is deployed on a cloud computing platform. The generated model parameters are sent back to the edge computing server for real-time anomaly detection.

3.5   Daisy-Chain Approach to Ensure the System Security

As a complex framework consisting of wireless sensor nodes, edge computing server and cloud computing platform, the whole system has heterogeneous security needs. Sensor nodes have to ensure the authenticity of messages transmitted while the edge computing server and cloud computing platform have to authenticate legal sensor nodes to join in the network and manage the correct access rights of users and applications. Different computing capabilities and resource limitations make it difficult to adopt a single security approach in the whole system.

In the SECC framework, we propose to apply the daisy-chain approach to satisfy different security needs of the system. In the system initialization phase, the cloud computing platform will first authenticate the edge computing server and establish security parameters used in the following cryptographic operations. Then the edge computing server will in turn authenticate sensors nodes, initializing security parameters used in light-weight message authentication algorithms. Through the daisy-chain approach, each part of the system can get a corresponding security level on-demand.

4   System Evaluation

At the system architecture level, the SECC framework uses edge computing technology and edge-cloud collaboration technology to realize the development and deployment of IoT applications. Compared with the traditional IoT infrastructure, it has the following advantages.

From the Perspective of Wireless Sensor Node
In this system framework, the wireless sensor nodes communicate with the edge computing server, and at the same time, the edge computing server acts as a relay to communicate with the cloud computing platform. First, the requirements for the communication capabilities of wireless sensor nodes are greatly reduced. Second, the edge computing server's advantage in data processing capabilities on the data edge side has been more embodied.

From the Perspective of Edge Computing Server
Compared with the IoT system based on wireless sensor network technology, the edge computing server is deployed on the edge of the network. The data is close to the preprocessing unit for data analysis, protocol conversion, and data collection to ensure the low latency of the system. It generally uses dedicated GPUs, DSP chips or general-purpose CPUs, and has strong computing capabilities in data storage, network security, and data transmission. Moreover, edge computing server can be embedded with artificial intelligence technology

and machine learning to bring higher service efficiency through edge intelligence, thereby enhancing service capabilities.

The edge server stores the sensitive data collected or generated in the wireless sensor nodes in a local device, which greatly improves security and privacy. In some application scenarios, such as smart homes, smart cities, etc., wireless sensor nodes will get some private data of users for intermediate processing purpose. The data do not need to be stored on the local device, or to be uploaded to the cloud computing platform. This greatly reduces the risk of data leakage and provides strong protection for user data security and user privacy.For private data that must be transmitted to the cloud computing platform, it can adopt necessary ways such as authentication, desensitization, and encryption to ensure the security of the data without revealing privacy.

From the Perspective of Cloud Computing Platform
Compared with the sole use of edge computing technology or cloud computing technology, the edge computing server in SECC framework can perform preliminary data processing, thereby reducing the amount of computing on the cloud computing platform, reducing the amount of data uploaded in the cloud computing platform, and cooperating with the cloud computing platform to reduce the backbone link bandwidth usage.

The edge computing server adopts a layered processing mechanism and works with the cloud computing platform. In order to improve the data processing efficiency of the cloud computing platform, only some complicated tasks that do not require low latency and require centralized control are placed on the cloud computing platform. It brings higher efficiency to the services provided by the system.

5   Conclusion

In this paper we propose a secure edge-cloud computing (SECC) framework for the Internet of Things. We divide the framework into three components: wireless sensor nodes, the edge computing server and the cloud computing platform. Through the collaboration of the edge computing server and the cloud computing platform, we can achieve a trade-off between computing capability and response delay. We further implement the edge computing server as a common basic service provider, including unified interfaces to connect wireless sensors and applications to the framework, basic services such as edge device orchestration, data processing and storage, communication management, authentication and authorization, environment sensing and situation analysis. To achieve the security in the framework, we propose a daisy-chain approach to meet the heterogeneous security requirements of the system. We demonstrate the efficacy of the SECC framework through comprehensive analysis.

Acknowledgement. This work was in part supported by the National Natural Science Foundation of China under Grant 61701019.

References

1. Liu, A., Cai, R.: Architecting cloud computing applications and systems. In: 2011 Ninth Working IEEE/IFIP Conference on Software Architecture, Boulder, CO, pp. 310–311 (2011)
2. Naveen, S., Kounte, M.R.: Key technologies and challenges in IoT edge computing. In: 2019 Third International conference on I-SMAC (IoT in Social, Mobile, Analytics and Cloud) (I-SMAC), Palladam, India, pp. 61–65 (2019)
3. Ghosh, A.M., Grolinger, K.: Deep learning: edge-cloud data analytics for IoT. In: 2019 IEEE Canadian Conference of Electrical and Computer Engineering (CCECE), Edmonton, AB, Canada, pp. 1–7 (2019)
4. Xu, J., Wang, S., Zhou, A., Yang, F.: Edgence: a blockchain-enabled edge-computing platform for intelligent IoT-based dApps. China Commun. **17**(4), 78–87 (2020)
5. Miraz, M.H., Ali, M., Excell, P.S., Picking, R.: A review on Internet of Things (IoT), Internet of Everything (IoE) and Internet of Nano Things (IoNT). In: 2015 Internet Technologies and Applications (ITA), Wrexham, pp. 219–224 (2015)
6. Raj, A., Prakash, S.: Internet of Everything: a survey based on architecture, issues and challenges. In: 2018 5th IEEE Uttar Pradesh Section International Conference on Electrical, Electronics and Computer Engineering (UPCON), Gorakhpur, pp. 1–6 (2018)
7. Evans, D.: The Internet of Things: how the next evolution of the internet is changing everything. In: Cisco White Paper, pp. 3–4 (2011)
8. Lpez Pea, M.A., Muoz Fernndez, I.: SAT-IoT: an architectural model for a high-performance fog/edge/cloud IoT platform. In: 2019 IEEE 5th World Forum on Internet of Things (WF-IoT), Limerick, Ireland, pp. 633–638 (2019)
9. Shi, W., Cao, J., Zhang, Q., Li, Y., Xu, L.: Edge computing: vision and challenges. IEEE Internet Things J. **3**(5), 637–646 (2016)
10. Zhao, P., Zhao, W., Bao, H., Li, B.: Security energy efficiency maximization for untrusted relay assisted NOMA-MEC network with WPT. IEEE Access **8**, 147387–147398 (2020)
11. Taleb, T., Samdanis, K., Mada, B., Flinck, H., Dutta, S., Sabella, D.: On multi-access edge computing: a survey of the emerging 5G network edge cloud architecture and orchestration. IEEE Commun. Surv. Tutor. **19**(3), 1657–1681 (2017)
12. Hu, L., Sun, G., Ren, Y.: CoEdge: exploiting the edge-cloud collaboration for faster deep learning. IEEE Access **8**, 100533–100541 (2020)
13. Xiao, Y., Jia, Y., Liu, C., Cheng, X., Yu, J., Lv, W.: Edge computing security: state of the art and challenges. Proc. IEEE **107**(8), 1608–1631 (2019)
14. Wu, W., Zhang, Q., Wang, H.J.: Edge computing security protection from the perspective of classified protection of cybersecurity. In: 2019 6th International Conference on Information Science and Control Engineering (ICISCE), Shanghai, China, pp. 278–281 (2019)
15. Caprolu, M., Di Pietro, R., Lombardi, F., Raponi, S.: Edge computing perspectives: architectures, technologies, and open security issues. In: 2019 IEEE International Conference on Edge Computing (EDGE), Milan, Italy, pp. 116–123 (2019)

An Enhanced Approach for Multiple Sensitive Attributes in Data Publishing

Haiyan Kang[✉], Yaping Feng, and Xiameng Si

Department of Information Security, Beijing Information Science and Technology University, Beijing 100192, China
kanghaiyan@126.com

Abstract. With the development of the e-commerce and the logistics industry, more and more personal information has been collected by the third-party logistics. The personalized privacy protection problem with multiple sensitive attributes is seldom considered in data publishing. To solve this problem, a method of Multi-sensitive attributes Weights Clustering and Dividing (MWCD) is proposed. Firstly, set the corresponding weight for each sensitive attribute value considering the different requirements of users and then cluster the data based on the weights. Secondly, divide the records by level rule to select record for l-diversity. Finally, publish data based on the idea of Multi-Sensitive Bucketization. The experimental results indicate that the release ratio of the important data though the proposed algorithm is above 95%, and the execution time is shorter.

Keywords: Data publishing · Multi-sensitive attributes · Privacy protection · Clustering · Dividing

1 Introduction

With the development of the Internet, e-commerce has achieved new growth and has driven the development of the logistics industry. Especially since 2011, China's express delivery business has increased at an average rate of more than 50% each year. In the end of 2017, the State Post Bureau announced that China's express delivery had reached 41 billion pieces, ranking the first in the world's express business for four consecutive years. The rapid development of the express delivery industry has improved people's lives to a certain extent and provided great convenience for people's lives. However, information sharing also leads to the leakage of personal private information, which is becoming serious. For example, there are more and more personal accidents in today's society, such as telephone or text message harassment, kidnapping, fraud. Therefore, studying the problem of privacy protection in data publishing can effectively reduce the risk of personal information disclosure.

In real applications, the published data has involved multiple sensitive attributes. Some attributes do not directly contain private information, but when combining with other attributes, they can further infer more private information. Based on the previous

© ICST Institute for Computer Sciences, Social Informatics and Telecommunications Engineering 2021
Published by Springer Nature Switzerland AG 2021. All Rights Reserved
Y.-B. Lin and D.-J. Deng (Eds.): SGIoT 2020, LNICST 354, pp. 79–94, 2021.
https://doi.org/10.1007/978-3-030-69514-9_8

work [1–4], we have presented an algorithm to decrease the leakage of private information. In this paper, we further study the multi-sensitive attribute privacy data release in the field of logistics and propose Multi-sensitive attributes Weights Clustering and Dividing method (MWCD).

Our main contributions are as follows:

(1) We pointed out the problem of privacy protection data publishing with multiple sensitive attributes.
(2) We propose Multi-sensitive attributes Weights Clustering and Dividing algorithm(MWCD), which can keep as much available information as possible, while maintaining data security.
(3) We compare our algorithm with the WMBF algorithm[5] on the real data set. The experimental results show that the release ratio of important data in our algorithm is higher (above 95%), and the execution time is shorter. Therefore, the published data through our algorithm had higher availability and achieved the effect of personalized privacy protection.

2   Related Work

In the study on privacy-preserving data publishing, based on grouping privacy protection have developed amounts of classic privacy protection models. Sweeney et al. firstly proposed k-anonymity model [6]. This model only cut off the connection between identifier and sensitive attributes, but it did not make corresponding requirement for sensitive attributes, and it was easy to produce homogeneity attack. Then, domestic and foreign scholars continue to improve the model, and l-diversity [7], p-sensitive k-anonymity model [8, 9], (a, k)-anonymous model [10], t-closeness model [11] and other models were proposed. The above privacy protection models are mainly for single sensitive attribute data, but in the actual situation, logistics data publishing involves multiple sensitive attributes. So data owners should pay more attention to privacy leakage for each sensitive attribute when publishing data. Yang Xiao-chun et al. proposed a Multi-Sensitive Bucketization (MSB) [12] based on lossy join for publishing data with multiple sensitive attributes, which is a breakthrough in this field. Tao Y et al. [13] proposed the (g, l)-grouping method, whose principle is: based on the MSB, in order to protect the personal privacy information in the data publishing with multiple sensitive attributes, the sensitivity concept of sensitive attributes was introduced, then the l-diversity and g-difference principles were used to constrain the value of each sensitive attribute in records. In 2010, Liu et al. [14] proposed the l-MNSA algorithm, which used anonymity to release data. In 2013, Han et al. [15] proposed a SLOMS algorithm to publish data for microdata with multiple sensitive attributes. Zhu et al. [16] proposed a new (w, y, k)-anonymity model and implemented it in a top-down approach. In 2014, Liu et al. [17] implemented the anonymous data publishing of multiple numerical sensitive attributes by adding noise. Xiao et al. [18] proposed a new privacy protection framework—differential privacy, to prevent any background knowledge attacking. In order to better prevent similarity attacks between multiple numerical sensitive attributes, in 2015, Sowmyarani and

Srinivasan [19] combined t-closeness technology with p-sensitive, k-anonymity technology to form a new privacy protection model for multiple sensitive attributes. Liu et al. [20] proposed the MNSACM method by using clustering and MSB for privacy preserving data publishing.

Some of the above data publishing methods are directed to the data with a single sensitive attribute, while others are directed to the data with multiple sensitive attributes. But they have some shortcomings in terms of algorithm efficiency, background knowledge attacks and others. Therefore, we propose Multi-sensitive attributes Weights Clustering and Dividing method.

3 Preliminary

3.1 Problem Description

Based on different application purposes (population statistics, income statistics, etc.), the third-party will publish data containing sensitive personal information. Once these data are used by attackers, it will lead to the disclosure of individual information and cause immeasurable consequences. Because the fact that different users have different application purposes, we need to protect the published data while meeting the needs of different users. But personalization issues are rarely considered in current data release studies.

The multi-dimensional bucket grouping model is still used in data publishing with multiple sensitive attributes. But, the multi-dimensional bucket of previous methods has the following shortcomings: (1) The grouping efficiency is lower. (2) The order of selecting buckets is improper, causing data suppressing problems. (3) They cannot meet the users' personalized needs. We propose relevant methods for resolving the above problems in the paper.

3.2 Problem Definition

It is assumed that the data table T $\{A_1, A_2,..., A_x, S_1, S_2,..., S_y\}$ is published by the data owner, where $\{A_1, A_2,..., A_x\}$ represents the quasi-identifier and $\{S_1, S_2,..., S_y\}$ represents the sensitive attribute. It is assumed that the number of data records is n in the data table T, then $|T| = $ n, and each data recorded as t_i ($1 \leq i \leq n$).

Definition 1 (Lossy join). Data publisher divide the data set into two data tables. One includes the Group ID of data record and the quasi-identifier, and the other includes Group ID of data record and sensitive attributes.

Definition 2 (Multidimensional sensitive attributes). In the data table T, all the sensitive attributes form multidimensional sensitive attributes, which can be denoted by S. S_i ($1 \leq i \leq y$) represents i-th sensitive attribute.

Definition 3 (Grouping). A group is a subset of the data records in the data table T. Each data record belongs to only one group in the data table T. The group of the data table T is denoted as $GT\{G_1, G_2,..., G_m\}$, and $(QI_i \cap QI_j =)$ $(1 \leq i \neq j \leq m)$, where QI is a quasi-identifier attribute.

Definition 4 (Multidimensional sensitive attributes' *l*-diversity) [16]. In the group G, if each dimension sensitive attribute value of all data records satisfy *l*-diversity respectively, then the group G satisfies *l*-diversity of multi-dimensional sensitive attributes. In other words, the group G satisfies multi-dimensional sensitive attributes' *l*-diversity.

Definition 5 (d-dimensional bucket). [12]. If there are d-dimensional sensitive attributes, the d-dimensional bucket is denoted as Bucket $(S_1, S_2, ..., S_d)(2 \le d \le n)$, and each dimension of the multi-sensitive attributes corresponds to a one-dimensional bucket. According to the values of each dimension, the records are mapped to the corresponding bucket.

Definition 6 (Weights clustering). Suppose that there are n records in the data table T, each data record has d-dimensional sensitive attributes. For the sake of simplicity, we ignore the identifier and the quasi-identifier when forming multiple clusters which is denoted as $T_c\{C_1, C_2, ..., C_q\}(|C_q| \ge 1, 1 \le q \le n)$. The weights of the sensitive attribute values of each dimension in the same cluster are equal or similar, and the weights of different clusters are quite different.

Definition 7 (Weighted average value). It represents the average of the weights all sensitive attribute in each record.

Definition 8 (Weighted standard value). It represents the degree of deviation between the weight of different sensitive attribute in each record. The greater the value is, the greater the degree of difference. On the contrary, the smaller the value is, the smaller the degree of difference.

Definition 9 (Suppression technology). Some records that cannot be released or some records that do not satisfy privacy protection are hidden.

4   Multi-sensitive Attributes Weights Clustering and Dividing Model (MWCD)

4.1   The Overall Framework of Data Publishing

In this paper we improve the MSB grouping technology to achieve safer and more available data release. The main framework of this paper is shown in Fig. 1. It consists of three modules: data collection layer, method layer and data publishing layer. Specific explanations are as follows:

Data Collection Layer
Data collection is obtained through enterprise survey and web crawlers. The enterprise survey aims to understand the storage and release of data information in the express company. Web crawlers use crawler technology to collect information from website pages. The collected information is built into the original database. In order to make the algorithm more convenient, the data is preprocessed and shown in Table 1.

Method Layer
We firstly divide different records into multiple categories by clustering. Then we build weighted multi-dimensional buckets for multi-sensitive attributes, and map the records in

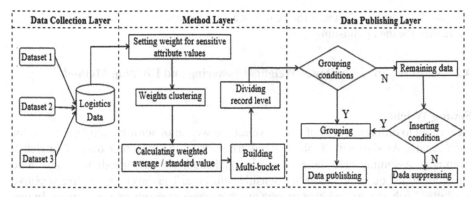

Fig. 1. The flow chart of data publishing.

Table 1. Part of the customer data of a logistics company.

Identifier	Quasi-identifier		Sensitive attribute			
ID	Zip	Age	Home address	Phone number	Name of goods	Credibility
t_1	0052	29	HeBei **(0.8)	132****7752(0.9)	Food	B
t_2	0029	31	TianJin**(0.6)	135****6851(0.2)	Clothing	A
t_3	0031	35	ShanDong**(0.5)	134****5612(0.7)	Phone	B
t_4	0058	28	HeBei **(0.1)	136****5762(1.0)	Toy	B
t_5	0062	32	TianJin**(0.5)	136****8623(0.1)	Clothing	A
t_6	0046	36	BeiJing(0.4)	137****6752(0.4)	Toy	A
t_7	0039	40	HeBei **(0.2)	139****4231(0.9)	Food	B
t_8	0075	30	ShanDong**(0.8)	187****1234(0.8)	Phone	C
t_9	0048	46	BeiJing**(0.6)	152****2564(0.2)	Book	A
t_{10}	0089	38	TianJin**(0.2)	136****8962(0.8)	Book	B

the data table to corresponding multi-dimensional buckets. Finally, we select important records by the hierarchical division method to satisfy the users' different needs.

Data Publishing Layer

By considering the max weight first selection algorithm, we select the data record in the multi-dimensional bucket to build a group satisfying l-diversity. Then we judge the data that do not satisfy the group for the first time. Finally, the quasi-identifiers of the groups that satisfy the condition are generalized. We suppress the remaining data and publish anonymous tables.

Our paper mainly improves the method layer and solves the following problems. (1) According to the weights that users set, we can meet the user's personalized privacy requirements. (2) Our core idea is clustering and dividing. We group the records that satisfy *l*-diversity by adopting record level strategy to protect data privacy. (3) We further process the clustered data and the remaining data to reduce data suppressing. Finally, we realize the data publishing.

4.2 Multi-sensitive Attributes Weights Clustering and Dividing Method

Setting Weight

According to different needs of users, we set the weight of sensitive attribute value for each record. As shown in Table 1, there are parts of the customer data of Logistics Company. Assuming that Table 1 is to be published, the data are divided into three parts: identifier, quasi-identifier and sensitive attribute. The data contains five sensitive attributes, such as home address, phone number, name of goods and credibility. In this paper, the first Two sensitive attributes are analyzed in Table 1, where the home address and phone number match corresponding weights for the user's requirements. For example, in Table 1, for the record t_1, the weight of the home address and phone number is 0.8 and is 0.9, respectively. For the record t_2, the weight of the home address and phone number is 0.6 and 0.2 respectively and so on.

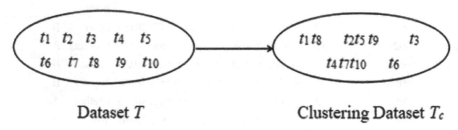

Dataset T Clustering Dataset T_c

Fig. 2. The process of clustering.

Weights Clustering

Based on the weight of sensitive attribute value in each record, all records are clustered to form multiple clusters, recorded as clustered dataset Tc. In each cluster, the corresponding weights of all records are similar or equal. As shown in Fig. 2, it is a simple process of clustering for Table 1.

In Fig. 1, ten records are clustered to form 5 clusters, C_1 {t_1, t_8}, C_2 {t_2, t_5, t_9}, C_3 {t_3}, C_4 {t_4, t_7, t_{10}}, C_5 {t_6}. It can bring benefits for the next step. The process not only reduces time to calculate the weighted average value and the weighted standard value, but also contributes to comparison and selection results between the records when grouping, thus improve the efficiency of the algorithm and reduce the running time of CPU.

Calculating the Weighted Average and Weighted Standard Value for Each Record

For Table 1, the records have four sensitive attributes, recorded as S_1, S_2, S_3, and S_4. In t_1, the weight of each sensitive attribute is recorded as $S_1{}^1$, $S_1{}^2$, $S_1{}^3$, $S_1{}^4$. In t_2, the weight of each sensitive attribute is recorded as $S_2{}^1, S_2{}^2, S_2{}^3, S_2{}^4$, and so on. The Weight Average Value ($WAve^n$) is denoted as

$$WAve^n = \frac{1}{d} \sum_{i=1}^{d} S_i^n \tag{1}$$

The Weight Standard Value ($WSve^n$) is denoted as

$$WSve^n = \frac{1}{d} \sum_{i=1}^{d} \left(S_i^n - WAve^n\right)^2 \tag{2}$$

After weight clustering, calculate the weighted average and weighted standard value of each record based on the Eq. (1) and (2), and then write the result of each record in the corresponding place.

Building Multi-sensitive Bucketization

The previous method for building a multi-sensitive bucketization is that every dimension of the multi-sensitive bucketization corresponds to the dimension of the multiple sensitive attributes, and the value of each dimension corresponds to different sensitive attribute values. However, in practical applications, some sensitive attribute values are mostly different or even completely different. If there are a big amount of data records, the previous method cannot work. In this case, we first generalize the sensitive attribute values in order to reduce the classification of sensitive attribute values. Then build a multi-sensitive bucketization. We built a multidimensional bucket for Table 1, showed in Table 2. In the first two sensitive attributes, the attribute values of the phone number are different. We generalize each sensitive attribute value, according to respective dimension of the multi-sensitive bucketization.

Table 2. 2-d bucket structure.

	Class 1	Class 2	Class 3	Class 4	Class 5
HeBei**	$\{t_1, t_7\}$				$\{t_4\}$
TianJin**		$\{t_2, t_5\}$		$\{t_{10}\}$	
ShanDong**			$\{t_3, t_8\}$		
BeiJing**				$\{t_9\}$	$\{t_6\}$

Dividing Record Level

We divide the records based on the weighted average value, then selects important records and builds a group that satisfies l-diversity. The larger the weighted average value, the more important the record is. As shown in Table 2, the record level represents the importance of the record, and all records are divided into three levels. 'A' represents important, 'B' represents mediocre and 'C' is not important. The purpose of the record level table is to judge the importance of the records. The important records are firstly released.

In order to release important data as much as possible, while satisfying the privacy requirements of users, we use the maximum weight first selection strategy (where the 'weight' is not the weight of each sensitive attribute but considering the weighted average and the weighted standard value synthetically) to select the record for group which satisfy multi-sensitive attributes l-diversity, which ensure that important data are released.

Four conditions between the weighted average and the weighted standard value of each record in the same cluster are listed as follows:

(1) Both the weighted average value and the weighted standard value are different.
(2) The weighted average value is different, but the weighted standard value is equal.
(3) The weighted average value is equal, but the weighted standard value is different.
(4) Both the weighted average value and the weighted standard value are equal.

Therefore, the steps for defining the maximum weight first selection strategy are as follows:

Step1: If there exists the cluster of $WAve^n \in [0.6, 1]$ in data set, these data are very important. Alternately select the record with larger weighted average and smaller weighted standard value to form group until all the records are traversed in the cluster. Otherwise, goto Step2.

Step2: If there exists the cluster of $WAve^n \in [0.4, 0.6)$ in data set, these data are important generally. Alternately select the record with larger weighted average and smaller weighted standard value to form group until all the records are traversed in the cluster. Otherwise, goto Step3.

Step3: If it exists the cluster of $WAve^n \in [0, 0.4)$ in data set, these data are not very important. In turn, select the record with larger weighted average and larger weighted standard value form group until all the records are traversed in the cluster.

Table 3. Record level table.

The range of the weighted average	Record level
[0.6, 1]	A
[0.4, 0.6)	B
[0, 0.4)	C

When $WAve^n \in [0, 0.4)$, firstly choose the record with larger weighted standard value. The reason is that in some records, the individual sensitive attributes have higher weights and other sensitive attributes have lower weights. In order to guarantee the release of sensitive attributes with higher weights, we, only choose the record with larger weighted standard value to join the group. For example, if the weighted average of two records is 0.3 in the cluster, but the sensitive attribute weights are (0.8, 0.1, 0.1, 0.2), (0.3, 0.2, 0.4, 0.3), respectively. It can be seen that the former contains a sensitive attribute with higher weight, and the weighted standard values are 8.5 and 0.5, respectively by calculation, so that the former is first selected to ensure that important data is firstly released, which further satisfies the users' personalized privacy requirements.

Publishing Data

It generalizes the quasi identifier of the data that satisfies l-diversity. The released data are divided into two data tables. One contains the records with the quasi identifier attributes and group number, called the quasi identifier attribute table QIT. The other contains the records with the sensitive attribute and group number, called the sensitive attribute table ST.

4.3 Multi-sensitive Attributes Weights Clustering and Dividing Algorithm

In this paper, we propose MWCD methods to release data, and we use Algorithm 1 to denote them. In this algorithm, we bring in clustering, division and generalization methods, and then select important records to release.

Take Table 1 as an example to illustrate the process of the proposed algorithm. We can see the weights of the first two-dimensional sensitive attributes and Table 3 shows the corresponding d-dimensional bucket ($d = 2$). By clustering, the dataset T_c contains 5 clusters: $C_1\{t_1, t_8\}$, $C_2\{t_2, t_5, t_9\}$, $C_3\{C_3\}$, $C_4\{t_4, t_7, t_{10}\}$, $C_5\{t_6\}$. According to the maximum weight first selection strategy, we first select record t_1 of cluster C_1 into group G_1, $G_1\{t_1\}$, while deleting t_1 in bucket; then t_8 is selected, and t_1 and t_8 satisfy multiple sensitive attributes l-diversity, so we insert t_8 into the group G_1, as $G_1\{t_1, t_8\}$, while deleting t_8 in bucket; the next step is to select record t_3 in cluster C_3. Due to multiple sensitive attributes l-diversity rule, t_3 cannot be inserted into the group G_1, so a new group G_2 is built, and denoted as $G_2\{t_3\}$, and deleting t_3 in bucket; then record t_4 in the cluster C_4 is selected, and record t_3 and t_4 satisfy multiple sensitive attributes l-diversity, so we insert t_4 into the group G_2, as $G_2\{t_3, t_4\}$, and deleting t_4 in bucket; Then we can get the groups $G_1\{t_1, t_8, t_{10}\}$, $G_2\{t_2, t_3, t_4\}$, $G_3\{t_5, t_7, t_9\}$, and the remaining record is t_6. Once again, determine whether the remaining data can be inserted into the group. At this time, the remaining record t_6 can be inserted into the group G_1, as $G_1\{t_1, t_6, t_8, t_{10}\}$. Therefore, the final groups are $G_1\{t_1, t_6, t_8, t_{10}\}$, $G_2\{t_2, t_3, t_4\}$, $G_3\{t_5, t_7, t_9\}$. The final released data is shown in Table 4 and Table 5.

Algorithm 1 Multi-sensitive Weights Clustering and Dividing

Input: Data table T, Diversity parameter l.

Output: Quasi-identifier attribute table QIT, Sensitive attribute table ST.

1: Setting weight;

2: Weights clustering;

3: Calculating the weighted average value and the weighted standard value for each record and save them in the record;

4: Building multi-sensitive bucket;

5: Dividing records level;

6: **while**

7:    Selecting the record t_i by the maximum weight first selection strategy;

8:    **if** (the record t_i satisfies l-diversity)

9:      Inserting t_i into the group and deleting t_i from the bucket;

10:    **else**

11:        creating a new l-diversity group and deleting t_i from the bucket;

12: **end while** (no record is selected)

13: **for each** the records which do not satisfy l-diversity group

15:    Selecting the record t_i by the maximum weight first selection strategy;

16:    **if** (a group G_i still satisfy l-diversity after adding the record t_i)

17:      Inserting t_i into the group G_i;

18: **else**

19:    Inserting t_i into the remaining dataset;

20: **end for**

21: Suppression all the remaining records;

22: Generalizing the quasi-identifier attributes of data in all groups;

23: Output QIT and ST;

---

5   Experimental and Analysis

5.1   Experimental Data and Environment

Experimental Data

The customer information of the logistics company is used as experimental data and we collect 7000 records. The description of partial data is shown in Table 1.

Experimental Environment

Processor Intel(R)Core(TM)i5-5200U CPU, memory 4GB, operating system Windows 10($\times$64), MATLAB and Java are used as the main test language.

5.2   Evaluation Criteria of the Algorithm

Release Ratio of Important Data

If the weighted average value of the record belongs to the range of [0.4, 1], it is defined as "important data", the release ratio of important record is defined as Eq. (3).

$$Relration = \frac{number'(WAve \in [0.4, 1])}{number(WAve \in [0.4, 1])} \tag{3}$$

In the Eq. (3), $number'(WAve \in [0.4, 1])$ represents the number of important records in the published data, and $number(WAve \in [0.4, 1])$ represents the number of important records in the initial data. The larger the Relratio, the more important the record is. Important records are released first, so that personalized demand of users can be satisfied.

Additional Information Loss
In data set T, if there exist multi-sensitive attribute l-diversity group $G\{G_1, G_2,...,G_m\}$, $|G_i| \geq l(1 \leq i \leq m)$, where m represents the number of groups, then the additional information is defined as Eq. (4).

$$AddInfo = \frac{\sum_{1 \leq i \leq m} |Gi - l|}{ml} \tag{4}$$

Suppression Ratio
When publishing data, if the number of suppression records is $|T_s|$ and the number of total data is $|T|$, then the suppression ratio is defined as Eq. (5).

$$Suppratio = \frac{|T_s|}{|T|} \tag{5}$$

Execution Time
The execution time means the time it takes to execute the proposed algorithm in the testing dada.

5.3 Experimental Analysis

The experiment will analyze the performance of the proposed algorithm from four aspects: release ratio of important data, additional information loss, suppression ratio, and execution time. With various data size $|T|$ ($k = 10^3$), various diversity parameters l, and various the number of sensitive attribute d, we compare algorithm 1 with WMBF algorithm, and the results are shown in the following chart.

Analysis for Release Ratio of Important Data
Figure 3(a–c) gives the release ratio of important data in two algorithms under different parameters. For example, Fig. 3(a) shows the release ratio of important data under different data size $|T|$, when l is 3 and d is 3.

Three phenomena can be acquired from the experiment results:(1)With the increase of different parameters, the release ratio of important data has been changed in two algorithms, but it always keep above 0.80; (2) In Fig. 3(b), there is a big gap for the release ratio of important data in two algorithms. The reason is that between MWBF algorithm, the bigger the diversity parameter is, the more l-diversity groups are, and the number of records in each bucket is less, then the random selection of the records becomes relatively large, which may lead to selecting the unimportant records preferentially. In contrast, important records are preferentially selected in the algorithm 1. Therefore, the release ratio of important data is higher. (3) For the algorithm 1, the release rate of important data is always higher than the algorithm MWBF, which can reach above 95%.

Figure 4(a–c) shows the additional information loss under different parameters in two algorithms.

We can see that (1) In Fig. 4(a), the additional information loss is below 0.12 for different data size when $l = 3$ and $d = 3$ and it takes a significant trend as the increasing number of data size; (2) From Fig. 4(b), it can be seen that with the increase of diversity parameter l, the additional information loss also increases when $|T| = 6$ k and $d = 3$; (3) The additional information loss generated in the two algorithms is small, which is below 0.03, and means that the algorithm is close to optimal.

Analysis for Suppression Ratio

Figure 5(a, b) shows the suppression ratio under different parameters in two algorithms. When the parameters are different, the suppression ratio changes, too. When the suppression ratio is the shortest, it also indicates that the algorithm is optimal under this condition.

Three phenomena can be acquired from the experiment results: (1) In Fig. 5(a), the suppression ratio decreases as the data size $|T|$ increasing, when $l = 3$, $d = 3$, and it will close to 0 when data size $|T| = 7$ k. The reason is that the greater the number of data size, the better the diversification of sensitive attribute values of the record, and then the effect of the grouping becomes better, and the number of suppressed data also gradually decreases. (2) In Fig. 5(b, c), with the increase of l and d, the suppression ratio continues to grow in two algorithm. With the increase of diversity parameter l, we need insert more records into the group. If the number of records in a group does not satisfy diversity parameter l, this group is incomplete and the remaining data will increase; (3) In Fig. 5(a, c), the suppression ratio is much lower than the results of Fig. 4(b).

Analysis for Execution Time

Figure 6(a–c) shows the execution time under different parameters in two algorithms.

Three phenomena can be acquired from the experiment results: (1) From Fig. 6(a, c), it can be seen that with the increase of the number of data $|T|$ (or the number of sensitive attributes d), the execution time also increases linearly, but below 25 s; (2) In Fig. 6(b), the execution time of the two algorithms are between 15 s and 20 s when $|T| = 6$ k and $d = 3$. (3)The efficiency of the algorithm 1 is higher than that of the algorithm WMBF. The algorithm 1 cost less time in the weights clustering process, and thus the total execution time of algorithm is lower.

Table 4. Algorithm 1 QIT.

Zip	Age	Group ID
[0050–0090]	[28–38]	1
[0020–0060]	[28–40]	2
[0020–0060]	[28–40]	2
[0020–0060]	[28–40]	2
[0030–0070]	[30–40]	3
[0050–0090]	[28–38]	1
[0030–0070]	[30–40]	3
[0050–0090]	[28–38]	1
[0030–0070]	[30–40]	3
[0050–0090]	[28–38]	1

Table 5. Algorithm 1 ST.

Group ID	Home address	Phone number
1	HeBei**	132****7752
	TianJin**	137****6752
	TianJin**	187****1234
	BeiJing**	136****8962
2	TianJin**	135****6851
	ShanDong**	134****5612
	HeBei**	136****5762
3	TianJin**	136****8623
	HeBei**	139****4231
	BeiJing**	152****2564

6 Conclusion

In this paper, we introduce data publishing for multi-sensitive attributes in logistics, and analyze the personalized privacy-preserving problem of multi-sensitive attributes values. Based on the idea of multi-sensitive bucketization, we proposed a method of Multi-sensitive attributes Weights Clustering and Dividing (MWCD) to satisfy the requirements of users. We adopted the clustering and dividing method to release data. Then we compared the proposed (MWCD) with WMBF algorithm. The experimental results show that the additional information loss and suppression ratio of two algorithms have a little difference, but the release rate of the important data in the proposed (MWCD) algorithm is above 95%, and the execution time is lower. Therefore, the published data

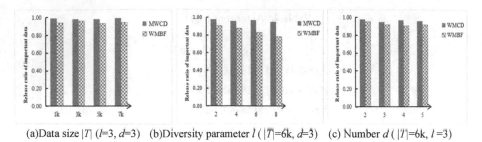

(a)Data size |T| (l=3, d=3)   (b)Diversity parameter l (|T|=6k, d=3)   (c) Number d (|T|=6k, l =3)

Fig. 3. Release ratio of important data under different parameters

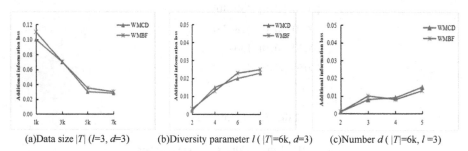

(a)Data size |T| (l=3, d=3)   (b)Diversity parameter l (|T|=6k, d=3)   (c)Number d (|T|=6k, l =3)

Fig. 4. Additional information loss under different parameters.

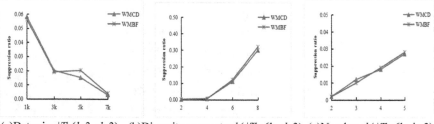

(a)Data size |T| (l=3, d=3)   (b)Diversity parameter l (|T|=6k, d=3)   (c)Number d (|T|=6k, l =3)

Fig. 5. Suppression ratio under different parameters.

in the proposed (MWCD) algorithm have high availability and achieved the effect of personalized privacy protection.

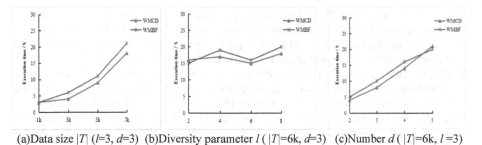

(a)Data size $|T|$ (l=3, d=3)   (b)Diversity parameter l ($|T|$=6k, d=3)   (c)Number d ($|T|$=6k, l =3)

Fig. 6. Execution time under different parameters.

Acknowledgment. This work is partially supported by Humanities and social sciences research project of the Ministry of Education (No. 20YJAZH046), fund of Bistu promoting the connotation development of universities and improving the scientific research level (No. 2019KYNH219), and Natural Science Foundation of China (No. 61370139).

References

1. Lu, Q.W., Wang, C.M., Xiong, Y., et al.: Personalized privacy-preserving trajectory data publishing. Chin. J. Electron. **26**(2), 285–291 (2017)
2. Li, J., Bai, Z.H., Yu, R.Y., et al.: Mobile location privacy protection algorithm based on PSO optimization. Acta Comput. Sinica **41**(05), 1037–1051 (2018)
3. Wang, H.Y., Lu, J.X.: Personalized privacy protection method for group recommendation. J. Commun. **40**(09), 106–115 (2019)
4. Zhou, C.L., Chen, Y.H., Tian, H., et al.: Network k nearest neighbor query method for protecting location privacy and query content privacy. Acta Softw. Sinica **31**(02), 229–250 (2020)
5. Lv, G.J.: Research on Privacy Protection Method of Multi Sensitive Attribute Data in Data Publishing. Chongqing University, Chongqing (2018)
6. Latanya, S.: k-anonymity: a model for protecting privacy. Int. J. Uncertainty Fuzziness Knowl.-Based Syst. **10**(05), 557–570 (2002)
7. Ashwin, M., et al.: L-diversity: privacy beyond k-anonymity. ACM Trans. Knowl. Disc. Data **2006**(1), 24–36 (2007)
8. Truta, T.M., Vinay, B..: Privacy protection: p-sensitive k-anonymity property. In: Proceeding of the 22th International Conference on Data Engineering 2006, pp. 94–103. ICDE (2006)
9. Sun, X.X., Wang, H., Li, J.Y., Ross, D.: Achieving P-sensitive K-anonymity via anatomy. In: Proceedings of the 2009 IEEE International Conference on e-Business Engineering 2009, pp. 199–205. ICEBE (2009)
10. Wong, R.C.W., Li, J., et al.: (α, k)-anonymity: an enhanced k-anonymity model for privacy preserving data publishing. In: Proceedings of the 12th International Conference on Knowledge Discovery and Data Mining 2006, pp. 754–759. ACM (2006)
11. Li, N.H., Li, T.C., Venkatasubramanian, S.: T-Closeness: privacy beyond k-anonymity and l-diversity. In: International Conference on Data Engineering 2007, pp. 106–115. IEEE (2007)
12. Yang, X.C., Wang, Y.Z., Wang, B., et al.: Privacy preserving approaches for multiple sensitive attributes in data publishing. Chin. J. Comput. **31**(04), 574–587 (2008)
13. Tao, Y., Chen, H., Xiao, X., et al.: Angel: enhancing the utility of generalization for privacy preserving publication. Trans. Knowl. Data Eng. **21**(07), 1073–1087 (2009)

14. Liu, T., Ni, W., Chong, Z., et al.: Privacy-preserving data publishing methods for multiple numerical sensitive attributes. J. Southeast Univ. (Nat. Sci. Ed.) **40**(04), 699–703 (2010)
15. Han, J., Luo, F., Lu, J., et al.: SLOMS: a privacy preserving data publishing method for multiple sensitive attributes microdata. J. Softw. **8**(12), 3096–3104 (2013)
16. Zhu, H., Tian, S., Xie, M., et al.: Preserving privacy for sensitive values of individuals in data publishing based on a new additive noise approach. In: Proceeding of the 3rd International Conference on Computer Communication and Networks 2014, pp. 1–6. IEEE (2014)
17. Liu, Q., Shen, H., Sang, Y.: A privacy-preserving data publishing method for multiple numerical sensitive attributes via clustering and multi-sensitive bucketization. In: Proceeding of the sixth International Symposium on Parallel Architectures, Algorithms and Programming 2014, pp. 220–223. IEEE (2014)
18. Guo, X.L., Zhang, J., Qu, Z.Y., et al.: MADARS: a method of multi-attributes generalized randomization privacy preserving. Int. J. Multimedia Ubiq. Eng. **10**(10), 119–126 (2015)
19. Sowmyarani, C.N, Srinivasan, G.N.: A robust privacy-preserving model for data publishing. In: 2015 International Conference on Computer Communication and Informatics 2015, pp. 1–6. IEEE (2015)
20. Liu, T.T., Ni, W.W., Chong, Z.H., et al.: Privacy-preserving data publishing methods for multiple numerical sensitive attributes. J. Southeast Univ. (Nat. Sci. Ed.) **40**(4), 699–703 (2010)

Secure Sharing Sensitive Data Based on Network Coding and Attribute-Based Encryption

Zhiqiang Xu[1][✉], Bo Shen[2], and Zhiyuan Zhang[2]

[1] School of Electronic and Information Engineering,
Beijing Jiaotong University, Beijing 100044, China
18120155@bjtu.edu.com
[2] Key Laboratory of Communication and Information Systems, Beijing Municipal Commission
of Education, Beijing, China
{bshen,zhangzhiyuan}@bjtu.edu.com

Abstract. The security of sharing sensitive information through a distributed information storage and sharing platform is required strictly in many situations. In this paper, we present a novel approach with the aim of increasing security of sharing sensitive information. The model improves security by exploiting Attribute-Based Encryption. In addition, we incorporate network coding to our model to improve the efficiency of transmitting information.

Keywords: Distributed information storage · Attribute-based encryption · Network coding

1 Introduction

With the development of information technology, people can quickly obtain valuable information from various types of data sources nowadays. We can easily facilitate cross-domain data sharing by a lot of means, such as Internet, massively parallel processing databases, distributed file systems, cloud computing platforms and scalable storage systems. Information acquisition and sharing is the fundamental purpose of the development of these communication and network technologies, and it is also an important technical means to build various information systems. At the same time, the distributed, cross-domain and dynamic transmission and sharing of information are also facing great security threats, which put great challenges to the traditional security model.

The security of sharing sensitive information is through a distributed information storage and sharing platform. Under the premise of ensuring information security, the sharing provider can share the required sensitive information according to a certain strategy, scope and target.

For the purpose of security, access control and data management are realized through security isolation between multiple domains in general information systems. On the other hand, cross-domain access is often required to maximize shared network and data resource services which are contradict to each other. Because cross-domain access

Y.-B. Lin and D.-J. Deng (Eds.): SGIoT 2020, LNICST 354, pp. 95–105, 2021.
https://doi.org/10.1007/978-3-030-69514-9_9

makes the management of users with different security domains and different security levels more and more complex, and various application layer protocol vulnerabilities give hackers opportunity to attack the network. Therefore, it is very important to study the security sharing theory and technology of sensitive data in view of the application scenario of multi-level security cross-domain sharing of data, and realize flexible cross-domain data access and improve the availability of data under the condition of protecting sensitive data from leakage.

In this paper, we describe a secure approach to share sensitive information with network coding and Attribute-Based Encryption in order to leverage the efficiency and security of information transmission.

2 Related Work

Shamir [1] first proposed the concept of Identity-Based Encryption. They introduce a novel cryptographic scheme, which enables any pair of users to communicate securely and to verify each other's signatures without exchanging private or public keys, without keeping key directories, and without using the services of a third party. However, it wasn't until much later that Boneh and Franklin [2] proposed the first fully functional Encryption scheme that was both practical and secure. Their solution made novel use of groups for which there was an efficiently computable bilinear map. The scheme had chosen ciphertext security in the random oracle model assuming an elliptic curve variant of the computational Diffie-Hellman problem.

Canetti et al. [3] rigorously defined a notion of security for forward-secure public-key encryption and also gave efficient constructions of schemes satisfying this notion. They proved semantic security of one scheme in the standard model based on the decisional version of the bilinear Diffie-Hellman assumption. Yao et al. [4] presented a scalable and joining-time-oblivious forward-secure hierarchical identity-based encryption scheme that allows keys to be updated autonomously. They also noted how their techniques for resisting collusion attacks were useful in attribute-based encryption. However, the cost of their scheme in terms of computation, private key size, and ciphertext size increased exponentially with the number of attributes.

Sahai and Waters [5] propose a new type of Identity-Based Encryption called Fuzzy Identity-Based Encryption as a new means for encrypted access control. In a Fuzzy Identity-Based encryption system ciphertexts are not necessarily encrypted to one particular user as in traditional public key cryptography. Instead both users' private keys and ciphertexts will be associated with a set of descriptive attributes or a policy over attributes. A user is able to decrypt a ciphertext if there is a "match" between his private key and the ciphertext.

Bethencourt et al. [6] provided the first construction of a ciphertext-policy attribute-based encryption (CP-ABE), and gave the first construction of such a scheme. In their system, a user's private key would be associated with an arbitrary number of attributes expressed as strings. On the other hand, when a party encrypted a message in the system, they specified an associated access structure over attributes. A user would only be able to decrypt a cipher-text if that user's attributes pass through the cipher-text's access structure. At a mathematical level, access structures in their system were described by a monotonic "access tree", where nodes of the access structure were composed of threshold gates and the leaves describe attributes. They noted that AND gates could be constructed as n-of-n threshold gates and OR gates as 1-of-n threshold gates. Furthermore, they could handle more complex access controls such as numeric ranges by converting them to small access trees.

Ahlswede et al. [7] proposed a new class of problems called network information flow which is inspired by computer network applications. Consider a point-to-point communication network on which a number of information sources are to be multicast to certain sets of destinations. We assume that the information sources are mutually independent. The problem is to characterize the admissible coding rate region. This model subsumes all previously studied models along the same line. In this paper, we study the problem with one information source, and we have obtained a simple characterization of the admissible coding rate region. Our result can be regarded as the Max-flow Min-cut Theorem for network information flow. Contrary to one's intuition, our work reveals that it is in general not optimal to regard the information to be multicast as a "fluid" which can simply be routed or replicated. Rather, by employing coding at the nodes, which we refer to as network coding, bandwidth can in general be saved. This finding may have significant impact on future design of switching systems.

3 Methodology

3.1 CP-ABE

First of all, we give the definitions of an access structure proposed by Bethencourt et al. [6]. Then we introduce how does the ciphertext-policy attribute-based encryption scheme work to guarantee the security of access control.

Definition (Access Structure): Let $\{P_1, P_2, \ldots, P_n\}$ be a set of parties. A collection $\mathbb{A} \subseteq 2^{\{P_1, P_2, \ldots, P_n\}}$ is monotone if $\forall B, C$ if $B \in \mathbb{A}$ *and* $B \subseteq C$ *then* $C \subseteq \mathbb{A}$. An access structure (respectively, monotone access structure) is a collection (respectively, monotone collection) A of non-empty subsets of $\{P_1, P_2, \ldots, P_n\}$, i.e., $\mathbb{A} \subseteq 2^{\{P_1, P_2, \ldots, P_n\}}$\empty set. The sets in A are called the authorized sets, and the sets no in A are called the unauthorized sets.

Setup. The input of setup algorithm is the implicit security parameter and the output are public parameters PK and a master key MK.

Encrypt(PK, M, A). The input of encryption algorithm are the public parameters PK, a message M, and an access structure A over the universe of attributes. The algorithm will encrypt the message M and output a ciphertext CT which contains A implicitly. The ciphertext CT can only be decrypted rightly when a user have a set of attributes that satisfy the access structure A.

Key Generation(MK, S). The input of key generation algorithm are the master key MK and a set of attributes S which gives some descriptions of the key. And the output of this algorithm is a private key SK which contains the set of attributes S implicitly.

Decrypt(PK, CT, SK). The input of decryption algorithm are the public parameters PK, a ciphertext CT, and a private key SK. As discussed in the former algorithms, we can see that the ciphertext CT contains access structure A implicitly and the private key SK contains the set of attributes S implicitly. When the set S of attributes satisfies the access structure A, the decrypt algorithm will decrypt the ciphertext rightly and output a message M.

Delegate(SK, S'). The input of delegate algorithm is a secret key SK of set of attributes S and a set S'⊆S. the output of this algorithm is a secret key S'K for the set of attributes S'.

There are several steps when we want to use CP-ABE. First of all, we need a implicit security parameter to generate the public parameters PK and a master key MK. Secondly, when we want to encrypt a message M, Encrypt(PK, M, A) can output a ciphertext CT. Then we should use Key Generation(MK,S) to generate private key SK for every users. Finally, user can use his private key SK to get the message M through the function Decrypt(PK, CT, SK) if the SK satisfies the access structure A.

3.2 Network Coding

Network coding is a novel technique proposed in 2000 which can improve throughput and performance of network. Many people think it will be a critical technology for future networks. With the appearance of network coding, a simple but important observation was made that in communication networks, we can allow nodes to process as well as forward the incoming independent information flows. When an intermediate node gets some independent data, it can make binary addition before transport them. Handling these independent data streams can greatly improve the efficiency of network information transmission. It is the cheap computational power that network coding utilizes to greatly increase network throughput. We will give a simple example to show how does the network coding improve network throughput when multicasting.

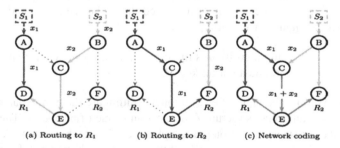

(a) Routing to R_1 (b) Routing to R_2 (c) Network coding

Fig. 1. Sources S1 and S2 multicast data to receivers R1 and R2.

As we can see in Fig. 1, a communication network represented as a directed graph, vertices represent terminals and edges represent channels. This communication network is commonly known as the butterfly network in the network coding. Assume that we have slotted time, and that through each channel we can send one bit per time slot. We have two data sources S1 and S2, and two data receivers R1 and R2. Each source produces one bit per time slot. Data x1 is produced by S1 and x2 is produced by S2.

If receiver R1 uses all the network resources by itself, it could receive both sources. As shown in Fig. 1(a), we can route the bit x1 from source S1 through the path {AD} and the bit x2 from source S2 through the path {BC, CE, ED}. In the same way, if we want the second receiver R2 with using all the network resources by itself, it could also receive both sources. As shown in Fig. 1(b), we can route the bit x1 from source S1 through the path {AC, CE, EF}, and the bit x2 from source S2 through the path {BF}.

We consider a situation called multicasting that receivers R1 and R2 want to receive the information from sources S1 and S2 at the same time. When comes to this situation, receiver R1 can receive x1 from source S1 through the path {AD} and receiver R2 can receive x2 from source S2 through the path {BF}. But we want receiver R1 can get x2 from source S2 and receiver R2 can get x1 from source S1 through the path {CE} simultaneously. However, we can only send one bit per time slot and we want to simultaneously send bit x1 to reach receiver R2 and bit x2 to reach receiver R1.

In the past, information flow was treated like fluid through pipes, and independent information flows were kept separate. In this case we would have to make a decision at edge CE: either use it to send bit x1, or use it to send bit x2. When we decide to send bit x2 using edge CE, then receiver R2 will only receive x2, at the same time receiver R1 will receive both x1 and x2.

The simple but important observation made by Ahlswede et al. [7] is that we can allow intermediate nodes in the network to process their incoming information streams instead of just forward them. In particular, node C can take bits x1 and x2 and xor them to create a third bit $x3 = x1 + x2$ which it can then send through edge CE (the xor operation corresponds to addition over the binary field). R1 receives {x1, x1 + x2}, and can solve this system of equations to retrieve x1 and x2. Similarly, R2 receives {x2, x1 + x2}, and can solve this system of equations to retrieve x1 and x2.

This example shows that when multicasting we can improve throughput through allowing intermediate node in the network to process information streams and receivers exacting the information.

In addition to the improvement of throughput, the security of network coding also has advantages. Instead of sending uncoded data, sending linear combinations of data can offer a natural way to use advantage of multipath diversity for security against wiretapping attacks. So we only need protection against other attacks with network coding.

However, there are some challenges to deploy the network coding. First of all, the complexity of employ network coding is high because the nodes in network need to have some additional functionalities. As we discussed in Fig. 1, the intermediate nodes C has additional memory and calculation requirements because instead of broadcasting streams immediately, it needs to store and process streams. The receivers D and F should be able to exact the information through what it receives. In fact, it is difficult to access the complexity of network coding. Secondly, with the rapid development of network technology, our demand for network security is becoming higher and higher. In our file sharing scheme, security is an important part and we need to guarantee protection against sophisticated attacks. Network coding need intermediate nodes to perform operations on the data. Thus, we should prevent intermediate nodes from maliciously tampering with the data. Finally, as communication networks' high speed development, a challenging task is to incorporate the emerging technologies such as network coding, into the existing network architecture. We want to profit from the network coding without incurring dramatic changes in the existing equipment and software. A related open question is, how could network coding be integrated in current networking protocols.

3.3 Model Description

We describe our model in this section. In our simulated file transfer system, we have one controller server and seven file servers, and the connection topology is shown in the Fig. 2. Each file server is connected to the controller server. These file servers are server nodes in different networks, representing system nodes which are located in different areas. Every server node stores a variety of encrypted files. In the initialization phase of the system, all the file server nodes first establish a connection to the controller and then transmit some information to it. The information is about all the local file directories and the connections to other file server nodes. When the controller receives feedback information from each node, it will summarize information. Through connections of each node, the controller can get the whole file system nodes' connection diagram. In the same way, after receiving every node's local file directory, the controller can generate a list of all the files existing in the system which consists of two parts. The first part is a map of in which nodes each file locates, the second is the directory of every node. In order to make our system has the ability of resisting some disasters, we follow the idea of Hadoop's mechanism which is making two copies of all files, that is to say for each file, has two backups distributed in different nodes of the system. This approach has great benefits for the system. Image a scene, if some special circumstances such as a node is damaged happen suddenly, we can still use the backup files stored in other nodes for file sharing and the recovery of damaged node. To achieve this, after the initialization process, system will start to maintain the list of files regularly. During list's maintenance, the controller sends a request to each server node. After receiving the request, server node will return the hash values of all the local files to the controller in the form of (file name, 32-bit md5 value). When received the files' hash values returned by each node, the controller compares the 32-bit md5 values of the same file, and there will be three different situations. In the first case, three backups of the same file have the same md5 value, which means that each file is right and no additional operations are required. The second case, two backups' md5 values are same, but are different from the last ones. Two files of same md5 value are right and the file which it's md5 value is different from the other two backups is damaged. The controller will notify the corresponding node stored damaged file to delete the damaged filed. Then it will randomly select a node which has same backup without error to transmit this file to the error node. Then we can ensure that there are two right backups of each file in our system all the time; Last case is that three backups' md5 value are different from each other which means at least two files are destroyed. We have no idea to distinguish which one is right. In this situation, the controller will notify the three server nodes to delete this file after which system will update the list of all files. But in fact the last kind of circumstance rarely happens.

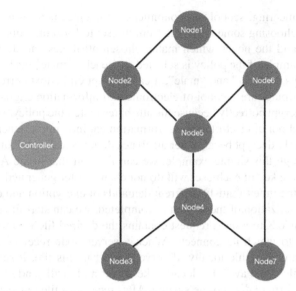

Fig. 2. Connection topology of simulated file transfer system

Another important task in the system's initialization phase is to assign private keys of ABE to each server node. We need to be aware of every server node's attributes due to use of attribute-based encryption in our system. We set default property set as the form of (node_id: id). For example, node 3 has attribute as a string of "node_id: 3". After determined attributes for each node, the controller generates private keys with the corresponding attributes of each node through key generation algorithm in ABE and then sends private keys to related server nodes.

When the controller assigns the private keys to server nodes, it is not allowed to send plaintext directly. Our system uses SSL (Secure Socket Layer) to distribute private keys. SSL is a protocol for the secure exchange of information between TCP connections which provides two basic security services: authentication and confidentiality. To use SSL for messaging, some preparations are needed on the controller side like installing openssl. First of all, an application for root certificate is generated using the private key, and root certificate will be produced using the self-signed method to sign the previous application. Then the private key of the server's authentication certificate is established. We are supposed to generate the certificate application file, and the root certificate is used to issue the server's authentication certificate. Finally, the private key of client's authentication certificate is established and certificate application is generated. Client's authentication certificate is issued by root certificate. After generating all the certificates, we assign the server-side certificate to the controller and the clients' certificates to the various file server nodes in the system. We can safely send the private keys of ABE to each file server node through the controller with SSL methods after finish preparatory work.

We will briefly make a explanation of ABE's encryption and decryption strategy. Suppose our attribute set is {student, teacher, male, female, school of electronic and information engineering, school of economics and management, school of science}. The first step is choosing some attributes from the set to form the policy of encryption and decryption and the nodes which match chosen attributes can decrypt ciphertext correctly. For example, if the policy is selected as {teacher, male}, as long as the user's attributes contains "teacher" and "male", it can decrypt ciphertext correctly. If there is a user whose attributes are {school of electronic and information engineering, teacher, male}, he can decrypt correctly because his attributes match the policy. If another user's attributes are {school of electronic and information engineering, teacher, female} then she cannot properly decrypt because her attributes do not satisfy attributes described in the policy. Through this simple example, we can find out that in the ABE encryption scheme, the private key of each user will do not change after generated. It is the policy that changes all the time to satisfy different demands of encryption and decryption.

After the initialization of the system is completed, we can start file sharing. If user needs a file, he needs to issue a request contains the desired file's name to the closest file server node to which he connects. When a server node receives request of file, first it will research that file locally. If server node has this file, it sends to the user directly. If this file is not available locally, the server node will send file request to the controller in the form of desired file's name. After receives a file request, the controller will search through the list of all files according to desired file's name to find where it is stored. When it comes to multicast, first of all the controller calls the minimum cut maximum flow algorithm of network coding to find out the path of transmission. Then the weight matrix is calculated by the weight calculation function in the network coding. In the following time, the configuration information will be sent to corresponding server nodes according to the path. After receiving configuration information, these nodes will prepare to receive and forward files as required. Controller can choose encryption policy according to attributes of user who requests files. The policy will be sent to first server node of the path. Starting node divide the file into some parts in setting size (for example, we set the block size of 100 MB). Every part will be encrypted by ABE with a header which recording the location of each part. UDP packet is used in the sending process, but only after receiving the confirmed message from receiver, the sending side can continue to send the next packet. Moreover, we have set up a simple verification and retransmission mechanism to ensure the high transmission quality of files. When get some bitstreams, receiver puts it into a queue and enables another thread to process bitstreams according to the configuration information of network coding and forwards it. Sending and receiving are separated. After receiving all the segmented parts, end server node extract information with network coding algorithm. Then it will decrypt segmented part using private key and recover complete file according to the header. This is what happens when files are transmitted in our system of multicast. If it is unicast, the controller finds the path according to the shortest path algorithm, and then sends the configuration information to related nodes. When server node is prepared well, the encryption policy is selected and sent to the starting node of path. The starting server node divides the file into some parts, encrypts these with ABE according to the policy, and then transmits the file. The intermediate node forwards the received bitstreams directly without any processing. After receiving each file part, the end server node will finish decryption and merge them into a complete file according to the header.

4 Experiment

We describe the evaluation tasks and report the experimental results in this section. We evaluate ABAE on two criteria:

1. Security
2. Effective of network coding

The system security of this paper mainly consists of two parts: the security of private key distribution and the security of file sharing. For key distribution, SSL is used to transmit private key securely because of its bidirectional authentication function. The related certificates are distributed to the controller node and the server nodes so that they can authenticate each other, and their communications will be encrypted when the authentication is completed. We use network sniffer tool to monitor the traffic which is found that all the data transmitted is garbled in the process of private key distribution. Then we can guarantee the security of key distribution process.

In addition to the security of key distribution, it is also necessary to ensure the security in process of sharing files. We use ABE to encrypt the transmitted content, because as required in distributed system, the data can be accessed correctly only if the user satisfies some particular attributes. However, there is a risk that the server node will be attacked if files are stored on it. Then we use Ciphertext-Policy Attribute-Based Encryption to ensure access control. The decryption policy is under the control of the controller node, so that even if the server where files are stored is attacked, data can be protected. [Ciphertext-Policy Attribute-Based Encryption] has proved that CP-ABE can resist collusion attacks.

We want to verify the efficiency of network coding in multicast. In this regard, we respectively transfer two different files from node 1 to node 3 and node 7 to record the speed. Each node stores 50 to 100 files, ranging in size from 1 MB to 5000 MB. We change size of the transferred files and recorded the time required for transferring two files under the two methods of using network coding and not using network encoding for comparison. The results are shown in the Table 1 when two files are in same size. The results are shown in the Table 2 when one file is half the size of the another.

Table 1. The time of transferring files (two files are in same size) using and not using network coding

	The size of files (MB)							
	1	5	10	50	100	500	1000	5000
With network coding (ms)	603	2912	5863	23829	52952	246922	508574	2297855
Without network coding (ms)	605	3115	6322	27176	57835	275357	565632	2582117

Table 2. The time of transferring files (one file is half the size of the another) using and not using network coding

	The size of bigger file (MB)							
	1	5	10	50	100	500	1000	5000
With network coding (ms)	449	2177	4510	18459	40998	193818	400105	1837972
Without network coding (ms)	457	2298	4801	20082	44019	206509	424324	1948675

As we can see in the experiment, the transferable efficiency of using network coding is higher than not using it by almost 11% when two files are in same size. But when one file is half the size of another the efficiency improvement is decrease to almost 6% because of the limitation of network coding which is that it is most efficient to transfer files of the same size. We can get the conclusion that using network coding can improve transferable efficiency in our system.

5 Conclusion

In this paper, we proposed a system for share sensitive data securely which was based on attribute-based encryption and network coding. Our system uses a new type of encrypted access control where user's private keys are specified by a set of attributes and a party encrypting data can specify a policy over these attributes specifying which users are able to decrypt. We also use network coding in our system to improve the efficiency of multicast.

One limitation of our system is that ABE is proved secure under the generic group heuristic. So the security of our system is limited in some situations. But we believe some more secure technologies which can be applied to our system would be proposed in future.

Acknowledgements. This work is supported by the National Key R&D Program of China under Grant 2018YFC0831300, China Postdoctoral Science Foundation under Grant 2018M641172, the National Natural Science Foundation of China under Grant 61701019.

References

1. Shamir, A.: Identity-based cryptosystems and signature schemes. In: Blakley, G.R., Chaum, D. (eds.) CRYPTO 1984. LNCS, vol. 196, pp. 47–53. Springer, Heidelberg (1985). https://doi.org/10.1007/3-540-39568-7_5
2. Boneh, D., Franklin, M.: Identity-based encryption from the weil pairing. In: Kilian, J. (ed.) CRYPTO 2001. LNCS, vol. 2139, pp. 213–229. Springer, Heidelberg (2001). https://doi.org/10.1007/3-540-44647-8_13
3. Biham, E. (ed.): EUROCRYPT 2003. LNCS, vol. 2656. Springer, Heidelberg (2003). https://doi.org/10.1007/3-540-39200-9

4. Yao, D., Fazio, N., Dodis, Y., et al.: ID-based encryption for complex hierarchies with applications to forward security and broadcast encryption. In: ACM Conference on Computer & Communications Security. ACM (2004)
5. Sahai, A., Waters, B.: Fuzzy identity-based encryption. In: Cramer, R. (ed.) EUROCRYPT 2005. LNCS, vol. 3494, pp. 457–473. Springer, Heidelberg (2005). https://doi.org/10.1007/11426639_27
6. Bethencourt, J., Sahai, A., Waters, B.: Ciphertext-policy attribute-based encryption. In: IEEE Symposium on Security and Privacy, 2007. SP '07. IEEE (2007)
7. Ahlswede, R., Cai, N., Li, S.Y.R., et al.: Network information flow. IEEE Trans. Inf. Theory **46**(4), 1204–1216 (2000)
8. Fragouli, C., Soljanin, E.: Network coding fundamentals. Found. Trends Netw. **2**(1), 1–133 (2007)
9. Gamal, A.A.E., Cover, T.M.: Achievable rates for multiple descriptions. IEEE Trans. Inf. Theory **28**(6), 851–857 (1982)
10. Roche, J.R., Yeung, R.W., Hau, K.P.: Symmetrical multilevel diversity coding. IEEE Trans. Inf. Theory **43**(3), 1059–1064 (1997)
11. Yeung, R.W., Zhang, Z.: Distributed source coding for satellite communications. IEEE Trans. Inf. Theory **45**(4), 1111–1120 (1999)
12. Agarwal, A., Charikar, M.: Manufacturing engineer - on the advantage of network coding for improving network throughput. In: IEEE 2004 IEEE Information Theory Workshop - San Antonio, TX, USA (24–29 Oct. 2004), pp. 247–249 (2004)

Machine Learning-Based Security Authentication for IoT Networks

Xiaoying Qiu$^{(\boxtimes)}$ (ID), Xuan Sun, and Xiameng Si

School of Information Management, Beijing Information Science and Technology
University, Beijing 100192, China
{20192329,Sunxuan,Sixiameng}@bistu.edu.cn

Abstract. In this paper, we propose a security authentication scheme
based on machine learning algorithms to detect spoofing attacks in the
Internet of Things (IoT) network. This authentication method exploits
the physical layer properties of the wireless channel to identify sensors and applies neural networks to learn channel fingerprints without
being aware of the communication network model. We propose a channel
differences-based security framework to provide lightweight authentication and a Long Short-Term Memory (LSTM) network-based detection
approach to further enhance the authentication performance for sinks
that support intelligent algorithms. Experiments and simulations were
carried out in an indoor conference room. The results show that our
strategy improves the authentication accuracy rate compared with the
existing non-learning security authentication methods.

Keywords: Wireless communication · Security authentication ·
Physical layer security · Machine learning

1 Introduction

A growing number of smart devices are being connected to large-scale heterogeneous networks at an unprecedented speed, realizing the concept of the Internet of Things (IoT) [1]. There are many application fields in which the IoT
plays a remarkable role, including smart home, smart grids, and smart industrial automation. Advanced communication technologies enable a wide variety
of devices to see, hear, talk, and share information. However, the heterogeneity of the IoT has brought huge challenges to existing security authentication
schemes [2,3]. In this complex scenario, traditional security standards and protocols may not be sufficient to completely protect wireless devices. In addition,
the overhead and complexity of available security algorithms greatly consume
the limited resources in IoT networks.

While digital key-based cryptographic methods already enjoy a large literature, they are still based on a promise that eavesdroppers lack the computational

Supported by school research foundation of BISTU (No.2035009).

power to successfully attack the network. Through impersonation, the attacker can modify the message so that it is mistaken for the message sent by a legitimate device. Due to the rapidly growing computational capability of wireless devices, it is becoming more and more feasible to crack the security key from the intercepted information by eavesdropping. For practical implementation, current classical security methodologies also require appropriate key management and distribution, which may cause excessive network communication delays. These problems exist in any communication networks and are not necessarily limited to wireless IoT networks.

Physical layer authentication (PLA), which safeguards communications by using the intrinsic characteristics of wireless channels, is a promising lightweight security method [4]. These kind of analog-domain attributes are essentially related to the unique defects of communication equipment and the corresponding wireless communication environment, which are difficult to impersonate or imitate by opponents [5–7]. Despite existing physical layer authentication have obvious advantages such as low power consumption, low network overhead and lightweight, most approaches are based on a single, static channel characteristic [8–11]. Therefore, they are unsuitable for providing accurate authentication in real time-varying environments. Incomplete channel estimation and interference errors constitute the main challenge factors in the authentication process.

In this paper, we propose a security authentication scheme that uses the physical layer properties of the wireless channel to improve the accuracy of spoofing detection. Specifically, the solution reuses the channel estimation result of the wireless device and extracts the received signal strength to construct channel vectors, which is compared with the channel record of the required communication device in a hypothesis test. The channel features extracted in the authentication scheme greatly affect the recognition effect of the classifier. The performance accuracy usually depends on the variation of the wireless channel, the spatial decorrelation characteristics, and the channel estimation method, which are difficult to predict in advance by the wireless devices in the IoT network. Therefore, this solution uses a deep learning method to extract channel characteristics based on the current received signal strength. We propose a Long Short Term Memory (LSTM)-based physical layer authentication scheme to enhance the detection performance of sinks that support deep learning, especially when the sink need to authenticate a large number of access nodes in the IoT network. Specifically, the proposed LSTM network is used to learn the deep features of each legitimate device automatically and authenticate the attacker simultaneously.

The proposed authentication scheme can be implemented on the Universal software radio peripheral in an indoor conference room to detect spoofing attacks. Experiments performed with universal software radio peripheral transceivers show that the proposed scheme have better anti-interference, higher authentication accuracy, and intelligent learning algorithm further improves the detection performance.

The rest of the paper is organized as follows. We present the system model in Sect. 2. The LSTM-based security authentication scheme is proposed in Sect. 3.

Following up from that, the simulation results of the proposed authentication solution are discussed in Sect. 4. Finally, Sect. 5 concludes the paper.

2 System Model and Problem Statement

2.1 System Model

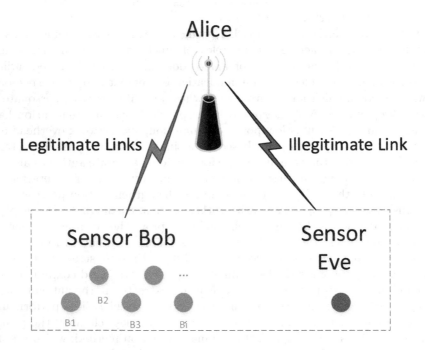

Fig. 1. The system model diagram describes the physical layer authentication scheme to consider.

As shown in Fig. 1, we consider three types of devices. The first type is smart device, which is capable of performing advanced tasks, such as data storage, transmission, and communication; in our security model, this type of device refers to smart device "Alice" for collecting data from other sensors. The second type is called "Bob", and its resources are limited. For the persistence of life, Bob spends most of his time on sensing and data recording. Once activated, Bob will run in data transfer mode, transfer its stored data to Alice, and clear memory for upcoming data. In our scenario, Eve is a potential spoofer who pretends to be a legitimate device Bobi, and then sends the false message to smart Alice. More explicitly, Eve not only tries to access the wireless network, but also to forge authorized identities for obtaining illegitimate benefits. Notably, since the presence of scatters and reflectors in the wireless communication environment, there will be multiple copies of the transmitted signal through different paths.

Therefore, the physical layer properties of the wireless channel between legitimate transceivers is independent of that between the spoofer and the receiver. The system model diagram describes the physical layer authentication scheme that needs to be considered, as shown in Fig. 1.

2.2   Problem Statement

We can reasonably assume that the initial transmission between Alice and Bobi was established before Eve arrived, which allowed smart Alice to obtain an estimate of the wireless channel. M estimates of the selected physical layer attributes of legitimate channel can be obtained during the initial authentication phase of the establishment, which are given by

$$\mathbf{H}_{Bobi} = [H_{Bobi,1}, H_{Bobi,2}, \cdots, H_{Bobi,M}]^T \tag{1}$$

where each $H_{Bobi,m}$ denotes the channel vector estimated from legitimate transmitter, $m \in \{1, 2, ..., M\}$ represents an time index, and M denotes the number of estimates during the initial authentication phase.

Smart Alice must verify the received message at time $t + 1$ and authenticate whether it is coming from Bob_i.

$$\mathrm{H_0} : |\mathrm{F}(\mathbf{H_{Bob_i}(t)} - \mathbf{H(t+1)})| \leq \gamma \tag{2}$$

$$\mathrm{H_1} : |\mathrm{F}(\mathbf{H_{Bob_i}(t)} - \mathbf{H(t+1)})| > \gamma \tag{3}$$

where $\mathrm{H_0}$ represents that the received message come from the sender Bob_i, $\mathrm{H_1}$ indicates the hypothesis that the sensor is spoofer Eve, F is the proposed learning authentication function, $\mathbf{H}(t)$ denotes the estimated physical properties of the channel at instantaneous time t, and γ is the threshold.

The main objective of the receiver Alice is to determine whether the source of the received message is Bobi by using the difference between the legitimate estimates $H_{Bobi,1}, H_{Bobi,2}, \cdots, H_{Bobi,M}$ and the newly estimated physical layer signatures. The problem with conventional physical layer authentication methods is that wireless channels are likely to be time-varying, but the channel estimates are static and incomplete, which greatly reduces the accuracy of the authentication scheme. It is for this reason that we use LSTM networks to learn time-varying channel features and perform spoofer detection concurrently. If the difference between the channel vectors is large, it is considered that the signal to be authenticated comes from a spoofing attacker, otherwise, from Bobi. We assume that the estimated noises of Bobi and Eve are independent and identically distributed, which is caused by interference factors, such as measurement errors and channel noises.

3   LSTM-based Physical Layer Authentication

In this section, we discuss the overall architecture of the physical layer authentication scheme based on the LSTM network. First, we quantify the difference between the legitimate channel vectors $H_{Bobi,1}, H_{Bobi,2}, \cdots, H_{Bobi,M}$ and the new estimates $\mathbf{H}_{t+1}$, which will be followed by the LSTM network. Finally, we discuss the implementation details. The step involved in physical layer authentication process based on LSTM network is shown in Fig. 2.

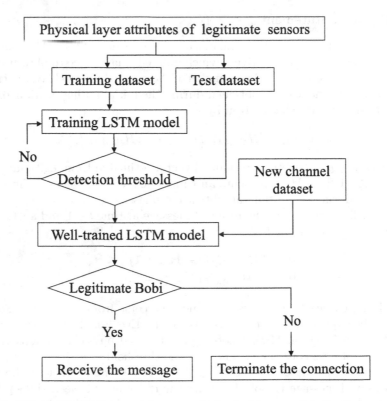

Fig. 2. Block diagram of proposed physical layer authentication.

As discussed in the overview, it is difficult to manually capture channel characteristics with high robustness, so the back-end utilizes the LSTM network to learn deep features. Inspired by image classification, the LSTM network is used to automatically extract channel characteristics and detect the attacker. One of the main advantages of the LSTM network is to ensure that our authentication model adapts to time-varying environments to provide reliable protection. Generally, the physical layer attributes have patterns according to the time-varying channel. These dynamic characteristics that do not appear in a single channel vector can be dispersed into multiple data vectors. Existing machine learning approaches for physical layer security authentication failed to track such attributes, and do not have the ability to extract time-varying characteristics that appear in multiple channel vectors.

Note that the transformation from the estimates into high-dimensional feature space is nonlinear. Therefore, to learn local characteristics and global features, the LSTM layer is used by introducing three gates (input, forget and output). The cell states CS_t in LSTM module can be formulated as

$$CS_t = Forg_t \odot CS_{t-1} + Inp_t \odot tanh(U * Hid_{t-1} + Wx_t + b) \qquad (4)$$

and the hidden states Hid_t is given by

$$Hid_t = Out_t \odot tanh(CS_t) \qquad (5)$$

where $\odot$ is the element-wise multiplication operation. As shown in Fig. 3, the input gate Inp_t, forget gate $Forg_t$ and output gate Out_t are expressed as

$$Inp_t = \sigma(W_{Inp} * x_t + U_{Inp} * Hid_{t-1} + b_{Inp}) \qquad (6)$$

$$Forg_t = \sigma(W_{Forg} * x_t + U_{Forg} * Hid_{t-1} + b_{Forg}) \qquad (7)$$

$$Out_t = \sigma(W_{Out} * x_t + U_{Out} * Hid_{t-1} + b_{Out}) \qquad (8)$$

where σ denotes the sigmoid function, U, W, and b represent parameters. The idea of the LSTM layer is to learn efficiently from variable channel vectors.

During training, each channel vector will be input to the LSTM network, and time-varying features will be obtained through the LSTM layer. The classifier following the LSTM layer will process the output of the LSTM and make decisions on the softmax loss function. The parameters of the authentication system we proposed are updated by the background propagation algorithm. After iteratively updating the learning model using the physical layer attributes, the loss value of eventually tends to zero gradually.

During the test, the test dataset is feed into the LSTM network, and the probability of the channel vectors belonging to different transmitters is calculated after network processing. The prediction used in the model can be expressed as

$$Pr = \frac{e^{V_{class}}}{\sum_{class'=1}^{2} e^{V_{class'}}} \qquad (9)$$

In conclusion, our security authentication scheme based on the LSTM network is summarized at a glance in Fig. 2. In summary, the channel vector is transformed from single dimensional to multi-dimensional features, the authentication is modelled as an intelligent system. Therefore, it dramatically maps the physical layer authentication to a intelligent process that can learn time-varying features and perform authentication tasks.

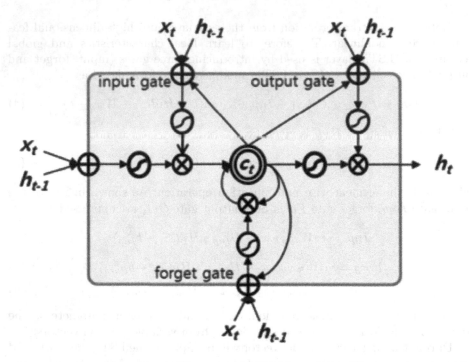

Fig. 3. Structure of LSTM layer [12].

4   Experimental Results

In this section, we first give the experimental setup of the LSTM network. Then, we verify the effectiveness of our authentication process through research and characterize the convergence. In addition, a brief comparison between our and other schemes is given. To emulate the learning-based physical layer authentication method, we set the Universal Software Radio Peripheral (USRP) transceiver to operate in IEEE 802.11a/g mode, working at 2.4 GHz and having a bandwidth of 20 MHz. We investigate the performance of the proposed intelligent model in the binary classification (Bob1 and Bob2). All estimates of received signal strength constitute a park with two classification targets. The sampled data set used for authentication provides a more realistic basis for theoretical verification. To automate the training model generation and detection authentication process, we created the script using the Python language.

We collect data for each transmitter-receiver combination. As shown in Fig. 4, two types of samples are involved in the proposed USRP data set, each of which contains 2000 × 256 channel feature sampling points, a total of 4000 × 256 samples. During the training process, 1000 × 256 sampling points are randomly selected for each type of channel feature data.

We train the LSTM network as a whole. Given the estimated channel vectors, as the input to our intelligent authentication model. First of all, one physical

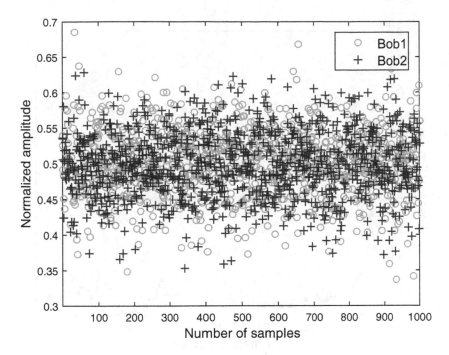

Fig. 4. Original channel estimation of different transmitters.

layer attribute, namely received signal strength is considered in the experiment to verify the viability of the LSTM network. The mathematical formulation of the received signal strength can be written as $P_{loss} = 75 + 36.1 \log(d/10)$, where P_{loss} represents the path loss, and d denotes the distance between the transceivers. We randomly set the initial parameters of the network model before training. Then, our intelligent process is validated in an indoor conference room to show its performance. Once the LSTM network is trained, we evaluate the model on the test subset. Then we verify the authentication performance of the proposed system by calculating the detection accuracy and the false alarm rate.

Figure 5 characterizes the training performance of the proposed LSTM network scheme (see Sect. 3) relying on the channel attribute. We consider the use of the received signal strength to authenticate malicious attackers. We can observe from Fig. 5 that with the increasing iteration index, the loss values of our intelligent process dramatically decrease. The reason for this trend is that the LSTM network is an adaptive algorithm that can update the system according to the dynamic characteristics of the channel, so as to adapt to the time-varying wireless network environment.

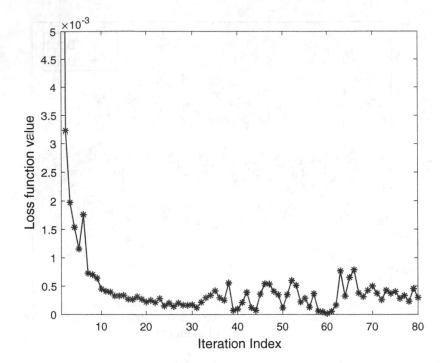

Fig. 5. Convergence performance of our intelligent authentication scheme.

Table 1. The authentication performance

Reference	Approach	False alarm rate	Accuracy
Scheme [14]	PCA + GMM	7.92%	94.50%
Scheme [13]	KLT + GMM	7.72%	92.80%
Scheme [15]	CNN	5.72%	95.81%
Our scheme	LSTM	0.80%	97.15%

In Table 1, we can observe the comparison results between our proposed solution and the existing methods using the USRP dataset. We can see that the proposed security authentication scheme has better performance in terms of accuracy and false alarm rate. Specifically, compared with the security method based on Gaussian mixture model, the recognition rate of the LSTM algorithm is greatly improved.

5   Conclusion

In this paper, we proposed a lightweight physical layer authentication scheme based on a long Short Term Memory network. Since manual selection of channel static characteristics will reduce the robustness of security authentication, we use the LSTM network to learn the channel characteristics while performing authentication tasks. To validate the effectiveness of utilizing the intelligent scheme, USRP prototype systems are set up in an indoor conference room. Furthermore, the rigorous security analysis and convergence of the proposed scheme are comprehensively evaluated.

References

1. Al-Fuqaha, A., Guizani, M., Mohammadi, M., Aledhari, M., Ayyash, M.: Internet of Things: a survey on enabling technologies, protocols, and applications. IEEE Commun. Surv. Tutor. **17**(4), 2347–2376 (2015). https://doi.org/10.1109/COMST. 2015.2444095
2. Xu, T., Darwazeh, I.: Design and prototyping of neural network compression for non-orthogonal IoT signals. In: IEEE Wireless Communications and Networking Conference (WCNC), Marrakesh, Morocco, vol. 2019, pp. 1–6 (2019)
3. Xu, T.: Waveform-defined security: a framework for secure communications. In: IEEE/IET 12th International Symposium on Communication Systems, Networks and Digital Signal Processing (CSNDSP2020), Porto, Portugal (2020)
4. Wang, N., Wang, P., Alipour-Fanid, A., Jiao, L., Zeng, K.: Physical-layer security of 5G wireless networks for IoT: challenges and opportunities. IEEE Internet Things J. **6**(5), 8169–8181 (2019)
5. Wang, N., Jiao, L., Alipour-Fanid, A., Dabaghchian, M., Zeng, K.: Pilot contamination attack detection for NOMA in 5G mm-wave massive MIMO networks. IEEE Trans. Inf. Forensics Secur. **15**, 1363–1378 (2020)
6. Gui, G., Liu, F., Sun, J., Yang, J., Zhou, Z., Zhao, D.: Flight delay prediction based on aviation big data and machine learning. IEEE Trans. Veh. Technol. **69**(1), 140–150 (2020)
7. Huang, H., et al.: Deep learning for physical-layer 5G wireless techniques: opportunities, challenges and solutions. IEEE Wirel. Commun. **27**(1), 214–222 (2020)
8. Wang, N., Jiang, T., Lv, S., Xiao, L.: Physical-layer authentication based on extreme learning machine. IEEE Commun. Lett. **21**(7), 1557–1560 (2017)
9. Qiu, X., Jiang, T., Wang, N.: Safeguarding multiuser communication using full-duplex jamming and Q-learning algorithm. IET Commun. **12**(15), 1805–1811 (2018)
10. Wang, N., Li, W., Jiang, T., Lv, S.: Physical layer spoofing detection based on sparse signal processing and fuzzy recognition. IET Signal Process. **11**(5), 640–646 (2017)
11. Wang, N., Jiang, T., Li, W., Lv, S.: Physical-layer security in Internet of Things based on compressed sensing and frequency selection. IET Commun. **11**(9), 1431–1437 (2017)
12. Moon, T., Choi, H., Lee, H., Song, I.: Rnndrop: a novel dropout for RNNs in ASR. In: ASRU, pp. 65–70 (2015). https://doi.org/10.1109/ASRU.2015.7404775
13. Qiu, X., et al: Wireless user authentication based on KLT and Gaussian mixture model. IEEE Wireless Communications and Networking Conference (WCNC), Marrakesh, Morocco, vol. 2019, pp. 1–5 (2019)
14. Qiu, X., Jiang, T., Wu, S., Hayes, M.: Physical layer authentication enhancement using a Gaussian mixture model. IEEE Access **6**, 53583–53592 (2018)
15. Qiu, X., Dai, J., Hayes, M.: A learning approach for physical layer authentication using adaptive neural network. IEEE Access **8**, 26139–26149 (2020)

CVSS Based Attack Analysis Using a Graphical Security Model: Review and Smart Grid Case Study

Tan Duy Le[1]([✉]), Mengmeng Ge[2], Phan The Duy[3,4], Hien Do Hoang[3,4], Adnan Anwar[2], Seng W. Loke[2], Razvan Beuran[1], and Yasuo Tan[1]

[1] Japan Advanced Institute of Science and Technology, Ishikawa, Japan
tanld@jaist.ac.jp
[2] School of Information Technology, Deakin University, Geelong, Australia
[3] Information Security Lab, University of Information Technology,
Ho Chi Minh City, Vietnam
[4] Vietnam National University Ho Chi Minh City, Ho Chi Minh City, Vietnam

Abstract. Smart Grid is one of the critical technologies that provide essential services to sustain social and economic developments. There are various cyber attacks on the Smart Grid system in recent years, which resulted in various negative repercussions. Therefore, understanding the characteristics and evaluating the consequences of an attack on the Smart Grid system is essential. The combination of Graphical Security Model (GrSM), including Attack Tree (AT) and Attack Graph (AG), and the Common Vulnerability Score System (CVSS) is a potential technology to analyze attack on Smart Grid system. However, there are a few research works about Smart Grid attack analysis using GrSM and CVSS. In this research, we first conduct a comprehensive study of the existing research on attack analysis using GrSM and CVSS, ranging from (1) Traditional Networks, (2) Emerging Technologies, to (3) Smart Grid. We indicate that the framework for automating security analysis of the Internet of Things is a promising direction for Smart Grid attack analysis using GrSM and CVSS. The framework has been applied to assess security of the Smart Grid system. A case study using the PNNL Taxonomy Feeders R4-12.47-2 and Smart Grid network model with gateways was conducted to validate the utilized framework. Our research is enriched by capturing all potential attack paths and calculating values of selected security metrics during the vulnerability analysis process. Furthermore, AG can be generated automatically. The research can potentially be utilized in Smart Grid cybersecurity training.

Keywords: Smart Grid · Graphical Security Model (GrSM) · Common Vulnerability Score System (CVSS) · Attack analysis · Attack tree · Attack graph

© ICST Institute for Computer Sciences, Social Informatics and Telecommunications Engineering 2021
Published by Springer Nature Switzerland AG 2021. All Rights Reserved
Y.-B. Lin and D.-J. Deng (Eds.): SGIoT 2020, LNICST 354, pp. 116–134, 2021.
https://doi.org/10.1007/978-3-030-69514-9_11

1   Introduction

Smart Grid is one of the application domains of the emerging Internet of Things (IoT). According to the US Department of Homeland Security (DHS) [1], it is one of the key technologies supporting essential services towards sustainable social and economic developments. The number of cyber attacks on the Smart Grid system has expanded in recent years. It has resulted in various negative impacts, such as blackouts, the loss of confidential data, and even physical destruction to electrical devices. Therefore, it is essential to understand the characteristics and evaluate the consequences of an attack on the Smart Grid system.

Vulnerability scanners are widely accepted to assess security threats by identifying the number, type, and location of the vulnerabilities within the network. Common Vulnerabilities and Exposures (CVE), maintained by MITRE, is a list of a reference-method for publicly known vulnerabilities and exposures [2]. This CVE glossary investigates vulnerabilities and uses the Common Vulnerability Score System (CVSS) to evaluate the severity level of vulnerabilities [3]. CVSS offers a systematic approach to capture critical features of vulnerabilities through numerical scores reflecting their severity. To support evaluation and prioritization of organization's vulnerability management processes by IT experts, security analysts, and cybersecurity professionals, CVSS scores can be converted into a qualitative representation, ranging from low, medium, high, and critical. Besides, these numerical scores can be taken as inputs to generate the Graphical Security Model (GrSM) [4].

GrSM is a significant technology to identify the security posture of networked systems and evaluate the effectiveness of security defenses. Since it provides a visualisation of how a system can be hacked through attack paths, countermeasures to prevent the attacks from reaching the target can be developed. Attack Tree (AT) [5] and Attack Graph (AG) [6] are two essential components of GrSM. The structure of an AT contains a root node as the attack goal and leaf nodes to represent different ways of achieving that goal. Each node represents a sub-target, and children of the node form the paths to accomplish this sub-target. There are two types of nodes, namely, AND nodes and OR nodes. Once an AT is built, CVSS values can be assigned to the leaf nodes; then, the calculation of security metrics can be conducted. An AG visualizes all paths through a system that results in a circumstance where attackers can successfully achieve their target. Cybersecurity professionals can utilize attack graphs for detection, defense, and forensics.

Several studies have proposed technologies to combine ATs and AGs in multiple layers to resolve the scalability issue of single-layered model [7,8]. GrSM with CVSS is an emerging technology to analyze attacks on Smart Grid system. However, there has been only a few works that focuses on Smart Grid attack analysis using GrSM and CVSS. In this context, we first provide an analytical literature review in current state-of-the-art attack analysis using GrSM and CVSS for (1) Traditional Networks, (2) Emerging Technologies, and (3) Smart Grid. We indicate that the framework for automating security analysis of the Internet of Things is a promising direction for Smart Grid attack analysis using GrSM and CVSS. We apply the framework to assess the security of the Smart Gid system. A case study with various attack scenarios was conducted to validate our applied framework.

The main contributions of this research are summarized as follows:

- A comprehensive study and comparison of the existing research on attack analysis using GrSM and CVSS ranging from (1) Traditional Networks, (2) Emerging Technologies, to (3) Smart Grid;
- Application of security assessment framework with automatic generation of AG for Smart Grid;
- A case study using the PNNL Taxonomy Feeders R4-12.47-2 and a simplified Smart Grid network model with gateways to validate the utilized framework.
- Classification of attack paths based on attack success probability and matching into five levels: Rare, Unlikely, Possible, Likely, and Almost Certain.

The remainder of this paper is organized as follows. Section 2 discusses the related research on attack analysis using GrSM and CVSS. A Smart Grid case study with various attack scenarios is provided in Sect. 3. Conclusion and future work are finally drawn in Sect. 4.

2   Attack Analysis Using GrSM and CVSS

In this section, we discuss the related studies on attack analysis using GrSM and CVSS based on three categories (1) Traditional Networks, (2) Emerging Technologies, to (3) Smart Grid. We examine numerous metrics of interest, including Attack Tree (AT), Attack Graph Generation (AGG), Attack Graph Visualization (AGV), Attack Success Probability (p), Attack Cost (ac), Attack Impact (aim), Attack Risk (r), Likelihood (lh), and Smart Grid Application (SG) to accomplish this goal. Table 1 chronologically presents the majority of the attack analysis using GrSM and CVSS that have been studied in recent years.

2.1   Attack Analysis for Traditional Networks

Nowadays, attacks targeting information systems are getting more sophisticated gradually. Attackers can combine and exploit multiple vulnerabilities to run an attack. The research [9] pointed out that probabilistic attack graphs can be used to analyze and draw all attack paths. This method can help mitigate risks and maximize the security of enterprise systems. The authors use available tools for generating attack graphs in enterprise networks to indicate potential steps that allow attackers to hit their targets. Besides, CVSS score, a standard that is used to evaluate the severity of security vulnerabilities of computer systems, is used to estimate the security risk.

HyunChul Joh et al. [10] indicated that a risk cannot be evaluated by a single cause. Independent multiple causes need to be considered to estimate the overall risk. Based on likelihood and impact values, a risk matrix is built to classify causes. The risk matrix is used to rate risks, and therefore, serious risks can be

Table 1. Attack analysis using Graphical Security Model (GrSM) and CVSS (Y: Yes, Blank: No)

No	Research	AT	Attack graph		Security metrics calculation				lh	SG
			AGG	AGV	p	ac	aim	r		
1	Security risk analysis of enterprise networks using probabilistic attack graphs [9]		Y		Y		Y	Y		
2	Defining and assessing quantitative security risk measures using vulnerability lifecycle and CVSS metrics [10]				Y		Y	Y		
3	Aggregating CVSS base scores for semantics-rich network security metrics [11]		Y				Y			
4	Dynamic security risk management using Bayesian attack graphs [12]	Y	Y		Y	Y		Y		
5	Determining the probability of smart grid attacks by combining attack tree and attack graph analysis [21]	Y	Y		Y					Y
6	Attack graph-based risk assessment and optimisation approach [13]	Y	Y		Y			Y		
7	A framework for modeling and assessing security of the internet of things [15]	Y	Y		Y	Y	Y	Y		
8	Security modelling and analysis of dynamic enterprise networks [16]				Y	Y	Y	Y		
9	A quantitative CVSS-based cyber security risk assessment methodology for IT systems [14]		Y		Y		Y	Y		
10	A framework for automating security analysis of the internet of things [17]	Y	Y		Y		Y	Y		
11	A comprehensive analysis of smart grid systems against cyber-physical attacks [22]	Y	Y		Y		Y	Y	Y	Y
12	CloudSafe: a tool for an automated security analysis for cloud computing [19]		Y		Y		Y			Y
13	Quantitative model of attacks on distribution automation systems based on CVSS and attack trees [18]	Y	Y		Y		Y	Y		
14	A Bayesian attack tree based approach to assess cyber-physical security of power system [23]	Y	Y		Y		Y	Y		Y
15	A framework for real-time intrusion response in software defined networking using precomputed graphical security models [20]	Y	Y		Y	Y	Y	Y		Y

recognized and mitigated. Their study also addressed the software vulnerability life cycle. From the method of risk evaluation for each single vulnerability using stochastic modeling, the authors defined conditional risk measures to evaluate risk by combining both the essence and accessibility of the vulnerability. They provided the mathematical basis and demonstrated this approach by experimental validation.

The existing approaches to assess a network security metric using aggregation of CVSS scores can result in valuable semantics of individual scores to be lost. The research [11] drilled down basic metric levels to get dependency relationships in order to obtain better semantics. These relationships are signified by an attack graph. This approach used three separate aspects of the CVSS score to explain and aggregate the basic metrics. This help maintained corresponding semantics of the individual scores.

The work in [12] used Bayesian networks to propose a risk management framework, called Bayesian Attack Graph (BAG). This framework allows administrators to estimate the possibility of network compromise at various levels. Security risk management with BAG comprises threat analysis, risk assessment, loss expectancy, potential safeguards, and risk mitigation analysis. This component enables administrators to execute static and dynamic risk assessments, and risk mitigation analysis. Security risk mitigation with BAG is formulated as a Multiobjective Optimization Problem (MOOP), having a low complexity for optimization.

In approaches of attack graph-based risk management, a study [13] proposed a framework of risk assessment and optimization to generate a graph using a genetic algorithm for drawing attack paths. The framework was presented by six steps: attack graph generation, likelihood determination, loss estimation, risk determination, optimization, and high-risk attack paths. The proposed genetic algorithm finds the highest risk for building a minimal attack tree. This also computed with huge graphs when very large attack paths are explored.

In a work of risk assessment for IT systems, Ugur Aksu et al. [14] proposed a quantitative methodology for evaluating the vulnerability in the system. Like other approaches, in this study, the CVSS metrics (base and temporal scores) are used to calculate the probability of attack success, attack risk, and the attack impact. The attack paths can be determined corresponding to the generation of the attack graph-based risk of a CVE on an asset. They measure risks not for only single CVEs but also for a collection of CVEs on the assets, elements, and attack paths in each IT system. But the authors did not evaluate the likelihood of potential attack when analyzing the cyber security risk that may occur inside the network.

2.2   Attack Analysis for Emerging Technologies

Internet of Things (IoT) brings many innovations in numerous domains; however, its security is a challenge. In order to analyze and address security issues in IoT, the work in [15] proposed a framework for security modeling and assessment, building graphs of security models, evaluating security levels, and recommending defense strategies. The framework can find attack scenarios in five stages: pre-processing, security model generation, visualization and storage, security analysis, and alterations and updates. This research demonstrated the ability of the framework in two cases of IoT networks in reducing impacts of possible attacks.

In the context of dynamic networks that the configuration changes over time, Simon et al. [16] presented the Temporal-Hierarchical Attack Representation Model (T-HARM) with two layers for analyzing the security problems in the network. Therein, the upper layer contains the temporal hosts reachability information whereas the lower layer shows the changes of vulnerabilities correlating with each host by defining AT and AG. The attack paths, attack cost, attack success probability, and the attack risk were calculated based on the metrics of CVSS base score. But the authors did not use the likelihood of exploitable vulnerability in investigating the security of a dynamic network.

In the study of automating security assessment for the IoT environment, Ge et al. [17] proposed a graphical security model which is used to find the potential attack before it occurs [15]. The authors conducted experiments with three different IoT networks in the context of smart home, environment sensor, healthcare wearable device monitoring. The 3-layer Hierarchical Attack Representation Model (HARM), an extended version of HARM, is used to find all potential attack paths. This extended one consists of an attack tree (AT) for each node in the network topology. They analyzed the security problems of IoT devices to specific vulnerabilities on various metrics like attack success probability, attack cost spent by hackers, attack impact and the time to compromise these vulnerabilities. To quantify the severity of vulnerabilities for network element, the CVSS is used to computed aforementioned metrics. They also supported the feature of choosing the most effective defense strategies for mitigating potential attacks. But this work neither discussed about the security likelihood nor visualized the attack graph.

Erxia Li et al. [18] presented a quantitative model in distribution automation systems (DASs) for attack analysis based on CVSS and ATs. To be more specific, their modeling method is considered from the perspective of attacker's behavior. Each step of complete attack processes is formed to calculate the node attack probability. Therein, the root tree is the ascertained component in the system while an attack which can be occurred in certain DASs is represented by each leaf node of the AT. Three metrics of CVSS, namely base, time, environment score, are used to compute the maximum probability of each potential path for intruding the network. The max score indicates the most vulnerable path to be patched with the most defense strategies. Although this framework can generate the quantitative attack graph, it does not support the feature of graph visualization.

Seongmo et al. proposed CloudSafe [19], a tool for automated security assessment in cloud environment which is implemented in the Amazon AWS. It consists of two phases: information collection and HARM generation. Firstly, they built a cloud information gathering interface for further data store and security analysis. Then, this module is integrated with HARM by modifying the security information retrieved from the first phase. In quantifying security, the probability of successfully exploiting a vulnerability is calculated by the metrics of CVSS on the Reachability Graph (RG) which is saved in a database after mapping inter-VM connections in cloud targets. Moreover, they also provided the Attack Cost, Risk, and Impact information correlating with each cloud vulnerability. Nevertheless, the graph visualization is not supported.

Meanwhile, a work by Taehoon Eom et al. [20], focused on the computation of possible attack graphs for real-time intrusion detection and response in Software-Defined Networking (SDN). They used HARM model with security metrics depending on the information of flow table, and SDN components. All possible attack paths which are pre-computed by HARM and full AG can evaluate the security issues of the network system prior to an attack detected. It is useful to estimate possible attack paths from the point of detection to formulate effective remedy. In detail, the authors used the base score (BS) of CVSS to measure the severity of vulnerabilities and the probability of an attack success in the network entities. The impact attack metric was directly inherited from CVSS. Additionally, in accordance with the reduction of scalability complexity, the authors also built attack graphs based on the modeling network nodes and their vulnerabilities onto multiple layers. The main reason for this is that the SDN consists of many components and network elements, causing security assessment to be not scalable in enumerating all possible attack scenarios. By leveraging from HARM, they generate 2-layer HARM, where each host in the higher layer has a corresponding AT in the lower layer. The lower layer is a collection of ATs, where each AT is the representative of the vulnerability information for each upper layer node, i.e SDN network node. Nonetheless, their work lacks the support of graph attack visualization and likelihood recommendation.

2.3   Attack Analysis for Smart Grid

An attacker collects information from the high-level aim of a target, and then takes low-level actions. Kristian Beckers et al. [21] delivered a method that can show steps of attackers. This method gathers information of a system at the low-level presentation to analyze high-level probabilistic attributes. The attacker's high-level aims are drawn as an attack tree and actions in low level as an attack graph. The research combined both the attack tree and attack graph for mapping aims of the attacker to actions. This combination was applied to a Smart Grid. This proposal helps system administrators prevent possible attacks.

The acceleration of the Smart Grid technologies makes the power delivery systems to be easily used as well as meet the intelligence and efficiency. However, insider and outsider attacks that may harm the Smart Grid system have recently occurred in the real case. Hence, there is more attention from researchers to deeply understand security levels in these systems in order to implement defense methods for disaster prevention to avoid the consequences of intrusion attacks.

To start with, the study [21] delivered a method that can show the steps of attackers. This method gathers information of a system at the low-level presentation to analyze high-level probabilistic attributes. The attacker's high-level aims are drawn as an attack tree and low-level actions as an attack graph. The research combined both the attack tree and attack graph for mapping aims of the attacker to actions. This combination was applied to a Smart Grid. This proposal helps system administrators prevent possible attacks.

Besides, Yatin et al. [22] presented the methodology of risk assessment for Cyber-physical attacks in Smart Grid system. They concentrated on one primary function which is power delivery to narrow down the number of attacks in the system. The Bayesian Attack Graph for Smart Grid (BAGS) tool is used to quantify the probability of attack success and the likelihood of attack relied on the CVSS base score when successfully exploiting vulnerabilities. The authors also considered the attack risk to help power engineers decide the security budget and patch management to protect system on which system component is being susceptible to easily get compromised by intruders. In addition, they applied reinforcement learning for resource allocation in the cyber domain of Smart Grid to generate the optimal policy which recommends whether to conduct the assessment and patching the vulnerability in the network. However, this work did not take into account the attack cost for hackers when attempting to compromise the cyber system. Graph visualization is also ignored in their implementation.

In [23], Rounak presented a Bayesian attack tree to model CPS vulnerabilities for SCADA's security assessment. This work concentrated on the perspective of prioritizing important vulnerabilities in SCADA to be first identified and generated attack paths to target element. This is to avoid comprehensive modeling of every element in the CPS. For each type of vulnerability, the probability of successfully exploiting is considered in accordance with the skill level of the intruder. Also, their skill level reflects on the time of compromising system which contains the vulnerability. The CVSS metric is used to calculate the probability that a vulnerability is successfully exploited. Besides, the impact on the power grid as well as the risk of cyber attack on each attack path is also assessed in the cyber-system. However, lack of attack graph visualization and likelihood is the shortcoming of this study.

2.4   Security Metrics Calculation

To compute the likelihood of compromise in a Smart Grid environment, Yatin et al. [22] used the base score of CVSS to compute the exploitability of a vulnerability. Based on the probability ranges, they matched each potential attack into the corresponding qualitative value of likelihood.

Besides, Ge et al. [17] proposed some metrics to analyze the security problems for an IoT-enabled system. In general, this framework takes IoT topology, vulnerability information and security metrics from security decision maker as its input to generate extended HARM model. Then, the graph visualization of IoT network topology with attack paths is produced. Subsequently, the security analysis is conducted relying on the set of IoT nodes, vulnerabilities and potential attack path information. The analysis result is then used to determine the most appropriate defense strategies for vulnerable nodes in the network. In this approach, a set of IoT nodes is defined as T. There is an attack tree

$at_t = (A, B, c, g, root)$ for each node $t \in T$. Attack success probability is the value to measure the probability of success when an attacker is attacking the target. At the level of node, attack success probability is measured for each inner node of an attack tree. The value of attack success probability at the node $t \in T$ is the attack success probability value of the root of the attack tree corresponding to the node. At the level of path, the value of attack success probability of an attack path is also measured. This value is the metric of the probability that an attacker can compromise the target over the attack path

Attack cost is the value of measuring the cost of an attack spent for successfully attacking a target. At the level of node, the values of attack cost are calculated for each inner node and node $t \in T$ of an attack tree. At the level of path, the measure is the cost spent by an attacker to compromise the target over the attack path. At the level of network, the measure is the minimum cost for an attacker compromising the target in the company of all possible paths.

Similarly, the attack impact value of an attack path is computed by taking the sum of attack values of each node. Then, at the network-level, the attack impact is the maximum value among all potential paths.

2.5 Summary

Among the related studies, the framework for automating security analysis of IoT proposed in [17] is the most advanced in terms of coverage, ranging from Attack Tree, Attack Graph Generation, p, ac, aim, r. Furthermore, the formulae to calculate security metrics were explained in detail. However, the scope of the framework focuses on the general IoT system. Therefore, there are still limitations in Attack Graph Visualization, Likelihood, and Smart Grid application. Attack Graph Visualization is a practical method for cybersecurity experts and even novices to examine the system activities and investigate all potential cyber attacks. By using Likelihood, the possibility of an attack can be ranked, which strongly supports the risk assessment process. Missing research on Smart Grid Attack Graph Visualization and Likelihood creates a gap in the field. Consequently, we utilize the framework to bridge the gap of current research.

3   Smart Grid Case Study

In this section, a Smart Grid case study with various attack scenarios is conducted. We first introduce the Smart Grid model, including the power grid and network models, followed by description of attack scenarios. Finally, attack analysis results are presented.

3.1 Smart Grid Model

There are two essential components of Smart Grid, including the power grid and network models. Various research has been completed to model each Smart Grid component. On the one hand, several distribution test feeders, which vary in the complexity, scale, and control data, are developed in recent decades. Among these test feeders, IEEE Feeders [24] and Pacific Northwest National Laboratory (PNNL) Taxonomy Feeders [25] are widely accepted in Smart Grid research community. On the other hand, numerous network architectural models were designed for the Smart Grid system [26, 27]. The IEEE Feeders have been applied in our previous research at [28] and [29]. Therefore, the selected PNNL Taxonomy Feeders for power grid and network models applied for the Smart Grid case study are discussed in the scope of this research.

Power Grid Model. The increasing integration of Smart Grid technologies in the U.S. electricity networks highlights the significance of test feeders' availability, which allows studying the impact of attacks for such cyber-physical models.

Due to its large size and the various utilities, the existing electricity grids in the US present a wide range of topologies and equipment. Therefore, test feeders should reflect these differences based on factors, for instance, the voltage level and climate region. To respond to this demand, PNNL introduced a set of 24-node radial distribution test feeders for taxonomy representing the continental region of the U.S. in 2009. These distribution test feeders have been developed with a clustering algorithm comprising of 17 different utilities and their 575 current feeders. The continental region was divided into five climate zones to perform this categorization, where 35 associated statistical and electrical characteristics were investigated.

Among 24 prototypical feeders, R4-12.47-2 has its advantage by representing a combination of a moderately populated urban area with a lightly populated suburban area. Besides, the less populous area is mainly comprised of single-family residences, which is ideal for our case study. The power grid infrastructure is shown in Fig. 1. There are 352 residential houses in the system. Each house was extended by a smart meter to collect electricity consumption data. In order to enhance the performance control, these houses are clustered into 5 smaller areas, namely, A, B, C, D, and E.

Network Model. The infrastructure of Smart Grid is divided into three major communication networks, namely Home Area Network (HAN), Neighbor Area Network (NAN), and Wide Area Network (WAN) [31]. The research at [32] introduced two distinct types of HAN architecture to represent its relationship with the utility. In the first architecture, the smart meter monitors all the house appliances to manage the grid. The disadvantage of this architecture is that all devices have to communicate through the same networking protocol. Therefore, the second architecture in which all the devices connect to the smart meter through a gateway is introduced to deal with the difficulty of multiple communication protocols.

We show the Smart Grid communication network with the gateway based on the selected structure of the power grid in Fig. 2. Note that the model was simplified for the purposes of our case study. The household in the network model reflects each house in the power grid model. Besides, these households

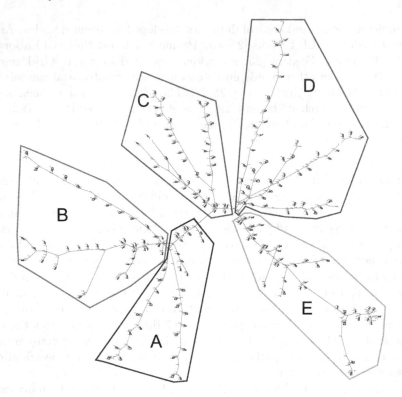

Fig. 1. The Pacific Northwest National Laboratory (PNNL) Taxonomy Feeders - R4-12.47-2 [30].

are clustered into smaller areas in the same way as the residential houses are clustered in the power grid model. Each house is equipped with five smart appliances, including a smart TV, a smart thermostat, a robot vacuum cleaner, a smart light, and an IP camera. The gateway handles incoming messages from the smart devices and forwards those relevant to the smart meter. Then, these data are transmitted from the smart meter to the area concentrator. Five area concentrators are corresponding with five areas A, B, C, D, E. They receive the data, then transfers to the central concentrator. Finally, these data are gathered at the SCADA system. In the considered scenario, the SCADA system is not covered.

Each device or node in the system is given an ID that follows a regular pattern including device name, area, and house ID. For instance, the ID of a smart TV belongs to house number 1 of area A is denoted as TV_{A_1}. Similarly, we have $Thermostat_{A_1}$, $Cleaner_{A_1}$, $Light_{A_1}$, Cam_{A_1}, $Gateway_{A_1}$, and $Meter_{A_1}$ as the IDs of the smart appliances of the area A's first house. In addition, $Concentrator_A$, $Concentrator_B$, $Concentrator_C$, $Concentrator_D$, and $Concentrator_E$ represent the concentrators for each area A, B, C, D, and E,

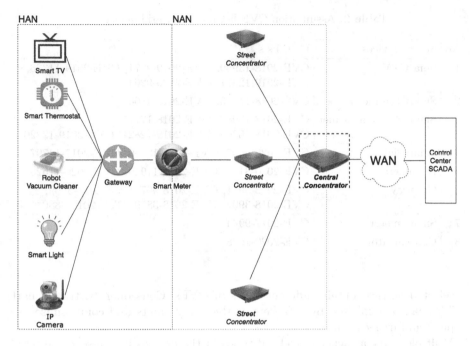

Fig. 2. Simplified network model (part of Smart Grid) with Gateway used in our case study.

respectively. Finally, *Central_Concentrator* serves as the ID for the central concentrator in the defined Smart Grid network model.

3.2 Attack Scenarios

We assumed that nearly 2% of 352 residential houses in the system, which are all of the smart devices inside seven households, contain vulnerabilities. In detail, there are two houses in each area A and B, as well as one house in each area C, D, and E, that have vulnerabilities.

A vulnerability is a weakness, flaw, or error detected inside a security system that can be taken advantage of by nefarious actors to compromise a secure network. By using sequences of commands, pieces of software, or even open-source exploit kits, hackers can exploit which vulnerabilities can be leveraged for malicious activity. In the considered circumstance, we assume that the CVE list shown in Table 2 was the vulnerabilities exploited by attackers. The hackers can use any HAN devices, including smart TV, smart thermostat, robot vacuum cleaner, smart light, and IP camera, one by one or even all of them as the entry points to start an attack. Three attack scenarios were considered in this research:

1. Single-entry attacker model: one type of devices has vulnerabilities in this model. Therefore, attackers can only exploit this kind of device inside the infected houses to conduct an attack. For instance, all smart TVs of seven

Table 2. Assumption CVE list for smart grid devices

No	Smart devices	CVE lists
1	Smart TV	CVE-2018-13989, CVE-2019-9871, CVE-2019-11336, CVE-2019-12477, CVE-2020-9264
2	Smart thermostat	CVE-2018-11315, CVE-2013-4860
3	Smart vacuum cleaner	CVE-2018-10987, CVE-2018-17177, CVD-2018-20785, CVE 2010 12821, CVE 2019-12820
4	Smart light	CVE-2020-6007, CVE-2019-18980, CVE-2017-14797
5	IP camera	CVE-2020-3110, CVE-2020-11949, CVE-2020-11623
6	Gateway	CVE-2018-3911, CVE-2018-907, CVE-2018-3909, CVE-2018-3902, CVE-2018-3879, CVE-2018-3880
7	Smart meter	CVE-2017-9944
8	Concentrator	CVE-2020-1638

selected houses contain different types of CVEs. Consequently, these smart TVs can be exploited by attackers as the entry points and compromised to perform further attacks.

2. Multiple-entry attacker model: all types of the devices in the seven selected houses have vulnerabilities. Accordingly, attackers can potentially exploit all of these devices to carry out an intrusion. This scenario can be considered as combining all available devices in the aforementioned single-entry attacker model.

3. Multiple-entry attacker model with patch: patching is used to fix the vulnerabilities in a specific type of devices. This scenario is the extension of the multiple-entry attacker model by integrating the patching as a defense strategy. For example, all vulnerabilities of all smart TVs inside the system have been fixed. Hence, they can not be used as the entry points by attacker to conduct the attack.

The attack goal is to control the central concentrator. If a Smart Grid device has more than one vulnerability, attackers can randomly select one vulnerability to conduct the attack. The considered attack scenarios are not the only solutions since more vulnerability rates can be selected and tested. Fortunately, the result at a 2% rate is visually significant.

3.3 Attack Analysis Results

We conducted a Smart Grid case study by applying the framework for automating IoT security analysis proposed in [17]. We calculate the security metrics values in node, attack path, and network level. These security metrics are Attack Success Probability (p), Attack Cost (ac), Attack Impact (aim), Attack Risk (r). The formulas to calculate these security metrics are extracted from Subsect. 2.4. Based on the range of p adapted by the research at [22] and [33], the attack

Table 3. Attack analysis results

Scenario	Entry point	Patch	p	ac	aim	r	Number of paths					
							Total	Rare enspace	Unlikely	Possible	Likely	Almost certain
1	Smart TV	No	1	21.6	35.8	35.8	25	1	10	0	7	7
2	Smart thermostat	No	0.65	23.6	35.8	23.27	25	0	5	14	6	0
3	Robot vacuum cleaner	No	0.86	21.6	32.2	27.69	25	3	12	0	8	2
4	Smart light	No	1	23.6	35.8	35.8	25	2	10	9	0	4
5	IP camera	No	0.8	23.6	35.8	28.64	25	2	9	5	6	3
6	All	No	1	21.6	35.8	35.8	125	8	46	28	27	16
7	All	Smart TV	1	21.6	35.8	35.8	100	7	36	28	20	9
8	All	Smart TV and Smart light	0.86	21.6	35.8	30.8	75	5	26	19	20	5

paths are classified into five categories, including Rare ($0.0 \leq p \leq 0.19$), Unlikely ($0.2 \leq p \leq 0.39$), Possible ($0.4 \leq p \leq 0.59$), Likely ($0.6 \leq p \leq 0.79$), and Almost Certain ($0.8 \leq p \leq 1$) paths. The network level analysis results are shown in Table 3. Accordingly, the scenarios from one to five denote the results for the single-entry attacker model, as well as scenario six represents the results for the multiple-entry attacker model, and the scenarios from seven to eight for results from multiple-entry attacker model with patch.

Single-Entry Attacker Model: We can see that attacking the smart TVs and smart lights have the maximum success probability from the metrics values 1. However, the attack cost by compromising the smart lights is higher than the smart TVs. Accordingly, there are 25 attack paths, which contain 7 Almost Certain paths, for attackers to reach the central concentrator via the smart TVs' entry points. Consequently, intruders are more likely to choose smart TVs as entry points.

At the network level, attack cost is the minimum cost, while attack impact is the maximum loss caused by an intruder to compromise the target among all potential paths. Therefore, an ideal path for attackers to compromise the central concentrator may not exist even in the single-entry attacker model. As an evidence, the path from TV_{A_1} to $Central\_Concentrator$, which is shown in the following, has the minimum attack cost at 21.6, maximum attack success probability at 1, and maximum attack risk and impact at 35.8:

– Attackers $\rightarrow$ TV_{A_1} $\rightarrow$ $Gateway_{A_1}$ $\rightarrow$ $Meter_{A_1}$ $\rightarrow$ $Concentrator_A$ $\rightarrow$ $Central\_Concentrator$

However, the following path from TV_{B_2} to $Central\_Concentrator$ has the maximum impact at 35.8:

– Attackers $\rightarrow$ TV_{B_2} $\rightarrow$ $Gateway_{B_2}$ $\rightarrow$ $Meter_{B_2}$ $\rightarrow$ $Concentrator_B$ $\rightarrow$ $Central\_Concentrator$

After analyzing the Smart Grid system, attackers can determine which paths to hack based on their intention. The knowledge can be used by security experts to protect the system against an attack. By using attack success probability metrics, the example of an attack graph generated automatically by the case study is shown in Fig. 3.

Multiple-Entry Attacker Model: By providing more entry devices, attackers possess more paths to conduct an attack. There is more likely that the Smart Gird system is hacked since among 125 paths, there are 16 Almost Certain, 27 Likely, and 28 Possible paths, respectively. In this scenario, attackers need to spend less cost at 21.6. However, the attack impact and attack risk are highest at 35.8. Similarly, smart TVs and smart lights should be protected at first in order to prevent the attackers from breaking into the system.

Multiple-Entry Attacker Model with Patch: We modify the vulnerability information for the smart TVs or both smart TVs and smart lights, separately.

Since the potential attack paths caused by both smart TVs and smart lights, the impact of patch function on smart TVs is not obvious. The attack success probability, attack impact, attack risk remain the same with multiple-entry attacker model. However, the total paths have been decreased. The Almost Certain paths are modified from 16 to 9.

By eliminating the vulnerabilities of both smart TVs and smart lights, we decrease the attack success probability, attack impact, and attack risk. However, the attack cost has not changed. The reason comes from the vacuum cleaners, which costs attackers less effort to compromise. The number of Almost Certain paths has been changed to 5. Therefore, based on the analysis results, it is evident that protecting both smart TVs and smart lights is more effective than protecting either of them.

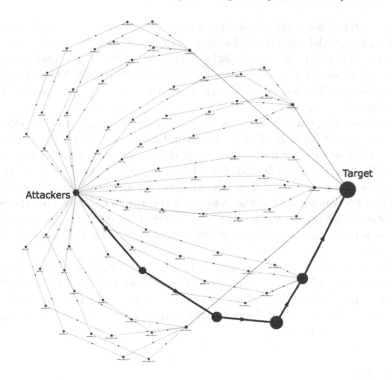

Fig. 3. An example of attack graph generated by a case study

4   Conclusion and Future Work

Cyber-security is at the core of modern technologies. In this research, we conducted a comprehensive and systematic survey of various attack analysis studies using the combination of Graphical Security Model and CVSS. We reviewed of the state-of-the-art techniques, ranging from traditional networks, emerging technologies, to Smart Grid. To accomplish this goal, numerous metrics of interest have been examined, namely, Attack Tree, Attack Graph Generation, Attack Graph Visualization, Attack Success Probability, Attack Cost, Attack Impact, Attack Risk, Likelihood, and Smart Grid Application.

As cyber attacks on the Smart Grid system can have serious issues, protecting the Smart Grid system safe from attackers is extremely important. Attack analysis is one of the advanced technologies to investigate and evaluate attackers' activities. This information is invaluable to defense the Smart Grid system. However, there is few research focus on Smart Grid attack analysis using Graphical Security Model.

We indicated that the framework for automating security analysis of the Internet of Things proposed in this paper is a successful solution which can be extended to Smart Grid system. By applying the PNNL Taxonomy Feeders R4-12.47-2, Smart Grid network model with gateway, a Smart Grid case study with three attack scenarios, including a single-entry attacker model, multiple-entry attacker model, and multiple-entry attacker model with patch, has been carried out. All potential attack paths have been determined, and the values of the selected security metrics have been calculated during the vulnerability analysis process. Besides, our research is enriched by the automated Attack Graph generation capacity.

This knowledge can be used for cybersecurity training of IT experts and cybersecurity professionals. Based on evaluating various security metrics, IT experts and cybersecurity professionals can determine all possible attack paths, then decide which devices included in the paths should be protected at first. Besides, the effectiveness of specific device-level strategies deployed for different devices can be compared. For the network-level, the performance of the Smart Grid system's defense strategies can be measured. Furthermore, our work can help system planners estimate the attack's damage cost on the proposed Smart Grid system.

We intend to extend our current work to a Cyber Attack Analysis Framework for Smart Grids, which integrates more power grid test feeders and network models for future work. We will also conduct case studies with the collection of various Smart Grid CVEs, different power grid and network models, to validate our extended framework.

References

1. Ghansah, I.: Smart Grid Cyber Security Potential Threats. Interim Project Report. California Energy Commission, Vulnerabilities and Risks (2012)
2. Christey, S., Martin, R.A.: Vulnerability type distributions in CVE (2007)
3. Scarfone, K., Mell, P.: An analysis of CVSS version 2 vulnerability scoring. In: 3rd International Symposium on Empirical Software Engineering and Measurement, pp. 516–525. IEEE (2009)
4. Hong, J.B., Kim, D.S., Chung, C.-J., Huang, D.: A survey on the usability and practical applications of graphical security models. Comput. Sci. Rev. **26**, 1–16 (2017)
5. Schneier, B.: Secrets and Lies: Digital Security in a Networked World. John Wiley & Sons, Hoboken (2015)
6. Sheyner, O., Haines, J., Jha, S., Lippmann, R., Wing, J.M.: Automated generation and analysis of attack graphs. In: Proceedings: IEEE Symposium on Security and Privacy, pp. 273–284. IEEE (2002)
7. Hong, J., Kim, D.-S.: Harms: hierarchical attack representation models for network security analysis (2012)
8. Hong, J.B., Kim, D.S.: Towards scalable security analysis using multi-layered security models. J. Netw. Comput. Appl. **75**, 156–168 (2016)
9. Anoop Singhal, X.O.: Security risk analysis of enterprise networks using probabilistic attack graphs, National Institute of Standards and Technology (NIST), Tech. Rep. (2011)
10. Hyunchul Joh, Y.K.M.: Defining and assessing quantitative security risk measures using vulnerability lifecycle and CVSS metrics. In: The 2011 International Conference on Security and Management (SAM 2011) (2011)

11. Cheng, P., Wang, L., Jajodia, S., Singhal, A.: Aggregating CVSS base scores for semantics-rich network security metrics. In: International Symposium on Reliable Distributed Systems (2012)
12. Poolsappasit, I.R.N., Dewri, R.: Dynamic security risk management using Bayesian attack graphs. IEEE Trans. Dependable Secur. Comput. **9**(1), 61–74 (2012)
13. Alhomidi, M., Reed, M.: Attack graph-based risk assessment and optimisation approach. Int. J. Netw. Secur. Appl. **6**(3), 31 (2014)
14. Aksu, M.U., et al.: A quantitative cvss-based cyber security risk assessment methodology for it systems. In: 2017 International Carnahan Conference on Security Technology (ICCST), pp. 1–8 (2017)
15. Ge, M., Kim, D.S.: A framework for modeling and assessing security of the internet of things. IEEE 21st International Conference on Parallel and Distributed Systems (2015)
16. Yusuf, S.E., Ge, M., Hong, J.B., Kim, H.K., Kim, P., Kim, D.S.: Security modelling and analysis of dynamic enterprise networks. In:. IEEE International Conference on Computer and Information Technology (CIT), vol. 2016, pp. 249–256 (2016)
17. Ge, M., Hong, J.B., SeongKim, W.G.D.: A framework for automating security analysis of the internet of things. J. Netw. Comput. Appl. **83**, 12–27 (2017)
18. Li, E.: Quantitative model of attacks on distribution automation systems based on CVSS and attack trees. Information **10**(8), 251 (2019)
19. An, S., et al.: Cloudsafe: a tool for an automated security analysis for cloud computing. In: 2019 18th IEEE International Conference on Trust, Security and Privacy in Computing and Communications/13th IEEE International Conference on Big Data Science and Engineering (TrustCom/BigDataSE), pp. 602–609 (2019)
20. Eom, T.H., Jin, B., An, S.P., Jong, S., Kim, D.S.: A framework for real-time intrusion response in software defined networking using precomputed graphical security models. Secur. Commun. Netw. (2020)
21. Beckers, K., Heisel, M., Krautsevich, L., Martinelli, F., Meis, R., Yautsiukhin, A.: Determining the probability of smart grid attacks by combining attack tree and attack graph analysis. In: Cuellar, J. (ed.) SmartGridSec 2014. LNCS, vol. 8448, pp. 30–47. Springer, Cham (2014). https://doi.org/10.1007/978-3-319-10329-7_3
22. Wadhawan, Y., Neuman, C., AlMajali, A.: A comprehensive analysis of smart grid systems against cyber-physical attacks. Electronics **7**(10), 249 (2018)
23. Meyur, R.: A Bayesian attack tree based approach to assess cyber-physical security of power system. In: IEEE Texas Power and Energy Conference (TPEC), pp. 1–6 (2020)
24. Schneider, K., et al.: Analytic considerations and design basis for the IEEE distribution test feeders. IEEE Trans. Power Syst. **33**(3), 3181–3188 (2017)
25. Schneider, K.P., Chen, Y., Chassin, D.P., Pratt, R.G., Engel, D.W., Thompson, S.E.: Modern grid initiative distribution taxonomy final report, Pacific Northwest National Lab. (PNNL), Richland, WA (United States), Tech. Rep. (2008)
26. Saputro, N., Akkaya, K., Uludag, S.: A survey of routing protocols for smart grid communications. Comput. Netw. **56**(11), 2742–2771 (2012)
27. Colak, I., Sagiroglu, S., Fulli, G., Yesilbudak, M., Covrig, C.-F.: A survey on the critical issues in smart grid technologies. Renew. Sustain. Energy Rev. **54**, 396–405 (2016)
28. Le, T.D., Anwar, A., Beuran, R., Loke, S.W.: Smart grid co-simulation tools: Review and cybersecurity case study. In: 2019 7th International Conference on Smart Grid (icSmartGrid), pp. 39–45. IEEE (2019)
29. Le, T.D., Anwar, A., Loke, S.W., Beuran, R., Tan, Y.: Gridattacksim: a cyber attack simulation framework for smart grids. Electronics **9**(8), 1218 (2020)

30. Cohen, M.A.: Gridlab-d taxonomy feeder graphs, GridLAB-D Taxonomy Feeder Graphs (2013)
31. Raza, N., Akbar, M.Q., Soofi, A.A., Akbar, S.: Study of smart grid communication network architectures and technologies. J. Comput. Commun. **7**(3), 19–29 (2019)
32. Clements, S.L., Carroll, T.E., Hadley, M.D.: Home area networks and the smart grid, Pacific Northwest National Lab. (PNNL), Richland, WA (United States), Tech. Rep. (2011)
33. Blank, R.M.: Guide for conducting risk assessments (2011)

Hybrid Encryption Scheme for Secure Storage of Smart Grid Data

Jie Deng[1] and Hai-Yan Kang[2(✉)]

[1] School of Computer Science, Beijing Information Science and Technology University, Beijing 100192, China
bistu_dengjie@163.com
[2] School of Information Management, Beijing Information Science and Technology University, Beijing 100192, China
kanghaiyan@126.com

Abstract. The wide application of smart grid improves the energy utilization rate and improves the power market, but at the same time, it also introduces many security problems, such as data storage, transmission, theft and other security problems in the process of smart grid data communication. Due to the special position of power system, how to ensure the security of data storage in smart grid is of great significance for the safe and stable operation of power grid system. This paper first analyzes the smart grid and its data characteristics, combined with the relevant technologies of cloud computing, gives a data security storage model of smart grid to strengthen the reliability and storage capacity of smart grid. Then, in order to ensure the security of user data storage in the cloud in smart grid, this paper studies the data encryption algorithm, and proposes a hybrid encryption scheme for smart grid data security storage. Finally, the scheme is compared with the traditional method. The experimental results show that the scheme has the advantages of good encryption and decryption effect, fast execution speed and high security. It is an ideal scheme for smart grid data security storage.

Keywords: Smart grid · Data encryption · DES · RSA · Hybrid encryption

1 Introduction

The wide application of new smart grid improves the energy utilization rate and improves the power market, but it also introduces many security problems [1–4]. Due to the large number and variety of communication equipment in smart grid, and most of them are embedded devices, wireless communication with low cost and high flexibility is adopted [5]. In the process of information transmission, it is faced with data eavesdropping, tampering, forgery and other security threats [6–8]. At the same time, with the continuous development of the power grid, its scale will continue to expand, the structure will become more and more complex, the interactive information between the business systems will increase, and the source and distribution of data will be more extensive, which will lead to the data in the power system will present a huge increase, and the form of data

Y.-B. Lin and D.-J. Deng (Eds.): SGIoT 2020, LNICST 354, pp. 135–156, 2021.
https://doi.org/10.1007/978-3-030-69514-9_12

will be more diversified. At the same time, it also puts forward higher requirements for the reliability and real-time of the data. The traditional power hardware facilities, data calculation and processing capacity will be difficult to meet the requirements of future smart grid development. As a new rising technology in recent years, cloud computing technology provides a new way for the development of smart grid. The unique distributed computing and storage characteristics of cloud computing, as well as the advantages of high reliability, strong fault tolerance and easy expansion, can provide effective solutions for the problems encountered in the development process of smart grid. Therefore, the integration of cloud computing technology into the smart grid can ensure that the power hardware infrastructure can integrate all kinds of resources of the current system with as few changes as possible, so as to improve the real-time requirements of the smart grid for data processing, and provide effective support for the development of smart grid technology [9].

At present, the standard symmetric encryption algorithm is still used in smart grid, but the number of wireless terminals in smart grid is large and widely distributed, so the key distribution and effective update is a challenge [10, 11]. In order to solve this challenge, scholars at home and abroad have done a lot of research. For example, Li et al. [12] proposed a privacy protection method of power consumption data based on empirical mode decomposition (EMD) and homomorphic encryption, which solved the risk of leakage of user privacy in the process of power grid load balance and power supply adjustment in order to collect user power consumption data. However, the scheme calls a third-party service to generate and manage the key, and based on mathematical problems, it does not fully consider the storage space and computing capacity of communication equipment in the smart grid, and is not applicable in the process of real-time communication, which will bring additional communication burden [13, 14]. Premnath et al. [15] used NTRU (number theory research u-nit) asymmetric encryption algorithm to realize data integrity protection and identity authentication in data acquisition and monitoring control system of smart grid. However, when the length of data acquisition and monitoring control data packet is large, the storage space of communication equipment in smart grid will be seriously insufficient, and even affect the computing power. Therefore, some scholars have studied a series of lightweight cryptographic algorithms based on algebra, number theory and other basic knowledge. For example, Gao [16] proposed a lightweight key management scheme based on Elliptic Curve Cryptography (ECC) to realize the key distribution and management between the data concentrator and the smart meter. However, due to the shortage of ECC algorithm, the security of ECC key can not be guaranteed. Kumar et al. [17] proposed a lightweight elastic protocol to protect the secure communication between smart meters and smart grid infrastructure. However, the premise of normal operation of the protocol is that the initialization key in the security module of smart meters is always safe and effective, and once it is leaked, it will directly affect the safe transmission of data.

Data encryption technology is known as the core technology of information security, which is mainly divided into symmetric encryption and asymmetric encryption. Data Encryption Standard (DES) algorithm [18] and Rivest Shamir Adleman(RSA) algorithm [19] are typical representatives. DES algorithm is a block encryption algorithm with high computational efficiency and fast encryption speed, but its security depends on the key. The RSA algorithm is based on the decomposition of large numbers. It adopts the double key system of public key and private key. Its cracking difficulty is equivalent to the decomposition of the product of two large prime numbers. It has high security, but it has high computational cost and slow encryption speed. Although there is no effective method to decipher them in a short time, with the continuous development of computer software and hardware, the performance of computer is changing with each passing day, and the traditional data encryption algorithm is no longer secure. Therefore, in order to better solve the security problem of user data stored in the cloud in smart grid, based on the traditional DES and RSA algorithm, this paper first analyzes the advantages and disadvantages of DES, and combines the advantages of Triple Data Encryption Algorithm (TDEA) and Independent Sub Key DES Algorithm (ISKDES), improves DES algorithm, and proposes a Hybrid double DES encryption algorithm (HDDES). Then, this paper makes a detailed study on the method of judging prime number which affects the operation speed of RSA algorithm. On the basis of not affecting the security of RSA, this paper improves the original method of prime number judgment, and proposes a RSA algorithm based on improved prime number decision (IPNRSA). Finally, this paper combines the HDDES encryption algorithm and IPNRSA encryption algorithm to form a hybrid encryption scheme based on HDDES and IPNRSA, which can effectively ensure the security of user data in the cloud.

2 Data Security Storage Model for Smart Grid

2.1 Symmetric Encryption Algorithm DES

Overview of DES. DES is a block encryption algorithm, which uses 64 bit block encryption mechanism to process binary data. Both packet length and ciphertext packet length are 64 bits, and there is no data extension. The system of DES is public, and the security of the system depends on the confidentiality of the key.

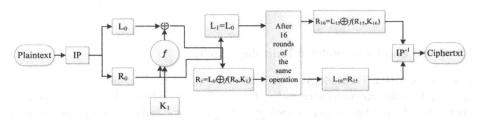

Fig. 1. Iterative flow chart of DES encryption.

The Principle of DES. The decryption process of DES algorithm adopts the same function as the encryption process, but the order of decryption key and encryption key is opposite. In DES algorithm, the key must be processed first. This step includes initial key mapping, 16 sub key calculation and key compression mapping. Then the plaintext is encrypted. The flow chart of DES iteration process is shown in Fig. 1.

2.2 Symmetric Encryption Algorithm RSA

Overview of RSA. RSA as an asymmetric encryption algorithm, one of the most important points is that when the data is transmitted in the network, the key used to encrypt the data does not need to be transmitted with the data, so it reduces the possibility of key leakage. Therefore, RSA is one of the most important encryption algorithms. It can resist most of the known key attacks so far, and ISO takes it as the public key data encryption standard.

The Principle of RSA. RSA algorithm is mainly based on the difficulty of decomposing large numbers, because it is easy to find the product of two large prime numbers, but it is difficult to decompose the product. Therefore, the product of two large prime numbers can be used as public key, and the prime number can be used as the private key generating factor. In this way, it is difficult to use public key and ciphertext to crack plaintext, which is equivalent to decomposing the product of two large prime numbers. Therefore, RSA algorithm is almost impossible to be brutally cracked, with high security. The encryption and decryption process of RSA is shown in Fig. 2.

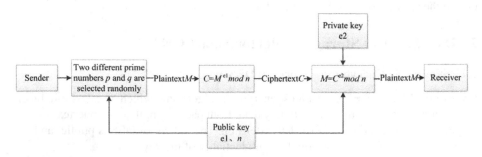

Fig. 2. RSA encryption and decryption process

2.3 Cloud Computing Related Technology Analysis

Cloud Computing Technology. Cloud computing [20] is a new data centric computing method. Its most important idea is to distribute on demand and provide dynamic services. Therefore, advanced computer technology is the pillar of cloud computing. Cloud computing includes virtualization technology, data storage technology, data management technology and some other unique key technologies.

According to different deployment methods, cloud computing has the following four deployment models [21]:

1) Private cloud, that is, a cloud platform built for an enterprise or institution to use alone, does not provide services to the outside world, and can avoid security risks and bandwidth constraints to a certain extent;

2) Public cloud refers to cloud computing services that can be obtained from third-party suppliers for free or at a lower cost, and the service objects have no special requirements;

3) Community cloud is a cloud platform constructed by many organizations with the same interests to support specific communities;

4) Hybrid cloud is composed of two or more public clouds and private clouds, which have the characteristics of the two and are independent of each other.

Hadoop Distributed File System (HDFS). Hadoop Distributed File System (HDFS) is a distributed file system, which is one of the two core technologies of Hadoop. As HDFS has the characteristics of high fault tolerance and high scalability [22], it can be designed and deployed on low-cost computer equipment, and applications can read data with higher efficiency, especially for programs with massive data.

HDFS adopts the Master/Slave structure model. An HDFS cluster is composed of a NameNode and several DataNodes, which undertake the work of Master and Worker respectively. The NameNode is the Master server, which is responsible for the allocation and scheduling in the cluster. The main work is to manage the file system's namespace and adjust the operation of client accessing files. DataNode is the execution node of the specific work in the Worker, which is mainly responsible for managing the data stored in the node. In addition, in order to store massive files reliably, each file in HDFS is stored in block form. This block is an abstract concept. By default, the size of the data block is 64MB. Users can also set data blocks of different sizes according to their actual situation [23]. The architecture of the Hadoop Distributed File System (HDFS) is shown in Fig. 3.

2.4 Construction of Data Security Storage Model for Smart Grid

Advantages of Cloud Computing Technology in Smart Grid. Cloud computing has the characteristics of distributed computing and storage, as well as high reliability, strong fault tolerance and easy expansion. Therefore, the application of cloud computing technology in smart grid can bring the following benefits [24–26]:

1) It can enhance the computing and storage capacity of smart grid. Due to the cloud computing technology in the cloud is through virtualization technology to build a large-scale cluster of computers with a large number of storage space and very efficient processing speed, which makes the massive data generated in each link of the smart grid can be calculated and stored in real time and reliably through cloud computing technology.

2) It improves the utilization rate of smart grid resources and reduces the maintenance cost. Because cloud computing provides a powerful computing and data storage capability for smart grid, all kinds of smart terminal devices in smart grid can be lightweight, without strong data processing capacity. At the same time, each region has system nodes responsible for management, maintenance and update. When a node fails, the processing tasks of this part can be assigned to other nodes to continue

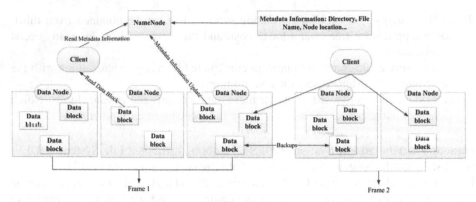

Fig. 3. Architecture of Hadoop distributed file system.

processing. Therefore, the utilization rate of resources is greatly improved and the maintenance cost is greatly reduced.

3) It improves the information and automation of smart grid. Due to the distributed computing and storage characteristics of cloud computing, the real-time and control-lability of smart grid data processing are improved. Real time monitoring and timely operation response can be obtained between power systems and user interaction.

4) It improves the reliability of smart grid. Cloud computing provides a safe and reli-able data storage center for smart grid. In the cloud storage system, the distributed storage mode is generally applied, and various data disaster recovery technologies and corresponding measures are used to ensure that the data in the cloud storage system can have high reliability.

Data Security Storage Model of Smart Grid (DSSMSG). According to the previous analysis, the introduction of cloud computing technology in smart grid and effective integration of existing software and hardware resources can make power system equip-ment as constant as possible, and greatly improve the processing and storage capacity of smart grid data [27]. As the hybrid cloud model has the characteristics of both private cloud and public cloud, Chen Jie [28] and others proposed a hybrid cloud structure for smart grid. At the same time, in order to ensure the security of data in the power system, the data with high security requirements should be stored and managed by the private cloud of the power system, while other data with low security requirements should be stored and managed by the public cloud of a third-party cloud service provider.

As the cloud service provider is not a fully trusted third party, the cloud service provider can obtain the first access to the grid related data by handing part of the power related data to the cloud service provider for storage [29]. In fact, there may be internal personnel's dereliction of duty (such as misoperation), hacker attacks, system failures and even the problems of application technology itself, which may have a certain impact on the security of data.

In this paper, we assume that the user is a secure user confirmed by the power service provider, and the operating environment of the private cloud of the power system is credible. This paper mainly studies the security of the data generated by the user in the public cloud storage. Therefore, based on the hybrid cloud structure of smart grid, this paper presents the data security storage model of smart grid under the deployment mode of hybrid cloud, as shown in Fig. 4.

After encrypting the required data, the data can be transferred to the third-party cloud service provider for storage. The key used by the user to encrypt the data is encrypted by the public key provided by the local power service provider, and then transmitted to the local power service provider for storage. As the trusted third party of users, local power service operators can provide key storage services for users and provide regular data integrity verification services for users. The third-party cloud service provider is mainly responsible for the storage of user data, receiving integrity verification requests from local power service operators, and sending the verification results back to local power service operators.

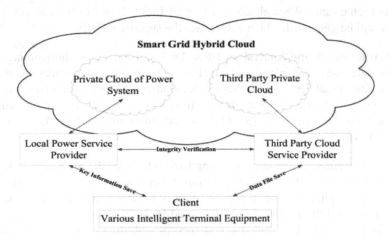

Fig. 4. Data security storage model of smart grid.

3 Hybrid Encryption Scheme for DSSMSG

3.1 A Hybrid Double DES Encryption Algorithm

Overview of DES Algorithm. DES algorithm is also called data encryption standard. It is a symmetric encryption algorithm developed by IBM in 1972. It was determined as the federal data processing standard (FIPS) by the National Bureau of standards of the federal government of the United States in 1976, and then widely spread in the world. Up to now, it still plays a very important role in the international information security stage.

DES is a block encryption algorithm, which adopts 64 bit block encryption mechanism for binary metadata. The length of data packet and ciphertext packet are both 64bit (8byte), without data expansion. The key length is also 64bit, of which 8bit is parity bit, and the remaining 56bit is the effective key length [30, 31]. The whole system of DES is public, and the security of the system depends on the degree of confidentiality of the key.

Analysis of DES's shortcomings

The Key Length is Too Short. The encryption unit of DES is only 64 bit binary, and 8 bits are used for parity check or other communication overhead, so the effective key is only 56 bits. Therefore, this will inevitably reduce the security of DES. With the development of computer performance, the method of brute force cracking des key has been found, and with the computer becoming more and more powerful, the DES with 56 bit key can not support the application with high security requirements. Due to these obvious shortcomings of DES, the National Institute of standards and technology in 1997 stopped studying DES, but studied its alternative method, namely Advanced Encryption Standard(AES) [32].

There is a Weak Key. Because the key is divided into two parts in the process of generating the sub key, if the two parts are divided into all 0 or all 1, the sub key generated in each round is the same. When all keys are 0 or all 1, or half of 1 or 0, weak key or semi weak key will be generated, which will reduce the security of DES.

The Latest Research and Analysis of DES. DES still has many shortcomings, such as its low data transmission rate, not suitable for long-term data protection, and vulnerable to differential key cracking. Therefore, scholars at home and abroad have made many attempts to improve DES algorithm. In this context, they have proposed more influential Triple DES algorithm [33] (TDEA) and independent sub key DES algorithm [34] (ISKDES).

Triple DES Algorithm. Because the key length of traditional DES algorithm is short and easy to be cracked, in order to make up for this deficiency, researchers have proposed a Triple DES Encryption Algorithm (TDEA), that is, the key length of DES is increased by three times, and three different keys are used for triple encryption and decryption. The encryption process is as follows: first encrypt with the first key $k1$, then decrypt with the second key $k2$, and finally encrypt again with the third key $k3$, that is, $C = Ek3(DK2(Ek1M))$. The decryption is in reverse order, that is, $M = Dk1(EK2(Dk3C))$. The core of TDEA is to use $k1$, $k2$, $k3$ to encrypt plaintext for many times, and the key length is three times of DES. The implementation process of TDEA algorithm is shown in Fig. 5.

Although this method increases the length of the key, improves the security strength of the algorithm, and effectively avoids brute force cracking, its calculation time is increased by n-1 times, so the operation efficiency is very low. In addition, although the key bits in TDEA are 168 bits, the threat of brute force cracking cannot be avoided for the current computer computing power.

Independent Sub Key DES Algorithm. The key of ISKDES algorithm depends on using different randomly generated sub keys for encryption, that is, the sub keys in each iteration are not generated by the same 56 bit binary key. Since 48 bit key is used in each round of 16 iterations, the modified DES key length of ISKDES becomes 768 bits. This method can greatly increase the difficulty of exhaustive decryption, so as to improve the encryption strength of DES. However, the length of key is too long and the cost is also increased.

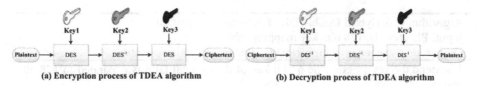

(a) Encryption process of TDEA algorithm   (b) Decryption process of TDEA algorithm

Fig. 5. Encryption and decryption process of TDEA.

Improvement Ideas of DES. Based on TDEA algorithm and ISKDES algorithm, this paper proposes a Hybrid Double DES Encryption Algorithm(HDDES). The algorithm extends the key of DES from 64 bits to 128 bits. After mapping through the mapping table (as shown in Table 1), it is divided into two sub keys (each sub key has 64 bits), which are respectively represented as key1 and key2. Then, 16 sub keys generated by key1 are used to encrypt plaintext to generate ciphertext 1, and then 16 sub keys generated by key2 are used to encrypt ciphertext 1 to generate ciphertext 2. In this way, the security strength is enhanced by double encryption. The specific process of HDDES algorithm is shown in Algorithm 1 and Fig. 6.

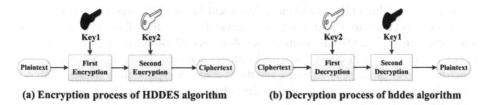

(a) Encryption process of HDDES algorithm   (b) Decryption process of hddes algorithm

Fig. 6. Encryption and decryption process of HDDES algorithm.

Table 1. 128 bits key mapping figure of TDEA.

97	98	52	21	101	86	103	54	105	3	107	23	109	83	89	112
17	18	19	20	100	22	108	24	25	26	27	28	29	30	31	32
49	50	51	9	53	104	55	56	57	123	59	60	61	62	63	64
81	82	110	84	85	102	87	88	111	90	91	92	93	94	95	96
65	35	67	68	69	37	71	72	40	74	75	76	117	127	79	80
43	116	106	4	114	6	125	8	9	10	121	12	13	118	15	16
113	5	115	2	77	14	119	41	11	122	58	124	7	126	78	128
33	34	66	36	70	38	39	73	120	42	1	44	45	46	47	48

Algorithm 1: A Hybrid Double DES Encryption Algorithm
Input: Plaintext M, 128 bits key mapping table
Output: double encrypted ciphertext C, double decryption plaintext M
1. Extend the key length: The 64 bit key of the original DES is expanded to 128 bit length.
2. Key mapping processing: Input the 128 bits key and map it according to the mapping table in Fig. 6 to get two sub keys key1 and key2, each of which has 64 bits.
3. Generation of sub key: Two sub keys key1 and key2 are processed to obtain 16 sub keys respectively.
4. Plaintext double encryption: After inputting plaintext, encrypting with key1 first, and then encrypting with key2 again to generate ciphertext C.
5. Output double encrypted ciphertext C.
6. Plaintext double decryption: After inputting ciphertext, first use key2 to decrypt once, and then use key1 to decrypt the second time to restore plaintext M.
7. Output double decrypted plaintext M.

Experimental Analysis of HDDES Algorithm. In order to prove the effectiveness of the HDDES algorithm proposed in this paper, the HDDES algorithm is compared with the Triple DES algorithm (TDEA) and the independent sub key DES algorithm (ISKDES). The experimental environment is set as follows: 1) CPU: Intel Core i5; 2) 2.8 GHz Main Frequency; 3) 24.0 GB Memory; 4) Windows 10 64 bit operating system; 5) Development software: Eclipse 2018 development platform. There are 5 groups in the experiment, each group runs 30 times, and the average encryption time is taken. Table 2 shows the time taken by three encryption algorithms to encrypt 10KB user data in smart grid when they are running separately.

Table 2. Comparison of short message encryption time between two encryption schemes

Operation time	TDEA algorithm	ISKDES algorithm	HDDES algorithm
The first time	1694 ms	1084 ms	1014 ms
The second time	1636 ms	996 ms	1036 ms
The third time	1679 ms	978 ms	1022 ms
The fourth time	1683 ms	984 ms	1039 ms
The fifth time	1668 ms	993 ms	1044 ms

As can be seen from Table 2, compared with TDEA, HDDES has obvious advantages in encryption efficiency, and is almost equal to that of ISKDES algorithm. This is because HDDES algorithm combines the advantages of TDEA and ISKDES. HDDES first expands the original 64 bits key to 128 bits, which reduces the risk of exhaustive attack if the key is too short. Then HDDES uses the advantages of TDEA algorithm to encrypt the encrypted information, which strengthens the security of the algorithm. Finally, referring to the characteristics of ISKDES algorithm, HDDES maps the 12 bits key to achieve local independence and avoid the threat of brute force cracking of the key. The two complement each other. Due to the only double encryption, the running efficiency of HDDES is higher than that of TDEA algorithm. Figure 7 shows the comparison of the encryption time of the three improved DES algorithms. It is obvious that the encryption efficiency of HDDES is better than that of TDEA.

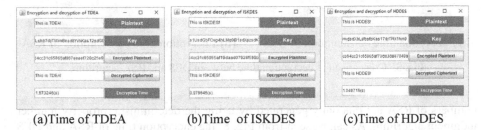

   (a)Time of TDEA   (b)Time of ISKDES   (c)Time of HDDES

Fig. 7. Comparison of encryption time of three improved DES algorithms.

3.2   A RSA Algorithm Based on Improved Prime Number Judgment

Overview of RSA Algorithm. Rivest Shamir Adleman (RSA) public key encryption algorithm was proposed by RonRivest, AdiShamir and LeonardAdleman in 1977. The algorithm was first published in 1987. RSA is asymmetric because the key used to encrypt the data is not the same as the key used to decrypt it.

RSA as an asymmetric encryption algorithm, one of the most important points is that when the data is transmitted in the network, the key used to encrypt the data does not need to be transmitted with the data. Therefore, this reduces the possibility of key disclosure. RSA is considered to be very secure, but its computing speed is much slower than DES.

Analysis of RSA's Shortcomings. At present, there are mainly the following ways to attack RSA: Forced cracking: try all private keys; Mathematical attack: factoring the product of two prime numbers; Timing attack: depends on the execution time of decryption algorithm. In order to prevent the RSA algorithm from being forced to crack, a super long key must be used. Therefore, the more bits of p and q are, the better. However, the speed of key generation, encryption and decryption is also slower and slower. For the remaining two attacks, the security of RSA is based on the difficulty of multiplication and integration of large prime numbers, so it is almost impossible to crack or the cost of cracking is very high.

Key Generation is Cumbersome. Because two large prime numbers p and q must be used to generate RSA key, it is difficult to use different key for each encryption because of the limitation of prime number generation technology.

Slow Encryption Speed. RSA algorithm not only has the high security which DES does not have, but also is very easy to understand. However, the high security is actually at the expense of encryption speed. In this paper, we compare the encryption time of DES algorithm and RSA algorithm for a group of simple data (2KB) to further illustrate their encryption speed gap, as shown in Fig. 8. In addition, the p, q and other large prime

   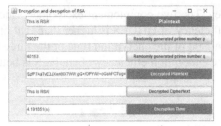

(a) Encryption time consumption of DES   (b) Encryption time consumption of RSA

Fig. 8. Comparison of encryption time between DES and RSA algorithm.

numbers of RSA are randomly generated by using the deterministic property number judgment algorithm. As can be seen from Fig. 8, the encryption time of RSA and DES is almost 100 times different.

The Latest Research and Analysis of RSA. RSA algorithm is a kind of algorithm based on large number decomposition. Because large number decomposition is a recognized mathematical problem, RSA has high security. Although the rapid update of computer hardware, computer performance continues to break through the limit, but the decomposition of large numbers still needs a lot of time to crack. In addition, in order to cope with the rapid development of computer computing power, RSA algorithm gradually increases the length of the key, but the encryption speed of RSA algorithm is just limited by the speed of key generation. In order to solve the encryption speed problem of RSA algorithm, researchers at home and abroad generally adopt two methods. The first method is to improve the implementation of key algorithm [35, 36], and take some measures to speed up its operation. This paper also studies how to improve the generation of RSA key and improve its operation speed. The second method is to find a new public key encryption algorithm to replace RSA, such as the public key encryption algorithm based on elliptic curve [37] (ECC). ECC has achieved a significant breakthrough in efficiency, but it has not been widely used, so a lot of research is still based on theory.

Improvement Ideas of RSA. Since the core algorithm of RSA is the modular power operation of large prime numbers, that is, large number self multiplication module. In order to improve the efficiency of RSA algorithm, it is necessary to solve the problem of operation speed of module power operation in RSA. The core complexity of modular power operation depends on the modular operation, which includes division operation. For a computer, a division operation requires several addition, subtraction and multiplication operations, which is quite time-consuming. Therefore, assuming that RSA algorithm can reduce or even avoid the operation of modulus taking, the performance of RSA algorithm will be significantly improved. Based on this, on the premise of ensuring the security of RSA algorithm, this paper makes a detailed study on the method of judging prime number which affects the operation speed of RSA algorithm module power, and carefully compares the advantages and disadvantages of deterministic and probabilistic prime number judgment algorithms. Then, this paper uses Montgomery fast power algorithm [38] to optimize the classic probability property number judgment algorithm (Miller-Rabin algorithm), and proposes an Improved fast prime number judgment algorithm (IFPNJA). Finally, this paper applies IFPNJA to RSA algorithm to form an RSA algorithm based on improved prime number decision (IPNRSA).

The Judgment Method of Prime Number. The judgment methods of prime number can be divided into two categories: one is deterministic prime number judgment algorithm, the other is probabilistic prime number judgment algorithm. Deterministic prime number judgment algorithm means its name, that is, the number generated through it is 100% prime, but with certain restrictions. Although the probabilistic prime number judgment algorithm can not guarantee 100% generation of prime number, there is no big restriction, and the speed of generating prime number is faster than that of deterministic prime number judgment algorithm. Generally speaking, the probabilistic prime number judgment algorithm is mostly used in real life. Although it can not guarantee 100% generation of prime number, the generation of non prime number is a small probability event after all, and the probabilistic prime number judgment algorithm can generate pseudo prime numbers quickly and irregularly, meeting most needs.

1) Deterministic prime number judgment algorithm. The most commonly used is divisibility algorithm, that is, the divisibility test. The principle of the algorithm is that all integers used as divisor are less than $\sqrt{n}$. If any of these numbers can be divisible by n, then n is a compound number. The efficiency of divisibility algorithm is very low, and its bit operation complexity is exponential growth.
2) Probabilistic prime number judgment algorithm. Among them, the more famous algorithms are: Miller-Rabin algorithm [39], Solovay-Strassen algorithm [40], Lehman algorithm [41], etc. Since this paper improves the Miller-Rabin probabilistic prime number judgment algorithm and is limited to space, only the Miller-Rabin algorithm is introduced in detail, and other famous algorithms are not described in detail.

Introduction of Miller Rabin Algorithm. If n is an odd prime number, then $n-1 = 2rm$. r is a nonnegative integer, m is a positive odd number, and a is any positive integer coprime with n, then $am \equiv 1 \pmod{n}$ or for some $h(0 \le h \le r-1)$, equation $aw \equiv -1 \pmod{n}$ holds, where $w = 2hm$. It can be proved that the error probability of Miller-Rabin algorithm is at most $4-1$. If n passes the t-test, the probability that n is not a prime number will be $4-t$, while the error probability of Solovay-Strassen algorithm and Lehman algorithm is $2-t$.

An Improved Fast Prime Number Judgment Algorithm. Because of the low efficiency and high complexity of the deterministic prime number judgment algorithm, it is not suitable for the modular power operation of RSA algorithm. Therefore, this paper uses the probabilistic prime number judgment algorithm to improve the modular power operation of RSA algorithm. According to the principle of each probability judgment algorithm, the probability of Miller-Rabin algorithm to judge prime number is much higher than the other two mainstream algorithms. Therefore, this paper selects Miller-Rabin algorithm to improve. This paper introduces Montgomery fast power algorithm, which can greatly reduce modular power operation, to optimize Miller-Rabin algorithm and form an improved fast prime number judgment algorithm (IFPNJA). The specific process is shown in Algorithm 2.

Algorithm 2: an improved fast prime number judgment algorithm
Input: large number A, B, Miller-Rabin algorithm, modulus N
Output: fast modular multiplication results of large numbers A and B

---

1. Initial Input. input two large numbers A, B and modulus N
2. Base selection: select a positive integer R which is coprime with N as the cardinal number. At the same time, when R is $2k$, N should meet the following requirements: $2k-1 \leq N \leq 2k$ and $GCD(R,N)=1$
   //Here R can be any base / / In this paper, in order to facilitate the processing, the power based on 2 is adopted
3. Montgomery fast power multiplication: use Montgomery fast power algorithm to simplify Miller-Rabin algorithm and carry out modular multiplication on large numbers A and B, namely Montgomery(A,B,N)=ABR-1(mod N)
4. Output the fast modular multiplication results of large numbers A and B

The main advantage of IFPNJA using Montgomery fast power algorithm is to transform division into shift operation, which not only simplifies the calculation process, but also improves the efficiency of large number power multiplication.

A RSA Algorithm Based on Improved Prime Number Judgment. In order to improve the judging efficiency of IFPNJA applied to RSA algorithm, in the initial stage of prime number generation, all even numbers and numbers divisible by 5 are directly eliminated, and 53 small prime numbers are selected to form a filter array for in-depth filtering, and then IFPNJA is applied to the module power operation of RSA algorithm for rapid screening. All the screening methods complement each other to form a RSA algorithm based on improved prime number judgment (IPNRSA). The specific improvement steps of IPNRSA are shown in Algorithm 3.

Algorithm 3: a RSA algorithm based on improved prime number judgment
Input: plaintext M, Miller-Rabin algorithm, random large array N
Output: encrypted ciphertext C, decrypted plaintext M

---

1. Random large number generation: randomly generates a large array N except even numbers and numbers divisible by 5
2. Large array screening: select 53 small primes and use the remainder method to filter large array N
3. Optimizing Miller-Rabin algorithm: using Montgomery fast power algorithm to optimize Miller-Rabin algorithm
4. Generate large prime numbers p and q: combine steps 1, 2, 3 and IFPNJA to generate two large prime numbers p and q
5. RSA encryption plaintext: input plaintext M, generate RSA key with two large prime numbers p and q to encrypt plaintext and generate ciphertext C
6. Output encrypted ciphertext C
7. RSA decryption plaintext: input ciphertext C, generate RSA key with two prime numbers p and q to decrypt ciphertext and generate plaintext M
9. Output decrypted plaintext M

Experimental Analysis of IPNRSA Algorithm

In order to verify the uncertainty of the probabilistic prime number judgment algorithm, the Miller-Rabin algorithm (three tests) is compared with the deterministic property number determination algorithm in the number range of 103, 105, 107 and 109. The results are shown in Table 3.

Table 3. Uncertainty of probabilistic judgment algorithm.

Algorithm	Prime number			
	103	105	107	109
Division Algorithm	168	9592	664579	50847534
Miller-Rabin Algorithm	168	9593	664582	50847546

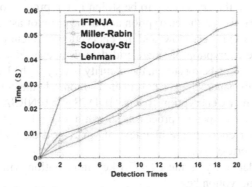

Fig. 9. Relationship between detection times and time of each algorithm.

As can be seen from Table 3, although the Miller-Rabin algorithm has a very high probability of judging a prime number, this probability will decrease with the increase of the number. In this paper, the IFPNJA judgment algorithm is compared with Miller-Rabin, Solovay-Strassen and Lehman three famous judgment algorithms. The experimental data range is [0,1000]. Finally, the relationship between the judgment times and the time is drawn in MATLAB, as shown in Fig. 9.

As can be seen from Fig. 9, the probability of IFPNJA judging prime numbers is not only higher than the other three algorithms, but also the time to generate prime numbers is greatly shortened. The improved prime number judgment algorithm is applied to RSA encryption algorithm to form a RSA algorithm based on improved prime number judgment (IPNRSA). The encryption and decryption time is compared with RSA algorithm. The running results are shown in Fig. 10.

As can be seen from Fig. 8, when producing the same bits of p and q, IPNRSA takes less time than RSA.

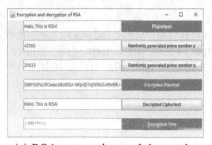
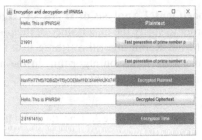

(a) RSA encryption and decryption   (b)IPNRSA encryption and decryption

Fig. 10. Comparison of encryption time between improved RSA algorithm and RSA algorithm.

3.3 Hybrid Encryption Scheme

Because the process of encryption and decryption of symmetric encryption algorithm (such as DES) is very fast, the encryption efficiency is very high, and it is very suitable for the encryption of smart grid data with fast update frequency and large amount of data. However, because the key is easy to be stolen in the process of transmission, the security is not high. However, the encryption and decryption of asymmetric encryption algorithm (such as RSA) is very slow, and the encryption efficiency is very low, which is not suitable for the encryption of smart grid data. However, due to the difficulty of cracking and the fear of key being stolen, the security is very high. Therefore, in order to solve this problem, this paper adopts a hybrid encryption scheme combining symmetric encryption and asymmetric encryption, that is, HDDES and IPNRSA are used to encrypt the data of smart grid. The specific process is shown in Fig. 11.

Step 1: The sender encrypts the plaintext of smart grid data with HDDES key to obtain encrypted ciphertext.

Step 2: The sender encrypts the HDDES key information with the public key of IPNRSA to get the encryption key.

Step 3: The sender sends the mixed information of encrypted ciphertext and encryption key.

Step 4: After receiving the mixed information, the receiver decrypts the encryption key with the private key of IPNRSA to obtain the HDDES key.

Step 5: The receiver decrypts the encrypted ciphertext with the decrypted HDDES key to obtain the plaintext of smart grid data.

The hybrid encryption strategy based on HDDES and IPNRSA not only improves the efficiency of encrypting user data in smart grid, but also ensures the security of user data transmission in smart grid.

3.4 Verification and Analysis of Hybrid Encryption Scheme

In order to verify the effectiveness of the proposed hybrid encryption scheme based on HDDES and IPNRSA, a detailed experimental comparison and result analysis are made between the proposed hybrid encryption scheme and the traditional hybrid encryption scheme based on DES and RSA in terms of encryption time efficiency and algorithm encryption and decryption performance efficiency.

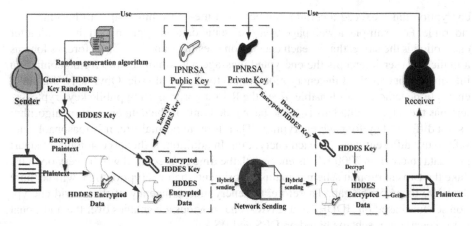

Fig. 11. Hybrid encryption scheme based on HDDES and IPNRSA.

Performance Verification and Analysis of Hybrid Encryption Scheme. This paper compares the key length and generation speed of the hybrid encryption scheme based on DES and RSA and the hybrid encryption scheme based on HDDES and IPNRSA. The length unit is bit, and the results are shown in Table 4.

Table 4. Comparison of key length and generation speed of two encryption schemes

Parameters	Hybrid encryption scheme based on DES and RSA			Hybrid encryption scheme based on HDDES and IPNRSA		
Key length	Secret key	Public key	Private key	Secret key	Public key	Private key
	64	1024	1024	128	1024	1024
Generation speed	Fast	Slow	Slow	Fast	Middle	Middle

The HDDES algorithm extends the 56 bits key of DES, that is, from 56 bits to 128 bits, but it only expands the key by one time, so it has little effect on the speed of key generation after expansion. In addition, RSA encryption algorithm uses 1024 bits key, while IPNRSA encryption algorithm uses improved fast prime number judgment algorithm (IFPNJA) to generate key, so the key generation speed is significantly faster than RSA.

Table 5 shows the comparison of the time spent on encrypting a small amount of smart grid data (200bit) when the two encryption algorithms are running separately. There are five groups of experiments, each group runs 30 times, and the average encryption time is taken.

As can be seen from Table 5, when encrypting short messages, the time difference between the two encryption schemes remains at the level of about 150 ms. Human beings can hardly perceive this subtle time gap, but it is only one encryption operation. If the encryption times exceed a certain number, the time-consuming gap will become considerable. For example, a web page user uses static data encryption, and the result after encryption is the same, that is, each encryption uses the same key. Therefore, as long as a malicious user intercepts the encrypted message and simulates the form submission information, it can cheat the encryption system to directly invade. Obviously, this static encryption method is not feasible. Even the RSA algorithm using public key cryptosystem has the same result. This risk can be avoided only if the data encryption algorithm uses a different key for each encryption. Therefore, in normal life, it is reasonable and safe to use different keys for each encryption. In addition, if the large amount of smart grid data (more than 2000 KB) is encrypted, the time gap required will be very obvious. Take the two encryption schemes in this experiment, their encryption time will be more than 100 times of the gap. Therefore, the encryption efficiency of the hybrid encryption scheme based on HDDES and IPNRSA has obvious advantages over the traditional hybrid encryption scheme based on DES and RSA.

Table 5. Time comparison of two encryption schemes for encrypting a small amount of data.

Operation time	Hybrid encryption scheme based on DES and RSA	Hybrid encryption scheme based on HDDES and IPNRSA
The first time	511 ms	362 ms
The second time	503 ms	364 ms
The third time	497 ms	359 ms
The fourth time	499 ms	361 ms
The fifth time	507 ms	356 ms

Verification and Analysis of Hybrid Encryption Scheme. In order to verify that the hybrid encryption scheme based on HDDES and IPNRSA can effectively encrypt the user's power data in smart grid, the real power department's user power data information is used for experiment. The experimental environment is set as follows: 1) CPU: Intel Core i5; 2) 2.8 GHz Main Frequency; 3) 24.0 GB Memory; 4) Linux CentOS6.4 operating system; 5) Developing software: Hadoop and Myeclipse Development platform; 6) Server: personal alicloud server. The user power data information collected by an electric power department is encrypted and stored in the cloud. Figure 12 [10] shows part of the original content of the stored data, and Fig. 13 shows part of the encrypted data content viewed in the cloud background.

Security of Data Transmission Process. Before transmission, the data has been authenticated by both parties, and the data to be exchanged has been encrypted, which can ensure the security of the data in the communication process.

Security of Stored Data. The data generated by users in smart grid is encrypted by HDDES and encrypted to produce ciphertext. Because the key and ciphertext of HDDES

CONS_NO	CONS_NAME			CONS_SORT_CODE	ELEC_ADDR			TRADE_TYPE_CODE	ELEC_TYPE_CODE	VOLT_CODE
1401687584	大风	沽	矿	01	元二	线1725		0610	401	AC00101
1401609322	赤峰	口 业有	壬公司	0106	元二	线		0610	100	AC00101
1402016369	赤峰	口 业有	壬公司	0105	兴二	线1036		0610	100	AC00101
1401681023	平庄	务 (古		01	平一	线728		0610	401	AC00661
1401681052	平庄	务 (东	矿)	01	元二	线1726		0610	401	AC00661
300743817	平庄	务 (元	矿) 1714反向	00	元二	线1714反向		0690	000	AC00661
1401680990	平庄	务 (元	矿)	01	元二	线1714		0610	401	AC00661
1401681821	平庄	业 团)	责任公司	01	平一	线路0700		0610	100	AC00661
1401681834	平庄	务 (元	露天矿)	01	元一	线123		0610	401	AC00661
1401681007	平庄	务 (红	)	01	元一	乙线124		0610	401	AC00661
1401681049	平庄	务 (风	矿)	01	元二	线1725		0610	401	AC00661
1401681010	平庄	务 (西	矿)	01	平一	线726		0610	401	AC00661

Fig. 12. Original power data information of an electric power department.

```
                              root@MyHadoop:~
 File  Edit  View  Search  Terminal  Help
[root@MyHadoop ~]# hadoop dfs -text /test/outputdata/Elec_DataTest.data
38c0m/N2FzfK6oABMCM/Dkg7K7XunQHAfc/mGBd3mwFYIYD6J6gNyA==
IyfDi02H9lofbCZvbr2a7bpccQopweaFvpkBV3fheQo4dW0w7JR/hS5dh7Ccpj36V6GruPtp3Yc39bQ89DJeYJ+WvM
uBBG2OjJkGFZGBbpV9LLcyPiGf8BRoqfrNcENRvNN7a2VSioN1QFk20dA4Dg==
I+vrpfTv6zaqb1DxTKZqb2cHL9ZjLW6JRNMNUH3Blh8=
MKdd4vDqAWF56SQ9wj+QzFRdiaAc6SltAUPMkd6Rcmovc2fgqVLvNz9GxT05IvLS+AVpFV0RsNuGqHmIMcMvW1HjvL
YTA/+moHU4Ku3wxn3fgsmfqgLbRKuv3nAF5ykt
pHWBS313SfZoCQfxbaHKXQ9uFh4qbEgYTN97ebN8t7M=
u70kCWI2UGOC4nR/O41L0SwL+KHLK3S5UPP2sDzHdntzDTNLVfQmovRZPnlcvcVMbQdnuo5ECND70Hn8Nxo5x0vGC2
RtX1MCaDqFm5HXZfirWaqEa16Lhabhj9JgwhKo
Se3pZH1KupUu/y1Lqs1KWqPl+pbQV9siLFjk+r7v24I=
0cTckU2TgdU1CmFzHHZgBbYuB7Gj8BXvq8+mTmKJBZmTB8EyfM204n+Xg2NlZhkWJMjVZiFTM6qiH2NPRbm5epdwfm
UYT6XLV5VQtsFGWp00269yfp70aUPFZ2VZdrtg
EA1vWmC2C8mff9NenvqhT4Y6DkA8vVW6WWALayua0Wc=
HZZ7L33pBHzQBLODF7mKvgvEj4MSLP5T14Ga0ATi1IiXc9qX/gfzbue9uWOL79/tyYMx2WVDPgi1+S7p6N83qp5L+Q
XhkFXWmZh+aoin96raGaXj85Fj0P6hpvVeceF0
EA1vWmC2C8n4Rwr94MslSoVfEJMH0ncqC0vFZeKRtpI=
d/+iZG2g9uglzoWobdUBP5C8KIineuBCsk6I9+sJXD5v5dSb6Bgwd7ke8qcbTwfYhP7CwGVBButsGrSKciPEfoNTDV
LImftdHX+xqXLRLCZxZNkeXNhBbXkGod8v4V6S
```

Fig. 13. Encrypted data information stored in alicloud.

are encrypted by IPNRSA, even if the malicious user obtains the ciphertext in the transmission process, it will not be cracked because there is no private key of the receiver. Moreover, the hybrid encryption scheme in this paper can use different keys for each encryption, which makes it very difficult for the attacker to crack the ciphertext. In addition, the key and ciphertext are kept separately, and the effective key length is at least 128 bits, which makes the search space of brute force cracking very large and the possibility of cracking is very small. Therefore, it can be considered that the stored data has high security.

To sum up, the hybrid encryption scheme based on HDDES and IPNRSA proposed in this paper can meet the requirements of data storage security in the development of smart grid, and has high operation efficiency.

4   Conclusion

With the further development of smart grid in the future, the scale of power grid is also expanding, and the data in smart grid is also showing a huge increase. The development of cloud computing technology provides a new direction for data storage and processing in smart grid. While cloud computing technology has helped the development of smart grid, data security in smart grid is also an important issue that can not be ignored. Because the data confidentiality is an important factor of smart grid data security, this paper makes a more in-depth study on the data encryption algorithm, respectively makes some improvements to the data encryption method, and puts forward two improved encryption algorithms and a hybrid encryption scheme, so that the data security can be effectively improved. Finally, simulation experiments and multi angle analysis are carried out to show that the proposed hybrid encryption scheme can improve the security of smart grid data storage. Of course, the hybrid encryption scheme proposed in this paper can improve the security of data storage, but the data is only pure text, and does not cover the encryption and decryption of pictures, audio and video. In the future, we will continue to study and improve from the above aspects.

Fund Projects. Humanities and social sciences research project of the Ministry of Education (No. 20YJAZH046); National Natural Science Foundation of China (61370139); scientific research level improvement project (2019KYNH219).

References

1. Rajagopalan, S.R., Sankar, L., Mohajer, S., et al.: Smart meter privacy: a utility-privacy framework. In: IEEE International Conference on Smart Grid Communications 2011, Brussels, Belgium, pp. 190–195. IEEE (2011)
2. Lu, Z., Lu, X., Wang, W., et al.: Review and evaluation of security threats on the communication networks in the smart grid. In: Military Communications Conference 2010, San Jose, pp. 1830–1835. IEEE (2010)
3. Liu, X.Y., Zhang, Q., Li, Z.M.: A survey on information security for smart grid. Electr. Power Inf. Commun. Technol. **12**(4), 56–60 (2014)
4. Amin, S.M.: Smart grid security, privacy, and resilient architectures: opportunities and challenges. IEEE Power Energy Soc. Gen. Meet. 2012, SanDiego, pp. 1–2. IEEE (2012)
5. Wang, X., Yi, P.: Security framework for wireless communications in smart distribution grid. IEEE Trans. Smart Grid **2**(4), 809–818 (2011)
6. Lim, H., Ko, J., Lee, S., et al.: Security architecture model for smart grid communication systems. In: International Conference on IT Convergence and Security 2013, Macao, pp. 327–330. IEEE (2013)
7. Li, X., Liang, X., Lu, R., et al.: Securing smart grid: cyberattacks, countermeasures, and challenges. IEEE Commun. Mag. **50**(8), 38–45 (2012)
8. Anandhi, A., Kalpana, G.: Securing smart grid communication against false data injection attacks. Wireless Commun. **8**(5), 211–215 (2016)
9. Bitzer, B., Gebretsadik, E.S.: Cloud computing framework for smart grid applications. In: Power Engineering Conference 48th International Universities 2013, pp. 1–5. IEEE (2013)
10. Nicanfar, H., Jokar, P., Beznosov, K., et al.: Efficient authentication and key management mechanisms for smart grid communications. IEEE Syst. J. **8**(2), 629–640 (2014)
11. Smart Grid Interoperability Panel Cyber Security Working Group: Introduction to NISTIR 7628 guidelines for smart grid cyber security [EB/OL], USA, NIST Special Publication (2010). https://www.nist.gov/smart-grid/upload/nistir-7628_total.pdf
12. Li, Y.C., Zhang, P., Zheng, S.Q.: Privacy protection of power consumption big data based on empirical mode decomposition and homomorphic encryption. Power Grid Technol. **43**(05), 1810–1818 (2019)
13. Dehalwar, V., Kalam, A., Kolhe, M.L., et al.: Review of IEEE 802. 22 and IEC 61850 for real-time communication in smart grid. In: International Conference on Computing and Network Communications 2015, Trivandrum, India, pp. 571–575. IEEE (2015)

14. Fu, G., Zhou, N.R., Wen, H.: The study of security issues for the industrial control system communication protocols in smart grid system. Inf. Secur. Technol. **5**(1), 36–38 (2014)
15. Premnath, A.P., Jo, J.Y., Kim, Y.: Application of NTRU cryptographic algorithm for SCADA security. In: 11th International Conference on Information Technology: New Generations 2014, Las Vegas, pp. 341–346, IEEE (2014)
16. Gao, K.T., Mao, Y.G., Xun, P., et al.: Light-weight key management solution for OSGP. J. Chin. Comput. Syst. **36**(10), 166–170 (2015)
17. Kumar, V., Hussain, M.: Secure communication for advance metering infrastructure in smart grid. In: Annual IEEE India Conference 2014, Pune, India, pp. 1–6. IEEE (2014)
18. Tuchman, W.: Hellman presents no shortcut solutions to the des. IEEE Spectr. **16**(7), 40–41 (1979)
19. Rivest, R.L., Shamir, A.,Adleman, L.: A method for obtaining digital signatures and public-key cryptosystems. Commun. ACM **21**(2), 120–126 (1978)
20. Feng, D.G., Zhang, M., Zhang, Y., Xu, Z.: Study on cloud computing security. J. Softw. **22**(1), 71–83 (2011)
21. Yi, Z.D., Duan, Y.Z., Xiao, C.W., et al.: Cloud computing security: concept, status quo and key technologies. Proceedings of the 27th National Conference on Computer Security (2012)
22. Gao, Y.Z., Li, B.L., Chen, X.Y.: Random detection algorithm of HDFS data theft based on MapReduce. J. Cryptologic Res. **39**(10), 15–25 (2018)
23. Sivapragash, C., Thilaga, S.R., Kumar, S.S.: Advanced cloud computing in smart power grid. In: Sustainable Energy and Intelligent Systems 2012. IET Chennai 3rd International, pp. 1–6 (2012)
24. Li, Q.L., Zhou, M.T.: Research on cloud computing in smart grid. Comput. Sci. **38**(B10), 432–433 (2011)
25. Cong, W., Qian, W., Kui, R., et al.: Ensuring data storage security in cloud computing. In: 17th International WorkShop 2009. Quality of Service IWQoS, pp. 13–15 (2009)
26. Hashmi, M., Hanninen, S., Maki, K.: Survey of smart grid concepts, architectures, and techno-logical demonstrations worldwide. In: 2011 IEEE PES Conference 2011 in Innovative Smart Grid Technologies, pp. 19–21 (2011)
27. Chen, J., Zhang, Y.Y.: Research on application and security of cloud computing in smart grid. ZTE Technol. **18**(6), 17–21 (2012)
28. Huang, J.F., Wang, H.G., Qiang, Y.: Smart grid communications in challenging environments. In: 2012 IEEE Third International Conference 2012 in Smart Grid Communications, pp. 552–557 (2012)
29. Wright, M.A.: The evolution of the advanced encryption standard. Netw. Secur. **1999**(11), 11–14 (1999)
30. Chen, Q.C.: A hybrid encryption algorithm based on DES and RSA algorithm. Yunnan University, China (2015)
31. Jain, N., Ajnar, D.S., Jain, P.K.: Optimization of advanced encryption standard algo-rithm (AES) on field programmable gate array (FPGA). In: International Conference on Communication and Electronics Systems 2019. IEEE (2020)
32. Gao, N.N., Li, Z.C., Wang, Q.: A reconfigurable architecture for high speed implementation of DES, 3DES and AES. Acta electronica Sinica **34**(8), 1386–1390 (2006)
33. Yu, W.: Research on key extension method and security of DES algorithm. Central China Normal University, China (2019)
34. Sepahvandi, S., Hosseinza, M., Navi, K., et al.: IEEE 2009 International Conference on Research Challenges in Computer Science (ICRCCS), 28 November 2009–29 November 2009, Shanghai, China, 2009 International Conference on Research Challenges in Computer Science - An Improved Exponentiation Algorithm for RSA Cryptosystem, pp. 128–132 (2009)

35. Li, D.J., Wang, Y.D., Chen, H.: The research on key generation in RSA public-key cryptosystem. In: Fourth International Conference on Computational & Information Sciences. IEEE (2012)
36. Zhou, J.Z., Gao, L.: Research on improved RSA algorithm based on multi prime number and parameter replacement. Comput. Appl. Res. **36**(02), 495–498 (2019)
37. Yan, S.Y.: Elliptic Curve Cryptography. Cybercryptography: Applicable Cryptography for Cyberspace Security (2019)
38. Li, F., Gong, Z.Y., Lei, F.F., et al.: Summary of fast prime generation methods. J. Cryptologic Res. **06**(04), 463–476 (2019)
39. Qin, X.D., Xin, Y.W., Lu, G.Z.: Research and optimization of Miller Rabin algorithm. Comput. Eng. **28**(10), 55–57 (2002)
40. Zhao, Y.W., Liu, F.F., Jiang, L.J., et al.: Multi core parallelization of Sch(o)nhage Strassen algorithm for large integer multiplication. J. Soft. **29**(12), 3604–3613 (2018)
41. Fu, X.Q., Bao, W.S., Zhou, C., et al.: Integer factorization quantum algorithm with high probability. Acta electronica Sinica **39**(01), 35–39 (2011)

Internet of Things, Ad Hoc, Sensor and RFID Networks

Classification of Uncertain Data Based on Evidence Theory in Wireless Sensor Networks

Yang Zhang[1]([☒]), Yun Liu[1], and Zhenjiang Zhang[2]

[1] Key Laboratory of Communication and Information Systems, Beijing Municipal Commission of Education, School of Electronic and Information Engineering, Beijing Jiaotong University, Beijing 100044, China
{zhang.yang,liuyun}@bjtu.edu.cn
[2] School of Software Engineering, Beijing Jiaotong University, Beijing 100044, China
zhangzhenjiang@bjtu.edu.cn

Abstract. In wireless sensor networks, the classification of uncertain data reported by sensor nodes is an open issue because the given attribute information can be insufficient for making a correct specific classification of the objects. Although the traditional Evidential k-Nearest Neighbor (EkNN) algorithm can effectively model the uncertainty, it is easy to misjudge the target data to the incorrect class when the observed sample data is located in the feature overlapping region of training samples of different classes. In this paper, a novel Evidential k-Nearest Neighbor (NEkNN) algorithm is proposed based on the evidential editing method. The main idea of NEkNN algorithm is to consider the expected value and standard deviation of various training sample data sets, and use normalized Euclidean distance to assign class labels with basic belief assignment (BBA) structure to each training sample, so that training samples in overlapping region can offer more abundant and diverse class information. Further, EkNN classification of the observation sample data is carried out in the training sample sets of various classes, and mass functions of the target to be tested under this class are obtained, and Redistribute Conflicting Mass Proportionally Rule 5 (PCR5) combination rule is used to conduct global fusion, thus obtaining the global fusion results of the targets. The experimental results show that this algorithm has better performance than other classification methods based on k-nearest neighbor.

Keywords: Evidence theory · Uncertain data · Target classification · Combination rule

1 Introduction

When using the sensor's observation data to carry out the local classification of targets, the sensor's observation data contains a lot of imprecise information due to various interferences [1]. For example, some sample data comes from different categories of targets but they are very similar, that is, the sample data of different categories may

Y.-B. Lin and D.-J. Deng (Eds.): SGIoT 2020, LNICST 354, pp. 159–168, 2021.
https://doi.org/10.1007/978-3-030-69514-9_13

partially overlap, which brings great challenges to traditional target classification tasks [2]. In the classification task with supervision, the sensor's observation data may be in the overlapping area of different categories of training samples, it is difficult for the traditional voting kNN classifier to accurately classify the target at this time. For this reason, many scholars have fully considered the distance relationship between the target and its neighbors, and proposed the fuzzy kNN (Fuzzy kNN, FkNN) classification algorithm [3]. This algorithm allows the target to belong to different categories with different fuzzy membership degrees, which obtains the better classification effect than voting kNN [4].

Dempster-Shafer evidence theory, also referred as evidential reasoning or belief functions theory, has been proved to be valuable as a solution for dealing with uncertain and inaccurate data [5], and it has been widely applied in sorts of applications, for example, state estimation [6], target recognition [7], data classification [2], and information fusion [8], and etc. As the extension of probability theory, evidence theory provides a series of functions and operations defined on the power set of the identification framework, which can effectively reason and model the uncertainty, and can provide more abundant category information than fuzzy membership [9]. Therefore, many scholars have combined evidence theory with traditional classification algorithms with supervision and developed a series of evidence classification algorithms. Among them, the most representative is the evidential kNN (Evidential k-Nearest Neighbor, EkNN) algorithm proposed by Scholars such as Denoeux, et al. [10, 11]. This algorithm is simple and direct with low error rate, so it is very suitable for the target classification task of sensor nodes. However, the EkNN algorithm only considers the factor of the distance between the target and the training samples, and does not treat all training samples differently [12]. It is assumed that the target sample is in the overlapping area of the training set, and the target data is far from the sample points of the same category, and closer to the sample points of other categories, if the EkNN algorithm is used at this time, the evidence formed by the sample points that are closer to the target will be given a large mass value, then when making the decision after the evidence is fused, it is easy to misjudge the target data into other categories. In [13], it is further pointed out that since the EkNN algorithm treats imprecise training samples from overlapping regions as training samples that truly represent the distribution of the target category, it will have a greater negative impact on the final classification effect. In order to solve this problem, it is necessary to preprocess the original training samples with the evidence editing method based on EkNN, and replace the category labels of the original training samples with basic belief assignment, it can better characterize the inaccuracy of the overlapping regions of categories. However, in [13], it is proposed that the evidence editing method will make the edited evidence have a higher correlation. When subsequently fusing the evidence constructed by the target's neighbors, it is necessary to evaluate the correlation between the evidences, and to search for the corresponding fusion rules according to the degree of correlation between the evidences. Therefore, this method has the problems of high algorithm complexity and excessive calculation, which is not suitable for sensor nodes with limited energy. In addition to the evidence editing method, in [14], it is pointed out that if a target falls in the overlapping area of the training set, to first consider using EkNN to classify the target in the training set of each category and then perform the evidence fusion of the classification results can also suppress the influence of other categories of training samples in the overlapping area on the fusion result. The improved EkNN algorithm (Improved Evidential k-Nearest Neighbor, IEkNN) was also proposed to improve the performance of the EkNN algorithm [15], however, IEkNN does not edit the samples, while directly uses the original training samples for classification [16].

In order to effectively model and reason about imprecise data, this paper proposes a NEkNN (New Evidential k-Nearest Neighbor, NEkNN) algorithm. The NEkNN algorithm proposes a simple evidence preprocessing method under the framework of evidence theory. This method only considers the expected value and standard deviation of the training sample sets of each category, thereby avoiding the evidence correlation that may be caused by the original evidence editing method. On this basis, by fusing the classification results of the target to be tested in the training sample set of each category, the EkNN obtain a more accurate identification and judgment of the target.

The other parts of this paper are arranged as follows. Section 2 fundamentally introduces the basis of evidence theory. Section 3 focuses on the original training data preprocessing method, and design the NEkNN classification algorithm after preprocessing. Section 4 comprehensively evaluates and analyzes the classification performance of the proposed NEkNN algorithm based on simulation data, and finally summarize the work of this paper in Sect. 5.

2 Basics of Belief Functions Theory

The Dempster–Shafer evidence theory introduced by Shafer is also known as belief functions theory [17]. In this theory, the frame of discernment Ω is a finite set, whose elements are exhaustive and mutually exclusive, and it is denoted as $\Omega = \{w_1, w_2, \ldots, w_i, \ldots, w_c\}$. 2^Ω is the power set of the frame of discernment, which represents the set of all possible subsets of Ω, indicated by $2^\Omega = \{\phi, \{w_1\}, \ldots \{w_n\}, \{w_1, w_2\}, \ldots, \{w_1, w_2, \ldots, w_i\}, \ldots, \Omega\}$. Given an object X, it can be classified as any singleton element and any sets of elements in 2^Ω with a basic belief assignment (BBA). The BBA is also known as the mass function, which is a mapping $m : 2^\Omega \rightarrow [0, 1]$ satisfying $\sum_{A \in 2^\Omega} m(A) = 1, m(\phi) = 0$. The function $m(A)$ is used to quantify the degree of belief that is exactly assigned to the subsets A of Ω. If $m(A) > 0$, the subset A can be called the focal elements of the mass function $m(\cdot)$. The mass values assigned to compound elements can reflect the imprecise observation of object X.

The mass function $m(\cdot)$ is always associated with three main functions, including the belief function $Bel(\cdot)$, the plausibility function $Pl(\cdot)$ and the pignistic probability function $BetP(\cdot)$, which are defined as follows, respectively:

$$Bel(B) = \sum_{A \subseteq B} m(A) \tag{1}$$

$$Pl(B) = \sum_{A \cap B \neq \emptyset} m(A) \tag{2}$$

$$BetP(w) = \sum_{w \in A, A \subseteq \Omega} \frac{1}{|A|} m(A) \tag{3}$$

where $m(\cdot)$ is the focal elements on Ω, and $|A|$ denotes the cardinality of focal elements A. All three functions can be employed to make a decision on an unknown object according to a few rules, such as selecting the class with maximum $BetP$.

Assuming that there are two pieces of evidence denoted by m_1 and m_2, the popular Dempster's combination rule can be used to combine them as follows:

$$m_\oplus(A) = m_1(B) \oplus m_2(C) = \begin{cases} 0, & B \cap C = \phi \\ \frac{\sum_{B \cap C = A} \forall B, C \subseteq \Omega m_1(B) \times m_2(C)}{1 - \sum_{B \cap C = \phi, \forall B, C \subseteq \Omega} m_1(B) \times m_2(C)} & B \cap C \neq \phi \end{cases} \quad (4)$$

where $\sum B \cap C = \phi$, $\forall B$, $C \subseteq \Omega m_1(B) \times m_2(C)$ represents the conflict between m_1 and m_2, which is used to redistribute the conflicting mass values. Dempster's combination rule is commutative and associative. It provides a simple and flexible solution for data fusion problems.

3   The New Evidential k-Nearest Neighbor Algorithm

In order to overcome the limitations of EkNN, a new EkNN classification algorithm is proposed in this section. The algorithm uses the method of preprocessing training samples to replace the category labels of the original samples with the basic belief assignment, so as to better describe the uncertainty of the training samples in the overlapping regions of the categories. In order to avoid the pre-processed evidence from generating greater correlation, the newly obtained category labels with the basic belief assignment structure for each sample are constructed based on the Mahalanobis distance from the evidence to the center of the corresponding category. In the subsequent classification of the target, it is first to find the k nearest neighbors of the input sample in each category of training sample set, construct k nearest neighbor evidence describing the respective classification information, and perform fusion to obtain the mass function under this category of condition, then the global fusion of evidence between categories is performed based on the mass function generated by each category, and the final classification result is obtained.

3.1   Preprocessing of Training Samples

In order to avoid evidence-related problems, this section focuses on the preprocessing method of training samples based on Mahalanobis distance. The concept of Mahalanobis distance belongs to the theory of multivariate statistical analysis [18]. It is a discriminant method that uses the distance between the sample to be judged and each population as the measurement scale to judge the attribution of the sample. When processing numerical data in wireless sensor networks, Mahalanobis distance comprehensively considers the two statistical characteristics of the expected value and standard deviation of each category in the true distribution. It avoids discussing the correlation caused by the specific distribution of sample data. At the same time, compared with Euclidean distance, Mahalanobis distance can also eliminate the interference of the correlation between attribute variables, which is more reasonable. The Mahalanobis distance used in this section can also be called the normalized Euclidean distance.

To consider a M-class problem, where the object may belong to M different classes, and $\Omega = \{w_1, \ldots, w_M\}$ is the set of all classes. It is supposed that the training sample set is $Y = \{y_1, \ldots, y_g\}$. First, the attribute information of each category of training sample can be used to calculate the center vector of the category. The center of $c_i (i = 1, \ldots, M)$ can be expressed as:

$$c_i = \frac{1}{s_i} \sum\nolimits_{y_j \in w_i} y_j \tag{5}$$

where s_i is the number of training samples of class w_i.

For each training sample $y_h (h = 1, \ldots, g)$, sample preprocessing is performed according to the distance from it to the center. The distance requires to fully consider the degree of dispersion of each category of sample distribution, that is, the size of the standard deviation. Therefore, the Mahalanobis distance is used as the measurement scale of distance here, which is:

$$d_h^{w_i} = \sqrt{\sum_{k=1}^{p} \left(\frac{y_h(k) - c_i(k)}{\delta_i(k)} \right)^2} \tag{6}$$

where $\delta_i(k)$ is the standard deviation of the training data set of class w_i, $y_h(k)$ and $c_i(k)$ are the values of the attribute vector y_h and center c_i on the k-th dimension respectively, and p is the number of dimensions.

The smaller the distance $d_h^{w_i}$ is, the more likely the training sample y_h belongs to the category w_i. If y_h is farther from the center c_i, the less likely it is that y_h belongs to category w_i. Therefore, the support of y_h belonging to category w_i is:

$$s_h(W_i) = e^{-d_h w_i} \tag{7}$$

The BBA m_h should correspond to the normalized $s_h(w_i)$, formally defined by:

$$m_h = \frac{s_h(w_i)}{\sum_{l=1}^{M} s_h(w_l)} \tag{8}$$

The above mass function m_h provides more powerful information to characterize the uncertainty for training sample y_h than the original class label $w_i \in \Omega$, and it can be consider as a new soft class label of the sample y_h. As a consequence, the new training sample set with soft class labels $Y' = \{y_1, \ldots, y_g\}$ is adopted for the target classification task in this paper.

3.2 Classification with Preprocessed Training Samples

After preprocessing, the next problem to be solved is how to classify the newly observed unknown target $x \in R^p$ based on the preprocessed training samples. Different from the general classification problem, the category of training sample used here is represented by the structure of basic trust distribution, so it is necessary to improve the original evidence kNN classification algorithm accordingly to enable it to classify x reasonably using the category label of this structure. For the target $\Omega = \{w_1, \ldots, w_M\}$ of categories

M, it is to first establish training sample sets for each category based on the total training samples, and then refer to the EkNN classification algorithm to generate evidence that can be combined in various training sets based on the training samples and the feature data of the target to be tested. The entire classification process can be divided into the construction and fusion of mass functions under each category, and the global fusion of the fusion results between categories, which will be introduced separately below.

The Construction and Fusion of Mass Functions

To consider the k nearest neighbor samples of the target x to be tested in the training samples of category $w_i(i = 1, \ldots, M)$, if one of the training samples is very close to the sample x to be tested, the training sample provides a more reliable evidence for the classification of the sample to be tested. Conversely, if the distance is far, the reliability of the evidence provided by the training sample is relatively small. According to the evidence kNN algorithm, it is to choose Euclidean distance as the measurement scale to calculate the distance between the target and the training sample. It is assumed that the set of k nearest neighbor samples of target x in category w_i is, $\Gamma_i = \{(y_1, d_1), \ldots, (y_k, d_k)\}$, $d_j(j = 1, \ldots, k)$ is the Euclidean distance between neighbor y_j and target x, m_j is the category label of y_j, β_j is the reliability of classifying x based on sample y_j, then the evidential mass function m'_j provided by y_j for the classification of target x can be expressed as:

$$\begin{cases} m'_j(w_i) = \beta_j m_j(w_i), i = 1, \ldots, M \\ m'_j(\Omega) = \beta_j m_j(\Omega) + (1 - \beta_j) \end{cases} \quad (9)$$

where the reliability β_j is determined by the Euclidean distance d_j between y_j and the target x. The greater the distance between the two, the lower the corresponding reliability, that is, the reliability β_j and d_j show a decreasing relationship, which can be expressed as:

$$\beta_j = e^{-\left(d_j / \overline{d}^i\right)} \quad (10)$$

where $\overline{d}^i$ is the average distance between all training samples in category w_i.

In order to classify the unknown target x, the k mass functions constructed by the k nearest neighbor samples $y_j(j = 1, \ldots, k)$ in the category w_i need to be fused to obtain the classification result of the target by the training samples of the category w_i. In the fusion process, considering that the mass functions provided by the same category of training samples have high consistency, the Dempster combination rule can be used directly for the fusion operation, it an be expressed as:

$$m_i = m'_1 \oplus m'_2 \oplus \cdots \oplus m'_j \quad (11)$$

where $\oplus$ is Dempster combination operation.

Considering that there are a total of M categories of targets, a set of M nearest neighbor samples of the target can be generated, namely. According to Eq. (11), the mass function set $\Gamma = m_1, \ldots, m_M$ under categories M can be obtained.

The Global Fusion of the Fusion Results Between Classes

For the mass function set of categories M targets, the mass value constructed by the samples of category w_i is mainly assigned to the corresponding focal element, that is $m_i(w_i)$. Therefore, it can be considered that the distribution of mass values of different categories is different, and there will be certain conflicts between the mass functions obtained by Eq. (11). At this time, if the Dempster combination rule is used for global fusion, a fusion result that contradicts the facts may be obtained. Therefore, when fusing between categories, this paper uses PCR5 (Redistribute Conflicting Mass Proportionally Rule 5, PCR5) combination rules to accurately and reasonably allocate conflict information. The PCR5 rule is an evidence fusion rule proposed by Desert and Smarandache for conflicting data. This rule can accurately distribute the conflict information proportionally according to the mass values of the two parties in the conflict, which is very suitable for combining high conflict evidence. While compared with the Dempster rule, it is a more conservative combination method, and the convergence speed of the fusion result is relatively slow. Assuming that B and C are two independent evidences to be combined, the corresponding focal elements are B_j and C_j, and the mass functions are m_1 and m_2 respectively, then the PCR5 rule can be expressed as [19]:

$$m(x) = \sum_{\substack{B_i, C_j \in 2^\Omega \\ B_i \cap C_j = x}} m_1(B_i)m_2(C_j) + \sum_{\substack{y \in 2^\Omega \\ x \cap y = \emptyset}} \left[\frac{m_1(x)^2 \, m_2(y)}{m_1(x) \, m_2(y)} + \frac{m_2(x)^2 \, m_1(y)}{m_2(x) \, m_1(y)} \right] \quad (12)$$

where x and y are two focal elements of evidence body B and C with conflicting information.

Example 1: The evidence body m_1 confirms that the mass value of that the target belongs to category w_1 is 0.9, and the mass value of that the target belongs to category w_3 is 0.1. The evidence body m_2 confirms that the mass value of that the target belongs to category w_2 is 0.9, and the mass value of that the target belongs to category w_3 is 0.1.

After combining m_1 and m_2 by the Dempster combination rule, it can be obtained that:

$$m_{Dempster}(w_1) = 0, m_{Dempster}(w_2) = 0, m_{Dempster}(w_3) = 1.$$

After combining m_1 and m_2 by the PCR5 combination rule, it can be obtained that:

$$m_{PCR5}(w_1) = 0.486, m_{PCR5}(w_2) = 0.486, m_{PCR5}(w_3) = 0.028.$$

It can be seen that the original two evidences respectively believe that the target belongs to w_1 and w_2, And the reliability values provided are all 0.9. The Dempster rule offers a fusion result contrary to m_1 and m_2, which is obviously not reasonable. While PCR5 believes that the mass values of that the target belongs to m_1 and m_2 are still the same and are much higher than the mass value of that the target belongs to w_3. The fusion result is more reasonable and credible than the result of Dempster's rule.

Therefore, considering the inconsistency of evidence between categories, for the mass function set of the categories M observation target, it is necessary to use the PCR5 combination rule for fusion, and it can be obtained that:

$$m = m_1 \overset{PCR5}{\oplus} m_2 \overset{PCR5}{\oplus} \cdots \overset{PCR5}{\oplus} m_M \quad (13)$$

$$\overset{PCR5}{\oplus}$$

where $\overset{PCR5}{\oplus}$ represents PCR5 combination operation.

The final fusion result m can be calculated according to Eq. (13). According to the mass value of each category assigned to it, the final recognition result can be made on the target x, that is, the unknown target x is assigned to the category with the maximum mass value.

4 Experimental Results

This section is to use simulation analysis to compare the NEkNN classification algorithm mentioned in this paper with voting kNN, EkNN, IEkNN, and to illustrate the effectiveness of NEkNN. In the experiment, the parameters in EkNN are optimized according to the existing method [20]. The experiment utilizes simulation data to compare and analyze the misclassification rate of the proposed method and other classification methods based on k-nearest neighbors.

In this target recognition simulation experiment, a classification problem of 3-class target $\Omega = \{w_1, w_2, w_3\}$ is considered. After the sensor's observation data is preprocessed by data association and feature extraction, the training database is used to classify the feature data containing these three categories of targets. Assuming that the feature data is a three-dimensional vector, and the observation data and training data are generated from three three-dimensional data sets that obey the Gaussian distribution, then its mean and standard deviation have the following characteristics:

Table 1. 3-class data set with 3D Gaussian distributions.

Label	μ_1	μ_2	μ_3	Standard deviation
w_1	1	1	1	1
w_2	−1	1	0	1
w_3	0	-1	1	2

In Table 1, the three characteristics of each category of data have the same standard deviation. For example, the probability density functions of the three attribute data of category w_2 are: $x_1|w_2 \sim N(-1, 1), x_2|w_2 \sim N(1, 1), x_3|w_2 \sim N(0, 1)$, their standard deviation is the same as 1, and it randomly generates 3×100 test samples and 3×200 training samples. It is to select kNN, EkNN, IEkNN to compare and analyze with NEkNN proposed in this paper, take the value of the adjacent number k from 5 to 15, and take the average of 10 simulation results as the error rate of the test data set. The classification results are shown in Table 2.

It can be seen from Table 2 that the EkNN and IEkNN methods are better than the traditional voting kNN and can effectively improve the classification accuracy. The NEkNN algorithm proposed in this paper can better characterize the imprecision of the sample data in the overlapping area of the category and improve the classification accuracy of the data by using the basic belief assignment to replace the original category

Table 2. 3-class data set with 3D Gaussian distributions.

k	kNN	EkNN	IEkNN	NEkNN
$k = 5$	32.73	29.12	25.12	23.60
$k = 6$	32.68	28.33	25.19	23.97
$k = 7$	31.19	27.87	25.38	24.06
$k = 8$	33.62	27.61	24.67	24.11
$k = 9$	31.44	27.59	24.71	23.86
$k = 10$	32.25	27.55	25.09	24.03
$k = 11$	31.28	27.43	25.02	23.79
$k = 12$	31.42	26.96	24.91	23.45
$k = 13$	30.99	26.93	24.47	23.52
$k = 14$	32.94	26.86	24.52	23.35
$k = 15$	32.17	26.98	24.59	23.35
$k = 16$	32.73	29.12	25.12	23.60

label. Therefore, compared with the EkNN and IEkNN algorithms, it has a smaller classification error rate, especially when the number of neighbors is small, the performance improvement is more significant. In addition, it can be found that compared with other classification methods based on k-nearest neighbors, NEkNN method is less sensitive to the value of k-nearest neighbor.

5 Conclusion

In order to effectively express and reason about imprecise data, this paper proposes an evidence editing classification method based on EkNN. Before identifying and classifying the sample to be tested, this method uses a class label with a basic belief assignment structure to replace the original numerical category of the training sample, so that the training sample in the class overlapping area can provide more abundant and more diverse category information. And lay a better foundation for the follow-up kNN classification process. From the comparative analysis of related experiments, it can be found that for imprecise sample data, the NEkNN algorithm can obtain better classification performance than other classification algorithms based on k-nearest neighbors. Our future work mainly involves the following two aspects: (1) finding a more efficient strategy to estimate the mass values to improve the classification accuracy; (2) designing more credible combination rules to deal with the uncertain data in IOT environment.

Acknowledgement. This work was supported by the Fundamental Research Funds for the Central Universities 2019RC044.

References

1. Izadi, D., Abawajy, J.H., Ghanavati, S., et al.: A data fusion method in wireless sensor networks. Sensors **15**(2), 2964–2979 (2015)
2. Liu, Z., Pan, Q., Dezert, J., et al.: Hybrid classification system for uncertain data. IEEE Trans. Syst. Man Cybern. Syst. **47**(10), 2783–2790 (2017)
3. Andrew, A.M., Shakaff, A.Y.M., Zakaria, A. et al.: Fuzzy K-nearest neighbour (FkNN) based early stage fire source classification in building. In: IEEE Conference on Systems Process and Control (2018)
4. Keller, J.M., Gray, M.R., Givens, J.A.: A fuzzy K-nearest neighbor algorithm. IEEE Trans. Syst. Man Cybern. **15**(4), 580–585 (1985)
5. Smets, P.: Analyzing the combination of conflicting belief functions. Inf. Fusion **8**(4), 387–412 (2007)
6. Zhang, Z., Zhang, W., Chao, H., et al.: Toward belief function-based cooperative sensing for interference resistant industrial wireless sensor networks. IEEE Trans. Industr. Inf. **12**(6), 2115–2126 (2016)
7. Zhang, W., Zhang, Z.: Belief function based decision fusion for decentralized target classification in wireless sensor networks. Sensors **15**(8), 20524–20540 (2015)
8. Shen, B., Liu, Y., Fu, J.: An integrated model for robust multisensor data fusion. Sensors **14**(10), 19669–19686 (2014)
9. Luo, J., Shi, L., Ni, Y.: Uncertain power flow analysis based on evidence theory and affine arithmetic. IEEE Trans. Power Syst. **33**(1), 1113–1115 (2018)
10. Denoeux, T.: A k-nearest neighbor classification rule based on Dempster-Shafer theory. IEEE Trans. Syst. Man Cybern. **25**, 804–813 (1995)
11. Denœux, T., Kanjanatarakul, O., Sriboonchitta, S.: A new evidential K-nearest neighbor rule based on contextual discounting with partially supervised learning. Int. J. Approximate Reasoning **113**, 287–302 (2019)
12. Faziludeen, S., Sankaran, P.: ECG beat classification using evidential K-nearest neighbours. Procedia Comput. Sci. **89**, 499–505 (2016)
13. Jiao, L., Denœux, T., Pan, Q.: Evidential editing K-nearest neighbor classifier. In: Destercke, S., Denoeux, T. (eds.) ECSQARU 2015. LNCS (LNAI), vol. 9161, pp. 461–471. Springer, Cham (2015). https://doi.org/10.1007/978-3-319-20807-7_42
14. Liu, Z., Liu, Y., Dezert, J., et al.: Classification of incomplete data based on belief functions and K-nearest neighbors. Knowl. Based Syst. **89**, 113–125 (2015)
15. Yang, Z.: A new evidential K-nearest neighbors data classification method. Fire Control Command Control **38**(9), 58–60 (2013)
16. Chen, X., Wang, P., Hao, Y., et al.: Evidential KNN-based condition monitoring and early warning method with applications in power plant. Neurocomputing **315**, 18–32 (2018)
17. Xu, X., Zheng, J., Yang, J., et al.: Data classification using evidence reasoning rule. Knowl. Based Syst. **116**, 144–151 (2017)
18. Zhang, Z., Liu, T., Zhang, W.: Novel paradigm for constructing masses in Dempster-Shafer evidence theory for wireless sensor network's multisource data fusion. Sensors **14**(4), 7049–7065 (2014)
19. Smarandache, F., Dezert, J.: Advances and Applications of DSmT for Information Fusion. viXra (2004)
20. Zouhal, L.M., Denoeux, T.: An evidence-theoretic k-NN rule with parameter optimization. IEEE Trans. Syst. Man Cybern. **28**, 263–271 (1998)

Text Summarization as the Potential Technology for Intelligent Internet of Things

Lijun Wei[1,2](✉), Yun Liu[1,2], and Jian Li[1,2]

[1] School of Electronic and Information Engineering,
Beijing Jiao Tong University, Beijing, China
{18120145,liuyun,lijian}@bjtu.edu.cn
[2] Key Laboratory of Communication and Information Systems, Beijing Municipal
Commission of Education, Beijing, China

Abstract. Applying automatic text summarization technology to Internet of Things can save network cost and improve computing speed. However, the models of generated text summarization are always using sequence-to-sequence model with attention mechanism. Unluckily, this method for abstractive summarization has two main shortcomings: first, they fail to address unknown words problems, second, their generated summaries are not very readable because of repetition. In our work, our goal is to enhance the semantic coherence of summaries for original texts. In order to this end, we propose a new model that augments the traditional model in two ways. First, we apply semantic relevance to pointer-generator network to get high similarity between source texts and our summaries. Second, we change the mechanism of coverage and use it to pointer-generator network to discourage repetition. Following other works, we apply our new model to Chinese social media dataset LCSTS. Our experiments suggested that our new model outperforms current abstractive baseline systems on the dataset.

Keywords: Intelligent Internet of Things · Text summarization · Attention mechanism

1 Introduction

We use text summarization in order to get a short representation of an input text which captures the core meaning of the original. In some Internet of Things scenarios, such as smart home and intelligent robot, text summarization can compress the obtained text information to save network cost and improve computing speed. Different from the extractive text summarization [1–3], which selects elements from original text to form summaries, the aim of abstractive text summarization is to produce summaries in a generated way. Extractive text summarization performs well when the source text is long, however, it doesn't apply to short text. Recently, most abstractive text summarization is depended on seq2seq models which have attention mechanism [4–6], and this way is superior to the traditional statistical methods.

© ICST Institute for Computer Sciences, Social Informatics and Telecommunications Engineering 2021
Published by Springer Nature Switzerland AG 2021. All Rights Reserved
Y.-B. Lin and D.-J. Deng (Eds.): SGIoT 2020, LNICST 354, pp. 169–177, 2021.
https://doi.org/10.1007/978-3-030-69514-9_14

Unfortunately, it is shown that there are prominent shortcomings in conventional attention mechanism. Lin pointed out that the attention based seq2seq abstract text summarization model has the problems of duplication and semantic independence, which leads to poor readability and can't tell source text's core point [6]. For example, in the summary produced by traditional model in Fig. 1, because attention mechanisms take note of words with high attention scores as usual, "钻研" is still behind "钻研".

Text:
11日下午，中共中央政治局常委、中央书记处书记刘云山登门看望了国家最高科技奖获得者于敏、张存浩。刘云山指出，广大科技工作者要学习老一辈科学家求真务实的钻研精神，淡泊名利、潜心科研，努力创造更多一流科研成果。
On the afternoon of 11th, Liu Yunshan, member of the Standing Committee of the Political Bureau of the CPC Central Committee and secretary of the Secretariat of the CPC Central Committee, paid a visit to Yu Min and Zhang Cunhao, the recipients of the State Preeminent Science and Technology Award. Liu Yunshan pointed out that scientists and technologists should study the pragmatic research spirit of the older generation, be indifferent to fame and fortune, devote themselves to scientific research, and strive to create more first-rate scientific research achievements.

Reference: 刘云山看望著名科技专家 Liu Yunshan paid a visit to prominent science and technology experts
Baseline: 刘云山：科技钻研钻研 Liu Yunshan: Science and technology research research

---

Fig. 1. A simple case got from the conventional attention-based seq2seq model. As we can see, the summary generated by the baseline contains repetition.

See and Paulus use a model with pointer-generator that uses interpolation of generation and replication probabilities to generate summaries [7, 8]. Moreover, the interpolation is controlled by a mixture coefficient that is predicted by the model. Theoretical analysis shows that the pointer-generator mechanism enables the model to get summary in a comprehensive method, which integrates the advantages of extraction summary and generative summary, in addition, it can solve the out-of-vocabulary (OOV) problem. However, in practice, compared to source text, the summaries we got have low semantic relevance.

We design a pointer-generator model with semantic relevance in order to solve the above problems, the main idea of our model is to get high relevance between generated summaries and original text. A semantic similarity evaluation factor is used in our proposed model, which can measure the correlation between original text and the generated summary. By maximize the score of similarity, our model can get high coherence between source articles and summaries during training stage. Finally, in order to reduce and avoid repetition problem, attention mechanism is introduced into our model. It can be shown that compared to current abstractive baseline systems, our model can generate better summaries which have high score.

2 Proposed Model

We describe (1) the baseline seq2seq model with attention mechanism, (2) our pointer-generator model with semantic relevance, (3) our coverage mechanism that can be added to both of the first two models in this section.

2.1 Attention-Based Seq2seq Model

The baseline model is a seq2seq model which is attention-based, and it is described in Fig. 2. Similar to that of Hu [9], our model consists of three parts, the first part is encoder, the second part is decoder and the last part is attention mechanism. The encoder can help us to condense long source texts into continuous vector representation, and the decoder can help us to generate short summary. The encoder is a single-layer bidirectional GRU that can get the sequence vector $\{h_1, h_2, h_3..., h_N\}$ from source text x. On every time step, the decoder part has a decoder state s_t, and the last character's word embedding is fed to it.

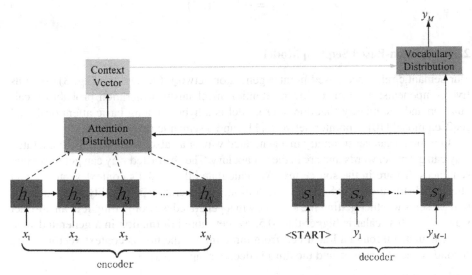

Fig. 2. Our attention-based seq2seq model. This model is made up of encoder (left), decoder (right) and attention mechanism.

Attention mechanism is used to inform our model to find the correct place which is used to get next word [4]. The context vector c_t is equal to the weighted sum of the hidden states of the encoder

$$c_t = \sum_{i=1}^{N} \alpha_{ti} h_i \tag{1}$$

where h_i is the hidden state of the i th input x, α_{ti} is the probability of x_i on t step:

$$\alpha_{ti} = \frac{e^{g(s_t, h_i)}}{\sum_{j=1}^{N} e^{g(s_t, h_i)}} \tag{2}$$

The correlation score between the decoder hidden state s_t and that of encoder is $g(s_t, h_i)$. The context vector c_t and the decoder state s_t are linked, and it is the input of the two linear layers, then we can get the vocabulary distribution P_{vocab}, which is a probability distribution to predict words w:

$$P(w) = P_{vocab}(w) \qquad (3)$$

During training stage, the loss for the whole input sequence is:

$$loss = \frac{1}{T} \sum\nolimits_{t=0}^{T} loss_t \qquad (4)$$

In which $loss_t$ is the loss for time step t:

$$loss_t = -\log P\left(w_t^*\right) \qquad (5)$$

2.2 Attention-Based Seq2seq Model

Our semantic relevance-based pointer-generator network (depicted in Fig. 3) contains five components: encoder, decoder, attention mechanism, generation probability calculation and a similarity function. Our model is a hybrid among basic attention-based seq2seq model [10], a pointer network [11], and a semantic relevance [12].

Our model can get summary in a generated way or an abstracted way. The generated way can get novel words that are in the vocabulary. The abstracted way can get important sentences that are in the source text. We calculated the model's context vector c_t and attention distribution α_t in Sect. 2.1. In addition, the generation probability p_{gen} is applied to represents whether getting the summary in a generated way or getting it in an abstract way. When this scalar is bigger than 0.5, we get more information in a generated way. It is calculated through a linear cell from three inputs, the first is context vector c_t, the second is decoder state s_t and the third is decoder input y_{t-1}:

$$p_{gen} = \sigma \left(w_{c*}^T c_t^* + w_s^T s_t + w_y^T y_{t-1} + b_{ptr} \right) \qquad (6)$$

where vectors w_{c*}, w_s, w_y and b_{ptr} are parameters which can be learned, the function σ is a sigmoid function. Then we use p_{gen} to get the final words distribution P_{final}:

$$P_{final}(w) = p_{gen} P_{vocab}(w) + \left(1 - p_{gen} \right) \sum_{i:w_i=w} \alpha_i \qquad (7)$$

The pointer-generator network can solve OOV problem easily. Suppose that w is a word that does not appear in the vocabulary, then $P_{vocab}(w)$ is zero, we can get the word through pointing.

We adapt similarity function to our model and we can receive a high semantic coherence between long original texts and short summaries. In order to get high semantic relevance, we select maximize the score computed by similarity function as our training object. Original text's semantic vector V_t is equal to the last output h_N. Previous work has proved that we can get the summary's semantic vector by simply subtracting h_N from s_M:

$$V_s = s_M - h_N \qquad (8)$$

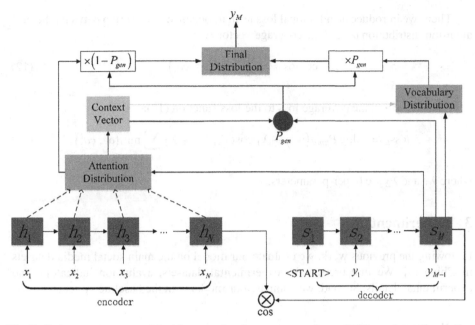

Fig. 3. Pointer-generator model with semantic relevance computing unit. It is made up of encoder, decoder, attention mechanism, generation probability calculation and cosine similarity function.

Cosine similarity is a measure of similarity between two non-zero vectors in the same space, and we use it to measure the similarity relevance:

$$\cos(V_s, V_t) = \frac{V_s \cdot V_t}{\|V_s\| \|V_t\|} \tag{9}$$

During training stage, we need to add similarity score to our loss function:

$$loss_t = -\log P_{final}(w_t^*) - \lambda \cos(V_s, V_t) \tag{10}$$

where λ is a hyperparameter [13].

2.3 Coverage Mechanism

Repetition is one of the big problems in abstractive text summarization [7], moreover, it is a universal question for sequence-to-sequence models [14, 15]. We use the coverage model [7] to solve the repetition problem. The idea is that we use the attention distribution to track what has been covered so far, and penalize the networks that participate in the same part again. On each time step t of the decoder, the coverage vector co_t is the mean of the sum of all the attention distributions α_j to data:

$$co_t = \sum_{j=0}^{t-1} \alpha_j \Bigg/ t - 1 \tag{11}$$

Then, we introduce an additional loss term to penalize any overlap between the new attention distribution α^t and the coverage vector co_t:

$$\text{covloss}_t = \sum_i \min\left(\alpha_i^t, co_i^t\right) \tag{12}$$

Finally, we add the coverage loss to the loss function (10):

$$\text{loss}_t = -\log P_{final}\left(w_t^*\right) - \lambda_1 \cos(V_s, V_t) + \lambda_2 \sum_i \min\left(\alpha_i^t, co_i^t\right) \tag{13}$$

where λ_1 and λ_2 are hyper-parameters.

3 Experiment

Following the previous work, we evaluate our model on the main social media datasets in China [9]. We first present the experimental datasets, evaluation indicators, and experimental details. Second, we compare our model with the baseline systems.

3.1 Dataset

LCSTS is a large-scale Chinese short text summarization dataset collected from Sina Weibo, a well-known Chinese social media website, consisting of over 2.4 million text-summary pairs [9]. The summaries are created manually, and the source texts are less than 140 Chinese characters. In addition, the dataset is divided into three parts, and all the text-summary pairs are manually scored, with associated scores ranging from 1 to 5. We just select pairs with scores more than 2, leaving 8,685 pairs in PART II and 725 pairs in PART III. In experiment, PART I is used for training, PART II for validation and PART III for testing.

3.2 Evaluation Metric

For evaluation metrics, we adopt ROUGE scores [16], which is widely used for summarization evaluation [17–19]. By calculating the overlapping units, the ROUGE metrics compare generated summary with the reference summary. Following previous work, we use ROUGE-1 (overlap of unigram), ROUNGE-2 (overlap of bigrams) and ROUNGE-L (longest common subsequence) as our evaluation metrics.

3.3 Experimental Details

We implement our experiments in TensorFlow [20]. The vocabularies are extracted from the training sets, and the summaries and the source contents share the same vocabularies. We split the Chinese sentences into characters to mitigate the risk of word segmentation errors. In order to covering most of the common characters, we trim the vocabulary to 50,000.

For all experiments, our model has 256-dimentional hidden states and 128-dimentional word embeddings. Unlike [10], we do not use transfer learning and the pre-trained word embeddings. Instead, they are learned during training. We use Adagrad [21] for training with a learning rate of 0.15 and an initial accumulator value of 0.1. The batch size is 32, and we do not use dropout [22] on this dataset. Following the previous work, we implement the beam search with a beam size 4 and gradient pruning with a maximum gradient norm of 2. To obtain our final coverage model with semantic relevance, we set $\lambda_1 = 0.0001$ and $\lambda_2 = 1$ (as described in Eq. 13).

3.4 Results

We compare our proposed model with the following baseline models:

Simple Seq2seq is the basic sequence-to-sequence model for abstractive summarization. The encoder is a bidirectional GRU and the decoder is a unidirectional GRU [9].

Attention-based Seq2seq is a sequence-to-sequence model with attention mechanism. The main difference between Attention-based Seq2seq and Simple Seq2seq is that attention mechanism is added to the first one, so it can pay different attention to the source words on each time step [9].

SRB is an encoder-decoder model that takes semantic relevance into account. This model adds a similarity function to attention-based sequence-to-sequence model in order to make sure that there is high semantic relevance between source texts and generated summaries [6].

Table 1. Comparison with baseline models on LCSTS test set.

Model	ROUGE-1	ROUGE-2	ROUGE-L
Simple Seq2seq (W[1]) [9]	17.7	8.5	15.8
Simple Seq2seq (C[2]) [9]	21.5	8.9	18.6
Attention-based Seq2seq (W) [9]	26.8	16.1	24.1
Attention-based Seq2seq (C) [9]	29.9	17.4	27.2
SRB (C) [6]	33.3	20.0	30.1
PGC (C)	38.5	20.3	32.4
PGCS (C)	39.1	20.2	33.3

[1] Word level
[2] Character level.

We denote PGC as our proposed pointer-generator network with coverage mechanism, and PGCS as our pointer-generator network with semantic relevance and coverage mechanism. Table 1 shows the results of our experiments. We can see that the ROUGE-1, ROUGE-2, and ROUGE-L scores keep rising among the models. Compared with SRB, the ROUGE-1, ROUGE-2, and ROUGE-L scores of PGCS improves 17.42%, 1% and

10.63% respectively, which shows that pointer-generator network and coverage mechanism play an important role in getting more coherent summaries. In addition, from the comparison of PGC and PGCS ROUGE scores, we can notice that the semantic relevance unit in the model improves the quality of generated summaries.

4 Related Work

The encoder-decoder architecture is the basic framework of our proposed model. Sutskever first proposed sequence-to-sequence model and used it for neural machine translation [23]. Bahdanau proposed attention mechanism, which allows the model to automatically select a part from the primitive text [4]. Rush first applied attention mechanism to text summarization task and the model performs better than the state-of-the-art sequence-to-sequence models [5]. Vinyals described pointer network than can learn the conditional probability of an output sentence in a new way [11]. Coverage mechanism is first applied to neural machine translation, then See used it for text summarization and it solves the problem of repetition at some level. Weber modified the pointer-generator network and the new model can control the amount of copying [24]. Ma pro-posed a neural model based on semantic relevance that can improve the semantic relevance between the source text and the generated summaries [12]. Ma used the semantic representation of standard summary to supervise the learning of that of source text [6].

5 Conclusion

In this paper, we propose an architecture that can get the summary in an automatically copied or generated way. The similarity computing unit can improve the semantic relevance between source text and generated summaries. Our coverage mechanism solves the problem of repetition to some extent. In addition, experimental results show that our PGCS (pointer-generator network with coverage and semantic relevance mechanism) outperforms the baseline models. As a result, when our PGCS is applied to many intelligent scenarios of Internet of Things, we can get more benefits about computing and network transmission.

Acknowledgments. This work is supported by the National Natural Science Foundation of China under Grant 61701019.

References

1. Dragomir, R., Timothy, A., Sasha, B.: MEAD - a platform for multidocument multilingual text summarization. In: Proceedings of the Fourth International Conference on Language Resources and Evaluation, LREC (2004)
2. Kristian, W., Mirella, L.: Automatic generation of story highlights. In: Proceedings of the 48th Annual Meeting of the Association for Computational Linguistics, ACL, pp. 565–574 (2010)

3. Cheng, J., Lapata, M.: Neural summarization by extracting sentences and words. In: Proceedings of the 54th Annual Meeting of the Association for Computational Linguistics, ACL, vol. 1: Long Papers (2016)
4. Dzmitry, B., Kyunghyun, C., Yoshua, B.: Neural machine translation by jointly learning to align and translate. CoRR, abs/1409.0473 (2014)
5. Alexander, M., Sumit, C., Jason, W.: A neural attention model for abstractive sentence summarization. In: Proceedings of the 2015 Conference on Empirical Methods in Natural Language Processing, EMNLP, pp. 379–389 (2015)
6. Ma, S., Sun, X., Lin, J., Wang, H.: Autoencoder as assistant supervisor: improving text representation for chinese social media text summarization. In:Proceedings of the 56th Annual Meeting of the Association for Computational Linguistics, vol. 2: Short Papers (2018)
7. Abigail, S., Peter, J., Christopher, D.: Get to the point: Summarization with pointer-generator networks. arXiv: 1704.04368 (2017)
8. Romain, P., Caiming, X., Richard, S.: A deep reinforced model for abstractive summarization. arXiv:1705.04304 (2017)
9. Hu, B., Chen, Q., Zhu, F.: LCSTS: a large scale Chinese short text summarization dataset. In: Proceedings of the 2015 Conference on Empirical Methods in Natural Language Processing, EMNLP, pp. 1967–1972 (2015)
10. Ramesh, N., Bowen, Z., Cicero, D.: Abstractive text summarization using sequence-to-sequence RNNs and beyond. In: Computational Natural Language Learning (2016)
11. Oriol, V., Meire, F., Navdeep, J.: Pointer networks. In: Neural Information Processing Systems (2015)
12. Ma, S., Sun, X., Xu, J.: Improving semantic relevance for sequence-to-sequence learning of Chinese social media text summarization. In: Proceedings of the 55th Annual Meeting of the Association for Computational Linguistics, ACL, pp. 635–640 (2017)
13. Wang, W., Chang, B.: Graph-based dependency parsing with bidirectional LSTM. In: Proceedings of the 54th Annual Meeting of the Association for Computational Linguistics, ACL, vol. 1: Long Papers (2016)
14. Tu, Z., Lu, Z., Liu, Y.: Modeling coverage for neural machine translation. In: Association for Computational Linguistics, ACL (2016).
15. Mi, H., Sankarab, B., Wang, Z.: Coverage embedding models for neural machine translation. In: Empirical Methods in Natural Language Processing (2016)
16. Lin, C.Y.: Rouge: A package for automatic evaluation of summaries. In: Text Summarization Branches Out (2014)
17. Chen, X., Chan, Z., Gao, S.: Learning towards abstractive timeline summarization. In: Proceedings of the Twenty-Eighth International Joint Conference on Artifificial Intelligence, IJCAI-19, pp. 4939–4945 (2019)
18. Gao, S.,Chen, X., Li, P.: How to write summaries with patterns? learning towards abstractive summarization through prototype editing (2019)
19. Lin, J., Sun, X., Ma, S.: Global Encoding for Abstractive Summarization (2018)
20. Abadi, M., Barham, P., Jianmin, C.: Tensorflflow: a system for large-scale machine learning. OSDI **16**, 265–283 (2016)
21. Duchi, J., Hazan, E., Singer, Y.: Adaptive subgradient methods for online learning and stochastic optimization. J. Mach. Learn. Res. **12**, 2121–2159 (2011)
22. Srivastava, N., Hinton, G., Krizhevsky, A.: Dropout: a simple way to prevent neural networks from overfifitting. J. Mach. Learn. Res. **15**, 1929–1958 (2014)
23. Sutskever, I., Vinyals, O., Le, Q.V.: Sequence to sequence learning with neural networks. In: Annual Conference on Neural Information Processing Systems, pp. 3104–3112 (2014)
24. Weber, N., Shekhar, L., Balasubramanian, N.: Controlling Decoding for More Abstractive Summaries with Copy-Based Networks (2018)

Design and Implementation of FPRP on FPGA for Internet of Things

Shuning Lei, Zhongjiang Yan[(✉)], Xiaojiao Hu, Mao Yang, and Bo Li

School of Electronics and Information, Northwestern Polytechnical University,
Xi'an, China
593154441@qq.com, {zhjyan,yangmao,libo.npu}@nwpu.edu.cn,
18392990273@mail.nwpu.edu.cn

Abstract. To guarantee low energy consumption and high efficiency for
the nodes of the Internet of Things (IoT), designing and implementing
the network protocols, e.g., routing and multiple access control (MAC)
protocols, on FPGA become significant issues. Aiming at designing and
implementing FPRP protocol on FPGA, this paper proposes a design
scheme of FPGA implementation of FPRP protocol. The overall architecture includes clock counting module, reservation module, data transmission module, algorithm module and reservation result generation module,
which are connected and restricted with each other. In order to verify,
we divide it into two parts, i.e., single node verification and double node
verification. Finally, the basic implementation of the five-step reservation
is initially completed which show that the design scheme is correct and
feasible.

Keywords: FPRP · Multi - access protocol · MAC · FPGA

1 Introduction

With the rapid development of communication technology and the improvement
of people's communication requirements, Internet of Things (IoT) has become
an important research hotspot of nowadays network. Medium Access Control
(MAC) protocol has great influence on the performance of wireless sensor networks and is one of the key protocols to ensure efficient communication for IoT.
Different from the contention based protocols, e.g., Carrier Sense Multiple Access
with Collision Avoid (CSMA/CA) [1–3] and ALOHA [4–6], the performance of
which may deteriorate when the network density becomes high. The joint contention and reservation-based protocol, e.g., Five-Phase Reservation Protocol
(FPRP) [7–11], has both flexible and high efficiency advantages. To guarantee
low energy consumption and high efficiency for the nodes of the IoT, how to
design and implement the joint contention and reservation-based protocol, e.g.,
FPRP, becomes a significant issue.

© ICST Institute for Computer Sciences, Social Informatics and Telecommunications Engineering 2021
Published by Springer Nature Switzerland AG 2021. All Rights Reserved
Y.-B. Lin and D.-J. Deng (Eds.): SGIoT 2020, LNICST 354, pp. 178–194, 2021.
https://doi.org/10.1007/978-3-030-69514-9_15

FPRP divides the channel into frames, and each frame contains two stage, i.e., the reservation stage and the data transmission stage. The nodes that need to transmit traffic initiate the reservation process with probability P in the reservation stage, and they interactively contend channel resources by controlling the grouped broadcasting type. Once the contention is successful, the node will reserve the broadcast information slot corresponding to the reservation slot and automatically occupy the certain slot for data transmission until the next reservation period comes. If the node still needs an information slot, the slot resource is re-competed in the next reservation phase.

The node completes the reservation of information slot after five information interactions in the contention cycle. The basic process of five handshake runs in FPRP is as follows.

- Reservation Request phase (RR): Requesting Node (RN) sends reservation request with probability P.
- Contention Report phase (CR): The nodes of the channel are monitored. If multiple RR are received, CR is sent to indicate that the channel contention occurred. If the RN does not receive CR, then its RR is sent successfully, and RN becomes Transmission Node (TN).
- Reservation Confirmation phase (RC): If TN does not receive CR, it means that the reservation is successful. After that, TN sends RC, and TN's neighbor node is informed that the slot is reserved by TN. Otherwise, do not send RC.
- Reservation Acknowledgement phase (RA): The node receiving RC replies to RA and tells its neighbor TN that its reservation has been successful. Nodes that cannot receive RA are isolated nodes. RA is also used to inform nodes beyond two hops that the slot is successfully reserved. The node receiving RA sets its own state to Blocked (BK).
- Packing/Elimination phase (P/E): The two-hop neighbor node of TN sends PP and tells the three-hop neighbor node of TN that the slot has been successfully booked. The three-hop neighbor node knows that its one-hop neighbor node will not compete for the slot, so the three-hop neighbor node can increase the competition probability P in its own two-hop network. At this stage, TN also sends EP to other potential TNs with a probability of 0.5 to solve the deadlock problem of non-isolated nodes.

The FPRP protocol uses Bayes-based algorithm to calculate the probability P to send messages. The algorithm stipulates that each node should estimate the number of resource competitors around it, n, and adjust its probability P.

$$P = \frac{1}{n}$$

At the end of each competition, the node updates its estimate n based on feedback.

- If the competition is successful or the competition is idle:

$$n = n - 1$$

– If contention happened:

$$n = n + (e - 2)^{-1}$$

In the research work of improving FPRP protocol, Bayes-based algorithm is taken as the focus, which is constantly updated and improved.

It has been proved by practice that the FPRP protocol adopts the five-steps handshake mechanism, which does not produce time slot waste and effectively solves the problem of hidden terminal and non-isolated deadlock. However, the FPRP protocol does not take into account such problems as unfair slot allocation caused by different node loads, low channel utilization and excessive access delay due to single channel communication. In recent years, aiming at the problems found in the application of FPRP protocol, many targeted improvement and research have been carried out. For example, in order to simplify the complexity of the implementation of FPRP protocol system, the node should have the ability to measure the signal-to-noise ratio of wireless communication link, judge whether the communication link is reliable according to the signal-to-noise ratio, and then choose whether to select the link. At the same time, it is necessary to distinguish the transmitting power in different stages. For example, in the RR and CR phases, the wireless transmitting power of the node sending RR packets can be appropriately increased to reduce interference and conflict. Besides, aiming at the problem that FPRP can not fully use some time slots in the information frame, an improved pseudo Bayesian algorithm is proposed. The improved FPRP contention access mechanism allows nodes to compete for multiple slots in the reserved frame according to a certain probability or priority, so as to improve the slot utilization.

Field Programmable Gate Array (FPGA) has a strong real-time capability to process signals in real time. In addition, it realizes various functions through software programming oriented to chip format instructions. Therefore, the original design scheme or original functions of the system can be improved by modifying the software code without changing the hardware platform, which is of great flexibility. Therefore, using FPGA as the platform to implement FPRP protocol is very convenient, practical and effective.

FPGA is a semi-custom circuit developed in recent years on the original hardware editable device. Using FPGA to implement MAC protocol can make the design products small, integrated, stable and reliable, which shorten the development cycle greatly. In addition, it is easy to debug and modify internally. In Ad Hoc networks, MAC protocol is required to be implemented on FPGA due to its advantages of high integration, fast speed and low power consumption. However, as FPGA is a hardware platform, it is a parallel working environment, while MAC protocol is usually a time-dimension sequential working process. Therefore, how to accurately describe the sequence working process of the designed MAC protocol on FPGA has become a breakthrough point that has been widely studied. In the implementation of various protocols with FPGA, for example, using FPGA to implement a subset of IEEE 802.15.4 protocol to realize point-to-point communication and compare the power consumption of wireless data transmission system [14]. Besides, a new MAC-PHY Interface (MPI) protocol is implemented with FPGA, which realize that the throughput is 1.21 Gbps [15].

How to use FPGA to implement FPRP protocol is the key content of this paper. The main contributions of this paper are as follows.

1 Proposed a design scheme to realize FPRP protocol. Proposed to divide FPRP protocol into several modules to realize different functions, including clock counting module, algorithm module, reservation module, reservation result generation module, data transmission module, and so on. And realized various functions with Verilog language simulation.
2 Carried out simulation design for clock counting module, algorithm module and reservation module. Successfully realized the receiving and sending of double nodes and obtained correct output waveform. Proved the feasibility of the whole scheme.

This paper is divided into six sections. Section 1 introduces the research background and innovation points of the paper. Section 2 designs and divides FPRP modules on the basis of the knowledge learned. Section 3 gives the realization ideas according to the module division, and Sect. 4 gives the final simulation results. Section 5 summarizes and looks forward to the future. Section 6 gives acknowledgement.

2 Overall System Architecture Design

In order to realize FPGA design and implementation, according to different functions and MAC protocol model, FPRP protocol is divided into several key sub-modules for design simulation and implementation.

Figure 1 shows the MAC layer networking protocol module system architecture. It is mainly divided into two parts, which are MAC protocol module and memory management module. The MAC protocol module mainly realizes the logic function of MAC protocol, and the memory management module caches and transmits data to the data transmission module or the upper module according to the requirements of MAC protocol. In addition, it supports data re-transmission.

As a kind of MAC protocol, the system framework of FPRP protocol is also the same as Fig. 1. However, in order to realize the function of FPRP simply, according to Fig. 1, the simplified FPRP system is divided into five main modules as shown in Fig. 2 in addition to the memory management module.

As shown in the Fig. 2, the five parts are introduced as follows.

1 Clock counting module. It is the master control module for sending and receiving data, which decides when to send corresponding frame signals.
2 Reservation module. It contains reservation sending module and reservation receiving module. It can realize the five-step reservation mechanism, send and receive each type of frame (RR, CR, RC, RA, PP/EP), and decide whether the five handshakes proceed smoothly.

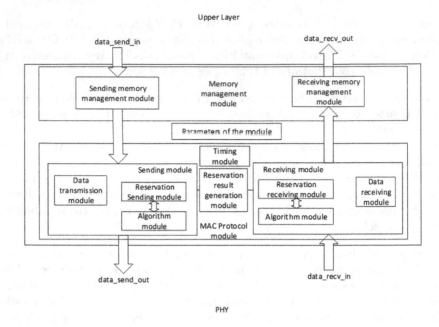

Fig. 1. MAC protocol module system architecture

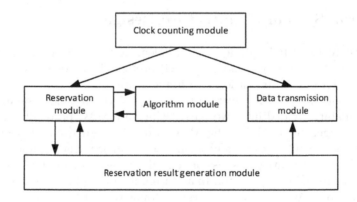

Fig. 2. Integral module division

3 Data transmission module. It contains data transmission sending module and data transmission receiving module. After the reservation is successful, the packet is transmitted.

4 Algorithm module. It can adjust the probability P to determine whether each node can make a reservation.

5 Reservation result generation module. It can generate reservation slot allocation table, which transmits the signal whether the reservation is successful.

These five modules are interrelated. Among them, the clock timing module counts according to the micro-slot of reservation and data transmission, outputs the micro-slot count, and jointly manages the reservation module with the algorithm module. The reservation results of the reservation module are saved in the reservation generation module and correlated with the algorithm module. Generate modules based on reservation results to provide relevant information for the data transfer module.

In this paper, the relationship among the reservation module, algorithm module and clock counting module is refined into several parts as shown in Fig. 3 for design.

As shown in Fig. 3, the reservation master module is composed of the total top-level module of reservation sending and reservation receiving master module. The total top-level module of reservation sending calls the sub-module of reservation sending module, the clock counting module and the algorithm module to realize the mutual restriction of the three. The sub-module of reservation sending calls the five-step reservation frame signal sending sub-module. The reservation receiving master module calls the five-step reservation receiving sub-module to realize the receiving of frames.

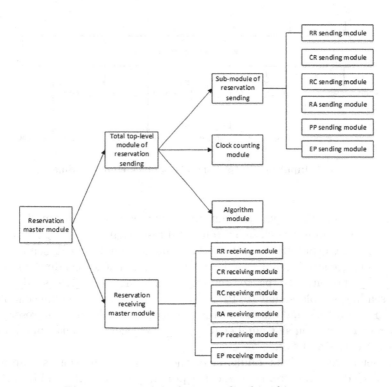

Fig. 3. The module design realized in this paper

3   Detailed Sub-module Design and Implementation

In this paper, the clock counting module, algorithm module and reservation module are presented.

3.1   Clock Counting Module

The main function of the clock counting module is to generate enabling signals needed in the Reservation Frame (RF) and Information Frame (IF), and to divide the whole time period orderly. The clock counting module is divided into two sub-modules, namely RF counting module and IF counting module. Each module generates corresponding enabling signals. The RF counting module outputs the enabling signals of the Reservation Slot (RS) counting module, which in turn outputs the enabling signals of the Reservation Cycle (RC) counting module, and then the RC module outputs the enabling signals of RR, CR, RA, RC, PP and EP phases. Each module works in an orderly manner according to the time slot.

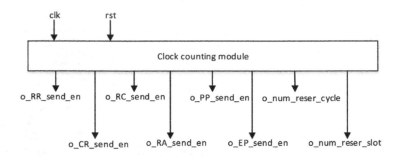

Fig. 4. Input and output signals of clock count module

Figure 4 shows the input and output of the clock counting module. Clock counting module inputs clock signal (clk) and reset signal (rst) to generate clock to set counter. Output RR packet sending enable signal (o_RR_send_en), CR packet sending enable signal (o_CR_send_en), RC packet sending enable signal (o_RC_send_en), RA packet sending enable signal (o_RA_send_en), PP packet sending enable signal (o_PP_send_en), EP packet sending enable signal (o_EP_send_en), and output current reservation cycle (o_num_reser_cycle) and current reservation slot number (o_num_reser_slot) to make time limits on reservation cycles and slots.

In order to realize this module, after the interface definition, set up a 3-bit counter, cycled counting from 0 to 4, corresponding RR, CR, RC and RA, PP/EP five time slot. At different time slot (different counter value), the corresponding frame can pull up the enable signal, e.g., o_RR_send_en, then the certain frame is allowed ti be sent. Set a reservation cycle count (o_num_reser_cycle) counter.

Every time the micro-counter counts to 4, add one. And keep counting from 0 to 2, indicating 3 reservation cycles. Set a reservation slot counter. Every time the number of reservation slots (o_num_reser_cycle) is added to 2 and then it added 1. The count from 0 to 9 is repeated, indicating 10 reservation slots.

3.2   Algorithm Module

According to the interaction of the reservation control group, the module adjusts the node's reservation probability based on the Bayes algorithm to improve the success rate of the reservation and accelerate the convergence rate of the protocol.

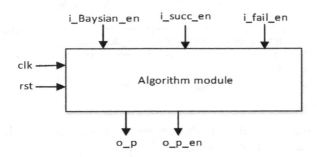

Fig. 5. Input and output signals of algorithm module

Figure 5 shows the input and output of the algorithm module. The algorithm module inputs clock signal (clk) and reset signal (rst) to generate the clock. The enable signal of the input algorithm module (i_Baysian_en) determines whether the algorithm module is called, that is, the algorithm module is called when the enabling signal of the algorithm module is high. Input the successful reservation enable signal (i_succ_en) and the failed reservation enable signal (i_fail_en) for conditional judgment, and calculate the probability P with different calculation methods according to the success or failure of the reservation. Output the send probability P (o_p) and the output P effective enable signal (o_p_en).

When the nodes receive RC group, RA group, PP group or EP group, they will generate reservation success signal to the algorithm module, that is, input i_succ_en to the algorithm module. The algorithm module will adjust the sending probability of its output through success or failure signal. If successful, refer to the formula $P = \frac{1}{n}$, $n = n - 1$. If it fails, refer to the formula $P = \frac{1}{n}$, $n = n + (e - 2)^{-1}$. Firstly, use an intermediate variable register to calculate the two formulas, such as $\frac{24}{n}$ and $\frac{2520}{n}$, so that it is still a positive integer. Then use ">> 2" operation to reduce the corresponding multiple to make it a decimal. Output probability P. Generate a random number. If the probability P is less than the random number, a reservation can be made. Otherwise, no reservation will be made.

3.3   Reservation Module

Reservation module should be able to make reservation according to the probability generated by the algorithm module. When reservation, different slots output by clock counting module and the deference of the received frames are taken into consideration in order to send the five - step reservation frame in order accurately. And it should judge the frame type when the frame comes, call the corresponding frame receiving module, and receive the frame accurately.

3.3.1   RR Module

The RR frame format is shown in Fig. 6.

Fig. 6. RR frame

Type: RR group, set to 0001. The previous bit 0 means that the frame is in the reservation stage and 001 means RR frame.

Src_Addr: The source address of reservation node S.

3.3.1.1 RR Sending

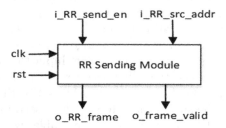

Fig. 7. Input and output signals of RR sending module

Figure 7 shows the input and output of the RR sending module. RR sending module inputs clock signal (clk), reset signal (rst) to generate the clock. Input i_RR_send_en enable signal to decide whether to call sending module. RR frame can be sent when i_RR_send_en is high. Enter i_RR_src_addr to display the source address of the node which sends the RR packet and tell the surrounding nodes who is sending the frame. Output RR packet (o_RR_frame) and the output signal display valid field o_frame_valid.

In order to realize this module, firstly set up the interface. Then define a 3-bit counter to count from 0 to 3, one for each clock cycle. When the enable signal is high, RR frames are sent in three clock cycles. The RR frame Type field is sent in the first clock cycle. The first 32bit of the source address is sent in the second clock cycle, and the last 16bit of the source address is sent in the third clock cycle and 0 is supplemented. Once 32bit is sent, pull the o_frame_valid high.

3.3.1.2 RR Receiving

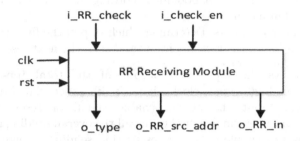

Fig. 8. Input and output signals of RR receiving module

Figure 8 shows the input and output of the RR receiving module. RR receiving module inputs clock signal (clk), reset signal (rst) to generated clock. Then input receive enable signal (i_check_en) determines whether the RR receive module is called, that is, when the receive enable signal is high, RR packet will be received. Input the received 32-bit RR group (i_RR_check) to receive. Output the type field extracted from the received RR group (o_type) and the source address that sent RR (o_RR_src_addr). After all the above points are received, the enable signal (o_RR_in) of RR group receiving is output.

In order to realize this module, firstly, set up the interface. Then define a 3-bit counter to count from 0 to 5, one clock cycle for each count. When the enable signal is high, RR frames are received in 4 clock cycles. The type field of RR group is extracted from i_RR_check in the first clock cycle. The second clock cycle extracts the first 32 bits of the sending node's source address from i_RR_check. In the third clock cycle, extract the last 16 bits of the source address of the sending node from i_RR_check and make up with 0. At the fourth clock cycle, RR group has been already received, and the enable signal (o_RR_in) is set to a high position.

3.3.2 Other Frame Types Send and Receive Modules

The design of CR, RC, RA, PP and EP sending and receiving modules are carried out in the same principle as those of RR sending and receiving module. However, the o_type of each frame is different. It is 0010 to CR, 0011 to RC, 0100 to RA, 0101 to PP and 0110 to EP.

3.3.3   Total Top-Level Module of Reservation Sending

This module call algorithm module, clock counting module and reservation sending module. Realize the normal delivery of the reservation frame under the following three constraints.

1 Time slot constraints. Call the corresponding frame sending sub-module in five steps to reserve the corresponding time slot.
2 Algorithm constraints. Start booking according to the probability generated by the algorithm module.
3 Received frame constraints. Determine which step of the five-step reservation is made according to the received frame and send the next reservation frame.

Figure 9 shows the input and output of the total top-level module of reservation sending. Input clock signal (clk), reset signal (rst) to generate the clock. Input the overall enable signal of reservation sending (i_reser_send_en) to determine whether to call the overall sending module. That is, when the overall enable signal of reservation sending is high, it is called. Input the source addresses (i_RR_src_addr, i_CR_src_addr, i_RC_src_addr, i_RA_src_addr, i_PP_src_addr, i_EP_src_addr). Input the enable signal of contend (i_contention_en) to simulate the occurrence of contend and send CR frame. Input the completion enable signals (o_RR_in, o_CR_in, o_RC_in, o_RA_in, o_PP_in, o_EP_in) of each frame, connecting to the receiving module, and determine which frame to send in the next handshake by the received frame. Output the frame signal that was sent (frame_out), and print out the frame's valid field (frame_invalid).

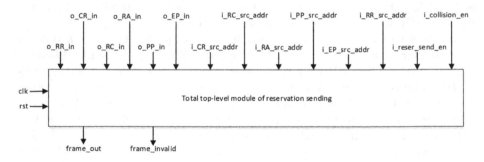

Fig. 9. Input and output signals of total top-level module of reservation sending

In order to realize this module, firstly set up the interface. Then input source address. Input contend enable signal (i_contention_en) to simulate contend situation. Input o_RR_in and so on to enable module to know which frame has been received. Call the timing module to integrate the constraint condition 1, time slot constraint, to send enable signals for each frame, that is, only the corresponding frames can be sent in the corresponding time slot. Call the sub-module of reservation sending, which indicates that only when the sending enable signal is high can the sending module of each frame be called to send the frame. The algorithm module is called to calculate the reservation probability and determine whether the node should make an appointment or not. In this overall module, another constraint condition to send enable signals of each frame is set, that is, sending according to the received packet. For example, if only the RC packet (i.e., the input o_RC_in is high) is received, the sending module of the next frame, i.e., RA frame, can be sent. Output the packages the node sent.

3.3.4 Reservation Receiving Master Module

It can judge the type of frame and then call the corresponding sub-module to receive the certain frame signal.

Figure 10 shows the input and output of the reservation receiving master module. Input clock signal (clk), reset signal (rst) to generated clock. Input the total enable signal of reservation receiving (i_reser_recv_en) to determine whether to call the total module of reservation receiving. Input the received frame signal (frame_in) and call each receiving sub-module to receive the frame. Output the completion enable signals (o_RR_in, o_CR_in, o_RC_in, o_RA_in, o_PP_in, o_EP_in) of each frame after receiving, which is connected to the sending module and determine which frame to be sent in the next handshake by the received frame.

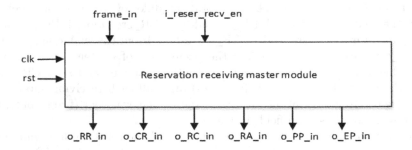

Fig. 10. Input and output signals of reservation receiving master module

In order to realize it, firstly set up the interface. Then set the frame signal received as the input. Every time one frame comes, the first 32bit of the incoming frame, namely the type code of the frame, is judged. And the receiving module of the corresponding frame is called according to the different type code and the receiving of the frame is carried out. After each frame is successfully received, output completion enable signals.

3.3.5 Reservation Master Module

The total top-level module of reservation sending and the Reservation receiving master module are called in this module to realize that after a node receives a frame, the sending master sends the next reservation frame according to the

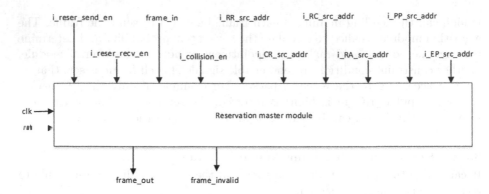

Fig. 11. Input and output signals of reservation master module

signals generated by the receiving master to realize the connection of sending and receiving.

Figure 11 shows the input and output of the reservation master module. Input clock signal (clk) and reset signal (rst) to generate the clock. Input the overall enable signal of reservation sending (i_reser_send_en) to determine whether to call the overall top-level module of reservation sending. Input the total enable signal of reservation receiving (i_reser_recv_en) to determine whether to call the total module of reservation receiving. Input the source addresses (i_RR_src_addr, i_CR_src_addr, i_RC_src_addr, i_RA_src_addr, i_PP_src_addr, i_EP_src_addr). Input the enable signal of contend (i_contention_en) to simulate the occurrence of contend, that is, when the enable signal of contend is high, contention happens and send CR frame. Input the received frame signal (frame_in) and call each receiving sub-module to receive the frame. Print out the frame signal that was sent (frame_out), and print out the frame's valid field (frame_invalid).

In order to realize it, set up the interface. Call the total top-level module of reservation sending and the Reservation receiving master module. After receiving each frame output by the Reservation receiving master module, completion enable signals, such as o_RR_in, etc., are connected to the input port of the total top-level module of reservation sending with several intermediate linear variables to connect the two modules. Output the frames sent by the overall sending module.

4   Performance Evaluation

4.1   Single Node Validation

4.1.1   Total Top-Level Module of Reservation Sending Module
Enable signal will be generated by three conditions – the clock module output enable signals, the algorithm module calculate probability to decided when to send the RR, the judging of the type of the received frame to decide the next

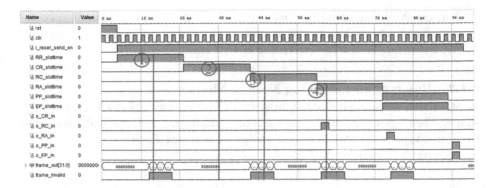

Fig. 12. Waveform of non-contention situation

handshake step and send certain frame. Integrated them into the overall module, input node source address, pull contention enable signal up, simulating the situation of contention, check the waveform. Pull down the contention enable signal to simulate the non-contention situation, and check the output waveform.

The results are shown as below.

– Non-contention situation in Fig. 12
  The result of this situation displays as Fig. 12 and the explanation of label 1 to 4 is shown as below.
  The label 1 shows that it send the corresponding frame in the corresponding slot. For example, send the RR frame in the RR slot. The label 2 shows that no CR frame is sent in non-contention situation. The label 3 shows that if no CR frame is received, the RC frame is sent in the RC slot. The label 4 shows that After receiving the RC frame, the RA frame is sent in the RA slot.
– Contention situation in Fig. 13

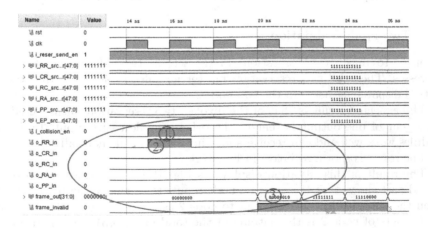

Fig. 13. Waveform of contention situation

The result of this situation displays as Fig. 13 and the explanation of the circled part shows that on the premise that the contention occurs(1) and the RR frame has been received(2), the CR frame is sent(3).

4.1.2   Reservation Receiving Master Module

In order to make a implantation, firstly pull up the reservation receiving enable signal. Then input the received signal frame (frame_in), automatically recognize the frame type to receive, and view the generated waveform.

The result is as below in Fig. 14.

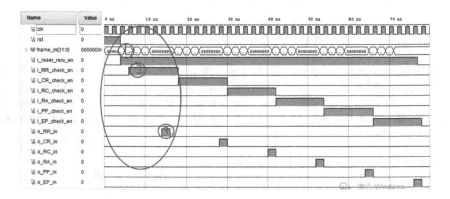

Fig. 14. Waveform of Reservation receiving master module

The result of this situation displays as Fig. 14 and the explanation of the circled part shows that for the incoming frame, firstly judge the frame type(1). Then call the corresponding frame receiving sub module to receive(2). After receiving, output the receiving completion enable signal (e.g. o_RR_in(3)).

4.2   Two-Node Validation

In order to make a implantation, firstly set up two different node source addresses. Then call two reservation master modules to simulate the state of mutual dispatching between the two nodes.

The expected result is that of the invoked two reservation master modules, frame_out of one output is sent to the other module as its input. Both submodules work well and can receive and send frame signals normally.

The result is shown as below in Fig. 15.

The result of this situation displays as Fig. 15 and the explanation of the circled part shows that the external node inputs the signal value to node 1 (1). Then the outputs of node 1 are sent to node 2 as the inputs of node 2 (2). And the outputs of node 2 is the outputs of the total module(3) and the display is normal.

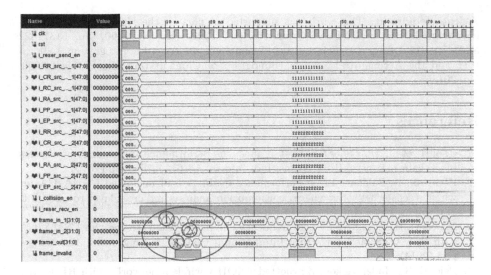

Fig. 15. Waveform of two nodes

5 Conclusion and Future Works

In this paper, the FPGA implementation scheme of FPRP protocol is presented. The design and simulation ideas of algorithm module, clock counting module and reservation module are detailed. And it is proved that this scheme is feasible.

In the simulation practice, we design a new signal to realize a contention. That is because that the principle shows that when multiple RR frames arrive, CR frames are sent to indicate contend. However, in the two-node validation, we receive at most one RR frame, and there will never be a contend. In this case, a contention signal is directly set in the simulation test file to indicate the occurrence of the contention. When the contention occurs, CR frame is sent under the simulate the occurrence of the contention. However, in fact, it cannot be realized. In the network, only when there are multiple RR frames coming or the node cannot parse out RR frames or fails to receive them successfully, the contend will be considered.

In addition, we would like to list the following points for the future work outlook.

In the following work, the result of fractional generation of algorithm module can be improved, and the remaining unrealized modules such as reservation result generation module and data transmission module can be fully realized. Besides, for some reasons, this paper does not calculate the maximum clock frequency and other parameters of the program, and hope to improve it in the future research work.

Acknowledgment. This work was supported in part by the National Natural Science Foundations of CHINA (Grant No. 61771392, No. 61771390, No. 61871322 and No. 61501373), and Science and Technology on Avionics Integration Laboratory and the Aeronautical Science Foundation of China (Grant No. 201955053002, No. 20185553035).

References

1. Cao, B., et al.: How does CSMA/CA affect the performance and security in wireless blockchain networks. IEEE Trans. Ind. Inform. **16**(6), 4270–4280 (2019)
2. El Korbi, I., Saidane, L.A.: Performance evaluation of unslotted CSMA/CA for wireless sensor networks: energy consumption analysis and cross layer routing. Int. J. Comput. Netw. Inf. Secur. **9**(6), 1–12 (2017)
3. Mawlawi, B., et al.: Analysis of frequency channel division strategy for CSMA/CA with RTS/CTS mechanism. In: International Conference on Sensing Technology, p. 5 (2014)
4. Pejoski, S., Hadzi-Velkov, Z.: Slotted ALOHA wireless networks with RF energy harvesting in Nakagami-m fading. Ad Hoc Networks **107**, 102235 (2020)
5. Baccelli, F., Blaszczyszyn, B., Muhlethaler, P.: An Aloha protocol for multihop mobile wireless networks. IEEE Trans. Inf. Theory **52**(2), 421–436 (2006)
6. Ishii, K.: Modified slotted ALOHA protocol for average consensus problem. In: IEEE 18th International Workshop on Signal Processing Advances in Wireless Communications (SPAWC), pp. 1–5. IEEE (2017)
7. Mustafa, M.M., Parthasarathy, V.: A design and implementation of polling TDMA with a comparative analysis with time division multiple access for sporting application. Wirel. Netw. **26**(3), 1897–1904 (2018). https://doi.org/10.1007/s11276-018-1879-9
8. Yang, Q., Zhuang, Y., Shi, J.: An improved contention access mechanism for FPRP to increase throughput. Etri J. **35**(1), 58–68 (2013)
9. Zhu, C., Corson, M.S.: A five-phase reservation protocol (FPRP) for mobile ad hoc networks. Wirel. Netw. **7**(4), 371–384 (2001)
10. Anuradha, B., Dutta, P.: Fuzzy-controlled power-aware routing protocol (FPRP) for mobile ad hoc networks. Int. J. Comput. Appl. **11**(7), 39–43 (2010)
11. Zhenghua, L., et al.: Improvement research on FPRP for MAC of wireless Ad Hoc network. J. Chengdu Univ. p. 2 (2015)
12. Bhatia, I.S., Randhawa, D.K.K.: Verilog-A modeling of a silicene-based p-n junction logic device: simulation and applications. J. Comput. Electr. **19**(1), 387–395 (2020)
13. Ciletti, M.D.: Advanced Digital Design with the Verilog HDL. Advanced digital design with the Verilog HDL =. Pub, House of Electronics Industry (2004)
14. Bhat, N.S.: Design and implementation of IEEE 802.15. 4 Mac protocol on FPGA. arXiv preprint arXiv:1203.2167 (2012)
15. Wang, G., Kang, G.X., Wang, H.: Design and FPGA implementation of MAC-PHY interface based on PCI express for next-generation WLANs. In: Wireless Communications, Networking and Mobile Computing (WiCOM), 2012 8th International Conference on, pp. 1–4. IEEE (2012)

QR Code-based Efficient Entry Method for Intelligent Files of Internet of Things

Wang Genwang[1,2](✉)

[1] School of Electronic and Information Engineering, Beijing Jiaotong University, Beijing, China
18120130@bjtu.edu.cn
[2] Key Laboratory of Communication and Information Systems, Beijing Municipal Commission of Education, Beijing, China

Abstract. In recent years, with the development and application of technologies such as the Internet of Things, cloud computing, and big data, file management, the originally complicated task, has become more intelligent and flexible. However, when recording files, the existing technology still uses the method of scanning one file at a time. Therefore, when massive file information needs to be recorded at the same time, additional time cost or equipment cost will be incurred. In order to shorten the time of file entry as much as possible and reduce unnecessary equipment costs, we propose to mark the key information of files with the QR code technology in the Internet of Things, and then design a special image segmentation method according to the characteristics of the file bag or file box. Thus, the segmentation and extraction of different archive information within the visual range of the input device can be realized, and the effect of simultaneously inputting multiple archive information can be achieved. The experimental results show that in an ideal situation, our method can input the information of 20 files at one time, which greatly improves the efficiency of file entry. It is expected that if this method is applied to the current file management system, it can solve the problem of time consuming and energy consuming, and realize a more intelligent file management system at the same time.

Keywords: QR code · File management · Internet of Things

1 Introduction

In recent years, with the development of information technology, archive management has gradually shifted from traditional manual management to intelligence. However, due to the limitations of archives, some file archives cannot be completely replaced by electronic archives. Therefore, there is an urgent need for a solution to achieve an efficient and intelligent file entry program while retaining complete file information. The Internet of Things [1], as a network of intelligent identification, monitoring, and management, has been widely applied in the fields of medical treatment [2], transportation [3] and logistics [4]. Therefore, if the Internet of Things technology can be applied to file management, a smart and efficient file management system can be constructed. QR code [5], as one

Y.-B. Lin and D.-J. Deng (Eds.): SGIoT 2020, LNICST 354, pp. 195–207, 2021.
https://doi.org/10.1007/978-3-030-69514-9_16

of the key technologies of Internet of Things, has been applied in smart library [6], smart locker [7], electronic payment and other fields in early years because of its fast decoding, high data storage, strong error correction ability and other characteristics, and has achieved very good results. Therefore, applying it to an intelligent file management system also has a certain application basis. The main work of the current file management system is mostly aimed at efficient retrieval and safe storage after electronic files have been obtained, while ignoring the necessity of traditional paper files in the process of converting paper files into electronic files. The time cost and equipment cost required, so there is still some room for optimization.

Aiming at the disadvantages of low input efficiency and high cost of the existing archive management system, this article makes full use of the advantages of the QR code and saves the key information of the file in the QR code. After that, multiple files were scanned at once, and images containing multiple files were obtained. In the process of extracting image information, referring to the common methods in face recognition in the CV field, the RGB image is converted into YCrCb image, and the Cr channel and Cb channel are used cleverly to eliminate the influence of uneven illumination when some images are collected. Thereby improving the accuracy of extracting information from multiple archives. In addition, when extracting the QR code containing the archive information, the binary image of multiple channels is merged, which eliminates the tiny interference areas and improves the efficiency of multiple archive information recognition. Finally, the transmission transformation is used to correct the distorted QR code containing the file information, and the information of multiple files is decoded. The experimental results show that our method can simultaneously enter the information of multiple files at one time, which greatly reduces the time for file entry. It is expected that this method can be applied to the existing file management system to make the existing file management system more efficient and intelligent.

The remainder of this paper is divided into four sections. Section 2 describes the related work. In Sect. 3 of this paper, we introduce the specific program implementation. The fourth section is the experiment and analysis of the program. Finally, we have summarized the work of this paper and made further prospects and improvement ideas for our method.

2 Related Work

File management system, as an intelligent and efficient solution for file management, has always been one of the focuses of research. In the context of the era of big data and cloud computing, Sui et al. [8] analyzed the problems existing in the archives of university endowment funds, and put forward suggestions for funding to improve the efficiency of archive utilization. Considering the prospect of cloud computing in the aspects of electronic archives management infrastructure construction, archives business platform construction and archives utilization, an electronic archives cloud platform based on Hadoop [9] was built to realize data information exchange and business collaboration. On the other hand, various new frameworks and technologies have also been applied to the construction of archive management systems. A device file management system [10] was constructed based on Struts2 + Hibernate + SiteMesh. This system uses a bridge-based page display method to reduce the coupling between programs, and has the advantages of good scalability and easy maintenance. Wang et al. [11] combined with the advantages of Ajax and ASP.NET technology, so as to make the file management system more reliable. In addition, some customized file management systems have been developed to take into account the functional differences between different agencies and units in file management. In view of the fact that the existing student file management system cannot solve high concurrent access, a hybrid database and message queue mechanism [12] is introduced into the student electronic file management system, which reduces the cost of system deployment and maintenance. Taking into account the need for confidentiality of file management in public security agencies, some encryption mechanisms [13] have been added to file management to ensure the security of files. In rural areas, it takes a lot of time to back up the electronic archives of land contracts. Therefore, Xu et al. [14] proposes a solution that can use multithreading and distributed storage to improve the efficiency of data sealing. Our work is aimed at the low efficiency of converting paper files into electronic files, and we have designed an appropriate method to improve the efficiency of file entry.

3   Our Approach

In this section, we will describe the design details of an efficient file entry method.

In the process of program design, we used the C++ programming language. In order to simplify our program, we used the open source image processing library OpenCV3.2 to locate the key areas in the captured image, and the open source barcode recognition library ZBar to extract the file information. According to different functions, we divide the designed program into four modules. Figure 1 shows the basic architecture of the program we designed.

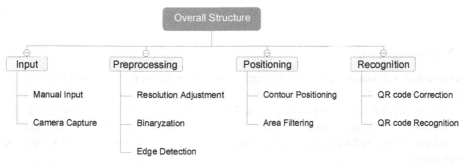

Fig. 1. Overall structure of the program

Considering that the image input and the QR code recognition can directly call the camera or manually input the image and call the QR code recognition library, so only the other two modules will be described in detail here.

3.1 Input

First, we extract the key information of the archive and encode it with a QR code (if security is required, a suitable encryption method can be selected). Then, attach the obtained QR code to the surface of the original file. In order to improve the efficiency of collection, multiple files are overlapped and the QR code information of each file is not blocked. After that, multiple files were scanned at the same time to complete the collection of information. We provide two input methods, automatic scanning and manual input, to facilitate subsequent function expansion.

Figure 2 shows the basic effect of archival information collection.

Fig. 2. An example of image acquisition

3.2 Preprocessing

Resolution Adjustment. Due to the high resolution of the input image, if it is processed directly, more CPU resources and time will be consumed. In order to reduce the time consumed by subsequent operations and improve the efficiency of the program, the resolution of the original image is adjusted. In this way, on the one hand, the amount of image data is reduced, and on the other hand, some tiny noises in the image are eliminated

Among the commonly used image scaling algorithms, there are three types: nearest interpolation, bilinear interpolation, and bicubic interpolation. Here we have tested them separately. The results show that bilinear interpolation achieves a good balance between time consumption and interpolation effect, so bilinear interpolation is used to reduce noise in the original image.

Here is a brief introduction to bilinear interpolation. For an image with a resolution of $w \cdot h$, if we want to change its resolution to $w\prime \cdot h\prime$, we use the nearest four points in the coordinates $P(x, y)$ in the original image to calculate the target point. $P/(x', y/)$ pixel value. The specific practices are as follows:

Let Q_{11}, Q_{12}, Q_{21} and Q_{22} be the nearest four integer points from the distance $P(x, y)$. First, we interpolate in the x direction to get the pixels at R_1, as shown in Eq. (1).

$$f(x, y_1) = \frac{x_2 - x}{x_2 - x_1}f(Q_{11}) + \frac{x - x_1}{x_2 - x_1}f(Q_{21}) \tag{1}$$

Similarly, we can get the pixels at R_2, as shown in Eq. (2).

$$f(x, y_2) = \frac{x_2 - x}{x_2 - x_1}f(Q_{12}) + \frac{x - x_1}{x_2 - x_1}f(Q_{22}) \tag{2}$$

After that, we use the coordinates of R_1 and R_2 to perform interpolation processing in the y direction, and then the pixel value of the target point $P/$ can be obtained, as shown in Eq. (3).

$$f(x, y) = \frac{y_2 - y}{y_2 - y_1}f(x, y_1) + \frac{y - y_1}{y_2 - y_1}(x, y_2) \tag{3}$$

Resolution adjustment can reduce redundant pixels, but it can also make the reduced image appear jagged. To solve this problem, we use mean filter, median filter and Gaussian filter to convolve the compressed image. Among them, compared with other methods, Gaussian filtering can preserve the edges of the image well and has lower distortion.

Binarization. Binarization is an important step of preprocessing. The quality of the processing result determines whether the QR code area and interference area can be accurately located. Since the foreground and background of the RGB image involved in this scene have good discrimination (black and white and other colors), the OTSU algorithm is suitable. The binary image we hope to obtain satisfies the following conditions: the separated QR code area has a regular shape and does not adhere to the background; the color of the QR code area is consistent with the surrounding area; and the interference area is as few as possible.

The commonly used binarization methods mainly include two categories. The first type is the global thresholding method. This method uses the same threshold for the entire image and has low complexity such as the OTSU method. Consequently, the foreground and background of the preprocessed image are also need to be obviously different; the second type of the methods is the adaptive thresholding method, which is also called a local thresholding method. When an image is processed, the thresholds of different coordinates are dissimilar, and thus it is suitable for processing complex backgrounds. Correspondingly, the complexity of the algorithm will be higher.

Here we briefly introduce the principle of commonly used local binarization.

First, for any point P in the image, its pixel is I. We take a neighborhood of the point, calculate the weighted average m of all point pixels in the domain, and take the difference as n. Then compare the size of I and $C = m - n$, so as to determine whether the pixel after the point P binarization takes 0 or 255.

What matters is that we can calculate the weights of the points in the neighborhood in two ways: one is to give the same weight to each point, and the other is to use the Gaussian convolution kernel to give different weight to each point according to the distance from each point to the center point.

Since both types of algorithms can only process single-channel pictures, we need to convert the original RGB image into a grayscale image. In this process, there are maximum value method, average value method, weighted average method, and so on.

Here we compare the traditional method with our method to show why our method works better.

Traditional Processing Methods. First, the image is converted to a grayscale image. Here, we choose a weighted average method and it works like Eq. (4):

$$Gray = 0.3R + 0.59G + 0.11B \tag{4}$$

After that, the OTSU algorithm and two adaptive threshold algorithms are used to obtain the binary image, as shown in Fig. 3, Fig. 4, Fig. 5:

Fig. 3. OTSU method

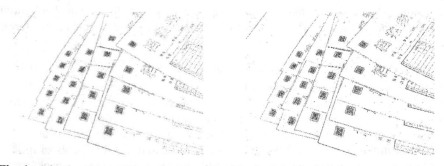

Fig. 4. Adaptive binarization method (gauss)   **Fig. 5.** Adaptive binarization method (mean)

It can be seen that the binarized images obtained in the above three cases do not meet our requirements, which is reflected in two aspects:

First, there are too many point-like interference regions in the image, and some of the interference regions are too close to the QR code, which is not conducive to the extraction of the QR code.

Second, the color of the QR code area and the background area in the image can't be divided clearly.

Our Method. In order to solve the above two problems, and considering the time complexity, we consider the global thresholding method, that is, to expand the difference between the foreground and the background in the grayscale image before using the OTSU algorithm.

Since the color of the portfolio is very close to the skin color in this scene, we use the method in skin color detection. First, the original RGB image color space is converted into YCrCb space, and then the image is separated into three channels of Y, Cr and Cb. Since the channel Y represents brightness, we abandon it to avoid the effects of uneven illumination. The QR code regions and the interference regions in the channel Cr and the channel Cb are clearly colored, so the two channels are used to replace the original grayscale image, and the OTSU algorithm is used for processing. The results show that both channels can separate the QR code area from the background area. As shown in Fig. 6, Fig. 7:

Fig. 6. Channel Cr

Fig. 7. Channel Cb

In the binary image obtained by the channel Cr, the boundary of the corresponding region of each QR code is smooth, but there are slightly more interference regions in the background.

In the binary image obtained by the channel Cb, there are fewer interference regions in the background, but there are certain burrs in the corresponding boundary of each QR code region.

In order to obtain a binary image with less interference area and smooth QR code region, we need to combine the advantages of the two channels, so we reverse the binary image obtained by the channel Cr, and then XOR the processed image with channel Cb, which combines the advantages of both images.

Since the obtained QR code image is black in the binary image and the background is white, and we hope that the background area can be connected as much as possible to eliminate the black holes in the background, the morphological closed operation is adopted.

Through the above operations, we can visually see the target area and the background area. Because there are obvious color mutations at the boundary, we can perform contour detection based on this feature, and obtain a binary image containing only the outline of each area. Here we test the commonly used edge detection operator Sobel operator, Laplace operator and Canny operator respectively. The results show that the Canny operator detects the edge of the contour and the pseudo edge.

3.3 Positioning

In the part of QR code positioning, because some complicated algorithms are involved, and these algorithms have been implemented in OpenCV, in the following part we only introduce the call of the corresponding function of each algorithm, if you want to understand the specific implementation of the relevant algorithm, please see the official OpenCV source code.

Contour Positioning. Since the image used may not be incomplete during the shooting process, the result of the contour detection may be discontinuous, so we need to do further processing. Our goal here is to close the contours so that each contour becomes a closed curve. The common method is a polygonal curve approximation, and the *approxPolyDP* function in OpenCV can help us. This has the advantage of reducing the number of vertices per contour, simplifies the image outline to a certain extent, and also makes the contour continuous.

First, we use the *findContours* function in OpenCV for contour detection. Since the outline of the hierarchy will include many layers, there is a nesting relationship between the layers. In this task, we only need to locate each target area, so we only need to detect an outline for each target area. In order to avoid missing defects in the corresponding position of the original image area, here we choose the outer contour. After using the *findContours* function, the coordinates of the points contained in each outline will be stored separately.

Since the image used may not be incomplete during the shooting process, the result of the contour detection may be discontinuous, so we need to do further processing. Our goal here is to close the contours so that each contour becomes a closed curve. The common method is a polygonal curve approximation, and the *approxPolyDP* function in OpenCV can help us. This has the advantage of reducing the number of vertices per contour, simplifies the image outline to a certain extent, and also makes the contour continuous.

Area Filtering. Next we filter the resulting contour and remove the contours that are not part of the QR code area.

Since our target area has an approximately quadrilateral shape, and the shape of other interference areas is mostly irregular, we can filter them according to this feature.

First, we obtain the minimum enclosing rectangle according to the vertices of each contour. Then we calculate the perimeter of each contour, the enclosed area and the perimeter and area of its enclosing rectangle. Table 1 and Table 2 show some measured data.

Table 1. The perimeters of the contours and the enclosing rectangles

Contour/pix			Rectangular/pix		
130.2	132.3	128.0	178.4	181.0	177.5
126.4	103.5	120.0	170.6	139.3	165.9
122.6	102.7	97.2	171.5	139.6	132.3
111.8	101.9	96.0	152.7	136.5	129.9
111.3	0.0	0.0	160.2	0.0	0.0
98.8	106.2	7.2	136.2	149.1	14.4
44.8	68.0	88.9	89.6	116.8	124.8
18.1	0.0	19.8	36.2	0.0	39.7
283.2	100.6	102.1	286.9	140.0	146.2
91.9	92.4	2057.0	125.1	128.7	2323.3

Table 2. The areas of the contours and the enclosing rectangles

Contour/pix^2			Rectangular/pix^2		
1893.0	1981.0	1904.5	1987.9	2043.5	1962.0
1754.0	1181.0	1604.0	1816.0	1211.8	1720.0
1734.0	1169.5	1019.5	1823.7	1217.5	1089.0
1402.0	1116.0	992.5	1453.1	1164.0	1050.5
1474.5	0.0	0.0	1594.8	0.0	0.0
1088.0	1257.5	0.0	1158.8	1386.7	0.0
0.0	149.5	903.0	0.0	492.0	973.0
0.0	0.0	0.0	0.0	0.0	0.0
31.0	1144.5	1190.0	4756.2	1225.0	1318.2
922.0	950.5	103.5	975.9	1034.6	289068

By Analyzing the Data in Tables 1 and 2, We Find that:

For a normal target area, the perimeter of the contour is not much different from the perimeter of the corresponding enclosing rectangle. However, for the interference area, a part of the contour perimeter is not much different from the perimeter of the enclosing rectangle, and the other part is half of the perimeter of the enclosing rectangle.

For a normal target area, the contour area is approximately equal to the area of the corresponding enclosing rectangle, but for the interference area, the areas of the two are different or both are 0.

Therefore, based on these results, we first filter out the area of the enclosing rectangle with a small length and width. Then, calculate the ratio of the area of the enclosing rectangle to the area of the contour. If the ratio is approximately 1, it is the target area. If the ratio is too large, then it is the interference area.

After the above operation, the interference area in the contour is basically filtered out, and if other interference areas still exist, it can be excluded in the QR code recognition process.

3.4 Recognition

QR Code Correction. Since the QR code recognition library ZBar we use has poor support for the deformation of the QR code, we initially get that the target area is not a standard square, so we need to get the contour area before the QR code recognition. The perspective transformation is performed to restore the shape of the inclined area to further improve the success rate of the QR code recognition.

Perspective transformation is a kind of nonlinear transformation, which can project the original image into a new plane of view, and then correct the image. Equation (5) shows how the transmission transformation is calculated

$$\left[x', y', z'\right] = [u, v, w] \begin{bmatrix} a_{11} & a_{12} & a_{13} \\ a_{21} & a_{22} & a_{23} \\ a_{31} & a_{32} & a_{33} \end{bmatrix} \tag{5}$$

In the above formula, $[x = x'/z', y = y'/z']$ represents the transformed pixel coordinates, $[u, v, w]$ represents the pixel coordinates before the transformation, and a is the matrix of the transmission transformation. Since we deal with the image transformation of a QR plane, w and a33 are always equal to 1.

According to the transmission transformation, we can calculate the corrected QR code area. First, we calculate the coordinates of the corresponding points in the original image according to the coordinates of the vertices in the contour and sort the vertices (because we have reduced the image during preprocessing), then we use the perspective transformation to deform the corresponding regions in the original image. Here we call the *getPerspectiveTransform* function in OpenCV to get the perspective transformation matrix, and then call the *warpPerspective* function to perform affine transformation, and finally get the corrected QR code region.

QR Code Recognition. After that, we call the open source QR code recognition library ZBar to detect the corrected QR code region, and coordinate the region where the QR code exists.

4 Experiments and Analysis

Parameter setting: In the resolution adjustment section, the resolution of the input image is 1440 * 1080, so the resolution is adjusted to 800*600. In the binarization part, the default parameter setting is adopted in the OTSU method, and the filter used by the adaptive binarization (Gauss) is 3 * 3. In the edge detection part, the lower limit of Canny operator is 80 and the upper limit is 240. In the area filtering section, filter out areas where the length and width of the enclosing rectangle are less than 25 pixels or the width and height ratio of the enclosing rectangle is less than 1.4, and areas where the ratio of the area of the enclosing circle to the area of the enclosing rectangle is less than 0.4.

Experimental setup: We selected 30 images taken from different angles, including different numbers of QR codes, to test the missing detection of the target area and the correct rate of decoding the QR code. Table 3 shows the test results.

Table 3. QR code recognition rate (recognized QR codes / total QR codes)

QR code recognition rate					
20/20	15/15	20/20	12/13	20/20	20/20
20/20	12/13	11/13	19/20	9/9	20/20
8/9	13/13	15/15	9/9	20/20	12/12
15/15	20/20	11/12	11/13	15/15	9/9
11/12	10/12	9/9	15/15	19/20	12/12

It can be seen from Table 3 that our algorithm has a good recognition effect on a variety of QR codes, but in some cases, the QR code cannot be recognized occasionally. After analysis, we found that when the portfolio is not empty and the shooting angle is too oblique, it will cause different degrees and types of distortion in the QR code in the captured image, which may result in the QR code not being decoded. Therefore, our algorithm applies to multiple QR code recognition that is less severely deformed.

Table 4. Regional omissions (missing areas/redundant areas)

Regional omissions					
0/0	0/0	0/0	0/1	0/0	0/0
0/0	0/1	2/0	1/1	0/0	0/2
0/0	0/0	0/1	1/2	0/1	0/0
0/0	0/0	2/0	0/1	0/0	0/0
0/0	0/0	0/1	0/0	0/0	0/1

As Table 4 shows, our algorithm can detect and separate all regions containing the QR code in most cases. For the extra interference area in the detection, we can eliminate it by detecting whether there is a QR code. For the missing QR code area in the detection, we suggest to put the QR code in the center of the image when the image is taken to help reduce the deformation of the QR code area.

5 Conclusion and Future Work

In this paper, we first propose the use of QR code to store key archive information, and design a method of simultaneously inputting multiple pieces of archive information, to solve the problem of low efficiency of document management information inputting in the Internet of Things era. The results show that, compared with the existing method of entering one file at a time, the method we designed can simultaneously enter the information of multiple files at the same time, and the number of simultaneous entries can also be adjusted, which has a good expansion. So our method not only improves the efficiency of file information entry, but also provides new solutions for data entry in the existing intelligent file management system.

Of course, our method still has some limitations. In our experiment, the QR codes of all file labels are of the same type and the same size, and when entering specific files, you may encounter situations where different types of files are simultaneously entered. In addition, when multiple files are overlapped, the types and degrees of deformation of different QR codes are not consistent, and how to correct the deformed QR codes becomes very challenging. Therefore, we will conduct further research on these issues in future work to build a more intelligent file management system.

Acknowledgment. This work is supported by the National Key R&D Program of China under Grant 2018YFC0831300, China Postdoctoral Science Foundation under grant number: 2018M641172 and the National Natural Science Foundation of China under Grant 61701019.

References

1. Limin, L.: IoT and a sustainable city. In: 5th International Conference on Energy and Environment Research (ICEER), pp. 23–27. Elsevier Ltd, Prague, Czech Republic (2018)
2. Rajithkumar, B.K.: IoT based integrated health monitoring system. Int. J. Eng. Sci. Res., 225–231 (2018)
3. Praveen, M., Harini, V.: NB-IOT based smart car parking system. In: 2019 International Conference on Smart Structures and Systems (ICSSS), pp. 1–5. Chennai, India (2019)
4. Zhi, L., Guo, L., Xinjun, L.: IoT-based tracking and tracing platform for prepackaged food supply chain. In: Industrial Management and Data Systems, pp. 1906–1916 (2017)
5. Tiwari, S.: An introduction to QR code technology. In: 2016 International Conference on Information Technology (ICIT), pp. 39–44. Bhubaneswar (2016)
6. Pandey, J., Kazmi, S.I.A., Hayat, M.S., Ahmed, I.: A study on implementation of smart library systems using IoT. In: 2017 International Conference on Infocom Technologies and Unmanned Systems (Trends and Future Directions) (ICTUS), pp. 193–197. Dubai (2017)
7. Sa-ngiampak, J., Hirankanokkul, C., Sunthornyotin, Y.: LockerSwarm: an IoT-based smart locker system with access sharing. In: 2019 IEEE International Smart Cities Conference (ISC2), pp. 587–592. Casablanca, Morocco (2019)
8. Jie, S., Linqian, D., Jing, S.: Management of university endowment fund archives under the background of big data. In: 2016 8th International Conference on Information Technology in Medicine and Education (ITME), pp. 584–586. Fuzhou, China (2016)
9. Wang, Y.: Design and implementation of electronic archives information management under cloud computing platform. In: 2019 11th International Conference on Measuring Technology and Mechatronics Automation (ICMTMA), pp. 154–158. Qiqihar, China (2019)

10. Guigui, Y., Gengguo, C., Kaomin, B.: Design and realization of equipment's archives management system based on Struts2 and Hibernate. In: 2010 Second International Conference on Information Technology and Computer Science, pp. 466–469. Kiev (2010)
11. Xiang, W., Yuhang, W., Kaiwen, H.: The Design of file management system based on website and Qr. In: 2019 International Conference on Smart Grid and Electrical Automation (ICSGEA), pp. 157–160. Xiangtan, China (2019)
12. Cui, Z., Cui, B.: Research on low cost student electronic archives management system in high-concurrency environment. In: 2020 IEEE 10th International Conference on Electronics Information and Emergency Communication (ICEIEC), pp. 248–252. Beijing, China (2020)
13. Zhi, L.: Design and implementation of the comprehensive archives information digital management system. In: 2012 2nd International Conference on Consumer Electronics, Communications and Networks (CECNet), pp. 1764–1767. Yichang, China (2012)
14. Xu, J., et al.: Archiving system of rural land contractual management right data using multithreading and distributed storage technology. In: 2019 8th International Conference on Agro-Geoinformatics (Agro-Geoinformatics), pp. 1–5. Istanbul, Turkey (2019)

OAuth-Based Access Control Framework
for IoT Systems

Min-Zheng Shieh[1]([✉]) [iD], Jui-Chun Liu[1] [iD], Yi-Chih Kao[1] [iD], Shi-Chun Tsai[2] [iD],
and Yi-Bing Lin[2] [iD]

[1] Information Technology Service Center, National Chiao Tung University,
Hsinchu, Taiwan
{mzshieh,g0737,ykao}@nctu.edu.tw
[2] Department of Computer Science, National Chiao Tung University,
Hsinchu, Taiwan
{sctsai,liny}@cs.nctu.edu.tw

Abstract. With the emergence of the Internet of Things (IoT) technology, the number of related devices has been increasing at a very rapid speed. The security of IoT systems has become a crucial issue. Due to the complex IoT environment and users' unawareness, such issues are usually hard to resolve. Many IoT systems lack proper access control mechanisms and suffer from various large scale attacks. We need a robust and effective secure access control to build IoT systems that retain user privacy and data integrity with high availability.

In this paper, we propose an access control framework based on OAuth 2.0, with which we constructed a remote control system for various devices. The secured authentication schemes prevent possible private data leaks. The proposed framework provides flexibility for further functional extensions with new IoT devices.

Keywords: Access control · Authentication · Internet of Things · OAuth

1 Introduction

An integrated system with IoT devices often consists of embedded sensors, actuators, communication hardware, and software. The devices collect various data from the built-in sensors and generally communicate over a heterogeneous network. IoT systems add much more value to their hardware by providing applications in automation, artificial intelligence, etc. However, IoT systems have many inherent security threats and challenges due to their system scale [1], the heterogeneity of networks [2], various communication protocols [3], and the lack of proper access control [4]. Open Web Application Security Project (OWASP)

This work was financially supported by the Center for Open Intelligent Connectivity from The Featured Areas Research Center Program within the framework of the Higher Education Sprout Project by the Ministry of Education (MOE) in Taiwan.

Y.-B. Lin and D.-J. Deng (Eds.): SGIoT 2020, LNICST 354, pp. 208–219, 2021.
https://doi.org/10.1007/978-3-030-69514-9_17

[5] lists the "top 10 things to avoid when building, deploying, or managing IoT systems" to show adversaries in diverging aspects. It is a crucial issue to create IoT systems against various attacks.

Khan et al. [2] pointed out one essential characteristic of IoT devices is the limit of resources, such as electricity, computing power, and memory. When the adversary attacks an IoT system, the devices consume much more and may deplete certain kinds of resources. Without proper security control, there are risks of system meltdown. Chiang et al. [6] and Cirani et al. [7] showed that it is unrealistic to deploy complex access control protocol or to perform encryption algorithms on IoT devices since the resources are too limited. There are practical needs for simple access control protocols and lightweight authentication mechanisms.

Chiang et al. [6] suggested that many IoT devices may have a long life cycle, but the threats will become more advanced with the development of new technology. Therefore, we should keep enhancing IoT systems against new threats. In Sicari et al. [8] and Anggorojati et al. [9], they both addressed that IoT applications must satisfy security and privacy requirements. After all, IoT devices pervasively involve human life. To protect privacy, we need proper access control and authentication mechanism to prevent unauthorized accesses of sensitive personal information.

In a pilot project at National Chiao Tung University, we have a dormitory [10] installed with several IoT systems, including laundry machines, drying machines, air conditioners. These systems are provided by different suppliers and developed with various protocols, including WiFi, TCP/IP, HTTP, TaiSEIA [11], etc. Moreover, none of the system providers integrates their system with an authentication system. To ensure proper access to the tenants, we have to incorporate these IoT systems into the smart campus system. In this paper, we focus on secure access control and privacy protection issues. We create a framework to integrate IoT systems with the campus authentication system via the OAuth 2.0 protocol.

The OAuth 2.0 protocol allows information systems to access the private data authenticated by the users. For example, the user may grant access to their room number to an agent software. The agent will provide access to the air conditioner controller system in the private networks and configure the air conditioner at the users' demand. With OAuth 2.0, we can even implement application without revealing information to client software, such as smartphone apps and web browsers. OAuth server synchronizes the user data with the other databases in the data center. Thus, there is no need to directly modify the architectures of IoT systems provided by the vendors.

Based on the proposed framework, we develop a universal remote control platform for smart home devices. Users may access the IoT devices properly via smartphone apps or web-based graphical user interface (GUI). We create an agent to deliver users' commands to the home appliances, such as air conditioners in a room. Developers can compose their client software over the HTTPS protocol and OAuth 2.0. There is no need to involve any underlying heterogeneous communications to IoT devices. The framework also creates a barrier between the users and the IoT systems. Therefore, we allocate private IP addresses to the IoT devices or their gateway. With such configuration, we prevent all direct communication and attacks from the public networks and among different IoT subsystems. Thus, the adversaries can only launch cyberattacks to the IoT devices in the same private networks, which are much harder to compromise.

Our approach is flexible to integrate new IoT subsystems into the existing systems. Adding an IoT subsystem means creating an agent to access it via its application programming interface (API) and the authentication system via the OAuth 2.0 protocol. Without modifying the IoT subsystem, it is much easier to maintain the software. We can also apply the framework for the smart appliance system in a residential facility. The facility will grant access to the tenants upon their check-in, and the facility will revoke their access rights when they checkout.

This paper is organized as follows. Section 2 reviews related background and works. Section 3 illustrates the proposed access control mechanism for IoT systems with a working example. Section 4 shows the security of the implementation. At last, we discuss future works and briefly conclude this paper in Sect. 5.

2   Background and Related Works

OAuth 2.0, often called OAuth in the following, is an open standard for open authorization. It enables third-party applications to obtain limited access to private data, without having to provide the access permission to third-party applications directly. RFC6749 [13] defines the roles of the OAuth authorization flow as follows.

- The resources owner authorizes the client to access the private data in the resource server.
- The authorization server is responsible for issuing an access token after obtaining authorization from the resource owner.
- The resource server is responsible for storing private data, allowing the clients to access private data according to the access token.
- The client accesses private data on behalf of the resource owner.

Many websites have adopted authorization and single sign-on (SSO) in recent years, with OAuth 2.0 being one of the most popular frameworks. Fett et al. [12] summarized that the prime identity providers, including Amazon, Facebook, Google, and GitHub, use OAuth 2.0. Being one of the most popular SSO systems on the web, OAuth enables billions of users to log in at millions of services and to authorize selected private data to applications.

There are many existing research results about IoT applications based on OAuth. Emerson et al. [14] utilized OAuth to provide a secure authentication mechanism for the IoT network. The security manager efficiently manages the database with a list of authorized users who can access the IoT network. In this approach, only authenticated users are allowed to access the IoT network, protecting the IoT network from unauthenticated users. However, this research does not present any testing and verification results. Performance issues may exist when applied to complex network environments. Cirani et al. [7] proposed an approach targeting HTTP/CoAP services to provide an authorization framework by invoking an external OAuth-based authorization service. The proposed framework can be integrated with IoT scenarios to provide security assurance for IoT. The research by Fremantle et al. [15] combines OAuth with MQTT to let OAuth as a part of the MQTT protocol flow and within an MQTT broker, making federated and user-directed control decisions. Siris et al. [16] presented models for utilizing blockchain and smart contract technology with the widely used OAuth open authorization framework to provide delegated authorization for constrained IoT devices.

3 Proposed Framework

In this paper, we propose an access control mechanism for the IoT remote control system in a dormitory based on the integration of OAuth 2.0 and user databases. With proper access control, we ensure that the connection between user devices and IoT devices is secure. OAuth authorizes legitimate third-party applications to access private data to ensure each tenant can only control corresponding IoT devices in their room after authentication. We had constructed the IoT remote control system for the air conditioner in a dormitory allowing users to configure air-conditioning functions and check IoT device status.

3.1 Architecture

Figure 1 depicts the architecture of the proposed access control framework for IoT systems. The main components include User Device, IoT Agent, IoT Subsystem, OAuth Server, and Database. In particular, IoT Agent, OAuth Server, and Database are located in the data center, whereas IoT Subsystem is in the private network.

User Device (Fig. 1a) could be any device that has access to the IoT remote control mobile apps or web browsers, such as smartphones, laptops, or any other mobile devices. The IoT remote control apps or web browsers provide web-based GUI for users to interact with the devices in the IoT Subsystem (Fig. 1c) via IoT Agent (Fig. 1b). IoT Agent resides in a virtual machine installed in the data center that systematically manages the features of the IoT Subsystem and allows users to access the IoT Subsystem properly. IoT Agent and IoT Subsystem interact via Application Programming Interface (API). Authenticated users can read the sensors and configure the IoT devices through the IoT Agent, which redirects the client software to the OAuth Server (Fig. 1d) to initiate the authorization code grant flow for the first access. After that, the User Device receives a token for accessing the IoT Subsystem.

User Device may communicate with the IoT agent and OAuth Server over public networks. The IoT subsystem can only interact with the IoT Agent by using its API. The separation guarantees that IoT Subsystem is immune from cyberattacks outside of its private network unless IoT Agent is compromised. For user privacy protection, the OAuth protocol allows users to decide which data in the database (Fig. 1e) is accessible by the IoT Agent. With the proper design of IoT Agent, we can control what data can be revealed to the IoT subsystem and the client software.

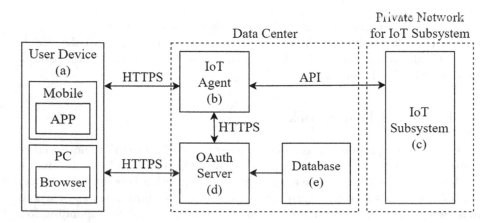

Fig. 1. Access control framework for IoT systems

3.2   Use Case

In this subsection, we show a use case of the proposed framework. We construct a remote control system for the air conditioners (Fig. 2) in the dormitory. Here, we use NCTU OAuth service (Fig. 2g) and Resident Database (Fig. 2h) to provide the user information. The air conditioner IoT subsystem consists of an IoT Gateway (Fig. 2c), one hundred Access Points (Fig. 2d), and two hundred air conditioners (Fig. 2f). We install an IoT Dongle (Fig. 2e) to each air conditioner.

The API used for the interactions between the IoT Agent and the IoT Gateway is based on WebSocket. The IoT Agent retrieves the information of the air conditioner system from the IoT Gateway, where the information contains underlying devices' name and type, managed device list, connected device list, device configurations, and sensor values. We can configure the air conditioners through the WebSocket API. Since IoT Agent itself maintains the information of the IoT subsystem and user binding tables, the status of each IoT Dongle will be updated simultaneously when the IoT Dongle connects to the IoT Gateway. The customized IoT Agent provides HTTP-based RESTful APIs for User Device to display or operate the air conditioner on the IoT remote control apps or web browsers.

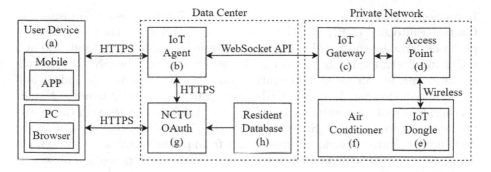

Fig. 2. Remote control system for air conditioners

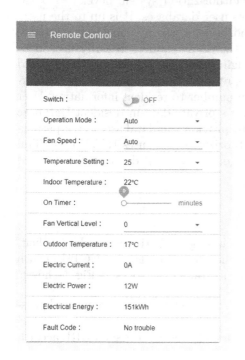

Fig. 3. IoT remote control web GUI

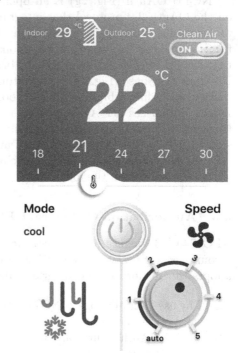

Fig. 4. IoT remote control app GUI

IoT Dongle is embedded in the air conditioner to control air-conditioning functions and possesses a control module that supports the TaiSEIA [11] protocol enabling smart appliances to be interconnected. This protocol features cross-vendor management that solves the vendor-dependent issue, providing optimized flexibility for IoT device management. IoT Dongle establishes Wi-Fi Protected Access (WPA/WPA2) connection to wireless Access Point (AP) (Fig. 2d) in each room via Wi-Fi, and the IoT Gateway gathers the traffic from each room's AP. After the connection is completed, IoT Dongle then establishes Transport

Layer Security (TLS) connection to IoT Gateway. By using secure Transmission Control Protocol (TCP), IoT Gateway sends control commands to IoT Dongle to perform air-conditioning functions. The IoT remote control web and app GUIs are illustrated in Fig. 3 and Fig. 4, users can adjust the ON/OFF switch, operation mode, fan speed, temperature, and can also monitor the indoor and outdoor temperature. With the GUIs, users can conveniently monitor the air conditioner's real-time status and configure control functions through the smartphone app or web browser. Since we deploy the air conditioner subsystem in the designated private network, all direct traffic from public networks are prevented. Thus, we keep the IoT system away from cyberattacks initiated in public networks.

NCTU OAuth (Fig. 2g) is an open authorization system developed based on the OAuth 2.0 protocol that integrates user databases. It is up to the users to determine whether their data is authorized for use by third-party applications, providing third-party applications the data required to verify user identity. NCTU OAuth is responsible for bridging the User Device, IoT Agent, and Resident Database (Fig. 2h), which stores resident information and room information, including a binding table of room number to resident information. User Device authorizes IoT Agent to access user's private data in Resident Database through NCTU OAuth without having to provide the database access permission to IoT Agent. The whole OAuth authorization flow uses HTTPS RESTful API for communication and data exchange, and we will describe the detailed authorization flow in the following.

3.3 Authorization Code Grant Flow

RFC6749 [13] defines four grant types, including authorization code, implicit, resource owner password credentials, and client credentials. The NCTU OAuth adopts the authorization code grant, and the grant flow works as Fig. 5 shows:

(a) The user initially logs in NCTU OAuth by entering the username and password on User Device.
(b) NCTU OAuth returns an authorization code and a redirected URL according to the required scope.
(c) The client software on User Device sends the authorization code to the IoT Agent after redirecting.
(d) IoT Agent uses the authorization code provided by the User Device to exchange an access token from NCTU OAuth via a POST request.
(e) NCTU OAuth issues an access token and returns to the IoT Agent.
(f) IoT Agent uses the access token to access device information and user information (e.g., room number and resident information) from NCTU OAuth via a GET request.
(g) NCTU OAuth returns device information and user information.
(h) IoT Agent sends a SESSION_TOKEN to User Device for further authentication.

(i) User Device gets the managed device list and device configurations via the SESSION_TOKEN.

(j) IoT Agent responses data.

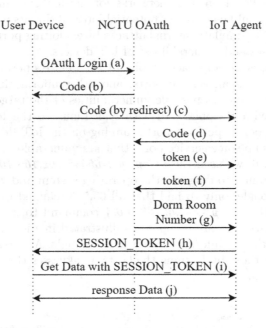

Fig. 5. Authorization code grant flow

Since NCTU OAuth only authenticates the identity of User Device, any other clients within the proposed architecture cannot access the information of User Device, ensuring confidentiality for the network environment and preventing private data leakage.

3.4 Summary

IoT Agent maintains a binding table associating each room to the devices under management. Therefore, when IoT Agent retrieves the binding table and resident information from NCTU OAuth, the devices in the room match with the room's tenant. In this way, the User Device can effectively and safely communicate with the IoT Dongle. It is easy to reconfigure the devices with the binding table and readjust the binding when the tenants move.

This paper proposes an access control framework for the IoT system based on OAuth. This framework only allows valid users to access resources and eliminates malicious adversaries and attackers. Authenticated users are limited in operating the devices they have the permission to; they can not tamper with other IoT devices deliberately, thereby ensuring the integrity of the data and enhancing the security of the network.

4   System Security and Discussion

4.1   Vulnerability Scanning

Even though we allocate private networks for the IoT system, which prevents cyberattacks from public networks, potential internal threats within private networks still exist. We simulate internal attacks by exploiting port scanning to find poooiblo weaknesses and vulnerabilities of IoT devices.

Port scanning is an approach to obtain the device operating system (OS) version, software version, service ports, and other information. Through this information, we can collect possible vulnerabilities of the target device. In this test, we connected a Raspberry Pi with Kali Linux to the IoT Gateway. We used Nmap [17] tool to perform port scanning on the IoT dongle to see if the IoT dongle opens up some service ports that are vulnerable to security attacks. As shown in Fig. 6, we used the *nmap -p 1-65535 192.168.100.4* command to perform port scanning to diagnose the operating system and various services of the target IoT dongle, only to find that all 65,535 scanned ports were filtered. Again, we used the *nmap -A 192.168.100.4* command to probe the OS information of the hosts that are mapped, as illustrated in Fig. 7. However, Nmap cannot interpret the OS information of the IoT dongle. As a result, the possibility of malicious attacks by learning the hosts' weaknesses through vulnerability scanning is reduced.

```
root@kali:~# nmap -p1-65535 192.168.100.4
Starting Nmap 7.80 ( https://nmap.org ) at 2019-12-24 06:19 UTC
Nmap scan report for 192.168.100.4
Host is up (0.0030s latency).
All 65535 scanned ports on 192.168.100.4 are filtered
MAC Address: 9E:█████████:3B (Unknown)

Nmap done: 1 IP address (1 host up) scanned in 1328.33 seconds
```

Fig. 6. Scanning all 65,535 ports using nmap -p 1-65535

4.2   Security Testing

Unlike many previous works, we send the implemented remote control system and its mobile app to a third party for verifying their security. Chunghwa Telecom Laboratories Testing Center tested the system with schemes based on "Basic Security Testing Baseline for Mobile Applications V3.0" [18] defined by the Industrial Development Bureau, Ministry of Economic Affairs, Taiwan. The security of the IoT remote control app and its back-end server is tested and certified by Chunghwa Telecom Laboratories Testing Center. The tests include but not limited to the following items.

```
root@kali:~# nmap -A 192.168.100.4
Starting Nmap 7.80 ( https://nmap.org ) at 2019-10-24 15:37 UTC
Nmap scan report for 192.168.100.4
Host is up (0.0039s latency).
All 1000 scanned ports on 192.168.100.4 are filtered
MAC Address: 9E:          :3B (Unknown)
Too many fingerprints match this host to give specific OS details
Network Distance: 1 hop

TRACEROUTE
HOP RTT     ADDRESS
1   3.91 ms 192.168.100.4

Nmap done: 1 IP address (1 host up) scanned in 43.77 seconds
```

Fig. 7. Scanning the OS information using namp -A

1. Authentication and authorization

   - The app offers an appropriate authentication mechanism to identify the user.
   - The app authorizes users by user's identity.
   - The app prevents users from entering common injection strings.

2. Transmission security

   - The app securely encrypted transmitted private data by using an appropriate and effective key length of the encryption algorithms.
   - The app avoids connecting and transferring private data to servers without a valid certificate.
   - The app avoids using regular SESSION_TOKEN, and the SESSION_TOKEN does not relate to time, regular numbers or strings, or anything related to the user's submission.

The implemented system fully complies both the security baselines for mobile applications and server-side defined in "Basic Security Testing Baseline for Mobile Applications V3.0". It means that the systems implemented under the same framework are likely to provide the same security and pass the same test.

4.3   Discussion

In previous subsections, we showed that the implementation of the remote control system for the dormitory air conditioner system, including the back-end and the client software, is resilient to major cyberattacks. The framework can isolate every single integrated IoT subsystem in a private network so that we can provide the same security to any new integrated IoT subsystem.

The proposed framework is not only suitable for applications on campus IoT systems. Some facilities, like hotels and fitness centers, have similar needs. Hotels may install several smart home appliance systems in the guest rooms and provide a mobile app as a remote controller for the guests. Nowadays, hotel chains like

Marriott International and Hilton Worldwide have their account system for their members. Using our proposed framework, one can build a remote control system with the authentication system without much effort. The guests may control the IoT devices in the room with their mobile phones upon check-in, and the system automatically revokes their access right after they check out.

5   Conclusion

In this paper, we proposed an OAuth-base framework for integrating IoT systems on campus or a similar facility. The framework enables us to use the campus authentication system to construct an access control system for the IoT systems; even the vendors do not provide such a function. The framework reduces the security risks by separating IoT subsystems into independent private networks. For privacy, the client software may only access the necessary information by using the OAuth authorization code grant flow.

We specifically built the remote control system for the air conditioners with the proposed framework. With the performance test results, we have shown that the remote control system is efficient. For security proof, it passed the security tests and obtained the certificate from Chunghwa Telecom Laboratories Testing Center. We are seeking new applications on more smart IoT devices and opportunities on similar facilities, such as chained hotels and fitness centers.

References

1. Andy, S., Rahardjo, B., Hanindhito, B.: Attack scenarios and security analysis of MQTT communication protocol in IoT system. 2017 4th International Conference on Electrical Engineering, Computer Science and Informatics (EECSI), pp. 1–6. IEEE, Yogyakarta, Indonesia (2017)
2. Khan, M.A., Salah, K.: IoT security: review, blockchain solutions, and open challenges. Future Gener. Comput. Syst. **82**, 395–411 (2018)
3. Ojo, M., Adami, D., Giordano, S.: A SDN-IoT architecture with NFV implementation. In: 2016 IEEE Globecom Workshops (GC Wkshps), pp. 1–6. IEEE, Washington, DC, USA (2016)
4. Ouaddah, A., Mousannif, H., Abou Elkalam, A., Ouahman, A.A.: Access control in the Internet of Things: Big challenges and new opportunities. Comput. Netw. **112**, 237–262 (2017)
5. OWASP Internet of Thing Top 10. https://owasp.org/www-project-internet-of-things/. Accessed 10 Aug 2020
6. Chiang, M., Zhang, T.: Fog and IoT: an overview of research opportunities. IEEE Internet Things J. **3**(6), 854–864 (2016)
7. Cirani, S., Picone, M., Gonizzi, P., Veltri, L., Ferrari, G.: Iot-oas: an oauth-based authorization service architecture for secure services in iot scenarios. IEEE Sens. J. **15**(2), 1224–1234 (2014)
8. Sicari, S., Rizzardi, A., Grieco, L.A., Coen-Porisini, A.: Security, privacy and trust in Internet of Things: the road ahead. Comput. Netw. **76**, 146–164 (2015)

9. Anggorojati, B., Mahalle, P.N., Prasad, N.R., Prasad, R.: Capability-based access control delegation model on the federated IoT network. In: The 15th International Symposium on Wireless Personal Multimedia Communications, pp. 604–608. IEEE, Taipei, Taiwan (2012)
10. Lin, Y.-B., Shieh, M.-Z., Lin, Y.-W.: DormTalk: edge computing for the dormitory applications on campus. IET Networks **8**(3), 179–186 (2018)
11. TaiSEIA 101 Interconnection protocol for devices in smart home. http://www. taiseia.org.tw/Affairs/. Accessed 10 Aug 2020
12. Fett, D., Küsters, R., Schmitz, G.: A comprehensive formal security analysis of OAuth 2.0. In: Proceedings of the 2016 ACM SIGSAC Conference on Computer and Communications Security, pp. 1204–1215. ACM, Vienna, Austria (2016)
13. The OAuth 2.0 Authorization Framework. https://tools.ietf.org/html/rfc6749. Accessed 10 Aug 2020
14. Emerson, S., Choi, Y.-K., Hwang, D.-Y., Kim, K.-S., Kim, K.-H.: An OAuth based authentication mechanism for IoT networks. In: 2015 International Conference on Information and Communication Technology Convergence (ICTC), pp. 1072–1074. IEEE, Jeju, South Korea (2015)
15. Fremantle, P., Aziz, B., Kopecký, J., Scott, P.: Federated identity and access management for the internet of things. In: 2014 International Workshop on Secure Internet of Things, pp. 10–17. IEEE, Wroclaw, Poland (2014)
16. Siris, V.A., Dimopoulos, D., Fotiou, N., Voulgaris, S., Polyzos, G.C.: OAuth 2.0 meets blockchain for authorization in constrained IoT environments. In: 2019 IEEE 5th World Forum on Internet of Things (WF-IoT), pp. 364–367. IEEE, Limerick, Ireland (2019)
17. Nmap: the Network Mapper - Free Security Scanner. https://nmap.org/. Accessed 10 Aug 2020
18. Basic Security Testing Baseline for Mobile Applications v3.0. https://www. mas.org.tw/spaw2/uploads/files/benchmark/Basic-Security-Testing-Baseline-for-Mobile-Applications-v3.0.pdf. Accessed 10 Aug 2020

A Multi-channel Anti-collision Algorithm in Multi-reader RFID Networks

Zhiyong Ding, Jianying Li, Mao Yang$^{(\boxtimes)}$, Zhongjiang Yan, Bo Li,
and Wenhui Chen

School of Electronics and Information,
Northwestern Polytechnical University, Xi'an, China
dingzhiyong@mail.nwpu.edu.cn, {yangmao,zhjyan,libo.npu}@nwpu.edu.cn

Abstract. In order to solve the problem of identification collision in multi-reader Radio Frequency Identification (RFID) systems, this paper proposes a multi-channel anti-collision algorithm based on grouping strategy named McAnCo. In this algorithm, the interference types among readers are classified and modeled, and then the vertex coloring algorithm in graph theory is used to group the readers with mutual interference. The readers in the same group can work at the same frequency and time slot, while the readers in different groups in the same set can work at the same time slot in different frequency, so that the maximum number of readers can work simultaneously without interference. Simulation results show that, compared with distributed color selection (DCS) algorithm, hierarchical Q-learning (HiQ) algorithm and neighborhood friendly anti-collision scheme (NFRA) algorithm, the proposed algorithm effectively prevent reader collision and raise the identification efficiency of the system.

Keywords: Anti-collision · RFID · Readers · Tags

1 Introduction

In recent years, the Internet of Things (IoT) [1] is developing rapidly and becoming increasingly popular. It has been found everywhere in our daily life, such as the Electronic the collection (ETC) system free of parking fees, the card swiping system on campus, the smart home system, and etc. According to official statistics, global Internet penetration increased from 12% in 2013 to 65% in 2019 [1]. The complete radio frequency identification (RFID) system includes reader and electronic tag application system [2,3]. As the core of IoT technology, RFID stores all kinds of data of physical infrastructure into tags, so as to integrate physical facilities and data center into an integrated platform and make the IoT run better [4].

In RFID technology, the core part is tag identification technology. The rate of tag identification determines the performance of RFID system. The configuration

Y.-B. Lin and D.-J. Deng (Eds.): SGIoT 2020, LNICST 354, pp. 220–238, 2021.
https://doi.org/10.1007/978-3-030-69514-9_18

scheme of single reader is difficult to overcome new challenges. In many new scenario, it is required to complete the identification of a large number of tags in a short time. Therefore, there is a configuration scheme of placing multiple readers in RFID system. But in the multi-reader RFID system, there has a new form of collision called Multi-reader collision [5]. In the process of tag identification, multi-reader system will cause a lot of packet loss and of course identification failure due to this collision, which will seriously affect the performance of the system [11].

There are three types of collisions in multi-reader system: 1) the collision between tags [6], 2) the collision between readers [7] and 3) the collision between tags and readers [8]. The collision between tags is caused by multiple tags replying to the reader at the same time after the reader sends information to all tags. At present, there are many mature anti-collision protocols between tags, among which the most important one is the anti-collision protocol based on Aloha [9] and that based on Binary tree [10]. They mainly solve the collision problem between tags under the coverage of a single reader in the read range.

In the multi-reader RFID system, with the increase of the number of readers and the number of tags, the collision between readers becomes increasingly serious, so there are some interesting solutions. Distributed color selection (DCS) [12,13], a multi-reader anti-collision algorithm based on time division multiplexing (TDMA), is based on the principle that in case of reader collision, the colliding reader selects time slots randomly to avoid collision. This algorithm needs a long time to complete the global optimization. In dense scenes, with the increase of the number of readers, the optimization effect of the algorithm becomes weaker. In order to improve the DCS algorithm, a hierarchical Q-learning (HiQ) algorithm [14] has been proposed. This algorithm introduces the scheduler Q-server to achieve the global optimal effect. The Q-learning algorithm is invoked in Q-server to learn the relevant collision information collected by the reader, and then the optimal allocation scheme is made according to the learning result, so as to achieve the maximum number of readers working at the same time and the reader collision rate to a minimum. When the number of readers increases, a huge amount of collision information needs to be processed, which may affect the efficiency of the system.

In order to solve the problem of low efficiency of multi-reader collision processing in dense environment, this paper proposes a multi-channel anti-collision algorithm for multi-reader RFID system named as McAnCo. McAnCo introduces the anti-collision grouping strategy to put the readers that may collide into different groups, so that the readers can run at different frequencies or time slots. After processed by the algorithm, the readers in this RFID system can avoid collision and make greater use of channel resources, so as to improve the tag identification efficiency of the multi reader system.

Section 2 we mainly introduce the existing work about multi-reader anti-collision and the motivation of this algorithm. Section 3 mainly introduces the basic ideas, implementation process and procedure of the algorithm. Section 4 evaluates the performance. Finally Sect. 5 is the summary and prospect.

2   Related Work and Motivation

2.1   Related Work

DCS. A DCS algorithm based on TDMA is proposed in [13], in which all readers have the same frame size. The reader randomly selects time slots in the frame to compete for the right to identify tags. In DCS algorithm, the frame size is called "Max color", and multiple time slots in the frame are called "colors". If the reader does not collide when the frame is running, the color selected by the reader this time will be used as the selection when the next frame is running, and will not be re selected. When the reader collides, the collided reader will re randomly select color in Max color. After selection, it will send the new selection result to the surrounding readers. The surrounding readers will compare with their own color after receiving it. If the color is the same, they will immediately randomly select the color.

HiQ. The HiQ algorithm proposed in [14] mainly includes R-servers, Q-servers, readers and tags to be identified. Q-server allocates time slots for R-servers. R-servers grant frequency and time slots for readers. Authorized readers can start to identify tags. When the reader works, record the collision times and types related to the reader, and wait for the completion of the reader to transmit these information to Q-server through R-servers. Q-server searches for more efficient frequency and time slot allocation by learning collision information from readers. This process is called Q-learning algorithm. The purpose of HiQ algorithm is to minimize the allocated consumption and make the maximum number of readers work without interference at the same time. When the success rate of the reader is large, the overall consumption of the system will be less. On the contrary, when the success rate of the reader is small, the overall consumption of the system will be more. HiQ algorithm is to use Q-learning to find the optimal allocation method to achieve the desired goal.

NFRA. In reference [15], a neighborhood friendly anti-collision scheme (NFRA) is proposed. The algorithm avoid reader to reader interference (RRI) and reader to tag interference (RTI) problems through centralized algorithms. Server broadcasts an array command (AC) that contains a random number range. Readers generate their 0wn random numbers by receiving AC. The server then issues a sort command (OC), and each reader compares the value in OC with its random number. If the numbers are equal, the reader issues a beacon to determine if a collision has occurred. After the beacon frame, they will send the frame to the adjacent readers when readers do not detect any conflicts. By the way the NFRA can prevent adjacent readers receiving the next OC from the server. The next OC is not identified due to of or the adjacent readers that detect beacon conflict are in the next AC. NFRA assumes that tag identification is not performed before using only one data channel, and it does not mention how the reader detects conflicts between beacons.

2.2 Motivation

With the rapid development of RFID technology and the continuous expansion of the application field, the number of tags in the RFID system is also growing exponentially. In the original RFID system, a single reader is used, and the algorithms are optimized. But the optimal tag identification efficiency is still limited, far from meeting the identification requirements of massive tags. Taking the algorithm based on Aloha anti-collision protocol as an example, the optimal value of tag identification efficiency in theory is 0.368/slot. For the scenario with thousands of tags, the maximum number of time slots in the frame is limited, which will cause serious tag collision. In addition, it is assumed that there is unlimited for the number of time slots in the frame. Due to the low efficiency of identification, the process of tag identification takes a long time and cannot meet the requirements of identification efficiency.

Therefore, using multiple readers in RFID system can solve this problem. When multiple readers are introduced, serious reader collisions will be introduced if reader's behaviors are not controlled. For the collision between readers, it is necessary focus distinguish the two concepts of read range and interference range. The read range is the tag can communicate and decode with the reader in the range, while the interference range is that the reader can interfere with the communicate of other tags or readers within this range. As shown in the Fig. 1, there are two readers R_1 and R_2, and two tags T_1 and T_2. The read range of the reader is represented by solid line, and the interference range is represented by dotted line. When multiple readers work at the same frequency, as shown in Fig. 1, R_1 sends commands first, T_1 receives commands from R_1 and then responds to R_1 after processing. At the same time, R_2 also sends a command. Since R_1 is in the interference range of R_2, the command from R_2 interferes with T_1's command, and the first type of collision occurs. In the same scenario where multiple readers work at the same frequency, as shown in Fig. 2, T_1 is within the read range of R_1 and the interference range of R_2. When reader R_1 sends a command, R_2 is also sending a command. At tag T_1, the command sent by R_1 cannot be received normally due to the interference of R_2 command, resulting in the second type of collision. In the scenario of multiple readers working at different frequencies, as shown in Fig. 3, T_1 is within the read range of R_1 and R_2. When reader R_1 sends the command, reader R_2 is also sending the command. Two effective read commands collide at tag T_1, which causes T_1 can not receive the command normally. This is the third type of collision.

In conclusion, in the RFID system with multiple readers, if the reader's behavior is not controlled, it will lead to serious collision, which will greatly reduce the identification efficiency. Then we will introduce the algorithm to avoid collisions.

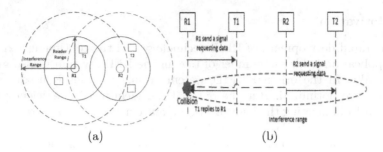

Fig. 1. (a) First type of collision and (b) procedure chart

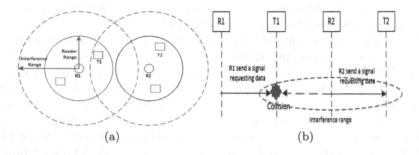

Fig. 2. (a) Second type of collision and (b) procedure chart

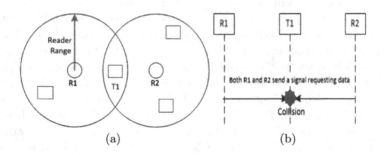

Fig. 3. (a) Third type of collision and (b) procedure chart

3   Grouping Multi-channel Algorithm Description

3.1   Basic Ideas

In the proposed McAnCo, polling server is introduced. As shown in Fig. 4, the effective range of signals broadcast by polling server can cover all readers. The readers only need to receive the commands sent by the polling server. The server and readers don't need to communicate with each other. In the practical application scenario, considering the cost and complexity, the arrangement of multiple readers is most likely to be arranged by fairly regular rules. As shown in Fig. 5, the rule in this paper is the readers are arranged in a square topology. The distance between two readers arranged in a straight line is $\sqrt{2}$ times the read range. And the distance between two readers on a diagonal line is twice the read range.

According to the read range and interference range, the collision of readers can be divided three types. The three types collisions is detailed introduction in Sect. 2.2. Then define Mutil-reader Interference Graph according to graph and network definition in graph theory. A graph G is an ordered pair (V(G), E(G)) consisting of two sets and an incidence function. The V(G) is the set of vertices, the E(G) is the set of edges. According to the definition of graph, each reader in multi-reader RFID system is represented by a vertex, all readers form a vertex set V(G), the interference between readers is represented by an edge, all the interference forms an edge set E(G). As shown in Fig. 5, build the reader topology graph as a Mutil-reader Interference Graph with $V(G) = [V_1, V_2, V_3]$, $E(G) = [e_1, e_2, e_3]$.

After obtaining interference graphs, we choose the classical vertex colouring algorithm in graph theory to process them. In the vertex colouring algorithm, a k vertex coloring of G refers to the assignment of k colors (1,2,3,...,k) to each vertex of G, so that any two adjacent vertices are assigned with different colors. If a graph G has a normal k vertex coloring, it is said that G is k vertex colorable. The chromatic number of G refers to the minimum value of the number k with normal vertex coloring of G, which is expressed by X(G) [16]. Given a k-coloring of graph G = (V,E), where V_i is the vertex set (i = 1,2,... k) colored with the i color in G, then each V_i is an independent set of G. Therefore a k-coloring of G corresponds to a partition of V(G) is $[V_1, V_2, ... V_k]$, where each V_i is an independent set. The vertex chromatic number X(G) of graph G is the minimum natural number k. The algorithm steps of finding the chromatic number X(G) of graph G are as follows: 1) make H = G, select a pair of different vertices u, v that are not adjacent to H, and draw H+uv and H·uv. 2) Let H be the two graphs obtained in 1). If H is a complete graph, for example, if there are k vertices, then X(H) = k. If H is not a complete graph, make G = H and turn to 1) to continue.

After processed by the vertex colouring algorithm, we can get the reader sets and reader groups. A set contains multiple groups, and different groups in the same set can work at different frequencies to avoid collision. There is no collisions between each group of readers. Readers in the same group can work at the same frequency and time slot. Through this grouping mechanism, the maximum number of readers can work simultaneously without interference. Then the polling server broadcasts commands to make readers start to identify tags in their frequency and time slot. After the processing of the algorithm, as many readers as can work simultaneously without interference and meet the needs of the increase of the number of tags and the development of the working speed.

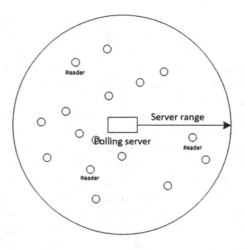

Fig. 4. The RFID system topology with polling server.

3.2   The Grouping Algorithm

For the three types of reader collisions, different measures can be taken to avoid these collisions. Set the read range are r_1, r_2, the interference range are i_1, i_2, and the distance between two readers to d. The first type and the second type of collisions are collectively called read range and interference range collision (RIC), the last type of collision is called read range and read range collision (RRC). RIC will occurs when:

$$d < r_1 + i_2 \tag{1}$$

So that readers with RIC can work at different frequencies to avoid the collision. RIC will occurs when:

$$d < r_1 + r_2 = 2r_1 \tag{2}$$

The readers with RRC can avoid collision only when they work in different time slots.

According to the analysis of reader collision, the algorithm uses the content of graph theory to model the interference between readers. When the distance between two readers is less than 2 times the read range, that is, when the RRC occurs, there must be RIC. Therefore, according to the special rule of interference

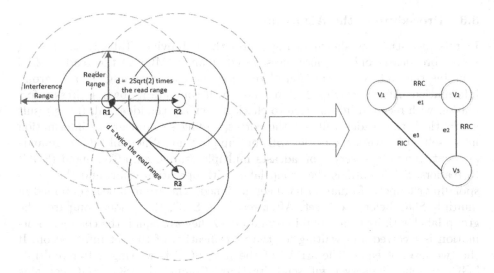

Fig. 5. The process generating interference graph.

graph, turn readers into hollow points and convert the collision between two readers to the solid line between two hollow points.

After getting the interference graph, the interference graph conforms to the concept of simple graph in graph theory, that is, there is only one solid line between two hollow points and the meaning of two points is not completely equal. The purpose of the interference graph is to divide the readers with interference into different groups. And the classical vertex coloring algorithm in graph theory can meet requirements. In the coloring algorithm, different colors represent different groups, and two points connected by solid lines are colored with different colors. The most important thing is to cover all points in the interference graph with the least colors. After processed by the algorithm, we can obtain the optimal grouping strategy and the least set number. This ensures that all readers can complete identification with a minimum of time slots.

In this algorithm, the concept of set is proposed. After RRC is completed, the number of colors needed for dyeing represents the number of sets. There is no RRC between readers in each set, and they can operate in the same time slot. There are still RIC between the readers in one set, that is, the distance between two readers is less than the sum of the read range and the interference range. Then the interference graph is constructed again for each reader in the set and processed by vertex coloring algorithm. The number of colors needed for dyeing represents the number of groups in each set. There is no reader interference between each group of readers. They can work at the same frequency and time slot, and different groups in the same set can work at different frequencies to avoid collision. This ensures that readers in a set can operation simultaneously with a minimum of channels.

3.3 Procedure of the Algorithm

In this algorithm, as shown in Fig. 6 and the abbreviate Table 1, the polling server broadcasts one or more message commands (MC) to the readers. MC contains the address information of readers, the corresponding set and group information. After receiving MC, a reader will compare its own address information with received information to check if they are the identical. If the result is identical, the reader will put the corresponding set and group information into itself. Otherwise, the reader will continue to wait. When all MC commands are sent, the polling server broadcasts multiple Start-Group-Command (SGC) to readers, SGC contains the group label with operation grant and the corresponding channel information has been assigned. The group labels contained in multiple SGC belong to a set. After receiving SGC, the reader compares the group label with its own group information. If they are equal, the channel information is received and waiting for the identification of the set information. If the two are not equal, the arrival of the next SGC is waiting. After multiple SGC are sent, the server will send Start-Sets-Command (SSC), SGC contains the set label that has the operation grant. After receiving the SSC, the reader that successfully matched the group information will compare the set information. If the comparison results are equal, it will start to identify tags according to the allocated channel. If the comparison results are not equal, it will wait for the SGC command. Readers that fail to match group information will not do anything after receiving SSC. After waiting for the communications between a reader and tags (CRTs), polling server will send multiple SGC containing group label and corresponding channel information. The rest of the process is similar to the previous process until all tags are identified.

Table 1. Abbreviate table.

Full name	Abbreviated name
Message command	MC
Start-Group-Command	SGC
Start-Sets-Command	SSC
Communications between a reader and tags	CRTs

3.4 Illustrative Example

Then, taking 36 readers in dense scenarios as an example to introduce the operation process of the algorithm. As shown in Fig. 7, the 36 readers are arranged in the special rule in the form of 6*6. In the rule, the distance between two readers arranged in a straight line is $\sqrt{2}$ times the read range. And the distance between two readers on a diagonal line is twice the read range The read range is 2 m, and the interference range is 6 m. The distance between two readers arranged

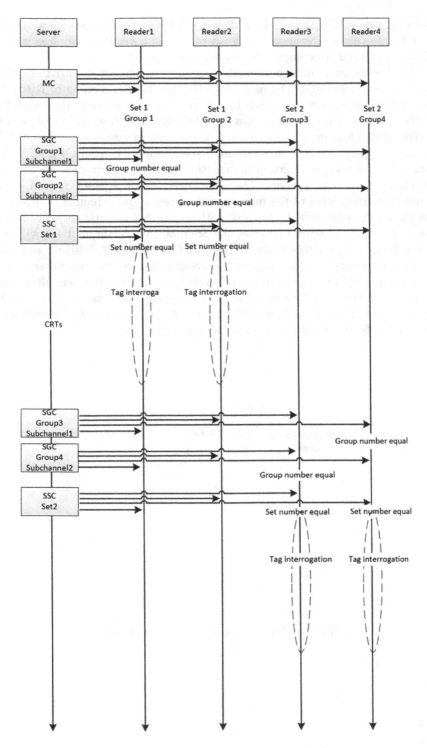

Fig. 6. Procedure chart of the proposed McAnCo.

in a straight line is $2\sqrt{2}$ m. And the distance between two readers on a diagonal line is 4 m. In this arrangement, the read range can cover the read area without omission, and no more complex overlapping occurs.

After the location information of 36 readers is imported into the polling server, the server grouping the readers for the first time according to RRC. The result is that the readers are divided into two sets, each set contains 18 readers, and the two sets of readers are cross distributed. Then, the readers of each set are divided into four groups according to the second grouping operation of RIC. The final grouping result is divided into 2 sets, each set contains 4 groups. The server adds the processed group information and set information to MC and broadcasts them to all readers. Then the server sends 4 SGC in turn, which contain four group label of the first set and corresponding channel information. After the server send all SGC, the SSC with set label of the first set will continue to be sent. After the reader receives the SSC, all tags of the first set will start to identification tags without any collisions in their channels. Wait for the CRTs time and start sending the command corresponding to the second set. After the processing of the algorithm, as many readers as can work simultaneously without interference and occupy the least channels, so as to achieve a higher identification efficiency, and meet the needs of the increase of the number of tags and the development of the identification efficiency.

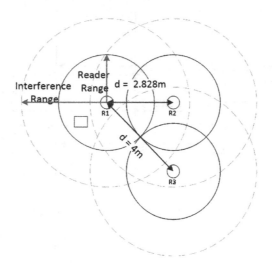

Fig. 7. Architecture of the illustrated example.

4   Performance Evaluation

4.1   Simulation Scenarios and Simulation Configurations

Next, the proposed McAnCo is compared with the typical DCS algorithm, HiQ algorithm and NFRA algorithm in the RFID system multi-reader anti-collision algorithm. The NS3 simulation platform is used to simulate the system efficiency, the number of control command collisions and the control command efficiency. The simulation parameters are shown in Table 2. The collision between tags is not considered in the anti-collision algorithm of multi reader in RFID system, so the time for readers to identify tags in the simulation process is fixed time. Using the type A tag identification algorithm, the time to identify 100 tags is 0.46 s. In the proposed McAnCo, the channel resource used is twice the comparison algorithms. Therefore, the McAnCo algorithm spend twice the time of the comparison algorithm when the readers and tags send commands. And the simulation result is the time for the reader to identify 100 tags is 0.58 s in the McAnCo. When the number of readers is less than 100, the time required for MC is 10 ms, and the time required for each additional 100 readers MC is 10 ms, a single SGC and SSC takes 1 ms.

Set up two kinds of simulation scenario, dense scenario and sparse scenario. In dense scenario, there are many readers, the number of which is from 100 to 1000, and the distance between two readers arranged in a straight line is $2\sqrt{2}$ m, and the distance between two readers in a diagonal line is 4 m. In the sparse scenario, there are few readers, the number of which is from 10 to 100. The distance between two readers arranged in a straight line is $4\sqrt{2}$ m, and the distance between two readers in a diagonal line is 8 m. In order to reduce the influence of accidental factors on the performance of the algorithm, the experimental results take the average data of 100 times of simulation.

Table 2. Simulation parameters.

Parameter	Value
Number of tags for each reader	100
Comparing algorithm	DCS, HiQ, NFRA
Time to identify 100 tags (Proposed McAnCo)	0.58 s
Time to identify 100 tags (Comparing algorithm)	0.46 s
Read range of a reader	2 m
Interference range of a reader	6 m
Number of channel	4
Dense reader scenario Number of readers	100, 200, 300, 400, ..., 1000
Sparse reader scenario Number of readers	10, 20, 30, 40, ..., 100

4.2 Simulation Results

The simulation results in Fig. 8 compare the system efficiency of different algorithms when the number of readers increases from 100 to 1000 in dense scenario. From the simulation results, we can see that when the number of readers is less than 200, the system efficiency of the proposed McAnCo is slightly lower than NFRA and HiQ algorithm. When the number of readers is greater than 200, the system efficiency of this algorithm is the highest, NFRA algorithm and HiQ algorithm are lower than the proposed McAnCo, and DCS algorithm is relatively low in this scenario. When the number of readers increases, the probability of reader collision of DCS algorithm increases, resulting in the increase of free time slots and the slight decrease of work efficiency. With the increase of readers, NFRA algorithm and HiQ algorithm can still deal with the relationship between adjacent readers and avoid collision. But there are some limitations in resource allocation and utilization, which leads to the final work efficiency tends to a fixed value. The proposed McAnCo maximizes the readers that can simultaneously work by using the operation of polling server. With the increase of readers, they can work without interference in each group increases correspondingly. Therefore, the efficiency of the proposed McAnCo is almost linear growth. In the case of limited channel resources, the McAnCo algorithm's efficiency of reader identify tags is lower than comparison algorithms. Therefore, when the readers is fewer, the efficiency gain brought by grouping cannot offset the efficiency drop caused by frequency division, result in the efficiency will be lower than NFRA algorithm and HiQ algorithm.

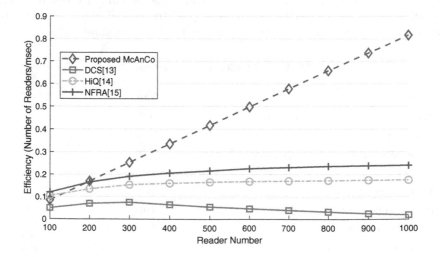

Fig. 8. Efficiency with the vary number of readers in dense scenario.

The simulation results in Fig. 9 compare the system efficiency of different algorithms when the number of readers increases from 10 to 100 in the sparse scenario. From the simulation results, we can see that when the number of readers is less than 30, the system efficiency of this algorithm is basically the same as NFRA algorithm and HiQ algorithm. When the number of readers is greater than 30, the system efficiency of this algorithm is the highest. NFRA algorithm and HiQ algorithm are basically the same, but slightly lower than this algorithm. The efficiency of DCS algorithm is the lowest. Because in the sparse scenario, the reader placement can reduce the occurrence of a collision. This algorithm can avoid reader collision by putting the reader in groups. NFRA algorithm and HiQ algorithm can also adapt to the changes of the scene very well, so the efficiency of these three algorithms is not much different. However, DCS algorithm can not avoid reader collision completely, which will still cause serious impact on efficiency.

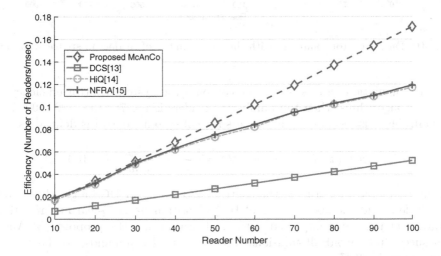

Fig. 9. Efficiency with the vary number of readers in sparse scenario.

The simulation results in Fig. 10 compare the failed number of control command of different algorithms when the number of readers is 25, 75, 150, 300, 500, 750, 1000 in dense scenario. When the control command cannot avoid reader collision, the control command is called failed. The simulation results show that the number of control command failures of DCS algorithm is the most. The number of failed command of HiQ algorithm is less, NFRA algorithm and the proposed McAnCo can completely avoid reader collisions, so the number of failed control command is 0. In DCS algorithm, when there is a collision, the color of adjacent readers will be updated to avoid collision, so when the readers number is large, the collision will inevitably be more. In the HiQ algorithm, the Q-learning algorithm can better allocate resources by learning the type and quantity of collisions. Therefore, there will be some collisions, but the collision probability will be much less than that of the DCS algorithm.

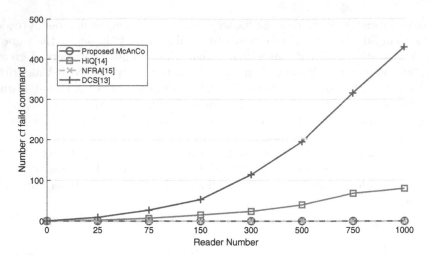

Fig. 10. Failed control command with the vary number of readers in sparse scenario.

The simulation results in Fig. 11 compare the system control efficiency of different algorithms when the number of readers is 25, 75, 150, 300, 500, 750, 1000 in the dense scenario. The success rate of system control is defined as:

$$System\ control\ efficiency\,(\%) = \frac{Command_{success}}{Command_{all}} * 100\,(\%) \qquad (3)$$

In the comparison algorithm, the control success rate of DCS algorithm is relatively low, and the success rate of HiQ algorithm using Q-learning real-time adjustment is greatly improved. NFRA algorithm and the proposed McAnCo can successfully avoid all collisions through control commands, so the control success rate is 100%.

The simulation results in Fig. 12 and Fig. 13 compare the system efficiency of different algorithms when channel resources are unlimited in dense and sparse scenario. In the proposed McAnCo and other algorithms, the time a reader to identify 100 tags is 0.46 s when the channel resources is enough to meet the demand. Other simulation parameters are consistent with the preceding part of the text. From the simulation results, we can see that the system efficiency of the proposed McAnCo algorithm is the highest, NFRA algorithm and HiQ algorithm are lower than the proposed McAnCo, and DCS algorithm is relatively low in dense and sparse scenario. When readers are fewer, the system efficiency of this algorithm is still superior to other algorithms due to the enough channel resources. Thus, it can be concluded, the efficiency gain brought by grouping can fairly improve the system efficiency.

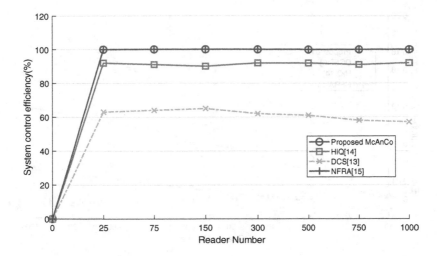

Fig. 11. System control efficiency with the vary number of readers.

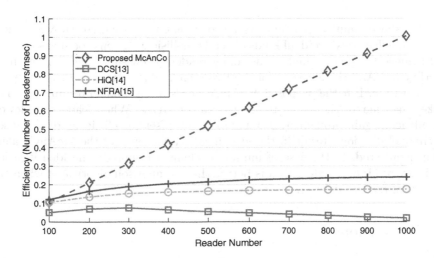

Fig. 12. Efficiency with the vary number of readers in dense scenario when the channel resources are unlimited.

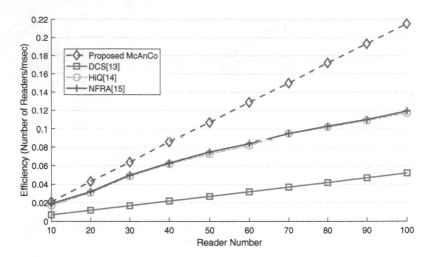

Fig. 13. Efficiency with the vary number of readers in sparse scenario when the channel resources are unlimited.

The above simulation results can prove that the proposed McAnCo algorithm can effectively avoid all kinds of reader collisions in dense or sparse scenes, and achieve the goal of making as many readers work simultaneously without interference. And the efficiency of the two scenarios is better than the comparison algorithm. But the proposed McAnCo needs more channel resources, which makes the time for the reader to identify tags increase. When readers are fewer, the efficiency gain brought by grouping cannot offset the efficiency drop caused by channel division. Result in the identification efficiency of the McAnCo algorithm is affected. In the case of unlimited channel resources, the identification efficiency of McAnCo algorithm is better than comparison algorithms when the number of readers is fewer.

5   Conclusions

This paper presents an efficient anti-collision algorithm for multi-channel RFID multi-reader named McAnCo. The algorithm uses polling server to process the interference graph with vertex coloring algorithm in graph theory, to get reader sets that can avoid interference, and then uses algorithm to process readers in each set to get multiple reader groups. There is no interference between the readers in one group, which can achieve the same frequency and time slot operation without interference. There are RIC among different groups in a set, and readers in different groups can work without interference by running in different channel of the same time slot. The readers with interference between different sets can only be avoided by running in different time slots. The maximum number of readers can work without interference in the same time slot by sending information to the readers through the polling server. Compared with DCS algorithm,

HiQ algorithm and NFRA algorithm, this algorithm groups readers by polling server, avoiding the possibility of reader collision. The simulation results show that the proposed McAnCo is better than other algorithms in system identification efficiency and system control efficiency. Therefore, this algorithm can be applied to RFID real-world scenarios where readers are sparse or densely distributed.

Acknowledgement. This work was supported in part by Science and Technology on Avionics Integration Laboratory and the Aeronautical Science Foundation of China (Grant No. 20185553035), the National Natural Science Foundations of CHINA (Grant No. 61871322, No. 61771392, No. 61771390, and No. 61501373), and Science and Technology on Avionics Integration Laboratory and the Aeronautical Science Foundation of China (Grant No. 201955053002).

References

1. Walshe, M., Epiphaniou, G., Al-Khateeb, H., Hammoudeh, M., Katos, V., Dehghantanha, A.: Non-interactive zero knowledge proofs for the authentication of IoT devices in reduced connectivity environments. J. Ad Hoc Netw. **95**(1), 549–575 (2019)
2. Ahuja, S., Potti, P.: An introduction to RFID technology. Commun. Netw. **2**(3), 183–186 (2010)
3. Rajaraman, V.: Radio frequency identification. J. Reson. **22**(6), 549–575 (2017)
4. Yu, Y., Yu, X., Zhao, Z., et al.: Image analysis system for optimal geometric distribution of RFID tags based on flood fill and DLT. IEEE Trans. Instrum. Meas. **67**(4), 839–848 (2018)
5. Du, J., Sugumaran, V., Gao, B.: RFID and multi-agent based architecture for information sharing in prefabricated component supply chain. IEEE Access **5**(1), 4132–4139 (2017)
6. Chen, H., Wang, Z., Xia, F., et al.: Efficiently and completely identifying missing key tags for anonymous RFID systems. IEEE Internet Things **5**(4), 2915–2926 (2018)
7. Rezaie, H., Golsorkhtabaramiri, M.: A fair reader collision avoidance protocol for RFID dense reader environments. Wireless Netw. **24**(6), 1953–1964 (2017). https://doi.org/10.1007/s11276-017-1447-8
8. Safa, H., El-Hajj, W., Meguerditchian, C.: A distributed multi-channel reader anti-collision algorithm for RFID environments. Comput. Commun. **64**(1), 549–575 (2015)
9. Zhang, Y., Yang, F., Wang, Q.: An anti-collision algorithm for RFID-based robots based dynamic grouping binary trees. Comput. Electr. Eng. **63**(1), 91–98 (2017)
10. Myung, J., Lee, W., Srivastava, J.: Adaptive binary splitting for efficient RFID tag anti-collision. IEEE Commun. Lett. **10**(3), 144–146 (2006)
11. Engels, D.W., Sarma, S.E.: The reader collision problem. IEEE Int. Conf. Syst. Man. Cybern. **3**(1), 641–646 (2002)
12. Waldrop, J., Engels, D.W., Sarma, S.E.: Colorwave: a MAC for RFID reader networks. IEEE Wireless Commun. Netw. **3**(1), 1701–1704 (2003)
13. Waldrop, J., Engels, D.W., Sarma, S.E.: Colorwave: an anticollision algorithm for the reader collision problem. IEEE Int. Conf. Commun. **2**(1), 1206–1210 (2003)

14. Ho, J., Engels, D.W., Sarma, S.E.: HiQ: a hierarchical Q-learning algorithm to solve the reader collision problem. Int. Symp. Appl. Internet Workshops **1**(1), 88–91 (2006)
15. Eom, B., Yim, B., Lee, T.: Colorwave: an efficient reader anticollision algorithm in dense RFID networks with mobile RFID readers. IEEE Trans. Industr. Electr. **56**(7), 2326–2336 (2009)
16. Mirsaleh, M.R., Meybodi, M.R.: A Michigan memetic algorithm for solving the vertex coloring problem. J. Comput. Sci. **24**(1), 389–401 (2018)

NOMA-Based RFID Tag Identification Method

Qingyuan Miao[1], Yong Fang[1] (ORCID), Mao Yang[2(✉)], Zhongjiang Yan[2], and Bo Li[2]

[1] School of Information Engineering, Chang' an University, Xian, China
{2018224013,fy}@chd.edu.cn
[2] School of Electronics and Information, Northwestern Polytechnical University, Xian, China
{yangmao,zhjyan,libo.npu}@nwpu.edu.cn

Abstract. RFID (radio frequency identification technology) is a non-contact automatic identification technology. During the Tag identification process, an effective anti-collision method will make a significant contribution to the RFID system in accelerating the identification speed. This paper proposes a method to improved RFID anti-collision protocol that incorporates a NOMA (non-orthogonal multiple access) technique, which is based on ISO 18000-6C standard. This paper simulates the method and compares it with traditional scheme of 18000-6C18000-6C. Through our simulations, NOMA-based RFID Tag identification method outperforms Traditional schemes in both the average access slot efficiency and time efficiency. It can solve serious collision under massive Tags numbers and improve system efficiency. It also can be conveniently applied to engineering implementations.

Keywords: Anti-collision · NOMA · RFID · ISO 18000-6C · Efficiency improvement

1 Introduction

As the Internet of Things equipment grows with each passing day, the amount of data therefrom advances swiftly and vigorously every year, the relevant theoretical research on the Internet of Things steps into the rapid development stage. RFID, one of the most central key technologies on the processing layer of application network of wireless networks, identifies an entity object with the Tag and receives the data of entity object with RFID Interrogator. Facing with the massive access request nowadays and the operation characteristics different from human communications, there are higher requirements on the performance of the Access terminal of the Internet of Things.

Radio Frequency Identification (RFID) ("UHF-RFID" for short) on the basis of goods management, defines two types of protocols, namely Type A and Type B. Later, it defines the Type C of the communication between 860MHz-960MHz in the Version II of the follow-up protocol. ISO/IEC 18600-6C can simultaneously read hundreds of Tags, it has not only larger user data field, but also high transmission rate of 40Kbps-640Kbps, therefore it applies to the scenarios requiring larger flow; due to the characteristics of low power consumption, low cost and high efficiency, it gradually develops to maturation

Y.-B. Lin and D.-J. Deng (Eds.): SGIoT 2020, LNICST 354, pp. 239–253, 2021.
https://doi.org/10.1007/978-3-030-69514-9_19

and occupies the main stream. Tag will be activated by the continuous wave (CW) RF signal transmitted by the Interrogator to it, and then reflect and scatter the signal to the Interrogator by modulating the reflection coefficient of its antenna; since the Interrogator and the Tag share the same wireless channel, there is channel contention, and ISO/IEC 18600-6C uses the ALOHA-based algorithm (Q- algorithm) on the basis of random number generator to reduce the probability of occurring collision, and then complete the Tag identification process.

In order to solve the collision when more than one RFID-Tag transmits their information to the Interrogator at the same time, the stack-like anti-collision algorithm, based on the ISO 18000-6C protocol, solves the fluctuation of Q value and thereby improves the system efficiency to some extent in [1]; In [2], the media access control algorithm adopted by ISO/IEC 18000-6C RFID on air interface protocol is analyzed and the process realizing the optimal identification efficiency is proposed. The above ones focus on the path optimization of Q-algorithm based on software and the realization of system's simple design, low cost and easy modification; however, the time delay is longer and the efficiency improvement is limited. In [3], an improved RFID anti-collision protocol is proposed, it is integrated with CDMA technology and does not cause bandwidth extension. It is an optimizing way combined by hardware and software, with less time delay and obvious improvement of efficiency, but it can increase the equipment complexity. Existing technologies are still facing with the issue that there is still severe collision under massive Tags numbers.

The 5th generation wireless systems are the latest generation of cellular mobile communication technology, the NOMA is one of the critical technologies of 5G. It can improve more network capacity, access user number and realize quicker access efficiency by stacking multiple users on the same time-frequency resource to achieve the doubled and redoubled user access.

For the severe identification conflict under massive Tags, this paper proposes a NOMA-based RFID Tag identification method. This method introduces NOMA technology to the Tag identification process, allowing the Tag at the different locations to reflect identification signal according to the different power, separate and identify multiple different Tags by receiving NOMA at the side of Interrogator. The method complying with ISO/IEC 18000–C6 protocol standard [4, 6] as designed therefrom is universal.

This article designs simulation and builds a NOMA-based RFID system, simulates and builds a traditional RFID system. Configures different simulation environments, and completes a large number of simulation results output. Its emulation proof is made on the NS3 software platform. According to the results of emulation proof, the NOMA-based RFID Tag identification method solves the identification conflict of massive Tags and thereby improves the identification efficiency of system.

The second section of this paper introduces Related Work and Motivation, the third section details the method of RFID Tag identification based on NOMA, the fourth section simulates and tests the method on the ns3 simulation platform, the fifth section summarizes the Results and Concluding Remarks, the last section is the Acknowledgement.

2   Related Work and Motivation

2.1   RFID Tag Identification Method Principle

The ISO/IEC 18000-6C protocol [4] adopts the Q-algorithm, its command set includes Query, QueryAdjust, QueryRep etc. The primary parameter is the slot counting parameter Q. The value Q in the protocol decides the slot number used by the anti-collision, the Interrogator completes the anti-collision job by issuing corresponding commands to the Tag to change the status of the Tag.

An inventory round starts when the Interrogator issues a Query command, the Query command contains the parameter Q, the Tag in the non-killed status receives the command and picks up a random value from the range $(2^Q - 1)$ and load it into the slot counter. The Tag with the slot counter as "0" converts into the Reply status and makes a reply immediately. Afterwards the non-zero Tag can be selected to convert into the Arbitrate status and then wait for issuing the command QueryAdjust or QueryRep. The steps when a Tag completes the identification are shown by Fig. 1 as follows:

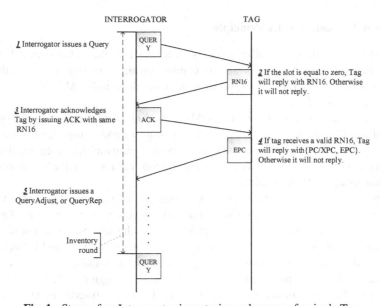

Fig. 1. Steps of an Interrogator inventories and access of a single Tag.

a)   The tag issues a reply first, and then backscatters the RN16 (16-bit random number or pseudo-random number) signal;

b)   The interrogator will acknowledge the Tag with an ACK containing the coincidence RN16;

c)   The acknowledged Tag switches to the acknowledged state and backscatters PC/XPC, EPC;

d) The Interrogator issues a QueryAjust or QueryRep, whichcauses the identified Tag transition to ready and another Tag to start a query-response dialog with the Interrogator since the Step (a) above;

After issuing the command Query to start an inventory round, the Interrogator will generally issue one or more QueryAdjust or QueryRep command. The QueryAdjust command will repeat the previous Query command, it can make the Q value appreciate or decrease, but the new Tag will not be introduced to the inventory round. The QueryRep command will repeat the previous Query command, the parameter will remain unchanged, and the new Tag will not be introduced to the inventory round. The inventory round can comprise multiple QueryAdjust or QueryRep command. The Interrogator will issue new Query command at a moment, and a new inventory round will start therefrom.

Through detecting and solving collision at the waveform level, the RN16 from one of Tags could be resolved by the Interrogator, then the solved Tags could be further acknowledged, whereas the unsolved Tags will receive the wrong RN16 and return to Arbitrate state instead of backscattering the reply EPC.

2.2 Power Domain NOMA Principle

The NOMA (non-orthogonal multiple access) is defined as follows: the identical resource can carry multiple data, it supports massive connection and ultra-large capacity; there are many solutions via different resources, such as power domain NOMA, SCMA, MUSA, PDMA, IDMA, BDM etc.

The core concept of power domain NOMA downlink is the one of using the superposition coding SC (superposition coding) at the transmitting end, using the SIC (successive interference cancellation) at the receiving end, and realizing multiple access in the power domain via different power levels on the same time-domain and frequency-domain, this is the mainstream NOMA solution.

The principle of power domain NOMA is shown by Fig. 2 as follows: where Sender 1 and Sender 2 adopt the identical signal transmitting power; considering the factors of path loss, noise interference etc., the Receiver makes the successive demodulation on the received signal by using the capture effect of wireless network. The SIC technology is used to realize cache for composite signal, the other signals and noises at the receiving end are deemed as the interference; firstly the Sender 1 signal with higher power is demodulated, then the demodulation data of Sender 1 is used to re-construct its simulation waveform, following, the cached signal is used to subtract the re-constructed Sender 1 simulation waveform to obtain a relatively clear Sender2 signal, it is then demodulated accordingly.

2.3 Motivation

As shown by the Fig. 3, if two or more Tags reply RN16 simultaneously, the Interrogator under Type C protocol can only identify one thereof at most, but can't realize the total identification. When there are more numbers of Tags, the value Q remains unchanged, so the probability of replying RN16 at the same time will increase as the number of

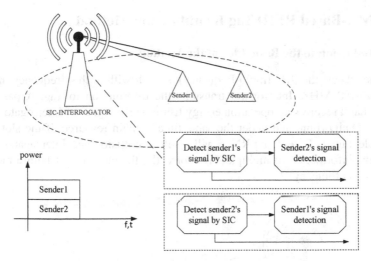

Fig. 2. Power domain NOMA Uplink Principle.

Tags increases, which will result in a severe collision. Moreover, it is not enough to only optimize the slot number (*i.e.*: the value Q) and the related algorithm since the number of slots has a slow dynamic regulation convergence, it takes a longer time for identification.

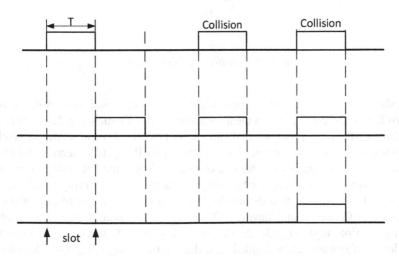

Fig. 3. Two or more Tags reply RN16.

3   NOMA-Based RFID Tag Identification Method

3.1   Introduction to the Basic Idea of the Method

RFID modulates the RF (radio-frequency) signal within the frequency range of 890 MHZ–960 MHZ, Interrogator transmits the information to Tag. A passive Tag signifies that it receives all operation energy from the RF signal of Interrogator.

In the Q-algorithm and under the same time-domain resource, if the slot counter of multiple Tags is 0, replying RN16 will result in collision and Interrogator will not identify the information of multiple Tags correctly, the current slot failure blocks the identification efficiency.

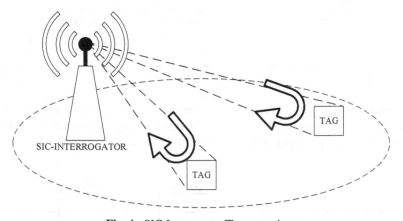

Fig. 4. SIC-Interrogator/Tag operations.

As shown by Fig. 4 as follows, Interrogator issues the continuous-wave (CW) RF signal to Tags and thereby receives the information issued by such Tag. Tags will respond by modulating the reflecting system of antenna and then reflect and scatter passively the information signal to Interrogator. Thus, within a RFID system, sender and receiver of signal can be deemed as the Interrogator itself; when using SIC-Interrogator, signal will be issued by SIC-Interrogator by using the identical transmitting power, and then be scattered to the Tags within the RF field, in such case Tags will respond the signal, whereas the SIC-Interrogator having NOMA uplink receiving capacity is capable of receiving multiple reply signals. As shown by Fig. 5 as follows, the distinguishable power levels of system can be divided according to the change of gray-scale color:

The signals returned by the Tag are at different power levels, and all signals are successfully identified. For instance, Tag1, Tag 2, Tag 3 and Tag 5 join in identification, so Tag 1, Tag 2, Tag 3 and Tag 4 at the slot are identified successfully.

If two or more Tags at same power level join in identification, all will fail to identify. For instance, Tag1, Tag 2, Tag 3 and Tag 5 join in identification, so Tag 1, Tag 2, Tag 3 and Tag 4 at the slot get identification failure. For certain related scenarios, see Table 1 as follows:

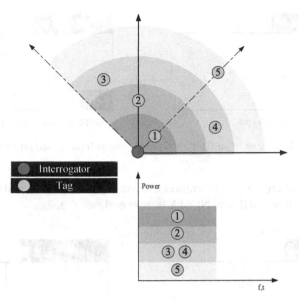

Fig. 5. Power level distinction.

Table 1. Identification results of different power levels.

Identify members	Success/fail
Tag1/Tag2/Tag3/Tag4/Tag5	Success
Tag1, Tag2, Tag3, Tag5	Success
Tag1, Tag2, Tag4, Tag5	Success
Tag3, Tag4	Fail
Tag1, Tag2, Tag3, Tag4, Tag5	Fail

3.2 Design of RFID-Type C Tag Identification Frame Based on NOMA

In the RFID -Type C system as shown by Fig. 6(a), multiple Tags backscatter its RN16 simultaneously to Interrogator, if the Interrogator can identify one RN16 signal thereof, such Tag will be acknowledged. As shown by Fig. 6(b), multiple Tags backscatter its RN16 signal simultaneously to Interrogator. In the NOMA-based circumstances, Interrogator can successfully detect multiple RN16 signals coming from different Tags via SIC and then scatter the ACK frame of multiple different corresponding Tags. The Tag monitor channels; when detecting certain ACK frame field containing the own RN16, the Tag will backscatter its EPC to Interrogator to complete its own identification process.

Within RFID system, RN16 of multiple Tags can be successfully received under the same time domain sometimes when Tag capacity is ultra-large, therefore making ACK reply to every Tag will affect the entire system performance and increase the burden of Interrogator. Tag needs to catch the ACK belonging to themselves from many similar

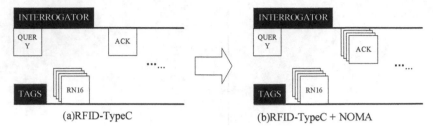

Fig. 6. Design of RFID-Type C identification frame based on NOMA.

ACK signals, so there are certain requirements on Tag performance, and thereby a design of ACK frame more suitable to NOMA is proposed, see Fig. 7.

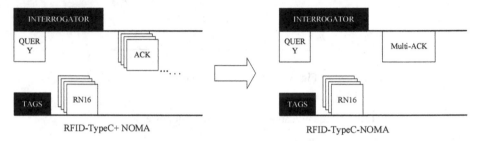

Fig. 7. Design of RFID-Type C Multi-ACK frame based on NOMA.

In the NOMA-based RFID-Type C Tag identification system, a Multi-ACK frame based on the number of RN16 to be received currently will be constructed, it contains all successfully received RN16 information; Tags will seek for the RN16 belonging to themselves from Multi-ACK and reply EPC.

3.3 SINR-Based Threshold and Power Control Method

If using SIC to carry out interference elimination, we need to know the signal meeting the given or required conditions is the usable signal. As we know, $SINR_{db} = Signal_{dbm} - Noise_{dbm}$, the larger SINR is, the better the quality of signal is; so we can deem the signal at the Lower power as the noise and assume the size of received power of Tag 1 ~ Tag N at the moment as follows, see Fig. 8:

Following, we can deem Tag2 ~ Tag N and noise as the interference of Tag 1, and select one threshold complying with the given conditions; when meeting $Power_{dbm}^{tag1} - Power_{dbm}^{tag2} > Threshold_{db}$, the Tag 1 and Tag 2 are identifiable under NOMA, the rest can be deduced by analogy like this.

$$Power_{dbm}^{tag1} - Power_{dbm}^{tag2} > Threshold_{db}$$

$$Power_{dbm}^{tag2} - Power_{dbm}^{tag3} > Threshold_{db}$$

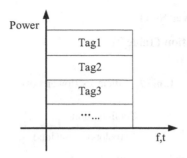

Fig. 8. Signal power received by the Interrogator at a certain moment.

$$Power_{dbm}^{tag3} - Power_{dbm}^{tag4} > Threshold_{db}$$

$$\cdots\cdots$$

$$Power_{dbm}^{tagN} - Power_{dbm}^{tag(N+1)} > Threshold_{db} \tag{1}$$

The signal meeting the relationships aforesaid is the usable signal. For different modulation styles and exterior environments, the setting values of power threshold are different, moreover the larger $Power_{dbm}^{tagN} - Power_{dbm}^{tag(N+1)}$ is, namely the larger SINA is, the better the receive signal is; the quality of signal may affect the parameters such as packet loss probability etc. The smaller the threshold is, the higher the performance requirement of SIC-Interrogator is, the better the NOMA identification efficiency is, and the larger the system overhead is. Therefore, the different thresholds are configured in different scenarios.

4   Simulation Platform Design and Implementation

NS3 and MATLAB 2018 is used for our simulations. NS3 is an open source, discrete event-based simulator. We use ns3 to build a NOMA-based simulation environment on LINUX, and then use MATLAB to process the simulation data.

Considering that in the simulation of RFID Tag identification based on NOMA, it is necessary to construct a similar situation in reality. Therefore, when using ns3 build a simulation environment, a radio propagation model with the propagation delay set to the speed of light is used, and use the shadowing Mode as wireless propagation loss model.

In this section of the simulation, we mainly focus on the number of tags connected in a unit time and the number of tags connected in a unit slot in different situations. Because time efficiency and slot efficiency can reflect the access efficiency of the system, this is our main consideration. Before the simulation, we set Interrogator to communicate with all tags with a constant transmission power of 17.0206dbm. Perform several simulations and take the average value as the simulation result.

4.1 NOMA Gain at Lower Slots

a) **Simulation configuration** (Table 2)

Table 2. Efficiency (lower slots).

Parameter	Configuration
Q (slots)	4 (16slots)/6 (64slots)
Interrogator communication radius	15m
Number of Tags	6–256
Threshold	6.9 db
Contrast variable	With or without NOMA
Cycles	5000
Output	Slot efficiency = All successful Tags/ Total number of slots Time efficiency = All successful Tags/ Total time (s)

b) **Simulation results**

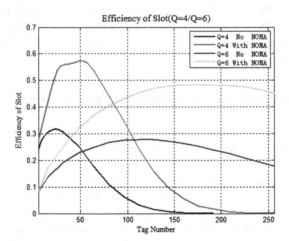

Fig. 9. Efficiency of Slot (Q = 4/Q = 6).

As shown by Fig. 9, it can be seen from the slot efficiency graphs with Q values of 4 and 6, that Type C with non-orthogonal multiple access function is more efficient than Type C in the whole process.

When the number of Tags is 24, the slot efficiency of Type C with a Q value of 4 reaches a peak of 0.320289. Compared with Type C with NOMA function, it can be seen that the slot efficiency reaches the peak when the number of Tags is 52, and its time slot efficiency value is 0.594048, the gain is about 185%.

As with Q = 4, it can be seen from the slot efficiency graph with Q = 6 that the efficiency of Type C with non-orthogonal multiple access function compared to Type C is gain in the whole process.

Type C reaches its peak at 112 Tags, and its slot efficiency is about 0.278183. Type C based on NOMA reaches its peak at 180 Tags, and its slot efficiency is about 0.484365. The slot efficiency peak gain is 0.484365/0.271183 about 178%.

As the Q value increases, the peak slot efficiency of RFID decreases from 0.320289 with a Q of 4 to 0.278183 with a Q of 6. The peak slot efficiency of NOMA-based RFID has decreased from 0.594048 with a Q of 4 to 0.484365 with a Q of 6.

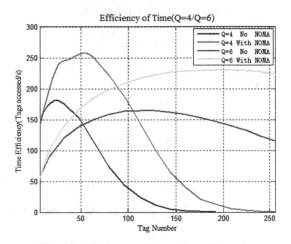

Fig. 10. Efficiency of Time (Q = 4/Q = 6).

As shown by Fig. 10, the number of Tags accessed per unit time with a Q value of 4 also reached peaks at 24 and 52, with values of 182.031 and 263.788, respectively, with a gain of 145%.

Type C with a Q value of 6 reaches a peak of 164.835 at 112 Tags, and a NOMA-based Type C with a Q value of 6 reaches a peak of 230.063 at 180 Tags. Its gain is about 140%.

As the Q value increases, the peak time efficiency of RFID decreases from 182.031 with a Q of 4 to 164.835 with a Q of 6. The peak time efficiency of NOMA-based RFID has been reduced from 263.788 with a Q of 4 to 230.063 with a Q of 6.

As the Q value increases, its peak gain will decrease slightly. For example, when Q is 6, the time slot efficiency peak gain is 178%, when Q is 4, the time slot efficiency peak gain is 185%, and the time slot efficiency gain is reduced by about 7%. When Q is 6, the time efficiency peak gain is 140%, and when Q is 4, the time efficiency peak gain is 145%, and the time efficiency gain is reduced by about 5%.

The peak access efficiency of RFID system is related to the number of slots and Tags. In each inventory round, when the number of slots is equal to the number of Tags, the access efficiency of the inventory round is the highest. Since a certain number of Tags will be stored in each inventory round, the access efficiency is a dynamic value for each different inventory round, So the number of Tags corresponding to the peak of the total RFID access efficiency is always greater than a value, which is the number of Tags equal the number of slots.

4.2 NOMA Gain at Higher Slots

a) **Simulation configuration** (Table 3)

Table 3. Efficiency (higher slots).

Parameter	Configuration
Q (slots)	8 (256 slots)
Interrogator communication radius	15 m
Number of Tags	6–354
Threshold	6.9 db
Contrast variable	With or without NOMA
Cycles	5000
Output	Slot efficiency = All successful Tags/Total number of slots Time efficiency = All successful Tags/Total time (s)

b) **Simulation results**

As the number of slots increases, the number of Tags that the RFID system can accommodate also increases. With the addition of the NOMA function, the slot efficiency and time efficiency of the system has been further improved on this basis. (Figs. 11 and 12)

4.3 Different Thresholds

a) **Simulation configuration** (Table 4)

b) **Simulation results**

Threshold is a problem that needs to be considered for NOMA-based RDIF Tag identification. According to Fig. 13, comparing the curves with thresholds of 10.3 db

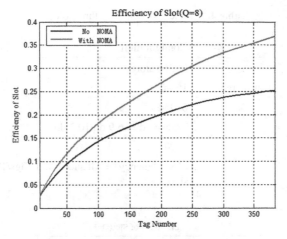

Fig. 11. Efficiency of Slot (Q = 8).

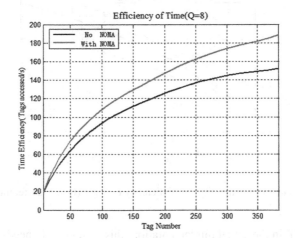

Fig. 12. Efficiency of Time (Q = 8).

and 6.9 db, as the threshold increases, the efficiency of the system also decreases. The gain of NOMA-based Tag identification system depends on the threshold setting, and different SINR thresholds can achieve different gain effects. In order to be more adaptable to engineering implementations, diverse SINR thresholds are configured according to the actual scene.

5   Results and Concluding Remarks

This article proposes the NOMA-based RFID Tag identification algorithm with the purpose of versatility increment and efficiency improvement for RFID systems. Through numerous simulations, we detect that the radio frequency identification system based on NOMA has a great performance improvement, which is undoubtedly very suitable for

Table 4. Efficiency (Different thresholds)

Parameter	Configuration
Q (slots)	8 (256 slots)
Interrogator communication radius	15 m
Number of Tags	6–354
Contrast variable	Threshold = 6,9 db/10.3 db
Cycles	5000
Output	Slot efficiency = All successful Tags/Total number of slots

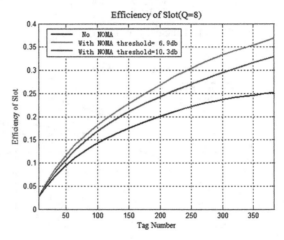

Fig. 13. Efficiency of Time (Q = 8). Efficiency of Time (Q = 8/Different threshold)

the upcoming 5G. In the actual implementation, this method only needs to consider the modification and update of the Interrogator device without considering the Tag device. Therefore, the method also has excellent versatility. The algorithm has higher access efficiency, larger system capacity, and higher peak Tag count Compared with traditional RFID system.

The peak Tag count of RFID system is related to the slots and Tags [5]. In each inventory round, when the number of slots is equal to the number of Tags, the access efficiency of the inventory round is the highest. H. Wang [1] and Y. Maguire [2] used two different algorithms to improve the system performance by changing the Q-value under different inventory round. Through simulation comparison, it is found that the algorithm complexity of our NOMA-based method is smaller and the performance gain is higher. And compared with T. Demeecha's algorithm [3], our method has better system overhead while ensuring the complexity of the algorithm. In summary, NOMA-based RFID Tag identification method has the best comprehensive performance.

Reader can grasp through the protocol design of Sect. 3.3 and the simulation of Sect. 4.3 in this article that a smaller SINR-threshold will bring better performance gains, but will increase the overhead of the system. How to select a threshold in combination with different actual conditions is also What we need to do in the future. we will try different SINR-threshold algorithms to obtain the best SINR-threshold under the current system overhead.

Acknowledgement. This work was supported in part by the National Natural Science Foundations of CHINA (Grant No. 61871322, No. 61771392, No. 61771390, and No. 61501373), and Science and Technology on Avionics Integration Laboratory and the Aeronautical Science Foundation of China (Grant No. 20185553035, and No. 201955053002).

References

1. Wang, H., You, X., Cui, Y.: A stack-like optimal Q-algorithm for the ISO 18000–6C in RFID system. In: 2012 3rd IEEE International Conference on Network Infrastructure and Digital Content, Beijing, pp. 164–168 (2012). https://doi.org/10.1109/ICNIDC.2012.6418735.
2. Maguire, Y., Pappu, R.: An optimal Q-Algorithm for the ISO 18000–6C RFID Protocol. IEEE Trans. Autom. Sci. Eng. **6**(1), 16–24 (2009). https://doi.org/10.1109/TASE.2008.2007266
3. Demeechai, T., Siwamogsatham, S.: Using CDMA to enhance the MAC performance of ISO/IEC 18000-6 Type C. IEEE Commun. Lett. **15**(10), 1129–1131 (2011). https://doi.org/10.1109/LCOMM.2011.082011.110848
4. ISO/IEC_CD 18000–6. Information Technology—Radio Frequency Identification (RFID) for Item management—Part 6: Parameters for Air Interface Communications at 860–930 MHz (2004)
5. Ko, Y., Roy, S., Smith, J.R., Lee, H., Cho, C.: RFID MAC performance evaluation based on ISO/IEC 18000-6 Type C. IEEE Commun. Lett. **12**(6), 426–428 (2008). https://doi.org/10.1109/LCOMM.2008.080254
6. EPC global: EPC Radio-Frequency Identity Protocols Class-1 Generation-2 UHF RFID Protocol for Communications at 860 MHz–960 MHz; Version 1.2.0, Brussels, Belgium (2008)

Computing Capacity Allocation for Hierarchical Edge Computing Nodes in High Concurrency Scenarios Based on Energy Efficiency Evaluation

Ziheng Zhou[1], Zhenjiang Zhang[1(✉)], Jianjun Zeng[2], and Jian Li[1]

[1] Beijing Jiaotong University, No.3 Shangyuancun, Beijing, China
zhangzhenjiang@bjtu.edu.cn
[2] Beijing Li'antong Information Technology Company, Beijing, China

Abstract. Edge computing could play an important role in Internet of Things (IoT). Computing capacity allocation has been researched a lot in mobile edge computing, which is task oriented. However, hierarchical edge computing also needs computing capacity allocation which is node oriented. This paper focusses on capacity allocation of nodes in hierarchical edge computing. We take energy efficiency and loss in high concurrency scenarios into consideration and work out a method to do allocation by weighing loss and energy efficiency. Simulation is under circumstances that nodes overload, which means that loss is inevitable. A new inspiration of deployment is also given after simulation.

Keywords: Edge computing · Energy efficiency · Computing capacity

1 Introduction

Edge computing should be deployed at the edge of the network in order to get better latency and reduce the pressure of core network. However, edge hold less computing capacity compared to cloud, which means that we need strategy to make full use of edge rather than appending servers like cloud. Network structure optimization might be a good idea before deploying. With appropriate deployment, we could use less power and weaker devices to satisfy the latency and data processing requirements.

A. Kiani, N. Ansari and A. Khreishah proposed a hierarchical structure for fog computing [1], they made a lot of work to prove and simulate. Inspired by them, we will move on to find a more specific solution of deployment in hierarchical edge computing. We focus on loss ratio and energy efficiency to make a strategy, so as to adjust a fixed-structure hierarchical edge network by modifying their computing capacity allocation. Assuming that we need some CPU cycles to deal with data which arrives continuously, different layers in this hierarchical network will provide diverse and distinct computing capacity, namely different CPU frequencies or service rate. By weighing loss and energy efficiency, we figure out a plan to do capacity allocation before deployment. Simulations are also given.

Y.-B. Lin and D.-J. Deng (Eds.): SGIoT 2020, LNICST 354, pp. 254–259, 2021.
https://doi.org/10.1007/978-3-030-69514-9_20

2 Related Work

A. Kiani et al. [1] investigated how and where at the edge of the network the computation capacity should be provisioned, and proposed a hierarchical model. They use queueing theory to analyze latency and solve the problem by stochastic ordering and upper bound-based techniques.

Y. Li et al. [2] studied the edge server placement problem in mobile edge computing. They focus on energy consumption and devise a PSO (particle swarm optimization) [3, 4] to find the solution. Z. Liu et al. [5] found that cooperation can contribute to the sum-capacity of a hybrid network. P. Yuan et al. [6] studied the capacity of edge caching systems. Y. Lin et al. [7] proposed a problem that how to allocate the traffic and capacity in the management plane in mobile edge computing. Queueing theory and latency are concerned. M. Noreikis et al. [8] focus on edge layer capacity estimation and provide a capacity planning solution which considers QoS requirements. H. Badri et al. [9] proposed a risk-based optimization of resource provisioning in mobile edge computing. M. Liu et al. [10] proposed a price-based distributed method to manage the offloaded computation tasks.

3 System Model

Hierarchical edge coming contains two types of computing nodes. Shallow nodes are deployed near the devices while deep nodes contact with a set of shallow nodes. Data generated from devices flow from shallow nodes to deep nodes, which probably reach cloud eventually.

Data from devices could need to be computed and each piece of such data can be casted to a task. Computing service could be provided from shallow nodes and deep nodes in the meantime because there could be an offloading scenario on the shallow nodes.

For shallow node i, λ_i is the arrival rate. If shallow nodes could not process the task timely, this task will be casted to deep nodes so that shallow nodes could handle the next task. So that the whole server rate is divided into two parts. Assuming that we need μ_t in total, $(1 - \alpha)\mu_t$ is deployed on shallow node and $\alpha\mu_t$ is on deep node. It is noted that the shallow rate is $(1 - \alpha)\mu_t$ but deep one is not. A deep node is linked to several shallow nodes, and it should be $\alpha n\mu_t$ while n is the number that is linked. α is distribution coefficient.

$$\mu_s = (1 - \alpha)\mu_t \tag{1}$$

$$\mu_d = \alpha n\mu_t \tag{2}$$

μ_s is the rate of shallow nodes while μ_d is the rate of deep ones. Regarding one deep node and its shallow nodes as a cluster, we focus on this cluster to solve the problem.

3.1 Loss

As previously noted, the arrival rate has an effect on the loss ratio. We assume that λ_i is known and certain over a period of time so that the problem is simplified, because we mean to decrease the loss rather than seeking an accurate solution of loss ratio. With a certain arrival rate λ_i and server rate μ_s, we can find the offloading work load λ_{ji} as a part of arrival rate of deep node j in time stationary, which is from shallow node i.

$$\lambda_{ji} = max\lfloor\lambda_i - (1 - \alpha)\mu_t, 0\rfloor \tag{3}$$

Notice that a deep node is linked to several shallow nodes, the total arrival rate of deep node j is definite. C_{ij} is a coefficient to indicate whether shallow node i is linked to deep node j. In addition, it is clear that $\sum_j C_{ij} = 1$.

$$\lambda_j = \sum_i \{C_{ij}*max[\lambda_i - (1 - \alpha)\mu_t, 0]\} \tag{4}$$

Focusing on this deep node and ignoring the situation that there is no loss, the lost portion is transformed into r. Thus, the lost portion on deep nodes can be expressed.

$$r = \sum_i \{C_{ij}*max[\lambda_i - (1 - \alpha)\mu_t, 0]\} - \alpha n\mu_t$$

$$= \sum_{k=1}^{m} [\lambda_k - (1 - \alpha)\mu_t] - \alpha n\mu_t$$

$$= \sum_{k=1}^{m} \lambda_k - (1 - \alpha)m\mu_t - \alpha n\mu_t \tag{5}$$

$\sum_{k=1}^{m} \lambda_k$ is independent of α so that we could regard it as a constant K. Therefore, a function is built after normalization.

$$r(\alpha) = \frac{K - (1 - \alpha)m\mu_t - \alpha n\mu_t}{\sum \lambda}$$

$$= \frac{K - m\mu_t + (m - n)\mu_t\alpha}{\sum \lambda} \tag{6}$$

With $r(\alpha)$, we can take its derivative easily.

$$r'(\alpha) = \frac{(m - n)\mu_t}{\sum \lambda} \tag{7}$$

It is clear that $r'(\alpha)$ is always no more than 0, which means that $r(\alpha)$ is a non-increasing function. We could also get the similar conclusion with intuition. With more provisioning or capacity allocated to deep node, the extent of multiplexing goes higher among these edge nodes so that the lost portion will be reduced.

3.2 Energy Efficiency

M. Dayarathna et al. have proposed that CPU consumes the most power in a certain device [11]. And the energy consumption of a server in idle state accounts for more than 60% in full state [11, 12]. We could also get the similar result when it comes to some lightweight devices such as Raspberry Pi and other IoT devices. Thus, some algorithms try to decrease amounts of idle server and succeed.

However, the problem in this paper talks about a different case. Those excellent methods are not appropriate because we could not modify the location or amounts of edge nodes. The whole network structure is definite and we could only adjust capacity allocation to optimize energy efficient. The total power should consist of idle power and working power, where working power is generated from CPU utilization.

$$P_{total} = P_{idle} + P_{working} \tag{8}$$

P_{idle} is certain once we determine the network. $P_{working}$ can be reduced by adjusting CPU utilization. In other words, adjusting its capacity, which means CPU frequency as known as server rate μ, can decrease power consumption. The relation of CPU frequency and power is sometimes approximately linear in some cases. However, we need more accurate evaluation but not approximation because $P_{working}$ is the only thing that we can optimize.

We can regard CPU as a set of FET (Field Effect Transistor) or CMOS (Complementary Metal Oxide Semiconductor). And we can try to figure a function of power [13].

$$P = CV^2 f \tag{9}$$

P is the power consumption and we use C to indicate some other constant which is independent of frequency f. V is the supply voltage. It seems that f and P is linear, but noting that there is a factor that V does influence f. Frequency f could not keep going higher without the increase of V because of gate delay. To simplify the problem, we can construct a function to measure power consumption. The argument is μ which is affected by f and V. And C is just a constant to amplify so that we can ignore it.

$$p' = \mu^3 \tag{10}$$

It should be noted that p' is a parameter to measure the level of power consumption but not itself. Thus, we have a function to indicate energy efficiency as long as we use allocated capacity to replace μ.

$$\begin{aligned} p' &= n\mu_s^3 + \mu_d^3 \\ &= n(1-\alpha)^3\mu_t^3 + \alpha^3 n^3 \mu_t^3 \end{aligned} \tag{11}$$

μ_t is definite at the beginning so it is not a variable. In order to simplification and normalization, assume that $\frac{p'}{n^3\mu_t^3} = p$.

$$p(\alpha) = n^{-2}(1-\alpha)^3 + \alpha^3 \tag{12}$$

It is obvious that $p(\alpha)$ is a convex function.

3.3 Capacity Allocation

With $r(\alpha)$ and $p(\alpha)$, we can do allocation easily. In order to weigh loss and energy efficiency, we create a new function using another coefficient β.

$$G(\alpha) = \beta*r(\alpha) + (1 - \beta)*p(\alpha)$$
$$= \beta*\frac{K-m\mu_t+(m-n)\mu_t\alpha}{\sum\lambda} + (1 - \beta)*[n^{-2}(1 - \alpha)^3 + \alpha^3] \tag{13}$$

β indicates the balance of loss and energy efficiency which ranges from 0 to 1. It is clear that we could find α to make $G(\alpha)$ minimum with given β, n, k, K, μ_t by taking derivative because $G(\alpha)$ is the sum of a non-increasing function and a convex function (Fig. 1).

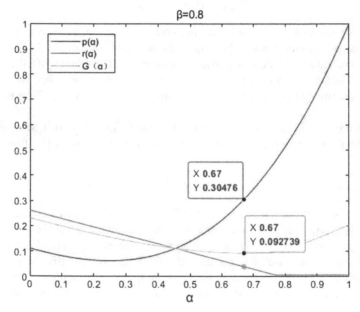

Fig. 1. $\beta = 0.8, n = 3$.

4   Simulation and Result Analysis

Taking $\mu_t = 1$ for instance, the upper bound capacity of this cluster is 3 because $\mu_{cluster} = n\mu_s + \mu_d$. In order to reveal loss, we make that $\sum\lambda > \mu_{cluster}$ so that there is always loss. λ is [1.57 0.23 1.22] in this experiment and $\sum\lambda = 3.02 > 3$.

When $\alpha = 0.67$, loss equals 0.03. Meanwhile, $p(\alpha)$ equals 0.30476, namely costing 30% power compared to methods without energy efficiency optimization.

With more nodes in one cluster, energy efficiency goes well when α is low, which makes solution of α shifts left. And $p(\alpha)$ did not increase. Moreover, there is inspiration that increasing β and n will help to reduce loss and energy cost.

5 Conclusion and Future Work

We find a method to simplify the problem and propose a model to do capacity allocation considering of weighing loss and energy efficiency in hierarchical edge computing. Simulation proves that it is easy to regulate parameter in accordance with the circumstances. Finally, we suppose a pattern to optimize hierarchical edge network structure.

In future, we will still work on hierarchical edge computing and try to figure out a method to adjust hierarchical structure dynamically.

Acknowledgements. This work was supported by the National Key Research and Development Program of China (grant number 2018YFC0831304).
The National Natural Science Foundation of China under Grant 61701019.

References

1. Kiani, A., Ansari, N., Khreishah, A.: Hierarchical capacity provisioning for fog computing. IEEE/ACM Trans. Netw. **27**(3), 962–971 (2019)
2. Li, Y., Wang, S.: An energy-aware edge server placement algorithm in mobile edge computing. In: 2018 IEEE International Conference on Edge Computing (EDGE), San Francisco, CA, pp. 66–73 (2018)
3. Kennedy, J., Eberhart, R.: Particle swarm optimization. In: Proceedings of the IEEE International Conference on Neural Networks (ICNN 1995), pp. 1942–1948 (1995).
4. Laskari, E.C., Parsopoulos, K.E., Vrahatis, M.N.: Particle swarm optimization for integer programming. In: Proceedings of the Congress on Evolutionary Computation (CEC 2002), pp. 1582–1587 (2002)
5. Liu, Z., Peng, T., Peng, B., Wang, W.: Sum-capacity of D2D and cellular hybrid networks over cooperation and non-cooperation. In: Proceedings of 7th International ICST Conference on Communications and Networking, China, pp. 707–711 (2012)
6. Yuan, P., Cai, Y., Huang, X., Tang, S., Zhao, X.: Collaboration improves the capacity of mobile edge computing. IEEE Internet Things J. **6**(6), 10610–10619 (2019)
7. Lin, Y., Lai, Y., Huang, J., Chien, H.: Three-tier capacity and traffic allocation for core, edges, and devices for mobile edge computing. IEEE Trans. Netw. Serv. Manag. **15**(3), 923–933 (2018)
8. Noreikis, M., Xiao, Y., Ylä-Jääiski, A.: QoS-oriented capacity planning for edge computing. In: 2017 IEEE International Conference on Communications (ICC), Paris, pp. 1–6 (2017)
9. H. Badri, T. Bahreini, D. Grosu and K. Yang: Risk-Based Optimization of Resource Provisioning in Mobile Edge Computing. In: 2018 IEEE/ACM Symposium on Edge Computing (SEC), Seattle, WA, pp. 328–330. (2018).
10. Liu, M., Liu, Y.: Price-based distributed offloading for mobile-edge computing with computation capacity constraints. IEEE Wirel. Commun. Lett. **7**(3), 420–423 (2018)
11. Dayarathna, M., Wen, Y.G., Fan, R.: Data center energy consumption modeling: a survey. IEEE Commun. Surv. Tutor. **18**(1), 732–794 (2016)
12. Wang, S., Liu, Z., Zheng, Z., Sun, Q., Yang, F.: Particle swarm optimization for energy-aware virtual machine placement optimization in virtualized data centers. In: Proceedings of the 19th IEEE International Conference on Parallel and Distributed Systems (ICPADS 2013), pp. 102–109 (2013)
13. Texas Instruments: CMOS Power Consumption and Cpd Calculation. SCAA.35B (1997)

An Intelligent Approach for Optimizing Energy-Efficient Packets Routing in the Smart Grid Internet of Things

Chih-Kun Ke[1]([⊠]), Mei-Yu Wu[2], and Chia-Yu Chen[1]

[1] Department of Information Management, National Taichung University of Science and Technology, North Dist, No.129, Sec.3, Sanmin Rd., 40401 Taichung, Taiwan, R.O.C.
ckk@nutc.edu.tw

[2] Department of Business Management, National Taichung University of Science and Technology, 40401 Taichung, Taiwan, R.O.C.

Abstract. This work proposes a multi-criteria artificial bee colony (MABC) algorithm to optimize the energy consumption problem in wireless sensor networks. The approach uses the artificial bee colony (ABC) algorithm to discover sensor nodes in a network as a cluster header combination. Different nodes are dynamically selected according to their current status in the network. The purpose is to cluster sensor nodes in the network in such a way that nodes can transmit packets to their cluster header, and then identify the most energy efficient packet routing from the cluster headers to the Internet of Things (IoT) base station. The routing strategy takes into account nodes' residual energy and energy consumption, routing distance, number of hops, and frequency, in order to assign decision scores to help the algorithm discover a better solution. The use case shows that the MABC algorithm provides energy-efficient packet routing, and thus extends the wireless sensor network lifespan, which is confirmed by the multi-criteria analysis evaluation of the candidate routing. The contribution of this research is its use of swarm intelligence algorithms in wireless sensor network routing, with a multi-criteria artificial bee colony algorithm used in a wireless sensor network to address the problem of fast convergence of the algorithm.

Keywords: Internet of Things · Packet routing · Energy-efficient · Artificial bee colony algorithm · Multi-criteria decision analysis

1 Introduction

The Internet of things (IoT) [1] provides a multitude of convenient services in daily life, and wireless sensor networks (WSN) are a key technology in IoT development. However, WSN sensors have some limitations and challenges, such as limited power, fewer instructions per second (IPS), less storage, and lower network bandwidth. The limited power of sensors, in particular, is a key challenge in IoT-enabled smart grid development. WSN sensors collect data from the sensing environment and communicate

© ICST Institute for Computer Sciences, Social Informatics and Telecommunications Engineering 2021
Published by Springer Nature Switzerland AG 2021. All Rights Reserved
Y.-B. Lin and D.-J. Deng (Eds.): SGIoT 2020, LNICST 354, pp. 260–269, 2021.
https://doi.org/10.1007/978-3-030-69514-9_21

that data to each other through radio signals, with each transmission consuming each node's limited store of energy [2]. In addition, general wireless sensors for environmental monitoring are often installed in areas that people cannot reach. If a wireless sensor's energy is depleted, it is thus difficult to provide power support, meaning the sensors will be abandoned, leaving gaps in the WSN and reducing its ability to warn of environmental threats [3]. A more flexible and faster programming method based on the status of each sensor in the network is thus crucial to extend the lifespans of both wireless sensors and WSNs.

Optimization problems related to engineering scheduling or mathematical sciences are very complex and challenging. The purpose of such problems is to identify the best and most feasible solution from all candidate solutions. However, current methods tend to become trapped in local optima, and require novel solutions to improve the problems [4]. In recent years, researchers have explored the use of optimization algorithms based on Swarm Intelligence (SI), using characteristics of swarms of creatures found in nature. SI algorithms decentralize control between swarms, and emulate self-organized collective behavior. Through these algorithms, each agent follows simple rules to perform operations locally, looking for the best solution for complex problems, and these rules, as the name implies, are inspired by nature. The algorithms tend to be flexible, easy to implement, and sufficiently versatile to handle different types of optimization problems. The artificial bee colony algorithm (ABC) is one such swarm intelligence algorithm [5]. ABC is inspired by the foraging behavior of honey-bee colonies. Various types of bees perform different activities according to their division of labor. By sharing and exchanging foraging information, they can find the optimal solution to a given problem. The main advantage of ABC is that it does not need to consider a specific solution, but rather compares all solutions; even information contained in a bad solution thus becomes useful. Through the local optimization of each type of bee, the optimal value of the problem becomes the solution for the entire bee colony, and the convergence speed is faster.

Multi-criteria decision analysis (MCDA) is decision-making analysis based on multiple conflicting criteria, and MCDA problems can be defined as finding multiple alternatives using multiple criteria [6]. This process can help decision-makers divide those multiple alternatives into a ranking order based on the nature of each alternative, and the characteristics of each criterion. They can then arrange the priorities, evaluate alternatives, and select a plan that is closest to the user's ideal solution. In MCDA, decision-making factors such as the properties, attributes, and criteria of alternatives can be processed using two types of MCDA: multi-objective decision making (MODM), and multi-attribute decision making (MADM). MODM is an alternative plan comprised of a set of restrictive conditions, which seeks the best solution for several objective functions, while MADM provides a set of alternative plans, considering multiple attributes (criteria) to evaluate the alternatives, with the best option determined by the order of the evaluation results [7]. A simple additive weighting method (SAW) was developed by Churchman et al. in 1954 [8]. In the SAW meth-od, each attribute (criteria) is assigned a weight, and then the performance value of each attribute (criteria) is converted into a number by multiplying it by the weight value. The preliminary priority order can then be arranged according to these scores [9–11].

This study proposes an intelligent approach to optimizing the problem of energy consumption in WSNs. The approach uses the ABC algorithm to discover sensor nodes in the network as a cluster head combination. Different nodes are dynamically selected according to their current status in the network. The purpose is to cluster the sensor nodes in the network in such a way that other nodes can transmit packets to their respective cluster headers, and then find the most energy-efficient packet routing from the cluster headers to the IoT base station. The routing method takes into account multiple attributes, including nodes' residual energy, energy consumption, routing distance, number of hops and frequency to derive decision scores, which are then used to discover a more energy-efficient routing solution.

The remainder of this paper is organized as follows. Section 2 presents the proposed intelligent approach for optimizing energy-efficient packet routing in the smart grid IoT. The use case demonstration follows in Sect. 3. Finally, Sect. 4 presents the conclusions.

2   The Proposed Approach

This section describes how the artificial bee colony algorithm (ABC) is combined with the simple additive weighting method (SAW) to solve the random selection problem. The proposed approach is called a multi-criteria artificial bee colony algorithm (MABC). Based on the rich attributes in packet transmission, the approach recommends the most energy-efficient routing for each cluster header. First, the MABC algorithm is described, and a detailed analysis and calculations are presented in Sect. 3. Table 1 presents the parameter definitions.

Table 1. The parameter definitions for the proposed MABC algorithm

Parameter	Definition
Cluster_Header_Set	The cluster header set;
Cluster_Set	The cluster set;
Best_Routing_Set	The best routing set calculated by ABC;
Routing _Set	The initial routing set;
Max_ Iter	The maximum iteration of ABC;
Limit	The maximum mining limitation of a food solution of ABC;
Bee_number	The number of bees in the ABC;
MCDA_Parameter	An MCDA parameter;
MCDA_Candidate	A candidate set calculated by MCDA

The pseudo-code of the proposed MABC algorithm is as follows.

Pseudo-code: MABC routing algorithm.
Input: The set of cluster and header information (`Cluster_Set`).
Output: The best routing set calculated by MABC (`Best_Routing_Set`).

```
00 MABC_Routing(Cluster_Header_Set, MCDA_Parameter){
01  Set the parameter Max_Iter, Limit and Bee_number
02  ABC(Routing_set, Max_liter, Limit, Bee_number){
03   Initialize food sources
04   Evaluate the food sources' the fitness
05   Iter_number ← 1
06    Do While (Iter_number < Max_liter)
07     For i =1:
08      Generate new routing solutions in Clus-
              ter_Header_Set.
09      Evaluate the new routing solutions' fitness
10      Apply greedy selection process
11      End for
12      MCDA_Candidate = SAW(MCDA_Parameter);
13      Sort(MCDA_Candidate);
14      //Onlooker bee process
15      For i=1:
16       Onlooker bees choose the best one in
              MCDA_Candidate.
17       Generate new routing solutions using onlooker
               bees
18       Evaluate the new routing solutions' fitness
19       Apply greedy selection process
20       End for
21      // Scout bee process
22      IF Limit_number > Limit:
23       Generate new CH solutions in
              Candiate_Sensor_Set.
24       Limit_number = 0
25       Memorize the best solution.
26        Iter_number ← Iter_number + 1
27      End While
28      Return best solution.
29  }
30   Return Best_Routing_Set.
31 }
```

The routing plan obtains the best cluster header solution and member node information of each cluster. It then uses the ABC algorithm to evaluate the most energy-efficient routing for the cluster header. The algorithm parameters include the number of bee colonies; the number of employee bees, onlooker bees and scout bees; the maximum number of iterations of the algorithm (Max_Iter); the maximum mining limitation (Limits) for each food solution; and the initial food source of the bees. The food source is the current best routing cluster and problem solution, as well as the best routing cluster reconciliation of each cluster header.

Since it is necessary to evaluate the pros and cons of the initial solutions before colony mining, this study calculates the fitness values of all solutions generated. The fitness value represents the total energy consumption of all routings in the problem solution. A smaller problem solution fitness value means that the routing cluster will consume relatively less energy, while a larger fitness value indicates greater energy consumption. Finally, the total value is added to derive the fitness value of the problem solution, and the evaluation step ends when all problem solutions are calculated.

After evaluating the fitness value of all problem solutions, the employee bees take the lead in mining each problem solution. Because the routing is modified, the energy consumption of the routing cluster must be re-evaluated as the new problem solution's fitness. The fitness value is the energy consumed by each cluster header in the routing in order to transmit packets to each other. The energy consumed by each cluster header in order to receive transmitted packets is included to obtain the overall fitness value. If the fitness value of the new problem solution is greater than that of the original solution, the employee bee adopts the greedy selection method to select a better solution. Therefore, the employee bee keeps the original problem solution and discards the new problem solution. If the solution has not been updated, the number of mining (Limits) will increase by one, until the maximum mining limitation is exceeded, and will be eliminated by the scout bee, and so on until the employee bee update is completed.

When all employee bees have updated the problem solution, they will inform the onlooker bees of the information they have mined so far. In the traditional artificial bee colony algorithm, the onlooker bee uses the roulette wheel selection method to select the employee bee position to follow. The purpose of onlooker bees searching for solutions is to find a better solution based on the current problem solution. Therefore, it is important to choose a better solution among the current candidates; however, the roulette selection method has some shortcomings. First, roulette uses the fitness value of each problem solution to calculate its probability of being selected. If the probability value is very different, the selection will be problematic. The current better problem solution will have a greater chance of being selected by the onlooker bee, and the introduction of bias into the solution is sought, leading to premature convergence and loss of diversity. On the other hand, the calculation of the probability value only considers the fitness value at a single level, which means that the pros and cons of the routing are considered at a single level; this may make it difficult to find a better routing problem solution with single-level evaluation routing.

Therefore, this study modified the roulette selection method to introduce MCDA. The multiple attributes in the routing are evaluated to help the onlooker bee search for better solutions. Based on [12, 13], this work takes into account routing attributes, including the total routing distance, total energy consumption, total number of hops, frequency, and remaining total energy, in order to evaluate the routing. Longer routing distances result in greater energy consumption for packet transmission. Total energy consumption consists of the energy consumed by each node in the transmission routing. The total hop count indicates the number of nodes through which a packet is passed from the cluster head node to the IoT base station in each routing, with more hops resulting in greater energy consumption. The remaining energy represents the remaining energy of each node after a packet is transmitted. The frequency represents the number of packets sent or forwarded by each node, and the higher the frequency, the faster the battery power will be consumed.

This work uses the simple additive weighting method (SAW) to set the weight value of each packet transmission routing according to the characteristic attributes, and to evaluate the recommended score of each routing solution. A higher score indicates a better solution. In this way, the onlooker bee chooses the best solution to the mining problem according to the recommended result evaluation, followed by further mining. The SAW calculation process is as follows. The onlooker bee intends to mine a food source. The goal is to find a better solution for each evaluation attribute among existing food solutions. The decision-making solution is based on the problem-solving content mined by the employee bee. The network administrator sets the weights of the evaluation indicators, where each weight is assigned to each evaluation indicator, and the total is 1. The routing solution and its evaluated attributes are converted into a decision matrix, which is then normalized. The normalized matrix is then used to calculate the direction normalization. This study calculated the direction normalization matrix using the minimization criterion. The weight matrix and the direction normalization matrix are comprehensively evaluated to obtain a comprehensive evaluation value. Finally, the comprehensive evaluation values are ranked from large to small, and the observation bee selects the better-ranked solution for updating, according to the sorted problem solution.

When the employee bee and the onlooker bee have finished their work, the scout bee will replace certain food solutions that exceed the mining times (Limits) by randomly generating new routing solutions to replace them with new food solutions, and increase the number of iterations by one. In this way, the algorithm stops computing until the number of loops exceeds the maximum number of iterations (Max_Iter), and returns the best solution after computing.

3   Use Case Demonstration

This study randomly generated the routing for each cluster header to transmit a packet to the base station. The routing included the cluster header. In the cluster header selection step, this study calculated the best cluster header combination in the network as [4, 7–9, 11] to generate six food sources, as shown in Table 2. The numbers 0 to 4 in the routing were represented as [4, 7–9, 11], and the number 5 was the base station. Each employee bee then visited various food sources for mining, and the food source was called the problem solution.

Taking Solution 1 as an example, the transmission routing of the 0th cluster header was [0, 1, 4, 5, 2, 3]. First, the cluster header needed to transmit five packets to the base station. The energy consumed by each cluster header in order to transmit the packets, as well as the energy consumed by each cluster header in order to receive packets, was

Table 2. Routing planning and solutions of the MABC

Solution	Routing
1	[[0, 1, 4, 5, 2, 3], [1, 2, 4, 0, 5, 3], [2, 3, 0, 4, 5, 1], [3, 2, 1, 4, 5, 0], [4, 5, 3, 1, 2, 0]]
2	[[0, 5, 3, 1, 2, 4], [1, 5, 3, 4, 0, 2], [2, 4, 3, 0, 5, 1], [3, 4, 0, 1, 5, 2], [4, 2, 3, 1, 5, 0]]
3	[[0, 2, 3, 1, 4, 5], [1, 3, 5, 0, 2, 4], [2, 1, 0, 4, 3, 5], [3, 4, 2, 0, 1, 5], [4, 2, 0, 1, 5, 3]]
4	[[0, 1, 4, 3, 5, 2], [1, 3, 4, 2, 5, 0], [2, 0, 1, 5, 4, 3], [3, 2, 0, 4, 1, 5], [4, 2, 0, 1, 5, 3]]
5	[[0, 3, 5, 4, 1, 2], [1, 5, 4, 2, 3, 0], [2, 3, 5, 4, 0, 1], [3, 1, 5, 4, 0, 2], [4, 5, 3, 0, 2, 1]]
6	[[0, 2, 3, 1, 4, 5], [1, 0, 5, 3, 2, 4], [2, 4, 1, 5, 3, 0], [3, 5, 1, 2, 4, 0], [4, 3, 5, 1, 0, 2]]

calculated as shown in Table 3, as $0.00002500026 + 0.00005313742 + 0.00005529074 = 0.00013342842$ J, and so on to calculate the energy consumed by other routings. The value was added as the fitness value of the problem solution, and the evaluation step ended when all the problem solutions were calculated.

Table 3. Routing energy consumption calculation of the MABC

Routing	Energy consumption calculation
$0 \rightarrow 1$	$500 \times 5e\text{-}8 + (4.47213595499958)^4 \times 500 \times 1.3e\text{-}15 = 0.00002500026$
$1 \rightarrow 4$	$500 \times 5e\text{-}8 + 500 \times 5e\text{-}8 + (46.87216658103186)^4 \times 500 \times 1.3e\text{-}15 = 0.00005313742$
$4 \rightarrow 5$	$500 \times 5e\text{-}8 + 500 \times 5e\text{-}8 + (53.41348144429457)^4 \times 500 \times 1.3e\text{-}15 = 0.00005529074$

Continuing the Solution 1 example, the routing was [[0, 1, 4, 5, 2, 3], [1, 2, 4, 0, 5, 3], [2, 3, 0, 4, 5, 1], [3, 2, 1, 4, 5, 0], [4, 5, 3, 1, 2, 0]], and the employee bee changed the transmission sequence of all routings to [1, 2] to form a new problem solution, so the new problem solution was [[0, 4, 1, 5, 2, 3], [1, 4, 2, 0, 5, 3], [2, 0, 3, 4, 5, 1], [3, 1, 2, 4, 5, 0], [4, 3, 5, 1, 2, 0]]. Because the routing was modified, the energy consumption of the routing cluster header to be recalculated. The fitness value was the energy consumed by each cluster header of the routing in order to transmit packets to each other, plus the energy consumed by each cluster header in order to receive packets. The total available energy was 0.0023852419407 J (J). The original fitness value was 0.00013342842 J (J), which was less than the available energy. If the fitness value of the new problem solution is greater than the original solution, the employee bee adopts a greedy selection method to select a better solution; it will thus keep the original problem solution and discard the new problem solution. If the solution is not updated, the Limits will be increased by one until the maximum mining limitation is exceeded; it will then be eliminated by the onlooker bee when the employee bee has updated.

In MCDA, the SAW method is used to assign weight values to criteria. The SAW calculation process is as follows. The onlooker bee intends to mine the food source.

Solution S = $\{S_1, S_2, S_3, \ldots, S_n\}$, where S includes total routing length, total energy consumption, total number of hops, total remaining energy of nodes, and frequency in the cluster header transmission routing combination set, as shown in Table 4.

Table 4. Candidate solutions of MCDA

No	Routing length	Energy consumption	Hops	Remaining energy	Frequency
1	926.932114095416	0.004265394907499999	12	9.995734605092501	47.4
2	1078.3434271204517	0.004638783719999999	16	9.99536121628	61.2
3	463.7951328053706	0.0024948649999999998	5	9.997505134999999	21.6
4	1117.8385570224605	0.0048117749407	13	9.9951882250593	55.6
5	1129.3773153600205	0.0047363974101	14	9.995263602589901	53.2
6	427.9026888159207	0.0018840385002000001	7	3, 9.9981159614998	12.6

There are five decision evaluation indicators used in MCDA. The decision evaluation indicators of this study refer to the routing attributes [12, 13], as shown in Table 5. C = $\{C_1, C_2, C_3 \ldots \ldots C_m\}$, where C_1, C_2, C_3 and C_5 are minimization criteria, and C_4 is the maximum criterion.

Table 5. Evaluation criteria

Criteria	Routing length (C_1)	Energy consumption (C_2)	Hops(C_3)	Remaining energy (C_4)	Frequency(C_5)
Weight	0.15	0.15	0.25	0.3	0.15

A weight matrix W is constructed, and the network administrator sets the weights of the evaluation indicators, where each weight is assigned to each evaluation indicator, and the total is 1:

$$W = \begin{bmatrix} 0.15 & 0 & 0 & 0 & 0 \\ 0 & 0.15 & 0 & 0 & 0 \\ 0 & 0 & 0.25 & 0 & 0 \\ 0 & 0 & 0 & 0.3 & 0 \\ 0 & 0 & 0 & 0 & 0.15 \end{bmatrix}$$

A decision matrix D is constructed, and then normalized to be a normalization matrix D':

$$\text{MCDA\_Candidate} = \begin{bmatrix} D_{11} & \cdots & D_{1j} & \cdots & D_{1m} \\ \vdots & & \ddots & & \vdots \\ D_{n1} & \cdots & D_{1j} & \cdots & D_{nm} \end{bmatrix} \times [W_1 W_2 W_3 W_4 W_5]$$

$$D = \begin{bmatrix} 926.932114095416 & 0.004265394907499999 & 12 & 9.995734605092501 & 47.4 \\ 1078.3434271204517 & 0.004638783719999999 & 16 & 9.99536121628 & 61.2 \\ 463.7951328053706 & 0.0024948649999999998 & 5 & 9.997505134999999 & 21.6 \\ 1117.8385570224605 & 0.0048117749407 & 13 & 9.9951882250593 & 55.6 \\ 1129.3773153600205 & 0.0047363974101 & 11 & 9.995263602589901 & 53.2 \\ 427.9026888159207 & 0.0018840385002000001 & 3 & 9.9981159614998 & 12.6 \end{bmatrix}$$

$$\frac{12}{12 + 16 + 5 + 13 + 11 + 3} = 0.190476193$$

$$D' = \begin{bmatrix} 0.18019013 & 0.18682263 & 0.190476193 & 0.16665899 & 0.18839428 \\ 0.20962359 & 0.20317691 & 0.25396825 & 0.16665277 & 0.24324324 \\ 0.09015903 & 0.10927411 & 0.07936508 & 0.16668851 & 0.08585056 \\ 0.21730121 & 0.21075386 & 0.20634921 & 0.16664988 & 0.22098569 \\ 0.21954428 & 0.20745235 & 0.22222222 & 0.16665114 & 0.21144674 \\ 0.08318176 & 0.08252015 & 0.04761905 & 0.1666987 & 0.05007949 \end{bmatrix}$$

The direction normalization matrix G is calculated using the minimization criteria. Finally, the weight matrix W and the direction normalization matrix are comprehensively evaluated to obtain a comprehensive evaluation value. The comprehensive evaluation values are then ranked from largest to smallest.

$$1 - D' = G = \begin{bmatrix} 0.81980987 & 0.81317737 & 0.80952381 & 0.83334101 & 0.81160572 \\ 0.79037641 & 0.79682309 & 0.74603175 & 0.83334723 & 0.75675676 \\ 0.90984097 & 0.89072589 & 0.92063492 & 0.83331149 & 0.91414944 \\ 0.78269879 & 0.78924614 & 0.79365079 & 0.83335012 & 0.77901431 \\ 0.78045572 & 0.79254765 & 0.77777778 & 0.83334886 & 0.78855326 \\ 0.91681824 & 0.91747985 & 0.95238095 & 0.8333013 & 0.9499205 \end{bmatrix}$$

0.81980987x0.15 + 0.81317737x0.15 + 0.80952381x0.25 + 0.83334101x0.3
+0.81160572x0.15 = 0.8221559891937644

$S_1 = 0.8221559891937644$ $S_2 == 0.891133617849319$ $S_3 = 0.8756477072779868$
$S_4 = 0.8063207016645405$ $S_5 = 0.8072234161938577$ $S_6 = 0.891133617849319$

$$S_6 > S_3 > S_1 > S_5 > S_4 > S_2$$

From the above, Solution S_6 is a better problem solution. The onlooker bee selects S_6 to update according to the problem solution rankings. The algorithm stops computing when the number of loops exceeds the maximum number of iterations (Max_Iter), and returns the best solution after computing.

4 Conclusion

This study uses an intelligent approach called the multi-criteria artificial bee colony (MABC) algorithm to optimize the energy consumption problem in wireless sensor networks. The use case shows that the MABC algorithm provides energy-efficient packet routing, extending the lifespan of the wireless sensor network; this is confirmed by the evaluation of the candidate routing using multi-criteria analysis. The contribution of this work is its use of swarm intelligence (SI) algorithms in wireless sensor network routing. The artificial bee colony algorithm based on multi-criteria decision analysis is used in a wireless sensor network to address the fast convergence problem. Future work will compare the performances of other swarm intelligence algorithms in wireless sensor networks with that of the proposed approach.

Acknowledgement. This research was supported in part by the Ministry of Science and Technology, R.O.C. with a MOST grant 107–2221-E-025-005-.

References

1. Kusek, M.: Internet of things: today and tomorrow. In: 2018 41st International Convention on Information and Communication Technology, Electronics and Microelectronics (MIPRO), pp. 0335–0338. IEEE, May 2018
2. Albreem, M.A., El-Saleh, A.A., Isa, M., Salah, W., Jusoh, M., Azizan, M.M., Ali, A.: Green internet of things (IoT): an overview. In: 2017 IEEE 4th International Conference on Smart Instrumentation, Measurement and Application (ICSIMA), pp. 1–6. IEEE, November 2017
3. Maksimovic, M.: Greening the future: green Internet of Things (G-IoT) as a key technological enabler of sustainable development. In: Internet of Things and Big Data Analytics Toward Next-Generation Intelligence, pp. 283–313. Springer, Cham (2018)
4. Yang, X.-S., Deb, S., Zhao, Y.-X., Fong, S., He, X.: Swarm intelligence: past, present and future. Soft. Comput. **22**(18), 5923–5933 (2017). https://doi.org/10.1007/s00500-017-2810-5
5. Karaboga, D.: An idea based on honey bee swarm for numerical optimization, vol. 200, p. 10. Technical report-tr06, Erciyes university, engineering faculty, computer engineering department (2005)
6. Triantaphyllou, E.: Multi-criteria decision making methods. In: Multi-criteria Decision Making Methods: A Comparative Study, pp. 5–21 (2000)
7. Guo, S., Zhao, H.: Fuzzy best-worst multi-criteria decision-making method and its applications. Knowl.-Based Syst. **121**, 23–31 (2017)
8. Abdullah, L., Adawiyah, C.R.: Simple additive weighting methods of multi criteria decision making and applications: a decade review. Int. J. Inf. Process. Manage. **5**(1), 39 (2014)
9. Zanakis, S.H., Solomon, A., Wishart, N., Dublish, S.: Multi-attribute decision making: a simulation comparison of select methods. Eur. J. Oper. Res. **107**(3), 507–529 (1998)
10. Fauzi, N., Noviarti, T., Muslihudin, M., Irviani, R., Maseleno, A., Pringsewu, S.T.M.I.K.: Optimal dengue endemic region prediction using fuzzy simple additive weighting based algorithm. Int. J. Pure Appl. Math **118**(7), 473–478 (2018)
11. Goodridge, W., Bernard, M., Jordan, R., Rampersad, R.: Intelligent diagnosis of diseases in plants using a hybrid Multi-Criteria decision making technique. Comput. Electron. Agric. **133**, 80–87 (2017)
12. Chithaluru, P., Ravi P., Subodh, S.: WSN structure based on SDN. In: Innovations in Software-Defined Networking and Network Functions Virtualization. IGI Global, pp. 240–253 (2018)
13. Djellali, H., Djebbar, A., Zine, N. G., Azizi, N.: Hybrid artificial bees colony and particle swarm on feature selection. In: IFIP International Conference on Computational Intelligence and Its Applications, pp. 93–105, Springer, Cham (2018)

WLAN, Wireless Internet and 5G

A Dynamic Priority Adjustment Scheme for the Next Generation WLAN Supporting Delay Sensitive Services

Ning Wang, Bo Li, Mao Yang$^{(\boxtimes)}$, and Zhongjiang Yan

School of Electronics and Information, Northwestern Polytechnical University,
Xi'an, China
ningwang22668800@mail.nwpu.edu.cn, {libo.npu,yangmao,zhjyan}@nwpu.edu.cn

Abstract. With the rapid development of wireless communications, Wireless Local Area Network (WLAN) has entered thousands of households and has become one of the most important ways of carrying data business. In recent years, delay sensitive applications and services such as real-time game and wireless meeting have been increasing sharply. These applications and services require low latency. However, the traditional WLAN can hardly satisfy the needs of this requirement. The next generation WLAN standard: IEEE 802.11be which was established in 2019 regards low latency as one important technical objective. In this paper, we propose a delay sensitive priority adjustment scheme for the next generation WLAN to improve the latency performance of delay sensitive services. In the Media Access Control (MAC) layer, if there is still some time left before deadline, the priority of delay sensitive packets will be normal. Conversely, as the deadline approaches, the priority of delay sensitive packets will be upgraded. The priority related mechanisms in MAC layer include queuing policy, channel access parameters, and Modulation and Coding Scheme (MCS) selection.

Keywords: WLAN · 802.11be · EDCA · Low latency

1 Introduction

With the popularization of wireless network and the rapid growth of global user business, Wireless Local Area Network(WLAN) has become one of the most important data service carriers. However, as the number and demand of users increases, the performance requirements for business transmission are also steadily increasing. In order to meet the increasing user demand, both academic and industrial circles are paying attention to the key technology research and standardization of next-generation WLAN.

With the rapid development of IEEE802.11 WLAN, the demand of users for Quality of Service(QoS) is increasing. As the diversity of service types and the number of delay-sensitive services increased, it is necessary for network

© ICST Institute for Computer Sciences, Social Informatics and Telecommunications Engineering 2021
Published by Springer Nature Switzerland AG 2021. All Rights Reserved
Y.-B. Lin and D.-J. Deng (Eds.): SGIoT 2020, LNICST 354, pp. 273–285, 2021.
https://doi.org/10.1007/978-3-030-69514-9_22

transmission to keep pace with the times and provide corresponding QoS guarantees for various services. Therefore, the improvement of QoS becomes the direction that the device business or the terminal mobile device is striving to improve. In 2005, IEEE 802.11e proposed a Hybrid Coordination Function (HCF) based on the Distributed Coordination Function (DCF) and Point Coordination Function (PCF) in the original IEEE 802.11 protocol, which included Enhanced Distributed Channel Access (EDCA) mechanism. EDCA can provide business priority service and provide QoS guarantee to some extent.

However, the EDCA mechanism has its limitations. Although it divides the business into 4 types and 8 priority levels, as new low delay business rises, its disadvantage has gradually exposed. At present, such network service as on-line game, VR and automatic drive, which have very high request to the low delay, are gradually increasing. The demand for such services is growing fast. But for these derived delay-sensitive services, the existing mechanisms cannot meet their transmission performance requirements, and there is no guarantee that they will complete the transmission within the specified time. Even in the transmission, there are often discarded packets and so on, resulting in an extremely bad result. Clearly, the EDCA does not provide sufficient protection for delay sensitive services.

The next-generation WLAN Protocol IEEE802.11be has taken low latency guarantee as a key technology target, aimed at solving the problem of low latency service in the EDCA mechanism of IEEE802.11e.

The current literature on WLAN delay performance and IEEE 802.11be standards for next-generation WLAN is as follows:

Hyame Assem Alameddine et al. [1] described the service types, development prospects and requirements of ultra-low latency, and then, based on the fifth generation of cellular network, proposed a method to enhance the performance of cellular network based on routing scheduling.

Yu Y U et al. [2] explored the delay problem in mobile and wireless networks, a FPP with spatial diversity and coding redundancy was proposed to enhance the delay performance as much as possible.

Engelstad P E et al. [3] proposed a method to predict the total packet transmission delay, which can be used to improve the performance of the EDCA priority scheme of IEEE 802.11e standard.

Khorov E et al. [4] analyzed hundreds of features proposed based on the new technology of IEEE 802.11be, including the description of low delay guarantee and real-time requirements.

In Yang M et al. [5], the key technologies such as delay and jitter guarantee of IEEE 802.11be are systemized and prospected.

The main features of IEEE 802.11be are described in detail in López-Pérez et al. [6] and the potential throughput gain it provides is evaluated.

However, the existing literature can not analyze the EDCA mechanism to find out its problems in low-delay guarantee. Then according to the solution of the problem, raise a dynamic priority adjustment in detail.

Based on the analysis of the EDCA mechanism of IEEE 802.11e, this paper proposes a dynamic access priority adjustment strategy for protecting delay-sensitive services. In this scheme, the delay-sensitive service packets are analyzed, and the priority of the service and the transmission scheme are dynamically adjusted according to the time threshold of the waiting time. Finally, the delay-sensitive service transmission requirement is guaranteed.

In the first part of this paper, we present IEEE 802. 11e is difficult to guarantee delay-sensitive services. We investigate the current research situation at home and abroad, and describes the work done in this paper. In the second part, the traditional EDCA is briefly introduced and its principle is briefly analyzed, and then the problems of traditional EDCA in delay-sensitive service are pointed out. The third part, on the basis of the previous, leads to the low-delay guarantee strategy proposed in this paper, and gives the concrete realization ideas. In the fourth part, simulation experiments are carried out on the delay-time guarantee model proposed in this paper, and the simulation results are compared and analyzed. The fifth part is the summary of the full text.

2   Background and Motivation

2.1   The EDCA Mechanism

In IEEE802.11, the DCF mechanism adopts contention access mode, which can not provide accurate delay and bandwidth guarantee. So, the DCF can not guarantee QoS at all.

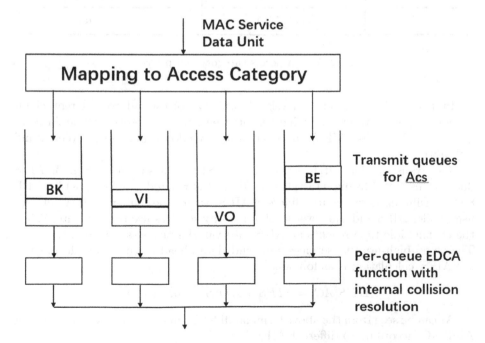

Fig. 1. Queue access for EDCA

To improve the QoS of the MAC protocol in IEEE802.11, IEEE802.11e raised EDCA which provides different levels of priority services. Figure 1 shows the basic queue access method for EDCA. The EDCA mechanism introduces the concept of Service Queue, which maps the service into four access categories. The four access categories are prioritized from top to bottom: voice (AC_VO), video (AC_VI), data (AC_BE), background flow (AC_BK). Four access categories were divided into eight priority. EDCA access categories and priorities are shown in Fig. 2.

Priority	AC	Designation Informative
1	AC_BK	Background
2	AC_BK	Background
0	AC_BE	Best Effort
3	AC_BE	Best Effort
4	AC_VI	Video
5	AC_VI	Video
6	AC_VO	Voice
7	AC_VO	Voice

Fig. 2. EDCA access category and priority

In IEEE802.11e, different levels of priority correspond to different channel intervention parameters. Channel intervention parameters include Arbitration Frame Intervals (AIFS) and Contention Windows (including CWmax and CWmin).

The transport backoff process of DCF/EDCA is shown in Fig. 3. AIFS does not use fixed frame intervals like DIFS (Distributed Frame Gaps) in IEEE 802.11. Different services use different AIFS, where the higher-priority services use smaller AIFS and the lower level of priority services use the opposite. When the channel idle time reaches an AIFS interval, the business can send the data. Therefore, high-priority services will send data ahead of time. The formula of the AIFS' calculation is as follows:

$$AIFS[AC] = SIFS + AIFSN * aSlotTime \tag{1}$$

As can be seen from the above formula, different businesses may have different AIFS[AC] according to different AIFSN.

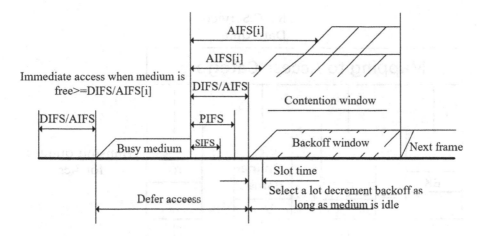

Fig. 3. Backoff Process of DCF and EDCA

Meanwhile, the higher the priority level is, the shorter the competition window will be. It also ensured that high priority services get better service.

Different types of traffic are differ in priority, so they can be transmitted according to different channel parameters and guarantee the QoS. In this way, EDCA provides a degree of QoS assurance to the business.

2.2   EDCA is Insufficient for Low Latency Service

With the development of network services, services with high requirements for low transmission delay have gradually become the mainstream. Such as online games, industrial control, VR, autopilot and so on, these services must be transmitted with very low delay to meet the users' needs. The question arises: for these low latency services, how should they be prioritized for transmission using traditional EDCA mechanisms?

We assume a simple scenario: during the transmission of an EDCA, the channel is in a relatively saturated state. At this point, there is a delay-sensitive packet to be sent, as shown in Fig. 4 below. To meet the needs of delay-sensitive businesses, it seems the easiest way is to configure all of these businesses to be high priority, such as VO.

If all delay sensitive services are treated as high priority services, the requirements of these services are guaranteed to some extent, but this will have a significant impact on the existing high priority services in the VO queue. As a result, the queue of high priority traffic is congested, which seriously affects the transmission quality. Furthermore, more business is assigned to the High Priority Queue, which means the high priority particularity is no longer existed. Obviously, this will have a bad effect on the transmission. So, it's not a viable strategy.

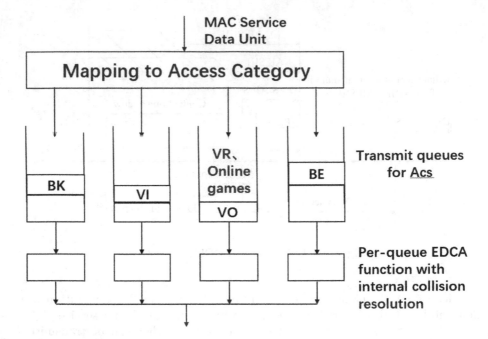

Fig. 4. Example

If the delay sensitive business is all set to low priority, such as BE. That doesn't work either. While this approach protects the transmission quality of traditional high-priority services, the problem of delay-sensitive Services has not been solved at all. Low-priority queues, which are inherently inefficient, will only become more crowded and will certainly not meet the needs of delay-sensitive services.

The above analysis is only a simple case. We can see that the EDCA mechanism has been unable to meet the transmission needs of a single delay-sensitive business. As a matter of fact, with the rise of delay-sensitive business, business is becoming more and more differentiated. Today, latency is no longer exclusive to certain packets. Packets of different services may have low latency demand, the only difference is the degree of the demand.

For example, an AC_BE type packet does not require much delay when entering the queue. But if it can not compete with the channel for a long time, and can not send, then its delay will become more and more sensitive. That eventually caused the packet to fail.

It is obvious that in reality, when more and more packets require low delay, the traditional EDCA will only fail more and more. A simple high-low priority configuration will only result in more and more serious errors. Clearly, it does not meet the needs of the user.

3   Low Delay Safeguard Strategy

3.1   Low Delay Guarantee Strategy for Dynamic Priority Adjustment

In this paper, a low delay guarantee strategy based on dynamic priority adjustment is proposed to provide dynamic priority adjustment for delay-sensitive services, so as to guarantee the emerging delay-sensitive services without affecting the transmission quality of the traditional four services as much as possible.

3.2   The Core Idea of Dynamic Prioritization

In order to simplify the analysis, high priority VO and low priority BE are set. The high priority VO and low priority BE are connected to a single channel in the EDCA way. Within the node, VO and BE are divided into two queues, which perform queuing and retreating access independently.

Supposing that packets of a delay-sensitive service need to be sent, in order to meet the needs of users, there is a time T as the deadline for dispatching. That is, after such packets are queued for sending, they must be dispatched within time T, otherwise the packets will be lost. Assuming that after a packet is queued, its waiting time in the queue is recorded from zero at t. It is obviously that the packet is sent at t<T according to business requirements.

The implementation process is shown in Fig. 5.

First of all, in order to save channel resources as much as possible, when the delay sensitive class packet just arrived, it was queued according to the traditional EDCA idea, placed in the low priority BE queue to wait for sending, and then executed the backoff according to the channel access parameters of the low priority service.

It is best if the delay-sensitive packets are sent successfully in the BE queue. More often than not, t (the waiting time) is near T (the deadline for sending), but there are still many packets in the queue ahead of delay-sensitive packets. If we don't act now, the delay-sensitive packets will not be sent in time.

Through many experiments, the parameter $\alpha(0< \alpha <1)$ is chosen as the threshold of the waiting time of delay-sensitive packets in the low-priority Queue. That is, when t arrives αT, if the delay-sensitive packet is still not sent in the BE queue, it is urgent. To ensure the demand of service transmission, dynamic adjustment should be taken. At this point, the channel access parameters of delay sensitive packets are changed from BE queue to high priority VO queue, which increases the possibility of receiving the packet delivery service.

When the delay sensitive packets enter the high priority VO queue, it is best if the packets can be sent smoothly. But if the waiting time t is very close to the deadline T, and at this point the delay sensitive packets are still queued in the VO queue, which makes it more urgent.

Through many experiments, the parameter $\beta(\alpha < \beta <1)$ is chosen as the threshold of the waiting time of delay-sensitive packets in the high-priority queue. That is, when t reaches βT, if the delay sensitive packet is still waiting to be sent

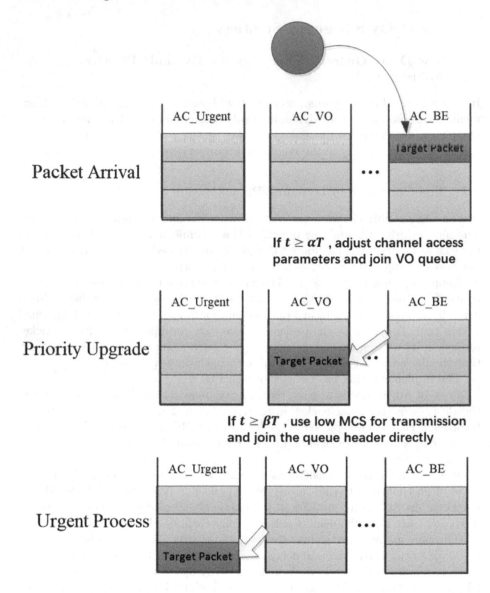

Fig. 5. Core idea

in the VO queue, it is more urgent. To ensure the service transmission requirement, dynamic adjustment measures should be taken again. The packet will be transferred to the head of the queue directly, and the low MCS(Modulation and Coding Scheme) is used for transmission to ensure that the delay-sensitive packets are sent before T time and to make the transmission more reliable.

The entire delay-sensitive business dynamic assurance process is shown in Fig. 6.

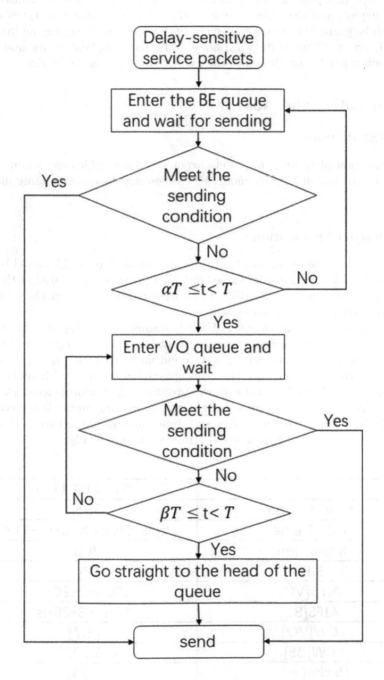

Fig. 6. Core idea' process

Through this process, the channel and slot resources can be utilized to a greater extent, and the transmission quality of the original four types of services can be guaranteed to guarantee the performance of the emerging low delay demand services. This strategy is undoubtedly more applicable now and in the future, when low latency becomes the mainstream of network services.

4   Simulation and Analysis

4.1   NS3 Platform

NS3 simulation platform is a discrete event simulator, which can simulate network transmission and service model by configuring the corresponding modules of it.

4.2   Design of Simulation

In order to meet the requirements of the experiment, the EDCA model is simulated on the NS3 platform, and three kinds of services are generated at the same time. One is VO, the other is BE, and another is low delay. Put them into the model to carry out simulation experiments.

The design of the experiment is UDP transmission. During the experiment, the low delay service was first processed according to the high priority VO type in the common EDCA mechanism at different data generation rates, which was used as the control. Then, the low-delay guarantee strategy with dynamically adjusted priority is used to deal with the problem. The performance of the delay and the change of the throughput of the two processing methods are collected respectively. Finally, the advantages and disadvantages of the two methods are compared and analyzed. Parameter Settings are shown in Fig. 7.

PHY	IEEE 802.11ax
MAC header	56bit
ACK frame	Physical layer header +112bit
a slot time	20μs
SIFS	10μs
AIFS[VO]	10μs+2*20μs
AIFS[BE]	10μs+3*20μs
CW[VO]	[3,7]
CW[BE]	[15,1023]
Packet size	1500Byte

Fig. 7. Parameter Settings

In the simulation of the dynamically adjusted model raised in this paper, the last contract period T of the low delay service is set to 10 ms. Through a large number of experiments, the optimal effect is selected, so that the configuration parameters $\alpha = 0.5$, $\beta = 0.92$. That is, before 5 ms, services with low latency requirements were transmitted as BE. After 5 ms, it's transmitted as VO. Transmission should be completed by 9.2 ms at the latest.

4.3   Analysis of Simulation Results

Using two different processing methods, when the packet rate is different, the transmission delay of the low-latency service are shown in Fig. 8.

Using two different processing methods, the total throughput of the network changes with different packet rates are shown in Fig. 9.

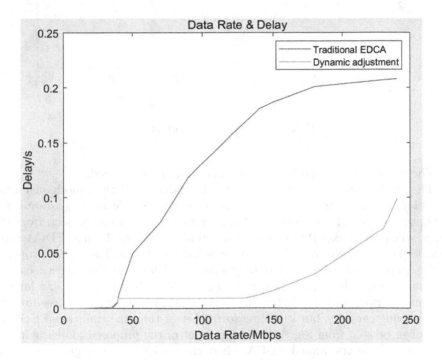

Fig. 8. Delay performance of delay-sensitive service

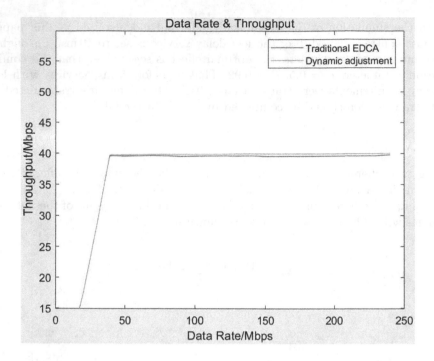

Fig. 9. Throughput performance

The results of the experiment were analyzed and compared.

The result shows that, compared with the traditional EDCA mechanism, the low delay guarantee strategy proposed in this paper can effectively guarantee the low delay demand of the service within a certain limit. As can be seen from the Fig. 8, when the packet rate is less than 130 Mbps, the traditional EDCA can't provide the delay guarantee for the delay sensitive service. The model proposed in this paper guarantees that data packets of delay sensitive service can be sent at 9.2 ms. When the data rate is higher than 130 Mbps, the low latency guarantee performance is affected due to the traffic increasing and exceeding the load carrying capacity, but it still performs better than the traditional EDCA.

As can be seen from Fig. 9, the throughput of the proposed model is higher than that of the traditional EDCA when the packet rate is higher than 39.5 Mbps. This is due to the low-delay dynamic adjustment strategy proposed in this paper, which can make use of both low-priority BE and high-priority VO. Therefore, the total throughput and transmission efficiency of the network are improved to a certain extent.

It is concluded that the dynamic priority adjustment model in this paper is effective, not only for the delay sensitive service, but also for network throughput efficiency.

5 Discussion

According to the simulation, the dynamic priority-based strategy proposed in this paper can provide better protection for the emerging low-latency services than the traditional EDCA. In the face of the booming low delay business, the traditional EDCA can't meet the needs of users. Using the strategy provided in this paper, the transmission of low delay traffic is guaranteed without affecting the traditional traffic.

6 Conclusions and Future Works

Based on the analysis of the latest progress of WLAN and the shortcomings of traditional EDCA mechanism in the new low-delay service transmission, a low-delay guarantee strategy with dynamically adjusted priority is proposed. This strategy not only guarantees the normal transmission of the traditional services, but also provides a solution to save the channel and slot resources for the emerging low-delay services. The results show that the low delay guarantee strategy proposed in this paper is better than the traditional EDCA mechanism.

Acknowledgement. This work was supported in part by the National Natural Science Foundations of CHINA (Grant No. 61771390, No. 61871322, No. 61771392, and No. 61501373), and Science and Technology on Avionics Integration Laboratory and the Aeronautical Science Foundation of China (Grant No. 20185553035, and No. 201955053002).

References

1. Alameddine, H.A., Qu, L., Assi, C.: Scheduling service function chains for ultra-low latency network services. In: International Conference on Network & Service Management. IEEE Computer Society (2017)
2. Yu, Y.U., Kucera, S., Lim, Y., et al.: Low-latency communication in LTE and WiFi using spatial diversity and encoding redundancy. Ice Trans. Commun. E101.B(4) (2018)
3. Engelstad, P.E., Osterbo, O.N.: Analysis of the total delay of IEEE 802.11e EDCA and 802.11 DCF. In: IEEE International Conference on Communications. IEEE (2006)
4. Khorov, E., Levitsky, I., Akyildiz, I.F.: Current Status and Directions of IEEE 802.11be, the Future Wi-Fi 7. IEEE Access **PP**(99), 1 (2020)
5. Yang, M., Li, B.: Survey and Perspective on Extremely High Throughput (EHT) WLAN - IEEE 802.11be. Mobile Networks and Applications 2020(2)
6. López-Pérez, D., Garcia-Rodriguez, A., Galati-Giordano, L., et al.: IEEE 802.11be Extremely High Throughput: The Next Generation of Wi-Fi Technology Beyond 802.11ax. IEEE Communications Magazine (2019)

Low-Latency Guarantee Protocol Based on Multi-links Scheduling Random Access in the Next Generation WLAN: IEEE 802.11be

Luoting Gan, Bo Li, Mao Yang[✉], and Zhongjiang Yan

School of Electronics and Information, Northwestern Polytechnical University, Xi'an, China
glt102288@mail.nwpu.edu.cn, {libo.npu,yangmao,zhjyan}@nwpu.edu.cn

Abstract. With the advent of artificial intelligence and big data era, the demands for wireless networks require increasingly high quality of service (QoS). In the next-generation wireless local area network (WLAN), the Institute of Electrical and Electronics Engineers (IEEE) 802.11 regards low-latency guarantee as one of the main technical goals. Multi-link operation (MLO) technology can effectively guarantee network delay. Based on this, this paper proposes a low-latency guarantee protocol based on multi-link scheduling random access. The specific process of the low-latency guarantee protocol is proposed and designed, and the frame format of the protocol is designed to make it compatible with the 802.11 frame format. The simulation results show that the random access protocol based on multi-link scheduling can effectively improve the QoS of the network compared with the traditional single link. It not only increases the throughput of the network, but also effectively reduces the data transmission delay. The addition of scheduling algorithms can effectively reduce the delay of high-priority services and reduce the packet loss rate of the entire network.

Keywords: QoS · WLAN · IEEE · MLO · Low-latency guarantee

1 Introduction

With the rapid development of mobile Internet and the widespread use of smart terminals, the amount of data carried by wireless networks has continued to increase sharply, and wireless services have gradually become diversified. Wireless local area networks (WLAN) has become the main carrier of wireless services. With the advent of the internet of everything, intelligent manufacturing and big data era, lifestyle changes on network performance requirements are also increasing. The requirement for low-latency guarantee of wireless network and improvement of network throughput is also imminent.

© ICST Institute for Computer Sciences, Social Informatics and Telecommunications Engineering 2021
Published by Springer Nature Switzerland AG 2021. All Rights Reserved
Y.-B. Lin and D.-J. Deng (Eds.): SGIoT 2020, LNICST 354, pp. 286–296, 2021.
https://doi.org/10.1007/978-3-030-69514-9_23

Based on the latest with the Institute of Electrical and Electronics Engineers (IEEE) 802.11ax specification of a new generation of more powerful Wi-Fi products Wi-Fi6 come out [1]. The Wi-Fi 6 will not only greatly improve people's lifestyle, but also bring great economic value to various industries [2]. In the next few years, video traffic will become the main traffic type (such as 4k and 8k video), and with the emergence of more advanced technologies, its throughput requirements will continue to grow to tens of gigabits per second (Gbps). At the same time, new applications requiring high throughput and low latency are also proliferating, such as augmented reality, virtual reality, giant games and remote office and so on. The IEEE 802.11 will have to further improve Wi-Fi to meet the needs of these specific scenarios with high throughput, low latency and high reliability. In order to continuously meet the rapid growth of the services and improve the user experience. The IEEE 802.11 discussed and revised the project approval of the next generation WLAN standard extremely high throughput (EHT) at the standards working group meeting held in March 2019. The next-generation WLAN standard EHT project authorization request (PAR) clearly requires that it support 30 Gbps throughput and improve the low-latency guarantee capability and jitter [3]. In order to achieve the technical goal of extremely high throughput, 802.11 be introduces a multi-band operation (MBO) mechanism, so that the device can work efficiently and coordinately on more frequency bands [4]. The multi-link operation (MLO) is one of the key MBO technologies that attracts the most attention. It runs multiple links independently or cooperatively at the same time to improve the limit throughput of the network [5].

Through the research of the literature, the author found that the previous WLAN standards mainly focused on designing the media access control (MAC) layer algorithm protocol to optimize the low-latency guarantee. In this paper, based on the introduction of multi-link operation mechanism of 802.11be, a low-delay guarantee algorithm based on multi-link scheduling random access is proposed. This algorithm mainly provides a multi-link scheduling algorithm that guarantees network delay. The access point (AP) performs effective coordinated scheduling on multiple links according to the current channel conditions. This can not only reduce network transmission delay, but also effectively improve network performance, such as throughput and packet loss rate.

In the remaining chapters of the article, the author will expand from the following aspects. In the second chapter, we mainly give an overview of the next-generation WLAN standard and introduce the MLO mechanism introduced by 802.11 be. The delay guarantee algorithm based on multi-link scheduling random access will be introduced in detail and the algorithm flow will be given in the third chapter. In the fourth chapter, the author will design the simulation scene according to the algorithm in this paper and compare it with the traditional low-delay guarantee algorithm and the scheme without scheduling algorithm. Finally, in the fifth chapter, draw conclusions.

2   Overview of the Next Generation WLAN Standards and MLO Operation

2.1   Overview of the Next Generation WLAN Standards

802.11be was formed in May 2018 to form the EHT topic interest group (TIG) [6], which is determined to enable the new MAC and physical layer (PHY) operation mode, which can support the maximum throughput of at least 30 Gbps. It also ensures backward compatibility and co-existence with older 802.11 devices in the 2.4 GHz, 5 GHz, and 6 GHz unlicensed bands. The EHT study group (EHT SG) was launched in July 2018 with the primary goal of forming an effective serialization development process. At the IEEE 802.11 standard working group meeting held in March 2019, the project document of the next-generation WLAN standard EHT working group was discussed and revised, and the project was named 802.11be [4]. In May 2019, the next-generation WLAN standard officially entered the working group stage from the study group. It is expected that the 802.11be standard will be launched around 2024.

In the 802.11be PAR approved by the IEEE standard protocol in March 2019, not only the throughput of the network is required to be improved, but also the delay guarantee capability of the network is clearly required to be improved [7]. The proposal of delay guarantee shows that the focus of the next generation WLAN will be devoted to the research and development of delay guarantee mechanisms. Low latency, low jitter, and high stability requirements have been valued by the 802.11 standardization organization, which shows that the standard development group has changed its mindset of focusing on the single characteristic of improving throughput (Fig. 1).

Fig. 1. 802.11be standardized timelines

2.2   Overview of MLO

In previous versions of IEEE 802.11, only one link was used between an AP and a station (STA) and worked on one frequency band, such as 2.4 GHz or 5 GHz. In order to achieve the technical goal of extremely high throughput, IEEE 802.11be introduced multi-link operation. IEEE 802.11be allows the device to have multiple sets of radios and work in multiple frequency bands such as 2.4 GHz, 5 GHz (high frequency band and low frequency band), 6 GHz at the same time. This greatly improves the limit throughput of the network [8].

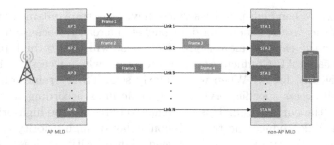

Fig. 2. Multi-link operation schematic

As shown in Fig. 2, an AP multi-link device (AP MLD) is similar to the role of the traditional AP, and the non-AP MLD (hereinafter referred to as STA MLD) is similar to the role of the traditional STA. But strictly speaking, there is a big difference in concept. An AP MLD can have multiple APs working in different frequency bands, such as AP1, AP 2, AP 3 until AP N in the figure, but these APs are located in the same device. A STA MLD can have multiple STAs working in different frequency bands, such as STA1, STA 2, STA 3 until STA N in the figure, and these STAs are located in the same device. Wherein, AP1, AP2 and AP3 work in different frequency bands, STA1, STA 2 and STA 3 work in different frequency bands, and AP1 and STA1, AP2 and STA2, AP3 and STA3 work in the same frequency band respectively. The links formed by them are called link 1, link 2, and link 3. Therefore, a link corresponds to a collection of APs and STAs working in the same frequency band. It can be seen from the figure that different links can work at the same time, such as data transmission. In addition, resources between links can be efficiently integrated. For example, the transmission of frame 1 on link 1 in the figure fails, and AP MLD chooses to retransmit the frame on link 3. It can be seen that, first of all, MLO enables APs and STAs to have more bandwidth resources, thereby laying an important foundation for achieving the goals of EHT. In addition, efficient coordination between different links can further improve the efficiency of access, transmission and retransmission.

In this paper, we design a delay guarantee protocol based on the multi-link scheduling random access design, which not only helps to reduce the network delay, but also has the advantages of increasing the network throughput rate and reducing packet loss rate.

3 The Low-Latency Guarantee Protocol Based on Multi-link Scheduling Random Access

3.1 Protocol Overview

Regarding how to ensure low-latency transmission in wireless networks, this paper proposes a low-latency guarantee protocol based on multi-link scheduling random access. When high-priority services have been transmitting data on a certain link, as the rate of generating data packets increases, because high-priority services enter the channel more aggressively, this will lead to high-priority services in the same AP Conflicts are prone to occur when accessing channels, as shown in Fig. 3(a) below. When we regularly send TSAF frames on each link, the node will access specific services to specific links according to the specific conditions of the current link. This can effectively reduce the high-priority push on a certain link, reduce the transmission delay of high-priority services and reduce the probability of conflicts between high-priority services, as shown in the following Fig. 3(b). This protocol not only improves the throughput of the network and reduces the transmission delay of the network, but also reduces the packet loss rate of the entire network.

3.2   The Process of the Low-Latency Guarantee Protocol

In order to effectively protect the low-latency data transmission in next generation WLAN. This paper proposes a scheduling random access protocol based on multiple links. The specific agreement process can be divided into the following steps:

Step 1: The AP periodically sends a traffic scheduling announcement frame (TSAF) on each link to indicate which link or links a specific service is transmitted on.

Step 2: After receiving the control frame, the STA performs data transmission on the link assigned to the specific service according to the control frame. For example, when performing downlink data transmission, the AP will put specific services into the queue of the assigned specific link to compete for current link resources. As shown in Fig. 4, the AP will assign high-priority services to the link 1 and link 2, and assign low-priority services to link 2. This greatly improves the efficiency of high-priority service access and helps reduce high-priority delay and throughput.

Step 3: When the destination node receives a packet over a link, it returns an acknowledgement (ACK) on that link.

Step 4: In each TSAF cycle, each node transmits a specific service on a specific link according to the information sent by the TSAF frame. Transmission based on the information carried in the TSAF frame helps to ensure that high-priority services minimize collisions, ensure the delay of high-priority services, and improve the throughput of high-priority services.

3.3   Scheduling Algorithm Design

In order to enable the AP to effectively schedule reliable link resources to transmit high-priority services, we have designed a scheduling algorithm based on service priority differences. Through this algorithm, our goal is to enable high-priority services to be transmitted on reliable links as much as possible, so as to

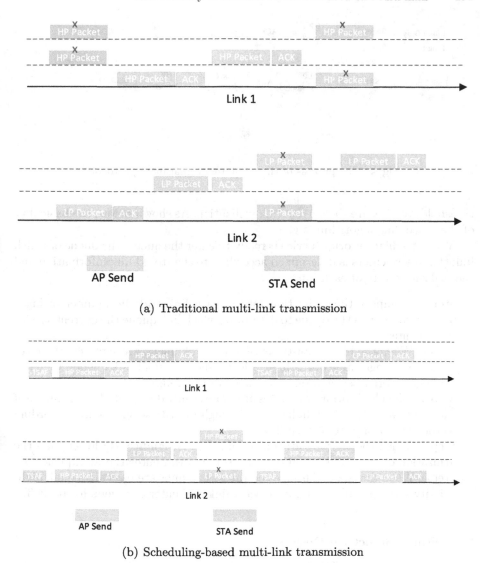

(a) Traditional multi-link transmission

(b) Scheduling-based multi-link transmission

Fig. 3. Data transmission under multiple links

ensure the delay and transmission of high-priority services. Based on this idea, this paper designs an algorithm based on link utilization and TSAF's information received by AP to effectively allocate link resources. The core idea is: when the AP receives the TSAF sent by the AP of other cells, it will store the link information carried by the TSAF. When the AP competes for a certain link, it will use the stored link information, Information such as channel utilization rate allocates link resources. For link utilization, we use parametric link utilization threshold (including two thresholds, high priority threshold and low priority

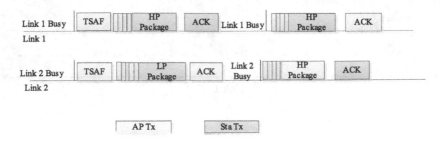

Fig. 4. The process of the low-latency guarantee protocol

threshold) to measure the current link utilization. As shown below, the basic flow of the scheduling algorithm is given:

When the high-priority service is ready to enter the queue, the queue of which link the service enters is determined according to the stored link information and the utilization rate of each link.

> Step 1: Compare the utilization rate of each link and the number of high-priority services in the queue to determine which link queue the current service should enter.
> Step 2: When the high-priority services in a link queue are significantly lower than the average value of the high-priority services in all link queues, we enter the high-priority services into the queue of this link.
> Step 3: When high-priority services are more evenly distributed in the queue of each link, we judge which link queue the high-priority services enter according to the utilization rate of each link.
> Step 4: When the channel utilization of a link is significantly lower than the utilization of other links, high-priority services will enter the link queue.
> Step 5: When the channel utilization rates of all links are basically equal, high-priority services will randomly select a link and enter its queue for backoff.

3.4   Frame Structure Design

The frame structure of TSAF is extended according to the frame format of the 802.11 traditional trigger frame (TF). As shown in the figure below, the author adds a Link Info field in the TSAF to indicate the link number, service type, and transmission duration in the link. The other fields are consistent with the traditional TF structure (Fig. 5).

Fig. 5. Frame structure of TSAF

4   Simulation Design and Implementation

How to guarantee delay has become an important research direction in the next-generation WLAN. So what is the effect of the delay guarantee protocol based on the random access method of scheduling multi-link designed in this paper? Based on this, we designed and implemented algorithms on the NS3 simulation platform and designed specific scenarios to verify our protocol. NS3 is a discrete event simulator, which is a software dedicated to learning and researching network simulation. Based on this platform, the author has realized the test and verification of the delay guarantee of this protocol and the traditional single link. First of all, we designed a basic single cell scenario to verify the performance of this protocol and the traditional single link to compare all aspects. We adjust the node's packet production rate to compare the network performance of this protocol which is different from the traditional single link mode. The specific parameters of the scene are shown in the following Table 1:

Table 1. The parameter of simulation one

Parameter	Value	Parameter	Value
The Number of AP	1	Service Type	High/Low Priority
The Number of STA	4	The Number of Link	2
Transfer Mode	Down Link	MCS Value	4

The purpose of this simulation is to compare the basic network performance of this protocol with the traditional single link (TSL), mainly from the network throughput and service transmission delay. As shown in the figure below, we can clearly find that compared to the traditional single-link mode, the multi-link scheduling protocol not only improves the throughput of the entire network, but also significantly reduces the transmission delay of the entire network. It not only reduces the delay of high-priority services, but also reduces the transmission delay of low-priority. This shows that compared with the traditional single link, our protocol can greatly improve the performance of the entire network. And with the increase of the node's packet production rate, this protocol improves the overall network performance more obviously than the traditional single link.

This paper designs a single-cell transmission scenario to verify whether the scheduling protocol can effectively reduce the transmission delay of high-priority services and improve network performance. The basic parameters of this scene are shown in the table below (Table 2). The simulation results are shown in the figure below. From the Fig. 6, we can see that the scheduling algorithm can effectively guarantee the high-priority transmission delay. As the data rate increases, the function of the scheduling protocol becomes more apparent (Fig. 7).

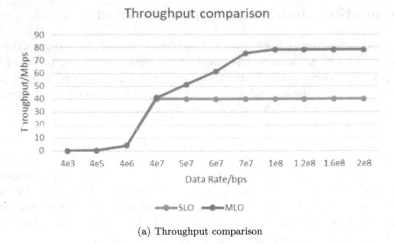

(a) Throughput comparison

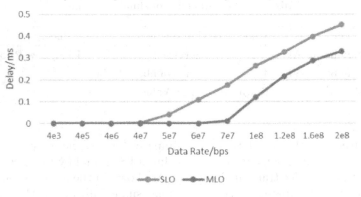

(b) Low priority services delay comparison

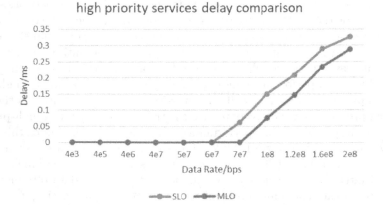

(c) High priority services delay comparison

Fig. 6. Scheduling algorithm comparison

Table 2. The parameter of simulation two

Parameter	Value	Parameter	Value
The Number of AP	1	Service Type	High/Low Priority
The Number of STA	4	The Number of Link	2
Transfer Mode	Down Link	MCS Value	4
Data Rate/Mbps	0.1–500		

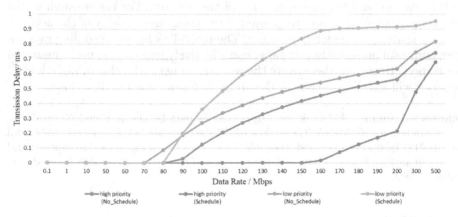

(a) Services delay comparison

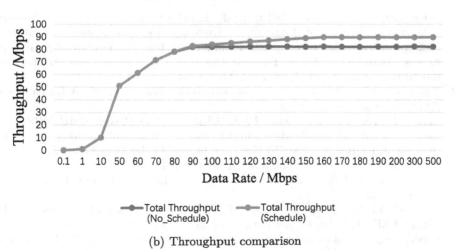

(b) Throughput comparison

Fig. 7. Scheduling algorithm comparison

5   Conclusions and Future Works

From the simulation results, we can see that compared with the traditional single link, this protocol can not only effectively improve the throughput of the entire network, but also significantly reduce the service transmission delay. The scheduling protocol significantly improves the communication quality of the entire network in the case of multiple cells, can effectively reduce the collision of data packets, thereby improving the throughput of the network and reducing the packet loss rate and transmission delay of the network. For the research of the next-generation WLAN, how to guarantee the transmission delay of the network is a very challenging research direction. The multi-link based scheduling random access protocol proposed in this paper can effectively improve the performance in this respect. How to further ensure the research of network delay in high-density scenarios will also become one of the author's future research directions.

Acknowledgment. This work was supported in part by the National Natural Science Foundations of CHINA (Grant No. 61771390, No. 61871322, No. 61771392, and No. 61501373), and Science and Technology on Avionics Integration Laboratory and the Aeronautical Science Foundation of China (Grant No. 20185553035, and No. 201955053002).

References

1. IEEE 802.11, P802.11ax - IEEE Draft Standard for Information Technology Telecommunications and Information Exchange Between Systems Local and Metropolitan Area Networks Specific Requirements Part 11: Wireless LAN Medium Access Control (MAC) and Physical Layer (PHY) Specifications Amendment Enhancements for High Efficiency WLAN (2018)
2. Telecom Advisory Services, LLC, The Economic Value of Wi-Fi: A Global View (2018 and 2023), August 2018
3. Cariou, L.: 802.11 EHT Proposed PAR, IEEE 802.11-18/1231r6, March 2019
4. Yang, M., et al.: AP coordination and full-duplex enabled multi-band operation for the next generation WLAN: IEEE 802.11 be (EHT). In: 2019 11th International Conference on Wireless Communications and Signal
5. Meng, K., et al.: IEEE 802.11 Real Time Applications TIG Report, IEEE 802.11-19/2009r6, March 2019
6. Yang, M., Li, B.: Survey and Perspective on Extremely High Throughput (EHT) WLANIEEE 802.11 be. Mobile Networks and Applications, pp. 1–16 (2020)
7. Lopezperez, D., Garciarodriguez, A., Galatigiordano, L., et al.: IEEE 802.11be extremely high throughput: the next generation of wi-fi technology beyond 802.11ax. IEEE Commun. Mag. **57**(9), 113–119 (2019)
8. Chen et al.: Discussions on the PHY features for EHT, IEEE 802.11-18/1461r0, September 2018

Coordinated TDMA MAC Scheme Design and Performance Evaluation for the Next Generation WLAN: IEEE 802.11be

Huanhuan Cai, Bo Li, Mao Yang$^{(\boxtimes)}$, and Zhongjiang Yan

School of Electronics and Information, Northwestern Polytechnical University, Xi'an, China
caihuanhuan@mail.nwpu.edu.cn, {libo.npu,yangmao,zhjyan}@nwpu.edu.cn

Abstract. The next generation Wireless Local Area Network (WLAN) standard: IEEE 802.11be focuses on achieving extremely high throughput (EHT). High-dense deployment network is still one challenging and important scenario for IEEE 802.11be. In order to improve quality of experience (QoE) of users in high-dense scenario, access point (AP) coordination is considered as a promising technology for IEEE 802.11be. Many researchers and engineers have proposed different specific AP coordination solutions, but the work on the performance verification of the proposed protocol is not yet fully validated. This article focuses on the detailed protocol design and performance of the Coordinated time division multiple access (co-TDMA), one type of AP coordination technologies. We design a specific simulation protocol implementation scheme, perform simulations based on the system-level and link-level integrated simulation platform, evaluate the performance of co-TDMA. Simulation results show that the co-TDMA protocol can improve the throughput and packet loss rate performance under certain network scenarios.

Keywords: WLAN · TDMA · AP coordination · MAC protocol

1 Introduction

Wireless communication technology plays an increasingly important role in our lives. Whether it is communication, entertainment or online office, wireless communication technology can bring us flexibility and convenience. With the increase of end users, the business volume of wireless communication has also increased dramatically. The ever-increasing demand for data services has also brought challenges to Wireless Local Area Network (WLAN) research. In order to bring users a better user experience, countless researchers are devoted to the research of wireless technology. The study of WLAN has always been the focus of academic and industrial attention. From the first WLAN standard released by IEEE in 1997, it has experienced more than twenty years of development [1]. IEEE 802.11ax, which is considered as the standard as WiFi 6 and will be probably

© ICST Institute for Computer Sciences, Social Informatics and Telecommunications Engineering 2021
Published by Springer Nature Switzerland AG 2021. All Rights Reserved
Y.-B. Lin and D.-J. Deng (Eds.): SGIoT 2020, LNICST 354, pp. 297–306, 2021.
https://doi.org/10.1007/978-3-030-69514-9_24

released in 2020, introduces a number of new technologies such as uplink and downlink Orthogonal Frequency Division Multiple Access (OFDMA) technology, uplink and downlink Multi-User Multiple-Input Multiple-Output (MU-MIMO) technology, spatial reuse (SR), and etc. [2–4]. It can be seen that WLAN has made great progress [5]. In order to make a better breakthrough in WLAN technology, the researchers are still persevering and are exploring and researching on the next-generation WLAN standard: IEEE 802.11be.

IEEE 802.11be aims to extremely high throughput (EHT). It is worth noting that high-dense deployment network is still one challenging and important scenario for IEEE 802.11be [6]. It means there are many cells and the cross-cell interferences is deteriorated. It will seriously affect the performance of the entire network and the quality of experience (QoE) of users without efficient solutions [7]. In this case, the objective of extremely high throughput can hardly be achieved.

Access point (AP) coordination is considered as a promising technology for IEEE 802.11be. This technology reduces link conflicts and improves network performance. In previous studies, there were similar related technologies. Some of the related AP coordination protocols are described below. Literature [8] proposes a trigger-based Distribute Multiple-Input Multiple-Output (D-MIMO) Media Access Control (MAC) protocol. This protocol is triggered by STAs. Multiple AP performs joint transmission in D-MIMO mode, combining the advantages of D-MIMO and joint transmission to achieve reliable concurrent transmission. The protocol can meet the needs of high-speed users. Literature [9] proposes a joint reservation and coordinative MAC protocol based on ALOHA, which combines channel reservation technology and joint transmission technology, and makes full use of the advantages of channel reservation technology under reliable joint transmission. This protocol realizes the improvement of network throughput in dense network scenarios. Literature [10–13] also introduced some different protocols for coordinative transmission between AP. Coordinated time division multiple access (co-TDMA) is that multiple APs share time resources during a Transmission Opportunity (TXOP) period, that is, multiple APs are scheduled by one AP called the master AP to perform data transmission in different time periods during this TXOP period. That is to say, in a coordinative transmission, only the master AP needs to compete for the channel, and the slave AP does not need to compete for the channel again, so it gets an opportunity for data transmission and can directly perform data transmission. The most important advantage of co-TDMA is easy to implement. But, there are few studies focusing on the performance evaluation of co-TDMA. In this paper, we design a detailed MAC protocol. After that, we fully evaluate the performance of co-TDMA by our designed simulation platform. Simulation results show that the protocol designed in this article can improve network performance in certain network scenarios.

The chapter structure of this article is as follows: Section 2 discusses the motivation of this article. Section 3 introduces the design details of the protocol. Section 4 designs protocol simulation scenarios and performs protocol simulation and performance evaluation. Section 5 summarizes the work done and prospects of this article.

2 Motivation

2.1 Principle of Coordinated AP

AP coordination, as the name implies, is that multiple APs coordinated with each other to jointly perform data transmission. AP coordination technology enables more than one AP to perform data transmission in a period of time. This technology requires master AP scheduling and each slave AP to obey the master AP's scheduling instructions. Generally, the master AP notifies the slave AP after competing for the channel, and can perform data transmission together with the master AP at the opportunity of the master AP competing for the channel to complete a coordinative transmission. The transmission scenario is shown in Fig. 1.

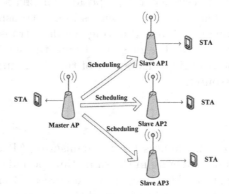

Fig. 1. AP coordination transmission scenario diagram

The link transmitted by the master AP is called the master link, and the link transmitted by the slave AP is called the slave link. The master link and slave link have equal opportunities for data transmission, and the two coordination with each other to jointly improve network performance. The basic transmission process is that at the beginning of transmission, each AP competes for the channel fairly through Carrier Sense Multiple Access with Collision Avoid(CSMA/CA). Once an AP competes for the channel, this AP is determined to be the master AP for this coordinative transmission. The master AP undertakes this scheduling leader role of coordinative transmission. Only if the master AP correctly implements the scheduling process, can the entire coordination process be carried out intact. Then the master AP according to network conditions, selects the slave APs for this coordinative transmission through a selection algorithm, and then the master AP sends a Trigger Frame (TF) to each slave AP to notify these slave APs and the master AP to transmit data together within a certain period of time. After receiving the TF from the master AP, it knows that it has been selected as the slave AP for this coordination transmission and starts to prepare for data transmission with the master AP. After a period of time, the master AP and the slave AP start data transmission simultaneously. Some of the proposed AP coordination protocols are described below.

Coordinated Beamforming/Null Steering (co-BF) Protocol, which proposes a beamforming/zero direction control cooperation method. The main idea of this protocol is to use beamforming technology to coordinate the use of space resources by APs and make full use of the available array. The degree of freedom in space allows data to be transmitted between the coordinating APs simultaneously with little interference between links.

Coordinated OFDMA (co-OFDMA) protocol, the main idea of this protocol is that in a transmission, multiple APs are scheduled to each other in a downlink/uplink Multi-User, and cooperate to transmit in OFDMA mode. Different APs coordinate and use different frequency resources to achieve sharing of frequency resources.

Co-TDMA is studied in some in the proposals. The main idea of this protocol is that multiple APs share the time resources in one transmission. The master AP can jointly schedule the slave AP during the data transmission time of the master AP. During this time, The master AP and the slave AP transmit data in different time periods during this period of time. The master and slave APs share all frequency resources.

2.2   Motivation

The co-TDMA protocol introduces the mechanism of AP coordination, which enables multiple APs to cooperate in the same time period. The co-TDMA protocol studies how multiple APs share time resources. Because the co-TDMA protocol is easy to implement, it has received the attention of many researchers. But there are few studies on the performance verification of co-TDMA protocol. This article conducts research on this protocol flow, focusing on the specific implementation of this protocol, that is, how to implement the co-TDMA protocol flow and co-TDMA protocol performance evaluation. This article designs a specific MAC implementation scheme, and emulates this protocol flow according to the designed scheme. According to the simulation results, the performance of this protocol is discussed and evaluated.

3   Detailed Protocol Design for co-TDMA

This protocol is mainly for the specific protocol design of how the master AP and the slave AP share time resources during AP coordination. Set some APs as a group, each AP in the group can be the master AP when competing for the channel. Each AP can compete for the channel regardless of whether there is a service to be transmitted or not. After the competition reaches the channel as the master AP, if the master AP has a service to transmit, the master AP service will be transmitted first, and the other slave AP services will be transmitted. If the master AP has no business to transmit, it will directly transmit other slave AP services. During the transmission time of a master AP, divide this time into different time periods. The master and slave APs occupy different time periods for data transmission. In this way, the master and slave APs share this transmission opportunity of the master AP. These slave AP does not need to compete for channels, and can directly send data when the allocated time period arrives. This protocol is compared with the scenario where AP does not perform joint transmission. Protocol process is:

(1) Each AP competes for the channel fairly. The AP competing for the channel sets itself as the master AP.
(2) The main AP sends a detection frame to obtain whether other APs have services to transmit.
(3) The other APs that have uplink or downlink data to send an ACK to the master AP, indicating that it has business to transmit.
(4) The master AP sends a co-TDMA TF to each slave AP. The co-TDMA TF carries the slave AP information and the time segment information transmitted from the slave AP.
(4) If the master AP has services to transmit, the master AP starts to transmit data within the time period allocated by itself. If not, go to step 4.
(5) After receiving the TF from the master AP, the slave APs obtain the time segment information of the transmission assigned by the master AP to itself. When the time segment arrives, the corresponding slave AP becomes the TXOP holder and starts uplink and/or downlink data transmission. The slave AP have to guarantee that the transmission should finished before the next time segment start time. The process is shown in Fig. 2. After the AP contends for the channel, set the master AP, obtain the slave APs, and share the time with the slave AP in the time period of the master AP's current transmission. Data transmission takes place in different time periods within a certain period of time.

In the process of implementing this protocol, the setting of NAV is extremely important, There are two ways to solve the NAV setting problem.

(1) Newly introduce a Group NAV and a one bit indication filed named IsGroup. After the master AP competes for the channel, The slave APs receives the TF of the master AP and sets its IsGroup to TRUE, if IsGroup of the filed is TRUE, the Group NAV is allowed to be ignored for slave AP. IsGroup is FALSE at this time, the Group NAV is not allowed to be ignored, and data transmission is not possible.
(2) Newly introduce a Group NAV and modify the TF frame, that is, add a 1bit co-TDMA Indication field to the TF frame. Since the information between the master AP and the slave APs is interoperable, it is mainly necessary to solve the NAV problem of the STA. First, if the STAs associated with

the slave AP receive other frames in a Group, they need to update the Group NAV. Then, if the STA receives the TF frame sent by the slave AP it is associated with and schedules it to send uplink data, if the co-TDMA Indication field in the TF frame is set to 1, the Group NAV can be ignored, and if it is set to 0, it is not allowed to be ignored. And Group NAV should not be ignored in other situations where the TF frame is not received.

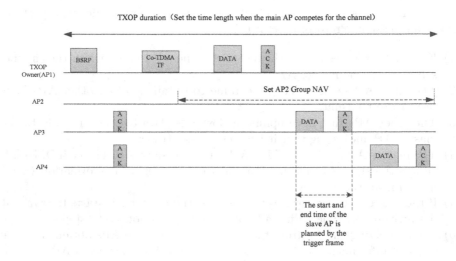

Fig. 2. Protocol process

4   Performance Evaluation

4.1   Simulation Scenario Configuration

Simulation on the system-level and link-level integrated simulation platform verifies the protocol proposed in this paper. By writing the MAC layer code, the MAC flow of the designed protocol is realized, the simulated network scenario is designed, and compared with the Enhanced Distributed Channel Access (EDCA) mechanism, the following simulation results are obtained, and the obtained simulation results are analyzed and evaluated. The set simulation scene configuration and parameter configuration is shown in Table 1.

4.2   Performance Analysis

Taking the EDCA mechanism as a comparison, under the same scenario configuration, using different simulation rates to obtain the average simulation throughput results of each cell of the two are shown in the figure. The result is shown in Fig. 3, Fig. 5, Fig. 7 and the average packet loss rate of the two is shown in Fig. 4, Fig. 6, Fig. 8.

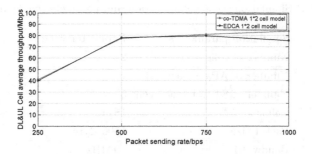

Fig. 3. Scene one throughput comparison.

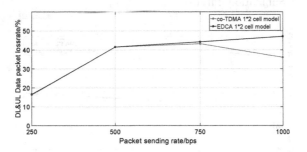

Fig. 4. Scene one comparison of packet loss rate.

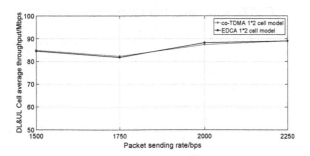

Fig. 5. Scene two throughput comparison.

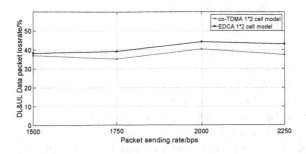

Fig. 6. Scene two comparison of packet loss rate.

Table 1. Simulation scene configuration and parameter configuration

Simulation parameters	Parameter value
Number of cells	2
Number of APs in each cell	1
Number of STAs in each cell	5
Cell size	15 m
Packet size	1500 Byte
Bandwidth	20 MHz
Protocol	Co-TDMA/EDCA
Simulation duration	5 s

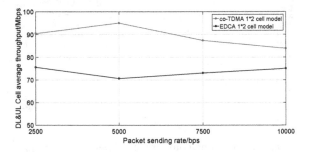

Fig. 7. Scene three throughput comparison.

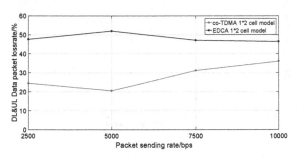

Fig. 8. Scene three comparison of packet loss rate.

It can be seen from the simulation results that under different simulation rates, the co-TDMA mechanism has different performance compared to the EDCA mechanism. When the simulation rate is between two hundred and fifty bps to one thousand bps, the result showns its cell network throughput and packet loss rate is basically consistent with the EDCA mechanism.

As the data packet sending rate increases, the simulation rate is between fifteen hundred bps to two thousand two hundred and fifty bps, Although the throughput of the network has increased, its network performance is still basically the same as the EDCA mechanism.

The rate of sending packets continues to increase, the simulation rate is between two thousand five hundred to ten thousand bps, the co-TDMA mechanism has a more obvious gain than the EDCA mechanism, indicating that the co-TDMA mechanism is more suitable for a network environment with relatively large competition.

5   Conclusion and Future Works

Based on the idea of co-TDMA protocol design, this paper designs a specific co-TDMA protocol implementation scheme, implements the co-TDMA protocol process, and evaluates the performance of this protocol. It can be seen from the simulation results that in scenarios where network traffic is relatively intensive, using the co-TDMA mechanism, compared with the EDCA mechanism, can alleviate link conflicts and improve network throughput. In scenarios where network traffic is relatively small, the co-TDMA protocol does not show any advantages. So this protocol is suitable for scenarios with dense networks. In future research, different simulation implementation schemes can be designed, and the performance of this protocol can be evaluated in multiple aspects.

Acknowledgement. This work was supported in part by the National Natural Science Foundations of CHINA (Grant No. 61871322, No. 61771390, No. 61771392, and No. 61501373), and Science and Technology on Avionics Integration Laboratory and the Aeronautical Science Foundation of China (Grant No. 20185553035, and No. 201955053002).

References

1. Maksutov, A.A., Kondrashkin, K.V., Durachenko, S.V., Matveeva, D.V.: Development of mesh networks based on the 802.11 family of standards. In: 2019 IEEE Conference of Russian Young Researchers in Electrical and Electronic Engineering (EIConRus) (2019)
2. Lei, E., Fan, M., Jia, L., Huimin, L., Guang, L.: The next generation WLAN technical standard 802.11ax. In: Information and Communications Technology and Policy (2019)
3. Hu, Z., Bo, L., Yan, Z., Mao, Y.: An OFDMA based multiple access protocol with QOS guarantee for next generation WLAN. In: IEEE International Conference on Signal Processing (2015)
4. Yalcin, A.Z., Yuksel, M., Bahceci, I.: Downlink MU-MIMO with QOS aware transmission: precoder design and performance analysis. IEEE Trans. Wirel. Commun. **18**(2), 969–982 (2019)
5. Machrouh, Z., Najid, A.: High efficiency WLANS IEEE 802.11ax performance evaluation. In: IEEE - 2018 International Conference on Control Automation and Diagnosis (ICCAD'18), March 19–21, 2018, Marrakech-Morocco (2018)

6. Yang, M., Li, B.: Survey and perspective on extremely high throughput (EHT) WLAN — IEEE 802.11be. Mob. Netw. Appl. **25**(5), 1765–1780 (2020). https://doi.org/10.1007/s11036-020-01567-7

7. Choi, M., Sun, W., Koo, J., Choi, S., Kang, G.S.: Reliable video multicast over Wi-Fi networks with coordinated multiple APS. In: IEEE INFOCOM 2014 - IEEE Conference on Computer Communications (2014)

8. Tan, P., Wang, D., Yang, M., Yan, Z., Li, B.: CRJT: Channel reservation based joint transmission MAC protocol for the next generation WLAN (2018)

9. Zhang, Y., Li, B., Yang, M., Yan, Z., Zuo, X.: An OFDMA-based joint reservation and cooperation MAC protocol for the next generation WLAN. Wirel. Netw. **25**(2), 471–485 (2017). https://doi.org/10.1007/s11276-017-1567-1

10. Bhalla, G., Karmakar,R., Chakraborty, S., Chattopadhyay, S.: CrowdAP: crowd-sourcing driven AP coordination for improving energy efficiency in wireless access networks. In: ICC 2016–2016 IEEE International Conference on Communications (2016)

11. Wong, C.N.E., Porat, R., Jindal, N., Fischer, M.J., Erceg, V.: Inter-AP coordination and synchronization within wireless communications (2014)

12. Barriac, G.D., Merlin, S., Zhou, Y., Sampath, H.: High efficiency wireless (HEW) access point (AP) coordination protocol (2015)

13. Yang, M., Li, B., Yan, Z., Yan, Y.: AP coordination and full-duplex enabled multi-band operation for the next generation WLAN: IEEE 802.11be (EHT). In: 2019 11th International Conference on Wireless Communications and Signal Processing (WCSP) (2019)

Survey of Routing Metric in Wireless Mesh Networks

Yunlong Wang, Zhongjiang Yan[✉], Mao Yang, and Bo Li

School of Electronics and Information, Northwestern Polytechnical University,
Xi'an, China
613349866@qq.com, {zhjyan,yangmao,libo.npu}@nwpu.edu.cn

Abstract. As an important technology in the construction of the next generation wireless communication system, Wireless Mesh Networks (WMNs) has the advantages of high bandwidth, flexible networking, wide coverage and low investment risk. Routing metrics have a great impact on network. Appropriate routing metrics can reduce intra-stream and inter-stream interference, improve throughput and reliability, achieve load balancing and eliminate network hot spots. At present, research on routing metrics for WMNs has made some progress. Relevant scholars have proposed various routing metrics, but no scholars have compared and classified these routing metrics. In this paper, the classical routing metrics in WMNs and the routing metrics proposed in the last ten years are studied. The following conclusions are drawn from these investigations. Firstly, delay, packet loss rate and bandwidth are the most commonly considered factors in routing metrics. Secondly, routing metrics separately describe the types of disturbances that lead to the introduction of variable constants. Thirdly, routing metrics often ignore the choice of gateway nodes. Finally, delay is the most important parameter of routing metrics. For example, the introduction of bandwidth and bottleneck channels is for more accurate calculation of delay. NS3 is used to simulate Hop Routing Metric (HOP) and Distance Routing Metric. The simulation results show that in a small network, Distance Routing Metric can effectively reduce the delay and increase the network throughput.

Keywords: Wireless Mesh Networks · Routing metric · NS3

1 Introduction

Since its birth in the 1960s, the development of network technology has been extremely rapid. Traditional Wireless Local Area Network (WLAN) provide stable network connections and large amounts of data traffic for billions of people around the world. With the rapid development of economy, users put forward higher requirements on the coverage, communication quality and carrying capacity of wireless network. However, in many cases, the existing wireless

Y.-B. Lin and D.-J. Deng (Eds.): SGIoT 2020, LNICST 354, pp. 307–325, 2021.
https://doi.org/10.1007/978-3-030-69514-9_25

basic network can not be fully covered or the infrastructure construction is difficult. Therefore, Wireless Mesh Networks (WMNs) with advantages of flexible deployment, multi-hop transmission, wide coverage, low investment cost and low risk have been developed rapidly [1]. WMNs is a new network technology that separates from Ad Hoc Network and inherits part of WLAN [2].

Routing metrics have a great impact on network quality. WMNs have the characteristics of wide coverage, non-line-of-sight transmission and high bandwidth. Therefore, these characteristics of WMNs should be fully considered when select routing metrics [3]. Now, the routing metric used in WMNs is Air Time Link Metric (ALM). Although ALM considers protocol overhead, packet loss rate and transmission rate [4], ALM can not meet the requirements for large-scale WMNs. Although scholars have proposed various routing metrics, no scholars have sorted out these routing metrics or made comparative analysis.

Although the concept of WMNs has been proposed since the mid-1990s, WMNs did not attract widespread attention [5]. Until 2005, Nokia, Nortel, Tropos, SkyPilot and other companies launched wireless mesh products, and WMNs entered a period of rapid development [6]. Expected Transmission Count (ETX) as an earlier WMNs routing metric was proposed in 2003 by Couto of the Massachusetts Institute of Technology's Computer Science and Artificial Intelligence Laboratory. ETX is easy to implement and the link with low packet loss rate can be selected as the data transmission link. Then R. Raves et al. proposed Expected Transmission Time (ETT) on the basis of ETX [7]. ETT considers the impact of packet size and data transmission rate on network quality. ETT is widely used in WMN and lays a foundation for other routing metrics. Due to the advantages of WMNs, WMNs have developed rapidly in recent decades. Corresponding routing metrics for WMNs are developing rapidly. For example, the Enhanced Air Time Link Metric (E-ALM) was proposed in literature [12]. Multirate Routing Metric (MRM) was proposed in literature [16]. Gateway Selection Based Routing (GSBR) was proposed in literature [19].

However, although many researchers have proposed various routing metrics, but to the best knowledge of the authors, there are no open references compared and classified these routing metrics. And this motivates us to survey the routing metrics of the WMNs. The main contributions of this paper are as follows.

(1) The classic routing metrics in WMNs are surveyed, and the routing metrics proposed in the last decade are detailed and summarized.
(2) The advantages, disadvantages and applicable scenarios of the investigated routing metrics are analyzed. According to the characteristics of routing metrics, routing metrics are divided into three categories. (1) Single channel routing metrics. (2) Multi-channel routing metrics. (3) Routing metrics in multi-gateway WMNs.
(3) NS3 is used to simulate Hop Routing Metric (HOP) and Distance Routing Metric. The simulation results show that in a small network, Distance Routing Metric can effectively reduce the delay and increase the network throughput.

The rest of this paper is organized as follows. Section 2 briefly introduces the definition and network structure of WMNs, and the factors often considered in routing metrics are briefly introduced. Section 3 introduces some routing metrics suitable for single channel networks. Section 4 introduces some routing metrics suitable for multi-channel networks. Section 5 introduces some routing metrics suitable for multi-gateway networks. Section 6 uses NS3 to simulate the HOP and Distance Routing Metric and analyze the simulation results. Section 7 summarizes the entire article.

2   System Model and Link Metric Methods

WMNs contain three types of nodes. Mesh Point (MP), Mesh Access Point (MAP), Mesh Portal Point (MPP). All devices that support WMNs functionality can be called MP. You can view MAP as a special kind of MP but pure terminals (non-MP nodes, such as STA) must through MAP connect to WMNs [8]. WMNs accessing to the Internet or other networks needs to be achieved through MPP. MPP can be connected to the Internet through wired or wireless manner [2], and all data accessing the external network needs to be forwarded through MPP.

In WMNs, not all types of nodes can form links with each other. MP can be linked with MP, MAP and MPP. But MP can not be linked with STA. MAP can be linked with MP, MAP, MPP and STA. MPP can be connected with MP and MAP to form a link. But MPP can not be connected with STA to form a link. The WMNs structure is shown in Fig. 1.

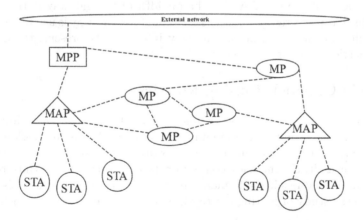

Fig. 1. WMNs architecture diagram

Link bandwidth, packet loss rate, packet length, transmission time, and queuing delay are all related to the link quality. Generally speaking, the wider the bandwidth, the higher the maximum transmission rate that the link can reach, and the better the quality of the corresponding link. Bandwidth is usually represented by the symbol B. The ratio of the number of packets lost to the total number of packets sent is the packet loss rate. The lower the packet loss rate, the better the quality of the link. The forward packet loss rate is often expressed by the symbol p_f and p_r represents the reverse packet loss rate. The data packet length is usually expressed by the symbol S. The time taken by the test packet from leaving one end of the link to being successfully received by the other end of the link is the transmission time. Queuing delay refers to the time from data enters the node packet queue to the data leaves the node.

Multi channel network is more complex than single network channel. Intra-stream interference, inter-stream interference, physical interference and available bandwidth have to be considered in multi-channel network. The intra-stream interference is described as follows. When two links are very close (within the interference range) and use the same channel, the two links cannot work at the same time because of serious interference. Inter-stream interference is caused by the links in the selected path because the links outside the path use the same channel as the links of the path. Available bandwidth or weighted accumulated Expected Transmission Time (ETT) is usually used to represent intra-stream interference and inter - stream interference. For detailed description, refer to Unified Description of Interference and Load Routing Metrics (MIL) or Multi-rate Network Routing Metric (MRM). Due to various disturbances, the actual bandwidth of the link is not equal to the theoretical bandwidth of the link. Physical interference refers to interference caused by environmental noise and equipment noise. Physical interference is usually expressed by the interference ratio.

In multi-gateway networks, the gateway is usually selected based on the bandwidth and load of the gateway. The bandwidth of the gateway is the effective bandwidth that the gateway can use. The load of the gateway is usually expressed by the buffer queue length at the gateway interface. At present, there are few routing metrics consider of gateways.

3   Single Channel Routing Metrics

For WMNs, single channel network refers that all nodes in the wireless network use only one channel for communication. Single channel network is usually found in early wireless communication networks. Most of the current wireless networks use multi-channels for communication. However, the study of single channel routing metrics is the foundation of the study of multi-channels routing metrics, so the study of routing metrics in single channel network is meaningful.

3.1   One-Dimensional Routing Metric for Single Channel

Hop Metric. Hop count is the number of data forwarding from the source node to the destination node. The path with the fewest hops is the transmission path [8]. The metric has the advantages of simple implementation and low overhead. However, the shortcomings of Hop Metric (HOP) are prominent. HOP does not consider the link delay, interference, load, packet loss rate and other factors. So HOP is likely to lead to poor performance of the selected path.

Round Trip Time. Round Trip Time (RTT) link metric uses the average round trip time between the two ends of the link as a reference for routing selection [8]. The process of obtaining Round Trip Time is shown as follows. Each node broadcasts a probe packet at an interval of 500ms, and adjacent nodes receive the probe packet and respond to the probe packet in a non-preemptive manner. The response message contains a time flag to calculate RTT.

Packet Pair Delay. Packet Pair Delay is an improved version of the RTT. Packet Pair Delay mainly comes from the media competition between the sending node and other nodes and the packet retransmission caused by channel changing. Packet Pair Delay does not include queuing delay and processing delay [8]. The implementation process of Packet Pair Delay is as follows. Before a long data packet (length is 1000Bit), a short data packet (length of 137Bit) is sent (continuous transmission). Each adjacent node is responsible for calculating the receiving time difference between the two packets. The average value of this time difference is the link cost.

Link Priority. Link Priority Metric (LP) considers the business priority level. Link weights are determined according to the number and priority of data passing through the link over a period of time. Each kind of data has a real-time priority R. The data group needing high real-time has a high R value, and the data needing low real-time has a low R value [9]. LP over a period of time can be calculated by Formula (1).

$$R_l = \sum_{u \in l, i=0}^{m} k_i R_i + \sum_{u \in l, j=0}^{n} k_j R_j \ u, v \neq s \ or \ d \tag{1}$$

u, v represent the nodes at each end of the link l. s represents the source node. d represents the destination node. m is the number of service request level types through the u node. n represents the number of service request level types through the v node. k_i represents the number of communication service requests with priority R_i within a period of time on node u. k_j represents the number of communication service requests with priority R_j during a period of time on node v. R_i represents the priority level of the transmission packet. The higher the priority, the stronger the real-time performance.

The path with the smallest LP value is the selected path. LP of router can be calculated by Formula (2).

$$LP(r) = \sum_{l \in r} R_l \tag{2}$$

R_l indicates the priority level of link l. It can be calculated by Formula (1).

The LP implementation process is as follows. Firstly, data are divided into different priorities according to their time and reality requirements. The higher the real-time requirement of data, the higher the priority of data. Secondly, recording the number of data passing through the link and data priority in a period of time. Thirdly, the priority (R_l) of link l is calculated by formula (1). Finally, selection path.

3.2   Single Channel Two-Dimensional Routing Metrics

Expected Transmission Count. Expected Transmission Count (ETX) uses the expected number of transmissions that successfully transmitted to the destination node as a measure of link quality. ETX comprehensively considers delay and packet loss rate [8].

The path with the smallest sum of ETX is the selected path. The ETT_i of link i can be calculated by Formula (3).

$$ETX_i = \frac{1}{(1 - P_f)(1 - P_r)} \tag{3}$$

P_f and P_r respectively represent the uplink and downlink packet loss rates of link i.

ETT_p of path p can be calculated by formula (4).

$$ETT_p = \sum_{i \in p} ETT_i \tag{4}$$

Quantified Packet Loss Rate. The Quantified Packet Loss Rate uses the end-to-end path loss probability as the routing cost. The influence of packet loss rate and delay on routing quality is considered comprehensively [8]. The Quantified Packet Loss Rate with logarithmic characteristics is not suitable for direct link cost, so the logarithm of the Quantified Packet Loss Rate of the link is selected as the link cost. The parameter allocation process is shown in Table 1.

Table 1. Parameter allocation table

Link Quality	Sending Rate	Re	-Log(Re)	Cost
Q_3	90% ~ 100%	0.95	0.05	1
Q_2	79% ~ 90%	0.85	0.16	3
Q_1	47% ~ 79%	0.65	0.43	8
Q_0	0% ~ 47%	0.25	1.39	28

Modified ETX. Modified ETX (mETX) is an improved version of ETX. mETX solves the defect caused by the lack of consideration of channel changing in ETX [8]. mETX comprehensively considers the influence of packet loss rate and channel changing on routing quality [8]. The path with the smallest sum of mETX is the selected path. mETX of a link can be calculated by formula (5).

$$mETX = \exp(u_\Sigma + \frac{1}{2}\sigma_\Sigma^2) \tag{5}$$

$\sum$ represents the bit error rate within the grouping time (frame length), which is related to device implementation. u_Σ and σ_Σ^2 represent the mean and variance of $\sum$ respectively.

Interference-Delay Aware. Interference-Delay Aware (IDA) comprehensively considers the impact of delay and physical interference on routing quality. Delay includes channel contention delay and transmission delay [10].

The average competition delay (ACD_i) of link i can be calculated by formula (6). The expected transmission time of link i (ETD_i) can be calculated by formula (7). The total delay of link i ($Delay_i$) is the sum of channel competition delay (ACD_i) and transmission delay (ETD_i). IDA of path p can be calculated by formula (9).

$$ACD_i = S_n \times \left(\frac{(1 - PEP)\left(1 - (2 \times PEP)^R\right)}{(1 - PEP^R)(1 - 2 \times PEP)} \times CW_{\min} + \frac{1}{2} \right) \tag{6}$$

$$ETD_i = ETX_i \times \left(\frac{L}{BW_a} \right) \tag{7}$$

$$Delay_i = ACD_i + ETD_i \tag{8}$$

$$IDA(p) = \sum_{i \in p}^{n} Delay_i \times (1 - IR_i) \tag{9}$$

S_n represents the average slot utilization of node n. $PEP = 1 - d_f \times d_r$ represents packet error probability. $CW_{\min}$ represents the minimum competition window. R represents the backoff order. ETX_i represents the expected transmission times of link i, which can be calculated by formula (3). L represents the packet length. BW_a represents the available bandwidth of link i. n represents the number of links of path p. $IR_i = \frac{SINR_i}{SNR_i}$ represents the interference rate of node i, SNR_i represents the signal interference noise ratio of node i, and SNR_i represents the signal noise ratio of node i.

3.3   Single Channel Three Dimensional Routing Metrics

Expected Transmission Time. Expected Transmission Time (ETT) is developed from ETX, adding two parameters, bandwidth and message length. ETT comprehensively considers the influence of packet loss rate, delay and bandwidth on routing quality. The path with the smallest sum of ETT is the selected path

[8]. The ETT_i of link i can be obtained by formula (10). ETT_i of path P can be calculated by formula (11).

$$ETT_i = ETX_i \times \frac{S}{B} \tag{10}$$

$$ETT_p = \sum_{i \in p} ETT_i \tag{11}$$

S represents the average data length, B represents the current actual data transmission rate.

Link Priority-Interference and Delay Aware. Link Priority-interference and Delay Aware (LP-IDA) integrates LP and IDA. LP-IDA comprehensively considers real-time service delay and inter-stream interference [9]. LP-IDA (p) of path p can be calculated by formula (12).

$$LP - IDA(p) = \alpha(IDA(p)) + (1 - \alpha)LP(p) \tag{12}$$

Interference-Aware Routing. Interference-aware Routing (IAR) is based on channel utilization [6]. IAR comprehensively considers the influence of inter-stream interference, delay and bandwidth on routing quality. The IAR (i) of link i can be calculated by formula (13). The IAR (p) of the path p can be obtained by formula (15).

$$IAR(i) = \frac{1}{1 - \alpha} \times \frac{S}{B} \tag{13}$$

$$\alpha = \frac{T_{wait} + T_{collesion} + T_{backoff}}{T_{wait} + T_{collesion} + T_{backoff} + T_{success}} \tag{14}$$

$$IAR(p) = \sum_{i \in p} IAR_i \tag{15}$$

T_{wait}, $T_{collesion}$, $T_{backoff}$, $T_{success}$ respectively represents the waiting, collision, back-off and successful transmission time of a data packet.

Airtime Link Metric. Airtime Link Metric (ALM) is an approximate measurement method. ALM's main purpose is to reduce the difficulty of specific implementation and interaction [11]. ALM considers the transmission rate, channel quality and packet loss rate. The airtime cost of link can be obtained by formula (16).

$$C_a = \left[\frac{O}{n} + \frac{B_t}{r} \right] \times \frac{1}{1 - e_f} \tag{16}$$

O represents channel access overhead, including frame header, training sequence, channel access protocol frame, etc. n depends on implementation. B_t represents the number of bits contained in the body of a data frame. r represents the data rate used under the current link conditions when the data frame (typical frame length is Bt) is transmitted. e_f represents the frame-error rate of data frame (typical frame length is Bt).

3.4   Four-Dimensional Routing Metrics for Single Channel

Enhanced-Airtime Link Metric. Enhanced- Airtime Link Metric (E-ALM) is improved on the basis of ALM. E-ALM introduced the Network Allocation Vector (NAV). E-ALM comprehensively considers the influence of channel over-head, protocol overhead, packet loss rate, node interference and bandwidth on network quality [12]. The cumulative average NAV value of links over a period of time can be calculated by formula (17). The average delay of links can be calculated by formula (18). The E-ALM of a path can be obtained by formula (19).

$$NAVC = \frac{\sum_{t_1=t_u}^{t_1=t_v} NAV_{t_1}}{t_v - t_u} \tag{17}$$

$$Delay\,(x) = \begin{cases} 2\ ms & if \quad x \leq 0.2 \\ 2 \times e^{7.9(x-0.2)^2} & if \ \ 0.2 \leq x \leq 0.65 \end{cases} \tag{18}$$

$$C_\alpha\,(p) = \sum_{node\ n \in p} \alpha C_n + (1-\alpha)\,D_n \tag{19}$$

$x = NAVC$ represents the cumulative average NAV value over a period of time. $Delay(x) = 14.16ms$ $(x > 0.65)$. C_n represents the air transmission time which can be calculated by formula (15). $D_n = Delay\,(x)$ represents the average delay, which can be calculated by formula (18), $0 \leq \alpha \leq 1$ the greater the α, the greater the proportion of the air delay in the criterion. The smaller the α, the greater the proportion of the time delay in the criterion.

3.5   Summary

Table 2. Comprehensive evaluation table of routing metric performance.

Routing metric	Packet loss rate	Delay	Interference	Real-time service	Channel change	Transmission rate	Channel protocol overhead	Reference label
Hop	–	–	–	–	–	–	–	[8]
RTT	–	Yes	–	–	–	–	–	[8]
LP	–	–	–	Yes	–	–	–	[9]
packet Pair Delay	–	Yes	–	–	–	–	–	[8]
ETX	Yes	Yes	–	–	–	–	–	[8]
Quantified packet loss rate	Yes	Yes	–	–	–	–	–	[8]
mETX	Yes	–	–	–	Yes	–	–	[8]
IDA	–	Yes	Yes	–	–	–	–	[10]
ETT	Yes	Yes	–	–	–	–	–	[8]
LP-IDA	–	–	–	Yes	–	–	–	[9]
IAR	–	–	Yes	Yes	–	Yes	–	[6]
ALM	Yes	–	–	–	–	Yes	Yes	[11]
E-ALM	Yes	–	Yes	–	–	Yes	Yes	[12]

In single channel networks, the most important considerations for routing metric is the delay and packet loss rate. Of course, interference, noise, transmission rate, channel bandwidth, etc. will also affect network quality. The comprehensive evaluation table of single-channel routing measurement performance is shown in Table 2

4   Multi-channel Routing Metrics

Currently, wireless networks often use multiple channels for data transmission. Multi-channel networks can enable nodes to use different channels to send and receive data at the same time without interference. Therefore, multi-channel can greatly increase network throughput and reduce delay.

4.1   Multi-channel Three Dimensional Routing Metrics

Multi-rate Dijkstra's Min-Cost. Multi-rate Dijkstra's Min-cost (MDC) is applied in a multi-rate network environment. MDC will determine the transmission rate of the node and the next hop sending node at the same time. MDC comprehensively considers the influence of channel interference, bandwidth and delay on routing quality [13]. The minimum path cost W_i from node i through forwarding node j to a given destination node d can be calculated by Formula (20). W_{ij}^r can be calculated by formula (21). In the case of using rate r, the link overhead can be calculated by formula (22).

$$W_i = \min_{r \in R, J \in G_P} \{W_{ij}^r\} \tag{20}$$

$$W_{ij}^r = w_{ij}^r + W_j \tag{21}$$

$$w_{ij}^r = \frac{1}{p_{ij}^r} \times \frac{s}{r} \tag{22}$$

R represents the set of available rates. G_p represents the set of all nodes that have completed the minimum path cost calculation. W_{ij}^r represents the path overhead of the node i using node j as the forwarding node and using the rate r as transmission rate. w_{ij}^r represents the link overhead of node i to the next-hop node j using rate r, which can represent the degree of channel interference. W_j represents the minimum path overhead of the next hop node j to the destination node. P_{ij}^r represents the delivery probability of the link using rate r between node i and node j, and the link delivery probability is the probability of successful packet transmission.

4.2   Multi-channel Four-Dimensional Routing Metrics

Metric Based on Uniform Description of Interference and Load. Metric Based on Uniform Description of Interference and Load (MIL) uses the combination of link average load, effective bandwidth and data packet size to calculate link weights. MIL comprehensively considers the influence of load, intra-stream interference, inter-stream interference and physical interference on routing quality [14].

The data transmission quality of links is affected by inter-stream interference and physical signal strength [15]. In the case of inter-stream interference and physical interference, the effective bandwidth of the link can be calculated by formula (23).

$$B_{Inter,i} = \left(1 - \frac{TotalTime - IdleTime}{TotalTime}\right) \times B_{bas} \times \left(1 - \frac{\sum\limits_{k \neq v} P_u(k)}{\frac{P_u(v)}{r} - N}\right) \quad (23)$$

$TotalTime$ is the total passive detection time CBT_i. $IdleTime$ is the back-off time and the idle time when no data packets occupy the channel. B_{bas} represents the standard data rate of the link. $P_u(v)$ represents the signal power received by node u from node v. $P_u(k)$ represents the interference power from node k. N represents the received background noise power. r is the preset SINR threshold.

When link $S - A$ and Link $A - B$ use the same channel, the available bandwidth $B_{S-A,A-B}$ of link $S - A$ can be calculated by formula (24). Based on the above equivalent bandwidth, the MIL_i of link i can be calculated by formula (25).

$$B_{S-A,A-B} = \frac{B_{Inter,S-A} \times B_{Inter,A-B}}{B_{Inter,S-A} + B_{Inter,A-B}} \quad (24)$$

$$MIL_i = \overline{L_i} \times \frac{S}{B_i} \quad (25)$$

S represents the packet size. B_i represents the effective bandwidth of link i, which can be calculated by Formula (24). $\overline{L_i} = (1 - \theta) \times L_{i-cur} + \theta \times L_{i-pre}$ represents the average load of link i. L_{i-cur} represents the current load value, and L_{i-pre} represents the previous load value.

4.3   Multi-channel Five-Dimension Routing Metrics

Multi-rate Routing Metric. Multi-rate Routing Metric (MRM) comprehensively considers the influence of inter-stream interference, delay, bandwidth and packet loss rate on routing quality [16]. In the network shown in Fig. 2, $ETT_{A-B}^{interflow}$ and $ETT_{A-B}^{intraflow}$ of link $A - B$ can be calculated by formula (26) and (27) respectively.

$$MRM_i = ETT_i^{interflow} + ETT_i^{intraflow} \quad (26)$$

$$ETT_{A-B}^{interflow} = ETT_{A-B} + ETT_{F-G} \quad (27)$$

$$ETT_{A-B}^{intraflow} = ETT_{A-B} + ETT_{B-C} \quad (28)$$

$ETT_i^{interflow}$ and $ETT_i^{intraflow}$ respectively represent inter-stream interference and intra-stream interference. ETT represents the expected transmission time.

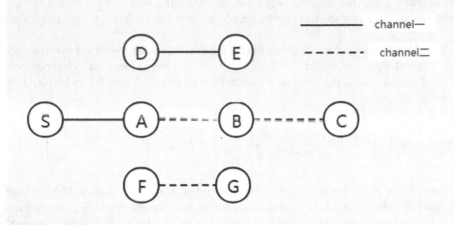

Fig. 2. Interference model diagram.

Weighted Cumulative Expected Transmission Time. Weighted Cumulative Expected Transmission Time (WCETT) is a routing metric specially designed for Multi-radio Link Quality Source Routing (MR-LQSR). WCETT is developed on the basis of ETT. WCETT comprehensively considers the impact of packet loss rate, bandwidth, intra-stream interference,delay and bottleneck channel on routing quality [8]. WCETT of a path can be calculated by formula (29) and (30).

$$X_j = \sum ETT_i \ (Hop \ i \ is \ on \ channel \ j) \ 1 \leq j \leq k \tag{29}$$

$$WCETT = (1-\beta) \times \sum_{i=1}^{n} ETT_i + \beta \times \max_{1 \leq j \leq k} X_j \ 1 \leq i \leq k \tag{30}$$

k represents the number of channels used by the path.

Interference Aware Routing Metric. Interference Aware Routing Metric (iAWARE) comprehensively considers the impact of packet loss rate, bandwidth, int-stream interference, delay and inter-stream interference on routing quality. The iAWARE of a path can be calculated by formula (31) [8].

$$AWARE = (1 - \alpha) \times \sum_{1}^{n} \frac{ETT_l}{\min(IR_j(u), IR_j(v))} + \alpha \times \max_{1 \leq j \leq k} X_j \tag{31}$$

$$IR_l(u) = \frac{SINR_{l(u)}}{SNR_{l(u)}} \tag{32}$$

Metric of Interference and Channel Switching. Metric of Interference and Channel Switching (MIC) is an improvement of WCETT. MIC solves the problem of WCETT's inability to capture inter-stream interference and out-of-order. MIC comprehensively considers the impact of packet loss rate, bandwidth, intra-stream interference, delay and inter-stream interference on routing quality [8]. The MIC of path p can be calculated by formula (33), (34) and (35).

$$MIC = \frac{1}{N \times \min(ETT)} \sum_{l \in p} IRU_l + \sum_{l \in p} CSC_i \tag{33}$$

$$IRU_l = ETT_l \times N_l \tag{34}$$

$$CSC_j = \begin{cases} \omega_1, CH\left(prv\left(j\right)\right) \neq CH\left(j\right) \\ \omega_2, CH\left(prv\left(j\right)\right) = CH\left(j\right) \end{cases} \tag{35}$$

N is the number of nodes in the network. IRU_l refers to the use of interference-aware resources on link l. IRU_l includes the delay in the path and the influence on the utilization rate of resources in the entire network. N_l represents the set of nodes within the interference range during data transmission on the link l. CSC_i is the channel switching overhead of link i. CH_i is the channel used by node j to the next hop. $CH(prv(j))$ represents the channel used by the previous jump node j.

4.4 Multi-channel Six-Dimensional Routing Metrics

WCETTR Metric. WCETTR is an improved version of WCETT. Compared with WCETT, WCETTR considers intra-stream interference and inter-stream interference. In other words, WCETTR comprehensively considers the impact of delay, bandwidth, intra-stream interference, inter-stream interference, packet loss rate and bottleneck channel on routing quality [18]. The newly defined parameter N can represent the degree of inter-stream interference and bottleneck channel in the flow. The N of path P can be calculated by Formula (36). When link i and link j use the same channel, the value of $I\left(C_i == C_j\right)$ is 1, otherwise it is 0. WCETTR can be calculated by formula (37).

$$N = \max\left((1 - \varepsilon) \sum_{j \subset In(i) \cap j \subset R} ETT_j \times I\left(C_i == C_j\right) + \varepsilon \times \sum_{k \subset In(i) \cap k \not\subset R} ETT_k \times I\left(C_i == C_k\right)\right) \tag{36}$$

$$WCETTR = (1 - \beta) \times \sum_{i=1} ETT_i + \beta \times N \tag{37}$$

4.5 Summary

In multi-channel networks, delay and packet loss rate are still research hot spots. However, compared with single channel, multi-channel has its own characteristics. Intra-stream interference and inter-stream interference are research hot

Table 3. Comprehensive evaluation table of routing metric performance.

Routing metric	Delay loss rate	Transmission Rate	Physical Interference	Intra-stream Interference	Inter-stream interference	Node load	Loss Rate	Bottle-neck channel	Reference label
MDC	Yes	Yes	–	–	–	–	–	–	[13]
MIL	–	–	Yes	Yes	Yes	Yes	–	–	[14]
MRM	Yes	Yes	–	Yes	Yes	–	Yes	–	[15]
WCETT	Yes	Yes	–	Yes	–	–	Yes	–Yes	[16]
LAWARE	Yes	Yes	–	Yes	Yes	–	Yes	–	[8]
MIC	Yes	Yes	–	Yes	Yes	–	Yes	–	[8]
WCETTR	Yes	Yes	–	Yes	Yes	–	Yes	Yes	[18]

spots for multi-channel networks. At the same time, severe intra-stream interference and inter-stream interference will greatly reduce network throughput. Of course, there are also scholars studying other aspects such as node load and bottleneck channels. The comprehensive evaluation table of multi-channel routing measurement performance is shown in Table 3.

5   Routing Metrics in Multi-gateway Mesh Networks

Gateway is necessary for backbone WMNs and hybrid WMNs to access to Internet. Gateways are also called protocol converters. Gateways are used for both WAN and LAN interconnections. However, there is often more than one gateway in a network, and the quality of the network is closely related to the quality of gateway, so the choice of gateway has great significance for the improvement of routing performance. Currently, in WMNs routing research, the bandwidth and load of the gateway are usually considered.

5.1   Multi-gateway Four-Dimensional Routing Metric

Gateway-Selection Based Routing. Gateway-Selection Based Routing (GSBR) is based on backbone WMN, which combines PM with CI. GSBR comprehensively considers the influence of gateway load, intra-stream interference, packet loss rate and inter-stream interference on routing quality [19]. In route selection, the path with the minimum GSBR value is selected, and the GSGB of path p can be calculated by formula (38). The capacity factor of gateway G can be calculated by formula (39). The path quality PM_p of path p from router to gateway can be calculated by formula (41).

$$GSBR_{(G,p)} = \beta(1 - CI_G) + (1 - \beta)PM_p \tag{38}$$

$$CI_G = \frac{\sum_{i \in I_G} \frac{1+\alpha_i}{2} C_{a_i}}{\sum_{i \in I_G} C_{\max_i}} \tag{39}$$

$$PM_p = \max_{i \in p}(LM_i) + \prod_{i \in p} LM_i \tag{40}$$

C_{max_i} is the maximum capacity of interface i of gateway G, assuming the maximum capacity is 100. C_{a_i} is the available capacity of interface i. α_i is an adjustable constant, which can be obtained by formula (40). I_G represents the interface set of gateway G.

The link quality LM_i of link L using channel C can be calculated by Formula (42).

$$LM_l = \left(1 - \left(\frac{1}{2}\right)^n\right) \times \frac{\sum_{i \in N} P_{vR}(v_i)}{P_{\text{max}}} + \left(\frac{1}{2}\right)^n \times \frac{1}{1 - p_f} \tag{41}$$

$$P_{\text{max}} = \frac{P_{vR}(V_S)}{T} \tag{42}$$

n is the number of adjacent nodes in a hop range sharing the same channel. T is the threshold value. $P_{vR}(v_s)$ is the sending power from the sending end to the receiving end. $P_{vR}(v_i)$ is the interference power of interfering node i. p_f is the data packet loss rate. N represents the set of interfering nodes within the interference range of the receiving end node.

Best Path to Best Gateway. Best Path to Best Gateway (BP2BG) comprehensively considers the effects of physical interference, packet loss rate, bottleneck channel and gateway capacity on routing quality. BP2BG is derived from Distribution Available Capacity Indicator (DACI) and Link Quality Metric (LQM). The $DACI_G = CI_G$ of gateway G can be calculated by Formula (39) [20]. (LQM) considers packet loss rate and physical interference. The LQM_i of Link i can be calculated by Formula (44). Path quality $PQ_{S \to G}$ from route S to gateway G can be calculated by Formula (45).

$$LQM_i = \frac{\beta \times IR_i + (1 - \beta)\frac{1}{d_f}}{2} \tag{43}$$

$$PQ_{S \to G} = \frac{Max_{k \in p}(LQM_k) + \prod_{k \in p} LQM_k}{2} \tag{44}$$

IR_i is the interference ratio of link i, the definition is the same as that of MIL. d_f represents the number of probe packets successfully transmitted.

$BP2BG_{(g,p)}$ can be calculated by formula (46).

$$BP2BG_{(g,p)} = \frac{\alpha(1 - DACI) + (1 - \alpha)PQ}{2} \tag{45}$$

5.2 Summary

Table 4. Comprehensive evaluation table of routing measure performance.

Routing metric	Gateway load	Packet loss rate	Intra-stream interference	Inter-stream Interference	Physical interference	Gateway capacity	Reference label
MDC	Yes	Yes	Yes	Yes	–	–	[19]
MIL	–	–	–	–	Yes	Yes	[8]

There is often more than one gateway in a network, so the choice of gateway is very important. Currently, in routing metric, the bandwidth and load of gateway are mainly considered. The capacity of the gateway is limited, and if the gateway is selected with heavy load, the network throughput will be limited. Therefore, the load of the gateway is also an aspect that should be considered in the multi-gateway network routing metric. The comprehensive evaluation table of multi-gateway routing measurement performance is shown in Table 4.

6   Routing Simulation and Performance Analysis

NS3 is a discrete event simulator. NS3 is a free software, an open source project written in C++. For windows systems, you can run NS3 by installing a virtual machine. Common virtual machines are Vmware, Virtualbox, VMLite WorkStation, Qemu, etc.

6.1   OLSR Simulation

Optimized Link State Routing (OLSR) provides the optimal path based on the number of route hops. Create Ad-hoc nodes, and the channel, physical layer and MAC layer all use the wifi protocol. There are 50 nodes randomly distributed in the area of 180×160. In the same network scenario, change the number of nodes to observe changes in throughput and delay, and compare the performance of the HOP and Distance Routing Metric. The resulting graph is shown in the Fig. 3 below.

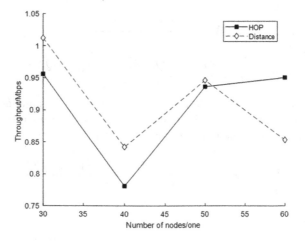

Fig. 3. A comparison of throughput between HOP and Distance Routing Metric.

By comparison, when the number of nodes is less than 50, Distance Routing Metric has a larger throughput. When the number of nodes is approximately

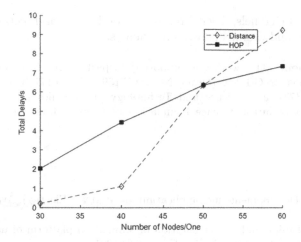

Fig. 4. A comparison of total delay between HOP and Distance Routing Metric.

greater than 50, HOP has a larger throughput and the performance of the HOP is better at this case (Fig. 3).

By comparison, when the number of nodes is approximately less than 50, the total delay of Distance Routing Metric is small, and the performance of Distance Routing Metric is better at this case. When the number of nodes is approximately greater than 50, the total delay of the Distance Routing Metric is greater than the total delay of HOP, and the performance of the HOP is better at this case (Fig. 4).

7   Summary and Prospect

As one of the evolution directions of the next generation wireless communication network, WMNs has the advantages of high bandwidth, easy deployment and maintenance, wide coverage, low cost and so on. Routing metric is a key technology in WMNs, which is of great significance for improving network performance. In this paper, the classical WMNs routing metrics and the recent ten years of WMNs routing metrics are carefully studied. According to the characteristics of each routing metric, the characteristics and applicable scenarios are described in this paper. NS3 simulation software was used to simulate HOP and Distance Routing Metric.

As a key technology of WMN, routing metrics should be diversified. The appropriate routing metrics should be selected for different scenarios. For different network quality requirements, it is also necessary to select appropriate routing metrics based on the focus of the requirements. At present, the consideration of routing metrics is relatively single, often focusing on factors such as delay, packet loss rate, and link quality. Less consideration is given to factors such as service priority, link priority, and inter-stream interference between some orthogonal channels. Therefore, it is a good research direction to combine routing metrics and channel allocation schemes.

Acknowledgment. This work was supported in part by the National Natural Science Foundations of CHINA (Grant No. 61771392, No. 61771390, No. 61871322 and No. 61501373), and Science and Technology on Avionics Integration Laboratory and the Aeronautical Science Foundation of China (Grant No. 201955053002, No. 20185553035).

References

1. Wang, N.: Development and application of WMNs. Electron. World (16), 110 (2019)
2. Zhang, Z.: Design and implementation of simulation platform of next generation WLAN's key technologies. Xidian University (2015)
3. Tu, S.: Research and simulation of interference sensing routing protocols for WMNs. Kunming University of Science and Technology (2013)
4. Wang, Q.: Research and application on anonymous communication critical technologies in WMNs. Northeastern University (2017)
5. Yang, S.: Research on channel interference of WMNs. Beijing Jiaotong University (2012)
6. Li, Z.: Research on load and interference-aware channel assignment and routing metric algorithm for multicast in WMNs. Jilin University (2016)
7. Qun, L., et al.: New mechanism to maximize capacity of WMNs. J. Electron. Meas. Instrum. **33**(10), 201–208 (2019)
8. Chai, Y.: Application of WMNs Technology, pp. 162–171. Publishing House of Electronics Industry, Beijing (2015)
9. Wu, Y.: Research on channel assignment and routing metric algorithm for multi-radio multi-channel WMNs. Liaoning University (2019)
10. Narayan, D.G., Mudenagudi, U.: A cross-layer framework for joint routing and resource management in multi-radio infrastructure WMNs. Arab. J. Sci. Eng. **42**, 651–667 (2017). https://doi.org/10.1007/s13369-016-2291-3
11. Wu, J.: Design and implementation of multi-gateway WMNs based on 802. 11s. Southeast University (2017)
12. Zhaohua, L., Yanqiang, H., Lin, Z.: Research on path selection metric based on HWMP. Comput. Eng. Des. **34**(03), 791–794 (2013)
13. Liu, J.: Research on joint routing metric and channel assignment in multi-rate WMNs. Jilin University (2016)
14. Wang, J.: Research on routing and partially overlapped channel assignment for multi-radio multi-channel WMNs. Jilin University (2016)
15. Wang, J., Shi, W., Xu, Y., Jin, F.: Uniform description of interference and load based routing metric for wireless mesh networks. EURASIP J. Wirel. Commun. Netw. **2014**(1), 1–11 (2014). https://doi.org/10.1186/1687-1499-2014-132
16. Yu, F.: Research of channel assignment and routing protocol in WMNs. University of Electronic Science and Technology of China (2015)
17. Li, H., Cheng, Y., Zhou, C., Zhuang, W.: Routing metrics for minimizing end-to-end delay in multiradio multichannel wireless networks. IEEE Trans. Parallel Distrib. Syst. **24**(11), 2293–2303 (2013)

18. Chen, D., Wang, S., Han, T.: Routing in 802. 11 based multi-channel WMNs. In: 2011 International Conference on Electronics, Communications and Control (ICECC), Ningbo, pp. 2264–2267 (2011)
19. Li, Y.: Research of channel assignment and routing algorithm in multi-radio multi-channel WMNs. Chongqing University of Posts and Telecommunications (2019)
20. Boushaba, M., Hafid, A.: Best path to best gateway scheme for multichannel multi-interface WMNs. In: 2011 IEEE Wireless Communications and Networking Conference, Cancun, Quintana Roo, pp. 689–694 (2011). https://doi.org/10.1109/WCNC.2011.5779216

Grouping Based Beamform Training Scheme for the Next Generation Millimeter Wave WLAN

Linlong Guo[1], Yong Fang[1] (ID), Mao Yang[2(✉)], Zhongjiang Yan[2], and Bo Li[2]

[1] School of Information Engineering, Chang'an University, Xi'an, China
{2020024012,fy}@chd.edu.cn
[2] School of Electronics and Information, Northwestern Polytechnical University, Xi'an, China
{yangmao,zhjyan,libo.npu}@nwpu.edu.cn

Abstract. The application of wireless local area network (WLAN) technology can make devices connected to the network move. On this basis, the millimeter wave WLAN protocol and beamforming (BF) technology enables wireless communication to support the transmission of services with ultra-high data rates. But the problem of conflict when station (STA) nodes perform BF training during the associated beamforming training (A-BFT) period is still unsolved. Therefore, this paper proposes a grouping based BF training scheme for the next generation millimeter wave WLAN to reduce conflict. The simulation results show that this scheme can effectively reduce the collision probability of STAs during BF training. Finally, it can improve the efficiency of information transmission and can be used in future improvements for the millimeter wave WLAN protocol.

Keywords: Millimeter wave WLAN · BF training · A-BFT period · Grouping based BF training · Collision probability of STAs

1 Introduction

With the development and application of millimeter wave technology [1], BF technology plays a major part in improving the quality of millimeter wave communications. Although BF technology enables millimeter waves to overcome high path loss, for STAs located within the beam coverage of the same sector, their conflict during BF training is still a crucial problem to be solved.

Based on the physical characteristics of millimeter wave and communication service requirements, WiGig Alliance first proposed the 802.11ad standard draft in 2009 and officially released it in 2013 [2,3]. In the same year, Chen Q proposed a new media Access Control (MAC) layer protocol for the directional multigigabit (DMG) transmission problem in IEEE 802.11ad [4]. In 2016, Assasa H implemented a model for IEEE 802.11ad and BF training technology in the network simulator ns-3 [5].

© ICST Institute for Computer Sciences, Social Informatics and Telecommunications Engineering 2021
Published by Springer Nature Switzerland AG 2021. All Rights Reserved
Y.-B. Lin and D.-J. Deng (Eds.): SGIoT 2020, LNICST 354, pp. 326–339, 2021.
https://doi.org/10.1007/978-3-030-69514-9_26

In IEEE 802.11ad standard [6,7], nodes (AP and STAs) get best transmission sector ID between nodes through the Beacon Transmission Interval (BTI) and Association Beamforming Training (A-BFT) by BF training [8,9]. However, in A-BFT period, multiple STAs may select the same A-BFT slot for BF training, which causes STAs to collide. This paper mainly proposes a new grouping based BF training scheme to improve the problem and reduce the collision probability and time overhead of BF training.

This scheme proposes that in A-BFT period, an access point (AP) divides STAs that belong to a same sector group into designated A-BFT slots, and these slots can only respond to BF training of the STAs. This method is called grouping based A-BFT slot response (G-ABFTRes). And AP sector scan mode is grouping based sector sweep from wide to narrow for carrying G-ABFTRes. The simulation results show that this scheme can successfully reduce the collision probability of STAs of BF training process in A-BFT period, and it is finally reflected in improving communication Throughput and Packet-Error-Rate (PER).

The rest of the paper is organized as follows: Section 2 introduces the basic theory of millimeter wave and BF training. Section 3 describes the mathematical logic analysis and flow chart of new scheme. For examining the proposed algorithms, results under different simulation environments are given in Sect. 4. And Sect. 5 summarizes the research questions, results, and innovations. Finally, acknowledgement and reference.

2   Background

2.1   802.11ad Frame Structure

In IEEE 802.11ad, Channel access process is mainly performed in Beacon Interval (BI), and sub-segments of the BI are called the access period. There are 4 periods: Beacon Transmission Interval (BTI), Association Beamforming Training (A-BFT), Announcement Transmission Interval (ATI), and Data Transfer Interval (DTI). They have different access rules and coordinate access time through schedules. This paper mainly studies a improvement schemes in A-BFT period for BF training (Figs. 1, 2, 3 and 4).

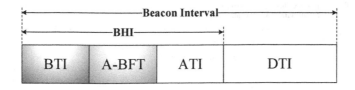

Fig. 1. IEEE 802.11ad BI structure

2.1.1 BTI

During BTI period, it is mainly realized that APs send directional multi-gigabit beacon (DmgBeacon) frames to STAs. The purpose is to enable STAs to obtain the best sending sector ID of APs and prepare to access A-BFT period.

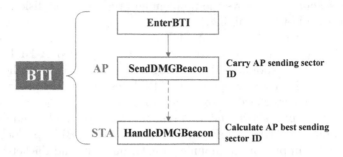

Fig. 2. BTI period

2.1.2 A-BFT

During A-BFT period, The main work is BF training. In IEEE 802.11ad, STAs randomly enter the pre-allocated A-BFT slots. In each A-BFT slot, a STA performs Sector Level Sweep (SLS) with all APs, and finally obtains the best sending sector/beam ID information of itself.

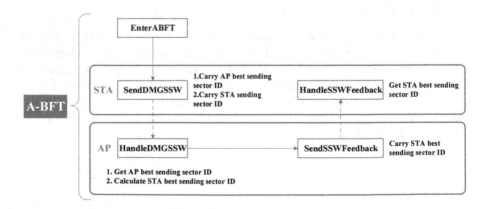

Fig. 3. A-BFT period

However, since different STAs may enter a same A-BFT slot. But only one STA can complete BF training in this slot. And other STAs affected by conflict only wait and enter the next A-BFT slot with the STAs that completed BF training. There are two scenarios to solve this problem:

1. Increasing the number of A-BFT slots. STAs will have a greater probability of entering different A-BFT slots. Scenario 1 can reduce the conflicts, but it will increase the time of BF training.
2. Using G-ABFTRes. STAs are divided into groups in advance. We stipulate that AP has multi-beam receiving capabilities, that is, AP can receive information frames from multiple sectors at the same time. And then, AP divides STAs that belong to a same group into designated A-BFT slots, and these slots can only respond to the BF training of this group. By comparison, scenario 2 is better than 1.

2.2 Beamforming Training

IEEE 802.11ad standard used BF training to solve the problem of high transmission loss in millimeter waves. Before antennas send data packets directionally, performing periodic BF training between initiator and responder nodes to find the best sending and receiving beams ID and achieve antenna alignment. This can effectively enhance the signal energy in the direction of demand link, and also suppress interference signals from other links.

In terms of workflow, BF training is divided into two stages: SLS and Beam Refinement Phase (BRP). Since BRP is not in this improvement, the following will mainly introduce SLS stage and sector sweeping method.

2.2.1 Sector Level Sweep

In SLS stage, transceivers (include AP and STAs) transmit control frames, which mainly contain information for adjusting antenna parameters of transceivers. When transceivers receive frames, they will adjust their antenna parameters, so as to optimize the beam direction.

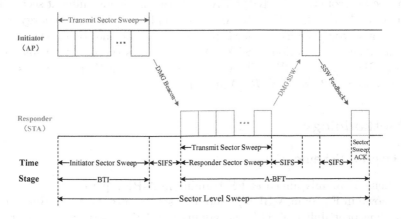

Fig. 4. Framework of SLS stage

When BF training initiator sends an information frame, the responder is in an omnidirectional receiving state; when initiator has finished sending, responder feeds back to initiator the best sending sector/beam ID information of initiator.

2.2.2 Sector Sweeping

In SLS, sector sweeping uses an exhaustive method in which initiator sweeps sectors from initial sector one by one until all sectors are swept.

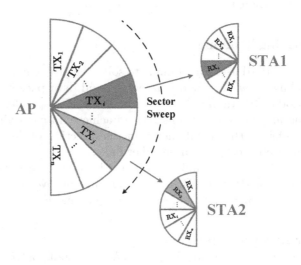

Fig. 5. Sector sweeping by exhaustive method

As shown in Fig. 5: AP uses n sectors/beams to cover cell. In SLS stage, AP sweeps sectors from the TX_1 to the TX_n in turn, and sends different sector/beam information. At the same time, STAs receive and measure signal energy emitted by different sectors/beams, and feeds back relevant information to AP. According to the feedback information of STAs, AP determines the best transmission sector/beam ID aimed at STAs. The best AP sector/beam ID pairs corresponding to STA1 and STA2 are (TX_i, RX_i) and (TX_j, RX_2).

3 Methodology

3.1 Overall Scheme

New scheme is mainly aimed at BF training in A-BFT period.

As shown in Fig. 6: in A-BFT period, this scheme uses G-ABFTRes to reduce the collision probability of STA and adopts G-SSW to perform sector grouping in BTI period.

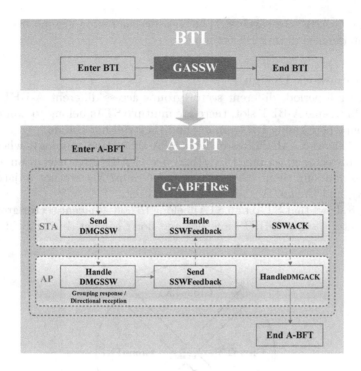

Fig. 6. New framework in overall scheme

3.2 Grouping Based A-BFT Slot Response

3.2.1 Theory

For G-ABFTRes, we stipulate that A-BFT slots are k, STAs in A-BFT period are l and all STAs are divided into $m(1 < m < l)$ sector groups. AP has multi-beam receiving capability, and STAs of non-adjacent sector groups can simultaneously access a same A-BFT slot.

When without using G-ABFTRes scheme, the probability of BF training collision between one STA and other STAs in A-BFT slot is $(l-1)/l$; when using G-ABFTRes scheme, the number of STAs in each sector group is l/m, and the probability of BF training collisions for STAs is:

$$\frac{\frac{l}{m}-1}{\frac{l}{m}} = \frac{l-m}{l}, \tag{1}$$

where $1 < m < l$,

$$\therefore \quad \frac{l-m}{l} < \frac{l-1}{l}. \tag{2}$$

As a result of using G-ABFTRes, the collision probability of STA is reduced in the A-BFT slot. In addition, because AP has multi-beam receiving capability, and STAs of non-adjacent sector groups can access a same A-BFT slot at the same time. G-ABFTRes avoids STAs in adjacent sector groups from causing mutual interference during BF training.

3.2.2 Framework Design

During A-BFT period, different sector groups access different A-BFT slots as required. In a same A-BFT slot, there are multiple STAs belong to non-adjacent sector groups performing BF training, and they will not collide.

Figure 7 shows G-ABFTRes in 1AP6STA simulation topology, where (a) is the result of sector grouping, (b.1)/(b.2) are G-ABFTRes execution stages in A-BFT slot. Among them, $GroupTX_A$ and $GroupTX_C$ are not adjacent, and $GroupTX_B$ and $GroupTX_D$ are also not adjacent.

Figure 8 shows that STAi and STAj belong to non-adjacent sector groups, but they can enter a same A-BFT time slot and don't conflict during BF training.

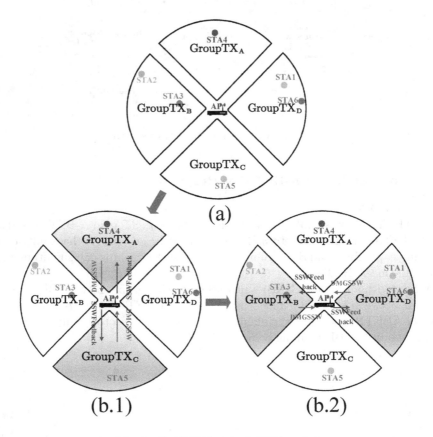

Fig. 7. G-ABFTRes in A-BFT period

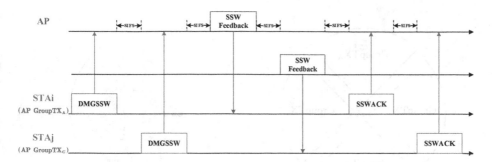

Fig. 8. New framework in A-BFT slot

3.2.3 Grouping Based Sector Sweep

G-SSW is proposed to assist G-ABFTRes in this paper. It has four phases: group sector division (GSD) phase, extra-group sector sweep (EGSSW) phase, request intra-group sector sweep (ReqIGSSW) phase, and intra-group sector sweep (IGSSW) phase.

Figure 9 shows G-SSW in 1AP6STA simulation topology, where (a) is GSD phase, (b.1)/(b.2) are EGSSW/ReqIGSSW phase, and (c) is IGSSW phase.

We stipulate that AP has n sectors, m group sectors and the number of STAs in BTI period are l and all STAs are divided into $m(1 < m < l)$ sector groups.

When without using G-SSW: each STA receives a total of n information frames containing information about different sectors of AP; when using G-SSW scheme, each STA receives a total of $m + \frac{n}{m}$ information frames from AP. When

$$m + \frac{n}{m} < n, \tag{3}$$

$$n > \frac{m^2}{m - 1}, \tag{4}$$

each STA receives fewer information frames from AP.

As shown in Fig. 10: AP sequentially enter different BTI slot, and interact with all STAs by G-SSW. In a BTI slot, AP first performs EGSSW phase (AP uses group sector to send the WideBeamDmgBeacon frame to each STA), and STAs feed back NarrowBeamRequest frame to AP in sequence. And then, AP judges whether STAs need to perform IGSSW phase through the feedback information. If necessary, AP uses intra-group sector to send a NarrowBeamDmgBeacon frame to STA. If not, skip this stage.

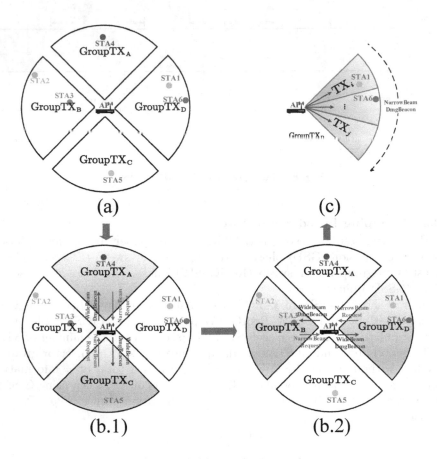

Fig. 9. G-SSW in BTI period

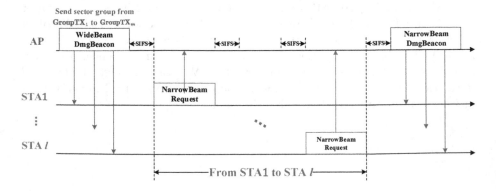

Fig. 10. New framework in BTI slot

4   Simulation Result

This experiment uses a network simulation platform based on ns-3 in 64 bit Ubuntu 4.4.3-4ubuntu5 operation system and is configured with Intel(R) Core(TM) i7-9750H CPU @ 2.60 GHz, 8 GB RAM. All above algorithms are developed in C++ environment.

4.1   Topology and Configuration

4.1.1   1AP6STA

In Fig. 11 and Table 1, there is 1 AP, 6 STAs and 6 A-BFT slots, and AP has 4 group sectors and multi-beam receiving capability. The first three A-BFT slots respond to BF training of STAs belonging to $GroupTX_A$ and $GroupTX_C$, and the last three A-BFT slots respond to the BF training of STAs belonging to $GroupTX_B$ and $GroupTX_D$ (refer to Fig. 9).

Table 1. 1AP6STA simulation parameters

Parameters	Configuration
Cell number	1
Number of nodes in cell	7
Sector number	12
Degree per sector	30°
Channel model	Calibrated SISO channel
Size of conference room scene	3 m * 4.5 m
Channel bandwidth	2.16 GHz
Packet size	40000 Byte
Simulation duration	1 s
Business	Up/Down Link+equal traffic-rate
BI duration	100 ms
DTI phase	Only SP
SP allocation rules	Priority fairness
Threshold of ReqIGSSW	−38 dB

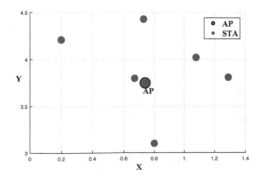

Fig. 11. 1AP6STA

4.1.2   6AP36STA

In Fig. 12 and Table 2, there is 6 AP, 36 STAs and 36 A-BFT slots, and AP also has 4 group sectors and multi-beam receiving capability. It is an extended simulation test and no different from 1AP6STA in the implementation of G-ABFTRes and G-SSW schemes.

Table 2. 6AP36STA simulation parameters

Parameters	Configuration
Cell number	6
Number of nodes in cell	7
Sector number	12
Degree per sector	30°
Channel model	Calibrated SISO channel
Size of conference room scene	3 m * 4.5 m
Channel bandwidth	2.16 GHz
Packet size	40000 Byte
Simulation duration	1 s
Business	Up/down link+equal traffic-rate
BI duration	100 ms
DTI phase	Only SP
SP allocation rules	Priority fairness
Threshold of ReqIGSSW	−38 dB

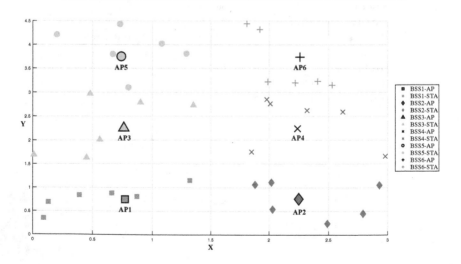

Fig. 12. 6AP36STA

4.2   Scheme Verification

4.2.1   Throughput

$$Throughput = \frac{successfully\ received\ Packets}{simulation\ duration} \tag{5}$$

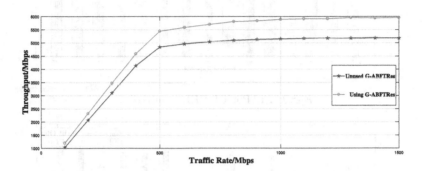

Fig. 13. 1AP6STA Throughput comparison

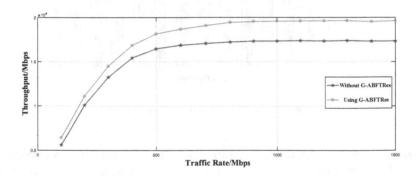

Fig. 14. 6AP36STA Throughput comparison

As shown in Fig. 13/14: when Throughput of 1AP6STA/6AP36STA reaches saturation, Throughput after using G-ABFTRes is about 6000/19000 Mbps and higher than unused G-ABFTRes. This is because G-ABFTRes reduces the probability of collisions between STAs in A-BFT slot, thereby reducing the time for re-BF training due to collisions. As a result, the number of successfully received packets are increased and throughput is also improved in same simulation time.

4.2.2   Packet-Error-Rate (PER)

$$PER = \frac{Error\ Packets}{Error\ Packets + successfully\ received\ Packets} \tag{6}$$

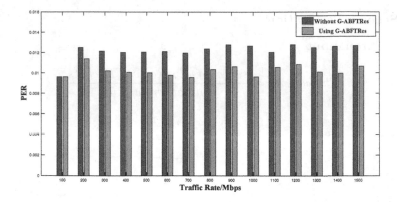

Fig. 15. 1AP6STA PER comparison

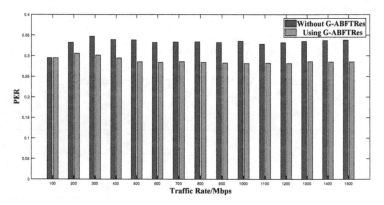

Fig. 16. 6AP36STA PER comparison

As shown in Fig. 15/16: when Throughput of 1AP6STA/6AP36STA reaches saturation, PER after using G-ABFTRes is about 0.01/0.29 and lower than unused G-ABFTRes. This is because Error Packets number has not changed and G-ABFTRes increases the number of successfully received Packets. As a result, PER is decreased in same simulation time.

5   Conclusion

In this paper, a grouping based BF training scheme has been proposed for solving a conflict problem when STAs perform BF training in A-BFT slot. The scheme can reduce conflict probability and improve Throughput and PER in millimeter wave communication.

Simulation results verify the correctness of G-ABFTRes and G-SSW. It is of some referenced and applicable significance in putting forward standard of next generation millimeter Wave WLAN. However, this scheme is limited to 802.11ad, and does not involve 802.11aj/ay. Hence, a future work would be to provide more analysis in other millimeter Wave WLAN standard.

Acknowledgement. This work was supported in part by the National Natural Science Foundations of CHINA (Grant No. 61871322, No. 61771392, No. 61771390, and No. 61501373), and Science and Technology on Avionics Integration Laboratory and the Aeronautical Science Foundation of China (Grant No. 20185553035, and No. 201955053002).

References

1. Park, M., Cordeiro, C., Perahia, E., Yang, L.L.: Millimeter-wave multi-Gigabit WLAN: challenges and feasibility. In: 2008 IEEE 19th International Symposium on Personal, Indoor and Mobile Radio Communications, Cannes, France, pp. 1–5 (2008). https://doi.org/10.1109/PIMRC.2008.4699890
2. Nitsche, T., Cordeiro, C., Flores, A.B., Knightly, E.W., Widmer, J.C.: IEEE 802.11ad: directional 60 GHz Communication for Multi-Gbps Wi-Fi. IEEE Commun. Mag. **52**(12), 132–141 (2014). https://doi.org/10.1109/MCOM.2014.6979964
3. Verma, L., Fakharzadeh, M., Choi, S.: WiFi on steroids: 802.11AC and 802.11AD. IEEE Wirel. Commun. **20**(6), 30–35 (2013). https://doi.org/10.1109/MWC.2013.6704471
4. Chen, Q., Tang, J., Wong, D.T.C., Peng, X.: Directional cooperative MAC protocol design and performance analysis for IEEE 802.11ad WLANs. IEEE Trans. Veh. Technol. **62**(6), 2667–2677 (2013). https://doi.org/10.1109/TVT.2013.2245352
5. Assasa, H., Widmer, J.: Implementation and evaluation of a WLAN IEEE 802.11ad model in ns-3. In: Workshop on NS-3, WNS3 2016, Seattle, WA, USA, pp. 57–64 (2016). https://doi.org/10.1145/2915371.2915377
6. Cordeiro, C., Akhmetov, D., Park, M.: IEEE 802.11ad: introduction and performance evaluation of the first multi-Gbps WiFi technology. In: Proceedings of the 2010 ACM International Workshop on mmWave Communications: From Circuits to Networks, mmCom 2010, Chicago, Illinois, USA, pp. 3–8 (2010). https://doi.org/10.1145/1859964.1859968
7. Perahia, E., Cordeiro, C., Park, M., Yang, L.L.: IEEE 802.11ad: defining the next generation multi-Gbps Wi-Fi. In: 2010 7th IEEE Consumer Communications and Networking Conference, Las Vegas, NV, USA, pp. 1–5 (2010). https://doi.org/10.1109/CCNC.2010.5421713
8. IEEE Standard for Information technology Telecommunications and information exchange between systems Local and metropolitan area networks Specific requirements - Part 11: Wireless LAN Medium Access Control (MAC) and Physical Layer (PHY) Specifications. IEEE Std 802.11-2016 (Revision of IEEE Std 802.11-2012), pp. 1–3534 (2016). https://doi.org/10.1109/IEEESTD.2016.7786995
9. Akhtar, A., Ergen, S.C.: Efficient network level beamforming training for IEEE 802.11ad WLANs. In: 2015 International Symposium on Performance Evaluation of Computer and Telecommunication Systems (SPECTS), Chicago, IL, USA, pp. 1–6 (2015). https://doi.org/10.1109/SPECTS.2015.7285289

Dynamic Time Slot Adjustment Based Beamform Training for the Next Generation Millimeter Wave WLAN

Zhaotun Feng[1], Yong Fang[1], Mao Yang[2(✉)], Zhongjiang Yan[2], and Bo Li[2]

[1] School of Information Engineering, Chang'an University,
Xi'an, People's Republic of China
{2018124076,fy}@chd.edu.cn
[2] School of Electronics and Information, Northwestern Polytechnical University,
Xi'an, China
{yangmao,zhjyan,libo.npu}@nwpu.edu.cn

Abstract. In recent years, people have put forward higher and higher requirements for high-speed communications within a local area. Millimeter-wave WLAN has attracted much attention from academia and industry by virtue of its ultra-large bandwidth and short-range coverage. Beam training is a key technology of millimeter wave WLAN. The quality of beam training is related to communication performance and even communication. However, as the number of nodes continues to increase, the beam training efficiency of the traditional millimeter wave WLAN is very low, which affects system performance. This paper proposes a beamforming training method based on dynamic time slot adjustment for the next generation millimeter wave WLAN. The beam training slot in the subsequent beacon interval (BI) can be adjusted according to the completion of the beam training in the previous BI, thereby improving the efficiency of beam training. The simulation results prove that the method proposed in this paper can effectively improve the beam training efficiency and has a small impact on the performance of the system.

Keywords: Millimeter wave · WLAN · 802.11ad · Beam training

1 Introduction

With the widespread use of WLAN, the unlicensed spectrum in the low frequency (LF) frequency band has been close to saturation. Therefore, the most commonly used 802.11 WLAN (such as 802.11n, 802.11ac, etc.) cannot meet the constantly updated wireless The data rate of the application. In order to provide users with a higher data transmission rate to meet the constantly updated data transmission requirements, in order to adapt to more complex network deployment scenarios, more usable spectrum and more cutting-edge technologies are required. Millimeter wave (mmWave) (i.e. 30 GHz–300 GHz) has more licensable spectrum, which

© ICST Institute for Computer Sciences, Social Informatics and Telecommunications Engineering 2021
Published by Springer Nature Switzerland AG 2021. All Rights Reserved
Y.-B. Lin and D.-J. Deng (Eds.): SGIoT 2020, LNICST 354, pp. 340–350, 2021.
https://doi.org/10.1007/978-3-030-69514-9_27

can provide more opportunities for emerging broadband applications [1]. Currently, millimeter wave communication has been applied to the fifth generation (5G) mobile communication system and some cutting-edge wireless communication systems (such as IEEE 802.15.3c 802.11ad and 802.11ay, etc.) [2]. Among these abundant unlicensed spectrum, both academia and industry suggest that the 60 GHz unlicensed mmWave frequency band should be given priority. IEEE 802.11ad uses the 60 GHz frequency band (i.e. 57–66 GHz). In the previous work [3], we have extensively evaluated the performance of IEEE 802.11ad, but there are still many problems to be solved under the high-density network deployment in the future.

Because millimeter wave propagation suffers from severe path loss and signal attenuation, it is almost impossible to achieve long-distance communication transmission when using traditional omnidirectional communication. Therefore, beamforming technology that can concentrate the transmit power and receiving area on a narrow beam is commonly used for directional transmission, and beamforming training (BFT) is a key process to realize directional communication. Therefore, the BFT process must be carefully designed in the protocol, and the best transceiver sector must be determined to be fully prepared for directional transmission. If the process of establishing directional communication transmission takes too much time, the communication delay will be too long. Quality of experience (QoE) is reduced [4]. However, because the BFT process in 802.11ad cannot be flexibly configured according to different requirements, this makes the BFT process very time-consuming and inefficient in communication. Therefore, it is very important to design a simple and effective BFT method, especially for WLANs that aim to reduce costs and complexity to provide high-quality services (QoS). The Association Beamforming Training (A-BFT) stage is the key to channel access and BFT, because in high-density user deployment scenarios, the number of nodes continues to increase or changes greatly, causing nodes to collide or not optimize when they enter a fixed number of time slots. Once the STA cannot complete the beam training in the A-BFT, it will not be allocated to the time slot to complete the data transmission, but will wait for another A-BFT in the next beacon interval (BI) to access the training again, which will seriously affect QoE.

At present, there are already some solutions to study the efficiency of BFT of millimeter wave WLAN. For example, some studies have proposed a multichannel A-BFT solution to reduce serious conflicts during A-BFT in high-density deployment scenarios. Other studies have proposed extending the number of time slots to adapt to high-density user scenarios. Although these solutions provide efficient and feasible solutions, they all create additional costs, which will affect the overall performance of the system more or less. Therefore, it is the key to present research to propose an efficient A-BFT scheme that can dynamically adjust the ABFT slots according to the beam training conditions of the nodes in the cell.

To efficiently improve the beamforming training performance, this paper proposes a method based on dynamic time slot adjustment, which dynamically determines the number of A-BFT time slots in the next BI according to the conflict in the A-BFT in the previous BI, thereby re-dividing the A-BFT time slots. And for the node that has completed the training, it is only necessary to save the training result for use in the next BI until the communication quality of the link drops, and then perform beam training for the node access. Save the time allocated for beam training. At the same time, the number of sector sweep frames (SSW frames) in ABFT Slot is reduced by determining the best receiving sector of the STA (obtained in the BTI phase), and using this as the center to do only 180° sector training. The simulation shows that the system greatly improves the efficiency of beam training while ensuring the overall performance is unchanged.

The Section 1 summarizes the research status of 802.11ad, the Sect. 2 introduces the principle and motivation of the method used, the Sect. 3 explains the principle and the frame structure design and program flow design, the Sect. 4.1 configures the simulation platform, and the Sect. 4.2 analyzes the simulation results. Section 5 summarizes the work of this paper.

2 Related Work and Motivation

2.1 BFT in IEEE 802.11ad/ay

In the 802.11ad/ay protocol, the A-BFT phase is allocated in each BI, and a certain amount of ABFT slots are set in the A-BFT phase. Before the beam training starts, that is, after the node receives the DMG beacon frame, the node in the cell randomly selects an ABFT slot It is used for beam training. In the ABFT slot, the AP receives the SSW frame sent by the STA rotating every sector omnidirectionally. Based on the received SSW frame, the AP determines the STA with the strongest transmission energy to send the sector, and sends the information It is stored in the sector sweep feedback frame (SSW-FBCK frame) and returned to the STA. This process completes the beam training of the STA's transmission sector. This process is shown in the following figure (Figs. 1, 2, 3, and 4):

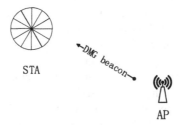

Fig. 1. AP sends DMG beacon frames in all directions

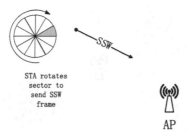

Fig. 2. STA rotates sector and sends SSW frame to AP

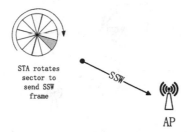

Fig. 3. The AP receives the SSW frame with the strongest signal energy

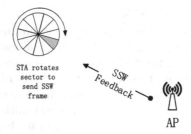

Fig. 4. The AP sends the STA's best sending sector information through the SSWF-BCK frame

In the A-BFT phase, the STA in the cell randomly selects the training time slot, which will cause several STAs to select the same time slot and cannot complete the training. (There are two cases where the training cannot be completed. One is although There are several nodes in the same time slot, but due to STA directional transmission, one node in the time slot finally completed the training, and the other is that all the nodes that choose the time slot cannot complete the training as shown in the figure). The node will try to access the training again in the next BI (Figs. 5 and 6).

In order to avoid such conflicts, it is common practice to preset free ABFT slots before the start of BI to ensure that the number of time slots is greater than the number of nodes. Although this method takes care of the success rate of beam training, it reduces the overall training efficiency. For a system where the nodes in a cell maintain a stable state, the less time the beam training takes, the

Fig. 5. Complete sector training of a STA in a time slot

Fig. 6. No node in the time slot has completed sector training

better. Considering this factor, this article introduces a beam training method based on dynamic time slot adjustment. This method only allocates time slots for nodes that have not completed beam training. For nodes that have completed beam training, save and use the trained sectors As a result, a link maintenance mechanism is also introduced to maintain the quality of the management link. If the quality of a link decreases (during the communication, the initiator does not receive an ACK frame or the receiver does not initiate an ACK frame), let the node of the link accesses the ABFT slot again for beam training.

2.2   Related Studies on BFT Improvement

There have been many studies aimed at improving the efficiency of BFT. For example, a multi-channel A-BFT scheme was proposed in [5], which allocates the same A-BFT to the STA on the secondary channel as the primary channel. Configuration to reduce serious conflicts during A-BFT in high-density deployment scenarios. For example, if two or more STAs choose to access the same ABFT slot, they are allocated to different master and slave channels respectively. Such a multi-channel scheme can effectively avoid conflicts. Since 8 ABFT slots are generally set in 802.11ad, in high-density network deployment scenarios, the number of time slots can be expanded to reduce training conflicts. [6] Provides a separate ABFT (SA-BFT) mechanism to expand the original 8 time slots to more, that is, an EA-BFT time slot is added to the DMG Beacon frame, which is expressed as an extended extra The number of time slots, therefore, the total number of time slots in the extended A-BFT is "A-BFT length+EA-BFT length". [7] and [8] can also effectively avoid the collision problem of A-BFT. Since A-BFT is divided into multiple time slots, when one STA performs receiving sector scanning in one of the time slots, other STAs can remain silent. In order to improve the efficiency of A-BFT, Akhtar and Ergenthe [9] proposed an intelligent monitoring (ILA) mechanism during A-BFT to reduce the BFT overhead between STAs. When a STA accesses the ABFT time slot for receiving sector scanning, other STAs keep listening in the quasi-omnidirectional mode instead of remaining idle. They will learn the approximate beam direction of the training STA by completing the training result of the beam training node. After a certain number of nodes have completed training, other STAs can infer the best sending sector direction of their peers. Therefore, STAs do not need to rotate 360° to send SSW frames to APs, which can significantly reduce the BFT overhead between STAs.

2.3 Motivation

The motivation of this paper is to solve the problem of training conflicts and the decrease of beamforming training efficiency due to the increase of the number of nodes during beamforming training. The beamforming training method in the A-BFT phase of the current 802.11ad protocol is not flexible enough, because it is usually necessary to set up enough ABFT slots in advance to cope with the nodes in the cell. Such a setting cannot meet future high-density network deployment scenarios. As the number of nodes in the cell increases, more and more STAs will inevitably In the beam training phase, conflicts are generated and the training cannot be successfully completed and thus cannot be served, which reduces the training efficiency of the entire A-BFT phase. The following figure shows that beam training conflicts occur with the increase of access nodes under a fixed number of ABFT slots (Fig. 7).

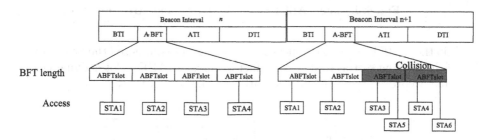

Fig. 7. Increased node access in cell leads to beamforming training collision

3   Scheme Description

The beam training method proposed in this paper dynamically adjusts the number of ABFT slots according to the number of nodes that have beam training conflicts at this stage to meet the training needs of all nodes in the cell. At the beginning of the simulation, an ABFT slot number is preset to perform beam training on the nodes in the cell. The beamforming training is first found The best receiving sector of the STA. Using this as the center, let the sector only scan 180°, then find the node that has completed the training and save the training result of the node, and count the conflicting time slots and conflicting nodes at the same time, and this The sum of the two values is set to the number of ABFT slots in the next BI. Assuming that there are 10 nodes in the cell preset 6 time slots, at most 4 of these 6 time slots will cause training conflicts, and at least 4 nodes will be unable to complete beam training due to conflicts (here the conflict is assumed to be In the first case, one node in the time slot has completed beam training). Then in the next BI, only 8 ABFT time slots need to be allocated to complete the training of all nodes in the cell, and no nodes are trained in the subsequent BI, unless the communication quality of some of the nodes is reduced (the communication quality can be reduced by The link maintenance mechanism detects that the receiving end has not received an ACK or the sending end has not initiated an ACK within a certain period of time). The following figure shows the frame structure design of this scheme (Fig. 8):

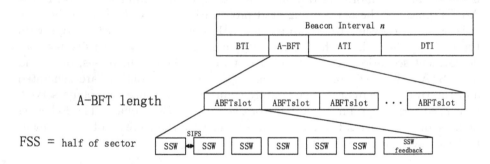

Fig. 8. Dynamic ABFT slot MAC layer frame structure

If in the A-BFT stage of the nth BI, a node has not completed the beam training of the sending sector, that is, a conflict occurs, the ABFT slot is dynamically adjusted according to the conflict situation in the n+1th BI (Fig. 9).

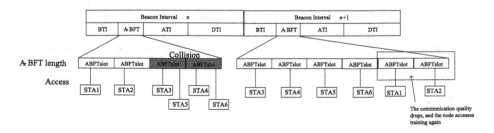

Fig. 9. Dynamically adjust ABFT time slot STA access training

As shown in the following figure, the sequence flow chart of STA performing beam training. First, AP broadcasts a DMG beacon frame to STA. After receiving it, STA in the cell selects an ABFT slot to access in order. After entering ABFT slot, STA rotates to receive the best The sector is the center 180° to send the SSW frame, the AP receives the SSW and makes a decision, selects the strongest energy among them, and returns the sector information to the SSW feedback frame to the corresponding STA. If two or more STAs are simultaneously accessed in the time slot, beam training cannot be completed. Therefore, in the ABFT phase of the next BI, first adjust the number of ABFT slots in the phase according to the conflict situation, and then train the nodes that have not completed beam training in the previous BI, and then consider whether the communication quality of the nodes that have completed the beam training is degraded, When the communication quality drops, beam training is performed for the node to access the time slot (Figs. 10 and 11)

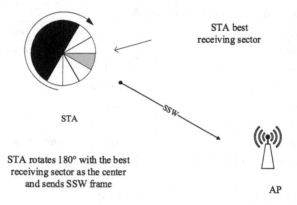

Fig. 10. STA rotates 180° to send SSW frame to AP

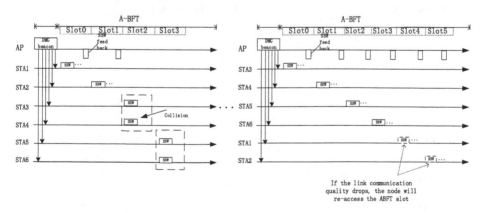

Fig. 11. Beam training sequence flow chart

4 Performance Evaluation

4.1 Simulation Settings

In this chapter, we use the configuration Intel®Core™i7-8750H CPU@2.20 GHZ main frequency, 8 GB memory and 64-bit Windows-10 operating system, all codes are developed under the NS3 simulation platform. The simulation configuration is a single cell scenario, with 1 AP and 6 STAs in the cell. Create cell congestion by reducing the number of preset ABFT slots to simulate high-density network deployment scenarios (Fig. 12 and Table 1).

Table 1. Parameter setting

Parameter	Configuration
Number of cells	1
Number of STA nodes in a single cell	6
Sector angle	30° (360° is divided into 12 sectors)
Channel model	Calibrated SISO channel
Meeting room scene size	3 m * 4.5 m
Channel bandwidth	2.16 GHz
Packet size	60000 bytes
Simulation duration	3 s
Link adaptation	According to simulation
MCS without link adaptation	DMG MCS24
BI length	100 ms
DTI stage configuration	Only SP
SP distribution principle	Fairness first
Physical layer	Phy Abstraction

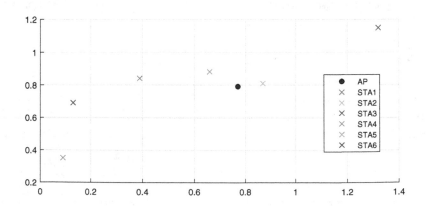

Fig. 12. Network topology diagram

4.2   Simulation Results and Analysis

According to the system throughput and packet loss rate, the simulation compares the script of adding dynamic time slot adjustment method and link maintenance mechanism with the original protocol script. As shown in the figure below, the blue solid line represents the original script without added functions, and the yellow The dotted line indicates the script with dynamic time slot adjustment added, and the red dotted line indicates the script with dynamic time slot adjustment and link maintenance mechanism added (Figs. 13 and 14).

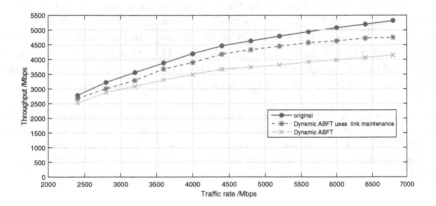

Fig. 13. Throughput comparison of various schemes

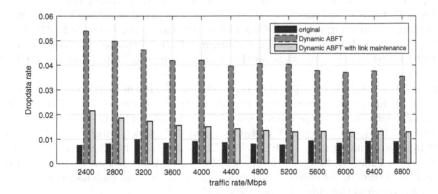

Fig. 14. Comparison of packet loss rate of each scheme

The simulation results show that, from the throughput curve, the performance of the curve with only dynamic time slot adjustment decreases more, and the link maintenance function can be better compensated. From the packet loss rate histogram, the packet loss rate with only dynamic time slot adjustment is higher, and the packet loss is mainly concentrated in the first few BIs. This situation is caused by the failure of the previous training conflict. Generally speaking, The dynamic time slot adjustment of link maintenance can not only improve the efficiency of beam training but also ensure the performance of the system.

5   Conclusions

This paper proposes a beam training method for the next generation millimeter wave WLAN based on dynamic time slot adjustment. In order to adapt to changes in the number of nodes in the cell and reduce beam training conflicts caused by changes in the number of nodes, the original fixed number of ABFT slots are set to a form that can be dynamically adjusted according to the beam training conflicts. The simulation results show that this method improves the efficiency of beam training while ensuring the overall performance of the system, and can better adapt to future high-density network deployments.

Acknowledgement. This work was supported in part by the National Natural Science Foundations of CHINA (Grant No. 61871322, No. 61771392, No. 61771390, and No. 61501373), and Science and Technology on Avionics Integration Laboratory and the Aeronautical Science Foundation of China (Grant No. 20185553035, and No. 201955053002).

References

1. IEEE: Status of project IEEE 802.11ay. IEEE P802.11 - Task Group ay - Meeting Update (2017). http://www.ieee802.org/11/Reports/tgay_update.htm
2. Zhou, P., Cheng, K., Han, X., et al.: IEEE 802.11ay based mmWave WLANs: design challenges and solutions. IEEE Commun. Surv. Tutor. **20**, 1654–1681 (2018)
3. Nguyen, K., Kibria, M.G., Ishizu, K., Kojima, F.: Performance evaluation of IEEE 802.11ad in evolving Wi-Fi networks. Wirel. Commun. Mob. Comput. **2019**, 11 (2019)
4. Shokri-Ghadikolaei, H., Gkatzikis, L., Fischione, C.: Beam-searching and transmission scheduling in millimeter wave communications. In: Proceedings of the International Conference on Communications (ICC), pp. 1292–1297 (2015)
5. Xue, Q., Fang, X., Wang, C.X.: Beamspace SU-MIMO for Future Millimeter Wave Wireless Communications. IEEE J. Sel. Areas Commun. **35**(7), 1564–1575 (2017)
6. Zhou, P., Fang, X., Fang, Y., Long, Y., He, R., Han, X.: Enhanced random access and beam training for mmWave wireless local networks with high user density. IEEE Trans. Wireless Commun. **16**(12), 7760–7773 (2017)
7. Kim, S.G., et al.: On random access in A-BFT. IEEE 802.11 documents (2016). https://mentor.ieee.org/802.11/documents?is_dcn=SSW&is_group=00ay
8. Johnsson, K., et al.: Scalable A-BFT. IEEE 802.11 documents (2016). https://mentor.ieee.org/802.11/documents?is_dcn=SSW&is_group=00ay
9. Akhtar, A., Ergen, S.C.: Efficient network level beamforming training for IEEE 802.11ad WLANs. In: Proceedings of the International Symposium on Performance Evaluation of Computer and Telecommunication Systems (SPECTS), pp. 1–6 (2015)

Latency Oriented OFDMA Random Access Scheme for the Next Generation WLAN: IEEE 802.11be

Zhaozhe Jiang, Bo Li, Mao Yang[⊠], and Zhongjiang Yan

Northwestern Polytechnical University, Xi'an 710129, China
jzz@mail.nwpu.edu.cn, {libo.npu,yangmao,zhjyan}@nwpu.edu.cn

Abstract. Real-time applications (RTA) develop rapidly these days. Latency sensitive traffic guarantee becomes increasingly important and challenging in wireless local area network (WLAN). In order to tackle the problem, this paper proposes a latency oriented random access scheme, which is compatible with IEEE 802.11 standards, based on orthogonal frequency division multiple access (OFDMA) in the next generation WLAN: IEEE 802.11be. AP utilizes trigger frame (TF) based OFDMA random access and reserves several resource units (RUs) for latency sensitive traffic only. According to the collision status in the past TF as well as the traffic arrival features, we theoretically analyze the estimated number of STAs who will have latency sensitive data to send during the next TF interaction. Thus, AP can allocate appropriate RUs for latency sensitive STAs dynamically. The simulation results show that the proposed dynamic RU adjusting algorithm outperforms the other schemes in both throughput and delay. The throughput utility of the proposed algorithm is 19.69% higher than that of IEEE 802.11ax. And the delay utility is 21.39% lower than that of IEEE 802.11ax, which validates the effectiveness of the proposed algorithm.

Keywords: Latency guarantee · Delay sensitive · Real-time application · WLAN · OFDMA

1 Introduction

In the past decades, with the rapid development of communication technology, wireless local area network (WLAN) has already penetrated into people's lives [1]. The number of terminals increases rapidly [2]. Meanwhile, live video streaming and online meeting have become more and more popular among people [3,4].

In recent years, lots of real-time applications (RTA) such as online game, virtual reality (VR) are becoming increasingly sensitive to delay [5,6]. Large delay will seriously influence the quality of experience (QoE) [7]. In order to improve quality of service (QoS) of RTA, schemes for latency guarantee need to

Y.-B. Lin and D.-J. Deng (Eds.): SGIoT 2020, LNICST 354, pp. 351–362, 2021.
https://doi.org/10.1007/978-3-030-69514-9_28

be well designed. Therefore, delay guarantee is considered to be a key issue of the next generation WLAN standard: IEEE 802.11be [8].

There are some existing latency guarantee algorithms for WLAN. Higuchi et al. [9] improved latency-rate (LR) scheduling method to guarantee a bounded delay for hybrid coordination function (HCF) controlled channel access (HCCA). His new scheduling algorithm can optimize the number of stations according to the token bucket and service interval (SI). Kuo et al. [10] put forward a contention-based scheme to guarantee Qos of both the upstream and downstream. A fixed contention window backoff scheme and the parameters optimization procedure help to mitigate the downlink bottleneck at the access point (AP). Through the analysis of the relationship between the optimal size of initial backoff competition window and the maximum aggregate throughput, an admission control algorithm is proposed by Gao et al. [11] for the purpose of maximizing the number of real-time nodes. Gao et al. [12] presented an accurate theoretical model which can predict the queueing delay of RTA in WLAN. According to the model, a decentralized scheme is put forward to minimize the traffic delay. Hurtig et al. [13] proposed the block estimation (BLEST) scheduler and the shortest transmission time first (STTF) scheduler for multi-path protocols. And multi-path protocols can optimize performance through load-balancing and link failures. However, few of the existing studies are well compatible with IEEE 802.11ax [14] or fully use the new features such as orthogonal frequency division multiple access (OFDMA).

In order to reduce the latency of RTA while maintain the compatibility of IEEE 802.11 standards [15], this paper proposes an OFDMA based random access latency guarantee scheme. AP can reserve appropriate resource units (RUs) for latency sensitive traffic dynamically through trigger frame (TF). It can be found that the proposed algorithm outperforms the other schemes on both throughput and delay.

The contributions of this article are summarized as follows:

- This article proposes an OFDMA based random access latency guarantee algorithm in the next generation WLAN: IEEE 802.11be, which is compatible with the framework of IEEE 802.11 standards.
- Meanwhile, the proposed algorithm has the highest throughput and the lowest delay compared with IEEE 802.11ax and the other methods. It has the best comprehensive performance.

The rest of this article is arranged as follows. Section 2 briefly describes the problem and puts up the key idea of the solution. In Sect. 3, we detailedly introduce and infer the proposed algorithm. Then, simulation results and analysis will show in Sect. 4. And the final section will summarize this article in the end.

2   Motivation

2.1   Problem Formulation

IEEE 802.11ax first introduced OFDMA in WLAN. Available channels are divided into multiple RUs. Users can select different RUs for information transmission [16].

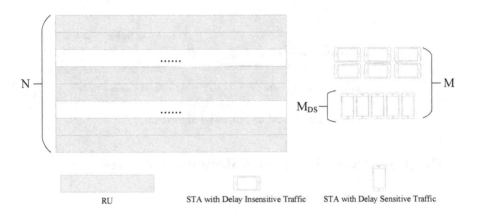

RU   STA with Delay Insensitive Traffic   STA with Delay Sensitive Traffic

Fig. 1. Communication scenario.

As Fig. 1 shows, there are N resource units for M stations (STAs) to compete. And there are M_{DS} stations with delay sensitive traffic within the M stations. Due to random access, the successful possibility of stations with delay insensitive traffic is the same as that of stations with delay sensitive traffic. Therefore, latency sensitive service cannot be well guaranteed.

2.2   Key Idea of Proposed Algorithm

For the sake of improving the comprehensive performance of latency sensitive service, a dynamic RU random access scheme is proposed. In the proposed algorithm, some RUs are reserved and allocated to STAs which have delay sensitive traffic. Then, STAs with delay sensitive traffic will have higher successful transmission possibility than that of STAs with delay insensitive traffic. Therefore, the QoS of RTA can be well protected (Fig. 2).

Every time before AP sends TF, AP will estimate volume of latency sensitive traffic [17]. And the queue information of STAs can be deduced according to the proposed algorithm. Then, AP can reserve appropriate RUs and put the RU configuration information into the TF, which means that proposed algorithm can adapt to the variable traffic rate.

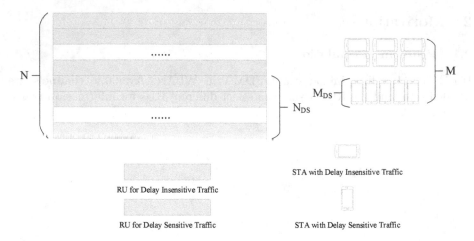

Fig. 2. Model of proposed algorithm.

3   Proposed Algorithm for Latency Guarantee

3.1   Procedures of Proposed Algorithm

Figure 3 shows procedures of the proposed algorithm. After a successful backoff, according to the collision status of RUs in the last TF interaction as well as the traffic arrival features, AP will estimate M_E, which is the number of STAs which will have latency sensitive data to send. Then, AP will configure appropriate N_{DS}, which is the RU number for latency sensitive STAs. And AP will send TF to STAs. A short interframe space (SIFS) after receiving TF, the STAs will send uplink (UL) data. A SIFS later, AP can respond block acknowledgment (BACK) frame to STAs. Table 1 shows the notations that will be involved in this paper.

3.2   Proposed Algorithm

A. Estimation
Because it is random for STAs to choose RU, there will be three states for a single RU. They are successful, idle and collided. A successful RU means that only one STA choose this RU. And an idle RU indicates that no STAs choose this RU. The situations of RUs can be utilized to estimate M_E.

When a collided RU occurs, it is obvious that there are at least two STAs choosing this RU. Cha et al. [18] pointed out that the estimated STA number is 2.39 times the number of collided RUs, which means that a collided RU is caused by 2.39 STAs on average. These STAs will retransmit data after receiving the next TF. In other words, STAs which chose collided RUs must send data at next transmission opportunity. However, it is not clear that whether the STAs which didn't choose collided RUs will send data at the next opportunity or not. In order to estimate M_E more accurately, we need to solve the above problem.

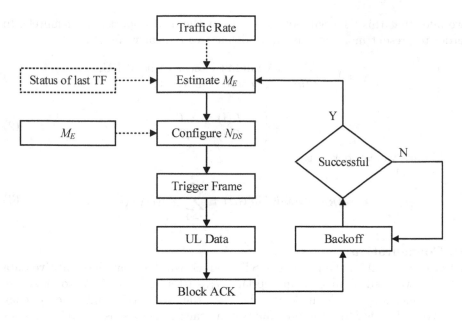

Fig. 3. Procedures of proposed algorithm.

Table 1. Notations.

Notations	Description
M	Number of all stations
M_{DS}	Number of stations with delay sensitive traffic
M_E	Estimated number of stations with delay sensitive traffic
N	Number of all resource units
N_{DS}	Number of resource units for delay sensitive traffic
N_S	Number of successful resource units within N_{DS} RU
N_I	Number of idle resource units within N_{DS} RU
N_C	Number of collided resource units within N_{DS} RU
T	Current time

Assume that the application traffic of STA i subject to Poisson distribution $P(\lambda_i)$ [19]. And the average traffic rate λ_i can be variable. AP is capable of recording the number of received packets $R(i)$ of station i. And AP also can extrapolate traffic rate of each STA. The detailed method is out of the scope of this paper. At the next transmission time T, an average of $\lambda_i T$ packets have been produced by STA i. If the number of received packets $R(i)$ is not larger than $\lambda_i T - 1$, STA i must send data at the next transmission. And if $R(i) > \lambda_i T - 1$, we infer that this STA will not send data at the next opportunity definitely. In order to present more intuitively, we define two indicative functions.

$$\chi_C(i) = \begin{cases} 1, & \text{STA } i \text{ didn't choose collided RU.} \\ 0, & \text{STA } i \text{ chose collided RU.} \end{cases} \tag{1}$$

$$\chi_T(i) = \begin{cases} 1, & R(i) \leq \lambda_i T - 1. \\ 0, & R(i) > \lambda_i T - 1. \end{cases} \tag{2}$$

Finally, we can derive that

$$M_E = round(2.39N_C) + \sum_{i=1}^{M_{DS}} \chi_C(i)\chi_T(i) \tag{3}$$

B. Configuration

After estimate M_E, the number of STAs which will have latency sensitive data to send, we need to allocate appropriate N_{DS} RUs for these STAs to maximize access efficiency. For a single RU, because the total RU number for latency sensitive STAs is N_{DS}, the probability that each latency sensitive STA chooses this RU is $1/N_{DS}$. Then, the probability of selecting the other RUs is $1 - 1/N_{DS}$. So, the probability that a latency sensitive STA can transmit successfully on this RU is given by:

$$P_S = \frac{1}{N_{DS}}\left(1 - \frac{1}{N_{DS}}\right)^{M_E - 1} \tag{4}$$

And there are N_{DS} resource units for latency sensitive traffic. The probability that a latency sensitive STA transmits data successfully is:

$$N_{DS}P_S = \left(1 - \frac{1}{N_{DS}}\right)^{M_E - 1} \tag{5}$$

Since there are total M_E STAs which will have latency sensitive traffic to transmit, the expected successful STA number M_S will be:

$$M_S = M_E\left(1 - \frac{1}{N_{DS}}\right)^{M_E - 1} \tag{6}$$

Therefore, the expected successful ratio η can be calculated as:

$$\eta = \frac{M_E}{N_{DS}}\left(1 - \frac{1}{N_{DS}}\right)^{M_E - 1} \tag{7}$$

In order to maximize η, calculate derivative of function η with respect to N_{DS}. And solve the equation that derivative value is equal to 0. Then, we can get that the optimal N_{DS} is equal to M_E. Therefore, after get M_E, AP will allocate M_E resource units for latency sensitive traffic.

3.3 Compatibility Analysis

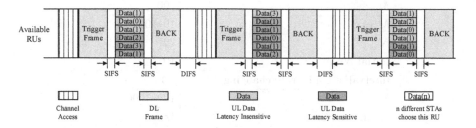

Fig. 4. Example of proposed algortithm.

Figure 4 presents an example of the proposed algortithm. There will be three types of frames in this system. They are trigger frame, data frame and block ACK frame, which are all included in IEEE 802.11ax standard. Data frame is used to transmit data. And block ACK frame is a kind of control frame, which indicates whether the data has been received correctly or not. Besides, we can put the configuration information of RUs into the TF, which is consistent with IEEE 802.11ax.

For latency sensitive traffic, we can set the user priority (UP) as 7. And put the packets into queue AC_VO, which has the highest transmission priority. As for latency insensitive traffic, the UP can be configured as 0. Packets will go into queue AC_BE, which has a lower priority.

4 Results and Analysis

NS3 [20] is used for our simulations. Suppose a STA only has one type of traffic. The traffic rate λ of all the STAs is the same and it can be time variant. The detailed configuration information is shown in Table 2.

In order to describe comprehensive performance of algorithms, weight coefficient α for delay sensitive STAs and β for delay insensitive STAs are defined to calculate utility. There are only two types of traffic. Thus, α and β need to meet the equation $\alpha + \beta = 1$. And for the reason that delay sensitive traffic has a higher priority, α will be larger than β.

Figure 5 shows the throughput of all delay sensitive STAs. IEEE 802.11ax performs uplink OFDMA (UORA) with total 72 RUs. The transmission opportunity for each STA is the same. And the throughput of each STA is equal. Therefore, the throughput has a linear relationship with the number of delay sensitive STAs. In the cases of fixed RU number mode, when the number of delay sensitive STAs is small, throughput will be higher as the delay sensitive STA number grows. And if the number of delay sensitive STAs is larger, the collision among delay sensitive STAs will be very serious. It also can be found that the maximum throughput achieves when the RU number is equal to the

Table 2. Simulation configuration.

Parameter name	Parameter value
M	100
M_{DS}	10–100
N	72
Initial N_{DS}	10
Interval of traffic rate changing	0.1 s
λ	100–1000
Simulation time	1s
Distributed interframe spacing (DIFS)	34 μs
Contention window (CW)	15
Slot time	9 μs
Physical layer preamble	40 μs
Trigger frame	108.8 μs
SIFS	16 μs
Packet size	1500 Bytes
Data Rate	11.8 Mbps
Block ACK	13.6 μs

number of delay sensitive STAs. The proposed dynamic RU algorithm can allocate appropriate RUs according to the current situation, so the throughput can be well guaranteed whatever the number of delay sensitive STAs is.

$\alpha = 0.8$ and $\beta = 0.2$ are chosen to calculate utility of throughput U_T, which is calculated by $\alpha T_{DS} + \beta T_{DI}$. T_{DS} is the throughput of delay sensitive STAs and T_{DI} is the throughput of delay insensitive STAs. From Fig. 6, we can find that the dynamic RU adjusting algorithm has the highest utility. The proposed algorithm's U_T can reach 123.99. It is 19.69% higher than that of IEEE 802.11ax. And it is 86.14% higher than that of fixed 30 RUs mode.

As Fig. 7 shows, the delay of IEEE 802.11ax is also a constant value because of its competition fairness for each STA. For fixed 30 RUs mode, as the number of delay sensitive STAs grows, the delay will be larger and larger due to the limited resource units. However, when the number of delay sensitive STAs is small, the delay of the proposed dynamic RU algorithm is nearly a constant due to the enough resource units. And the system will be saturated when the number of delay sensitive STAs is larger than 50. Therefore, the delay will increase if delay sensitive STAs is more than 50.

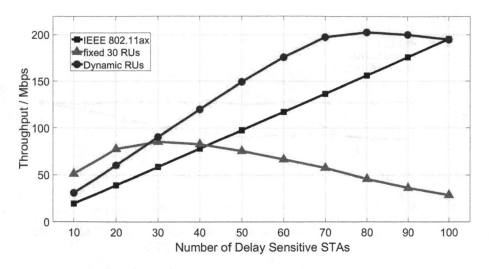

Fig. 5. Throughput of delay sensitive STAs.

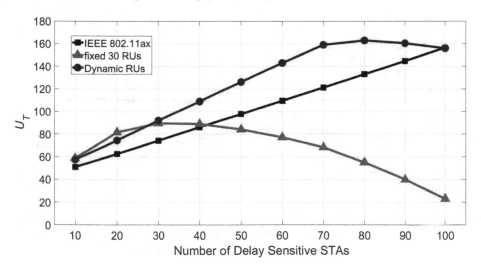

Fig. 6. Utility of throughput.

To calculate utility of delay U_D, we also choose $\alpha = 0.8$ and $\beta = 0.2$. Then, U_D can be calculated by $\alpha D_{DS} + \beta D_{DI}$. D_{DS} is the delay of delay sensitive STAs and D_{DI} is the delay of delay insensitive STAs. Figure 8 show the U_D of different algorithms. We can find that the proposed dynamic RU algorithm's U_D is 0.2227, which is the lowest among these algorithms. It is 21.39% lower than that of IEEE 802.11ax. And it is 15.93% lower than fixed 30 RUs mode.

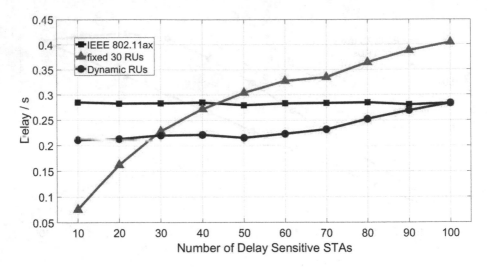

Fig. 7. Delay of delay sensitive STAs.

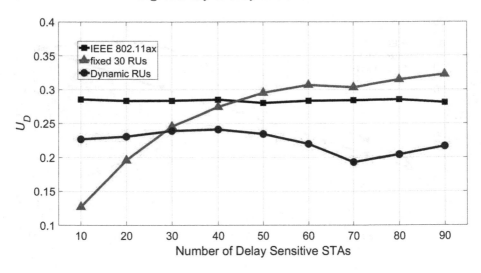

Fig. 8. Utility of delay.

5   Conclusion

For the purpose that guarantee the latency sensitive traffic better, this article proposes an OFDMA random access scheme for the next generation WLAN: IEEE 802.11be. According to the traffic rate and situations of last transmission, AP is capable of estimating the number of STAs which will have latency sensitive data to send. Then, AP can reserve appropriate RUs for latency sensitive traffic dynamically. Through our simulations, it can be found that the proposed dynamic RU adjusting scheme outperforms the other methods. U_T of proposed algorithm is 19.69% higher than that of IEEE 802.11ax. And it is also 86.14% higher than that of fixed 30 RUs mode. Besides, the proposed algorithm's U_D is 21.39% lower than that of IEEE 802.11ax. And it is also 15.93% lower than fixed 30 RUs mode. The proposed algorithm doesn't interrupt the transmission of delay insensitive traffic while latency sensitive traffic is guaranteed. Therefore, the proposed dynamic RU adjusting algorithm has the best comprehensive performance.

Acknowledgement. This work was supported in part by Science and Technology on Avionics Integration Laboratory and the Aeronautical Science Foundation of China (Grant No. 20185553035), the National Natural Science Foundations of CHINA (Grant No. 61871322, No. 61771392, No. 61771390, and No. 61501373), and Science and Technology on Avionics Integration Laboratory and the Aeronautical Science Foundation of China (Grant No. 201955053002).

References

1. Yang, M., Li, B., Yan, Z., Yan, Y.: AP Coordination and Full-duplex enabled multi-band Operation for the next Generation WLAN: IEEE 802.11be (EHT). In: 2019 11th International Conference on Wireless Communications and Signal Processing (WCSP), Xi'an, China, pp. 1–7 (2019)
2. Lepaja, S., Maraj, A., Efendiu, I., Berzati, S.: The impact of the security mechanisms in the throughput of the WLAN networks. In: 2018 7th Mediterranean Conference on Embedded Computing (MECO), Budva, pp. 1–5 (2018)
3. Tian, Y., Babcock, R., Taylor, C., Ji, Y.: A new live video streaming approach based on Amazon S3 pricing model. In: 2018 IEEE 8th Annual Computing and Communication Workshop and Conference (CCWC), Las Vegas, NV, pp. 321-328 (2018)
4. Yoshioka, T., et al.: Advances in online audio-visual meeting transcription. In: 2019 IEEE Automatic Speech Recognition and Understanding Workshop (ASRU), SG, Singapore, pp. 276-283 (2019)
5. Li, T., Guo, Y.: Stability and optimal control in a mathematical model of online game addiction. Filomat **33**(17), 5691–5711 (2019)
6. Deb, S., Carruth, D., Hudson, C.: How communicating features can help pedestrian safety in the presence of self-driving vehicles: virtual reality experiment. IEEE Trans. Hum. Mach. Syst. **50**(2), 176–186 (2020)
7. K. Umadevi, M. Gupta and S. Subodh. A modeling and analysis of delay sensitive scheduling in wireless network. In: 2017 International Conference on Microelectronic Devices, Circuits and Systems (ICMDCS), Vellore, pp. 1-4 (2017)
8. Yang, M., Li, B.: Survey and Perspective on Extremely High Throughput (EHT) WLAN–IEEE 802.11 be. Mobile Netw. Appl. **25**(5), 1765–1780 (2020)
9. Higuchi, Y. et al.: Delay guarantee and service interval optimization for HCCA in IEEE 802.11e WLANs. In: 2007 IEEE Wireless Communications and Networking Conference, Kowloon, pp. 2080–2085 (2007)
10. Kuo, Y., Tsai, T.: Design and evaluation of a contention-based high throughput MAC with delay guarantee for infrastructured IEEE 802.11 WLANs. J. Commun. Netw. **15**(6), 606–613 (2013)

11. Gao, Y., Dai, L., Hei, X.: Throughput Optimization of non-real-time flows with delay guarantee of real-time flows in WLANs In: 2015 IEEE International Conference on Communications (ICC), London, pp. 1541–1546 (2015)
12. Gao, Y., et al.: Characterization and optimization of delay guarantees for real-time multimedia traffic flows in IEEE 802.11 WLANs. IEEE Trans. Mobile Comput. 15(5), 1090–1104 (2016)
13. Hurtig, P., et al.: Low-latency scheduling in MPTCP. IEEE/ACM Trans. Networking **27**(1), 302–315 (2019)
14. IEEE Draft Standard for Information Technology - Telecommunications and Information Exchange Between Systems Local and Metropolitan Area Networks - Specific Requirements Part 11: Wireless LAN Medium Access Control (MAC) and Physical Layer (PHY) Specifications Amendment Enhancements for High Efficiency WLAN, in IEEE P802.11ax/D6.0, pp. 1–780 (2019)
15. IEEE Standard for Information technology–Telecommunications and information exchange between systems Local and metropolitan area networks–Specific requirements - Part 11: Wireless LAN Medium Access Control (MAC) and Physical Layer (PHY) Specifications, in IEEE Std 802.11-2016 (Revision of IEEE Std 802.11-2012), pp. 1–3534 (2016)
16. Bai, J., et al.: Adaptive Uplink OFDMA random access grouping scheme for ultra-dense networks in IEEE 802.11ax. In: 2018 IEEE/CIC International Conference on Communications in China (ICCC), Beijing, China, pp. 34–39 (2018)
17. Mangla, T., et al.: eMIMIC: estimating HTTP-based video QoE metrics from encrypted network traffic. In: 2018 Network Traffic Measurement and Analysis Conference (TMA), Vienna, pp. 1-8 (2018)
18. Cha, J., Kim, J.: Novel anti-collision algorithms for fast object identification in RFID system. In: 11th International Conference on Parallel and Distributed Systems (ICPADS), Fukuoka, pp. 63–67 (2005)
19. Yang, A., Li, B., Yang, M., Yan, Z.: Spatial clustering group-based OFDMA multiple access protocol with carrier sensing for the next-generation WLANs. In: 2018 IEEE International Conference on Signal Processing, Communications and Computing (ICSPCC), Qingdao, pp. 1–6 (2018)
20. The network simulator ns. https://www.nsnam.org

Power Control Based Spatial Reuse for LAA and WiFi Coexistence

Duoduo Hang, Mao Yang$^{(\boxtimes)}$, Zhongjiang Yan, and Bo Li

School of Electronics and Information, Northwestern Polytechnical University,
Xi'an, China
1714348511@qq.com, {yangmao,zhjyan,libo.npu}@nwpu.edu.cn

Abstract. A rising demand for larger network capacity is leading to the
rapid development of the 5th Generation Mobile Communications System (5G). Due to the scarcity of spectrum resources of the conventional
licensed band, 3GPP launched the research project of Licensed-Assisted
Access using LTE (LAA) in September 2014, aiming to design a single
global solution framework and protocol to ensure the efficient operation
of LAA on unlicensed band (e.g. 5 GHz spectrum band). However, existing studies indicate that it is difficult to improve the performance of
LAA and WiFi at the same time. In this paper, we propose a Power
Control based Spacial Reuse scheme (PC-based SR) aiming at increasing the probability of concurrent transmissions in coexisting scenarios
of LAA and WiFi. For LAA network, after recognizing existing WiFi
signal, it should raise its Energy Detection (ED) threshold and transmit
with adjusted power, and vice versa. Our simulation results show that,
using the proposed method, the performance of both LAA and WiFi are
improved and the fairness to WiFi is enhanced, with respect to throughput and latency.

Keywords: LAA · LBT · Network coexistence · Channel access ·
Spatial Reuse

1 Introduction

With the rapid increase in the number of mobile users and the diversification
of mobile service requirements, a rising demand on network capacity is generated, which promotes the rapid development of the 5th Generation Mobile
Communications System (5G). To garantee a better Quality of Service (QoS),
it is necessary to increase the licensed spectrum efficiency using new 5G technology. Due to the scarcity of spectrum resources of the conventional licensed
band, the unlicensed frequency band has raised public awareness. In comparison
to the expensive and crowded licensed band, the unlicensed band has superior
in rich spectrum resources, and possess good openness and propagation performance [1]. In September 2014, 3GPP launched the research project of Licensed-
Assisted Access using LTE (LAA). The target of LAA is to design a single

Y.-B. Lin and D.-J. Deng (Eds.): SGIoT 2020, LNICST 354, pp. 363–384, 2021.
https://doi.org/10.1007/978-3-030-69514-9_29

global solution framework and protocol to ensure the efficient operation of LAA in unlicensed band. In 2017, 3GPP R16 established the project group for 5G New Radio in Unlicensed Spectrum (5G NR-U), introducing LAA technology into 5G networks.

Although licensing is not compulsory, operations on unlicensed band are still required to obey regional regulations. In addition to various requirements such as indoor-only use, maximum in-band output power, etc., LTE operations in some unlicensed spectrum should also implement Dynamic Frequency Selection (DFS) and Transmit Power Control (TPC) to avoid interfering with radars [2].

Besides, a large number of wireless systems and protocols, such as WiFi, Bluetooth and Zigbee, have already been operating on unlicensed band, among which the most significant one is the WiFi system. Therefore, the deployment of LAA has to consider the fair coexistence with the existing WiFi system. According to 3GPP TR36.889, the impact of an LAA network to WiFi networks shall not be more than that of an additional WiFi network to the existing WiFi services concerning throughput and latency [3].

LTE-U technology is the first version on the market of LTE operating on unlicensed band, proposed by Qualcomm and Ericsson in 2013. Based on Duty-cycle Muting (DCM) scheme, it requires a muting period in LTE for fair coexistence with WiFi. This method is easy for deployment as the conventional LTE frame structure remains the same. But a high probability of collision may still exist at the beginning of each LTE-ON stage.

The present coexistence scheme used in LAA is Listen-before-talk (LBT) scheme, which implements similar function of carrier sensing and backoff procedure as Carrier Sense Multiple Access/Collision Avoidance (CSMA/CA) used in WiFi. The basic principle of LBT is to perform transmission(s) after the channel being idle and the backoff counter decremented to zero by Clear Channel Assessment (CCA). The downlink LAA was defined in 3GPP R13, and was extended to the uplink in R14. R.Kwan et al. [4] proved by simulation that LBT greatly improves the performance of WiFi in coexisting scenario.

MulteFire is another promising technology for fair coexistence with WiFi. It is a part of 5G NR-U project, requiring LBT scheme, Discrete Transmission (DTX), etc. The major advantage of MulteFire is to operate on unlicensed band independently without a primary carrier on licensed band. The technical detail of MulteFire has not been published yet, LAA is still a hotspot as an important unlicensed LTE technology.

Works have been done aiming to optimize the LBT scheme in LAA system. In [5], a dynamic contention window adaptation method was proposed based on measurement of current buffering length, but the problem of fairness was overooked. In [6–8], the fairness to WiFi is the major concern, yet a trade-off was found inevitable between the two systems.

In this paper, we concern downlink only and propose a Power Control based Spatial Reuse (PC-based SR) scheme for LAA-WiFi coexistence, which increases the probability of concurrent transmissions in coexisting scenarios. An LAA node should raise its Energy Detection (ED) threshold after recognizing WiFi signal and transmit with adjusted power, and vice versa. Simulation results show that, both LAA and WiFi are improved in performance and the fairness to WiFi is enhanced, with respect to throughput and latency.

The rest of this paper is organized as follows. In Sect. 2, we take a deep dive into LAA downlink channel access procedure and give an overview of present studies on LAA-WiFi coexistence. In Sect. 3, we present the MAC protocol and timing analysis of the proposed scheme. Then, we validate performance improvements with simulation results based on NS3 simulator. Finally, in Sect. 5, we conclude the paper and offer a prospect.

2 Related Work

2.1 Downlink Channel Access Procedure for LAA

LAA system uses Cat-4 LBT for transmission(s) including PDSCH (Physical Downlink Shared Channel), PDCCH (Physical Downlink Control Channel) and EPDCCH (Enhanced Physical Downlink Control Channel) [3].

The flowchart of DL LAA channel access procedure with Cat-4 LBT is shown in Fig. 1. An LAA-eNB goes to ICCA (Initial CCA) stage before the first transmission and loops in ECCA(Extended CCA) stage otherwise. During ECCA, LAA transmissions are performed after the channel is sensed to be idle during a defer duration of T_d; and after the counter N is decremented to zero [9]. N stands for the number of slots during which the channel shall be sensed idle; otherwise, an extra defer duration T_d shall be taken for channel sensing.

a) *CCA defer duration T_d:* $T_d = T_f + m_p \cdot T_{sl}$, where $T_f = 16$us, $T_{sl} = 9$us.
b) *Contention Window CW_p:* $CW_{min,p} \leq CW_p \leq CW_{max,p}$. The procedure of CW adjustment is as follows [9]:

step 1: for each priority class $p \in \{1, 2, 3, 4\}$, set $CW_p = CW_{min,p}$;

step 2: if more than or equal to 80% of the feedback of HARQ-ACK values in reference subframe k are NACK, increase CW_p to the next higher allowed value and remain in step 2; otherwise, go to step 1.
c) *Energy Detection Threshold X_{Thres}:* A channel is determined to be idle if the energy detected is less than X_{Thresh}. For coexistence scenarios, the maximum ED threshold is:

$$X_{Thres\_max} = \max \left\{ \min \left\{ \begin{array}{c} -72 + 10 \cdot log10(\text{BWMHz}/20\,\text{MHz}) \\ T_{max} \\ T_{max} - T_A + (P_H + 10 \cdot log10(\text{BWMHz}/20\,\text{MHz}) - P_{TX}) \end{array} \right\} \right\}$$

(1)

where $T_A = 10$ dB (for PDSCH); $P_H = 23$ dBm; P_{TX} is the maximum eNB output power in dBm. $T_{max}(dBm) = 10 \cdot log10(3.16228 \cdot 10^{-8} \cdot BWMHz)$; BWMHz is the single carrier bandwidth in MHz.

d) *Maximum channel occupation time $T_{mcot,p}$:* An LAA-eNB shall not occupy the channel for more than the duration of $T_{mcot,p}$.
e) *Downlink Channel Access Priority Class* See Table 1.

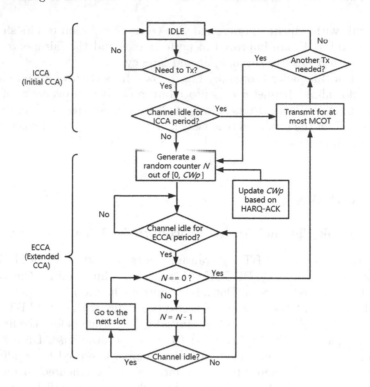

Fig. 1. Flowchart of DL LAA channel access procedure with Cat-4 LBT

Table 1. Downlink channel access priority class

Channel access priority class	m_p	$CW_{min,p}$	$CW_{max,p}$	$T_{mcot,p}$	Allowed CW_p
1	1	3	7	2 ms	{3,7}
2	1	7	15	3 ms	{7,15}
3	3	15	63	8 ms or 10 ms	{15,31,63}
4	7	15	1023	8 ms or 10 ms	{15,31,63,127,255,511,1023}

2.2 Present Studies on LAA-WiFi Coexistence

In terms of performance evaluation, Markov chain is often used to model LAA and WiFi and to analyse the system performance through different KPIs (Key Performance Indicators). The trade-off between channel occupancy time and throughput was analysed in [10]. Success rate of transmission and average throughput with each priority were analysed in [11]. Ref. [12] discussed the conflict probability and channel occupancy rate based on 3GPP R13. Ref. [13] and Ref. [14] set up new frameworks to study the effective capacity and system overhead of LAA respectively. Ref. [15] evaluated the influence of transmit power control and ED threshold. The optimal CW combination of LAA and WiFi was sought in [16], but no corresponding simulation was performed for verification. Ref. [17] compared LBT with DCM, and concluded that the drawback of LBT is the high overhead. Ref. [18] suggested that LAA achieves higher throughput by "suppressing" WiFi as the number of nodes increases.

Researches also conducted abundant of studies on system optimization. In terms of CW adjustment strategies, a CW adaptive adjustment strategy was proposed based on the exchange of QoS information between nodes in [19,20]. However, this method needs the QoS information of each AP (Access Point) and STA (Station), adding extra overheads and complexity. Ref. [6] designed CW adjustment schemes based on air time ratio. In terms of ED threshold, simulation results show that when LAA uses higher detection threshold, the overall network throughput may be improved at the cost of sacrificing WiFi performance [21]. Ref. [22] analysed the influence of ED threshold under imperfect Spectrum Sensing in coexistence scenario. Ref. [23] proposed a distributed algorithm based on downlink collision probability. Another adaptive mechanism based on Unimodal Bandits algorithm was proposed in [24]. Ref. [25] suggested that LAA adopting a higher ED threshold for LAA nodes while a lower one for WiFi nodes improves the fairness to WiFi as well as increases spacial utilization of LAA.

3   Power Control Based Spacial Reuse Scheme

3.1   Basic Idea of Our Proposal

Present studies iindicate the difficulty to improve the performance of both LAA and WiFi at the same time. In this paper, we propose a Power Control based Spacial Reuse scheme (PC-based SR) to increase the probability of concurrent transmissions. We assume that LAA and WiFi networks are able to recognize the signal of each other. A new parameter of Maximum Energy Detection Threshold is added apart from the Normal Energy Detection Threshold.

Take LAA as an example. If an LAA base station recognizes the signal from WiFi node(s) and the energy detected is between the two thresholds, the channel is declared to be idle and transmission(s) shall be performed with a lowered transmit power; otherwise, the transmit power remains the same and the channel state is determined based on the normal energy detection threshold. The power control procedure is same for WiFi.

In this paper, we use ED_{normal} and ED_{max} to represent the normal energy detection threshold and the maximum energy detection threshold respectively; we use $txPower$ and $rxPower$ to represent transmit power and receive power of energy detection in dBm respectively; and P_0 stands for the initial transmit power (not including antenna gain). Figure 2. shows the basic principle of the proposed method. According to Fig. 2, for operator B, when the signal of operator A is detected on a sharing carrier and the energy of which is between ED_{normal} and ED_{max}, it shall lower its transmit power to:

$$txPower = P_0 - (rxPower - ED_{normal}) \tag{2}$$

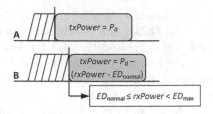

Fig. 2. Basic principle of PC-based SR

and transmit after backoff process, rather than wait until operator A's transmission is finished.

3.2 Protocol Description

The channel access and transmission procedure of LAA/WiFi with PC-based SR in a coexistence scenario is shown in Fig. 3.

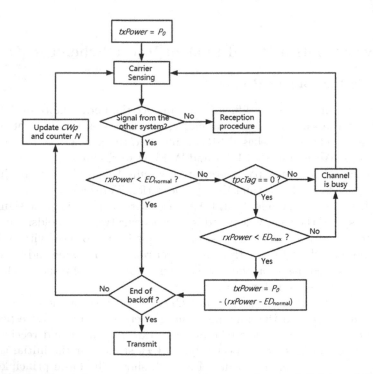

Fig. 3. Channel access and transmission procedure with PC-based SR

In our proposal, a transmit power control tag (i.e., $tcpTag$) is used to avoid the situation that transmissions with lowered power always occur to a certain network. Taking operator B as an example as is shown in Fig. 4. In order to enhance fairness to both systems, a setted *tcpTag* shall be sent along with each packet when using a lowered transmit power, and LAA/WiFi shall compete to access the channel after transmitting with lowered power.

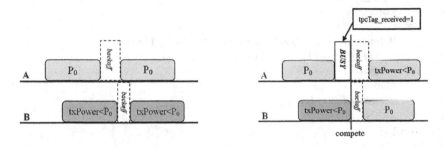

Fig. 4. Transmit without *tcpTag* (left) and with *tcpTag* (right)

LAA and WiFi share a similar transmit power adjustment procedure. Here we take LAA system as an example. If LAA has consecutive packets to transmit with initial *txPower*, during ECCA period,

Step 1: if $rxPower < ED_{normal}$, declare the channel to be idle, and set *tpcTag* to 0 and go to step 4; else, go to step 2;

Step 2: if receives no *tcpTag* from WiFi or the received *tcpTag* equals zero, go to step 3; else, declare the channel to be busy and go to step 1;

Step 3: if $rxPower < ED_{max}$, declare the channel to be busy, and adjust the transmit power to be:

$$txPower = P_0 - (rxPower - ED_{normal}) \tag{3}$$

and set *tpcTag* to be 1, then go to step 4; else, go to step 1;

Step 4: transmit after backoff procedure (if there is one). If another channel access request is required, go to step 5; else go to step 3;

Step 5: reset *txPower* to be P_0, go to step 1.

According to our proposal, for an LAA net device, transmit power adjustment is allowed before transmitting each packet; for an WiFi net device, transmit power adjustment is allowed before transmitting each MPDU. Mention that when using frame aggregation, an A-MPDU of WiFi is carried on one PHY Protocol Data Unit (PPDU), thus all the MPDUs share the same transmit power. To support the proposed scheme, we assume that each PPDU carries one MPDU and several PPDUs transmit consecutively with no or short interframe space. With the development of WiFi-PHY layer, it is expected that MPDUs carried on the same PPDU could use different transmit power in the future.

Algorithm 1. PC-based SR scheme for LAA-WiFi Coexistence

1: set $txPower \leftarrow P_0$
2: **procedure** CHANNEL SENSING
3: *Listening*:
4:     **if** $rxPower < ED_{normal}$ **then**
5:         $tcp_{send} \leftarrow 0$
6:         **goto** *Idle*
7:     **else**
8:         **if** $tcp\Gamma ay_{receive} - 0$ && $rxPower < ED_{max}$ **then**
9:             $txPower \leftarrow P_0 - (rxPower - ED_{normal})$
10:             **goto** *Idle*
11:         **else**
12:             **goto** *Listening*
13:         **end if**
14:     **end if**
15: *Idle*:
16:     **if** $N = 0$ **then**
17:         transmit
18:     **else**
19:         **goto** *Listening*
20:     **end if**
21: **end procedure**

As is recommended by 3GPP and WiFi Alliance, an LAA network shall use a lower energy detection threshold than that of a WiFi network to ensure the fairness to WiFi. When transmitting with initial power P_0, the receive power of energy detection (or channel sensing) can be:

(1) $rxPower \geq ED_{wifi\_max}$
(2) $ED_{laa\_max} \leq rxPower < ED_{wifi\_max}$
(3) $ED_{wifi\_normal} \leq rxPower < ED_{laa\_max}$
(4) $ED_{laa\_normal} \leq rxPower < ED_{wifi\_normal}$
(5) $rxPower < ED_{laa\_normal}$

where ED_{laa_max} and ED_{wifi_max} stand for the maximum energy detection threshold of LAA and WiFi respectively; ED_{laa_normal} and ED_{wifi_normal} stand for the normal energy detection threshold of LAA and WiFi respectively.

We consider the scenario of the coexistence of an LAA cell and a WiFi cell. If an LAA/WiFi base station sends one packet with same size each time after accessing the channel, and if LAA accesses the channel first, Fig. 6, 7, 8, 9 and Fig. 10 present the sequence diagrams by using different color blocks as in Fig. 5.

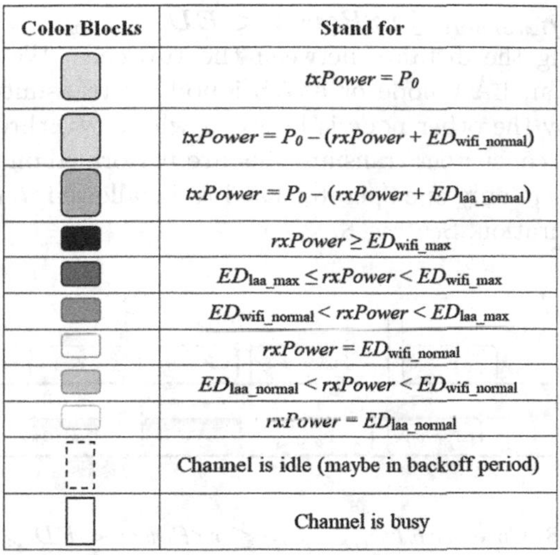

Color Blocks	Stand for
	$txPower = P_0$
	$txPower = P_0 - (rxPower + ED_{wifi\_normal})$
	$txPower = P_0 - (rxPower + ED_{laa\_normal})$
	$rxPower \geq ED_{wifi\_max}$
	$ED_{laa\_max} \leq rxPower < ED_{wifi\_max}$
	$ED_{wifi\_normal} < rxPower < ED_{laa\_max}$
	$rxPower = ED_{wifi\_normal}$
	$ED_{laa\_normal} < rxPower < ED_{wifi\_normal}$
	$rxPower = ED_{laa\_normal}$
	Channel is idle (maybe in backoff period)
	Channel is busy

Fig. 5. Legend

Case I. $rxPower \geq ED_{wifi\_max}$

In this case, the base stations of LAA and WiFi are very closed to each other. Therefore, when LAA is sending packets with P_0, the $rePower$ of WiFi is beyond $ED_{wifi_{max}}$ and the channel is determined to be busy, vice versa. See Fig. 6.

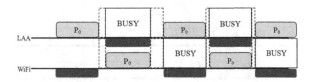

Fig. 6. Case I: $rxPower \geq ED_{wifi\_max}$

Case II. $ED_{laa\_max} \leq rxPower < ED_{wifi\_max}$

Then, we increase the distance between the two cells. In this case, if LAA is transmitting with P_0, the $rxPower$ of WiFi is between its two thresholds and a concurrent transmission with lowered transmit power may be performed. However, if WiFi is transmitting with P_0, the $rxPower$ of LAA is beyond ED_{laa_max} because LAA has lower ED thresholds. See Fig. 7.

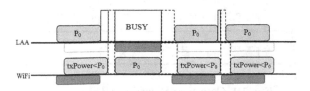

Fig. 7. Case II: $ED_{laa\_max} \leq rxPower < ED_{wifi\_max}$

Case III. $ED_{wifi\_normal} \leq rxPower < ED_{laa\_max}$

Keep on increasing the distance between the two cells. We come to the case where no matter an LAA node or a WiFi node is transmitting with P_0, the energy detected by the other node is between whose two thresholds. Using the proposed method, concurrent transmissions are performed on the shared carrier in the scenario where only one operator used to be allowed to transmit based on traditional configuration. See Fig. 8.

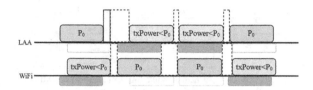

Fig. 8. Case III:$ED_{wifi\_normal} \leq rxPower < ED_{laa\_max}$

Case IV. $ED_{laa\_normal} \leq rxPower < ED_{wifi\_normal}$

In case IV, when LAA is transmitting with P_0, the $rxPower$ of WiFi is below ED_{wifi_normal}, the channel is determined to be idle and the initial transmit power shall be used for transmission. If WiFi is transmitting with P_0, the $rxPower$ of LAA is beyond ED_{laa_normal} but below ED_{laa_max}, thus LAA shall declare the channel to be idle and transmit with lowered $txPower$. See Fig. 9.

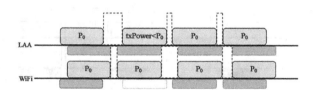

Fig. 9. Case IV:$ED_{laa\_normal} \leq rxPower < ED_{wifi\_normal}$

Case V. $rxPower < ED_{laa\_normal}$

In this case, the LAA cell and the WiFi cell are independent to each other, where the existence of the other network's transmissions cannot be detected based on ED_{laa_normal} or ED_{wifi_normal}. See Fig. 10.

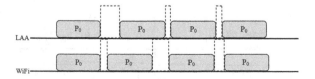

Fig. 10. Case V:$rxPower < ED_{laa\_normal}$

In conclusion, from case II to IV, the probability of concurrent transmissions is increased and the system is expected be improved based on timing analysis.

4   Performance Evaluation

4.1   Simulation Platform

In this paper, we use NS3 Simulator for performance evaluation of the proposed scheme. NS3 is an open source project written in C++ and run primarily on GUN/Linux (such as CentOs, Ubantu, Fedora, etc.) [20]. It is similar to a program library in which a variety of Application Programming interfaces (APIs) are provided for simulating different networks. After downloading and compiling the source code, users can simulate by writing scripts and running scripts (Fig. 11).

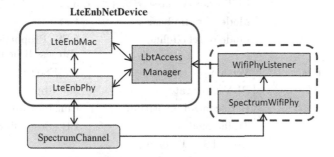

Fig. 11. Structure of LAA

According to the LAA-WiFi-Coexistence platform, elements from WifiNetDevice modeling the lower layer (PHY and lower MAC) are attached to the same SpectrumChannel as a modified LTE device, the main function of which is for carrier sensing and energy detection. A ChannelAccessManager is also added in LteEnbNetDevice. For LBT-based LAA, LbtAccessManager is used for achieving LBT procedures as a subclass of ChannelAccessManager.

4.2   Simulation Scenarios

The basic scenario used in this paper consists of an LAA cell and a WiFi cell (see Fig. 12). Table 2 and Table 3 show the scenario configurations and ED thresholds.

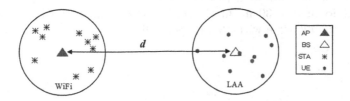

Fig. 12. Basic scenario

Table 2. LAA-WiFi coexistence scenario

Scenario and application layer configuration	Number of cells of LAA/WiFi	1
	Size of each cell (radius)	10 m
	Distance between BSs (d)	Changable/25 m/30 m
	Protocol of application layer	UDP
	Application layer rate	1.2 Mbps/changable
	Size of packet	1000 Bytes
	Transmission mode	Full-buffer transmission (continuous transmission)
LAA parameters	Version	3 GPP R13
	PHY layer Rate	9.9 Mbps
	Rate control algorithm	Constant Rate
	LBT priority class	3
	Mode of radio bearers	UM
	Mode of scheduling	PFS (Proportional Fairness Scheduling)
WiFi parameters	Version	IEEE802.11n
	PHY layer rate	9.9 Mbps
	Rate control algorithm	Constant rate
	Traffic mode	BE (Best Effort)
	Use RTS/CTS or not	Yes
	Maximum size of A-MPDU	65535 Bytes

Table 3. Energy detection threshold for LAA/WiFi with different configurations

	ED Threshold of LAA	ED Threshold of WiFi
Configuration 1	−72 dBm	−62 dBm
Configuration 2	−65 dBm	−62 dBm
Configuration 3 (proposed scheme)	$ED_{laa\_normal} = -65$ dBm $ED_{laa\_max} = -60$ dBm	$ED_{wifi\_normal} = -62$ dBm $ED_{wifi\_max} = -57$ dBm

(1) **Scenario 1:** $d = 15$ m−40 m, 10 UEs per cell;
(2) **Scenario 2:** $d = 25$ m, firstly change the number of UEs per cell; then change the *udpRate* with 10 UEs per cell;
(3) **Scenario 3:** $d = 30$ m, firstly change the number of UEs per cell; then change the *udpRate* with 10 UEs per cell;

4.3   Simulation Results

In this subsection, we show the simulation results based on NS3 and in scenarios mentioned before.

Scenario 1: performance comparison with different distances between BSs
With the distance $d = 20$ m$- 35$ m, there is an overall system performance improvement in terms of throughput and latency when using our proposed scheme of PC-based SR; and with $d = 25$ m$- 30$ m, the improvement is the most significant, as is shown in Fig. 13.

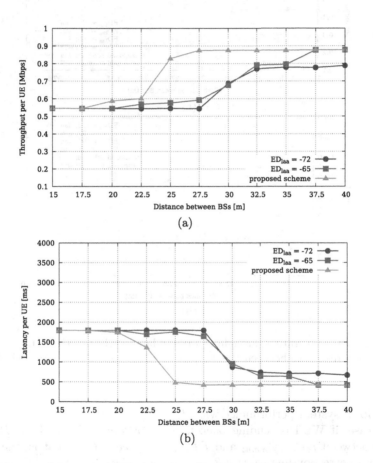

(a)

(b)

Fig. 13. Average latency per UE of the overall system with different distances between BSs ($udpRate = 1.2$ Mbps, $ED_{wifi} = -62$ dBm).

We also analyse the performance of LAA and WiFi in the same scenario separately as is shown in Fig. 14. It can be seen that both systems achieve performance improvements using the proposed scheme. For WiFi, the performance improvement is more significant when the distance between BSs is

$d = 25$ m$-30m$, while for LAA, the improvement is more significant when $d = 27.5$ m-35 m.

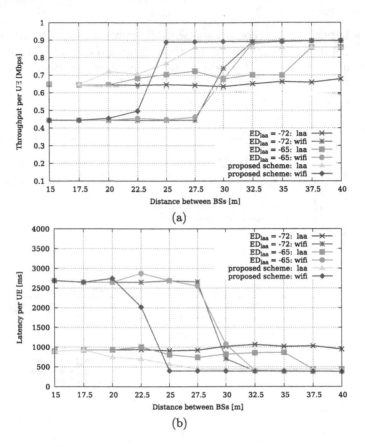

(a)

(b)

Fig. 14. Average saturation throughput (a) and latency (b) per UE of LAA and WiFi with different distances between BSs ($udpRate = 1.2$ Mbps, $ED_{wifi} = -62$ dBm).

Scenario 2: system performance with $d = 25m$

In this case, if WiFi is sending packets with $txPower = P_0$, the $rxPower$ of LAA is between ED_{laa_normal} and ED_{laa_max}, vice versa. That is, the present scenario is corresponding to *case 3* mentioned in Sect. 3.

The number of UEs per cell indicates the level of traffic in a cell. With a certain amount of the total resources, the more UEs in a cell, the less resources can be allocated to each UE, indicating the higher density of the cell and leading to a lower average saturation throughput of each UE.

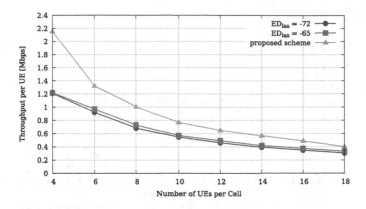

Fig. 15. Average saturation throughput per UE of the ovrall system ($d = 25m$, $ED_{wifi} = -62dBm$).

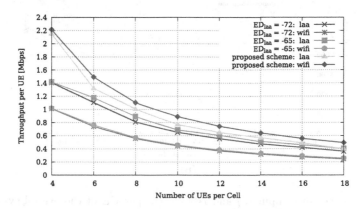

Fig. 16. Average saturation throughput per UE of LAA and WiFi ($d = 25m$, $ED_{wifi} = -62dBm$).

As can be seen from Fig. 15 and Fig. 16, this method can increase the saturation throughput of LAA and WiFi in both low-density scenarios (e.g., 4 UEs per cell) and high-density scenarios (e.g., 18 UEs per cell). The improvement can be even more significant for cells with fewer UEs. When the number of UEs is 4 for each cell, the average saturation throughput is increased by about 83.3%.

With 10 UEs in each cell, compared to the traditional configuration where $ED_{laa} = -72dBm$ and $ED_{wifi} = -62dBm$, using a higher ED threshold for LAA (i.e., $ED_{laa} = -65dBm$) brings a slight increase in overall system performance, while using the proposed scheme increases the performance greatly by about 53.7% of saturation throughput (see Fig. 17).

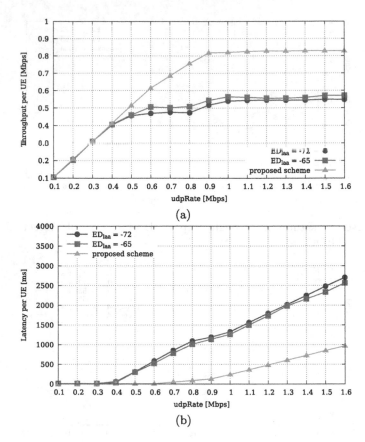

Fig. 17. Average throughput (a) and latency (b) per UE of the overall system ($d = 25\text{m}$, $ED_{wifi} = -62\text{dBm}$).

In view of performance comparison between LAA system and WiFi system, Fig. 18 shows that both LAA and WiFi are improved in throughput and latency, the saturation throughputs of which grow by 20.3% and 102.3% respectively, enhancing the fairness to WiFi. Table 4 lists the average saturation throughput per UE of LAA cell, WiFi cell and on average.

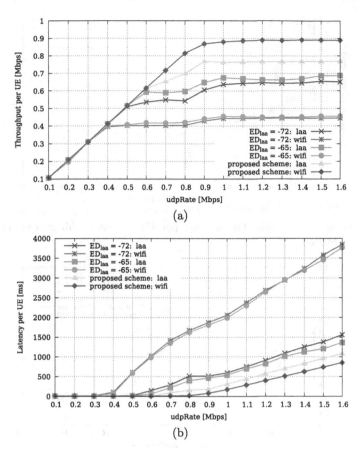

Fig. 18. Average throughput (a) and latency (b) per UE of LAA and WiFi ($d = 25$m, $ED_{wifi} = -62$dBm).

Table 4. Average saturation throughput per UE ($d = 25m$)

	LAA	WiFi	On average
Using traditioanl configuration/Mbps	0.64	0.44	0.54
Using PC-based SR/Mbps	0.77	0.89	0.83
Increased by	20.3%	102.3%	53.7%

Scenario 3: performance comparison with $d = 30m$
In this case, if WiFi is sending packets with $txPower = P_0$, the $rxPower$ of LAA is between ED_{laa_normal} and ED_{laa_max}; if LAA is sending packets with $txPower = P_0$, the $rxPower$ of WiFi is below ED_{laa_normal}. That is, the present scenario is corresponding to *case 4* mentioned in Sect. 3.

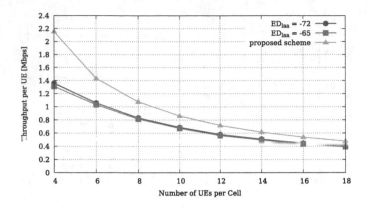

Fig. 19. Average Saturation Throughput per UE of the ovrall system ($d = 30$m, $ED_{wifi} = -62$dBm).

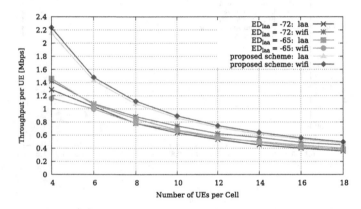

Fig. 20. Average Saturation Throughput per UE of LAA and WiFi ($d = 30$m, $ED_{wifi} = -62$dBm).

As can be seen from Fig. 19, this method can increase the saturation throughput of LAA and WiFi in both low-density scenarios (e.g., 4 UEs per cell) and high-density scenarios (e.g., 18 UEs per cell). The improvement can be even more significant for cells with fewer UEs. When the number of UEs is 4 for each cell, the average saturation throughput is increased by about 57.1% (Fig. 20).

When each cell has 10 UEs, compared to the traditional configuration where $ED_{laa} = -72dBm$ and $ED_{wifi} = -62dBm$, using a higher ED threshold for LAA(i.e., $ED_{laa} = -65dBm$) increases the overall system performance slightly, while using the proposed scheme increases the performance greatly by about 27.5% of saturation throughput (see Fig. 21).

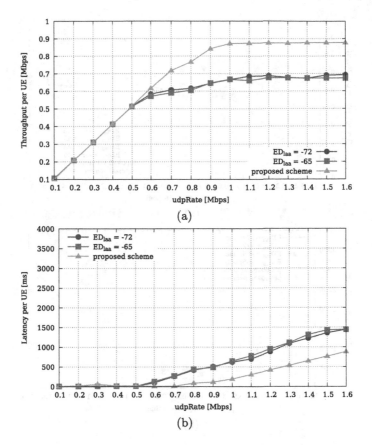

Fig. 21. Average throughput (a) and latency (b) per UE of the overall system ($d =$ 30m, $ED_{wifi} = -62$dBm).

In view of performance comparison of LAA and WiFi, Fig. 22 shows that both LAA and WiFi are improved in throughput and latency, the saturation throughputs of which grow by 36.5% and 20.3% respectively. Table 5 lists the average saturation throughput per UE of LAA cell, WiFi cell and on average.

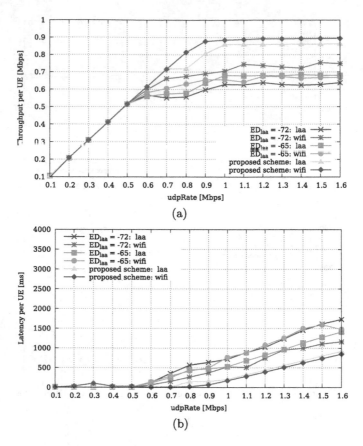

Fig. 22. Average throughput (a) and latency (b) per UE of LAA and WiFi ($d = 30$m, $ED_{wifi} = -62$dBm).

Table 5. Average saturation throughput per UE comparison ($d = 30m$)

	LAA	WiFi	On average
Using traditioanl configuration/Mbps	0.63	0.74	0.69
Using PC-based SR/Mbps	0.86	0.89	0.88
Increased by	36.5%	20.3%	27.5%

5   Conclusions and Future Works

In conclusion, simulation results prove the enhancement of system performance and fairness of our proposal, regardless of traffic density. Specifically, when the distance between the two BSs is $d = 25$m and $d = 30$m, the saturation throughput of overall system is increased by 53.7% and 27.5% respectively; both LAA and WiFi achieve performance improvement in throughput and latency. Future works can be done in LAA uplink access, interaction between cells, hidden node problems between systems, etc.

Acknowledgement. This work was supported in part by Science and Technology on Avionics Integration Laboratory and the Aeronautical Science Foundation of China (Grant No. 20185553035), the National Natural Science Foundations of CHINA (Grant No. 61871322, No. 61771392, No. 61771390, and No. 61501373), and Science and Technology on Avionics Integration Laboratory and the Aeronautical Science Foundation of China (Grant No. 201955053002).

References

1. Zhou, K., Qin, Z., Li, A., Sun, J.: Overview on coexistence technologies of unlicensed band LTE and WiFi. Coll. Commun. Eng. Army Eng. Univ. PLA. **52**(6), 1289–1298 (2019)
2. Kwon, H.J., et al. Licensed-assisted access to unlicensed spectrum in LTE release 13. In: IEEE Communications Magazine, pp. 201–207 (2017)
3. 3GPP TR 36.889. 3rd Generation Partnership Project; Study on Licensed-Assisted Access to Unlicensed Spectrum; (Release 13). Sophia Antipolis Valbonne, France (2015)
4. Kwan, R., et al.: Fair co-existence of Licensed Assisted Access LTE (LAA-LTE) and WiFi in unlicensed spectrum. In: 2015 7th Computer Science and Electronic Engineering Conference (CEEC), pp. 13–18. Colchester (2015)
5. Yan, X., Tian, H., Qin, C., Paul, A.: Constrained stochastic game in licensed-assisted access for dynamic contention window adaptation. IEEE Commun. Lett. **22**(6), 1232–1235 (2018)
6. Wang, W., Xu, P., Zhang, Y., Chu, H.: Network-sensitive adaptive LAA LBT strategy for downlink LAA-WiFi coexistence. In: 2017 9th International Conference on Wireless Communications and Signal Processing (WCSP), pp. 1–6. Nanjing (2017)
7. Alhulayil, M., López-Benítez, M.: Contention window method for improved LTE-LAA/Wi-Fi coexistence in unlicensed bands. In: 2019 International Conference on Wireless Networks and Mobile Communications (WINCOM), pp. 1–6, Fez, Morocco (2019)
8. Alhulayil, M., López-Benítez, M.: Dynamic contention window methods for improved coexistence between LTE and Wi-Fi in unlicensed bands. In: 2019 IEEE Wireless Communications and Networking Conference Workshop (WCNCW), pp. 1–6, Marrakech, Morocco (2019)
9. 3GPP TS 36.213. 3rd Generation Partnership Project; Physical layer procedures (Release 14). Sophia Antipolis Valbonne, France (2016)
10. Tuladhar, S., Cao, L., Viswanathan, R.: Throughput and channel occupancy time fairness trade-off for downlink LAA-Cat4 and WiFi coexistence based on Markov chain (poster). In: 2018 IEEE Conference on Cognitive and Computational Aspects of Situation Management (CogSIMA), pp. 129–134, Boston, MA (2018)
11. Ma, Y.: Analysis of channel access priority classes in LTE-LAA spectrum sharing system. In: 2018 27th International Conference on Computer Communication and Networks (ICCCN), pp. 1–7. Hangzhou (2018)
12. Pei, E., Jiang, J.: Performance analysis of licensed-assisted access to unlicensed spectrum in LTE release 13. IEEE Trans. Veh. Technol. **68**(2), 1446–1458 (2019)

13. Cui, Q., Gu, Y., Ni, W., Liu, R.P.: Effective capacity of licensed-assisted access in unlicensed spectrum for 5G: from theory to application. IEEE J. Sel. Areas Commun. **35**(8), 1754–1767 (2017)
14. Yi, J., Sun, W., Park, S., Choi, S.: Performance analysis of LTE-LAA network. IEEE Commun. Lett. **22**(6), 1236–1239 (2018)
15. Xia, P., Teng, Z., Wu, J.: Transmit power control and clear channel assessment in LAA networks. In: 2015 European Conference on Networks and Communications (EuCNC), pp. 210–213. Paris (2015)
16. Song, Y., Sung, K.W., Han, Y · Coexistence of Wi-Fi and cellular with listen-before-talk in unlicensed spectrum. IEEE Commun. Lett. **20**(1), 161–164 (2016)
17. Cano, C., Leith, D.J.: Unlicensed LTE/WiFi coexistence: is LBT inherently fairer than CSAT?. In: Proc. IEEE International Conference on Communications (ICC), pp. 1–6 (2016)
18. Bitar, N., Al Kalaa, M.O., Seidman, S.J., Refai, H.H.: On the coexistence of LTE-LAA in the unlicensed band: modeling and performance analysis. In: IEEE Access, vol. 6, pp. 52668–52681 (2018)
19. Tao, T., Han, F., Liu, Y.: Enhanced LBT algorithm for LTE-LAA in unlicensed band. In: 2015 IEEE 26th Annual International Symposium on Personal, Indoor, and Mobile Radio Communications (PIMRC), pp. 1907–1911. Hong Kong (2015)
20. Hao, F., Yongyu, C., Li, H., Zhang, J., Quan, W.: Contention window size adaptation algorithm for LAA-LTE in unlicensed band. In: 2016 International Symposium on Wireless Communication Systems (ISWCS), pp. 476–480. Poznan (2016)
21. Dama, S., Kumar, A., Kuchi, K. Performance evaluation of LAA-LBT based LTE and WLAN's co-existence in unlicensed spectrum. In: 2015 IEEE Globecom Workshops (GC Wkshps), pp. 1–6, San Diego, CA (2015)
22. Pei, E., Lu, X., Deng, B., Pei, J., Zhang, Z.: The impact of imperfect spectrum sensing on the performance of LTE licensed assisted access scheme. IEEE Trans. Commun. **68**(3), 1966–1978 (2020)
23. Li, L., Seymour, J.P., Cimini, L.J., Shen, C.: Coexistence of Wi-Fi and LAA networks with adaptive energy detection. IEEE Trans. Veh. Technol. **66**(11), 10384–10393 (2017)
24. Gao, X., Qi, H., Wen, X., Zheng, W., Lu, Z., Hu, Z.: Energy detection adjustment for fair coexistence of Wi-Fi and LAA: a unimodal bandit approach. In: 2019 IEEE 5th International Conference on Computer and Communications (ICCC), pp. 1086–1091. Chengdu, China (2019)
25. Hong, S., Lee, H., Kim, H., Yang, H.J.: Lightweight Wi-Fi frame detection for licensed assisted access LTE. IEEE Access **7**, 77618–77628 (2019)

An OSPF Based Backhaul Protocol for 5G Millimeter Wave Network

Zhanyu Zhang, Xindai An, Zhongjiang Yan$^{(\boxtimes)}$, Mao Yang, and Bo Li

School of Electronics and Information, Northwestern Polytechnical University,
Xi'an, China
592582711@qq.com, axdaxd@mail.nwpu.edu.cn,
{zhjyan,yangmao,libo.npu}@nwpu.edu.cn

Abstract. This paper proposes an Open Shortest Path First (OSPF) based Backhaul Protocol for 5th Generation (5G) mobile communication millimeter wave network (OBPG). This protocol includes the establishment stage and the transmission stage of the millimeter wave backhaul network. During the establishment stage, all millimeter wave micro base stations use fixed time division. The method is based on the OSPF protocol to establish the backhaul path between millimeter wave micro base stations. In the transmission stage, based on the network topology formed by millimeter wave micro base stations, the coloring method is used to allocate data transmission time slots. After that, the micro base station polls and schedules users for data transmission in the allocated data transmission time slot. The simulation results show that when the blocking probability of the millimeter-wave directional link is 30%, and along with the number of multiple associations between users and millimeter-wave micro base stations increases, the network throughput performance is about 20% higher than the performance of the number which is one less.

Keywords: 5G millimeter wave · Backhaul network · OSPF

1 Introduction

High capacity, large bandwidth, high speed and low energy consumption have become the main trends of wireless mobile communication networks in the future. A report predicts that by 2022, the global terminal monthly business transmission volume will reach 60PB, and this data is several times the current monthly data. Therefore, in order to meet the above-mentioned network requirements, studying future wireless mobile communication networks are imminent. The 5th Generation Mobile Communication (5G) communication system is definitely the mainstream of development. As one of the important components of 5G communication system, 5G millimeter wave (mmWave) network is also a research hot spot. To promote the further development of millimeter-wave mobile communications, the European Union launched the Millimetre Wave Evolution for Backhaul and Access (MiWEBA), EU-Japan joint project, Millimeter-Wave Small

© ICST Institute for Computer Sciences, Social Informatics and Telecommunications Engineering 2021
Published by Springer Nature Switzerland AG 2021. All Rights Reserved
Y.-B. Lin and D.-J. Deng (Eds.): SGIoT 2020, LNICST 354, pp. 385–399, 2021.
https://doi.org/10.1007/978-3-030-69514-9_30

Cell Access and Backhauling (MiWaves) project and mmWave-based Mobile Access network for fifth Generation Integrated Communications (MMMAGIC) project. In addition, in the beyond 5G (B5G) research initiated by the EU within the framework of H2020, one of the key technical is also using the millimeter wave frequency band from 30 GHz to 300 GHz. In China, the National 863 Program has already launched the implementation of 5th Generation Mobile Communication System Evaluation and Test Verification Technology Research and 5th Generation Mobile Communication System Large-capacity Millimeter Wave Indoor Wireless Access Technology Research And verification and other project research.

Among them, in this paper, the application scenario of millimeter wave communication based on large-scale multiple-input and multiple-output (MIMO) mainly introduces the millimeter wave integrated access and backhaul network (mmWave IABN). In mmWave IABN, IAB micro base stations provide user equipment (UE) accesses and backhaul services, and micro base stations are divided into two categories, fiber-enabled small cell station (FSCS) and integrated small cell station (ISCS). FSCS provides wireless backhaul function, and the interface between the UE and the core network. ISCS is connected to FSCS through the backhaul link, and then connected to the core network. Therefore, it is important to establish a backhaul path between millimeter wave micro base stations.

Backhaul technology is mainly responsible for providing backhaul path planning and management, network management and other content, which are important functions of mmWave IABN. The original intention of mmWave IABN is to ensure the access to resources and make full use of idle or redundant communication resources to realize the backhaul of data. The industry and academia have carried out some related research work with the verification and use of 60 GHz millimeter wave backhaul network. Regarding the optimization of the backhaul path between millimeter wave micro base stations, for the backhaul path planning in the millimeter wave wireless backhaul network, Ref. [5–7] was optimized, and new algorithm was proposed to improve the overall network service quality in every literature. For the user association and path optimization, Ref. [8,9] proposed problem discovery and solution, and proposed different algorithms to increase the user rate and improve energy efficiency.

For the backhaul routing problem of mmWave IABN, some researches [12,15] had proposed and verified some backhaul path planning and routing design schemes. From the perspective of backhaul, mmWave IABN is essentially a static mesh network, which needs to directionally transmit different data streams between relay nodes. The main problem with the design and application of existing routing protocols is the current designed routing protocols do not fully utilize the advantages of directional transmission. Therefore, cross-layer designs related to resource scheduling needs to be considered when designing directional routing to improve the overall performance of the network. The existence of these problems provides guidance for designing new routing protocols in mmWave IABN. Therefore, considering the distribution and scheduling of data transmission in access and backhaul network, the number of nodes and link allocation, it is very helpful to improve the overall network service quality and improve the user experience by designing active routing protocols. Therefore, the Open Shortest Path First (OSPF) routing protocol is a good choice, and it is of great reference significance to divide each micro cell to save resources and simplify the base station.

The main contributes to this paper are as follows. An OSPF based Backhaul Protocol for 5G millimeter wave networks (OBPG) is proposed. A coloring method used to allocate transmission time slots was proposed. The simulation results show that when the blocking probability is 30%, when the number of multiple associations with users and millimeter-wave micro base stations increases, the network throughput performance is about 20% higher than the performance of the number which is one less.

The remainder of this paper is organized as follows. In Sect. 2, the system model of 5G millimeter wave backhaul network is proposed. It will be introduced from multiple levels, specifically introducing various parts of the 5G millimeter wave backhaul network, including micro base station links. Section 3 proposes OBPG. The two parts of how to use OSPF to establish a backhaul path between millimeter wave micro base stations and time slot allocation are introduced in this chapter. Section 4 is the simulation part. Based on the C/C++ programming language, the impact of network throughput in the 5G scenario with OSPF protocol is observed. Section 5 concludes this paper.

2   System Model

mmWave IABN has the following characteristics. One of the characteristics is access and backhaul resource sharing. Although the sum of available resources on the access and backhaul links of mmWave IABN is fixed, the allocation of available resources between access and backhaul can be freely changed, so as to meet the needs of the network's instant service transmission. Another characteristic is free and flexible network deployment configuration. It can use self-backhaul integrated with access to simplify the network establishment and transmission stage. It can use millimeter wave communication. Most of the existing work is focused on millimeter wave communication in the 28 GHz, 38 GHz, 60 GHz and E-band (71 GHz–76 GHz, 81 GHz–86 GHz) frequency bands. Therefore, mmWave IABN is considered to be a viable and effective solution for 5G mobile communication networks to fully meet the flexible and self-organizing characteristics of the integrated access and backhaul in the 3rd generation partnership project (3GPP) technical report. The 5G millimeter wave architecture can be seen in the Fig. 1.

At first, the entire 5G millimeter wave network is roughly divided into two parts. micro base stations and link. The so-called integrated access and backhaul base station (IAB) is that the base station integrates a wireless access link and a wireless backhaul link, where the access link is the communication link between the UE and the IAB base stations. The wireless backhaul link is a communication link between various optical fiber and non-optical IAB base stations. These links

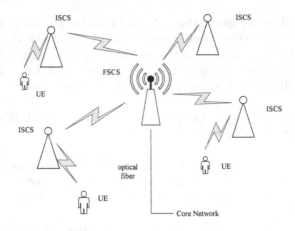

Fig. 1. 5G millimeter wave network structure

are used for data backhaul. Therefore, in addition to the wired connection with the core network, the IAB base station does not require a wired transmission network for data backhaul. Based on this, IAB base stations are easier to deploy in dense scenarios, which alleviates the burden of deploying wired transmission networks to some extent.

Among the specific nodes, there are the following three types of nodes. They are FSCS connected to the core network with a dedicated fiber, ISCS without fiber, and UE. Among them, FSCS provides the wireless backhaul function, and provides the interface between the UE and the core network. Other ISCSs transmit their UE services back to the FSCS in single-hop or multi-hop millimeter wave wireless communication. The UE will be distributed randomly and movably in the communication network, and each user equipment will be connected to more than one base station to prevent the link with the ISCS from being disconnected. The UE does not have the function of data forwarding.

Each mmWave ISCS has multiple electronically steerable directional antennas (ESDA), which are used to send or receive access and backhaul data. Because data transmission on one link interferes with data transmission on another link, directional communication reduces interference between links, allowing us to use concurrent transmission to greatly increase network capacity. Moreover, the sectorized antenna also has better main lobe antenna gain and better anti-interference effect. As for the loss during path transmission, unlike microwave frequency band transmission, the highly directional transmission of millimeter waves using antenna arrays is an effective method to overcome severe path loss. Although millimeter wave transmission has extremely high sensitivity to blocking and shadows, mmWave ISCS is statically installed on tall outdoor buildings, making the directional line of sight (LOS) transmission environment between mmWave ISCS relatively good.

In the entire data transmission operation phase, several types of streams can be distinguished in space, mainly four types. These are the downlink backhaul transport stream from FSCS to ISCS, the uplink backhaul transport stream from ISCS to FSCS, the downlink accesses transport stream from FSCS/ISCS to its associated UE, and the uplink access from UE to FSCS/ISCS Transport stream. The scheduling cycle on the network can be Uplink Scheduling (US) cycle and downlink scheduling (DS) cycle. According to Enhanced Cochannel Reverse Time Division Duplexing (ECR-TDD), each US and DS is divided into segments that do not overlap each other. For any US and DS, there are two stages of the scheduling and resource allocation stage and the data transmission stage. All transmission requirements and resource allocation will be calculated in a unified manner, so as to decide different transmission time slots and broadcast them in the entire network, thus completing the allocation of time slots.

3   OSPF-Based Backhaul Protocol for 5G Millimeter Wave Network

We detail the proposed OSPF-based Backhaul Protocol (OBPG) in this section. Particularly, the basic ideas of the proposed OBPG is overviewed in Sect. 3.1, which consists of two main stages. The first stage, i.e., the network backhaul paths establishment stage, is detailed in Sect. 3.2. And the second stage, i.e., the user access and backhaul data transmission stage, is presented in Sect. 3.3.

3.1   Basic Ideas of OBPG

For the backhaul protocol, there are two main functions, which are backhaul paths establishment and backhaul data transmission. Therefore, the proposed OBPG can be divided into two main stages, which are the backhaul routing path establishment stage, and the user access and backhaul data transmission stage.

In the backhaul routing path establishment stage, the time slots of the mmWave IABN can be statically allocated to each micro base station after deployment. Then within these allocated time slots, ISCSs can establish the backhaul routing path to the FSCS based on the OSPF routing protocol, such that each ISCS can hold the whole network topology and establishes at least one backhaul path to the FSCS.

In the user access and backhaul data transmission stage, based on the whole network topology obtained in the backhaul routing path establishment stage, each ISCS can run a coloring algorithm to allocate the user access time slots and the backhaul time slots in a distributed method. And ISCS can polling and scheduling the associated UEs to transmit data and backhaul them to the core network. From Fig. 2, we can know the composition of OSPG.

3.2   Network Backhaul Paths Establishment Stage

In the backhaul routing path establishment stage of OBPG, time division multiple access (TDMA) is used for access to the network. The time is divided into

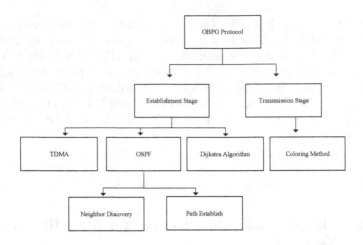

Fig. 2. OBPG protocol introduction

multiple time frames, and each frame is divided into multiple time slots according to different factors such as network size. Time slot allocation refers to the allocation of time slot resources to the traffic in the network according to different network environments. They do not interfere with each other and each takes up a certain amount of time. For example, in a scheduling period, as far as the FSCS is concerned, the FSCS does not send the access transport stream to the UE at the same time when sending the backhaul transport stream to the ISCS.

After the allocation of time slots, the next step is the specific transmission of OSPF data packets. The search and relationship confirmation of the three different base stations in this paper are based on the content of the OSPF routing protocol, and also include issues such as the way, the data packet and the format of the data packet. The basic principles of the OSPF routing protocol are introduced below.

OSPF is a relatively mature and very stable dynamic routing protocol. The entire protocol flow is based on 5 data packets (Hello, data base description (DBD), link state request (LSR), link state update (LSU), link state acknowledge (LSAck)) and 3 relationship tables (neighbor table, topology table, and routing table). The main operating mechanisms of the OSPF protocol are as follows.

One of the main mechanisms is neighbor discovery. The purpose of neighbor discovery is synchronization of the link state database. Among them, the steps related to neighbor discovery are as follows. Discovery and two-way communication, which is the most basic operation. The other mechanism is maintaining neighbors, maintain the determination of neighbors by periodically sending HELLO packets. If the neighbors have not received for a period of time, it means the connection is disconnected and the neighbor is invalid. Designated router (DR) and backup designated router (BDR) election, OSPF protocol defines DR, acts as the core-all routers in the entire network topology only send information to the DR, and the DR is responsible for forwarding the content. OSPF also proposed the concept of BDR to prevent DR failure. The routers other than DR and BDR are called DR Others, which only establish adjacency with DR and BDR, and do not exchange any link information between DR Others. The route calculation can only be performed after the link state database of each node is synchronized. The state of the neighbor needs to be confirmed in seven steps (as shown in Fig. 3) to achieve true adjacency.

(1) The first state is down. It's the initial state where the communication has not started.
(2) The second state is init. The node received Hello message sent by the neighbor, indicating that the neighbor already knows its existence.
(3) The third state is two-way. In this state, two-way communication has been established, and DR and BDR elections are started in the network.
(4) The fourth state is exstart. In this state, the master-slave router is elected by sending a DBD that does not carry the link state advertisement (LSA) header. During subsequent database synchronization, the master-slave router is used to decide who initiates the exchange first.
(5) The fifth state is exchange. The router sends the DBD carrying the LSA header to the neighbor to tell the neighbor node its own link state information.
(6) The sixth state is loading. In this state, LSR is sent to the neighbor to request the updated link information to be filtered in Exchange.
(7) The seventh state is full. In this state, the two neighboring nodes have reached the complete adjacency state and can perform route calculation.

The above states only guarantee the consistency of the link state data base (LSDB) between neighbors at the initial moment. When the network topology changes, the corresponding link state will need to be updated throughout the network. The realization process is the transmission of the link state update packet and the reception of the link state update packet.

With the help of the OSPF protocol, a millimeter-wave micro base station can establish a shortest path from any micro base station that is not connected to the optical fiber to the micro base station that is connected to the optical fiber. Among them, the algorithm we use is Dijkstra algorithm, which has been improved to a certain extent in the traditional algorithm.

The implementation of Dijkstra algorithm in the OSPF protocol involves the following steps.

(1) The router draws a network topology diagram according to the neighbor table of each node in the network. This diagram contains the positions of the points and the connected edges.
(2) The router takes itself as the root of the tree and performs Dijkstra algorithm on the entire topology graph to construct a shortest path tree from the root of the tree to each node in the graph, and the weight from the root to any other node is always the smallest. The weight is calculated by time, energy consumption, distance, etc.

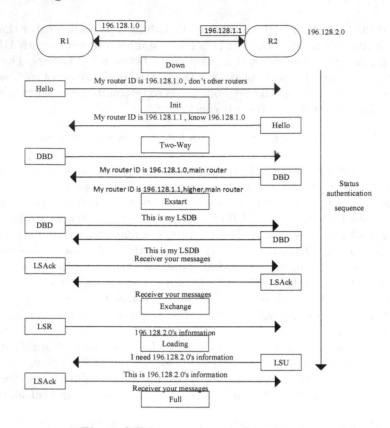

Fig. 3. OSPF protocol status determination

(3) Then add network information to each node in the tree, called "leaf node", add the cost and next hop from the root to these networks to the routing table, and finally get the root to the network routing cost is sum of distance from root to network node and cost from network node to leaf node.

Suppose that a network node and link distribution can be drawn as a directed connected topology diagram as shown as follows.

R5 executes the Dijkstra algorithm, draws the trunk of the shortest path tree with itself as the root, as shown in Fig. 5 and Fig. 6. Finally, the network information is added to the nodes of the tree as leaves, and the entire shortest path tree is constructed.

In addition, the traditional Dijkstra only calculates a path from the local node to the destination node, but this protocol needs to obtain multiple paths. From any micro base station that is not connected to the optical fiber, a shortest path to each micro base station that connects to the optical fiber is established. Then it will choose one of multiple paths as the best path.

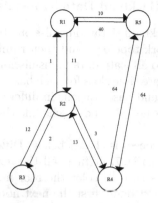

Fig. 4. Cost of nodes in a example

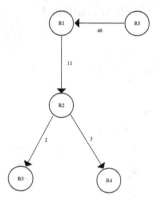

Fig. 5. Shortest path tree generation

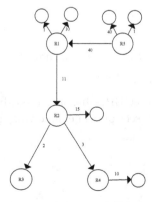

Fig. 6. Leaf nodes in the path tree

3.3   User Access and Backhaul Data Transmission Stage

In the user access and backhaul data transmission stage, each base station has established a global network topology, and then running a coloring method on such a network topology to allocate data transmission time slots. The so-called coloring method is to allocate time slots for each base station, and assign them to different link nodes, users and base stations in different transmission time slots, but two nodes that are not neighbors can schedule the same time slot (with the same color).

The specific coloring process is shown below. Different time slots are set to different node colors. From Fig. 7, at first, all the nodes have no color. At the beginning, the first color is used to color the root node. The coloring must be effective. Then go to the next node, first the next node will be colored with the first color, and then judge whether this node is the same as the adjacent node. If they are the same, it is judged as invalid, and then the second color is used until the coloring is effective. If it is different, it is determined as effective coloring, and the coloring of the next node is continued.

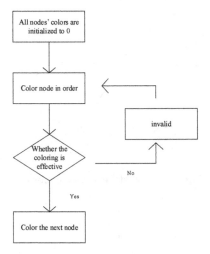

Fig. 7. Coloring process

At this point, the entire OBPG has been established. This section is an overview of the theoretical section. The following is the introduction of the simulation section.

4   Simulation

This section is the content of simulation. The simulation of multi-hop backhaul technology in cellular networks is based on the C/C++ programming language.

It adopts a sub-module approach and first writes OSPF protocol related data packet modules and data transmission modules. With the basic infrastructure, the next step is to build a 5G scenario. The 5G scenario includes the division of nodes, the connection of links, and the allocation of time slots. Connecting the two modules in series is the entire 5G millimeter wave based on the OSPF routing protocol. Back to the network simulation, and get the corresponding simulation results.

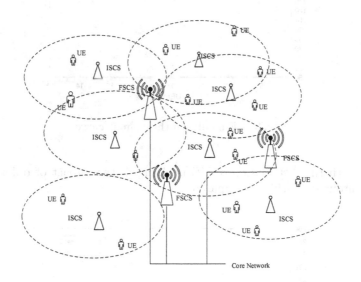

Fig. 8. 5G scene construction

In the Fig. 8, it can be seen that 10 mm-wave micro base stations are deployed within a range of 20×20. These millimeter-wave micro base stations have 7 mm-wave micro base stations that are not connected to optical fibers, and 3 mm-wave micro base stations that are connected to optical fibers. What's more, the probability p of the directional link being blocked is simulated by random numbers in the program.

Now suppose several situations, simulation output of 5G millimeter wave network scenarios with the impact of various factors will be given in the next simulations.

Assuming that the deployment of the base station has been determined, k refers to the number of base stations to which the user is connected, when the $k = 2$ and $k = 3$, and the number of UE is continuously added to the network, the following curve can be obtained.

Obviously from Fig. 9, the increase of users will inevitably lead to an increase in the amount of data, and user access is more frequent and huge, which requires higher throughput of the network. It further confirmed the higher requirements for mobile bandwidth in 5G scenarios and solutions for ultra-dense deployment to meet higher user density.

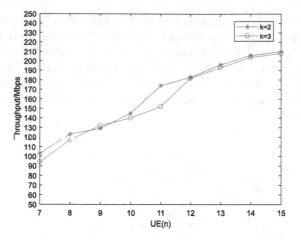

Fig. 9. UE number n-throughput curve

Next, with the distribution of UE unchanged, the impact of different k on network throughput will be compared.

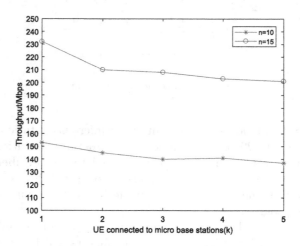

Fig. 10. Number of UE connected base stations k-throughput curve

In order to avoid accidents, the tests were conducted under the conditions of the number of UE $n = 10$ and $n = 15$. From Fig. 10, through the simulation curve, we can see that the more the number of base stations finally selected, the lower the network throughput. This is because it improves the tendency of the better link when selecting the link, and reduces the probability of data retransmission to a certain extent. Thereby it reduces the requirements for network throughput.

The directional link also has a blocking probability. According to theory, the greater the blocking probability, the more data should be retransmitted. This will definitely increase the throughput of the node. Assuming that there are fifteen users in the network, the distribution of users and the deployment of base stations have been determined, and the impact of the probability of the link being blocked on the throughput of the network is shown in the following figure.

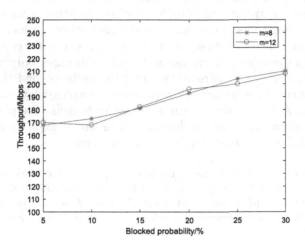

Fig. 11. Link blocking probability p-throughput curve

As shown in the Fig. 11, this is indeed the case. When the number of base stations $m = 8$ and $m = 12$ and the number of user equipment $n = 15$ are tested, you can see that the higher the probability of the link being blocked, the more data needs to be retransmitted, which greatly increasing the amount of data generated in the network is in line with our expectations, reducing the transmission efficiency, making the network require higher throughput to carry the normal operation of access and backhaul.

5 Conclusion

This paper is a simulation study of OBPG. First, in the introduction section, the current status of 5G millimeter wave networks and the current research status at home and abroad are investigated, which leads to some shortcomings in the routing protocol of 5G millimeter wave backhaul networks. The OSPF protocol is linked to try to solve this problem. Next, the specific combination of the OSPF mechanism and the operation of the 5G millimeter wave backhaul network are introduced, including in the establishment stage and the transmission stage, not only this but also the combination of slot allocation, coloring method, improved Dijkstra algorithm. With theoretical foreshadowing, it was implemented in simulation according to the process sub-module, and simulated more realistic 5G scenarios, such as three types of base stations, directional communication, blocked probability and other factors involved. It also observes the influence of factors such as the number of users or the number of connected base stations or the total number of base stations or blocking probability under other circumstances on network throughput. It was found that OSPF can well adapt to the construction of 5G millimeter wave access and backhaul integrated networks, and the purpose and significance of the research are obtained. In summary, this paper contributes the OBPG routing algorithm, which mainly refers to OSPF, and integrates a coloring method and other mechanisms. It has a good performance in simulation and has reference value. Of course, it can be more perfect in the subsequent research. Because this paper only mainly studies the network throughput requirements under the protocol, and there are many indicators that can describe network performance, such as delay, round-trip time, utilization, etc. A single indicator cannot completely define the pros and cons of a network's performance. The conclusions drawn after simulation are considered to be more reliable. These all require further research.

Acknowledgment. This work was supported in part by the National Natural Science Foundations of CHINA (Grant No. 61771392, No. 61771390, No. 61871322 and No. 61501373), and Science and Technology on Avionics Integration Laboratory and the Aeronautical Science Foundation of China (Grant No. 201955053002, No. 20185553035).

References

1. Cisco: Visual Networking Index (V.N.I.) Global Mobile Data Traffic Forecast Update, 2018–2023, White Paper (2020)
2. Zhang, G.: Fundamentals of heterogeneous backhaul design-analysis and optimization. IEEE Trans. Commun. **64**(2), 876–889 (2016)
3. Wu, X., Wang, C.X., Sun, J.: 60-GHz millimeter-wave channel measurements and modeling for indoor office environments. IEEE Trans. Antennas Propag. **65**(4), 1912–1924 (2017)
4. Yue, G., Wang, Z., Chen, L.: Demonstration of 60 GHz millimeter-wave short-range wireless communication system at 3.5 Gbps over 5 m range. Sci. China Inf. Sci. **60**(8), 70–76 (2017). https://doi.org/10.1007/s11432-017-9059-y
5. Liu, H., Hao, S., Li, J.: Routing and heuristic scheduling algorithm for millimeter wave wireless backhaul networks. In: IEEE 2nd Information Technology, Networking, Electronic and Automation Control Conference (ITNEC), pp. 300–304 (2017)
6. Ge, X., Tu, S., Mao, G.: Cost efficiency optimization of 5G wireless backhaul networks. IEEE Trans. Mob. Comput. **18**(12), 2796–2810 (2019)
7. Seppanen, K., Kapanen, J.: Fair queueing for mmWave WMN backhaul. In: IEEE 27th Annual International Symposium on Personal, Indoor, and Mobile Radio Communications (PIMRC), pp. 1–8 (2016)
8. Mesodiakaki, A., Zola, E., Kassler, A.: User association in 5G heterogeneous networks with mesh millimeter wave backhaul links. In: IEEE 18th International Symposium on A World of Wireless, Mobile and Multimedia Networks (WoWMoM), pp. 1–6 (2017)

9. Pateromichelakis, E., Samdanis, K.: Context-aware joint routing & scheduling for mmWave backhaul/access networks. In: 2018 IEEE Global Communications Conference (GLOBECOM), pp. 1–6 (2018)
10. Dahlman, E., Parkvall, S., Skold, J.: 5G NR : The Next Generation Wireless Access Technology. Academic Press, London (2018)
11. Islam, M.N., Subramanian, S.: Integrated access backhaul in millimeter wave networks. In: IEEE Wireless Communications and Networking Conference, pp. 1–6 (2017)
12. Chiang, Y.H., Liao, W.: mw-HierBack: a cost-effective and robust millimeter wave hierarchical backhaul solution for HetNets. IEEE Trans. Mob. Comput. **16**(12), 3445–3458 (2017)
13. Ogawa, H., Tran, G.K., Sakaguchi, K.: Traffic adaptive formation of mmWave meshed backhaul networks. In: IEEE International Conference on Communications Workshops (ICC Workshops), pp. 185–191 (2017)
14. de Mello, M.O.M.C.: Pinto: improving load balancing, path length, and stability in low-cost wireless backhauls. Ad Hoc Netw. **48**, 16–28 (2016)
15. Kim, J., Molisch. A.F.: Quality-aware millimeter-wave device-to-device multi-hop routing for 5G cellular networks. In: IEEE International Conference on Communications (ICC), pp. 5251–5256 (2014)

Protocol, Algorithm, Services
and Applications

The Relationships Among Perceived Severity of Negative Publicity, E-Service Quality, Perceived Risk, and Advocacy Intention in Social Network Sites

Chih-Hu Hsiao[1] and Kuan-Yang Chen[2]($\boxtimes$) (iD)

[1] National Chiayi University, 60054 Chiayi City, Taiwan
[2] National Taipei University of Nursing and Health Sciences, 11219 Taipei City, Taiwan
kuanyang@ntunhs.edu.tw

Abstract. Despite the importance of customers' perception and behavior intention in online travel agency, there has been little theoretically research on perceived severity of negative publicity for tourism purposes. This study is based on the online comparison price website: Trivago, and explores the impact of consumer satisfaction, E-service quality, perceived severity of negative publicity and perceived risk on consumers' advocacy intention to embrace after the impact of Trivago's negative publicity. This research collected a total of 300 valid questionnaires, and verified the research results: E-service quality was positively related to consumer satisfaction and negatively related to perceived risk; perceived severity of negative publicity was positively related to perceived risk; consumer satisfaction mitigates the positively influence of perceived severity of negative publicity on perceived risk; perceived severity of negative publicity was negatively related to advocacy intention. When detailing the effect of perceived risk on advocacy intention, psychological risk, performance risk and financial risk were negatively related to advocacy intention; social risk and time risk were not negatively related to advocacy intention.

Keywords: Perceived severity of negative publicity · Consumer satisfaction · E-service quality · Perceived risk · Advocacy intention

1 Introduction

1.1 Research Background

According to statistic report over 4.33 billion people were active internet users as of July 2019, encompassing 56% of the global population [1]. Internet technology has transformed distribution all across, hotel product being no exception. Internet removes the hurdle of marketplace, making distribution network more accessible [2].

Scholars advocated that the boom in internet technology has led to the tremendous growth in digital marketing and e-commerce and stated that flexibility, accessibility,

Y.-B. Lin and D.-J. Deng (Eds.): SGIoT 2020, LNICST 354, pp. 403–413, 2021.
https://doi.org/10.1007/978-3-030-69514-9_31

speed and comparisons, among others have boosted the growth of internet as the preferred distribution platform for customers [3]. Taking online travel agency as example, information exchange, pre-booking over the internet, with the abundant information now made easily available, which include not just visuals of hotels, guest rooms, public areas, outlets, menus etc., but importantly also independent holidaymaker reviews, should take the risk out of the process.

Traditionally, the logic of quality-value-intention is well recognized as academic model to describe consumers' behavior and even applied into online social network sites, such as FB or social communities [4]. The mediating role, perceived value, might be exchanged as perceived risk, satisfaction, trust, etc. [5–7].

This study assumes that when consumers have a good perception of quality on a social network and are satisfied with the community, will they change their feelings of satisfaction if they hear related negative news? And whether their advocacy intention will be affected by the negative news. Taking the work of Yu, Liu, Lee, and Soutar [8] as example, they noted that brand blame and information severity have differential effects on consumer evaluations of the affected brand. Specifically, brand blame negatively impacted attitudes and purchase intentions, but not brand image. In contrast, information severity negatively impacted brand image, but not attitudes or intentions. Therefore, it is necessary to explore the answer from these inconsistent results.

This study identified Trivago as the current research field. Trivago is a search engine that aggregates online hotel offers from online travel agents, hotel chains and independent hotels. Trivago's main source of revenue is the cost-per-click (CPC) payments it receives, where advertisers are charged a fee each time a user clicks on one of their offers. However, Trivago may have to pay several million dollars in fines after admitting it misled customers with its advertising. The hotel booking website was accused in August 2019 by an Australian authority of breaching the country's consumer laws with allegedly misleading ads said to exaggerate savings and hide the cheapest deals. The claims of misleading customers include Trivago leading customers to believe its search results page had the lowest prices, when cheaper options were located in a "more deals" section that wasn't obvious. Trivago is also said to have compared luxury rooms with standard rooms and guided consumers to hotels that paid them more commission than others or "prioritized advertisers who were willing to pay the highest cost per click fee", said the Australian Competition and Consumer Commission (ACCC) in a statement. Lawyers believe Trivago may have to pay AU$10 million (NZ$10.7 million) or more after admitting to some of the accusations by the ACCC.

Accordingly, this article will explore consumers' perceptions of online quality and satisfaction, whether they will affect their perception of risks by severity of negative publicity, and then impact their advocacy intention on online community.

2   Literature Review

2.1   E-Service Quality

According to Parasuraman et al. [9], service quality can be defined as an overall judgment similar to attitude towards the service and generally accepted as an antecedent of overall customer satisfaction.

Trivago is an online booking website example of this study to discuss the service quality, hence I take electronic service quality (E-service quality) as the variable. In general, that E-service quality is defined as the perceived discrepancy between customers' expectations and their evaluation of what they get [10]. This study defined e-service quality as the extent to which a website facilitates efficient and effective shopping, purchasing and delivery of products and services.

2.2 Perceived Severity of Negative Publicity

Van Hoye and Lievens [11] indicated that public report is not information that companies can manipulate directly. In other words, consumers are more convinced by public reports than information such as advertisements that can be directly manipulated by companies. Therefore, if negative news of the brand is transmitted to consumers by the form of public reports. At that time, based on the long-standing trust of most consumers in public publicity, consumers will likely have a negative perception of the brand [12]. Negative publicity will have a negative impact on the company's image [13]. Pullig et al. [14] concluded that negative publicity reduce customer satisfaction, willingness to buy, evaluation of the company, and brand equity. Thus, negative publicity could make the company a monitoring target for stakeholders.

2.3 Perceived Risk

Perceived risk is that when consumers purchase products and services, because consumers cannot expect results, in the face of such uncertain situations, perceived risk arises [15]. In other words, perceived risk is the uncertainty that consumers face in the decision-making procession. Scholars believe that perceived risk is the consumer's uncertainty perception that the purchase decision may have positive or negative results, and the degree of consumer awareness of the risk will affect their purchase decision. At this time, the risk is not real risk, but the risk felt by consumers themselves [16].

2.4 Consumer Satisfaction

According to the literature, there are many different definitions in the research on customer satisfaction. Customer satisfaction is a kind of emotional response to things, which comes from the surprise of purchase experience [17]. Scholars considered it as the evaluation of customers' experience and reaction after using goods [18]. Thus, satisfaction is the extent to which customers' expectations are realized or exceeded before purchasing. Accordingly, satisfaction is defined as an emotional response to the evaluation of service providers by customers after purchase.

2.5 Advocacy Intention

Although the advocacy intention plays a key role in attracting new tourists, this structural model is still rare in the tourism industry. When consumers enthusiastically make positive suggestions for products, services, or brands, they are the supporters of the object

[19]. Advocacy is an important step in the sustainable development of relationships between organizations and consumers. Therefore, support can be regarded as the top of the pyramid [20]. Advocacy refers to any action that advocates, recommends, argues, supports, defends or defends on behalf of others [21, 22]. According to the definitions of several studies above, the current study proposes a concept—advocacy intention and define it as the intent of tourists to support their destination.

2.6 Hypotheses

Scholars stated that the quality of relationship focuses on the degree of appropriateness of a relationship to meet the needs of customers associated with the relationship [23, 24]. Therefore, relationship quality captures the positive nature of the relationship, which in turn is expected to provide a positive benefit to the customers. Synthesizing the above literatures, it is concluded that the research hypothesis is as follows:

H1: E-Service quality is positively related to consumer satisfaction.

Doolin, Dillon, Thompson and Corner [25] suggested that shopping websites should enhance service quality and reduce perceived risks when investigating the impact of perceived risks on the online purchasing behaviors. This is because of that consumer behavior involves risk in the sense that any action of a consumer will produce consequences that the consumer cannot anticipate with any approximating certainty, and some of those consequences are not likely to be happy. Accordingly, as service quality increases, the risks perceived by consumers will be reduced. The study hypothesize that:

H2: E-Service quality is negatively related to perceived risk (2a psychological risk, 2b social risk, 2c performance risk, 2d financial risk, and 2e time risk).

Pullig et al. [14] in their research on a case of negative brand publicity points out that when negative publicity matches or aligns with the basis of a brand attitude, certainty in that attitude will interact to determine the effect of the negative publicity on brand evaluations. Van Hoye and Lievens [11] points out that public reporting is not information that companies can manipulate directly. In other words, consumers believe in public reports more than information that can be directly manipulated by companies, such as advertising. Therefore, if a brand's negative message is delivered to consumers in the form of a public report, based on the consumer's trust in public reports, consumers will have a negative perception of the brand. The hypothesis proposed in this study is as follows:

H3: Perceived severity of negative publicity is positively related to perceived risk (2a psychological risk, 2b social risk, 2c performance risk, 2d financial risk, and 2e time risk).

Previous studies agree that the relationship of consumer satisfaction and performance of suppliers, of consumer trust and suppliers, and of consumers' commitment and suppliers are the key variables underlying perceived relationship quality [26]. Perceived risk can be explained as the perceived cost of the consumption for the customer. Consumers' perceived risk when they realize that a purchase goal cannot be satisfied [27].

Based on the previous literature and inference, the hypothesis is presented as follows:

H4: Consumer satisfaction mitigates the positively influence of negative publicity severity on perceived risk.

Mattila [28] claimed that highly emotionally bonded customers might magnify the immediate negative effects of service failures on post-recovery attitudes. Overall, advocacy can lead to increased sales and greater profit margins because advocacy gives extra value for an organization. Zhu and Chang [13] studied the impact of negative publicity on the unethical behavior of company founders on the company's image, and pointed out that the perceived severity of this type of negative publicity has a negative impact on the positive corporate image. Based on the literature review, therefore the study hypothesize that:

H5: Perceived severity of negative publicity is negatively related to advocacy intention.

In the virtual environment of online booking website, consumers need to overcome their personal perception risks in order to increase consumers' intentions.

Srinivasan and Ratchford [29] find that experience in purchasing the product influences the behavior of information searching. If the former experience is negative, then the volume of the information to be collected may increase. Risks in the process of customer's purchase decision-making cannot be avoided in that when the perceived risk is high, then the purchase intention is much easier discouraged [15]. Sheth and Parvatiyar [30] point out that once the customer holds a higher perceived risk toward the future decision, he is inclined to preserve his loyalty to the original seller. The hypothesis is presented as follows:

H6: Perceived risk (6a psychological risk, 6b social risk, 6c performance risk, 6d financial risk, and 6e time risk) is negatively related to advocacy intention.

Based on these hypotheses proposed, this study provide the research model (see Fig. 1).

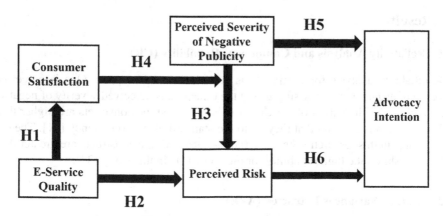

Fig. 1. The conceptual framework

3 Method

3.1 Sample

According to the judgments of valid samples and the general rules for collecting samples, this study received total of 413 questionnaires; the invalid sample has 113 which represents the overall valid response rate is about 72.6%. In the sample characteristics, females account for the largest responder demographic for 50.7%; male occupy for 49.3%; the age range from under 25 occupy the highest rate 32.3%; The second place of age range from 46 to 55 account for 29% for the valid samples; Bachelor's degree takes up the largest proportion for 39.7% invalid samples; master's degree (or higher) occupy the rate of 35.3%; The students is the majority occupations of the samples who answer the questionnaire. It is about 32.3%. The second place is the commerce account which covered for 31.3% of the valid samples. In order to exclude the searching experience in Trivago might cause bias, this study acquired that 72.6% of responders had the experience of searching in Trivago. And discovered the significant higher satisfaction and advocacy intention when consumers had the experience searching in Trivago before.

3.2 Statistic

All the variables used in the study were operationalized using multi-item instruments. Because the measurement scales were established in the West and the surveys were administered in Chinese, back translation was performed to ensure the accuracy of the translation. For statistical testing, SPSS (version 22.0) software is used.

4 Results

4.1 Reliability Analysis and Component Reliability (CR)

The reliability analysis for formal items is divided into two parts. One is perceived severity of negative publicity strong, and the other one is perceived severity of negative publicity weak. The values of the Cronbach's α of most the constructs are higher than 0.740, which representing that they up to the standard of the consistency [31]. The CR value range in this research is between 0.853–0.956. All the constructs are greater than 0.6 which shows the high reliability for the constructs in this study [32].

4.2 Average Variances Extracted (AVE)

In the view of the validity of the construct, if the results of AVE are higher than 0.5, it represents the constructs consist of convergent validity [32]. The value of the AVE of the constructs is between 0.500 and 0.950. The AVE value of all of the constructs is greater than 0.5, which represents the high validity of the formal questionnaire in this study.

4.3 Hypothesis Testing

This study explores the relationship between E-service quality and consumer satisfaction through regression analysis, and $R^2 = 0.289$, which means that the E-service quality of this study has a predictive power of 28.9% on consumer satisfaction. As shown in Fig. 1, E-service quality has a significant impact on consumer satisfaction ($P < 0.01$), and E-service quality is positively correlated with consumer satisfaction ($\beta = .538$). Therefore, H1 is approval.

For the relationship between E-Service quality and perceived risk, the R^2 is 0.222. It can be seen from Fig. 1. That the E-service quality has a significant impact on perceived risk ($P < 0.01$), and the E-service quality is negatively correlated with perceived risk ($\beta = -.471$). This study further explores the impact of E-service quality on the perceived risk of five different dimensions through regression analysis, and $R^2 = 0.236$, as shown in Fig. 1, we can see that E-service quality has a significant impact on all perceived risk impact ($P < 0.01$), and there is a negative correlation between E-Service quality and psychological risk ($\beta = -.437$), social risk ($\beta = -.354$), performance risk ($\beta = -.445$), financial risk ($\beta = -.446$), time risk ($\beta = -.441$). Therefore, Therefore, H2 (H2a, H2b, H2c, H2d, H2e) are all approval.

Next, the relationship between the perceived severity of negative publicity and perceived risk through regression analysis is tested and R^2 is 0.306, which means that the perceived severity of negative publicity in this study has a predictive power of 30.6% on perceived risk. It can be seen from Fig. 1. That the perceived severity of negative publicity has a significant impact on perceived risk ($P < 0.01$), and the perceived severity of negative publicity is positively correlated with perceived risk ($\beta = .553$). Therefore, H3 is supported.

As shown in Fig. 1, perceived severity of negative publicity has significant impact ($P < 0.01$) on all perceived risk impact and R^2 is 0.328. The perceived severity of negative publicity showed a positive correlation with psychological risk ($\beta = .533$), social risk ($\beta = .394$), performance risk ($\beta = .519$), financial risk ($\beta = .503$) and time risk ($\beta = .495$). Therefore, H3a to H3e are all supported.

For The moderation of Consumer Satisfaction (H4), this study explores the relationship between the perceived severity of negative publicity and perceived risk through hierarchical regression analysis, and consumer satisfaction plays a moderating role, and $R^2 = 0.377$, which means that the perceived severity of negative publicity in this study has a predictive power of 37.7% on perceived risk. It can be seen that the perceived severity of negative publicity has a significant effect on perceived risk ($P < 0.01$), and the perceived severity of negative publicity is positively correlated with perceived risk ($\beta = .534$). After the inclusion of consumer satisfaction, the estimated value of the unstandardized coefficient β of the perceived severity of negative publicity decreases, which means that it is disturbed by consumer satisfaction. Therefore, H4 is approval.

For the relationship between perceived severity of negative publicity and advocacy intention, the antecedent has a predictive power of 15.1% ($R^2 = 0.151$) on advocacy intention. It can be seen from Fig. 1. That the perceived severity of negative publicity has a significant effect on the advocacy intention ($P < 0.01$), and the perceived severity of negative publicity is negatively correlated with the advocacy intention ($\beta = -.389$). Therefore, H5 is confirmed.

Finally, this study explores the relationship between perceived risk and advocacy intention through regression analysis, and R^2 is 0.422, which means that the perceived risk of this study has a predictive power of 42.2% on advocacy intention. It can be seen from Fig. 1. That perceived risk has a significant effect on the advocacy intention (P < 0.01), and that perceived risk is negatively correlated with the advocacy intention (β = −.650). Therefore, H6 is approval.

This study also explores the impact of five different facets of perceived risk on advocacy intention through regression analysis, and R^2 = 0.458. Psychological risk, social risk, performance risk and financial risk have significant impact on advocacy intention (P < 0.01), and there was a negative correlation in psychological risk (β = −.346), performance risk (β = −.217) and financial risk (β = −.298) and advocacy intention. Therefore, psychological risk (H6a), performance risk (H6c) and financial risk (H6d) were negatively related to advocacy intention; social risk (H6b) and time risk (H6e) were not negatively related to advocacy intention (Fig. 2).

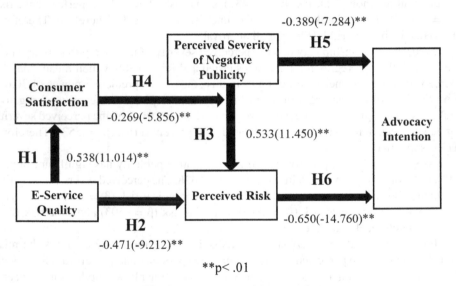

Fig. 2. The conceptual framework

5   Conclusion

5.1   Discussion

The results of this study show that the quality of information perceived by consumers positively affects the quality of services perceived by consumers, and that information quality also positively affects customer satisfaction. Also, when consumers feel good service quality, they will enhance the value perception of the enterprise; therefore, there is a significant correlation between service quality and perceived risk.

The negative publicity used in this study is that Trivago misleads consumers. This study inferred that information collection affects perceived risk, which in turn affects purchase decisions. In this study, negative publicity is a form of negative information that will have different effects on perceived risk depending on the content of the report. Moreover, when consumers receive negative severity from companies, consumer satisfaction will mitigate the positive impact of the severity of negative severity on perceived risk. Consumers may choose to reduce the messages conveyed by negative severity because they already have a very high degree of satisfaction with the company or brand, so that the company or brand still maintains a good image in their hearts.

Scholars noted that after several consecutive negative publicity, the company may reduce consumer recognition of the company. Consumers may see negative publicity and reduce their advocacy intention to the company or brand [33].

5.2 Academic Contribution

Negative publicity in different fields and different events may form different results. Public opinion in Taiwan is quite open and the news media always make negative publicity everywhere, so that the impact of negative report should be taken seriously. In addition, this research found that the interference effect of consumer satisfaction does exist.

The literature on negative publicity did not clearly indicate that the research should be conducted under the same event. Therefore, this study explores items that are not discussed in the past literature. In past, there has never been any research on the actual negative publicity of the tourism industry, this article makes up for the shortcomings in a timely manner.

5.3 Practical Contribution

This study suggests that when companies face negative publicity, they should pay attention to the perspective of consumers. Whether the perceived severity of negative publicity is strong, and follow-up remedial strategies are properly formulated to appease the consumers' negative feelings caused by the negative publicity and reduce the perceived risk.

In summary, this study believes that due to the different nature of the reported negative news or incidents, it will affect consumers' perception at different levels. Therefore, it is recommended that when companies face negative publicity, they should analyze what consumers are facing based on different incidents. Perceived risk of various aspects, and accordingly formulate strategies to reduce the perceived risk, and then maintain consumers' advocacy intention.

References

1. Statista report: Global digital population as of April (2020). https://www.statista.com/statis tics/617136/digital-population-worldwide/
2. Jain, S., Prabhu, A.: Study of the determinants that influence online hotel bookings. J. Res. Commer. Manag. 7(2), 118–124 (2018)
3. Liu, C.H., Chih, H.C., Tang, Y.C.: Marketing changes under the emergence of internet of things. Ind. Manag. Forum 22(1), 30–54 (2020)

4. Wu, L.Y., Chen, K.Y., Chen, P.Y., Cheng, S.L.: Perceived value, transaction cost, and repurchase-intention in online shopping: a relational exchange perspective. J. Bus. Res. **67**(1), 2768–2776 (2014)
5. Arshad, S.: Influence of social media marketing on comsumer behavior in Karachi. Int. J. Sci. Res. Publ. **9**(2), 547–557 (2019)
6. Jin, C.H.: Self-concepts in cyber censorship awareness and privacy risk perceptions. Comput. Hum. Behav. **80**, 379–389 (2018)
7. Sinha, P., Singh, S.: Comparing risks and benefits for value enhancement of online purchase. Int. J. Dus. **19**(3), 1 1 (2017)
8. Yu, M., Liu, F., Lee, J., Soutar, G.: The influence of negative publicity on brand equity: attribution, image, attitude and purchase intention. J. Prod. Brand Manag. **27**(4), 440–451 (2018)
9. Parasuraman, A., Zeithaml, Valarie A., Berry, L.L.: SERVQUAL: a multiple-item scale for measuring consumer perceptions of service quality. J. Mark. 41–50 (1988)
10. Zeithaml, V.A., Parasuraman, A., Malhotra, A.: Service quality delivery through web sites: a critical review of extant knowledge. J. Acad. Mark. Sci. **30**(4), 362–375 (2002)
11. Van Hoye, G., Lievens, F.: Recruitment-related information sources and organizational attractiveness: can something be done about negative publicity? Int. J. Sel. Assess. **13**(3), 179–187 (2005)
12. Dean, D.H.: Consumer reaction to negative publicity effects of corporate reputation, response, and responsibility for a crisis event. J. Bus. Commun. **41**(2), 192–211 (2004)
13. Zhu, D.H., Chang, Y.P.: Negative publicity effect of the business founder's unethical behavior on corporate image: evidence from China. J. Bus. Ethics **117**, 111–121 (2013)
14. Pullig, C., Netemeyer, R.G., Biswas, A.: Attitude basis, certainty, and challenge alignment: a case of negative brand publicity. J. Acad. Mark. Sci. **34**(4), 528–542 (2006)
15. Garretson, J.A., Clow, K.E.: The influence of coupon face value on service quality expectations, risk perceptions and purchase intentions in the dental industry. J. Serv. Mark. **13**(1), 59–72 (1999)
16. Stone, R.N., Grønhaug, K.: Perceived risk: Further considerations for the marketing discipline. Eur. J. Mark. **27**(3), 39–50 (1993)
17. Oliver, R.L., Desarbo, W.: Response determinants in satisfaction judgments. J. Consum. Res. **14**(4), 495–507 (1988)
18. Homburg, C., Stock, R.: Exploring the conditions under which salesperson work satisfaction can lead to customer satisfaction. Psychol. Mark. **22**(5), 393–420 (2005)
19. White, S., Schneider, B.: Climbing the commitment ladder: the role of expectations disconfirmation on customers behavioral intentions. J. Serv. Res. **2**, 240–253 (2000)
20. Susanta, S., Alhabsji, T., Idrus, M.S., Nimran, U.: The effect of relationship quality on customer advocacy: the mediating role of loyalty. J. Bus. Manag. **12**(4), 41–52 (2013)
21. Harrison-Walker, L.J.: The measurement of word-of-mouth communication and an investigation of service quality and customer commitment as potential antecedents. J. Serv. Res. **4**(1), 60–75 (2001)
22. Fullerton, G.: Creating advocates: the roles of satisfaction, trust and commitment. J. Retail. Consum. Serv. **18**(1), 92–100 (2011)
23. Hennig-Thurau, T., Klee, A.: The impact of customer satisfaction and relationship quality on customer retention: a critical reassessment and model development. Psychol. Mark. **14**(8), 737–765 (1997)
24. Kuo, C.W., Tang, M.L.: Relationships among service quality, corporate image, customer satisfaction, and behavioral intention for the elderly in high speed rail services. J. Adv. Transp. **47**(5), 512–525 (2013)

25. Doolin, B., Dillon, S., Thompson, F., Corner, J.: Perceived risk, the internet shopping experience and online purchasing behavior: a New Zealand perspective. J. Glob. Inf. Manag. **13**(2), 66–88 (2005)
26. Garbarino, E., Johnson, M.S.: The different roles of satisfaction, trust, and commitment in customer relationships. J. Mark. **63**, 70–87 (1999)
27. Hsiao, C.H., Shen, G.C., Chao, P.J.: How does brand misconduct affect the brand–customer relationship? J. Bus. Res. **68**(4), 862–866 (2015)
28. Mattila, A.S.: The impact of service failures on customer loyalty: the moderating role of affective commitment. Int. J. Serv. Ind. Manag. **15**(2), 134–149 (2004)
29. Srinivasan, N., Ratchford, B.: An empirical test of a model of external search for automobiles. J. Consum. Res. **18**, 233–242 (1991)
30. Sheth, J.N., Parvatiyar, A.: The evolution of relationship marketing. Int. Bus. Rev. **4**(4), 397–418 (1995)
31. Nunnally, J.C., Bernstein, I.H.: Psychometric Theory, 3rd edn. McGraw-Hill, New York (1994)
32. Fornell, C., Larcker, D.F.: Evaluating structural equation models with unobservable variables and measurement error. J. Mark. Res. **18**(1), 39–50 (1981)
33. Einwiller, S.A., Fedorikhin, A., Johnson, A.R., Kamins, M.A.: Enough is enough! When identification no longer prevents negative corporate associations. J. Acad. Mark. Sci. **34**(2), 185–194 (2006)

Constructing a Customized Travel Scheduling Recommendation Service Based on Personal Preference and Special Requirements

Chia-Ling Ho[1]([✉]), Pei-Syuan Li[2], Ying-Ching Wang[2], Peng-Yu Chou[2], Yan-Ling Pan[2], and Shi-Ting Chen[2]

[1] National Taipei University of Nursing and Health Sciences, No. 365, Ming-te Road, Peitou District, 112 Taipei, Taiwan R.O.C.
chialingho@ntunhs.edu.tw
[2] Taipei City University of Science and Technology, No. 2, Xueyuan Road, Beitou, 112 Taipei, Taiwan R.O.C.

Abstract. With the rapid development of the Internet, a variety of Internet services can break national and language boundaries, such as airline ticket booking, hotel booking, Airbnb, ticket booking, car rental service, and travel experience sharing. These online services help self-guided travelers collect data and compare prices or services as they plan their trips, but there still lack a one-stop automated travel planning services on the Internet. The purpose of this study is to design a set of personalized travel itinerary recommendation services based on personal preferences, in the hope that users can save time of data collection and maintain tourism quality when planning their self-guided travel itinerary to foreign countries. The system selects the recommended travel itineraries according to the expert-recommended travel database, personal preference, and travel restrictions, and users can modify the suggested travel itineraries according to personal needs in order to obtain their final travel itineraries.

Keywords: Travel itinerary · Personalized travel itinerary · Personal preferences · Travel restrictions

1 Background

With the gradual improvement of the national living standard, people's demand for tourism has increased year by year. Due to the limited tourism area in Taiwan and low-cost airlines competing in the aviation industry, ticket prices have dropped significantly, leading to a huge increase in the demand for travel to neighboring countries. According to statistics from the Tourism Bureau of MOTC as shown in Fig. 1, in 2018 the number of Taiwanese traveling abroad reached 16.64 million, and the rate of traveling abroad increased year by year from 20.6% in 2012 to 33.9% in 2018, setting a new record.

In terms of destination, as shown in Fig. 2, in 2018 most Taiwanese travelled abroad for short trips. Among them, most of them visited Asian countries (90%), including

Y.-B. Lin and D.-J. Deng (Eds.): SGIoT 2020, LNICST 354, pp. 414–425, 2021.
https://doi.org/10.1007/978-3-030-69514-9_32

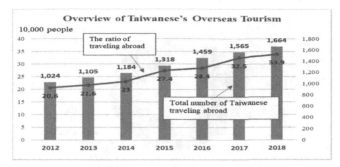

Fig. 1. Statistical chart of the number of people going abroad and ratio of traveling abroad by Taiwanese people over the years Source: National Statistics Report No. 163, Directorate General of Budget, Accounting and Statistics

4.83 million people visited Japan (29%), followed by 4.17 million people visited Mainland China (accounting for 25.1%), and then Hong Kong and Macao (together accounting for 13.8%). Nearly 70% of people visited China, Hong Kong, and Macao. As the most popular destination for Taiwanese to travel abroad is Japan, the simulation model of this study selected the recommended itinerary for Japan's self-guided tour.

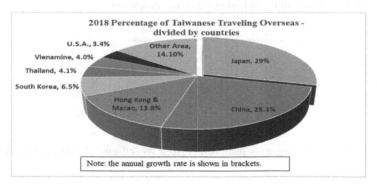

Fig. 2. The percentage of Taiwanese going abroad in 2018 – based on the destination Source: National Statistics Report No. 163, Directorate General of Budget, Accounting and Statistics

In terms of the type of tourism, Taiwanese prefer self-guided tours. As shown in Fig. 3, nearly 75% of the people mainly adopt self-guided tours, 25% of the people participate in group tours, and 10% of the people travel in other ways. Therefore, this study focuses on self-guided travel.

For the self-guided travel planning of overseas travel, this study applies the mind map to analyze the websites and Apps used by tourists. As shown in Fig. 4, the online query data about the planning of Taiwanese self-guided overseas travel involves airline tickets, hotels, scenic spots, means of transportation, admission tickets, etc. In addition, to ensure the quality of tourism, people also refer to the advice or instructions of tourism experts or tourism information websites to reduce the risk of incomplete planning before traveling. At present, tourism-related professional websites have been thriving, with

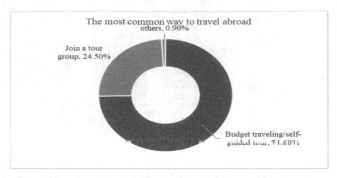

Fig. 3. Percentage chart of the most common ways for Taiwanese to travel abroad Source: Taiwan Trend Research (TTR)

rich data and large-scale diversified choices. However, a self-guided trip requires a lot of information collection before traveling. Air ticket booking, hotel reservations, transportation information, scenic spot information, or ticket booking all require careful planning. The neglect of one link may lead to the decline of tour quality. Therefore, a travel plan that can be completed without too much thought and time is a service that self-guided tourists urgently need. At present, research on self-guided travel itinerary recommendation is still in the initial stage of development.

Fig. 4. Analysis chart of network platforms or Apps for self-guided overseas travel planning

Self-guided travelers have various needs when planning their trips, including accommodation, transportation, attractions, shopping, food, and other activities. Some of these requirements can be met selectively, while others must definitely be met. For example, the requirements on the number of days, number of tourists, and tourist destinations must be met, while the requirements for scenic spots and food can be met according to the situation. This study applies a mind map to analyze the travel itinerary planning needs of Taiwanese for self-guided overseas travel, and there are three items: preferences, restrictions, and special needs, as shown in Fig. 5. Preferences refer to those of self-guided travelers in tourist destinations and places where they will stay. The possible options include shopping, famous scenic spots, and five-star hotels. Preferences are the items that can be possibly reached among the currently available tourism contents and are not necessary conditions for tourism. Restrictions refer to conditions that must be met for the self-guided traveler during the trip. They are necessary conditions of travel, including possible options such as the limited number of people, region, budget, and climate. Special needs refer to needs that are not generated by ordinary self-guided travelers, such as car rental for the self-guided tour and WiFi hotspots for the query of travel information. Options for winter travel may include ski travel arrangements, clothes rental, vegetarian arrangements, car rental services, and so on. Special needs are those items that can be possibly reached among the current tourism contents available for selection and are not necessary conditions for tourism.

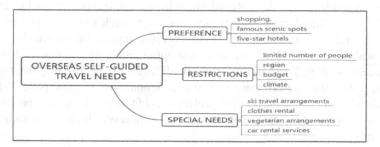

Fig. 5. Analysis chart of itinerary planning demand of self-guided overseas travel

To sum up, the number of Taiwan people traveling abroad has reached new highs, and the demand for self-guided travel-related services is increasing. At present, the relevant services available on the Internet mostly belong to a certain professional field, such as airline tickets, hotels, and admission tickets, showing a lack of integrated self-guided travel services. In addition, the planning of self-guided overseas travel is laborious, and foreign languages and unfamiliar environments increase the risk of self-guided travel. Therefore, a set of services with fewer risks and planning time that meet the needs of personal self-guided travel and can automatically generate or modify the itinerary is an urgent need for self-guided travelers. The purpose of this study is to design a set of self-guided travel itinerary recommendation services according to the necessary or non-necessary conditions of personal self-guided tourism, so as to reduce the time required for planning and tourism risks and improve tourism quality.

2 Related Work

As for the existing products, according to the research, as shown in Table 1, there are tourism websites/Apps in Taiwan that provide tourism planning services, such as TripPacker, KKDAY, Trip Case, Trip Hugger, Pintogo, and Good Luck Trip Japan.

KKDAY and TripCase are widely known, have rich service content, and see quite a lot of users. TripCase also has the function of sharing itineraries. Trip Packer is moderately known and has recommended itineraries for users. While Good Luck Trip Japan, Trip Hugger, and Funliday are not used as much as the three Apps mentioned above, they have features such as offering coupons and sharing articles. One can use Funliday to share a travel itinerary with friends and plan a travel destination. Although the above Apps have their own features and strengths, none of them can arrange travel itineraries according to personal preferences and provide customized travel services. Therefore, this study designs a set of services for self-guided tourists when planning their trips, and these services can help automatically generate customized itineraries according to personal preferences or needs, so as to reduce the time and energy consumed of self-guided tourists in planning their itineraries.

Many researchers have published papers related to the Personalized Travel Itinerary Recommendation. The research literature on route scheduling algorithm includes [1–5], and the research literature about automatic travel planning covers [6–8]. The route algorithm originated from a study of the salesman travel problem and gradually developed into the study of travel route optimization, including such factors as limited budget, location, arrival time, and stay time. However, these studies did not take into account the personal preferences of tourists, such as shopping itineraries, skiing itineraries, and experience itineraries. These factors seriously affect the quality of self-guided travel. In addition, most of the studies on automatic travel planning still focus on point-of-interest. Few studies have included the personal preferences of tourists. Therefore, personal preferences are incorporated into the considerations for the travel itinerary recommendation in this study.

3   System Framework

Because compared with other destination countries, a higher proportion of Taiwanese people travel to Japan when travelling independently, this study used independent travel in Japan as the basis for developing a service system that can automatically generate independent travel itineraries to reduce the time and effort required to plan independent travel in Japan.

3.1   Procedure of the Personalized Travel Itinerary Recommendation Service

The research framework of this study is displayed in Fig. 6. Itinerary recommendation comprises two offline stages. In the first stage, preliminary recommendation routes are produced, and in the second stage, the primary recommendation routes are produced. Subsequently, users revise the itineraries to generate the final itinerary recommendation. In the first screening stage, the system compares the screening constraints specified by the user with the expert-recommended itinerary database and accommodation level database. Itineraries and accommodation locations that match the screening constraints are added to the preliminary recommendation routes. In the second screening stage, the preliminary recommendation routes corresponding to the user input preferences are further screened to generate primary recommendation routes. Finally, the user adjusts the primary recommendation routes, and the remaining recommendation routes are output as the final itinerary recommendation results.

3.2   User Input Item

This study divided travelers' needs into conditions that must be satisfied and conditions that can be optionally satisfied. The conditions that must be satisfied are the screening

Table 1. Analysis of travel service websites/Apps

Name	Number of downloads	Feature	Service	Marketing
KKDAY	1 million times	The conversion of various languages	Charter cars, booking air tickets, and other services	TV ads, websites
Trip Case	1 million times	1. You can keep track of the travel status at any time 2. You can share the itinerary with others. 3. You can edit your personal information after logging into the website	1. If you input the reservation code and last name, you can search automatically 2. You can quickly switch the use function	Websites
Trip Packer	500,000 times	It provides scenic spots and itineraries recommended by users	Charter cars, book air tickets, and other services	Websites
Good Luck Trip Japan	100,000 times	1. You can add the content of Notes to My Favorite, browse, and share posts 2. The content can also be displayed offline	Currency exchange rate conversion	Websites
Japani	100,000 times	1. You can easily search popular scenic spots and shops 2. You can check other people's comments on sellers as a travel reference	Coupons of the most popular local stores	Websites
Funliday	100,000 times	You can create, share, and edit your own itinerary	Itinerary sharing	Websites

(continued)

Table 1. (*continued*)

Name	Number of downloads	Feature	Service	Marketing
Trip Hugger	1000 times	1. You can make friends. 2. There is a voting function In the app, and you can choose where you want to go	1. It can be used offline 2. It provides a tourist map	Websites

Source: Compiled by this study.

constraints of the proposed system. By contrast, the conditions that can be optionally satisfied are considered during itinerary planning when suitable options are available in the itinerary after the screening constraints have been satisfied. Therefore, the screening constraints are higher priority than the optional conditions. Screening constraints include days of travel (i.e., travel duration), accommodation conditions, and travel destination. In the first screening stage, the screening constraints must be applied. For example, the days of travel must be a positive integer greater than 1. Accommodation level is classified into luxury, mid-range, and budget. The travel destinations are Hokkaido, Honshu, Shikoku, Kyushu, and other islands. Among the constraints, days of travel is the only item that must be input; accommodation level and travel destination are optional input items. Conditions that can be optionally satisfied in the second screening stage are user preferences such as points of interests and types of activities. The points of interest are renowned attractions in a region, and the user can select multiple attractions. Types of activities include nature and ecology, sports and recreation, culture and the arts, shopping, and gourmet. The user can select multiple items in this condition. Input of these two conditions is optional. The user can input the conditions depending on their personal preferences.

3.3 Expert-Recommended Itinerary Database

The expert-recommended itinerary database was established to mitigate difficulty in itinerary searching. The database also aims to improve the quality of tourism. Some independent travelers share their travel itinerary on the Internet, but the quality of these itineraries is not guaranteed. Some challenges may have been encountered in the travel process, but the travelers may not mention them when sharing their itinerary. To minimize the uncertainty in travel quality, this study proposed an expert-recommended itinerary database detailing attractions recommended by many major travel agencies and tourism associations to ensure the quality of travel. Expert-recommended itineraries are provided according to the input tourism region and days of travel. A greater number of days of travel results in more travel destinations.

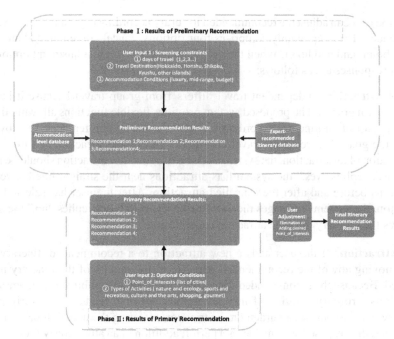

Fig. 6. Architecture of an automatic travel itinerary recommendation system

3.4   Accommodation Level Database

Excellent accommodation considerably contributes traveler satisfaction with a travel itinerary. Thus, this study used accommodation level as a screening constraint. To help screen accommodation sites suitable for the user, an accommodation level database was established. For each hotel included in the database, their accommodation levels are luxury, mid-range, or budget. Luxury hotels are those with four or more stars. Hotels with 2.5–3.5 stars are ranked as mid-range. Hotels with two or fewer stars, including hostels and private lodges, are considered budget hotels. Budget hotels that have received numerous negative reviews are not listed in recommendations. Regarding the selection of hotel location, the system prioritizes selection of a hotel near the final attraction of the day to save time spent on driving to the hotel.

3.5   User Adjustment Items

At the end of the second stage, the primary recommendation routes are generated. The recommended content may not necessarily satisfy the user. For example, the user may have been to some of the recommended attractions or hotels or want to leave blanks in the itinerary, visit some unrecommended attractions, adjust the times at which they visit the attractions, arrange accommodation independently, or adjust, cancel, or add to the itinerary abruptly for other reasons. Many factors can cause the user to adjust the recommended itinerary. To ensure user satisfaction with the recommended itineraries, the itinerary settings must be flexible. Therefore, the proposed system includes a step in which the user can adjust the recommended itinerary according to their personal needs or preferences. This step mainly comprises four options: cancel attraction, add attraction, cancel hotel, and add hotel. When the user selects any of these adjustment options, the system responses are as follows:

Cancel Attraction. Independent travel differs from group travel because it has customizable itineraries. The proposed system provides flexible functions allowing the user to delete part of an itinerary according to their stamina and preferences, thereby facilitating the goal of recreational travel. The user cancels one attraction at a time. Upon cancellation of an attraction, the system asks the user if a new attraction should be added. If the user replies "yes," the system lists attractions near the straight line between the attractions before and after the cancelled attraction. After the user has selected a new attraction, the system rearranges the day's itinerary. If the user replies "no," the system displays the itinerary after the attraction cancellation.

Add Attraction. If the user adds a new attraction to a recommended itinerary without removing any of the recommended attractions, the quality of the itinerary may be affected. Because the recommended itinerary is the optimal combination recommended by experts, arbitrary addition of new attractions not only leads to an overly packed itinerary but also puts on a burden on the traveler, affecting the overall tourism quality. Therefore, the proposed system does not permit addition of an attraction without removal of an attraction. Once the user has canceled an attraction, the system lists attractions near the straight line between the attractions before and after the cancelled attraction. After the user has selected a new attraction, the system rearranges the day's itinerary.

Cancel Hotel. The user may stay in a different hotel every day or in one hotel for consecutive days. If the user dislikes a recommended hotel stay on consecutive days, they can cancel it. If the user is not satisfied with the hotels in the recommended itinerary, they can cancel them. After cancellation of a hotel, the system displays a message to add a hotel. The user must select a new hotel; otherwise, the user may forget to add a hotel and have nowhere to stay. The system requires the user to add a new hotel whenever they cancel a hotel.

Add Hotel. In the itinerary, one hotel per day is reserved. To avoid more than one hotel being reserved for one day, the system limits the user to select only one hotel for one day in the itinerary. The "add hotel" function is only presented when the user cancels a hotel. Thus, the "add hotel" function is not visible in the menu. After the function is revealed, the user must select a hotel for accommodation; if they do not, the original hotel cannot be cancelled. Two methods are available for selection of a new hotel: First, a hotel of comparable level to the cancelled hotel is selected from the area near the cancelled hotel. Second, a hotel near the straight line between the final attraction of the day and first attraction of the next day is selected. The first method has higher priority than the second method. If the user is unsatisfied with the hotel recommended through the two methods, they can link to other dedicated hotel websites to select a hotel. The "add hotel" function also provides the option to allow the user to stay in a friend or relative's house to satisfy the requirement of flexibility in independent travel itineraries.

4 Simulation Model

The goal of the system proposed by the present study is to help independent travelers save time and effort on planning independent travel itineraries and improve the overall quality of independent travel. To achieve these goals, the quality of the core expert-recommended itinerary database is the key to success. In preliminary planning, the system is associated with professional travel agencies, who provide recommendations regarding itinerary planning, to ensure the quality and size of the expert-recommended itinerary database. In the following simulation model, the expert-recommended itinerary database is constructed for a single city, and the recommendations of hotels and attractions are limited to this city.

The flow of mobile application use is shown in Fig. 7. The user is asked to first provide personal information. Subsequently, the travel constraints and personal preference items can be input. The system then generates recommended itineraries. The user can customize a recommended itinerary before finalizing it. The user interface for adjusting the recommendation itinerary is displayed in Fig. 8. The system requires a hotel to be canceled before a new hotel is added; therefore, the "add hotel" function is only presented after hotel cancellation. No "add hotel" item is available in the itinerary adjustment stage. Once the user has adjusted the itinerary, they must confirm the itinerary; consequently, the final travel itinerary customized by the user is generated.

Fig. 7. Explanation of the flow of mobile application use.

Fig. 8. User interface for adjustment of the recommended itinerary.

5 Conclusion

Thanks to the Internet and low-cost airlines, the number of Taiwanese traveling to neighboring countries has reached a record high year by year. Japan is the top destination for

Taiwanese, followed by the Chinese mainland, and then Hong Kong and Macao. Self-guided tourism is the main method when Taiwanese travel abroad, accounting for nearly 3/4 of all travel modes. Because the largest number of Taiwanese travel to Japan, there is a growing demand for services related to travel planning to Japan. However, due to the limitation of national boundaries and language, self-guided overseas travel often leads to the decline of tourism quality or the increase of risks due to many uncertainties. While there are many travel-related websites or Apps that offer a single professional service, such as air ticket booking and hotel booking, there are few professional services for travel itinerary planning. Planning an overseas trip is not easy. In addition to language barriers, airline ticket booking, hotel booking, admission ticket booking, car rental, scenic spot selection, route planning, transportation planning, food, and other factors test the patience and carefulness of self-guided travelers. They are afraid that one of the links may be overlooked and ruin their overseas travel.

The purpose of this study is to provide a set of travel planning services for self-guided tourists to Japan. According to users' preferences and travel restrictions, this service selects high-quality and flexible travel itineraries recommended by experts. Its feature is that users can quickly complete travel planning without spending time collecting travel-related information, and that it can meet the needs of individuals in travel itineraries. The system can provide a travel itinerary recommended by experts, because of the establishment of a database regarding travel itinerary recommended by experts. The more perfect the database is, the higher the quality of the recommended travel itinerary will be. However, due to the limitation of research funds, the simulation model established in this study can only provide tourism suggestions for people who plan to go to Japanese metropolises and cannot provide travel itinerary suggestions of all Japanese cities for tourists. In the future, we plan to add special needs to the screening conditions, so as to better meet the demands of self-guided tourists in planning itineraries.

References

1. Li, C., Ma, L., Wang, J., Lu, Q.: Personalized travel itinerary recommendation service based on collaborative filtering and IEC. In: 2010 2nd IEEE International Conference on Information Management and Engineering, Chengdu, pp. 161–164 (2010). https://doi.org/10.1109/ICIME.2010.5477771
2. Li, X., Zhou, J., Zhao, X.: Travel itinerary problem. Transp. Res. Part B Methodol. **91**, 332–343 (2016). https://doi.org/10.1016/j.trb.2016.05.013
3. Yochum, P., Chang, L., Gu, T., Zhu, M., Chen, H.: A genetic algorithm for travel itinerary recommendation with mandatory points-of-interest. In: Shi, Z., Vadera, S., Chang, E. (eds.) IIP 2020. IAICT, vol. 581, pp. 133–145. Springer, Cham (2020). https://doi.org/10.1007/978-3-030-46931-3_13
4. Yang, L., Zhang, R., Sun, H., Guo, X., Huai, J.: A tourist itinerary planning approach based on ant colony algorithm. In: Gao, H., Lim, L., Wang, W., Li, C., Chen, L. (eds.) WAIM 2012. LNCS, vol. 7418, pp. 399–404. Springer, Heidelberg (2012). https://doi.org/10.1007/978-3-642-32281-5_39
5. Qing, L., Liang, C.-Y., Huang, Y.-Q., Zhang, J.-L.: Interactive multi-agent genetic algorithm for travel itinerary planning. Appl. Res. Comput. **25**, 3311–3313 (2008). CNKI:SUN:JSYJ.0.2008-11-034

6. Kim, J.K., Oh, S.J., Song, H.S.: A development of an automatic itinerary planning algorithm based on expert recommendation. J. Korea Ind. Inf. Syst. Res. **25**(1), 31–40 (2020)
7. Chen, G., Wu, S., Zhou, J., Tung, A.K.: Automatic itinerary planning for traveling services. IEEE Trans. Knowl. Data Eng. **26**(3), 514–527 (2014). https://doi.org/10.1109/TKDE.2013.46
8. De Choudhury, M., Feldman, M., Amer-Yahia, S., Golbandi, N., Lempel, R., Yu, C.: Automatic construction of travel itineraries using social breadcrumbs. In: Proceedings of the 21st ACM Conference on Hypertext and Hypermedia, pp. 35–44 (2010)

A Data Scheduling Algorithm Based on Link Distance in Directional Aviation Relay Network

Weiling Zhou, Bo Li, Zhongjiang Yan$^{(\boxtimes)}$, and Mao Yang

School of Electronics and Information, Northwestern Polytechnical University,
Xi'an, China
2018261692@mail.nwpu.edu.cn, {libo.npu,zhjyan,yangmao}@nwpu.edu.cn

Abstract. A data scheduling algorithm based on link distance is proposed in this paper, aiming at the problem of low data transmission throughput caused by the unequal link distance between aircraft relay nodes and ground nodes in a directional aviation relay network. Firstly, the aircraft node acquires the data transmission request of the ground node during the data transmission request collection stage, and measures the transmission distance and the data transmission delay with the ground node. Secondly, a data scheduling algorithm based on downlink first uplink, long distance first and short distance is designed, which fully utilizes the communication delay expansion gain brought by the unequal link distance. Finally, the simulation results show that when the network traffic is saturated, compared with the distributed scheduling (DS) algorithm, the algorithm named link distance data scheduling (LDDS) proposed in this paper improves the network throughput by 7.4%.

Keywords: Data scheduling algorithm · Unequal link distance · Directional aviation relay network

1 Introduction

The communication network composed of pure ground nodes will cause multi-hop routing to complete the information exchange due to factors such as the ground environment occlusion and the small communication range of the node itself [1]. At this time, there is the problem of complex network topology and poor anti-destructive performance. The directional aviation relay network is a network where a ground node communicates, and it is reasonable to deploy an air node at a higher position in the central area of the network that can be line-of-sight with the ground node [2]. Let this air node relay information for the distant ground node. Among them, the directional transmission method adopted by the air node only receives and sends electromagnetic waves in a specific direction, which can increase the effective utilization of radiated power, increase confidentiality, and at the same time enhance the signal strength and increase the anti-interference

Y.-B. Lin and D.-J. Deng (Eds.): SGIoT 2020, LNICST 354, pp. 426–440, 2021.
https://doi.org/10.1007/978-3-030-69514-9_33

ability [3,4]. However, in the directional aviation relay network, as the number of ground nodes in the network increases, the problem of low data transmission efficiency due to the difference in the link distance between the ground node and the air node will be particularly prominent.

The unequal link distance means that there are multiple ground nodes in the directional working beam of the air node, and the line-of-sight distance between each ground node and the air node is unequal, resulting in unequal data propagation delay. At this time, the communication sequence of air nodes will significantly affect the overall communication efficiency of the network. The reason for the unequal link distance is the wide distribution range of ground nodes, the large number and the long distance between nodes [5,6]. In the traditional TDMA mode, the length of each time slot is the same [7]. At this time, the length of the time slot will be determined by the maximum time extension and a lot of time is wasted on the close-range nodes. For example, in a circular communication area with a radius of 300 km, the air node is located at 3 km above the center of the circle, and the distance between the two ground nodes at 30 km and 150 km from the center of the circle and the air node are: 30.15 km and 154.43 km. The one-way signal propagation delay brought by the link is: 0.1 ms and 0.515 ms respectively. The length of the transmission slot will be set to 0.515 ms, and the nearest node only needs 0.1 ms to complete the transmission, and 0.415 ms of time is wasted, resulting in a lower data transmission efficiency of the node. The same time wasted in underwater acoustic communication. The typical propagation rate of sound waves near the sea surface is 1.52 km/s, and the propagation delay caused by the reduction of the propagation rate increases [8–10].

In a wider communication area, because the distance between the air node and the ground node is very large, that is, about hundreds of kilometers, the propagation time of the wireless signal is close to the data transmission time. Studying a data scheduling algorithm makes it necessary to reasonably arrange the order of interaction between air nodes and ground nodes to reduce the delay of the entire network due to distance transmission without controlling packet collisions.

Therefore, this paper proposes a data scheduling algorithm based on unequal link distance named LDDS in directional aviation relay networks. The basic idea of the LDDS algorithm is that the air relay node collects the service requirements from the ground nodes, and combines the link distance with each ground node to reasonably integrate the uplink and downlink transmissions, and calculates the packet sending time of each node in the uplink and downlink stages. This data scheduling algorithm can shorten data transmission time and improve network transmission efficiency.

This article will first introduce the system model, introduce the communication protocol description and link inequality problems used by the network, and then specifically talk about LDDS, the newly proposed data scheduling algorithm based on link distance. Finally, the LDDS algorithm and the comparison algorithm are used to compare the simulation performance and analyze the results.

2   System Model

In a directional aviation relay network, an aircraft node relays data packets for ground nodes, which can greatly reduce the multi-hop transmission time between ground nodes. In this network, the ground nodes are stationary and evenly distributed in the circular communication area with the aircraft node as the center (the aircraft node height is H) and the network coverage radius R. Moreover, all ground nodes can reach the air node in a single hop. The clocks of all nodes are synchronized, and the directional beam of the air node rotating in all directions is divided into B beams. The communication distance of air nodes is D_{Air} $(D_{Air} > R)$, and the communication distance of ground nodes is D_{Ground} $(D_{Ground} < D_{Air})$, as shown in Fig. 1.

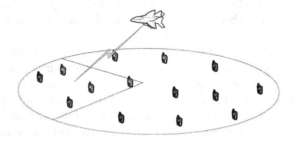

Fig. 1. Directional aviation relay network

2.1   Communication Protocol Description

The air-to-ground MAC time frame is divided into three stages, as shown in Fig. 2:

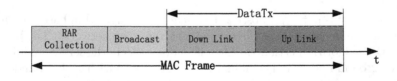

Fig. 2. MAC frame

RAR collection phase: The aircraft node and the ground node exchange data transmission requests in a Trigger-Response (Trg-Res) manner, as shown in Fig. 3. Downlink service: The aircraft node informs some ground nodes in the Trg frame that the downlink service is about to be sent. After being informed by the Trg frame that the ground node receives the Trg frame, it responds to the Res frame and prepares to receive the downlink service. Uplink service: If the ground node has uplink service that needs to be sent to the aircraft node, regardless of whether the node is included in the Trg frame, the Res frame is immediately answered after receiving the Trg frame. And in the Res frame, the local node's uplink service request is sent to the aircraft node.

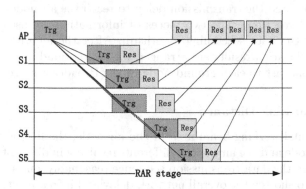

Fig. 3. RAR collection stage

Broadcast stage: After the aircraft node receives all the uplink and downlink service transmission requests, it allocates resources and broadcasts the results of the resource allocation to all nodes in the network, as shown in Fig. 4. The aircraft node sends the broadcast data packets routed by this node to the ground node, and allocates time slots for the broadcast data packets routed by the ground node.

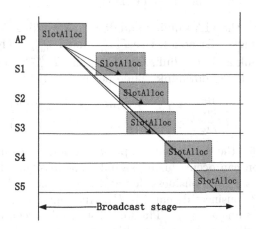

Fig. 4. Broadcast stage

Data stage: According to the result of the resource allocation algorithm, the data transmission between the aircraft node and the ground node is completed.

The duration of the uplink and downlink is dynamically adjusted according to the business situation.

The data scheduling algorithm based on link distance proposed in this paper works between the RAR collection stage and the Broadcast stage. First of all, through Trg-Res information interaction, we can know the service requirements of various nodes and the transmission delay to reach the air nodes (also the link distance of the reaction). The two pieces of information are used as the input parameters of the data scheduling algorithm. After the algorithm calculation, the resource allocation results are arranged for each ground node, and then the results are broadcast to each ground node in the Broadcast stage.

2.2   Unequal Link Distance

In the directional working beam area of the air node, the line-of-sight between each ground node and the air node is different, resulting in different transmission delays. Arrange the data transmission sequence reasonably, and use the unequal link distance to shorten the overall network delay and increase network throughput. Suppose there is two ground nodes i and j in the current working area of aerial node a, where node i is closer to aerial node a than node j. The total traffic in the network (including uplink and downlink services) is B_{UpLink}. Data transmission consumes time is T_{Data}. Then the throughput of the network is $W_{ThroughPut}$:

$$W_{ThroughPut} = \frac{B_{UpLink}}{T_{Data}} \tag{1}$$

When the network traffic is constant, the shorter the transmission time required, the higher the unit throughput of the network. At the same time, the following three constraints must be met:

* Conditions where the STA's uplink and downlink working time periods cannot conflict (for a single STA node). Use T_{Start}^{Up} and T_{Start}^{Down} to represent the start time of the uplink and downlink. Use T_{End}^{Up} and T_{End}^{Down} to represent the end time of the uplink and downlink. Time needs to satisfy:

$$\begin{cases} (T_{Start}^{Up} > T_{Start}^{Down}) and (T_{End}^{Up} > T_{End}^{Down}) \\ (T_{Start}^{Down} > T_{Start}^{Up}) and (T_{End}^{Down} > T_{End}^{Up}) \end{cases} \tag{2}$$

* The condition for the AP to receive packets uplink does not conflict is that no data collision can occur during signal transmission. The packet sending time of node i is T_i^{Data}, business demand is B_i. The packet sending time of node j is T_j^{Data}, business demand is B_j. And the data transmission rate of all nodes is the same as v_{Data}. The link distance between node a and node i is d_{ai}. The link distance between node a and node j is d_{aj}.

$$T_i^{Data} + \frac{B_i}{v_{Data}} + \frac{d_{ai}}{c} \geq T_j^{Data} + \frac{d_{aj}}{c} \tag{3}$$

* AP and STA can finish the business within the designated time slot.

3   Data Scheduling Algorithm Based on Link Distance

The core idea of LDDS algorithm used in directional aviation relay network:

The downlink has higher scheduling priority than the uplink: In a directional aviation relay network, the main role of an aircraft node is an air relay node, that is, an aircraft node is generally not a source node or a destination node of data. Therefore, the algorithm adopts the principle of prioritizing downlink data transmission. In this way, if the downlink data can be transmitted preferentially, the storage unit at the aircraft node can be released first, and then it is convenient to store the uplink data information newly sent by the ground node.

The long-distance link traffic has higher scheduling priority than the short-distance link: From the perspective of time slot allocation based on link distance, during downlink data transmission, if the aircraft node preferentially sends data to the long-distance node, it can opportunistically send data to close nodes within the time slot for the long-distance node to reply. Thereby improving the time slot utilization rate and the efficiency of the multiple access protocol.

3.1   Overall Algorithm Design

The directional aviation relay network is a single-AP multi-STA network. Due to the existence of a central control node in the network, it is possible to statistically analyze the uplink data request carried by the response from the air node (hereinafter referred to as AP). The transmission arrangement is obtained through a scheduling algorithm, and this time slot arrangement is sent to all ground nodes (hereinafter referred to as STAs) through broadcast control packets.

In order to make efficient use of time resources, the data scheduling algorithm proposed in this paper will obscure the uplink and downlink data transmission stages of the entire network in the general protocol flow. Instead, it is considered from the AP node, so that the AP can be continuously down and up as much as possible, as shown in the Fig. 5.

When the uplink and downlink services are symmetrical, this algorithm will not overlap the packet sending and receiving times at the STA node. But for a more general situation: when the uplink and downlink services are asymmetric, there may be overlap of uplink and downlink working hours at the STA, and further adjustment and optimization are needed. The general flow of this scheduling algorithm is as follows:

step 1   Based on the start time T_{Base}^{Start} of the AP sending packets to the farthest STA, first calculate the subsequent relative time;

step 2   Using the downlink algorithm mentioned in Sect. 3.3, calculate the AP's packet sending schedule for each STA, and in this case the STA's packet receiving schedule;

step 3   Use the uplink algorithm mentioned in Sect. 3.2 to calculate the timetable for each STA to send packets to the AP, and in this case, the AP's timetable for receiving packets corresponding to the data of each STA;

step 4 According to the link distance, the working area of each STA is detected sequentially from far to near, and whether there is an overlap of uplink and downlink working time. If there is overlap, go to step 5, otherwise go to step 6;

step 5 Advance the AP's packet sending time to the min (packet sending schedule) it maintains, and synchronously modify the AP packet sending schedule;

step 6 If the packet sending schedule has been modified, need to skip back to step 4 and check again whether there is any overlap in the working area of each STA.

step 7 After the collision detection is completed, the true packet sending time of AP and STA is re-determined by the following formula:

$$T_{Real}^{Start} = min(min(APtimetable), min(STAtimetable)) \qquad (4)$$

The data transmission stage calculated at the end of the algorithm flow is shown in Fig. 5:

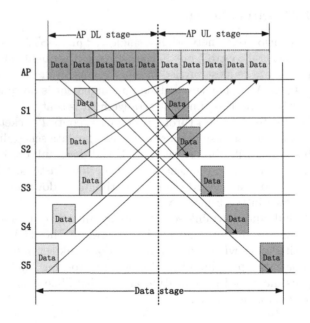

Fig. 5. Data transmission stage

3.2 Uplink Algorithm Design

In order to make the receiving end of the uplink data get the maximum throughput within a certain period of time, the best way is to arrange the sending time of each STA reasonably, so that the AP can continuously receive and process data without gaps, as shown in the Fig. 6:

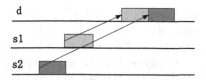

Fig. 6. Schematic diagram of AP receiving package

In the RAR stage, each STA writes its own data uplink request in the Res control packet and sends it to the AP. The AP end can calculate and know the transmission delay between each STA and the AP from the sending timestamp of Res and the current time. The data length of the data request carried by Res and the predetermined data transmission rate determine the data transmission duration. Figure 7 shows the uplink scheduling arrangement of the LDDS algorithm.

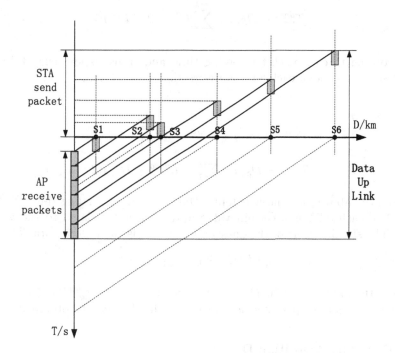

Fig. 7. Uplink algorithm diagram

In order of increasing transmission delay ($D_{S_1d} < D_{S_2d} < ... < D_{S_nd}$), the following data information table is organized: (Where N is the total number of STAs in the current network, and n is the number of STAs in the current AP's working sector).

The input parameters of this algorithm are: the service request of each STA. Under the condition that the data transmission rate is known, it is equivalent to the data transmission time $L_{Ul_i}^{data}(1 \leq i \leq n)$, transmission delay $D_{S_i d}(1 \leq i \leq n)$, and the beginning of the data uplink phase is T_{start}. Calculate and output the packet sending time $T_k^{data}(1 \leq k \leq n)$ of each STA.

The algorithm flow is as follows: Firstly, the data sent from the closest STA node S_1 is set to the time when the AP starts to work. Assuming that T_1^{data} is a certain constant, then the start time of receiving the first packet is:

$$T_1^{data} + D_{S_1 d} \tag{5}$$

The start time of receiving the second packet:

$$T_1^{data} + D_{S_1 d} + L_1^{data} \tag{6}$$

...

Start time of receiving the i-th packet:

$$T_1^{data} + D_{S_1 d} + \sum_{j=1}^{i-1} L_j^{data} (2 \leq i \leq n) \tag{7}$$

According to each packet receiving time and transmission delay table, the packet sending time of each STA is reversed:

$$\begin{cases} T_1^{data} \\ T_2^{data} = T_1^{data} + D_{S_1 d} + L_1^{data} - D_{S_2 d} \\ ... \\ T_k^{data} = T_1^{data} + D_{S_1 d} + \sum_{j=1}^{k-1} L_j^{data} - D_{S_k d}(2 \leq k \leq n) \end{cases} \tag{8}$$

From the above formula, it is found that the packet sending time $T_k^{data}(1 \leq k \leq n)$ of each STA is a certain value and is directly related to the value of T_1^{data}. The starting time of the data uplink phase is the known data. T_{Start}^{Ul}

$$min(T_k^{data}(1 \leq k \leq n)) = T_{Start}^{Ul} \tag{9}$$

From the above formula, T_1^{data} can be solved, so that $T_k^{data}(1 \leq k \leq n)$ can be solved, so that the packet sending time of all STAs can be obtained.

3.3   Downlink Algorithm Design

In the downlink data transmission phase, the air AP node sends data packets to the ground STA node. In the downlink data transmission, if the aircraft node preferentially sends data to the long-distance node, it can opportunistically send data to the short-distance node within the time gap waiting for the long-distance node to reply. In this way, the time slot utilization rate and the efficiency of the multiple access protocol can be improved. Figure 8 shows the downlink scheduling arrangement of the LDDS algorithm.

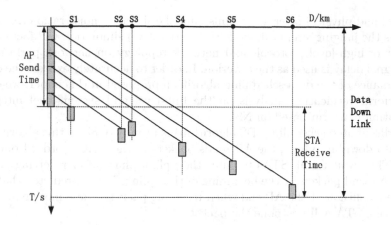

Fig. 8. Downlink algorithm diagram

Start time of the downlink phase: (T_{BEnd} is the end time of the broadcast phase of the current time frame):

$$T_{Start}^{Dl} = T_{BEnd} \tag{10}$$

The data information table maintained by the AP node itself records the service transmission requirements of the AP for each STA. Then, according to the data transmission rate v_{data}, the transmission duration $L_{Dl_i}^{data}$ of the downlink transmission data, the transmission delay $D_{S_i d}$ obtained from the RAR stage, and the strategy of giving priority to the transmission of the remote STA can calculate the packet sending time of the AP to each STA:

$$\begin{cases} T_1^{data} = T_{Start}^{Dl} \\ T_2^{data} = T_1^{data} + L_{Dl_1}^{data} \\ \dots \\ T_k^{data} = T_1^{data} + \sum_{j=1}^{k-1} L_{Dl_j}^{data} (2 \le k \le n) \end{cases} \tag{11}$$

And calculate the duration of the shortest downlink phase that can get the network:

$$L_{Dl}^{data} = max(T_1^{data} + D_{S_1 d} + L_{Dl_1}^{data}, ..., T_n^{data} + D_{S_n d} + L_{Dl_n}^{data}) \tag{12}$$

For AP, its uplink end time is its downlink start time, and the two phases will work without interruption.

4 Simulation and Results

At present, the simulation of wireless communication systems is generally divided into two categories: link-level simulation and system-level simulation. Among them, the link-level simulation mainly focuses on the performance of wireless channel and physical layer algorithms, and the signal-to-noise ratio error rate is used as the judging standard; while the system-level simulation will focus on the impact of high-level protocols and network topology on network performance. The signal delay is used as the criterion. In order to accurately express the overall performance of the data scheduling algorithm proposed in this paper, we choose to perform verification analysis on the link-level and system-level integrated simulation platform based on NS3.

A distributed scheduling (DS algorithm) is proposed [8]. In this algorithm, in the data downlink phase, the AP sends packets to the STA in order from far to near. Then wait for all STAs to enter the uplink phase after receiving packets. All STAs send packets at the beginning of the uplink. If it is predicted that there will be a collision at the AP end when receiving packets, the remote node in the conflicting STA will postpone the packet.

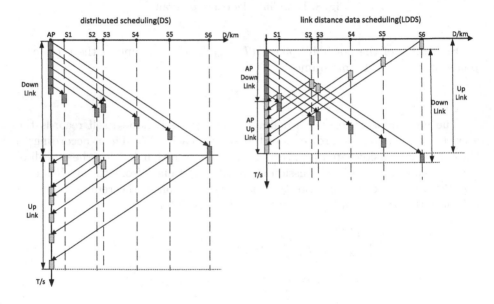

Fig. 9. DS and LDDS scheduling algorithms

Figure 9 represent the principles of DS and LDDS scheduling algorithms. T_{Data} represents the total time required for the transmission of all services on the network; T_{trans} represents the propagation delay caused by the maximum link distance in the network; T'_{Data} is the length of time required to represent the traffic transmission of a single node (in this analysis, set all nodes to have the same uplink and downlink traffic).

Test scenario: Design a directional aviation relay network so that 128 communication nodes are located in a circular area with a radius of 300 km. The only air node is 3 km above the center of the circle, and the remaining 127 ground nodes are evenly and randomly distributed inside the circle. The air nodes use directional beam communication, which is divided into 16 hemispherical coverage beams. An air node can reach any ground node in the circular communication area in a single hop. The size of a single data packet is $256B$, the data transmission rate is $54\,\text{Mbps}$, all nodes are stationary and the clocks are synchronized. Test the performance of various networks that communicate with each other through the assistance of air node relay forwarding between ground nodes.

Let the air node be a node relay node of the ground area in a directional beam, and for a circular uniformly distributed network, the number of ground nodes near the circular air node is less, and the number of ground nodes closer to the edge of the network is greater. Therefore, in the working beam of the AP node, there are 8 ground nodes on average and the distribution form relative to the AP is from sparse to dense. Under this scenario, simulation test was conducted to verify the performance characteristics of LDDS algorithm and DS algorithm.

In the case of network transmission of the same traffic, the time-consuming situation of the two algorithms is shown in Table 1.

Table 1. Algorithm time-consuming comparison

Business volume	DS time consuming	LDDS time consuming	LDDS saves time
$T_{Data} < T_{trans}$	$2T_{trans} + 2T'_{Data}$	$2T_{trans} - T_{Data} + T'_{Data}$	$T_{Data} + T'_{Data}$
$T_{Data} = T_{trans}$	$2T_{trans} + 2T'_{Data}$	$T_{trans} + T'_{Data}$	$T_{Data} + T'_{Data}$
$T_{Data} > T_{trans}$	$2T_{Data} + 2T'_{Data}$	T_{Data}	$2T'_{Data}$

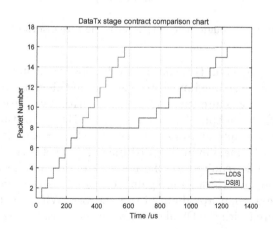

Fig. 10. The number of packets sent in a single Data phase varies with time

The x-axis of Fig. 10 is the time-consuming situation of the algorithm, and the y-axis is the number of packets sent (all nodes send a unit-length data packet).

It can be seen from the figure that the performance of the two algorithms is the same in the initial AP downlink phase; but in the AP uplink phase, the time required by the new algorithm is significantly better than the comparison algorithm. This is because after the LDDS algorithm enters the Data transmission phase, the STA will prepare to send packets uplink. In the DS algorithm, the uplink and downlink are completely separated. The STA must wait for the AP to complete the downlink phase before it can start the uplink transmission. This will cause all the packets to be sent or are in the link transmission state during the start of the uplink phase, and the AP will have a period of idle time, resulting in a waste of time. The LDDS algorithm proposed in this paper makes good use of link inequality information to arrange STA to send packets in advance, avoiding the time resource consumption of AP here.

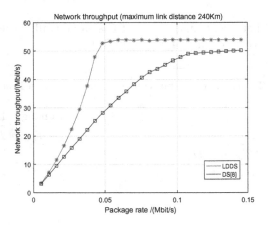

Fig. 11. Network throughput changes with the rate of production packets

The x-axis of Fig. 11 is the packet production rate, and the y-axis is the network throughput (the maximum link distance in this test scenario is 240 km). It can be seen from the figure that the LDDS algorithm can reach the saturation point of network throughput faster than the LDDS algorithm. It is easy to see through the principle analysis table of the LDDS algorithm and the DS algorithm. When the maximum link distance of the network is consistent with the transmission time required for the network data, the LDDS algorithm will have the most obvious throughput gain compared to the DS algorithm, and also reach the maximum throughput of the network. When the network traffic is saturated, compared with the DS algorithm, the network throughput is improved by 7.4%

The x-axis of Fig. 12 is the maximum link distance in the network, and the y-axis is the network throughput. Under the condition that the total traffic to be transmitted by the network is fixed, when the distance between the links in the network is small, the LDDS algorithm transmits all the services in one time, which is roughly equal to the service transmission time, and there is no

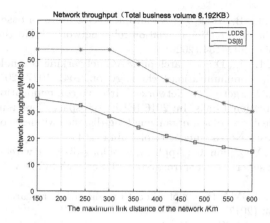

Fig. 12. Network throughput changes with the rate of production packets

additional link propagation delay. Will get the maximum network throughput. When the distance between the links in the network is large, the LDDS algorithm will increase the time it takes to transmit network services and the DS algorithm will increase the long-distance propagation cost. However, the total time consumption of the LDDS algorithm will always be less than that of the DS algorithm, so the network throughput of the LDDS algorithm is always better than the DS algorithm.

5   Conclusion

A data scheduling algorithm based on link distance is proposed in the directional aviation relay network, which blurs the uplink and downlink stages of the overall network, and keeps the relay nodes in working state as much as possible. Therefore, the air nodes and the ground nodes can communicate efficiently, improve the utilization rate of network resources, and increase the network throughput. And through simulation tests, verification shows that using this data scheduling algorithm in directional aviation relay networks, the network will have better throughput.

Acknowledgement. This work was supported in part by Science and Technology on Avionics Integration Laboratory and the Aeronautical Science Foundation of China (Grant No. 201955053002), the National Natural Science Foundations of CHINA (Grant No. 61871322, No. 61771392, No. 61771390, and No. 61501373), and Science and Technology on Avionics Integration Laboratory and the Aeronautical Science Foundation of China (Grant No. 20185553035).

References

1. Xu, Z., Yuan, J., et al.: Multi-UAV relay network supporting mobile ad hoc network communication. J. Tsinghua Univ. (Nat. Sci. Ed.) **51**(2), 8–13 (2011)

2. Yan, Z., Li, Q., Li, B., Yang, M.: A multiple access protocol based on link distance and ring splitting in directional aviation relay network. J. Northwestern Polytechnical Univ. **38**(1), 147–154 (2020)
3. Jing, Z., Zeng, H., Li, D.: Research on MAC networking technology of directional ad hoc network. Communication technology, pp. 1041–1047 (2014)
4. Macleod, R.B., Margetts, A.: Networked airborne communications using adaptive multi-beam directional links. In: 2016 IEEE Aerospace Conference (2016)
5. Liang, L.: Node design of self-organizing long-distance wireless communication system. Ph.D. thesis, North University of China (2011)
6. Lou, H.P., Sun, Y.Q., Fan, G.: Application of long-distance wireless communication technologies in supervisory control system. J. Sci-Tech Inf. Dev. Econ. **16**(17), 235–237 (2006)
7. Mo, P., Li, S.: TDMA time slot allocation algorithm research and Qt platform implementation (2017)
8. Zhang, J., Lai, H., Xiong, Y.: Concurrent transmission based on distributed scheduling for underwater acoustic networks. Sensors **19**, 1871 (2019)
9. Miguel-Angel, L.N., Jose-Miguel, M.R., Pablo, O., Javier, P.: Optimal scheduling and fair service policy for STDMA in underwater networks with acoustic communications. Sensors **18**(2), 612 (2018)
10. Hu, T., Fei, Y.: DSH-MAC: medium access control based on decoupled and suppressed handshaking for long-delay underwater acoustic sensor networks. In: 2013 IEEE 38th Conference on Local Computer Networks (LCN 2013) (2013)

A Probing and p-Probability Based Two Round Directional Neighbor Discovery Algorithm

Xiaojiao Hu, Qi Yang, Zhongjiang Yan$^{(\boxtimes)}$, Mao Yang, and Bo Li

School of Electronics and Information, Northwestern Polytechnical University,
Xi'an, China
18392990273@mail.nwpu.edu.cn,
{yangqi,zhjyan,yangmao,libo.npu}@nwpu.edu.cn

Abstract. Neighbor node discovery is one of the important steps in a wireless directed ad hoc network. Improving the efficiency of neighbor node discovery can not only reduce the collision during node communication, but also improve the performance of the wireless ad hoc network as a whole. In the Ad-hoc network of directional antennas, by analyzing and summarizing the deficiencies of the neighbor discovery algorithm, this paper proposes a probing and p-probability based two round directional neighbor discovery algorithm (PPTR). The second round adjusts the probability of neighboring neighbor nodes competing for slots based on the number of free slots, successful slots, and collision slots in the first round, thereby reducing the collision of neighboring nodes to reach the maximum number of neighbors discovered within a fixed time. We verified the protocol through network simulation. The simulation results show that the PPTR algorithm and the traditional neighbor discovery algorithm have the same neighbor discovery efficiency when the number of network nodes and the number of time slots are consistent. But The neighbor discovery efficiency increases on average 81.3% when the number of nodes increases to five times the number of timeslots.

Keywords: Ad-hoc · Neighbor discovery · Probabilistic optimization · Two rounds

1 Introduction

The wireless self-organizing network makes it minimally affected by geographical location through its self-configuration method, and its flexible structure makes the wireless self-organizing network in emergency communication, exploration and disaster relief, maritime communication and military communication, such as individual soldier communication systems on the battlefield, etc. All have irreplaceable positions and advantages. The directional antenna [1] is widely used in modern wireless communication because of its flexible structure, extremely high multiplexing rate, wide coverage, and reduced interference.

© ICST Institute for Computer Sciences, Social Informatics and Telecommunications Engineering 2021
Published by Springer Nature Switzerland AG 2021. All Rights Reserved
Y.-B. Lin and D.-J. Deng (Eds.): SGIoT 2020, LNICST 354, pp. 441–452, 2021.
https://doi.org/10.1007/978-3-030-69514-9_34

The addition of directional antennas to the wireless self-organizing network improves network transmission performance and enhances anti-interference, making it have better communication performance in military communications and emergency communications. However, in the wireless communication system, the problem of low discovery efficiency caused by the difficulty of neighbor node discovery and the collision of neighbor nodes must first be solved.

Neighbor node discovery is a key part of a wireless ad hoc network [2]. An effective neighbor node discovery algorithm is indispensable for most MAC protocols based on wireless networks. When the time slot is fixed, the number of neighbor nodes will greatly affect the discovery efficiency of neighbor nodes. Therefore, improving the efficiency of neighbor discovery is an extremely important process. Reference [3] sets the beam selection probability for each node and continuously adjusts this value during the neighbor node search process, thereby reducing the neighbor node discovery time as a whole and improving the search efficiency. In addition, by setting a special packet format for the discovery and transmission of neighboring nodes, it simplifies information exchange and makes searching easier and more efficient. However, it is only suitable for moving neighbors, and only for a certain beam, it cannot effectively reduce the discovery time of neighbors. Reference [4] proposes to add feedback information in the neighbor node discovery algorithm. The node uses the feedback information of the other party to avoid the repeated transmission of information. Although the collision of neighbor nodes is reduced, it is difficult to apply to multi-hop networks and it cannot solve directional antennas's neighbors found the problem. Reference [5] proposes that all nodes send and receive information in accordance with the specified order of sending and receiving, so that neighbor node discovery is deterministic. Although the collision of neighbor node discovery is reduced, the algorithm is not universal for self-organizing networks. Reference [6] proposes an ALOHA algorithm based on binary tree timeslots. Neighboring nodes randomly compete for timeslots. If conflicts occur in some neighboring nodes, the conflicting tags will be resolved through binary tree splitting. The protocol uses dynamic, adaptive, and segmentation methods to adjust the time slot to the estimated number of neighbor nodes each time. Reference [7] proposes to determine whether to find the neighbor node in each scan by determining whether it is the sending or receiving mode in the next scan. That is, the selection probability of the scan initiating node and the responding node is adjusted by an algorithm to improve neighbor node discovery efficiency, the algorithm requires multiple rounds of interaction to achieve its purpose. It is an adjustment algorithm with memo function. Although the efficiency of neighbor node discovery is improved, it also wastes network resources and time.

Synthesizing the existing research of neighbor node discovery in directional self-organizing network, in order to reduce the competition and conflict of neighbor nodes in fixed time slots and improve the utilization of time slots, this paper proposes a probing and p-probability based two round directional neighbor discovery algorithm. In this protocol, the original neighbor node scanning discovery is changed from one round to two rounds, that is, the scanning time slot is divided into two parts for scanning. In the second round, according to the number of successful slots, idle slots and collision slots in the previous round, and then based on the slots of the second round, the neighbor nodes in the second round calculate the probability of competing for slots by the slave nodes in the current round, and then the slave nodes respond with this probability, so as to reduce the collision of adjacent nodes and improve the efficiency of adjacent nodes discovery [8]. This protocol can improve the utilization rate of time slot and reduce the collision between adjacent nodes when the time slot is fixed. The neighborhood discovery algorithm should have certain stability and universality [9].

The contribution of this paper is as follows:

(1) This paper proposes a new directional neighbor discovery algorithm of PPTR, which improves the efficiency of neighbor node discovery. The algorithm learns and verifies the method of estimating the actual number of neighbor nodes based on the occupied status of the scan time slot, and adjusts the probability of the next round of neighbor nodes competing for the time slot, which make it possible to find as many neighbor nodes as possible within a fixed time, reduce time slot conflicts, and improve time slot utilization.

(2) The algorithm has good portability and can be applied to most wireless networks. Especially in the case of a large number of nodes, this algorithm has obvious advantages.

The rest of this paper is arranged as follows. In the second chapter, the shortcomings of neighbor node scanning algorithm in Directional Transmission and Reception Algorithms (DTRA) are briefly introduced. The third chapter introduces the neighbor node discovery protocol based on probability adjustment. The fourth chapter introduces the simulation results and analysis. The fifth chapter summarizes this paper.

2 Motivation

2.1 Brief Introduction to Neighbor Scan of DTRA

DTRA protocol is a MAC protocol that uses specific scanning mode to carry out pure directional communication. DTRA protocol divides communication into three stages, as shown in Fig. 1, each stage is composed of several time slots of the same size, and each time slot is divided into several micro time slots of the same size. The first stage is the scan discovery stage, in which the nodes discover the neighbor nodes and establish the neighbor table around the nodes.

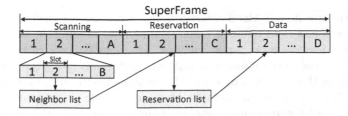

Fig. 1. Three step handshake in DTRA scanning phase.

This stage is the next two stages to solve the problem of adjacent node discovery and maintenance. The second stage is the reservation stage. According to the neighbor node table in the first stage, the resource reservation is made between nodes, and then the data communication between nodes is carried out in the third stage.

It can be seen that the adjacent node scanning phase of DTRA protocol is a key step for resource reservation and data transmission. However, due to its specific scanning mode, the efficiency of the protocol is low. When the number of adjacent nodes is far more than the communication time slots, the probability of collision is very high, which leads to the low efficiency of the nodes to discover the neighboring nodes [10].

2.2 Motivation

When scanning adjacent nodes, the time slot of node communication is fixed, but the number of adjacent nodes in current beam contention time slot is unknown [11]. As shown in Fig. 2, when the number of adjacent nodes is far greater than the number of current slots, the probability of collision increases, resulting in the number of adjacent nodes found by the current beam is very small [12]. Therefore, we need an algorithm that can adjust the probability of adjacent nodes competing for slots according to the number of adjacent nodes and slots, so as to improve the efficiency of neighbor node discovery [13].

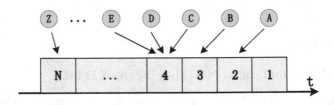

Fig. 2. Multiple neighboring nodes select the same time slot.

3 Proposed Probability Adjustment Algorithm

3.1 Key Idea

Based on the traditional Aloha algorithm, literature [14,15] proposed that when the number of slots and nodes is equal, the number of adjacent nodes found is the largest. Most research papers such as [16] focus on how to determine the relationship between the number of slots and the number of adjacent nodes, in order to adjust the time slots to achieve the maximum efficiency of neighbor node discovery. In each round, the number of adjacent nodes is estimated according to the results of the previous round of scanning, and then the current slot is dynamically adjusted for scanning again until the estimated number of adjacent nodes is consistent with the number of current slots. It can be considered that all the neighboring nodes are basically found and the current scanning is finished.

In the scanning phase of DTRA, the number of slots t is fixed. Therefore, the improved neighbor node discovery algorithm in this paper is to increase the number of adjacent nodes from one round to two rounds, as shown in Fig. 3. The first round of scanning is conducted according to the original set mode. According to the free slot En, successful slot Sn and collision slot Fn after the first round of scanning, the number of adjacent nodes around the current beam is estimated, According to the relationship between the number of adjacent nodes and the number of time slots, the probability Ps of neighboring nodes competing for slots in the second round is adjusted, so as to maximize the discovery efficiency of neighboring nodes [17]. Therefore, this paper focuses on how to find as many nodes as possible in a fixed time.

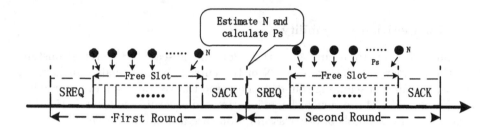

Fig. 3. Adjust competition probability.

In reference [18], a novel algorithm for estimating the adjacent nodes is proposed. Assuming that the discovery process of adjacent nodes is multinomial distribution, the probability P_e that a slot is idle when the total slot length is T is:

$$P_e = \left(1 - \left(\frac{1}{T}\right)\right)^N \tag{1}$$

The probability P_s that a slot is a successful slot is:

$$P_s = \left(\frac{N}{T}\right)\left(1 - \left(\frac{1}{T}\right)\right)^{N-1} \tag{2}$$

The probability P_f that a slot is a collision slot is:

$$P_f = 1 - P_e - P_s \tag{3}$$

Then the probability $P(E_n, S_n, F_n)$ of E_n free slots, S_n successful slots and F_n collision slots in one round is:

$$P(E_n, S_n, F_n) = \frac{T!}{E_n!S_n!F_n!} P_e^{E_n} P_s^{S_n} P_f^{F_n} \tag{4}$$

When the total time slots are t and there are N adjacent nodes to be discovered in the current beam, when there are E_n free slots and S_n successful slots, there are F_n collision slots:

$$P\left(N|E_n, S_n, F_n\right) = \frac{T!}{E_n!S_n!F_n!} \times \left[\left(1 - \frac{1}{T}\right)^N\right]^{E_n} \times \left[\frac{N}{T}\left(1 - \frac{1}{T}\right)^{N-1}\right]^{S_n}$$

$$\times \left[1 - \left(1 - \frac{1}{T}\right)^N - \frac{N}{T}\left(1 - \frac{1}{T}\right)^{N-1}\right]^{F_n} \tag{5}$$

According to the posterior distribution, when the value of $P(N|E_n, S_n, F_n)$ is reached to maximum, the estimated value of adjacent nodes is the best. Therefore, according to the number of free slots, successful slots and collision slots of the previous round, the optimal number of adjacent nodes E_e can be estimated.

3.2   Competition Probability

Assuming that the total number of time slots in the scanning phase is constant and the number of adjacent nodes N of the current beam remains unchanged, then the number of scanning rounds is increased to two rounds, and the number of adjacent nodes of the current beam is estimated according to formula (5). The parameters and symbols of other assumptions are as follows (Table 1):

Table 1. Parameter table

Notation	Description
T	Total number of time slots in scanning phase
T_s	The total number of slots used to reply from the node
N_s	Number of successful nodes in competition

In the scanning phase, each round of SREQ-SRES-SACK neighbor node discovery process includes one SREQ packet sending time slot, Ts SRES time slot and one sack packet reply time slot:

$$T = 2 + T_s \tag{6}$$

The discovery efficiency of neighbor nodes means that any slot can become a successful time slot among the Ts slave node reply slots.

When N slave nodes compete for SRES slots T_s with probability P_s, i nodes decides to participate in the competition probability:

$$P_{contend}(N, P_s, i) = \binom{N}{i} P_s{}^i(1 - P_s)^{N-i} \tag{7}$$

When i nodes decide to compete for T_s slots, the probability that any slot can become a successful slot is as follows:

$$P_{success}(T_s, i) = \binom{i}{1} \frac{1}{T_s} \left(1 - \frac{1}{T_s}\right)^{i-1} \tag{8}$$

According to formula (8), $P_{success}(T_s, i)$ can reach the maximum value when $i = T_s$.

Therefore, when N slave nodes compete for T_s slots with probability P_s, the probability that any slot can become a successful slot is as follows:

$$
\begin{aligned}
P_{slotsuccess}(N, P_n, T_n) &= \sum_{i=1}^{N} P_{contend}(N, P_s, i) \times P_{success}(T_s, i) \\
&= \sum_{i=1}^{N} \binom{N}{i} P_s^{\,i} (1 - P_s)^{N-i} \binom{i}{1} \frac{1}{T_s} \left(1 - \frac{1}{T_s}\right)^{i-1} \\
&= \frac{P_s}{T_s} \sum_{i=1}^{N} i \binom{N}{i} (1 - P_s)^{N-i} \left(P_s - \frac{P_s}{T_s}\right)^{i-1}
\end{aligned}
\tag{9}
$$

Then, when N slave nodes compete for T_s slots with probability P_s, the expectation of the number of successful nodes N_s is as follows:

$$
E[N_s] = \begin{cases}
N \times \left(1 - \frac{1}{T_s}\right)^{i-1}, & P_s = 1 \\
\sum_{i=1}^{N} i \binom{N}{i} (1 - P_s)^{N-i} P_s^{\,i} \left(1 - \frac{1}{T_s}\right)^{i-1}, & 0 < P_s < 1
\end{cases}
\tag{10}
$$

Then the discovery efficiency of neighbor nodes in a single round is as follows:

$$\eta = \frac{E[N_s]}{T_s} \tag{11}$$

When the number of slots in a single round is fixed, if the discovery efficiency of adjacent nodes is maximized η, that is, the number of successful neighboring nodes in a single round is expected to be the maximum. From formula (10), when the probability of competing slots is $P_s = min\left(1, \frac{T_s}{E[N]}\right)$, the maximum expectation can be obtained.

Therefore, through the scanning results of the first round of the current beam, the optimal number of adjacent nodes Ne is estimated. In the second round, let $N = N_e$, and the probability P_s of the slave node competing for time slot in the round is obtained, so that the number of adjacent nodes found in the second round is the largest.

4   Simulation and Results

In order to evaluate the performance of PPTR, the enhancement algorithm proposed in this paper is simulated and verified on C++ simulation platform, and the simulation result is the average value of 10000 simulations. In the simulation environment, we set that the beam of the scanning response node and the initiating node is always aligned, that is, when the neighboring node competes for the communication time slot, the master node can be regarded as successful in discovering the neighbor node as long as the competition is successful.

4.1   DTRA and PPTR Simulation Comparison

In DTRA protocol, when the number of adjacent nodes is more than the number of available slots, all nodes compete for fixed slots at the same time, which is prone to conflict, resulting in the discovery of very low number of neighboring nodes. In the first round, all nodes compete freely. In the second round, the probability of the current round of competitive slots is estimated according to the results of the first round of competition, and then the neighboring nodes are scanned. Note that the nodes that have been detected in the first round of scanning do not participate in the second round of competition. Compared with DTRA and this protocol, the simulation results of neighbor node discovery efficiency with the increase of the number of neighboring nodes are shown in Fig. 4. The parameters in the simulation are shown in the Table 2 below.

As shown in Fig. 4 shows the neighbor node discovery efficiency of different algorithms. The number of time slots is 15 and the number of neighboring nodes is 30. At the beginning, the two algorithms have little difference in neighbor discovery efficiency. With the increase of network node density, the probability of node collision in DTRA algorithm increases, so the adjacent node discovery efficiency becomes lower and lower. However, PPTR will be relatively gentle, from the initial growth of 10.4% to the final 882.1%, it can be seen that PPTR has more advantages in the case of dense network nodes. In the later stage, the curve of the number of neighbor nodes found is relatively gentle, because when the number of neighbor nodes increases, the probability of competition slot decreases, and the probability of collision also decreases, so that the discovery value of adjacent nodes will maintain a fixed value.

Table 2. Simulation parameter index

Parameter	Value
Number of scans	10000
Number of time slots	15
Slot ratio of the first round	1/5
Slot ratio of the second round	4/5

4.2   Comparison of Simulations with Different of Time Slots

In the same time slot, the different number of slots in each round will also affect the efficiency of neighbor node discovery. As shown in Fig. 5, with the different density of network nodes and the difference of two rounds distribution in different time slots, the number of final adjacent nodes found is different. The total number of time slots is 30, the blue line indicates that all time slots are divided in half, that is, the first round used to estimate the number of network nodes accounts for 1/2 of all time slots, and the second round based on probability competition time slot also accounts for 1/2 of all time slots. In this case, with the increase of the number of network nodes, the number of adjacent nodes found drops sharply. In the other two cases, the discovery efficiency of adjacent nodes will not be greatly reduced due to the change of the density of neighboring nodes.

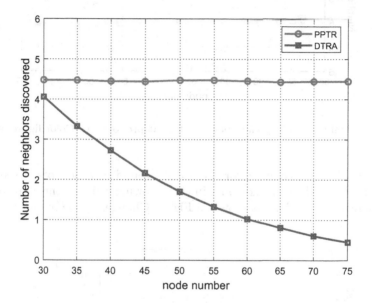

Fig. 4. DTRA vs PPTR.

For the green line, the first round accounts for 1/5 of all time slots and the second round takes up 4/5 time slots. In the first round, the number of neighboring nodes and the competition probability of the next round can be estimated by scanning competition. In the second round, compared with the other two situations, the number of slots available for competition is more, so the discovery probability of adjacent nodes will be relatively stable.

In the discovery of neighbor nodes with fixed time slots, all time slots are divided into several rounds. The first round is used to estimate the number of neighbor nodes, and the subsequent rounds are used by undiscovered nodes to continuously adjust the probability Ps to compete for time slots. As shown in Fig. 6, the time slots are divided into 2 rounds, 3 rounds and 4 rounds, respectively. When the round number is divided into 4 rounds, the number of neighboring nodes is estimated in the first round, and the undiscovered nodes

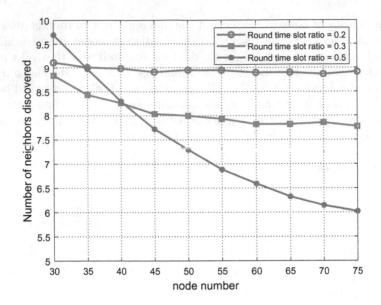

Fig. 5. Neighbor discovery efficiency of different proportion. (Color figure online)

in the second round compete for the second round of time slots based on the probability Ps, and so on, the nodes in the following rounds continuously adjust Ps to compete Time slot. As shown in Fig. 6, Changes in the number of rounds

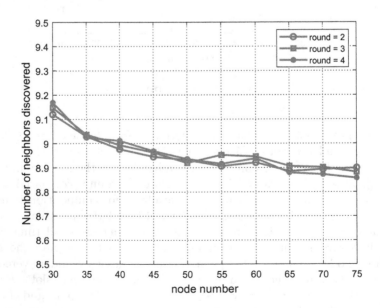

Fig. 6. Neighbor discovery efficiency of different proportion.

have no effect on the simulation results. This is because under a fixed time slot, although the number of rounds increases, the number of time slots per round decreases, and then Ps also decreases, and there are fewer nodes competing for time slots, so the total number of neighbors found no change.

5   Conclusion and Future Works

This paper proposes A Probing and P-probability based two round directional neighbor discovery algorithm. Its purpose is to improve the efficiency of neighbor node discovery. Readers can estimate the information of surrounding nodes and calculate the probability of competing slots in other projects according to the design of the protocol. Simulation results show that PPTR improves the number of adjacent nodes found in a certain period of time, reduces the probability of slot collision, and greatly improves the utilization of time slots. Moreover, the algorithm is not only suitable for DTRA, but also can be extended to other wireless ad-hoc network protocols with good compatibility.

Acknowledgement. This work was supported in part by Science and Technology on Avionics Integration Laboratory and the Aeronautical Science Foundation of China (Grant No. 201955053002), the National Natural Science Foundations of CHINA (Grant No. 61871322, No. 61771392, No. 61771390, and No. 61501373), and Science and Technology on Avionics Integration Laboratory and the Aeronautical Science Foundation of China (Grant No. 20185553035).

References

1. Felemban, E., Murawski, R., Ekici, E., Park, S.: SAND: sectored-antenna neighbor discovery protocol for wireless networks. In: IEEE Communications Society Conference on Sensor (2010)
2. Carty, J., Jayaweera, S.K.: Distributed network, neighbor discovery and blind routing for mobile wireless ad-hoc networks. In: 2019 12th IFIP Wireless and Mobile Networking Conference (WMNC) (2019)
3. Zhang, Y.J., Lei, L., Zhu, G., Dong, T.: Distributed neighbor discovery mechanism based on analytical modeling for ad hoc networks with directional antennas. J. Chin. Comput. Syst. **37**(10), 2226–2231 (2016)
4. Benssalah, M., Djeddou, M., Dahou, B., Drouiche, K., Maali, A.: A cooperative Bayesian and lower bound estimation in dynamic framed slotted ALOHA algorithm for RFID systems. Int. J. Commun. Syst. **31**(13), e3723.1–e3723.13 (2018)
5. Liu, A.F., Xian-You, W., Zhi-Gang, C., Wei-Hua, G.: Research on the energy hole problem based on unequal cluster-radius for wireless sensor networks. Comput. Commun. **33**(3), 302–321 (2010)
6. Wu, H., Zeng, Y., Feng, J., Gu, Y.: Binary tree slotted ALOHA for passive RFID tag anticollision. IEEE Trans. Parallel Distrib. Syst. **24**(1), 19–31 (2013)
7. Huang, S., Mo, L., Liang, Z.: An intelligent neighbor discovery algorithm for Ad Hoc networks with directional antennas. In: 2013 International Conference on Mechatronic Sciences, Electric Engineering and Computer (MEC) (2013)

8. Nguyen, D., Garcialunaaceves, J.J., Obraczka, K.: Collision-free asynchronous multi-channel access in ad hoc networks (2017)
9. Jia, X., Feng, Q., Yu, L.: Stability analysis of an efficient anti-collision protocol for RFID tag identification. IEEE Trans. Commun. **60**(8), 2285–2294 (2012)
10. Lee, J.C., Shin, M.K., Jeong, S., Kim, H.J.: Method of transmitting neighbor discovery protocol message in IEEE 802.16/WiBro network (2008)
11. Chen, W.T.: An accurate tag estimate method for improving the performance of an RFID anticollision algorithm based on dynamic frame length ALOHA. IEEE Trans. Autom. Sci. Eng. **6**(1), 9–15 (2008)
12. Cai, H., Liu, B., Gui, L., Wu, M.Y.: Neighbor discovery algorithms in wireless networks using directional antennas. In: IEEE International Conference on Communications (2012)
13. Mbacke, A.A., Mitton, N., Rivano, H.: A survey of RFID readers anticollision protocols. IEEE J. Radio Freq. Identif. **2**, 38–48 (2018)
14. Deng, D.J., Tsao, H.W.: Optimal dynamic framed slotted ALOHA based anti-collision algorithm for RFID systems. Wireless Pers. Commun. **59**(1), 109–122 (2011). https://doi.org/10.1007/s11277-010-0193-3
15. Zhang, X.H., Zhang, L.Y.: Research on RFID anti-collision algorithm of slot responding in real-time and co-processing. Acta Electronica Sinica **42**(6), 1139–1146 (2014)
16. Chu, C., Wen, G., Huang, Z., Su, J., Han, Yu.: Improved Bayesian method with collision recovery for RFID anti-collision. In: Sun, X., Pan, Z., Bertino, E. (eds.) ICAIS 2019. LNCS, vol. 11633, pp. 51–61. Springer, Cham (2019). https://doi.org/10.1007/978-3-030-24265-7_5
17. Kohvakka, M., Suhonen, J., Kuorilehto, M., Kaseva, V., Haennikaeinen, M., Haemaelaeinen, T.D.: Energy-efficient neighbor discovery protocol for mobile wireless sensor networks. Ad Hoc Netw. **7**(1), 24–41 (2009)
18. Xiong, T.W., Tan, X., Yan, N., Min, H.: Modeling and simulation of RTLS based on UHF RFID. J. Syst. Simul. **23**(1), 212–216 (2011)

An Optimal Channel Bonding Strategy for IEEE 802.11be

Ke Sun, Zhongjiang Yan$^{(\boxtimes)}$, Mao Yang, and Bo Li

School of Electronics and Information,
Northwestern Polytechnical University, Xi'an, China
sunke22@mail.nwpu.edu.cn, {zhjyan,yangmao,libo.npu}@nwpu.edu.cn

Abstract. Although there are a large number of available channels that can be bonded together for data transmission in the next generation WLAN, i.e., IEEE 802.11be protocol, it may cause long data transmission time to transmit large files due to the inefficient channel bonding strategies. This paper proposes an optimal channel bonding strategy based on the optimal stopping theory. Firstly, under the constraint of the number of available channels, the problem of minimizing the transmission time of large files is formulated as an optimal stopping problem, where the time duration of large file transmission is defined as the sum of channel accessing time and data transmission time after successful access into the channel, Secondly, the threshold of successful bonded channel number is derived based on the optimal stopping theory. When the channel access is successful, data transmission is performed if the number of bondable channels is larger than the threshold. Otherwise this data transmission opportunity is dropped and channel competition is resumed. The simulation results show that, compared with the traditional EDCA if access-success then-transmit strategy and the fixed bonding channel number threshold strategy, the data transmission completion time of large file is shortened by more than 40%.

Keywords: Channel bonding · IEEE 802.11be · Optimal stopping theory

1 Introduction

The concept of channel bonding technology is proposed from the IEEE 802.11n standard, the purpose is to improve the transmission rate and throughput. In IEEE 802.11 a/b/g, the bandwidth of each channel is 20 MHz. In IEEE 802.11n, two consecutive 20 MHz sub-channels can be bonded to form a 40 MHz bandwidth channel for data transmission. That is 40 MHz = 20 MHz + 20 MHz. These two channels are defined as a primary channel and a secondary channel, respectively, where the primary channel is mainly used as a broadcast channel to transmit broadcast frames to provide services for wireless connections. In 802.11be, the multi-channel bonding technology has been further developed, supporting the bonding of more adjacent channels (up to 16), and at the same time, the

© ICST Institute for Computer Sciences, Social Informatics and Telecommunications Engineering 2021
Published by Springer Nature Switzerland AG 2021. All Rights Reserved
Y.-B. Lin and D.-J. Deng (Eds.): SGIoT 2020, LNICST 354, pp. 453–467, 2021.
https://doi.org/10.1007/978-3-030-69514-9_35

primary and secondary channels are no longer distinguished Ref. [1,2]. That is, a node can access any channel, and then bond all other currently idle channels, which further reduces the difficulty of channel bonding and improves the feasibility of channel bonding, but still faces the problem of long and unstable transmission of large files. In the environment of rapid development of network technology, users' requirements for transmitting large files (such as 4k video) become more frequent, so it is necessary to design an effective channel bonding strategy to minimize the total data transmission time of large files.

In view of the existing problems, domestic and foreign scholars have carried out relevant research. Overall, these studies can be divided into two categories: channel bonding and optimal stopping. Sami Khairy et al. studied the performance of distributed and opportunistic multi-channel bonding in IEEE 802.11ac WLAN where existing IEEE 802.11a/b/g users coexist in Ref. [3], and proposed a method for Reduce competition in the network and obtain maximum network throughput. Eng Hwee Ong et al. in Ref. [4] proposed that increasing the bonded channel bandwidth to 160 MHz may not be an effective option, and the throughput no longer increases with increasing bandwidth. Wei Wang et al. proposed for the first time in Ref. [5] a scheme based on adaptive Clear Channel Assessment (CCA) for managing IEEE 802.11 WLAN channel bonding. Compared with the traditional channel bonding scheme and the default CSMA/CA, the throughput is increased by 37% and 46%, respectively. The above studies are all about the channel bonding research before IEEE 802.11ax, but now a channel bonding method suitable for IEEE 802.11be is needed.

In general, the optimal stopping model analysis problem often divides the problem into two parts, profit and cost. Ref. [6–11] The cost is a set of observable random variables $\{C_1, C_2, ...\}$, The cost C and profit Y at each observation may change, when C_n is observed and you choose to stop, you will get a profit Y_n, as shown in Fig. 1:

The purpose of the optimal stopping rule is to obtain the highest net profit, that is, the profit minus all costs. It can be expressed as:

$$\max\left\{Y_n - \sum C_n\right\}$$

Since future benefits and costs are generally unknown, all need to use existing observations to make predictions, and the solution to the optimal stopping rule is expressed as a set of thresholds composed of a series of observable values.

In the field of WLAN, the optimal stopping model has some applications, As applied in Ref. [12], it is applied to the problem of maximizing network throughput in the system model of multi-packet reception (MPR) WLAN with multi-round competition. In Ref. [13], it is used in wireless ad hoc networks to select the next-hop relay selection problem as a sequential decision problem. In Ref. [14], it is applied to consider distributed opportunity scheduling (DOS) in wireless ad hoc networks. However, there are still very few studies on the optimal access timing combined with channel bonding.

The purpose of this study is to propose a more optimized rule based on the channel bonding technology, so that the time required for file transfer is shorter. In IEEE 802.11be channel bonding, each channel can be used as the main channel to access the node, and then bond other idle channels to increase the transmission bandwidth and reduce the transmission time. However, due to the transmission of the node in the channel, etc. the number of idle channels is a random variable, and there may be few available channels after access.

In response to this problem, this article applies the idea of optimal stopping theory, combined with statistical laws, an optimal sending strategy can be obtained, so that file sending can be completed faster. On the premise of assuming that the file transmission speed is proportional to the number of bonded channels; the probability of occurrence of idle time slots in each channel is independently and identically distributed. The strategy in this article adds a judgment after the node accesses the channel to judge whether the current channel status is worth sending. Through analysis of factors such as channel conditions and file size to be sent, the strategy uses the method of minimizing expectations to dynamically obtain a threshold for the minimum number of successfully bonded channels, That is, when the STA accesses the channel, if the number of successfully bonded channels is not less than the threshold, it is selected to send, otherwise it will give up the access and re-compete for the channel to obtain the opportunity to bond more channels. The simulation results show that the file transfer completion time is significantly shortened compared to the traditional access-on-demand and fixed bonded channel number thresholds.

The rest of this paper is organized as follows. Section 2 describes the network topology model and problem modeling of the communication system concerned in this paper. Section 3 carries on the theoretical analysis and derivation of the proposed problem model. Section 4 is the simulation result analysis and error analysis. Section 5 is the summary and outlook.

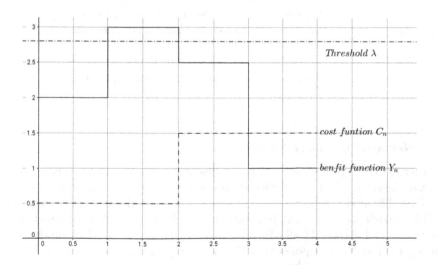

Fig. 1. Schematic diagram of the general optimal stopping model

2 System Model

See Table 1.

Table 1. Symbol notation and meanings

Symbol notation	Symbol meanings
H	Total number of channels
M	Average number of sSTAs in a BSS
h	The number of idle channels cSTA observed
m	The threshold of successful bonded channel number
n	cSTA access channel attempts
x	Number of channels successfully bonded when cSTA accesses
N	Number of access to channels while waiting
A_m	Average waiting time for access channel when threshold is m
S_m	Average sending time when the threshold is m
T_m	The total duration when the threshold is m
λ_m	Maximum file size for threshold m
F	The size of file to be sent
p	Probability of occurrence of free time slots in separate channels
p_h	When observing a channel, the probability that the number of channels that can be bonded is h
$P(m)$	When accessing a channel, the probability that the number of successfully bonded channels is at least m
f	Time required for file transmission on a single channel
s	Transmission rate of a single channel
τ	Probability of sSTA in the channel starting to send
P_{cl}	Probability that cSTA will collide on one of the channels when accessing the channel
P_{ac}	Probability of cSTA accessing the channel
$E[P]$	The average time for each sSTA to send a packet

2.1 Network Topology Model

In order to make the research content of this article more concise, this article will analyze the scene of a basic service set in a wireless local area network. As shown in Fig. 2, The nodes in this basic service set are divided into three categories.

This article divides STAs into two types: sSTA and cSTA, of which sSTAs are traditional STAs, M sSTAs are evenly distributed on H channels, which are regarded as the components of the channel environment in this article, and they are regarded as the background without considered separately when analyzing. And cSTA is a new type of STA using 802.11be. This article will focus on analyzing its behavior (Table 2).

Table 2. The number of each node in the BSS

Nodetype	Number of nodes in a BSS
AP	1
cSTA (STA with Channel bonding capability)	1
sSTA (STA without Channel bonding capability, only working on single channel)	M

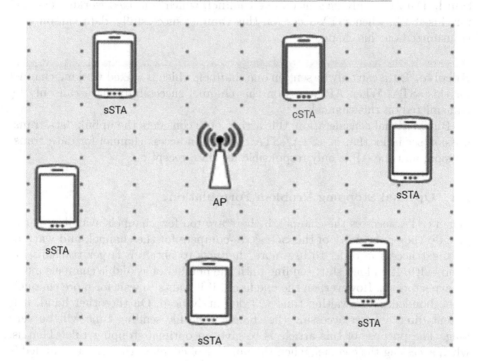

Fig. 2. Schematic diagram of network topology

2.2 Channel Access Method

In the process of accessing the channel, AP and cSTA can bond all current idle channels for transmission after accessing the channel, while traditional sSTAs can only send and receive on a fixed channel, and sSTAs are evenly distributed on all H channels. The specific channel access methods for each node when sending and receiving are as follows.

a) AP and cSTA can work on all H channels, that is.

Send. Data can be send on m $(1 \leq m \leq H)$ channels at the same time, Where m is the number of idle channels when AP/cSTA accesses the channel successfully.

Receive. Data can be received on $m\,(1 \leq m \leq H)$ channels at the same time, Where m is the number of idle channels when AP/cSTA accesses the channel successfully.

b) sSTAs can work on a fixed one of all channels, but cannot bond other idle channels, that is.

Send. Data can only be sent on one channel, which is a fixed working channel for this sSTA, when sSTA access on this channel successfully, data can only be transmitted on this channel.

Receive. Data can only be sent on one channel, which is a fixed working channel for this sSTA, When AP access on this channel successfully, data can only be transmitted on this channel.

But in actual consideration, this article only considers the uplink data transmission scenario, that is, cSTA/sSTA contention access channel for data transmission, and the AP is only responsible for data reception.

2.3   Optimal Stopping Problem Formulation

When cSTA accesses the channel, if there are too few channels available, it can give up the opportunity of this access, re-compete for the channel, and wait for the next access in order to use more channels to obtain a larger transmission bandwidth. It will not start sending until the number of available channels meets its expectations. However, on the one hand, if it wants to wait for more channels to be bonded, more waiting time will definitely need, On the other hand, if it is sent directly after accessing the channel, the file sending time will be very long. The purpose of this article is to give an optimal stopping rule, That is, when accessing the channel, when the number of channels that can be bonded is greater than that, stop waiting, bonding the existing channel to start sending, so as to achieve the minimum total time for cSTA to transfer files.

As with the general optimal stopping problem, in the channel bonding problem, we also need to consider the benefits and costs of the problem, but in fact, The object of the optimal stopping problem is when to stop waiting for the opportunity to access more channels, Once sending starts, no matter how many channels are bonded to send, the final income is consistent, that is, Complete the sending of the file. And the cost of the channel bonding problem only considers the time cost, that is, users want to transmit as quickly as possible. So we divide the time axis into two segments, with the sign of stopping waiting for the opportunity to bond more channels to start sending. As shown in Fig. 3, before the Nth access to the channel and stop waiting, there will be multiple attempts to access the channel, and the time for the nth wait for access to the channel is A_n, Therefore, a set of random variables can be obtained, $\{A_1, A_2, ..., A_N\}$, It follows a geometric distribution $GE\left(1/\left(1 - (1-p)^H\right)\right)$, So you can get the waiting time for access to the channel $A = A_1 + A_2 + ... + A_N$, Start sending after stopping waiting. The sending time is a function related to the file size and the number of successfully bonded channels m, the sending time is $S = F/ms$, But the number of successfully bonded channels is a random variable, $m = \{0, 1, .., h\}$, It satisfies the binomial distribution $B(h, p)$, Where h is the number of idle channels found while monitoring the channel, The purpose of the optimal stopping rule is to make the total sending time the shortest, that is, $\min\{A + S\}$, Since this is a random process, this article will use minimization expectations as a criterion for evaluating the optimal stopping.

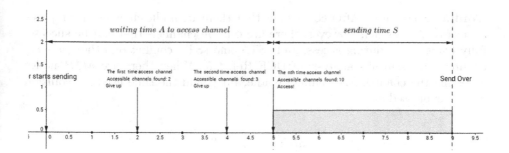

Fig. 3. Schematic diagram of the optimal stopping model in channel bonding

In the channel bonding problem, The only values that can be observed by cSTA are the number of free channels after each access to the channel h and the size of the file to be sent by cSTA F, In addition, it can know the channel idle probability p, and the current number of sSTAs in the BSS M and the number of channels H, Therefore, under the assumptions of this article, the solution of the optimal stopping model in channel bonding will be expressed as: After accessing the channel, the number of successfully bonded free channels x is greater than the threshold m of successfully bonded channels before sending is allowed, The minimum number of successfully bonded channels m is jointly influenced by F, p and the known BSS basic parameters M, H.

3   Optimal Channel Bonding Strategy Derivation

3.1   Channel Analysis

Idle and Busy Situation. According to the assumptions of this article, The channels are independent of each other and do not affect each other, The probability of an idle time slot in all channels is p, According to these conditions, we can get the probability P_{ac} that an accessible slot appears in the channel, that is The probability that each channel is not busy.

$$P_a c = 1 - (1 - p)^H$$

According to the conditional probability formula.

$$P(B|A) = \frac{P(AB)}{P(A)}$$

We can get the probability P_h that the number of available channels is h when cSTA accesses the channel.

$$p_h = C_H^h \frac{p^h (1-p)^{H-h}}{P_{ac}} - C_H^h \frac{p^h (1-p)^{H-h}}{1 - (1-p)^H} \tag{1}$$

Conflict Situation. After cSTA finds that there are h idle channels, it prepares to access the channel, However, there are only m channels that can be successfully transmitted during access, and cSTA and sSTA conflict on other $(h - m)$ channels, In Bianchi's analysis of DCF Ref. [15], When there are M/H nodes accessing the channel, the channel is idle, busy, and the time used for collision can be expressed as,

$$Idle : (1 - \tau)^{M/H}$$

$$Busy : (M/H) \cdot \tau (1 - \tau)^{(M/H)-1} \cdot E[P]$$

$$Collision : \left(1 - (1 - \tau)^{M/H}\right) + (M/H) \cdot \tau (1 - \tau)^{(M/H)-1}$$

where $E[P]$ is the average time for each sSTA to send a packet, τ is the probability of a node sending packets in a certain time slot, According to the definition of p as the channel idle probability in this article, the relationship between τ and p can be obtained.

$$p = \frac{(1 - \tau)^{M/H}}{1 + (E[P] - 1) \cdot (M/H) \cdot \tau (1 - \tau)^{(M/H)-1}} \tag{2}$$

Therefore, the collision probability of cSTA on any channel can be obtained.

$$P_{cl} = 1 - (1 - \tau)^{M/H} \tag{3}$$

Thus, the probability that cSTA will eventually access m channels after finding h idles is,

$$P(m|h) = C_h^{h-m} \cdot (1 - P_{cl})^m P_{cl}^{h-m} \tag{4}$$

3.2   Waiting Time for Access Channel Analysis

According to the assumptions in this article, each time slot on the channel can only have 2 states, accessible or inaccessible, And the probability of an idle slot appearing is p, Therefore, the channel can be regarded as an infinite number of Bernoulli experiments. In the n times Bernoulli experiment, try the kth time to get the first chance of success. In detail, it is expressed as, the probability of the first k−1 times all fail, but the kth success. Therefore, we can use the expectation of geometric distribution $E(X) = 1/p$ to represent the waiting time for the first occurrence of an event.

Take the example that more than channels must be bonded to allow sending. When accessing a channel, the probability that more than m channels are idle is,

$$P(m) = \sum_{i=m}^{H} \sum_{h=i}^{H} p_h \cdot P(i|h) \tag{5}$$

Expressed in Bernoulli's experiment, that is, The probability of being able to access the channel is $P(m)$ and the probability of not being able to access is $1 - P(m)$. Then use the geometric distribution of the expectations to indicate that the average number of attempts to access the channel when more than m channels are idle is.

$$N = \frac{1}{P(m)} = \frac{1}{\sum_{i=m}^{H} \sum_{h=i}^{H} p_h \cdot P(i|h)} \tag{6}$$

Similarly, the time interval between two access channels can be obtained as $1/P_{ac}$, It can be obtained that the average waiting time required for more than m channels to be idle is.

$$A_m = \frac{N}{P_{ac}} = \frac{1}{\left(1 - (1 - p)^H\right) \cdot \sum_{i=m}^{H} \sum_{h=i}^{H} p_h \cdot P(i|h)} \tag{7}$$

3.3   Sending Time Analysis

Sending time in this article refers to the time required for file transmission through the bonded channel after the channel has been accessed, Due to the difference in the number of bonded channels, the transmission speed will be different, resulting in different transmission time. If the size of the file to be sent is F, The speed of each individual channel is s, And according to the assumption of this article, the file transfer speed is proportional to the number of bonded channels, Then the transmission time required for bonding m channels can be obtained as F/ms. The stopping rule specifies the minimum number of bonded channels, so the average transmission time is expressed in the desired form. Taking as an example that more than m channels are allowed to be idle, the average transmission time S_m can be obtained as.

$$S_m = \sum_{i=m}^{H} P(i) \cdot \frac{F}{i \cdot s} \tag{8}$$

3.4 Threshold Analysis of the Number of Optimal Stopping Channels

According to the content of the previous two sections, it can be obtained that when the threshold of successful bonded channel number is m, the length of time that cSTA needs to wait for access to the channel and the length of sending files, Therefore, it can be obtained that the total time required by the cSTA when the threshold of successful bonded channel number is m.

$$T_m = A_m + S_m = \frac{1}{\left(1 - (1-p)^H\right) \sum_{i=m}^{H} \sum_{h=i}^{H} p_h P(i|h)} + \sum_{i=m}^{H} P(i) \frac{F}{i \cdot s} \tag{9}$$

Observe the formula (9), F/s is a constant, For convenience, let $f = F/s$, The physical meaning of f is the time required for the file to be transmitted on a single channel, Therefore, the expression for the total time can be written as.

$$T_m = \left(\sum_{i=m}^{H} \frac{p_i}{i} \right) \cdot f + \frac{1}{P_{ac}P(m)} \tag{10}$$

It can be seen that in the case of channel determination (p, H is a constant) and stopping rule determination (m is a constant), The total time T_m required by cSTA is a linear function of f.

Similarly, Expressions of total time can be written when the threshold of successful bonded channel number is $m + 1$.

$$T_{m+1} = \left(\sum_{i=m+1}^{H} \frac{p_i}{i} \right) \cdot f + \frac{1}{P_{ac}P(m+1)} \tag{11}$$

Comparing formulas (10) and (11), we can find.

$$\left(\sum_{i=m+1}^{H} \frac{p_i}{i} \right) - \left(\sum_{i=m}^{H} \frac{p_i}{i} \right) = \frac{p_m}{m} > 0$$

$$\frac{1}{P_{ac}P(m)} - \frac{1}{P_{ac}P(m+1)} = \frac{-\sum_{h=m}^{H} p_h \cdot P(m|h)}{P_{ac}P(m)P(m+1)} < 0$$

So as shown in Fig. 4, There must be an intersection λ_m between T_m and T_{m+1}, Similarly, There must be an intersection λ_m between T_{m+1} and T_{m+2}. Subtract the formulas (10) and (11) to get the expression about the intersection point λ_m.

$$\frac{p_m}{m}\lambda_m = \frac{1}{\left(1-(1-p)^H\right)} \cdot \frac{\sum_{h=m}^{H} p_h \cdot P\left(m|h\right)}{P(m)P(m+1)} \tag{12}$$

Simplifying formula (12) can get.

$$\lambda_m = \frac{m \cdot \sum_{h=m}^{H} p_h \cdot P\left(m|h\right)}{\left(1-(1-p)^H\right) P(m)P(m+1) \cdot p_m} \tag{13}$$

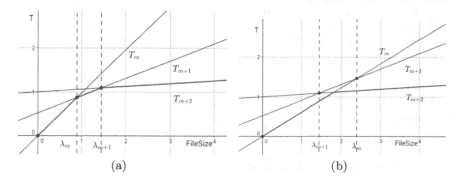

(a)   (b)

Fig. 4. Schematic diagram of stopping rules m and $m+1$ must have an intersection (Color figure online)

As shown in Fig. 4, the time spent corresponding to the best threshold of successful bonded channel number corresponding to different file sizes is shown by the red line in the figure, It can be clearly seen that there will be 2 situations.

Case 1. As shown in Fig. 4(a) In the case of $\lambda_m < \lambda_{m+1}$, when $f < \lambda_m$, the threshold of successful bonded channel number is m, when $\lambda_m < f < \lambda_{m+1}$, the threshold of successful bonded channel number is $m+1$, when $\lambda_{m+1} > f$, the threshold of successful bonded channel number is $m+2$.

Case 2. As shown in Fig. 4(b) In the case of $\lambda_m > \lambda_{m+1}$, The elapsed time (red line) corresponding to the best successful bonding channel number threshold is not related to T_{m+1}, The file size threshold corresponding to the threshold for switching the best successful bonding channel is the intersection of T_m and T_{m+2}, Therefore, in this case, you can directly delete T_{m+1}

Based on the above analysis, this article will use the following method to solve the optimal successful bonding channel threshold m corresponding to different file sizes.

Algorithm 1. FMT(Find Minimum Threshold) According to the total transmission time of files of different sizes under all fixed thresholds from 1 to H, find the corresponding Number of channels successfully bonded.

Input: H, p, τ, M
Output: $\lambda[]$
Begin procedure
$\quad i = 2$
$\quad rst[] = 0, \lambda[] = 0$ //Initialize to an array of all zeros
$\quad m = 1:1:H$ //Array 1 to H
$\quad \lambda[1] = T_{m[1]} \cap T_{m[2]}$ //$\lambda[1]$is the intersection of $T_{m[1]}$ and $T_{m[2]}$, Where T_m is related to H, p, τ, M
$\quad$**repeat**
$\quad\quad$ set $\lambda[i] = T_{m[i]} \cap T_{m[i+1]}$
$\quad\quad$ //Determine whether the situation
$\quad\quad$ **if** $\lambda[i] < \lambda[i-1]$ **then**
$\quad\quad\quad m[i+1] = []$ //Delete $T_{m[i+1]}$
$\quad\quad$ **else**
$\quad\quad\quad i = i+1$
$\quad\quad$ **end if**
$\quad$**until** $m[i+1] < H$ //Traverse channel
End procedure

---

4   Performance Evaluation

4.1   Simulation Results and Analysis

In the case of different channel busyness (p is different), Compare the performance of different successfully bonded channel threshold m with the optimal stopping rule proposed in this article, cSTA uses different rules to transfer files of different sizes, Perform a simulation analysis of the total time required, and the simulation results are shown in Fig. 5.

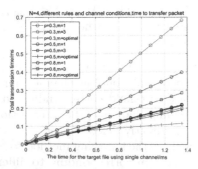 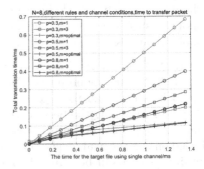

Fig. 5. When $N = 4, 8$, the time chart required to transfer files of different sizes under several stopping rules in different channel conditions

As shown in Fig. 5, the simulation results are consistent with the derivation of the threshold in 3.4, The smaller the threshold of successful bonded channel number, the shorter the time to wait for access to the channel, but the slower the speed of sending files, Therefore, the larger the file to be transmitted, the more suitable it is to wait for more channels to be bonded. On the other hand, the busier the channel, the more time it takes to bond multiple channels.

The optimal stopping rule proposed in this article needs to consider the waiting time and the sending time comprehensively, and select the best threshold for the number of successfully bonded channels according to the file size and the busy state of the channel, so that the sending time of the cSTA is the shortest.

As shown in Fig. 5, when files of the same size are transmitted under various channel conditions, the optimal stopping rule proposed in this article requires the least time compared to rules with fixed thresholds or no thresholds. According to the algorithm proposed in 3.4, we can get the optimal stopping rule for the transmission of files of different sizes under different channel conditions. The specific results are shown in Fig. 6.

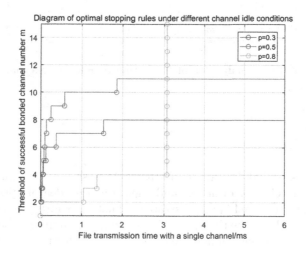

Fig. 6. Diagram of the optimal stopping rules corresponding to different file sizes under different channel conditions

As shown in Fig. 6, under different channel busy conditions, as the file size changes, the threshold m of the number of successfully bonded channels continuously changes. The larger the file to be sent, the greater the threshold m of the number of successfully bonded channels. Among the abnormal results at $p = 0.8$, there are no steps to rise because. Although the channel is idle ($p = 0.8$), the average sending length of sSTA is very short, and the sending frequency is high, The cSTA access probability is extremely high, which is not conducive to bonding too many channels.

4.2 Error Analysis

Since the sending time S_m is a function, When the number of bonded channels is fixed, it will not change, The waiting time A_m for access is a random value, so the error analysis is performed here. As shown in Fig. 7, the absolute error is all within 0.5 time slots. When analyzing the relative error and comparing the absolute error, it can be found that the absolute error is almost 0 when $m = 1, 2$, so the relative error at this time should be discarded, in addition, the relative error is within 1%.

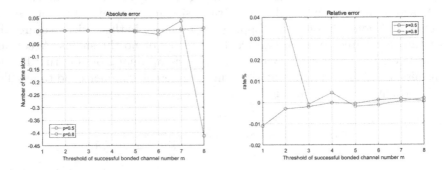

Fig. 7. Error analysis graph of waiting time for access channel

5 Conclusion

This article uses probability and expectation to describe the channel situation and the random behavior of nodes, and then uses the idea of optimal stopping theory to design a channel bonding strategy. That is, before accessing the channel, the node calculates the threshold of the minimum number of bondable channels based on the channel condition and the size of the file to be sent. Then, after the node accesses the channel, it is determined whether the bondable channel is greater than the threshold to determine whether to send. Through simulation, the time taken to transfer files using this channel bonding strategy can be obtained, which is smaller than the traditional channel bonding and fixed threshold channel bonding strategies. Moreover, the error between the simulation and the theoretical results is within 0.5 time slots, so it has a higher reliability.

In the analysis of this article, the channel is assumed to be a very ideal situation, there is no conflict, no impact on each other, and the busyness of each channel is exactly the same, and only one cSTA is considered. This has only a certain reference value for the resolution of practical problems. In one step, we will apply the knowledge of game theory to analyze the behavior of a large number of cSTAs, and analyze the impact of different types of cSTA on the channel. Based on this article, we will find a more general optimal stopping rule.

Acknowledgement. This work was supported in part by the National Natural Science Foundations of CHINA (Grant No. 61871322, No. 61771392, No. 61771390, and No. 61501373), and Science and Technology on Avionics Integration Laboratory and the Aeronautical Science Foundation of China (Grant No. 201955053002, No. 20185553035).

References

1. Lopezperez, D., et al.: IEEE 802.11be extremely high throughput: the next generation of Wi-Fi technology beyond 802.11ax. IEEE Commun. Mag. **57**(9), 113–119 (2019)
2. Avdotin, E., et al.: Enabling massive real-time applications in IEEE 802.11be networks. In: Personal Indoor and Mobile Radio Communications, pp. 1–6 (2019)
3. Khairy, S., et al.: Enabling efficient multi-channel bonding for IEEE 802.11ac WLANs. In: International Conference on Communications, pp. 1–6 (2017)
4. Ong, E.H., et al.: IEEE 802.11ac: enhancements for very high throughput WLANs. In: Personal, Indoor and Mobile Radio Communications, pp. 849–853 (2011)
5. Wang, W., Zhang, F., Zhang, Q.: Managing channel bonding with clear channel assessment in 802.11 networks. In: International Conference on Communications, pp. 1–6 (2016)
6. Lorden, G.: Procedures for reacting to a change in distribution. Ann. Math. Stat. **42**(6), 1897–1908 (1971)
7. Moustakides, G.V.: Optimal stopping times for detecting changes in distributions. Ann. Stat. **14**(4), 1379–1387 (1986)
8. Karatzas, I.: Optimization problems in the theory of continuous trading. SIAM J. Control Optim. **27**(6), 1221–1259 (1989)
9. Van Moerbeke, P.: On optimal stopping and free boundary problems. Rocky Mt. J. Math. **4**(3), 539–578 (1976)
10. Ramaiyan, V., Altman, E., Kumar, A.: Delay optimal scheduling in a two-hop vehicular relay network. Mobile Netw. Appl. **15**(1), 97–111 (2010)
11. Yan, Z., et al.: Optimal traffic scheduling in vehicular delay tolerant networks. IEEE Commun. Lett. **16**(1), 50–53 (2012)
12. Zhang, Y.J.: Multi-round contention in wireless LANs with multipacket reception. IEEE Trans. Wireless Commun. **9**(4), 1503–1513 (2010)
13. Ai, J., Abouzeid, A.A., Ye, Z.: Cross-layer optimal decision policies for spatial diversity forwarding in wireless ad hoc networks. In: 2006 IEEE International Conference on Mobile Ad Hoc and Sensor Systems. IEEE (2006)
14. Zheng, D., Ge, W., Zhang, J.: Distributed opportunistic scheduling for ad-hoc communications: an optimal stopping approach. In: Mobile Ad Hoc Networking and Computing, pp. 1–10 (2007)
15. Bianchi, G.: Performance analysis of the IEEE 802.11 distributed coordination function. IEEE J. Sel. Areas Commun. **18**(3), 535–547 (2000)

An Optimal Multi-round Multi-slot Hello-Reply Directional Neighbor Discovery Algorithm

Xinru Li, Zhongjiang Yan[✉], Mao Yang, Bo Li, and Hang Zhang

School of Electronics and Information, Northwestern Polytechnical University, Xi'an, China

1069769987@qq.com, {zhjyan,yangmao,libo.npu}@nwpu.edu.cn, 80090385@qq.com

Abstract. To solve the problem that multi-round and multi-slot Hello-Reply scheme takes a long time to discover all neighbors due to its multiple parameters and difficulty in optimization, this paper proposes an optimal multi-round and multi-slot (o-MRMS) Hello-Reply algorithm, which theoretically proves and reduces the total time and round number of the algorithm for neighbor discovery, effectively reducing discovery time, and combined with the existing discovery protocol. Simulation results show that compared with a fixed slot number Hello-Reply algorithm, the total neighbor discovery time in the proposed optimal multi-round and multi-slot Hello-Reply algorithm is reduced by about 50%. Compared with the DANDi protocol [3], discovery efficiency increased with the node number, when the node number is 256, the discovery time reduced by approximately 25%. It can be combined with the existing neighbor discovery protocol, which verifies its feasibility and efficiency.

Keywords: Neighbor discovery · Directional antenna · Dynamic slot number

1 Introduction

The directional wireless Ad Hoc network combines the directional antenna and the wireless Ad Hoc network. It has the characteristics of strong independence, high damage resistance and high spatial reuse, and can optimize the transmission performance of the network as a whole. It is widely used in military field, disaster relief and other occasions. Neighbor discovery is the premise of network communication, and the efficiency of neighbor discovery will directly affect the network performance. At present, more and more network researchers focus on wireless networks. Most of the relevant literature researches directly or indirectly talk about neighbor discovery, and many neighbor discovery protocols are constantly proposed. With the purpose of "shortening the total time of neighbor discovery", this paper focuses on the time slot optimization of neighbor discovery Hello-Reply phase in directional wireless Ad Hoc network.

© ICST Institute for Computer Sciences, Social Informatics and Telecommunications Engineering 2021
Published by Springer Nature Switzerland AG 2021. All Rights Reserved
Y.-B. Lin and D.-J. Deng (Eds.): SGIoT 2020, LNICST 354, pp. 468–486, 2021.
https://doi.org/10.1007/978-3-030-69514-9_36

According to the neighbor discovery protocols designed by scholars for wireless network discovery in recent years, it can be classified according to the following five conditions: (1) neighborhood discovery range; (2) antenna mode; (3) message reply mode; (4) clock state; (5) transmission/listening mode selection.

According to different neighbor scopes that nodes can discover, neighbor discovery protocols can be divided into direct and indirect neighbor discovery protocols. Ref. [4–6,10] all adopt direct neighbor discovery, that is, nodes can only discover their 1-hop neighbors through information exchange. A typical indirect neighbor discovery algorithm is the algorithm based on Gossip, and Ref. [16] is proposed on the basis of Gossip algorithm.

According to type of antenna in the network, neighbor discovery protocols can be divided into omnidirectional antenna, directional antenna and hybrid antenna protocols [15]. Hybrid antenna pattern is divided into directional-omnidirectional pattern and omnidirectional-directional pattern, the directional-omnidirectional pattern and omnidirectional pattern is two of the most common antenna combinations in wireless network, such as Ref. [4, 7] adopt directional antenna patterns, Ref. [8,10,17] involves the hybrid antenna pattern.

According to the way nodes respond to Hello messages, neighbor discovery protocols can be divided into Handshake-based and periodic poll response protocols. At present, Handshake-based methods account for the majority. In Ref. [4,6,9,13], two-way handshake are adopted, while in Ref. [14,17], three-way handshake are adopted.

According to clock state of nodes, neighbor discovery protocols can be divided into synchronous and asynchronous neighbor discovery protocols. Ref. [6–8,14,17] are all synchronous neighbor discovery algorithms. Nodes in the network need time synchronization. In asynchronous algorithm, the clock or interval sequence of different nodes is out of sync, so it is unnecessary to start neighbor discovery process at the same time, as shown in Ref. [11–13].

According to how nodes choose transmission or listening mode, neighbor discovery protocols can be divided into stochastic and deterministic neighbor discovery protocols. Ref. [4,8,17] are all stochastic algorithms, and certain probability is introduced in node state selection. Ref. [5] is a deterministic algorithm based on Disco protocol. Nodes select their own state according to pre-set rules. Neighbor discovery protocols in most literature can be divided into multiple categories simultaneously.

In the existing neighbor discovery protocol, it is also different in setting slot number per round in Hello-Reply phase. In SAND [1] and Q-SAND protocol [2], slot number is fixed. The slot number and discovery round are set in advance, and do not change with neighbor nodes. DANDi protocol [3] proposed a dynamic slot number adjustment algorithm, adopting the idea of exponential retreat, the initial slot number is 1. When collision slot number in this round is 0, discovery is completed. When collision slot number in this round is not 0, slot number in the next round is twice that of the current round, the round number is also constantly changing. Compared with the fixed slot number, the utilization rate of slot using the exponential retreat method is higher. Finding the same node requires less time slot, but there is still room for efficiency improvement.

In this regard, this paper proposes an optimal multi-round and multi-slot Hello-Reply algorithm, theoretically proves and deduces the total time and round number of neighbor discovery algorithm, effectively reducing the total neighbor discovery time, and combines the multi-round and multi-slot Hello-Reply algorithm with existing protocols to verify its feasibility and discovery efficiency. Combined with the simulation results, we give a simple fitting expression for discovery round number and time.

The rest of article is arranged as follows. In Sect. 2, we briefly introduce the system model and put forward the core issues to be solved in this paper. Section 3 introduces the multi-round and multi-slot Hello-Reply algorithm in this paper. After that, Sect. 4 conducts simulation and result analysis, and Sect. 5 summarizes this paper (Table 1).

2   System Model and Problem Modeling

Table 1. Symbol notation and meanings

Symbol notation	Symbol meanings
N	Total slave node number
S	Total slot number
R	Round number required by discovering all nodes
r	Current neighbor discovery rounds, $1 \leq r \leq R$
n_r	Slave node number in round r
s_r	Slot number in round r
n	Node number in the single round neighbor discovery
s	Slot number in the single round neighbor discovery
T	The total time required to discover all the nodes
t_h	The duration of the hello slot
t_r	The duration of the reply slot
N_E	The idle slot number after one round neighbor discovery
N_S	The success slot number after one round neighbor discovery
N_C	The collision slot number after one round neighbor discovery

2.1   System Model

In the Hello-Reply process of neighbor discovery, the master node establishes the connection between the two by sending hello message to slave node and receiving slave node's reply message. In the process of each Hello-Reply round, a Hello slot and several Reply slots form a frame. The frame length is determined by the Reply slot number N. Total rounds R of Hello-Reply is also a variable, which depends on slave node number to be found and Reply slot number in each round. Slot number per round is usually a series of discrete integers, for example, S could be $S = 2^k$, $S_1 < S_2 < \cdots < S_k < \cdots < S_K$, $1 \leq k \leq K$.

After the start of Hello-Reply in round r, the master node first transmits a Hello message to slave node in hello slot, which carrys the discovered slave node number and reply slot number s_r in this round. When the slave node receives the Hello message, it will check whether it has been found. If not, the slave node will randomly select a slot to reply Reply message in s_r reply slot, otherwise it will remain silent in this round.

After the slave node replies the Reply message, a reply slot may have three states:

Success: only one node selects this time slot to reply;

Idle: no node selects this time slot to reply;

Collision: two or more nodes select this time slot to reply.

When collision slot number is 0, it means that all slave nodes have been discovered by the master node, and the multiple rounds of Hello-Reply process neighbor discovery ends.

2.2 Problem Modeling

Assuming that hello slot duration is t_h and reply slot duration is t_r, the total time used by the Hello-Reply mechanism after round R can be expressed as

$$T = \sum_{x=1}^{R} (t_r s_x + t_h) = t_r \sum_{x=1}^{R} s_x + R t_h. \tag{1}$$

where t_h is one hello slot time required in round x, t_r is one reply slot time, and s_r is reply slot number required in round x. Our question is how to dynamically adjust the reply slot number per round to minimize time T needed to discover all neighbors.

3 Optimal Strategy

Theorem 1. *When reply slot number s_r per round is equal to remaining undiscovered slave node number n_r, the total time T required to find all slave nodes is minimum. At this point, the theoretical derivation of time T can be expressed as:*

$$\begin{cases} \text{Known } n_1 \text{ and } s_1 = n_1 \text{ (total number of slave nodes to be discovered)} \\ s_{r+1} = n_{r+1} = n_r - \sum_{x=0}^{n_r} x \cdot Q_x(n_r, s_r) \\ \text{if } n_{r+1} = 0 \text{ , then } R = r \\ T = \sum_{x=1}^{R} (t_r s_x + t_h) = t_r \sum_{x=1}^{R} s_x + R t_h \text{ .} \end{cases} \tag{2}$$

By fitting, time can be approximately expressed as

$$\begin{aligned} FittingTime = &round(2.702 \times N - 4.963) \times t_r \\ &+ round(0.045 \times N + 5.2728) \times t_h \text{ .} \end{aligned} \tag{3}$$

where, "round" means round off.

In the case that reply slot number s_r per round is equal to remaining undiscovered slave nodes number n_r, the theoretical derivation of round number R required to find all neighbors is as follows:

$$R = round\left(\frac{\lg(1/N)}{\lg(1 - 1/e)}\right). \tag{4}$$

Through data fitting, round number can be approximately expressed as

$$R = round(0.4581 \times (\lg N)^2 + 3.561 \times \lg N + 1.01). \tag{5}$$

where, "round" means round off.

In single-round neighbor discovery problem, if slave node number to be found is known, the maximum slot utilization and relationship between slot number and node number can be obtained by changing reply slot number S, that is, when $S = N$, the maximum slot utilization can be obtained. By popularizing the node discovery in a single round, we can get the value of reply slot number s_r in each round in the multi-round neighbor discovery, which can maximize total utilization rate of slot and minimize node discovery time, thus, the round number needed to find all nodes and the required minimum time can be derived theoretically.

It can be proved that in the single-round neighbor discovery, when reply slot number S is equal to slave node number N to be found, utilization rate of slot is the highest, and the maximum slot utilization decreases from 1 to $\frac{1}{e}$ with the node number increasing, as shown in Lemma 1. Extended to multi-round neighbor discovery, it can be proved that when reply slot number s_r per round is equal to the remaining undiscovered slave nodes number n_r, total slot utilization rate is the highest and node discovery time is the minimum, as shown in Lemma 2, and the theoretical derivation expression of round number required for discovery of all nodes and the minimum time required can be obtained. For the convenience of representation, it can be simulated and fitted, as shown in Lemma 3 and Lemma 4.

3.1 Neighbor Discovery of Single Round

Lemma 1. *In the single-round neighbor discovery problem, when reply slot number S is equal to slave node number N to be found, slot utilization is the highest, and the maximum slot utilization gradually decreases from 1 to $\frac{1}{e}$ as the node number increases. When $n \to \infty$, slot utilization approaches $\frac{1}{e}$, and when $n \to 1$, slot utilization approaches 1.*

Given the slot number S and the node number N, the probability of any slot being selected by the node and successfully sending reply packet can be shown, that is, the utilization rate of slot. By changing slot number and analyzing slot utilization rate expression, the relationship between slot number S and node number N can be obtained when slot utilization is at its maximum.

We use n to represent the node number to be discovered and S to represent the slot number available for the Reply message in the Hello-Reply process. When the master node sends Hello packet, the slave node receiving Hello packet will choose any slot to reply. There are three states of slot: success, collision and idle, among which the successful slot is also called discovery slot, so the probability of any slot is discovery slot $P(n, s)$ is

$$P(n, s) = \binom{n}{1} \left(\frac{1}{s}\right) \left(1 - \frac{1}{s}\right)^{n-1} . \tag{6}$$

$\frac{1}{s}$ means the possibility that a node randomly chooses one of s slots.

From $\frac{\partial P(n,s)}{\partial s} = 0$ and $\frac{\partial P(n,s)}{\partial s^2} < 0$, when $s = n$ and $n > 1$, $P(n, s)$ gets the maximum. Substitute $s = n$ into $P(n, s)$:

$$P(n, s)|_{s=n} = n \cdot \frac{1}{n} \cdot (1 - \frac{1}{n})^{n-1} = (1 - \frac{1}{n})^{n-1} . \tag{7}$$

When $n \to \infty$, let $\frac{1}{n} = -x$, get:

$$\lim_{n \to \infty} (1 - \frac{1}{n})^n \times (1 - \frac{1}{n})^{-1} = \lim_{x \to 0} (1 + x)^{-\frac{1}{x}} = \frac{1}{e} . \tag{8}$$

When $n \to 1$,

$$\lim_{n \to 1} (1 - \frac{1}{n})^{n-1} = \lim_{n \to 1} e^{(n-1)\ln(1-\frac{1}{n})} = e^{\lim_{n \to 1}(n-1)\ln(1-\frac{1}{n})} = e^0 = 1 . \tag{9}$$

That is, when slot number is equal to node number to be discovered, the probability of any slot to be discovery slot is the highest, and when n approaches ∞, the probability of any slot to be discovery slot is equal to $\frac{1}{e}$. As n approaches 1, the probability of any slot to be discovery slot gradually increases to 1.

Let $num(n, s)$ represent the maximum node number that is found in one round when node number to be discovered is n and slot number is s. $num(n, s)$ is expressed as

$$num(n, s) = \begin{cases} n & \text{if } n \le s \\ s - 1 & \text{if } n > s . \end{cases} \tag{10}$$

In the round of Hello-Reply containing s slots, the probability of discovering one node among n nodes is

$$Q_1(n, s) = C_s^1 P(n, s) L(n - 1, s - 1) . \tag{11}$$

$L(n - 1, s - 1)$ means the probability that all other $(s - 1)$ slots are not discovery slot, $P(n, s)$ means the probability that any slot is discovery slot, and C_s^1 is the way that this slot is selected. In one round of Hello-Reply, the probability of finding x nodes ($1 \le x \le num(n, s)$) is expressed as

$$Q_x(n, s) = \begin{cases} 1 & \text{if } n = 1 \\ 0 & \text{if } n \le s \ \& \ x = n - 1 \\ C_s^x \left[\prod_{k=0}^{x-1} P(n - k, s - k)\right] & \\ \times L(n - x, s - x) & \text{Otherwise .} \end{cases} \tag{12}$$

where, $L(n - x, s - x)$ represents the probability that no slot is discovery slot in the remaining $(s - x)$ slots, which can be expressed as:

$$L(n - x, s - x) = Q_0(n - x, s - x) = 1 - \sum_{j=1}^{num(n-x,s-x)} q_j(n - x, s - x) .\quad (13)$$

The expected node number to be found in an average round is:

$$E[n] = \sum_{x=0}^{n} x \cdot Q_x(n, s) .\quad (14)$$

The slot utilization of one round can also be expressed as

$$\eta_s = \frac{\sum_{x=0}^{n} x \cdot Q_x(n, s)}{s} .\quad (15)$$

The relationship between slot utilization and the probability that any slot is a discovery slot:

The probability that any one slot can successfully discover a node is $P(n, s)$, then discovery node number per round is $P(n, s) \times s$, and slot utilization rate is $\frac{P(n,s) \times s}{s} = P(n, s)$. Therefore, the probability that any one slot is a discovery slot is the slot utilization rate. In the same way, when the slot number is equal to node number to be discovered, slot utilization rate is the largest, and when n is large enough, the probability that any one slot is a discovery slot is equal to $\frac{1}{e}$.

3.2   Neighbor Discovery Efficiency of Multiple Rounds

Lemma 2. *In the multi-round neighbor discovery, when reply slot number s_r per round is equal to the remaining undiscovered slave node number n_r, the total utilization rate of slot is the highest and node discovery time is the shortest.*

Neighbor discovery often cannot end in one round. In the case of multiple rounds, r represents the total round number required, n_r represents the node number to be discovered corresponding to round r, and s_r represents the slot number required for round r. The node number that can be found in round r can be expressed as

$$E[n_r] = \sum_{x=0}^{n_r} x \cdot Q_x(n_r, s_r) .\quad (16)$$

Then the slot utilization rate in round r is

$$\eta_{sr} = \frac{\sum_{x=0}^{n_r} x \cdot Q_x(n_r, s_r)}{s_r} .\quad (17)$$

It can be known from the derivation in Sect. 3.1 that the probability that any one slot is a discovery slot is the slot utilization rate, so the slot utilization rate in round r can also be expressed as

$$P(n_r, s_r) = n_r \times \frac{1}{s_r}\left(1 - \frac{1}{s_r}\right)^{n_r-1}. \tag{18}$$

Then the slot utilization of multiple rounds of neighbor discovery is

$$\eta = \frac{\sum\limits_{r=1}^{R} s_r \times P(n_r, s_r)}{\sum\limits_{r=1}^{R} s_r}. \tag{19}$$

where $\sum\limits_{r=1}^{R} s_r \times P(n_r, s_r)$ represents the total number of nodes, denoted by N, then the above formula can be written as

$$\eta = \frac{N}{\sum\limits_{r=1}^{R} s_r}. \tag{20}$$

where, N is the total node number, and it is a fixed value. From single-round neighbor discovery process, when $s_r = n_r$, the slot utilization $P(n_r, s_r)$ is the largest, the discovery of same node number requires fewer slots. For multiple rounds Neighbor discovery, for the same reason, when the total node number to be discovered N is equal, when each round $s_r = n_r$, the total slot number required to discover all nodes is the least, the slot utilization is the highest, and the required discovery time is the shortest.

It is known from Sect. 3.1 that when $s_r = n_r$, the slot utilization rate of each round is the largest, and the maximum slot utilization maximum value is 1, the minimum value is $\frac{1}{e}$. As the node number increases, the slot utilization rate gradually decreases and approaching $\frac{1}{e}$. That is, in the slot utilization rate found by multiple rounds of neighbors, the slot utilization rate $P(n_r, s_r)$ of each round satisfies

$$\frac{1}{e} \leq P(n_r, s_r) \leq 1. \tag{21}$$

Assuming the total slave node number is ∞, that is $n_1 = \infty$, then

$$\eta = \frac{\frac{1}{e}\sum\limits_{r=1}^{R} s_r k_r}{\sum\limits_{r=1}^{R} s_r}. \tag{22}$$

$$e \geq k_r = \frac{P(n_r, s_r)}{1/e} \geq 1 (r = 1, 2, \cdots, R), 1 = k_1 < k_2 < \cdots < k_r = e. \tag{23}$$

Therefore, the efficiency of neighbor discovery in multiple rounds

$$\frac{1}{e} < \eta < 1 . \tag{24}$$

In actual applications, the total slave node number tends not to tend to ∞. In this case, the actual multi-round node discovery efficiency will be larger.

3.3   Neighbor Discovery Round of Multiple Rounds

Lemma 3. *When the reply slot number s_r per round is equal to remaining undiscovered slave node number n_r, the theoretical derivation of the round number required to find all nodes can be expressed as $R = round\left(\frac{\lg(1/N)}{\lg(1-1/e)}\right)$ and can be fitted as $R = round\,(0.4581 \times (\lg N)^2 + 3.561 \times \lg N + 1.01)$.*

Let the total node number to be discovered be N, and slot number s_r and node number to be discovered n_r of each round remain the same, that is $n_r = s_r$. As can be seen from Sect. 3.1, when n_r of each round is large enough, the slot utilization rate of each round is $\frac{1}{e}$, then the node number that is found in the rth round is s_r/e, which can also be expressed as n_r/e, and the remaining node number to be found is $n_r(1-1/e)$. After R rounds, the remaining nodes number to be found is $N(1-1/e)^R$. If all nodes are discovered after neighbor discovery ends, it should satisfy

$$N(1 - 1/e)^R < 1 . \tag{25}$$

that is

$$R > \frac{\lg(1/N)}{\lg(1 - 1/e)} . \tag{26}$$

Since round number R is an integer, the above formula can be rounded to obtain

$$R = round\left(\frac{\lg(1/N)}{\lg(1 - 1/e)}\right) = round(5.02 \times \lg N) . \tag{27}$$

where, "round" means round off.

In order to facilitate the representation and application of neighbor discovery time and round number, the simulation data of discovery time and round number obtained by simulation is fitted.

As the round number grows slowly with nodes number, it is generally in a step shape. In order to facilitate fitting, Node number N is the logarithm to base 10, total round number is represented by R, and the linear fitting expression of $\lg N$ and round number R is

$$R = 4.771 \times \lg N + 0.3413 . \tag{28}$$

The quadratic fitting expression is

$$R = 0.4581 \times (\lg N)^2 + 3.561 \times \lg N + 1.01 . \tag{29}$$

3.4   Neighbor Discovery Time of Multiple Rounds

Lemma 4. *When reply slot number in each round is equal to node number to be found in this round n_r, hello slot duration is t_h and reply slot duration is t_r, then the minimum time required by discovering all nodes can be fitted as*

$$
\begin{aligned}
FittingTime = & \ round(2.702 \times N - 4.963) \times t_r \\
& + round(0.045 \times N + 5.2728) \times t_h .
\end{aligned}
\tag{30}
$$

When the slot number s_r in each round changes with the remaining node number n_r, and $n_r = s_r$ is maintained, the node number to be found in the next round and slot number required are

$$
s_{r+1} = n_{r+1} = n_r - \sum_{x=0}^{n_r} x \cdot Q_x(n_r, s_r) .
\tag{31}
$$

n_r and s_r are the node number to be discovered and the required slot number corresponding to the rth round.

When $n_{r+1} = 0$, it indicates that node number to be found in the next round is 0, that is, all nodes have been discovered, and r at this time is the round number R required to find all nodes.

Suppose the duration of the hello slot is t_h, the duration of the reply slot is t_r, the time required to pass the R round is

$$
T = \sum_{x=1}^{R} (t_r s_x + t_h) .
\tag{32}
$$

The pseudo-code is used to represent the above discovery time calculation process. The algorithm is as follows.

First of all, we set the time slot length of both sending request packet and receiving reply as 1. After simulation, the time and round number needed for node discovery of different numbers are obtained, and node discovery time is fitted with known data. We can get linear fitting time at this point is

$$
T_1 = 2.747 \times N + 0.3098 .
\tag{33}
$$

N is total node number.

The fitting time T_1 at this point includes slot used by Hello package and slot used by Reply package. Since each round the primary node sends a Hello packet, neighbor discovery round number is the slot number used by the Hello packet.

Subtract round number from the total discovery time to get the time used without Hello package, and then conduct the fitting again. At this point, the fitting discovery time is

$$
T_2 = 2.702 \times N - 4.963 .
\tag{34}
$$

The total fitting discovery time expression is

$$
FittingTime = T_2 \times t_r + (T_1 - T_2) \times t_h .
\tag{35}
$$

Algorithm 1. DiscoveyTime (Notes, Slots) : For a given n and S, when slot number per round is equal to node number to be discovered, the round number and time required by discovering all nodes and the slot number per round.

Input: $N_{initial}$, t_r, t_h
Output: SumTime, Slots[], Round

1: **begin procedure**
2: Notes[1] = $N_{initial}$
3: /*The array format stores the number of slots required per round*/
4: Slots[1] = Notes[1]
5: x = 1
6: /*Round number in a while loop*/
7: **while** ($Notes[x] \neq 0$) **do**
8:      /*Node number to be found in the next round = node number to be found in the current round - node number already found in the current round*/
9:      /*round off*/
10:     Notes[x+1] = Notes[x] - round($\displaystyle\sum_{j=0}^{Notes[x]} k \times q_j(Notes[x], Slots[x])$)
11:     Slots[x+1] = Notes[x+1]
12:     x = x + 1
13: **end while**
14: Round = x - 1 /*Get round number needed*/
15: SumTime = 0
16: **for** r = 1:Round **do**
17:     /*Calculate the total time*/
18:     SumTime = SumTime + (Slots(r) * t_r + t_h)
19: **end for**
20: **end procedure**

By substituting the specific expressions of T_1 and T_2, it can be obtained that:

$$FittingTime = round(2.702 \times N - 4.963) \times t_r$$
$$+ round(0.045 \times N + 5.2728) \times t_h . \tag{36}$$

where: t_r is the length of a reply slot and t_h is the length of a hello slot.

3.5   Application of Multi-round and Multi-slot Hello-Reply Algorithm

In order to verify the application of Hello-Reply algorithm in this paper, this section applies the multi-round and multi-slot Hello-Reply algorithm on the basis of Q-SAND protocol [2]. In Hello-Reply phase of the Q-SAND protocol, a fixed pattern with 5 rounds of neighbor discovery and 5 reply slots per round is used. The DANDi protocol [3] adopts the idea of exponential retreat and the initial number of slots is 1. When collision slot number in this round is 0, node discovery is completed; when collision slot number in this round is not 0, the slot number in the next round is twice that of the current round, and the node discovery round is not set. When using the dynamic slot number selection algorithm in this article, the reply slot and node discovery round numbers are set as follows: The first round of node discovery reply slots in the Hello-Reply phase is set to 5, which is consistent with Q-SAND, in each subsequent round of node discovery, the slot number is determined by the previous round of node discovery, that is, the total node number is estimated by the successful number, idle, and collision slots for node discovery, thereby determining the next round of response number of slots. Another way to set slot number is to set slot number in the first Hello-Reply round to 1, consistent with DANDi, and the slot number per subsequent round is decided by the exact total node number minus the discovered node number. The node discovery round number is not set in advance. When all nodes are discovered, the node discovery process ends.

The node estimation method adopts Chen estimation method [18]. That is, in a round of node discovery with the slot number L, after the node discovery is completed, there are N_E idle slots and N_S successful slots, and the probability of N_C collision slots is:

$$P(N_E, N_S, N_C) = \frac{L!}{N_E! N_S! N_C!} p_e^E p_s^S p_c^C . \tag{37}$$

Among them, p_e, p_s, p_c respectively represent the idle, successful and collision slot probability when a node is discovered, and its expression is:

$$p_e = (1 - (1/L))^n . \tag{38}$$

$$p_s = (n/L)(1 - (1/L))^{n-1} . \tag{39}$$

$$p_c = 1 - p_s - p_e . \tag{40}$$

For a node discovery round with a slot number of L, the posterior distribution probability can be obtained. Under the environment of n nodes to be discovered, when there are N_E idle slots and N_S successful slots, collision slot number N_C can be obtained, and its expression is as follows:

$$P(n|N_E, N_S, N_C) = \frac{L!}{N_E! N_S! N_C!} \times \left[\left(1 - \frac{1}{L} \right)^n \right]^{N_E}$$

$$\times \left[\frac{n}{L} \left(1 - \frac{1}{L} \right)^{n-1} \right]^{N_S} \times \left[1 - \left(1 - \frac{1}{L} \right)^n - \frac{n}{L} \left(1 - \frac{1}{L} \right)^{n-1} \right]^{N_C} . \tag{41}$$

According to the posterior distribution, when the above formula reaches the maximum, the estimated value of the node is the best.

The pseudo codes for node estimation and slot number selection are as follows.

Algorithm 2. Node estimation and slot number selection.

1: Round = 1, Slots[1] = 5, After a round, get N_E, N_S and N_C
2: **if** $N_C = 0$ **then**
3:     Node discovery complete.
4: **else**
5:     Calculate the maximum value of n for $P(n|N_E, N_S, N_C)$.
6:     Round = Round + 1
7:     /*Remaining node number to be discovered, and rounded up*/
8:     Slots[Round] = [n N_S]
9: **end if**

---

4   Simulation and Analysis

In the Sect. 3, in order to facilitate the representation and application of the discovery round number and discovery time of multiple round nodes, it is fitted according to the simulation data. In this section, compare the dynamic slot selection method in this paper with the fixed slot number per round, that is, the slot number always takes the initial slave node number to be found. For example, when the total node number is 100, slot number in each round is 100, and specific round number is determined by the neighbor discovery situation. Finally, the Hello-Reply proposed in this paper is applied to the Q-SAND protocol to verify its neighbor discovery efficiency. This paper uses C++ simulation platform.

4.1   Neighbor Discovery Rounds Simulation

Firstly, fitting round number at different node counts is compared with actual rounds obtained by simulation to verify rationality of the fitting formula. The results are shown in Fig. 1.

As shown in Fig. 1, in the case that the slots number s_r is fixed, except that the number of slots s_r in the first round is equivalent to the number of nodes n_r, the rest of the slot each round number compared with the node number is larger, so while the slot utilization rate each round is low, but the node number can be found in each round is more than $s_r = n_r$, so neighbor discovery need less number of rounds, but the overall trend is consistent with the $s_r = n_r$, with the increase of the nodes number and ladder shaped growth. In the case of $s_r = n_r$, when the node number N is small, the rounds number fitting value and simulation value is appropriate, when N is large, there will be an error value of 1 in the round number of some nodes, and compared with those of linear quadratic has higher accuracy, namely when the node number is equal to the slot number per round, the node number and round relations can be expressed as follows:

$$R = 0.4581 \times (\lg N)^2 + 3.561 \times \lg N + 1.01 . \tag{42}$$

4.2   Neighbor Discovery Time Simulation

Let $t_r = 1$ and $t_h = 1$. Compare the fitting slots and simulation slots to verify the rationality of the fitting formula. The results are shown in Fig. 2.

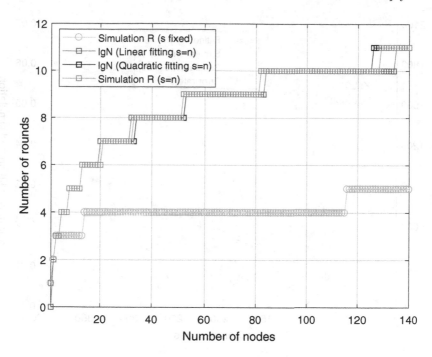

Fig. 1. Number of fitting rounds and simulation rounds at different nodes number

As shown in Fig. 2 that when slot number per round is equal to node number to be found per round, the node discovery time is far less than the number of fixed slot, and the performance is improved by about 50%. When the slot number is fixed, when the node number increases to a certain value, the discovery round number will increase by one round, causing the node discovery time to jump, as shown in the figure with the node number 110 and 120. When $s_r = n_r$ in each round, when $N = 20$, error rate of fitting time is the largest, the maximum error rate is 0.0587. According to the theoretical derivation in Sect. 4.2, slot utilization ratio is equal to $\frac{1}{e}$, which is obtained under the premise of $n \to \infty$. When N is small, there will be a certain error, and when N is small, node discovery time is small, and a small error will also cause a large error rate. Therefore, when N is small, error rate of fitting and simulation results is high. When N is greater than 90, error rate is basically stable below 0.01, that is, the fitting time formula has high accuracy.

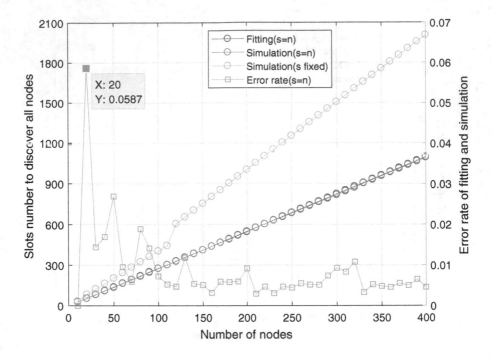

Fig. 2. Comparison of fitting time and simulation time and error rate for different number of nodes ($t_h = 1$, $t_r = 1$)

4.3   Application of Multi-round Multi-slot Hello-Reply Algorithm in Q-SAND

In this section, the application of the proposed multi-round and multi-slot Hellow-Reply algorithm in Q-SAND is simulated and verified, and compared with the Q-SAND protocol and DANDi protocol. The simulation parameters and network scenario settings in the protocol are shown in Table 2 and Table 3 respectively.

The node position is randomly set in a certain region. When neighbor discovery is conducted, the randomly generated nodes are required to form a connected network topology. If there are random isolated nodes, or if there is more than one network topology, the resulting network topology is discarded and does not count in the statistical results.

Under the same simulation parameters and network scenes, the node number is changed to simulate the neighbor discovery time in network.

Figure 3 shows the simulation discovery time with fixed slot number, DANDi, and variable slot number under Q-SAND protocol for different node number. To ensure the universality of the results, we randomly generate 20 kinds of network topologies for the same node number, and average the simulation results.

Table 2. Protocol simulation parameters

The stage of the node	Parameter	Value
FastScan mode	t_{switch}	3 ms
Hone-In mode	t_{HoneIn}	1.5 ms
	h	12
Hello-Reply mode(Q-SAND)	N_{slots}	5
	N_{rounds}	5
	t_{slots}	1.5 ms
Token Passing mode	$t_{GoToFastScan}$	1.5 ms

Table 3. Network scene parameter setting

Network scene setting	Value
Node distribution region	500 * 500
Maximum single hop communication distance	100
Number of sectors per node	6
Network simulation times with same nodes number	20

As can be seen from Fig. 3, compared with the original Q-SAND protocol with fixed slot, the node discovery time of Q-SAND protocol using the slot number variable algorithm proposed in this paper is reduced by about 50%, which is consistent with the neighbor discovery time in Hello-Reply phase in Sect. 4.2. Node discovery efficiency of the network is greatly improved. Meanwhile, when the node number is accurate, compared with DANDi, when the total node number in network topology is small, the number of neighbor node will also be small, the discovery time is both similar. As the neighbor node number increased, advantage of time-slot number variable algorithm presented in this paper gradually emerged, and discovery time is lower than DANDi protocol, and the gap increases gradually. When the node number in topology is 256, compared with DANDi protocol, the neighbor discovery time of slot number variable algorithm in this paper is reduced by approximately 25%. When node estimation is introduced, due to the large impact of estimation error when the node number is relatively small, the o-MRMS neighbor discovery time is slightly larger than DANDi, and with the node number increasing, the o-MRMS node discovery time is gradually smaller than DANDi protocol.

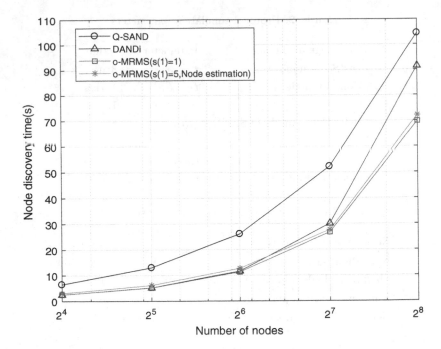

Fig. 3. Comparison of discovery time of various time slot selection methods under Q-SAND protocol

5   Summary and Future Outlook

In this article, we have conducted study on the neighbor discovery. Theoretical deduction proves that when the reply slots number per round is equal to the node number to be discovered, the slot utilization is the highest and the node discovery time is the shortest. Through simulation, the fitting expression of node discovery round and node discovery time is given, and the fitting expression is compared with the simulation data to verify the accuracy of the fitting expression. At the same time, we combine the proposed o-MRMS algorithm with existing protocols to verify its feasibility. Compared with Q-SAND protocol, node discovery efficiency is improved by about 50%. Compared with the DANDi protocol, which node discovery to be more efficient, when the network node number is greater than 250, efficiency can be increased by more than 25%, and the greater the node number, the greater the efficiency increase.

In wireless self-organizing network neighbor discovery, in order to improve the efficiency of discovery, often need to dynamically change the Reply time slot number in Hello-Reply phase, but there are so many ways to change, so how to choose is a question. Through this paper, reader can get an optimal selection method for slot number. Through the node number in the network, we can calculate the reply slot number each round and obtain the optimal way for dynamic change of slot, so as to improve the efficiency of system. Under the condition of known node number, this paper gives the fitting formula of discovery round number and total discovery time, can do not need to simulation, only for simple operation, convenient to calculate round and time for discovering all nodes roughly, so as to serve as a reference.

For the node discovery time fitting formula, there will be some error when the node number is small. Whether the accurate expression of neighbor discovery time can be obtained is an issue we need to consider in the future.

Acknowledgement. This work was supported in part by Science and Technology on Avionics Integration Laboratory and the Aeronautical Science Foundation of China (Grant No.201955053002), the National Natural Science Foundations of CHINA (Grant No.61871322, No.61771392, No.61771390, and No.61501373), and Science and Technology on Avionics Integration Laboratory and the Aeronautical Science Foundation of China (Grant No.20185553035).

References

1. Felemban, E., Murawski, R., Ekici, E., et al.: SAND: sectored-antenna neighbor discovery protocol for wireless networks. In: 2010 7th Annual IEEE Communications Society Conference on Sensor. Mesh and Ad Hoc Communications and Networks (SECON), Boston MA, pp. 1–9 (2010)
2. Gammarano, N., Schandy, J., Steinfeld, L.: Q-SAND: a quick neighbor discovery protocol for wireless networks with sectored antennas. In: 2018 Ninth Argentine Symposium and Conference on Embedded Systems (CASE), Cordoba, pp. 19–24 (2018)
3. Gammarano, N., Schandy, J., Steinfeld, L.: DANDi: dynamic asynchronous neighbor discovery protocol for directional antennas. In: VIII Brazilian Symposium on Computing Systems Engineering, pp. 16–23 (2018)
4. Ji, D., Wei, Z., Chen, X., et al.: Radar-communication integrated neighbor discovery for wireless ad hoc networks. In: 2019 11th International Conference on Wireless Communications and Signal Processing (WCSP), Xi'an, China, pp. 1–5 (2019)
5. Gao, M., Shen, R., Mu, L., et al.: An anti-collision neighbor discovery protocol for multi-node discovery. In: 2019 11th International Conference on Wireless Communications and Signal Processing (WCSP), Xi'an, China, pp. 1–5 (2019)
6. Yang, A., Li, B., Yan, Z., et al.: A bi-directional carrier sense collision avoidance neighbor discovery algorithm in directional wireless ad hoc sensor networks. Sensors **19**(9), 2120–2138 (2019)
7. Liu, B., Rong, B., Hu, R., et al.: Neighbor discovery algorithms in directional antenna based synchronous and asynchronous wireless ad hoc networks. IEEE Wirel. Commun. **20**(6), 106–112 (2013)
8. Mir, Z., Jung, W., Ko, Y.: Continuous neighbor discovery protocol in wireless ad hoc networks with sectored-antennas. In: 2015 IEEE 29th International Conference on Advanced Information Networking and Applications, Gwangiu, pp. 54–61 (2015)
9. Cai, H., Liu, B., Gui, L., et al.: Neighbor discovery algorithms in wireless networks using directional antennas. In: 2012 IEEE International Conference on Communications (ICC), Ottawa, ON, pp. 767–772 (2012)
10. Mir, Z., Ko, Y.: Self-adaptive neighbor discovery in wireless sensor networks with sectored-antennas. Comput. Stand. Interfaces **70**, 1–16 (2020)

11. Murawski, R., Felemban, E., Ekici, E., et al.: Neighbor discovery in wireless networks with sectored antennas. Ad Hoc Netw. **10**(1), 1–18 (2012)
12. Wang, Y., Liu, B., Gui, L.: Adaptive scan-based asynchronous neighbor discovery in wireless networks using directional antennas. In: WCSP 2013: Proceedings of the International Conference on Wireless Communications and Signal Processing, Piscataway, N.J., pp. 1–6. IEEE (2013)
13. Tian, F., Hu, R., Qian, Y, et al.: Pure asynchronous neighbor discovery algorithms in ad hoc networks using directional antennas. In: 2013 IEEE Global Communications Conference (GLOBECOM), Atlanta, GA, pp. 498–503 (2014)
14. Li, J., Peng, L., Ye, Y., et al.: A neighbor discovery algorithm in network of radar and communication integrated system. In: 2014 IEEE 17th International Conference on Computational Science and Engineering, Chengdu, pp. 1142–1149 (2014)
15. Dai, H., Ng, K., Li, M., et al.: An overview of using directional antennas in wireless networks. Int. J. Commun. Syst. **26**(4), 413–448 (2013)
16. Astudillo, G., Kadoch, M.: Neighbor discovery and routing schemes for mobile ad-hoc networks with beam width adaptive smart antennas. Telecommun. Syst. Model. Analy. Des. Manag. **66**(1), 17–27 (2017)
17. Zhang, Z., Li, B.: Neighbor discovery in mobile ad hoc self-configuring networks with directional antennas: algorithms and comparisons. IEEE Trans. Wirel. Commun. **7**(5), 1540–1549 (2008)
18. Chen, W.T.: An accurate tag estimate method for improving the performance of an RFID anticollision algorithm based on dynamic frame length ALOHA. IEEE Trans. Automat. ENCE Eng. **6**(1), 9–15 (2009)

Develop an Intelligent Hierarchical Alert Mechanism for Elderly Residential Institutions

Lun-Ping Hung[1]([⊠]), Zong-Jie Wu[1], Chiang-Shih Chun[1], Shih-Chieh Li[1], and Chien-Liang Chen[2]

[1] Department of Information Management, National Taipei University of Nursing and Health Sciences, Taipei, Taiwan, R.O.C.
lunping@ntunhs.edu.tw
[2] Department of Innovative Living Design, Overseas Chinese University, Taichung, Taiwan

Abstract. The tsunami of aging is coming making the population structure in Taiwan to change drastically. The elderly population with disability quickly rising which is accompanied by the doubling of the problem care. Family members who cannot be there with their elders due to economic burden send them to boarding typing institutions. Traditional medical care model cannot effectively manage due to limitations in deficient professional medical labor and medical resources resulting in the enigma of increasing social cost. In light of the fast development of information technology, that many innovative and cross-field applications can now be effectively placed into clinical institutions to enhance medical treatment efficiency and expand the scope of policy have become an important key. The research will bring in the basic concept of IoT and deploy medical grade IoT modules combined with communication transmission technology through edge computing connecting phasal warning mechanism to attempt to deploy deeply into clinical situation simulation to help the elderly self-examine their own health status on a regular basis in order to construct an appropriate model for health care and to reduce the waste of overcentralized social resources in large medical institutions for creating a life-protecting, protection, health care elderly care life environment so the institutional caring quality can be increased and that the combination of medical care for establishing a healthy elderly society.

Keywords: Internet of Things · Edge computing · Long-term care · Institutional care · Multichannel gateway

1 Introduction

The aging tsunami has brought about drastic changes in Taiwan's population structure. According to the assessment report released by the National Development Council in August 2020 [1], it is estimated that the elderly population over 65 years old will reach 20.6% of the total population in 2025, which means that one in every five people will be elderly over 65 years old. A rapid increase in the number of elderly people leads to a growing shortage of care resources. Many families send elders to care institutions

Y.-B. Lin and D.-J. Deng (Eds.): SGIoT 2020, LNICST 354, pp. 487–499, 2021.
https://doi.org/10.1007/978-3-030-69514-9_37

because they cannot live with them due to work or other factors. Due to the shortage of professional medical personnel and the limited use of medical resources, the traditional medical model cannot bear the impact of the aging trend, and the failure to effectively manage will lead to the increase of social costs. In recent years, information and communication technology and Internet of Things technology have made continuous progress. Innovative and cross-disciplinary applications of ICT will be effectively applied in the clinical care environment. In addition to improving the efficiency of medical care, it can also expand the application scope of medical information in line with policies.

According to the development of IoT applied in healthcare technology, Delghith et al. divided Medical IoT into application IoT and service IoT [2]. Sensors are embedded in health devices, and data are transmitted to professional medical care personnel through wireless transmission, so as to make analysis or provide suggestions for users. The universality and convenience of IoT can be effectively applied in the medical field to help the elderly solve problems in life, such as care.

However, there is no significant benefit to the care environment only through the intervention of existing IoT equipment. At present, there are different brands of equipment on the market, so it is not easy to combine them. When data tracking of physiological monitoring is needed, there are a variety of different brands of equipment to choose from, and the wireless communication mode among equipment manufacturers is different, resulting in the consumption of more human resources in the management and use. Therefore, it is the most urgent task to standardize the management of healthcare-related devices, to pay attention to the status of the elderly at any time by virtue of the real-time monitoring achieved through the IoT, and to construct a healthy and safe care environment.

This study intends to use a multi-dimensional gateway to establish a universal wireless communication transmission switching mechanism and design the edge computing effect, so as to disperse the real-time data received. This will not only reduce the burden on cloud systems, but also enable important data related to life safety to be processed, judged and analyzed quickly. The medical-level IoT module can be combined with communication transmission technology to gradually deploy into the clinical setting. In addition to the regular health examination, the care unit can also track the physiological status of the elderly at any time. Moreover, a real-time warning can be achieved through the edge computing effect to build an appropriate medical care model and reduce the excessive concentration of social resources in large medical institutions, thus improving the quality of care, and providing a friendly living environment for the elderly combined with medical care.

2   Literature Review

2.1   Smart Medicine

The development of IoT has brought powerful effects to the new medical environment. For example, in a general medical clinic or nursing environment, IoT technologies have been used for intervention and monitoring through the public network. Although these devices face the challenges of security and privacy, they will bring significant benefits to the medical field [3]. Tarouco et al. proposed in 2012 that in the home-based care/monitoring project for patients with chronic diseases of REMOA, the interoperability and security of the Internet of Things can be used to transmit the data to the cloud care system through the bridge equipment of the gateway intermediary layer for data calculation and threshold policy alarm, so as to effectively protect the real-time and low-cost healthcare environment of patients, family members and medical units [4].

2.2 Multichannel Wireless Transmission

The diversity of communication protocols in the Internet of Things leads to the dilemma of wireless communication between devices and the cloud. To realize barrier-free communication between different protocols for data transmission and communication exchange in clinical practice, Wi-Fi, BLE, ZigBee and Sigfox protocols were mainly used in this study. In order to achieve interoperability through four kinds of communication transmission, relevant foreign successful cases were found. For example, Amiruddin et al. built three kinds of communication protocol tools in a multi-communication gateway. After the IoT device is connected to the gateway, corresponding wireless transmission selection is made for the communication protocols used by various IoT devices, and data received by the three different communication protocols are integrated after selection [5]. In 2018, Vargas et al. proposed the design of the gateway interface layer. The interface layer contains (1) data conversion: JSON is used as the data format standard; (2) data processing: message processing is used to reduce delay time; (3) protocol conversion: corresponding, selecting and using is carried out according to different communication protocols; (4) data storage: the device data is uploaded to the cloud, and the data is uploaded to the database for cloud computing and data storage on the server through the Ethernet communication protocol using the TCP/IP transmission mode [6]. In 2015, Al-Fuqaha et al. introduced the technology, protocol and procedure of the Internet of Things, and explained the cooperation between different communication protocols and their application in the Internet of Things service [7]. In 2016, Marinčić described the problem of signal interference in different communication protocols. To ensure that these communications did not interact with each other leading to signal loss or confusion, SMAMCAT was used to analyze the sensitivity differences among these communications [8].

2.3 Edge Computing

With the rapid growth of IoT services, the amount of data used in sensing devices for healthcare has increased and become more complex. Based on the decentralized execution effect of edge computing, it uses similar functions of devices to help respond to critical needs and eliminate redundant data before cloud computing, and sends the filtered data to the cloud for complex analysis or permanent storage. This can not only reduce the complexity of data transmission, but also save power and reduce latency [9, 10]. In the field of healthcare, it is necessary to ensure the stable physiological state of users at any time, which is very sensitive to the response time. Therefore, it is necessary to use edge computing to build a communication architecture with high real-time response, so as to provide a fast, convenient and efficient notification mechanism.

In 2017, based on the concept of the Internet of Things, Gia et al. used the health monitoring system to track personal physiological status, and embedded edge computing effect into the gateway to enhance the physiological data obtained by the system from the sensor, and transmit the data to the gateway through specific wireless communication to solve the delay problem, and then transmit the complex tasks to the cloud server for calculation and processing. The results show that edge computing intervention is helpful to improve system efficiency and provide a real-time response with low latency to network edge architecture [11].

Table 2 shows a comparison between cloud computing and edge computing [12, 13]. Although cloud computing has good analytical capability and hardware resources, edge computing is more suitable for the environment of healthcare IoT due to its characteristics of the distributed load and fast response. It can speed up emergency notifications by spreading out tasks, and effectively reduce the burden of centralized computing in the cloud.

Table 1. Comparison table of cloud computing and edge computing

	Cloud computing	Edge computing
Response time	Minutes to weeks	Milliseconds to minutes
Data analysis	Aggregate analysis	Partial analysis
Geographical coverage	Global	Region
Hardware resources	Sufficient computing resources and storage space	Limited computing resources and storage space
Distributed load	No	Yes
Deployment mode	Centralized mode	Distributed mode

According to the above literature on elderly care, smart medicine, edge computing and so on, we understand that the shortage of medical personnel in the current healthcare industry leads to the problems of patient and equipment management. Therefore, the main goal of this study is to establish an intelligent institutional care environment of IoT. Through the real-time monitoring of the front end equipment of IoT, the edge computing alarm processing of the middle-end gateway and the data access and comprehensive processing of the back end platform and database, the tracking and management of the medical-level platform can reduce the security concerns of patients, the medical burden of family members and the management cost of the institution, so as to improve the effectiveness and quality of the care environment.

3   Application of EWMA Combined with Edge Computing in Long-Term Care Institutions

Based on the concepts of the IoT sensing layer, network layer and application layer, this study established an intelligent distributed alarm service mechanism. The sensing layer is the IoT device and gateway, and the network layer is the multi-communication switch, as shown in Fig. 1. The content includes a multi-channel switching mechanism, edge computing secure encryption mechanism, adaptive threshold alarm mechanism, as described in the following section in detail.

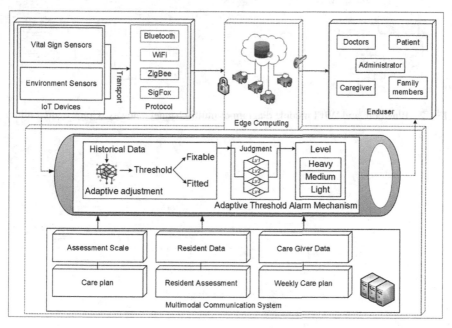

Fig. 1. Plan structure chart

3.1 Multichannel Switching Mechanism

In this study, a cross-communication gateway was built to combine Bluetooth and WIFI communication in wireless communication mode into the same module. The TXD green part is the signal transmitting point, and the RXD blue part is the signal receiving point (Fig. 2).

Sigfox and Zigbee are combined into the same module (Fig. 3). The RXTX/RFMOD orange part is the wireless signal receiving point, corresponding to the internal RF wireless signal, and MOSI blue part is the wired signal transmitting point. The MISO green part is a wired signal receiving point, and the SPI data transmission module (Fig. 4) is used to exchange data between two integrated modules. The wireless signal is transmitted to the Bluetooth-WIFI module and data is uploaded using MQTT, a lightweight transmission protocol based on TCP/IP over the wireless network.

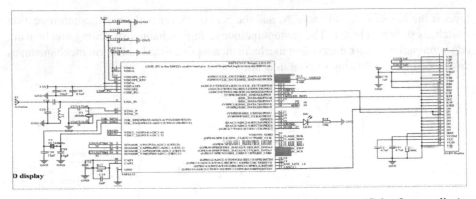

Fig. 2. Bluetooth and WIFI module diagram of multi-channel gateway (Color figure online)

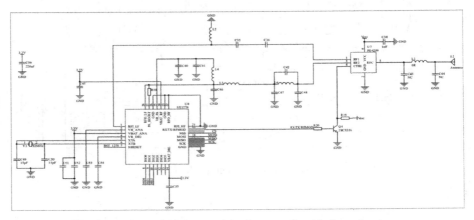

Fig. 3. Sigfox and Zigbee module diagram of multi-channel gateway

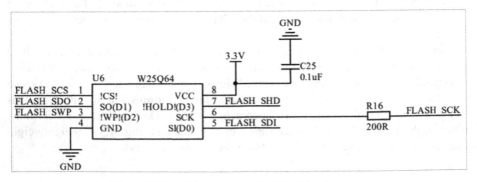

Fig. 4. SPI module diagram of multi-channel gateway

3.2 Security Encryption Edge-Computing Distributed Mechanism

In the clinical practice of care institutions, the data collected by IoT devices contain physiological signals and environmental values and different devices have different packet sizes, so the transmission in a fixed packet size will result in a waste of bandwidth and memory. In order to reduce the above problems and ensure the security of data, it is necessary to strengthen data identification. Therefore, this study adopted Prasad Calyam's optimal encryption mode and the packet cutting scheme after verification in both TLS and DTLS. AES256 encryption algorithm was adopted in the former, while CHACHA20 encryption algorithm was adopted in the latter. In practice, there have been many verification examples of the two encryption algorithms. It can effectively protect the data and make the data not easy to be falsified and retrieved, and can be applied to establish the pre-shared key for communication between the two parties for authentication among edge devices, gateways and cloud servers [14].

The distributed computing flow of signal transmission is shown in Algorithm 1. First, the data size is taken as the judgment benchmark for choosing TLS and DTLS, and data are transmitted through the streaming or package mode. When the 1024-bit packet is used as the transmission case, the data packet is $[1024/128] = 8$. But using 130 bits as the standard results in 126 blank bits for the second packet. Then, in the encryption process of TLS, the four steps including AddRoundKey, SubBytes, ShiftRows, and MixColums are repeated with 14 encryption cycles, until the MixColumns is omitted in the last encryption cycle, and replaced by AddRoundKey. During the encryption process of DTLS, the matrix is repeatedly changed in 20 encryption cycles and the shift operation is performed with quarter-round.

Algorithm 1 : Signal encryption distributed operation mode

Data: Data to be transmitted, data
Data: Protocol to be used for transmission, protocol
Data: Cipher to be used for encryption, mac
Data: encryption algorithm, enc
Result: *The best security scheme is chosen*
/* data.PACKET_SIZE in bits */
if data.PACKET_SIZE >= 128 **then**
    protocol ← TLS
    mac.TYPE ← BLOCK
    enc == AESGCM256
    for Times = 1,....,14 (256bytes) **do**
      AddRoundKey ( )
      SubBytes ( )
      ShiftRows ( )
      MixColums ( )
      If Times == 14 then
        AddRoundKey ( )
        SubBytes ( )
        ShiftRows ( )
        AddRoundKey ( )
      end
    end for
else
    protocol ← DTLS
    mac.TYPE ← STREAM
    enc == Chacha20
    for Times = 1,....,20 **do**
      InitialMatrix ( )
      QuarterRound ( )
    end for
end

3.3   Adaptive Threshold Alarm Mechanism

In the long-term care institutions, the elderly attach the most importance to emergencies. If the front-line staff can be notified immediately when an incident occurs, the crisis can be safely averted. However, not every incident will result in serious injury or death. Therefore, phased alarms should be conducted according to the risk level of the incident. The weight of the hazard level can be judged by the threshold setting of the related IoT equipment. The accuracy of the threshold will help to exclude false alarms and missed alarms. A single threshold setting will cause many false alarms and missed alarms, and a single threshold cannot be adjusted flexibly according to the situation, which will have a negative effect on caregivers, emergency units and family members.

Therefore, we use EWMA to adjust the threshold value and the physiological data of people receiving care appropriately. EWMA has been used for many years by scholars to adjust the mobility threshold. Aslansefat adjusts the threshold through this mode in gas engines and obtains a practical application of the adaptive threshold [15]. In this case, an adaptive threshold alarm mechanism that is suitable for the current situation of the care institutions is proposed.

In most cases, the threshold value is usually fixed as the basis for judging whether the event is normal or abnormal. The threshold value is set as Eq. (1), where m is the average value of all data, v is the variance of marked signals in all data, and α is the parameter exponential that can be freely adjusted by the designer.

$$T = \updownarrow \mp \alpha v \tag{1}$$

In situational design, if an alarm occurs under normal conditions, it is called a False Alarm Rate (FAR), as shown in Eq. (2). On the contrary, if there is no alarm under abnormal conditions, it is called Missed Alarm Rate (MAR), as shown in Eq. (3), where x_{tim} represents a fixed threshold. For the clinical application of care institutions, the health of the care receiver and the environment of the institution is different, so the threshold value of the IoT should be adjusted flexibly according to the different situations, and the customized monitoring condition judgment is the core element.

$$FAR = \int_{x_{tim}}^{+\infty} q(x)dx \tag{2}$$

$$MAR = \int_{-\infty}^{x_{tim}} p(x)dx \tag{3}$$

To minimize the False Alarm Rate and the Missed Alarm Rate, this study referred to the extended adaptive threshold method proposed by Koorosh to significantly reduce FAR and MAR. The main difference is that when the data is cut into normal and abnormal parts, the adaptive threshold is applied to each part, and it is adjusted according to the upper limit of normal data and the lower limit of abnormal data. Combined with a multi-objective constrained genetic algorithm, the threshold is optimized and adjusted to evaluate the accuracy of the alarm. Finally, the FAR and MAR are calculated according to the corrected threshold repeatedly to determine whether the threshold conforms to the site conditions and then consider the correction requirements.

Many studies and schemes related to threshold adjustment were referenced in the study, and differences among various methods were compared (see Table 2). Due to the good effect of the application of Exponentially Weighted Moving-Average (EWMA) in business, finance and other aspects, this mechanism is applied to reduce the occurrence of false alarms and the missed alarms. Moderate threshold adjustment is the core of a care facility using an IoT device for monitoring. In the simulation application, such a mechanism not only has a good effect of automatic monitoring for accurate notification, but also accurately guarantees the safety of the person receiving care and provides a good care environment for the family members.

Table 2. Threshold adjustment method table

	EWMA control chart	T-COV control chart	Adaptive threshold method of Monte Carlo
Examples	Sensor fault alarm system in large industrial system	It is used to detect false alarm for coronavirus and gear manufacturing errors	It is used for fault diagnosis of coal-burning turbine in industrial equipment
Advantages	It has been used in various financial and economic fields, and can be accurately and effectively used in various data analysis fields	Compared with the past CT control chart, it has better effect	It has a good performance of identification accuracy for equipment diagnosis in nonlinear state
Disadvantages	It is not suitable for the analysis of small amount of diverse data	Only in a few cases can it give reasonable results of error alarm correction	A large amount of data is needed to train the model and verify the effectiveness of threshold adjustment
Reference	[15]	[16]	[17]

4 Application

In this study, the IoT equipment was divided into physiological equipment, and environmental equipment, and field subdivision was carried out. Taking the clinical situation of the institution as the main analysis target, the physiological and environmental data were collected according to the IoT equipment in the actual field. Physiological equipment includes the sphygmomanometer, forehead thermometer, etc. Environmental equipment includes an intelligent floor mat, control socket, temperature and humidity sensor and multi-communication edge computing gateway. Through the gateway in the clinical field, the data signals of all IoT equipment are integrated. After preliminary data judgment and processing, the data are uploaded to the cloud healthcare information platform for analysis and storage, so as to reduce the cost of IoT equipment construction and provide a more friendly long-term healthcare environment for family members and the elderly.

As shown in Fig. 5, the back-end healthcare information platform presents the measured data with a graphical interface, and analyzes the data according to the different IoT devices used by the elderly. In order to let the nursing staff quickly understand the situation of the institution, we designed some functions for the system interface, including the management of personnel and equipment, as shown in the solid box (A), and with no more than two clicks as the humanized design goal. The section box is the data graph of the environment device. Block B is the sensor data record of the smart mattress, from which we can know the time of the elderly getting up and down the bed and going to the toilet at night. Block C is the use record of the control socket, from which the use status of the socket can be grasped to further understand the practicability of the socket in the mechanism. The dashed box is the data chart of the physiological measurement device. Block D is the sphygmomanometer measurement record. In addition to setting the systolic pressure at 130mmHg and diastolic pressure at 80mmHg in accordance with the latest treatment guidelines provided by the American Heart Association in 2017, the system also considers that blood pressure varies slightly depending on individual conditions. A fixed threshold setting will cause many false alarms or missing alarms, leading to the anxiety of nursing staff. Therefore, the adaptive threshold design is used to adjust the appropriate threshold flexibly, and the FAR and MAR are calculated continuously to get the most appropriate threshold setting. Block E is the measurement data record of the forehead thermometer. According to the body temperature standard of the Ministry of Health and Welfare, a fixed threshold was set, such as the normal forehead temperature between 35.0 and 37.5 °C. This chart can be used to quickly understand the temperature changes of the elderly, allowing caregivers to judge whether the elderly have a fever trend. Caregivers can click on an elderly person's name for detailed data, and use the platform to remotely operate specific IoT devices.

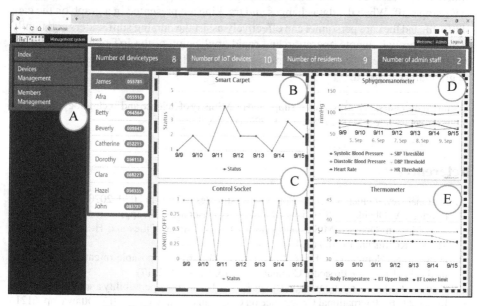

Fig. 5. Data map of the healthcare information platform

5 Conclusion

To ensure that the care system and IoT equipment can help nursing staff, family members and patients, this study designed the IoT environment with innovative concepts. The threshold setting of traditional IoT equipment is fixed, such as the standard blood pressure, blood sugar, heartbeat and other professional biomedical data set by the Ministry of Health and Welfare. In this study, physiological sensing equipment in accordance with medical standards was used, and the flexible adjustment mechanism of environmental sensing equipment was also designed. The data generated in various locations in the institution vary with different environments. For example, the toilet is damp, so the humidity is high; the fire is often used in the kitchen, so the room temperature is high; and the aerosols in the social hall need to be accurately grasped. Therefore, we used the adaptive computing mechanism to set the threshold, so as to get the appropriate notification threshold.

The phased alarm notification mechanism can not only effectively help the elders to get rescue from professional nurses in real time through intelligent notification technology or alarm functions, but also enable the fixed configuration of IoT equipment to be flexibly adjusted according to different factors of time and space through adaptive threshold technology, so as to reduce the interference of false alarms and missed alarms to the nursing staff. In addition, in order to solve the delay and bandwidth problems of data transmission from a large number of IoT devices to the cloud, an edge computing system was added to the gateway in the study, so that the data could be quickly determined and processed by distributed technology and more processing time could be given to nursing staff. When the data changes and tracking are presented in a graph on the care platform, and the care personnel can effectively assist the nursing staff, elders and family members through remote operation and rapid application of the IoT device, so that the patients can get better care and the nursing service efficacy of various institutions can be gradually expanded.

Acknowledgments. This research is supported by Ministry of Science and Technology of Taiwan, under research Project MOST108–2622-E-227–001-CC3.

References

1. National Development Council, Population estimates of Taiwan 2020–2070 (2020)
2. Belghith, A., Obaidat, M.S.: Chapter 2 - Wireless sensor networks applications to smart homes and cities. In: Obaidat, M.S., Nicopolitidis, P. (eds.) Smart Cities and Homes, pp. 17–40. Morgan Kaufmann, Boston (2016)
3. Darwish, S., Nouretdinov, I., Wolthusen, S.D.: Towards composable threat assessment for medical IoT (MIoT). Procedia Comput. Sci. **113**, 627–632 (2017)
4. Tarouco, L.M.R., et al.: Internet of Things in healthcare: Interoperatibility and security issues. In: 2012 IEEE International Conference on Communications (ICC). 2012, Ottawa. pp. 6121–6125 (2012)
5. Amiruddin, A., et al.: Secure multi-protocol gateway for Internet of Things, in 2018 Wireless Telecommunications Symposium (WTS). Phoenix, pp. 1–8 (2018)
6. Vargas, D.C.Y., Salvador, C.E.P.: Smart IoT gateway for heterogeneous devices interoperability. IEEE Latin Am. Trans. **14**(8), 3900–3906 (2016)
7. Al-Fuqaha, A., et al.: Internet of Things: a survey on enabling technologies, protocols, and applications. IEEE Commun. Surv. Tutorials **17**(4), 2347–2376 (2015)
8. Marinčić, A., Kerner, A., Šimunić, D.: Interoperability of IoT wireless technologies in ambient assisted living environments. In: 2016 Wireless Telecommunications Symposium (WTS), London, pp. 1–6 (2016)
9. Aazam, M., Huh, E.-N.: Fog computing: the Cloud-IoT/IoE middleware paradigm. In: IEEE Potentials, pp. 40–44 (2016)

10. Shi, Y., et al.: The fog computing service for healthcare. In: 2015 2nd International Symposium on Future Information and Communication Technologies for Ubiquitous HealthCare (Ubi-HealthTech), Beijing, pp. 1–5 (2015)

11. Gia, T.N., et al.: Fog computing in healthcare internet of things: a case study on ECG feature extraction. In: 2015 IEEE International Conference on Computer and Information Technology; Ubiquitous Computing and Communications; Dependable, Autonomic and Secure Computing; Pervasive Intelligence and Computing, Liverpool. pp. 356–363 (2015)

12. Luan, T., et al.: Fog Computing: Focusing on Mobile Users at the Edge. Comput. Sci., p. 11 (2015)

13. Pan, J., McElhannon, J.: Future edge cloud and edge computing for internet of things applications. IEEE Internet Things J. 5(1), 439–449 (2018)

14. Mukherjee, B., Neupane, R.L., Calyam, P.: End-to-End IoT Security Middleware for Cloud-Fog Communication. In: 2017 IEEE 4th International Conference on Cyber Security and Cloud Computing (CSCloud), New York, pp. 151–156 (2017)

15. Aslansefat, K., et al.: Performance evaluation and design for variable threshold alarm systems through semi-Markov process. ISA Trans. 97, 282–295 (2020)

16. Abdella, G.M., et al.: Phase-I monitoring of high-dimensional covariance matrix using an adaptive thresholding LASSO rule. Comput. Ind. Eng. 144, 106465 (2020)

17. Amirkhani, S., Chaibakhsh, A., Ghaffari, A.: Nonlinear robust fault diagnosis of power plant gas turbine using Monte Carlo-based adaptive threshold approach. ISA Trans. 100, 171–184 (2020)

Cell Cooperation Based Channel Access Mechanism for LAA and WiFi Coexistence

Peilin Liu, Mao Yang$^{(\boxtimes)}$, Zhongjiang Yan, and Bo Li

School of Electronics and Information, Northwestern Polytechnical University, Xi'an, China
lpl2016301996@mail.nwpu.edu.cn, {yangmao,zhjyan,
libo.npu}@nwpu.edu.cn

Abstract. In 2014, the 3rd Generation Partnership Project (3GPP) proposed the "Licensed-Assisted Access using LTE" (LAA) research project, with the intention to further improve LTE network capacity by deploying LTE system in 5GHz unlicensed frequency band. But deploying LAA in unlicensed band will inevitably affect other existing wireless systems such as WiFi and increase the risk of data collision. Therefore, the research of coexistence between LAA and WiFi is of great significance to facilitate the fair sharing and efficient utilization of unlicensed spectrum sources. However, the existing studies consider the relationship between LAA and WiFi in the coexistence scenario from the perspective of contention. In this paper, we proposed a cell cooperation based channel access mechanism. The basic idea of the proposed scheme is let an LAA cell and a WiFi cell establish a pair of cooperative relationship. Once LAA node accesses the channel, it will notify its cooperated pair WiFi node to share the transmission opportunity, and vice versa. After the transmission of the LAA node, the WiFi node can access the channel without performing backoff again. Simulation results manifest that the proposed cell cooperation based channel access mechanism improves the communication performances of both LAA and WiFi as well as the spectrum efficiency in the coexistence scenarios with high channel resources demand.

Keywords: LBT-Cat4 · CSMA/CA · Cell cooperation

1 Introduction

In the era of mobile Internet advancement, the number of mobile devices is increasing rapidly, together with mobile applications showing a trend of diversification. Mobile devices transmit a large amount of data through interconnection, and the traffic carried by cellular network systems is greatly increased, which makes wireless operators experience explosive data traffic growth. This brings a great challenge for operators on how can further enhance the capacity of mobile communication systems, satisfy the increasing demands of users, especially the reliability of mobile communication and business continuity. However, the licensed frequency spectrum resources are insufficient, and the research on the utilization of the licensed frequency resources is deep enough to make

© ICST Institute for Computer Sciences, Social Informatics and Telecommunications Engineering 2021
Published by Springer Nature Switzerland AG 2021. All Rights Reserved
Y.-B. Lin and D.-J. Deng (Eds.): SGIoT 2020, LNICST 354, pp. 500–515, 2021.
https://doi.org/10.1007/978-3-030-69514-9_38

further breakthrough, which makes the service pressure of the licensed frequency band raised sharply, difficult to guarantee higher service quality.

In response to the above phenomenon, the research of LTE network system deployed in unlicensed frequency bands has become an important part to improve the performance of communication network [1]. In 2014, 3GPP (3rd Generation Partnership Project) launched the research project "Licensed-Assisted Access using LTE (LAA)". LAA provides a feasible way for major operators to make reasonable use of unlicensed frequency band resources and helps to improve the overall performance of mobile communication networks. LAA extends the spectrum of LTE to unlicensed frequency bands to enhance the network performance of LTE and LTE-A (LTE-Advance), as well as effectively alleviate the shortage of spectrum resources in the licensed frequency band of LTE systems. Especially in areas with heavy service demands, various data services in LTE can be effectively offloaded to unlicensed spectrum resources, thereby improving the service capacity of LTE operators. LAA is mainly deployed in 5 GHz unlicensed band [2], affecting WiFi systems' operating, and will increase the risk of data collision. Therefore, how to establish a suitable coexistence access mechanism is a significant research direction to help LAA system and WiFi system coexist fairly in the unlicensed frequency band.

In order to minimize the interference, 3GPP introduced LBT mechanism into the standard, hoping to realize the protection of WiFi system under the influence of LAA as well as guarantee the performance of LAA system [3]. Literature [1] shows that simply introduce LTE system to the LTE-WiFi coexistence scenario will affect the performances of both WiFi and LTE; the performance of LTE system is slightly influenced by the coexistence while WiFi is greatly impacted by LTE. LTE-U (LTE-Unlicensed) takes a duty cycle based channel access mechanism and literature [4] suggests that LTE-U performance is closely related to duty cycle parameters and it may lead to more flexible resource sharing between systems with adaptive solutions like CSAT (carrier sensing adaptive transmission) added. Literature [5] tests two proposed channel sensing schemes for LTE-U, simulation shows that both of them can provide a promising tradeoff between WiFi and LTE-U in the coexistence scenario. Literature [4] also states that LAA can be a kind resource sharer for WiFi because the LBT mechanism of LAA is a reasonable solution for coexistence scenarios. In [6], it is concluded that LBT is essential for fair coexistence between WiFi and LAA, but the LBT scheme and scheme settings also matter. However, the studies all consider the relationship between WiFi and LAA in the coexistence scenario from the contention aspect. The performance improvement of one system and the whole scenario are achieved by sacrificing the performance of the other system.

To improve the efficiency of the coexistence scenarios, make the two systems as fair as possible in channel access and data communication, an LAA-WiFi cell cooperation based channel access mechanism is proposed in this paper. Under the condition that LAA devices and WiFi devices are aware of each other, once LAA node access the channel, it will inform its cooperated pair AP (Access Point) to share the transmission opportunity, and vice versa. The shared transmission opportunity allows the AP or the eNB (eNodeB) to access the channel after the former transmission is complete. Simulation results reveal that the cell cooperation scheme improves the performance of WiFi system as well as the efficiency of the coexistence especially in the scenarios with high traffic density and heavy channel access demands.

The following chapters are organized as follows. Section 2 elaborates the channel access mechanisms of LAA and WiFi in unlicensed frequency bands. And the research literature on LAA and WiFi coexistence is investigated. Section 3 introduces the idea of proposed cell cooperation based access method, with the protocol described in detail. Section 4 evaluates the proposed cell cooperation scheme by simulation. The LAA-WiFi coexistence simulation platform is firstly introduced and the results analysis of adopting and not adopting cell cooperation mechanism is carried out in two coexistence scenarios. Section 5 summarizes the content of this paper and puts forward the prospect of future work.

2 Related Work

2.1 LAA-LBT Access Mechanism

When deploying LTE systems to 5 GHz unlicensed frequency band, a problem that cannot be overlooked is how to make it coexist with WiFi system without affecting its performances. As a result, LAA system implements the LBT mechanism which requires clear channel assessment (CCA) before LAA transmit data, it needs to determine whether the channel can be accessed according to the channel state before data transmission.

According to whether backoff is required and how to adjust the contention window, the downlink LBE-LBT can be divided into four types:

No LBT (Cat-1): No channel monitoring before data transmission.

LBT without random backoff (Cat-2): The time at which the channel is monitored as idle before transmission is fixed.

Static backoff LBT (Cat-3): Before transmitting, the node randomly selects an integer N in a fixed contention window, and uses the random number N to determine the backoff time before the is channel is available for transmission.

Exponential backoff LBT (Cat-4): Before transmitting, the node randomly selects an integer N in the contention window, and use the random number N to determine the backoff time before the channel is available for transmission. The contention window size adjustment follows the exponential law during the LBT process.

The downlink Cat-4 LBT access mechanism and its contention window adjustment procedure are described in details [7].

Cat-4 LBT Procedure for Downlink Transmission. For downlink data transmission, if the eNB detects the channel is idle within the defer duration of Initial Clear Channel Assessment (ICCA) state, it can directly transmit data. otherwise the eNB enters the Extended Clear Channel Assessment (ECCA) backoff state, which means it defers its access, and the channel needs to be monitored within a delay time T_d. In this state, CW is used to indicate the size of contention window. the backoff counter N is the number of idle CCA slots monitored by the eNB before transmission, and the value is a randomly chosen integer between 0 and CW (Fig. 1).

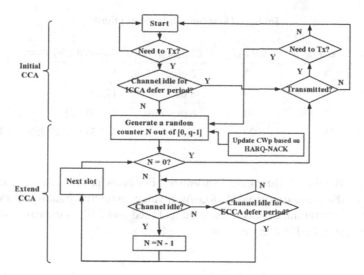

Fig. 1. LBT access procedure.

The adjustment steps of the backoff counter N in ECCA stage are as follows:

Step1: let $N = N_{init}$, with N_{init} the initial random counter selected in the domain from 0 to CW_p;
Step2: if $N > 0$, decrease the backoff counter by 1, that is, $N = N - 1$;
Step3: monitor another slot, if the slot is idle, go to Step4; otherwise go to Step5;
Step4: if $N = 0$, eNB can transmit data; otherwise go to Step5;
Step5: detect another delay time T_d;
Step6: if the delay time is idle, go to Step2; otherwise go to Step 5.

If eNB does not transmit immediately after completing Step4, eNB continues to detect at least one additional delay time T_d. If the channel is idle, eNB can transmit data.

For each priority, there are defined values for m_p, $CW_{min,p}$, $CW_{max,p}$, maximum channel occupation time $T_{m\,cot,p}$, and delay duration T_d. Delay time T_d includes $T_f = 16\,\mu s$ and m_p successive time slots, and the length for each time slot is $T_{slot} = 9\,\mu s$, thus

$$T_d = T_f + m_p * T_{slot} = 16\mu s + m_p * 9ms \tag{1}$$

CW_p is the size of the contention window, with the relation $CW_{min,p} < CW_p < CW_{max,p}$. The value of m_p, $CW_{max,p}$ and $CW_{min,p}$ is determined by eNB according to the transmitting access priority. The eNB shall not continuously transmit on a carrier, where the LAA transmission is conducted, for a time period exceeding the maximum channel occupation time $T_{m\,cot,p}$. Under certain conditions, $T_{m\,cot,p}$ can reach 10 ms for $p = 3$ and $p = 4$.

The lower the value of p, the higher the priority, and the shorter the waiting time when data needs to be sent (Table 1).

Table 1. Downlink LBT access priority.

p	m_p	$CW_{min,p}$	$CW_{max,p}$	$T_{m\,cot,p}$	Allowed CW_p sizes
1	1	3	7	2 ms	{3,7}
2	1	7	15	3 ms	{7,15}
3	3	15	63	8 or 10 ms	{15,31,63}
4	7	15	1023	8 or 10 ms	{15,31,63,127,255,511,1023}

Contention Window Adjustment Procedure. For every priority class p, Let $CW_p = CW_{min,p}$. If 80% or more received HARQ-ACK values in reference subframe are HARQ-NACK, the data transmission is considered as failed and CW_p is increased to the next higher value specified in every p.

2.2 WiFi CSMA/CA Access Mechanism

CSMA/CA Access Procedure. WiFi device gets the opportunity to transmit data through competing the channel according to DCF mechanism based on CSMA/CA.

When WiFi device has data to transmit, it firstly monitors the channel. If the channel is idle for DIFS (Distributed InterFrame Space) duration, it can perform backoff and send data frame. If the destination device correctly receives the data, it sends an ACK frame to the source device after SIFS (Short InterFrame Space) duration. Then if the source device does not receive the ACK frame, it will re-transmit the data frame after waiting for a period of time. DIFS is expressed as

$$DIFS = 2 * SlotTime + SIFS \qquad (2)$$

where *SlotTime* is time length of a slot.

When the channel is busy, the device delays the sending of data. After the channel becomes idle, device delays DIFS time and waits for a random backoff time before sends the data. The expression of backoff duration is

$$BackoffTime = N * SlotTime \qquad (3)$$

where N is the generated backoff counter, which is a random integer uniformly distributed in the domain of $[0, CW]$. Contention window size CW is in an integer between CW_{min} and CW_{max}.

The binary exponential backoff (BEB) algorithm is used in DCF to lower the collision probability between stations transmitting at the same time. The backoff counter randomly selects a positive integer value as the initial value in the interval. The backoff process and contention window size adjustment of BEB are as following steps:

Step1: randomly select an integer N in the contention window $[0, CW_1]$, where CW_1 is the contention window size of the first try, and the integer N is backoff counter.

Setp2: keep monitoring the channel. If the channel is idle during DIFS duration, the backoff counter then begins to decrease according to the number of idle slots.
Step3: transmit frames when backoff counter reaches 0.
Setp4: if the transmission fails, double the contention window size.
Step5: when contention window size CW_i in the i th try reaches CW_{max}, maintains the value of CW_{max}.
Step6: the data is discarded after twice unsuccessful transmission with the competition window size of CW_{max}, then the contention window is reset to CW_{min} to compete the channel for other data frames.

Enhanced Distributed Channel Access (EDCA). DCF mechanism treats all data equally, and all types of data will be put into the same queue. Therefore, some services with higher real-time requirements cannot be immediately served. EDCA is an optimized version of DCF Access mechanism, which is also based on competition but provides differentiated services to guarantee QoS (Quality of Service).

Table 2. Parameters of different ACs.

Priority	AC	CW_{min}	CW_{max}	AIFSN
Lowest	Background	CW_{min}	CW_{max}	7
	Best effort	CW_{min}	CW_{max}	3
	Video	$(CW_{min} + 2)/2 - 1$	CW_{min}	2
Highest	Voice	$(CW_{min} + 1)/4 - 1$	$(CW_{min} + 1)/2 - 1$	2

Four access categories (AC) are specified in IEEE 802.11e protocol, and the transmission priority of each AC is different. Data of different types enter the corresponding queue respectively. The priority of the four access categories is Voice (AC_VO) > Video (AC_VI) > Best Effort (AC_BE) > Background (AC_BK).

Different ACs use different AIFS (Arbitration InterFrame Space) to replace the single DIFS in DCF. The expression of AIFS is

$$AIFS[i] = SIFS + AIFSN[i] * SlotTime \tag{4}$$

where $AIFSN[i]$ is the number of idle time slots for a certain AC that have to defer after SIFS when the channel is idle. $AIFS[i]$ times of different ACs can be obtained from Eq. 4. Different ACs also have different contention windows size CW. The expression of backoff time in EDCA is the same as in DCF, while the value of CW changes. It can be seen from Table 2 that the queue with high priority has a smaller contention window size, so the randomly generated backoff counter and the calculated backoff time are smaller. Figure 3 shows the transmission schematic of the EDCA mechanism (Fig. 2).

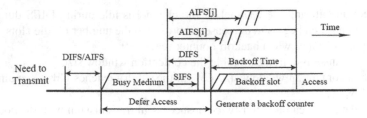

Fig. 2. Access schematic of EDCA mechanism.

2.3 Literature Research

A large number of literature studied the access method of LAA under the scenario of LAA and WiFi coexistence, hoping to get better coexistence performance.

To provide foundations for LAA standardization, literature [8] analytically derives a dynamic switch based optimum access method for LAA between random access and scheduling. However, it overlooks the impact of the proposed LAA scheme on the WiFi performance. In [9], the linear backoff LBT is used to modify the channel usage and the communication performance of the overall scenario with the validation provided by simulations. But the evaluation of WiFi performance is not taken into its consideration. In [6], LAA with and without LBT and LBT are analyzed and simulated. It is concluded that LAA without LBT may have a significant performance impact to WiFi, which is much greater to that of introducing another WiFi system. It also demonstrates that including LBT in LAA is the necessary condition but not the sufficient condition for fair coexistence between LAA and WiFi, the LBT scheme and parameter settings of LBT must be carefully selected to be more WiFi like to ensure fairness. Aiming to analyze and compare the effect of different LBT schemes, literature [10] studies the fixe, linear and the 3GPP specified exponential LAA coexistence schemes. Both theoretical expects and simulation results reveal that the 3GPP specified LAA scheme is the fairest one among the three LAA schemes when coexist with WiFi system, while the fixed LAA scheme is more beneficial to LAA but more unfriendly to WiFi.

And there also literature to modify the LBT channel access mechanism. Literature [11] and [12] studies the performance of adaptive contention window size based on the Cat-4 LBT mechanism. [11] focuses on enhancing the access scheme with the contention window size adjusted to a reasonable value by collecting the QoS information from neighbor nodes so as to achieve the access fairness as well as QoS fairness. [12] calculates the slot utilization rate in a short time duration and adjust the contention window size accordingly to achieve fairness and higher throughput gain. Literature [13] finds out that the fairness largely depends on the energy detection threshold used by LAA. The higher the sensing threshold of LAA, the better the overall system throughput at the cost of WiFi performance; whereas lower threshold results in better WiFi performance but degrades the overall network performance. Thus, there is a tradeoff in the selection of LAA energy sensing threshold. In [14], the relationship of fairness and TXOP (transmission opportunity) of LAA is studied. It summarizes that if the TXOP exceeds a certain threshold, an LAA-WiFi coexistence scenario can realize a higher maximum sum rate of the coexistence network than the single WiFi network. [15] quantifies the

WiFi throughput as the function of LAA transmission time, from which the constrains of LAA transmission time can be determined in order to achieve different protective targets of WiFi system. Under the constrains, the maximum overall channel rate can be optimized by properly setting LAA transmission time.

Above researches all consider the LAA-WiFi coexistence scenarios from the contention aspect. The performance improvement of one system and the whole scenario is achieved by sacrificing the performance of the other system.

3 Cell Cooperation Based Channel Access Mechanism

3.1 Basic Idea of Proposed Scheme

Considering that the performance of the WiFi system is always inferior to that of LAA in the scenario where the mutual influence of LAA and WiFi is serious, the scheme of cell cooperation is proposed to help improve the performance of WiFi system, so as to improve the data transmission capacity and spectrum efficiency of coexistence scenario by treating the two systems from the collaborative perspective.

The basic idea of cell cooperation is to establish cooperative cells with LAA and WiFi on the premise that the LAA and the WiFi device can understand the signal from each other. An LAA-eNB and a WiFi AP form a pair of cooperative relationship. During the channel access and transmission of the LAA-eNB, the LAA-eNB notifies the paired WiFi AP to share the transmission opportunity with the information piggybacked in the header of the transmitted frame. Then, the WiFi AP as well as the STAs who are associated with this AP and successfully received the information need to update its NAV with time duration equal to the transmission time of the ongoing LAA frame. Later, after the LAA-eNB completes the transmission, the WiFi AP can directly access the channel for data transmission, no longer need to perform backoff. Similarly, when WiFi transmits frames, the cooperating LAA-eNB gets the shared transmission opportunity information from the WiFi frames and updates its NAV with the time duration equal to the information exchange time of WiFi system. Then, when WiFi finishes the transmission, the LAA-eNB accesses the channel and transmits data frames.

It has to be noted that this cooperative relationship should be finished after the cooperation completes, and then the two cells need to compete for the channel resources if they have data to send. After competing for the channel and one of them successfully access the channel, they can cooperate again by informing the other one the shared transmission opportunity. The above cooperative access process is cyclical. In short, after a cooperative transmission, the two cells cannot cooperate again immediately and need to compete for the channel. When one of the cells gets the channel resources, they can cooperate again. This suspension is necessary, otherwise if the paired cells always have data to send, these two cells will always occupy the spectrum resources, affecting the communication of other cells.

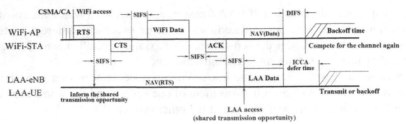

Fig. 3. Cooperation diagram for LAA.

3.2 Protocol Description

For LAA-ENB. For cooperating LAA cell, the backoff access process of LAA-ENB is basically the same as that of LAA-ENB not involved in cooperation, that is, ICCA and ECCA monitoring and LBT process are also required. The protocol is described as follows.

Every time the eNB notices that the channel enters a busy state, it needs to figure out which station is sending data. If it is the paired WiFi AP that is transmitting, the eNB gets the shared transmission opportunity and the WiFi data exchange time duration from the frame header, and updates its NAV with the time duration informed.

After the transmission of AP, the NAV time expires. The eNB uses its shared transmission opportunity and accesses the channel directly after the channel is idle for SIFS time.

For WiFi AP. For cooperative WiFi cell, the backoff process of AP is basically the same as that of WiFi AP not involved in cooperation, that is, channel monitoring and CSMA/CA process are also required. The protocol is described as follows.

When the cooperating LAA-eNB is transmitting, it notifies the AP and the relevant STAs with the shared transmission opportunity and time duration needed for LAA data transmission. Then the WiFi devices update their NAV with the informed time duration.

After the paired LAA-eNB finished transmission, and the channel is idle during the SIFS time, the cooperating AP can access the channel directly due to the shared transmission opportunity from the LAA-eNB.

Considering that there are four queues with different priorities in the EDCA mechanism, before transmitting, AP needs to determine which of the four queues has the shortest waiting time duration (the sum of the AIFS duration and the remaining backoff time), and let the chosen queue to access the channel and transmit data right after the channel is idle for SIFS time. Other queues remain the default backoff procedure (Fig. 4).

Cooperation Procedure. If eNB completes the transmission and AP follows eNB to transmit directly using the shared transmission opportunity, the AP finishes the cooperation, which means the eNB cannot follow the AP that to send data again. If they still have

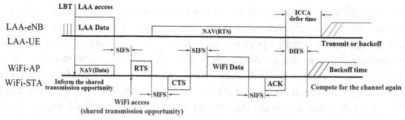

Fig. 4. Cooperation diagram for WiFi.

data frames in the buffer, they need to compete the channel resources After the coop-eration is finished to guarantee transmission opportunities for other cells in the whole coexistence scenario. And it is also the case when AP transmits first in a cooperative pair.

If the cooperation is not finished after the use of the shared transmission opportunity, the two cells in cooperation will continuously occupying the spectrum resources when they always have data to transmit, which will affect the communication of other cells. So the interaction between the two cells in a pair of cooperative relationship is described as following steps.

Step1: LAA-eNB and WiFi AP do the contention to access the channel;
Step2: LAA-eNB/WiFi AP access the channel and transmit;
Step3: WiFi AP/LAA-eNB gets the shared transmission opportunity;
Step4: WiFi AP/LAA-eNB access the channel and transmit follows the Step2's transmission after the channel is idle for SIFS duration, then go to Step1.

4 Performance Evaluation

4.1 Simulation Platform

All the simulations in this paper is implemented on the NS-3 network simulation platform.

The LAA and WiFi coexistence module [16] provides support to simulate the WiFi and variant LTE systems coexistence scenarios in the 5 GHz frequency band. This module develops LAA models for LBT defined in LTE Release-13 by 3GPP, and will not affect the function of original LTE module and WiFi module.

In order to modify an LTE network device into an LAA network device, the link between the MAC layer and the physical layer of LTE device is disconnected and an intermediate object, ChannelAccessManager, is added between to realize information synchronization and control between LAA and WiFi devices. ChannelAccessManager monitors the channel state by registering a listener of WiFi physical layer, and it could also be extended for receiving the Network Allocation Vector (NAV) from the lower MAC layer. The default ChannelAccessManager allows the LTE device to transmit at all times. The LbtAccessManager class, which is specialized from ChannelAccessManager, implements the function of sensing the channel as well as providing the necessary exponential backoff procedure specified in Release-13. To configure the type of channelaccessmanager, a new global value called channelaccessmanager need to be selected form three possible values: default, dutycycle, and LBT. When configuring the LAA network device, WiFi physical layer is attached to the LAA-eNB device with reception of WiFi frames disabled to ensure the information synchronization between the LAA and WiFi. The LAA network device and WiFi network device are connected to the same SpectrumChannel.

4.2 Scenario Design

Scenario Settings. Deploy two kinds of LAA-WiFi scenarios to run the downlink transmission simulation. All the parameters, except the standard and testing variables, are set to be as similar as possible to evaluate the performances of two operators and the proposed accessing mechanism. The detailed scenario design is as follows (Fig. 5 and Tables 3 and 4).

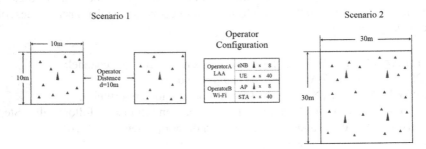

Fig. 5. Coexistence scenarios.

Table 3. Scenario configurations.

Two scenarios	2 * 8 * 5 LAA-WiFi downlink transmission
Operator number	2
Cell number each operator	8
UE/STA number each cell	5
Cooperative pair number	8
Number of nodes need to transmit	16

Varying Parameters. Compare the network performance with different WiFi carrier sensing threshold between −82 dBm and −62 dBm. Since the proposed cell cooperation scheme may shows its advantages in scenarios with higher channel access demands, let

Table 4. Parameter settings.

Parameters	LAA	WiFi
Access standard	Cat-4 LBT (Release 13)	CSMA/CA (802.11n)
Access priority	3	AC_BE
Carrier sensing threshold	−72 dBm	variable
Scheduling	proportional Fairness	/
Radio bearer	UM	/
RTS/CTS	/	Yes
A-MPDU	/	65535 Bytes
Working frequency	5 GHz	
Bandwidth	20 MHz	
Physical layer data rate	9.9 Mbps	
Rate control algorithm	constant rate	
Packet size	1000 bytes	
Buffer size	always full buffer	
Service type	constant bit flow with UDP protocol	
Propagation loss model	log distance propagation loss model	
Tx power	18 dBm	
Tx gain	5 dB	
Antenna mode	SISO	

the required UDP rate of a UE or STA varying from 0.05 Mbps to 0.4 Mbps, and observe the communication performances of the two systems.

Performance Metrics. Calculate the throughput and average time delay per packet of the two operators respectively in the scenarios. If necessary, calculate and compare the total throughput of the scenario, that is, the sum throughput of the two systems. All the simulation figures use the UDP rate (unit: Mbps) as horizontal axis.

4.3 Results Analysis

Results of Scenario 1. The operator throughput and average time delay per packet of scenario 1 are shown in the following Fig. 6 and Fig. 7.

After the implementation of cell cooperation based channel success mechanism, performance of WiFi in the coexistence scenario is greatly improved especially when WiFi is in a more conservative state. In Fig. 6, when the carrier sensing threshold of WiFi is −82 dBm, the throughput is increased about 1 Mbps in average before the channel is saturated (namely the UDP rate is less than 0.1 Mbps) and about 1.5 Mbps in average

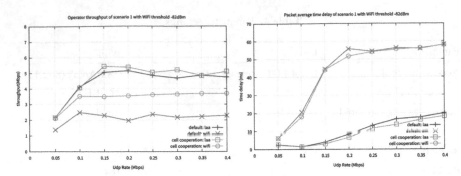

Fig. 6. Performance of scenario 1 with WiFi threshold −82 dBm.

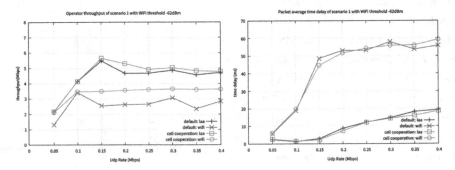

Fig. 7. Performance of scenario 1 with WiFi threshold −62 dBm.

after the saturation of channel with the average time delay per packet gets shortened. In Fig. 7, even when WiFi is radical with a carrier sensing threshold of −62 dBm, WiFi can get a throughput increment by about 1Mbps in average. Meanwhile, the performance of LAA also benefits from the proposed cell cooperation scheme. The throughput of LAA slightly increases and average time delay slightly decreases.

Results of Scenario 2. The operator throughput and average time delay per packet of scenario 2 are shown in the following figures. The simulation results of scenario 2 (Fig. 8 and Fig. 9) are similar to that of scenario 1, with throughput of WiFi and LAA both increased and average Time delay per packet slightly decreased. And the performance improvement of LAA in scenario 2 is more obvious than that in scenario 1.

Total Throughput Comparison. The total throughput comparison of scenarios with/without cell cooperation scheme are shown in Fig. 10 and Fig. 11.

According to above results analysis of the two scenarios, since both LAA operator and WiFi operator get better communication performance in throughput and average time delay per packet, the total throughput of the coexistence scenario is raised about 2 Mbps in average and almost reaches the maximum allowed data rate in the parameter settings due to the proposed cell cooperation based channel access mechanism, which also means the spectrum resources are utilized in a more efficient way.

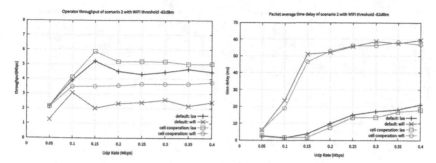

Fig. 8. Performance of scenario 2 with WiFi threshold −82 dBm.

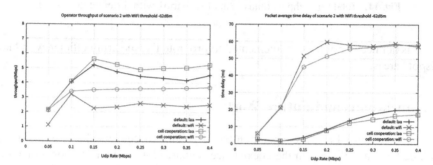

Fig. 9. Performance of scenario 2 with WiFi threshold −62 dBm.

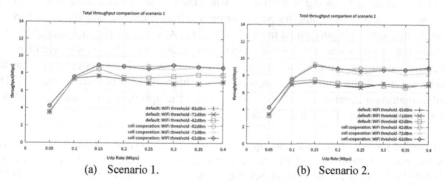

Fig. 10. Total throughput comparison of scenarios with/without cell cooperation scheme.

The simulation is also conducted in scenario 1 with a larger operator distance under the condition of a −62 dBm WiFi carrier sensing threshold to evaluate the effectiveness of the proposed cell cooperation scheme when the mutual influence between the two operators is not severe. However, simulation results in Fig. 11 show that the throughput improvement effect of the proposed scheme reduces when the distance between two operators increases, which means the proposed scheme can better reveal its advantages in the coexistence scenarios with higher traffic density and more channel access demands.

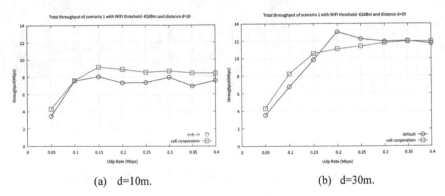

(a) d=10m.   (b) d=30m.

Fig. 11. Total throughput comparison of scenario1 with different distance d.

And it is not necessary to be implemented to promote the spectrum efficiency in "non-hotspot" areas.

5   Conclusions and Future Works

This paper proposed a cell cooperation based channel access mechanism, making an LAA cell and a WiFi cell in the coexistence scenario form a pair of cooperative relationship. If one in the cooperative relationship accesses the channel, it will notify the other cell the shared transmission opportunity. Then the latter cell can access the channel directly without performing backoff again when the former transmission is finished and channel is detected to be idle for SIFS duration. Simulation and analysis of cell cooperation mechanism is performed in two kinds of LAA-WiFi coexistence scenarios. The simulation results show that the cell cooperation based channel access mechanism can improve the throughput and time delay performances of the WiFi system as well as the entire system of the coexistence scenario with a high channel resources demand. The cell cooperation scheme will be more complex in the uplink transmission coexistence scenarios which will be included in our future work.

Acknowledgement. This work was supported in part by Science and Technology on Avionics Integration Laboratory and the Aeronautical Science Foundation of China (Grant No. 20185553035), the National Natural Science Foundations of CHINA (Grant No. 61871322, No. 61771392, No. 61771390, and No. 61501373), and Science and Technology on Avionics Integration Laboratory and the Aeronautical Science Foundation of China (Grant No. 201955053002).

References

1. Cavalcante, A.M., Almeida, E.,Vieira, R.D., et al.: Performance evaluation of LTE and Wi-Fi coexistence in unlicensed bands. In: 2013 IEEE 77th Vehicular Technology Conference (VTC Spring), pp. 1–6. IEEE, Dresden (2013)

2. Kwon, H., Jeon, J., Bhorkar, A., et al.: Licensed-assisted access to unlicensed spectrum in LTE release 13. IEEE Commun. Mag. **55**(2), 201–207 (2017)
3. Rupasinghe, N., Güvenç, I.: Licensed-assisted access for WiFi-LTE coexistence in the unlicensed spectrum. In: 2014 IEEE Globecom Workshops (GC Wkshps), pp. 894–899. IEEE, Austin, TX (2014).
4. De Santana, P.M., De Lima Melo, V.D., De Sousa, V.A.: Performance of license assisted access solutions Using ns-3. In: 2016 International Conference on Computational Science and Computational Intelligence (CSCI), pp. 941–946. IEEE, Las Vegas (2016)
5. Jia, B., Tao, M.: A channel sensing based design for LTE in unlicensed bands. In: 2015 IEEE International Conference on Communication Workshop (ICCW), pp. 2332–2337. IEEE, London (2015)
6. Kwan, R., Pazhyannur, R., Seymour, J., et al.: Fair co-existence of licensed assisted access LTE (LAA-LTE) and Wi-Fi in unlicensed spectrum. In: 2015 7th Computer Science and Electronic Engineering Conference (CEEC), pp. 13–18. IEEE, Colchester (2015)
7. TSGRAN. Study on Licensed-Assisted Access to Unlicensed Spectrum. In: 3GPP TR 36.889 V13.0.0 (2015)
8. Lien, S., Lee, J., Liang, Y.: Random access or scheduling: optimum LTE licensed-assisted access to unlicensed spectrum. IEEE Commun. Lett. **20**(3), 590–593 (2016)
9. Mushunuri, V., Panigrahi, B., Rath, H.K., Simha, A.: Fair and efficient listen before talk (LBT) technique for LTE licensed assisted access (LAA) networks. In: 2017 IEEE 31st International Conference on Advanced Information Networking and Applications (AINA), pp. 39–45. IEEE Taipei (2017)
10. Pei, E., Jiang, J.: Performance analysis of licensed-assisted access to unlicensed spectrum in LTE release 13. IEEE Trans. Veh. Technol. **68**(2), 1446–1458 (2019)
11. Tao, T., Han, F., Liu, Y.: Enhanced LBT algorithm for LTE-LAA in unlicensed band. In: 2015 IEEE 26th Annual International Symposium on Personal, Indoor, and Mobile Radio Communications (PIMRC), pp. 1907–1911. IEEE, Hong Kong (2015)
12. Hao, F., Chang, Y., Li, H., Zhang, J., Wei, Q.: Contention window size adaptation algorithm for LAA-LTE in unlicensed band. In: 2016 International Symposium on Wireless Communication Systems (ISWCS), pp. 476–480. IEEE, Poznan (2016)
13. Dama, S., Kumar, A., Kuchi, K.: Performance evaluation of LAA-LBT based LTE and WLAN's co-existence in unlicensed spectrum. In: 2015 IEEE Globecom Workshops (GC Wkshps), pp. 1–6. IEEE, San Diego (2015)
14. Gao, Y.: LTE-LAA and WiFi in 5G NR unlicensed: fairness, optimization and win-win solution. In: 2019 IEEE SmartWorld, Ubiquitous Intelligence & Computing, Advanced & Trusted Computing, Scalable Computing & Communications, Cloud & Big Data Computing, Internet of People and Smart City Innovation (SmartWorld/SCALCOM/UIC/ATC/CBDCom/IOP/SCI), pp. 1638-1643. IEEE, Leicester (2019)
15. Han, S., Liang, Y., Chen, Q., Soong, B.: Licensed-assisted access for LTE in unlicensed spectrum: a MAC protocol design. IEEE J. Sel. Areas Commun. **34**(10), 2550–2561 (2016)
16. NS-3 LBT Wi-Fi Coexistence Modules Documentation. https://www.nsnam.org/~tomh/ns-3-lbt-documents/html/lbt-wifi-coexistence.html, Accessed 20 June 2020

The Claim-Based Channel Access (CCA) Method for IEEE 802.11ah

Chung-Ming Huang[1], Rung-Shiang Cheng[2(✉)], and Yan-Jia Pan[1]

[1] Department of Computer Science and Information Engineering, National Cheng Kung University, Tainan, Taiwan
{huangcm,panyj}@locust.csie.ncku.edu.tw
[2] Department of Information Technology, Overseas Chinese University, Taichung, Taiwan
rscheng@ocu.edu.tw

Abstract. This work proposed the Claim-based Channel Access (CCA) method for IEEE 802.11ah, which is designed for Internet of Things (IOT). The proposed CCA method uses the newly devised Claiming RAW to let those stations having uplinked data frames to claim their intentions for uplinking data frames to reduce collisions. In addition, this work adopted the registered backoff time mechanism, for which a station registers its next backoff time to AP when its current channel access is finished. In this way, AP is able to schedule stations according to their registered backoff time in advance to avoid collisions more effectively. Comparing with the traditional IEEE 802.11ah, the proposed CCA method has the lower collision rate and higher throughput in the network environment having the more number of stations in each time slot for accessing the channel.

Keywords: IEEE 802.11ah · Internet of Things · Throughput improvement · Collision reduction

1 Introduction

Due to the development and advancement of sensor and wireless network technologies, the emergence of the Internet of Things (IOT) [1] has brought a new way of life, which allows devices to communicate with each other whenever and wherever, using the Machine to Machine (M2M) communication method. The IEEE Task group (TGah) therefore define a new protocol called IEEE 802.11ah, which is also known as Wi-Fi HaLow [2], for IOT. WiFi HaLow combines the advantages of (1) low-power communication technologies and the original WiFi's features and (2) possessing the higher throughput than LPWAN and higher transmission range than WPAN.

Since an IEEE 802.11ah AP is allowed to connect with up to 8192 stations, IEEE 802.11ah devises (i) the hierarchical organization through association identifier (AID) and (ii) the Traffic Indication Map (TIM) and Restricted Access Window (RAW) mechanisms to cluster stations into some groups and each group's stations can access the channel on different time. The AP can accurately determine each station through the AID, IEEE 802.11ah adopts the concept of Restricted Access Window (RAW), for

Y.-B. Lin and D.-J. Deng (Eds.): SGIoT 2020, LNICST 354, pp. 516–526, 2021.
https://doi.org/10.1007/978-3-030-69514-9_39

which each TIM period is divided into several RAWs, to alleviate the conflict of a large number of stations competing for channel access at the same time. In this way, hopefully, it can reach the goal of avoiding collision, improve throughput, power saving, etc., and ensure smooth operation [3].

However, the legacy IEEE 802.11ah still cannot avoid collisions even with the afore-mentioned devised mechanisms because many stations in a time slot may still need to access the channel at the same time, which causes collisions and decreases throughput. The main problem is stations' spontaneous actions, i.e., uplinking data frames from stations to the IEEE 802.11ah AP. Thus, how to have a method that can schedule stations' uplinking data frames is the key problem to be resolved.

This paper proposed a method called Claim-based Channel Access (CCA) for avoiding collision and improving throughput for IEEE 802.11ah. Two key ideas of the proposed CCA method are as follows: (1) A station generates the new backoff time for its next channel access when it finishes its current uplinking or downloading data frame and then registers the new backoff time in AP, i.e., a station generates its backoff time before accessing the channel and lets AP know in advance [4]. (2) The 1st RAW in a TIM period becomes the Claiming RAW, for which those stations having uplinked data frames to be transmitted can make claims in the Claiming RAW to notify their desire of uplinking data frames to the AP. In this way, the AP can thus know (i) the backoff time of each station in advance and (ii) which stations have uplinked data frames to be transmitted and then schedule stations' channel accesses accordingly. As a result, the collision rate can be reduced and the throughput can be improved.

The remaining part of this paper is organized as follows. Section 2 presents related works. Section 3 introduces the functional scenario of the proposed CCA method. Section 4 presents the proposed CCA method in details. Section 5 shows the performance analysis. Finally, conclusion remarks are given in Sect. 6.

2 Related Work

This Section presents related works of improving the performance of 802.11ah.

In [5], the authors considered that the performance of grouping is closely related to the demand of device traffic, thus they proposed a grouping algorithm for traffic-aware sensors. Based on the observation of analysis, a traffic-aware grouping algorithm was proposed to partition the sensors considering (i) the sensors' heterogeneous traffic patterns and (ii) dynamic channel condition. Then, a regression-based model is derived to estimate the competitive success's probability of sensors with heterogeneous traffic requirements. Compared with the unified random grouping, the proposed grouping algorithm improves the average channel utilization for about 6%.

In [6] the authors analyzed a new strategy for grouping stations in the dense network. The authors applied the Max-Min fairness standard to achieve the goal of improving stations' performance and fairness. In addition, the authors applied the ant colony optimization method to avoid the problem of hidden nodes. The proposed method can increase the total throughput for about 40%, and reduce the number of hidden terminals by 11%.

In [7], the authors analyzed a station regrouping algorithm based on competing WLANs to minimize potential transmission collisions caused by the hidden node problem. Information about the traffic demand of (1) potential hidden node pairs and (2) stations in the network is obtained through the AP. Stations are then redistributed into different groups according to a centralized Viterbi-like algorithm or a decentralized iterative update method. The simulation results shown that the collision situation can be reduced significantly through the regrouping algorithm.

In [8], the authors proposed a method to reduce the maximum delay by preferentially assigning those stations that cannot access the channel to reserved slots. The authors set the first slot of each RAW group as the reserved slot, which gives the opportunity of being able to send data to those nodes that cannot access the channel due to collisions. Furthermore, an algorithm was proposed to dynamically change the reserved slot time according to the traffic.

3   The Functional Scenario

This Section introduces the functional scenario of (i) the traditional IEEE 802.11ah and (ii) the proposed CCA method.

Figure 1 depicts an illustrated transmission process used in the traditional 802.11ah. Let station (STA) 1 and STA7 be in the same slot, and they have the same backoff value 5. After the DIFS time, they start to count down their backoff value until to 0, and then begin to uplink data. At this time, since they uplink data simultaneously, the collision has happened. Since stations didn't receive ACK from AP, after a DIFS time, STA 3 and STA 7 generate a new backoff value 7 and 5, respectively, after a DIFS time period and then continue to contend for the channel.

In this work, stations are divided into two categories: (1) known station and (2) unknown station. A known station means that AP knows the station having data to receive/send in its corresponding time slot, i.e., (i) the stations that have downlinked data frames in the AP and (ii) the stations that have more data frames to be transmitted after successfully uplinking a data frame. An unknown station means that AP doesn't know whether the station having data to send in its corresponding time slot or not, i.e., the stations having data to be uplinked are classified as unknown stations.

In the proposed CCA method, when a station finishes (i) receiving a downlinked data frame or (ii) transmitting an uplinked data frame, it generates a backoff value, which is called registered backoff value, for the next data communication, which can be uplinking or downlinking data, and registers the value in the AP. If the station's currently processing data is the uplinked data, the new backoff value will be piggybacked on the station's uplinked data frame and then delivered to AP. If the station's currently processing data is the downlinked data, the new backoff value is piggybacked on the station's PS-Poll frame and then delivered to AP. If a known station has both uplinked data and downlinked data at the same time, it performs the uplinking data at first and then the downlinking data. When a station is associating with an AP, it generates a registered backoff value and it is piggybacked on the association request and then delivered to the AP. AP records the registered backoff value and schedules it when the station intends to uplink its data frame immediately after the association processing, i.e., it is marked as the known station.

A new RAW called "Claiming RAW" is allocated in the 1st RAW of each TIM period such that those stations that have data frames to be uplinked can make claims about their intensions of uplinking data frames in the Claiming RAW. When the AP receives a claim from a station, it marks the station as the known station, and then schedules the station' uplinking data during the data communication stage. In the communication stage, if there are some known stations in a time slot, AP schedules these known stations according to their registered backoff time and informs them to send/receive data immediately by directly modifying the corresponding station's backoff value to 0. In this way, stations don't have to wait for backoff values' countdown to send/receive uplinked/downlinked data frames. In other words, the registered backoff values of these known stations are the reference values for AP scheduling.

Figure 2 depicts an example of the station's transmission and AP's notification behaviors. Let three known stations 4, 7 and 10 be in the same slot and their registered backoff values be 8, 5, 3. According to the order of backoff values, the AP sequentially informs known station 10, station 7 and station 4 to access channel. The station that is informed by the AP changes its backoff value to 0 and then uplinks its data frame immediately.

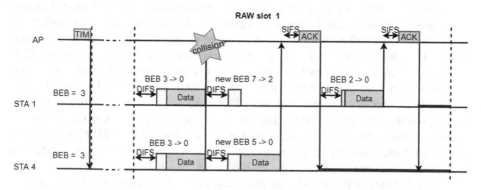

Fig. 1. An example of the collision situation.

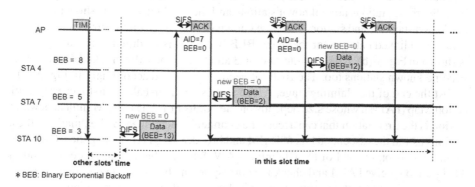

Fig. 2. An example of the station's transmission behavior.

4 The Proposed Claim-Base Channel Access (CCA) Method

The proposed CCA method is divided into three stages: (i) the association stage, (ii) the claiming stage and (iii) the communication stage.

4.1 The Association Stage

In the association stage, when a station is entering into the signal coverage of an AP, it needs to have some actions to associate with the AP. The station will randomly generate a backoff value from the contention window and put it in the association request message as the registered backoff value for its future channel access, and then sends the request to the AP. If the AP accepts the association of this station, it assigns an AID to this station and records its registered backoff value in the Binary Exponential Backoff (BEB) bit-vector for the scheduling of channel access.

4.2 The Claiming Stage

Please note that the first paragraph of a section or subsection is not indented. The first paragraphs that follows a table, figure, equation etc. does not have an indent, either.

In this work, a BEB bit vector is used to record the registered backoff value of each station. The BEB bit vector is stored in the AP: each time slot is associated with a BEB bit vector, which indicates a backoff value's state in the corresponding time slot, and bit x in the bit vector represents the registered backoff value x. In the BEB bit vector, each bit, e.g., the xth bit, is associated with an AID list, for which each one y in the AID list denotes that the registered backoff value of the corresponding station y is x. When one or more known stations have registered backoff value x, bit x of the BEB bit vector is set to 1. When there is not any station registered backoff value x or only unknown stations registered backoff value x, bit x of the BEB bit vector is set to 0.

Figure 3 shows an illustrated example of the BEB bit vector, in which there are six stations whose AID is 1, 3, 5, 7, 9 and 11, respectively, assigned to the same time slot. The registered backoff values for these six stations are 7, 10, 13, 4, 10 and 13, respectively. Initially, these stations are unknown stations and the BEB bit vector is shown in Fig. 3-(a). When station 1 and station 9 become known stations, e.g., the AP finds that there are some downlinked data are for them, the BEB bit vector is modified accordingly, which is shown in Fig. 3-(b). After a while, station 3 and 5 have some downlinked data and they become known stations too. The BEB bit vector is modified accordingly in Fig. 3-(c).

At the end of the claiming stage, AP generates a bitmap called First Accessor Indication Map (FAIM), whose size depends on the number of AIDs. FAIM indicates which station is the first station that can access the channel in each time slot, i.e., marking these stations as 1 in the associated bits of FAIM and broadcasting FAIM using the ACK frame to all stations on the end of the Claiming RAW. Stations that belong to corresponding TIM period receive FAIM and check the corresponding bit associated with themselves; if the bit is equal to 1, the station changes its backoff value to 0. At the same time, those unknown stations whose registered backoff values are 0 and belong to the same time slot should change their backoff values to avoid collision with the first accessor.

An example of using FAIM is depicted in Fig. 4.

Let there be 12 stations in a RAW, which has 4 time slots, and be evenly assigned in these 4 time slots, which is depicted in Fig. 4-(a). The station marked with a star is the known station with the minimum backoff value in each time slot, i.e., stations 4, 5, 7 and 10. The AP marks these four stations as the first station that can access the channel in their assigned time slot, and sets their corresponding bits in FAIM to 1, which is depicted in Fig. 4-(b). However, it is observed that most of the bits of the FAIM are 0. Thus some compressing scheme is needed. The compression rule is as follows:

- Each 8 bits are grouped together and concentrated in one bit.
- The first 8 bits of the bitmap indicate a total of 8 groups.
- When the group's bit is 1, it means that one or more stations in the group are set to 1, and then the details of the group are added after the bitmap.
- Otherwise, it doesn't need to add any information.

Thus, the aforementioned FAIM example depicted in Fig. 4 can be compressed, which is depicted in Fig. 4-(c).

Figure 5 depicts the situation at the end of the Claiming RAW. The AP sends the bitmap of FAIM on the end of the Claiming RAW using the ACK frame. Those stations belonging to this TIM can receive it. After receiving the bitmap of FAIM, those stations belonging to the first station for accessing the channel, i.e., those stations whose associated bits are marked as 1 in FAIM, can change their backoff values. The illustrated FAIM depicted in Fig. 5 denotes that stations 1, 4 and 12 can change their backoff value to 0.

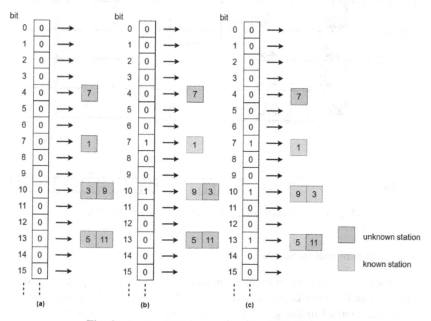

Fig. 3. An illustrated example of the BEB bit vector.

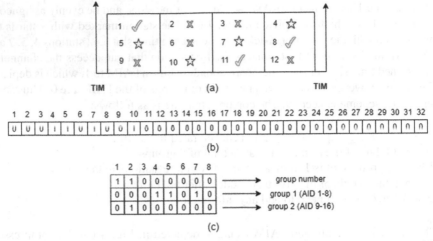

Fig. 4. An illustrated example of using the FAIM; (a) slot assignment, (b) the FAIM without compression and (c) the FAIM with compression.

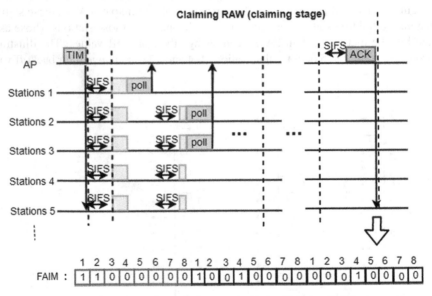

Fig. 5. An example of using FAIM in the Claiming RAW.

4.3 The Communication Stage

There are two phases in the communication stage: (i) the scheduling phase and (ii) the uplinking data and downlinking data phase. The AP schedules and notifies which station can access the channel in the scheduling phase. The selected and notified station can uplink or downlink its data frame, and also deliver its next registered backoff value to AP in the uplinking data procedure or the downlinking data procedure.

Since AP will calculate to which RAW sub-group each station belongs and record the stations' expected backoff values based on their previously registered backoff values, regardless of the station has or does not have data to send/receive, AP can know all of the registered time of all involved stations in a time slot. Thus, AP can arrange the channel access's sequence and time accordingly. Note that both the known and unknown stations can generate backoff values for registration, but the AP only schedules the known stations for the channel access.

When a station sends an uplinked data frame, it generates a new registered backoff value for its next channel access and piggybacks it on the data frame and sends it to the AP. After the AP has received the uplinked data frame, the AP is switched to the scheduling phase to select the next station for accessing the channel and indicates it in the ACK frame. When the AP selects a station to receive its downlinked data frame in the scheduling phase, the selected station generates a new registered backoff value for its next channel access and piggybacks it on the PS-Poll frame, which indicates its readiness to receive its downloaded data frame, and then delivers it to the AP. Note that if the backoff value of an unknown station is the same as the known station's backoff value notified by the AP, this unknown station will generate a new backoff value to avoid collision. The AP does not know the backoff value's change of the unknown station at this time. If the unknown station has downlinked data in the future, the AP schedules it according to its originally registered backoff value, which is recorded in the BEB bit vector.

5 Performance Evaluation

This Section presents the performance evaluation of the proposed CCA method. The proposed CCA method is compared with the traditional IEEE 802.11ah. The simulator uses a network model based on the IEEE 802.11ah infrastructure and uses the C++ programming language to implement the TIM and the RAW mechanisms. The simulation environment and simulation results are presented in detail in this Section.

5.1 The Simulation Environment

The simulation environment deployed an AP and 512 stations to build the 802.11ah network. At the beginning, all stations associated with the AP, and each station randomly generated 0 to 4 data frames. The proposed CCA method can reduce the chance of collision and let known stations' uplinked/downlinked data frames to be sent/received as earlier as possible. Table 1 lists the parameters and their values used in the simulation environment.

Table 1. The parameter setting.

Parameter	Value
CWmin	16
CWmax	1024
Number of stations	512
Payload size	128 bytes
MAC header type	Legacy header
DTIM Interval	1.2.8 s
Number of RAW	2
Number of slots	4
Wi-Fi Mode	MCS10, 1 MHz

5.2 Results of the Performance Analysis

Hereafter, "traditional" means using the traditional IEEE 802.11ah protocol, "RCA" means using the RCA method [4] and "CCA" means using the CCA method. In the following Figures, the x-axis denotes the number of TIM groups and the y-axis denotes the performance metrics.

Figure 6 depicts the simulation results of the throughput and collision rate using the RCA method and the traditional IEEE 802.11ah, and the CCA method. In the case of fewer TIM groups, the number of stations allocated to each time slot is more than that for the situation of more TIM groups, i.e., the number of known and unknown stations in each time slot is increased. Referring to Fig. 6-(a), when the number of groups increases, the throughput increases and the collision rate decreases, which is depicted in Fig. 6-(b). Since the number of stations in each slot is reduced, the collision rate is reduced and stations have more time to access the channel. Comparing with the traditional IEEE 802.11ah, the proposed CCA method has higher throughput, and has almost no collision. The reason is that, through the use of the Claiming RAW, stations having uplinked data frames to be transmitted can do claims to AP to become known stations using the CCA method. AP informs these known stations to transmit data sequentially to reduce collision. However, the collision situation still exists using the proposed CCA method because AP cannot predict unknown stations' behaviors and thus it may cause some collisions, which result from the same backoff value between some unknown stations.

The performance results shown that in a more crowded network environment (1 TIM groups), the throughput of using the CCA method is 27.49% better than that of using the RCA method and 295.06% better than that of using the traditional IEEE 802.11 ah, and the collision rate of using the CCA method is 28.02% of that of using the RCA method and 10.41% of that of using the traditional IEEE 802.11ah; in a sparse network environment (32 TIM groups), the throughput of using the CCA method is 30% better than that of using the RCA method and 52.94% better than that of using the traditional IEEE 802.11 ah, and the collision rate of using the CCA method is 6.48%of that of using the RCA method and 0.75% of that of the traditional 802.11ah.

Figure 7 depicts the simulation result with 16 groups. Referring to Fig. 7, when the number of stations increases, the collision rate and transmission time increases and the throughput decreases. The CCA method has the lower collision rate than that of using the RCA method and the traditional IEEE 802.11ah because the CCA method uses the Claiming RAW to let the stations having uplinked data frames to be transmitted do claims to become known stations and thus AP can schedule them to transmit data frames earlier and sequentially to avoid collision. Furthermore, the transmission time using the CCA to be transmitted is lower than that of using the RCA method and the traditional IEEE 802.11ah.

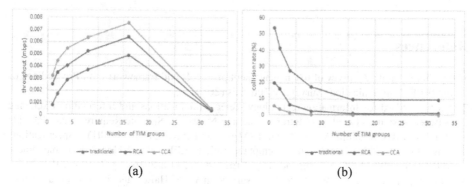

(a)   (b)

Fig. 6. The results with 512 nodes: (a) the throughput, and (b) the collision rate.

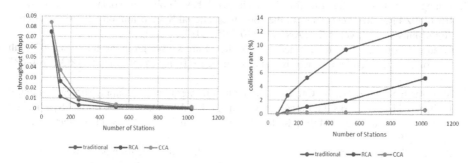

Fig. 7. The results of the environment with 16 groups: (a) the throughput, (b) the collision rate, and (c) the transmission time.

6   Conclusion

This paper has proposed a claim-based control scheme called Claim-based Channel Access (CCA) to schedule stations' channel access. Based on the registered backoff time mechanism, each station can register a random backoff value after its current channel access is finished. The proposed CCA method allows stations that have uplinked data frames to be transmitted sending claims to AP through the proposed Claiming RAW. AP can thus (i) know which stations have data to be processed and (ii) be able to schedule their channel access sequence. Simulation results have shown that the proposed CCA method is better than the traditional IEEE 802.11ah in terms of throughput, collision rate and transmission time. For the future work, it can consider how to have the dynamic distribution of stations to different TIM groups and different RAW groups such that the collision rate, transmission time and throughput can be further improved.

Acknowledgment. This work was supported by the Ministry Of Science and Technology (MOST), Taiwan (R.O.C.) under the grant number MOST 108-2221-E-006-036-MY3 and MOST 108-2221-E-240-002.

References

1. Sinche, S., et al.: A survey of IoT management protocols and frameworks. In: Proceedings of the IEEE Communications Surveys & Tutorials (2019)
2. IEEE Standard for Information technology–Telecommunications and Information Exchange between Systems - Local and Metropolitan Area Networks–Specific Requirements - Part 11: Wireless LAN Medium Access Control (MAC) and Physical Layer (PHY) Specifications Amendment 2: Sub 1 GHz License Exempt Operation. IEEE Std 802.11ah-2016 (Amendment to IEEE Std 802.11–2016, as amended by IEEE Std 802.11ai-2016), pp. 1–594 (2017)
3. Qiao, L., Zheng, Z., Cui, W., Wang, L.: A survey on Wi-Fi HaLow technology for internet of things. In: Proceedings of the 2nd IEEE Conference on Energy Internet and Energy System Integration (EI2), Beijing, pp. 1–5 (2018)
4. Huang, C.M., Cheng, R.S., Li, Y.M.: The registration-based collision avoidance mechanism for IEEE 802.11ah. In: Proceedings of the 16th International Symposium on Pervasive Systems, Algorithms and Networks (I-SPAN), pp. 240–255 (2019)
5. Chang, T., Lin, C., Lin, K.C., Chen, W.: Traffic-aware sensor grouping for IEEE 802.11ah networks: regression based analysis and design. IEEE Trans. Mob. Comput. **18**(3), 674–687 (2019)
6. Mosavat-Jahromi, H., Li, Y., Cai, L.: A throughput fairness-based grouping strategy for dense IEEE 802.11ah networks. In: Proceedings of the 30th IEEE Annual International Symposium on Personal, Indoor and Mobile Radio Communications (PIMRC), 8–11 September 2019, pp. 1–6 (2019)
7. Zhu, Z., Zhong, Z., Fan, Z.: A station regrouping method for contention based IEEE 802.11ah wireless LAN. In: Proceedings of the 13th IEEE International Conference on Wireless and Mobile Computing, Networking and Communications (WiMob), 9–11 October 2017, pp. 1–6 (2017)
8. Kim, J., Yeom, I.: QoS enhanced channel access in IEEE 802.11ah networks. In: Proceedings of the 17th International Symposium on Communications and Information Technologies (ISCIT), 25–27 September 2017, pp. 1–6 (2017)

Optimization of the Deposition Condition for Improving the Ti Film Resistance of DRAM Products

Yun-Wei Lin[✉] and Chia-Ming Lin

College of Artificial Intelligence, National Chiao Tung University, Tainan, Taiwan
jyneda@nctu.edu.tw

Abstract. Dynamic random access memory (DRAM) products are the key parts in consumer products. To fulfill the current market's strict specifications, various customers have asked DRAM manufacturers to continue improving the quality of DRAM products. The resistance of the Ti film directly affects the electrical quality of DRAM products. At present, the DRAM products developed by the case company have caused customer returns due to abnormal resistance value of Ti film. Process engineers always adjust the engineering parameters based on experience, which resulted in slow improvement and inability to determine the setting of engineering parameters. Consequently, shipments of DRAM products are delayed. This study adopts the Ti film resistance of DRAM products as the main research object for improvement and applies the response surface method, neural networks, and genetic algorithms to help process engineers analyze and improve DRAM products. This work assists the case company in achieving a significant improvement in Ti film resistance from 210.33 Ω (the origin made by the case company) to 185.28 Ω (the improvement made by this work) where the specified target value is 185 Ω. The results are effective in shortening the improvement time and reducing customer returns.

Keywords: DRAM · Response surface method · Neural networks · Genetic algorithms

1 Introduction

Dynamic random access memory (DRAM) is typically used for the data or program code needed by mobile computing devices, workstations, servers and more. Ti film resistance is an important quality characteristic for the yield of DRAM products. An ideal Ti film resistance target value is, e.g., 185 Ω. A case company makes effort to improve the process to tune the Ti film resistance to the target value. If the Ti film resistance of a DRAM product is more closed to the target value, the quality of the DRAM product is better. If Ti film resistance is far from the target value, the quality of DRAM products will be low as well as the yield.

This case study considers DRAM products developed by a semiconductor company in Taiwan. During production, the DRAM products had an electrical abnormality, which

© ICST Institute for Computer Sciences, Social Informatics and Telecommunications Engineering 2021
Published by Springer Nature Switzerland AG 2021. All Rights Reserved
Y.-B. Lin and D.-J. Deng (Eds.): SGIoT 2020, LNICST 354, pp. 527–542, 2021.
https://doi.org/10.1007/978-3-030-69514-9_40

was caused by product defects. Figure 1 shows the defect items of the DRAM products. The Ti film resistance value is the primary defect of the DRAM products, and it accounts for 46.7% of the total number of defects. Figure 2 shows a cross section of a DRAM product. The upper layer is the subject Ti film. To achieve quality control, the case company measured the Ti film resistance at 22 positions on each wafer. The measured positions are shown in Fig. 3. Figure 4 illustrates the daily average of the Ti film resistance of DRAM products in the case company during Jun. 1, 2019 and Aug. 28, 2019, where the total average resistance is 210.33 Ω.

The Ti film resistance of DRAM products has different measurement data because of different settings of engineering parameters. With the increase in the complexity of the manufacturing process, multiple engineering parameters need to be considered simultaneously when improving the quality of DRAM products. Using the experience of process engineers to perform experiments in the improvement stage would consume time and delay the product shipment schedule. Given the limited recourse of the case company, the optimal setting of engineering parameters should be determined within a short time. However, the case company cannot conduct numerous experiments. Therefore, this study integrates the response surface method (RSM), neural network (NN), and genetic algorithm (GA) to improve the Ti film resistance of DRAM products to enhance the electrical quality of the products.

The paper is organized as follows. Section 2 refers to related literature presenting fractional factorial design, response surface method, artificial neural network and genetic algorithm. Section 3 outlines a proposed approach for improving DRAM products. Section 4 presents a case study, the proposed approach was used to improve the resistance of DRAM products. Section 5 summarizes our conclusions.

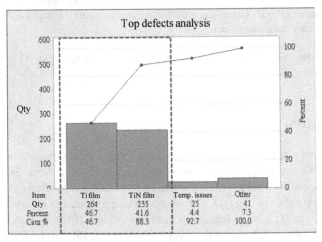

Fig. 1. The top defects in a DRAM product

Fig. 2. The cross section of a DRAM product

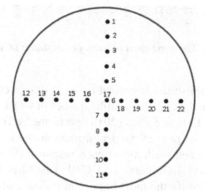

Fig. 3. The positions of the measured resistance for the quality control

2 Related Work

The design of experiment (DOE) methodology was developed to find the optimal engineering parameters in an experiment by Fisher in the early 19th century [1]. Full factorial design examines all of the engineering parameters in the experiment. As the number of engineering parameters increases, the number of examinations and cost in a full factorial design also increase. For example, for an experiment with seven 2-level parameters, $2^7 = 128$ times of examinations should be performed to find the optimal engineering parameters. The cost is also exponential growth. To solve this problem, Box and Hunter proposed the fractional factorial design in 1961 [2]. Fractional factorial design is part of the full factorial design experiment. The engineering parameters that are similar to those of the full factorial design can be found but with the fewer number of examinations. The main idea of the fractional factorial design is to select the important engineering parameters with the major impact on the results of the experiment. If an experiment with seven 2-level parameters has 5 important engineering parameters, the number of examinations is reduced to $2^{7-2} = 32$ using the fractional factorial design. Therefore, the fractional factorial design has great help in selecting important engineering parameters and saving cost, and it has been widely used in various product and process improvement.

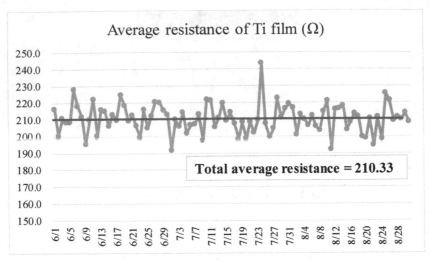

Fig. 4. The trend chart of average resistance of Ti film

Arévalo et al. (2019) established a fractional factorial design concluded in a total of 28 experiments to determine the critical variables values in which the matrix tablets reach the required quality [3]. Dias and Dias (2018) performed a fractional factorial design (24 − 1) to evaluate the contrasts of the dealumination variables (temperature, humidity, dealumination degree and washing) in each response (Si/Al ratio, number of acid sites, catalytic conversion) [4]. Harborne et al. (2018) used fractional factorial design for protein engineering to identify the most important residues involved in the interaction between AcrB and nickel resin [5].

Box and Wilson [6] proposed an experimental design method called response surface method (RSM) that provides a series of analysis steps to optimize the response of products, processes, and systems. RSM integrates a statistical regression model to predict the response value under different engineering parameters [7]. The principle is to construct the relationship between engineering parameters and response variables, and determines the optimal engineering parameters of the system. In practical applications, the RSM has been widely used in many enterprise improvement activities. Sharifi et al. (2018) applied a response surface methodology to determine the optimum synthesis parameters which are related to the paper sheets revealed that adding PANi decreases the amounts of breaking length, and tear and burst factors [8]. Tuzen et al. (2018) They adapted response surface methodology to combine both the high surface area and the active sites to enhance adsorption of the dye [9]. Most of practical applications used the second-order RSM model to construct the non-linear relationship of the input control factors and response variable. To further improvement, we try to use an artificial neural network to model the non-linear relationship of the input control factors and response variable in the paper.

The implementation of RSM generally requires at least two continuous engineering parameters to construct a response surface.

If $E[y] = E[f(x_1, x_2, \ldots x_n) + \varepsilon]$, where ε is the error observed in response value y, is used to present the expected response value, then the formed surfaces on $E[y]$ under different combinations of $x_1, x_2, \ldots x_n$ are called response surface, and the point with the best response value usually has the largest curvature.

The response surface can be used to estimate the response value, determine the best setting of engineering parameters, and find the optimal solution value. For RSM, an appropriate mathematical relationship should be established between the engineering parameters and response variable, and this can be achieved by using low-order polynomials of engineering parameters in certain region, such as a first-order model. However, when the relationship in the system has curvature, it must be expressed by a higher-order polynomial, such as a second-order model [10].

If the response value can be obtained as a linear function, the function is a first-order model, as shown in the following formula.

$$y = \beta_0 + \beta_1 x_1 + \beta_2 x_2 + \ldots + \beta_k x_k + \varepsilon, \tag{1}$$

where β_0 represents the intercept of the response surface and $\beta_1, \beta_2, \ldots \beta_k$ is the coefficient of each control variable.

If the system requires a model with curvature to estimate the response value, then a second-order model must be used. In addition to the items of the first-order mode, the second-order mode has interaction term $x_i x_j$ and quadratic term x_i^2, as shown in the following formula.

$$y = \beta_0 + \sum_{i=1}^{k} \beta_i x_i + \sum_{i=1}^{k} \beta_{ii} x_i^2 + \sum \sum_{i<j}^{k} \beta_{ij} x_i x_j + \varepsilon \tag{2}$$

In RSM experimental design, a screen experiment (fractional factorial design) is initially used to select the important engineering parameters that affect the response value, and these important engineering parameters are utilized to construct the response surface. Then, a first-order response surface is established to determine whether the optimal solution falls within the current region of engineering parameters. To confirm that the experimental region already contains the optimal solution value, we can use the center-point experiment design and analysis of variance (ANOVA) to determine is the significance of curvature in this experimental region. If the curvature is significant, then the optimal solution value may be within this region, and we can continue to construct the second-order response surface to determine the optimal setting of engineering parameters. However, if the curvature is not significant, then the steepest path that can increase or decrease the response value should be identified from the current experimental region, and the path to the optimal solution value should be advanced. The most common search method is the method of steepest descent or ascent, which is used to find the new experimental region of engineering parameters that may contain the optimal solution; then, the second-order response surface is constructed to determine the optimal setting of engineering parameters.

3 The Proposed Approach

This study initially uses the fractional factorial experimental design to assist the case company in selecting important engineering parameters and then adopts the center-point experimental design to confirm the presence of curvature within the region of engineering parameters. When curvature exists in the region of engineering parameters, the RSM is used for modeling; when no curvature exists, the steepest descent method is required to determine the new experimental region that may contain the optimal solution. Afterward, RSM is implemented for the region of engineering parameters where the optimal solution may exist, and some applicable experimental data are collected by RSM experiment. Artificial neural network (ANN) is modeled with RSM experimental data to establish the relationship between each engineering parameter and Ti film resistance of DRAM products. Finally, genetic algorithm (GA) is used to find the global optimal setting of engineering parameters. After finding the optimal setting of engineering parameters, confirmation experiments are required to verify the effectiveness of the proposed approach. The flow of proposed approach is shown in Fig. 6.

ANN training involves adjusting the link value continuously [12, 13]. The link value is a kind of weight; the larger the value is, the more likely the connected neuron is to be excited (the more important it is to the output variable). When multiple neurons are combined, they can create an ANN. Figure 5 shows an ANN composed of three layers of neural-like units. The first layer is an input layer composed of input units (engineering parameters). These input units are initially connected to the nodes of the hidden layer and then connected to the output units of the output layer through adjustable weights. Afterward, each output unit corresponds to a specific engineering feature.

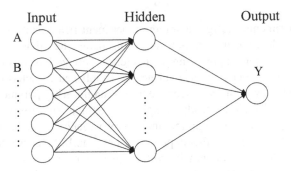

Fig. 5. Structure of ANN

ANN must be trained repeatedly so that each input engineering parameter can correctly correspond to the required output variable. Before ANN training, a training dataset must be prepared to offer a reference template for the network in the learning process. The purpose of ANN training is to make the output value of ANN close to the target value so that the error between the two becomes increasingly small [14]. When the error between the two hardly changes, the ANN has reached convergence and completed training. When the neural network is trained through the training samples, although the output of the neural network is close to the required value, we do not know what output results will be obtained for inputs that are not generated by the training samples. Therefore, another set of untrained samples must be used for the neural network to confirm the error between the predicted value and the known feature value. This sample is called the testing dataset.

The learning rate is a crucial parameter in an ANN training. The learning rate affects the convergence speed of ANN. If the learning rate is large, then the convergence of ANN will become fast. Conversely, a small learning rate makes the convergence of ANN slow. Fausett [15] and Hagan et al. [16] demonstrated the process of selecting appropriate ANN parameters.

Recent studies have used neural networks to elucidate the ability to learn the complex relationships between the engineering parameters and response variable, usually for process and quality control. Wang et al. (2019) used a two-layer neural network and genetic algorithm to established a fast approach to cavitation optimization and a parametric database for both hub and shroud blade angles for double suction centrifugal pump optimization design [17]. Mukherjee and Rajanikanth (2019) applied an artificial neural network to predict the variation of nitric oxide/nitrogen dioxide when the exhaust is subjected to discharge plasma [18]. Hu et al. (2019) developed an artificial neural network to predict polarization curves under different complex sea environments [19].

GA simulates the natural selection rule of the biological world, the natural elimination rule of the fittest, leaving only ethnic groups that best meet the living conditions. GA differs from conventional search techniques that conduct a point-to-point search in the solution space. GA is a robust adaptive-optimization technique that allows an efficient probabilistic search in high-dimensional space [20]. Many experts and scholars have invested in further exploration and research on the evolution of GA and confirmed the feasibility of this algorithm. Hosseinabadi et al. (2019) investigated genetic algorithms for solving Open-shop scheduling problem (OSSP), which could generate better solutions compared to other developed algorithms in terms of objective values [21]. Alipour-Sarabi et al. (2019) used genetic algorithm to minimize total harmonic distortion of the output signals, and consequently the estimated position error in concentrated coil wound field resolvers [22].

GA treats each engineering parameters in the engineering problem as a biological gene, transforms each variable in a binary encoding, and combines them into chromosomes. Each chromosome represents an independent population. GA generates the first generation in a random manner as the initial condition of the algorithm search, and each generation has multiple independent populations. The objective function of the engineering problem is then converted into a fitness function. The higher the fitness function value of population is, the stronger its adaptive capacity is and the greater the probability of producing offspring is. The evolution process of GA includes three major steps, namely, reproduction, crossover, and mutation of chromosomes. The evolution process occurs in the solution space of the engineering problem until the most adaptive solution (the optimal solution) that meets all the constraints is obtained. The chromosome with the highest fitness function value is determined after multiple generations of reproduction (multiple iterations). This chromosome is the global optimal solution we wish to find [23].

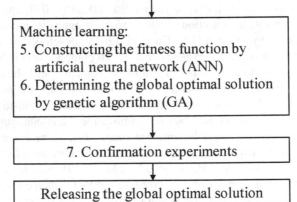

Fig. 6. Proposed approach

4 Case Study

The manufacturing process that affects the Ti film resistance in DRAM products includes five main processes, namely, via etch, Ti deposition, structure film deposition, CMP, and etching, as shown in Fig. 7. Six engineering parameters were selected based on the practical experience of process engineers; these six engineering parameters were AC bias power, backside Ar flow, backside pressure, heater temperature, E-chuck voltage, and composition time. The levels of the engineering parameters are shown in Table 1, where Level (+1) represents a high level and Level (−1) represents a low level. Through a fractional factorial design, 2^{6-2} DOE was selected as a screen experiment for selecting important engineering parameters. The engineering parameters (A–F) are arranged in the 2^{6-2} DOE.

The experimental results of 2^{6-2} are shown in Table 2. The factor response table, factor response chart, and ANOVA results of the resistance analysis results are presented in Table 3, Fig. 8, and Table 4, respectively. Table 3 shows that the contribution of each engineering parameter from high to low is E(21.62) > A(8.76) > D(6.32) > F(2.40)

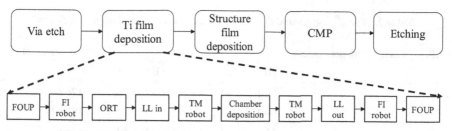

Fig. 7. The manufacturing process of the Ti film of DRAM products

Table 1. Engineering parameters and their levels for the fractional factorial design

Factor	Ac bias power (W)	Backside Ar flow (sccm)	Backside pressure (mTorr)	Heater temperature (°C)	E-chuck voltage (V)	Deposition time (sec)
	A	B	C	D	E	F
Level (s−1)	350	2	4000	250	285	3
Level (+1)	450	6	6000	260	385	5

> C(0.64) > B (0.35). Table 4 shows that the p-value of engineering parameters B, C, and F on Ti film resistance was not significant and can be ignored. In Fig. 8, a better combination of the engineering parameters could be set at A = 350 W, D = 250 °C and E = 300 V. In the next step, three important engineering parameters, namely, A (AC bias power), D (heat temperature), and E (E-chuck voltage), were used to design the center-point experiment for confirming whether the experimental region of engineering parameters contains curvature, that is, whether the experimental region contains the global optimal solution.

Due to check the better combination of the engineering parameters in previous factorial experimental design (A = 350 W, D = 250 °C and E = 285 V). We re-arranged a center-point experiment that contained full factorial experimental design and performed experiments with center points. Through full factorial design, 2^3 DOE is selected as the experimental arrangement for this step. Then, engineering parameters A, D, and E are arranged in the 2^3 DOE, and five center points are planned.

Through the first-order mode (e.g., Formula (1)), response value also changes when the level of engineering parameters changes. Each effect of engineering parameters depends on its main effect coefficient, that is, $\beta_1, \beta_2, \ldots \beta_k$. To reduce the response value effectively, we must find the direction that decreases response value the fastest and proceed toward this path. This path is called the path of steepest descent. The procedure of the sequential movement refers to the experiment in existing experiments of first-order model, which is performed along the steepest descent path until the response value no longer increases. The results of successive experiments can confirm that the optimal point has been reached. If it has already been reached, the more accurate second-order model is needed to obtain the optimal solution.

Table 2. The 2^{6-1} array and data for the fractional factorial design experiment

EXP	Engineering parameters						Resistance (Ω)
	A	B	C	D	E	F	
1	−1	−1	−1	−1	−1	−1	176.56
2	1	−1	−1	−1	−1	1	190.71
3	−1	1	−1	−1	−1	1	176.61
4	1	1	−1	−1	−1	−1	189.92
5	−1	−1	1	−1	−1	1	182.63
6	1	−1	1	−1	−1	−1	187.83
7	−1	1	1	−1	−1	−1	187.22
8	1	1	1	−1	−1	1	185.99
9	−1	−1	−1	1	−1	1	182.69
10	1	−1	−1	1	−1	−1	200.07
11	−1	1	−1	1	−1	−1	183.10
12	1	1	−1	1	−1	1	198.77
13	−1	−1	1	1	−1	−1	189.00
14	1	−1	1	1	−1	1	190.56
15	−1	1	1	1	−1	1	191.36
16	1	1	1	1	−1	−1	197.73
17	−1	−1	−1	−1	1	1	205.97
18	1	−1	−1	−1	1	−1	212.90
19	−1	1	−1	−1	1	−1	200.35
20	1	1	−1	−1	1	1	211.85
21	−1	−1	1	−1	1	−1	199.79
22	1	−1	1	−1	1	1	206.40
23	−1	1	1	−1	1	1	201.85
24	1	1	1	−1	1	−1	216.53
25	−1	−1	−1	1	1	−1	213.42
26	1	−1	−1	1	1	1	213.90
27	−1	1	−1	1	1	1	205.04
28	1	1	−1	1	1	−1	216.76
29	−1	−1	1	1	1	1	207.37
30	1	−1	1	1	1	−1	221.09
31	−1	1	1	1	1	−1	210.63
32	1	1	1	1	1	1	212.80

Table 3. Factor response table of average resistance of Ti film for the fractional factorial design experiment

Level	A	B	C	D	E	F
Level (−1)	194.60	198.81	198.66	195.82	188.17	200.18
Level (+1)	203.36	199.16	199.30	202.14	209.79	197.78
Effect	8.76	0.35	0.64	6.32	21.62	2.40
Rank	2	6	5	3	1	4

Using the regressed equation in ANOVA Table, the first-order model as follows:

$$\text{Resistance} = 200.068 + 4.08\,A + 3.41\,D + 11.09\,E. \tag{3}$$

Then, the steepest descent method is used to make the response estimate move forward along the steepest descent path from the current center point (A = 0, D = 0, E = 0) to obtain the optimal response value. The moving direction is determined by the maximum value of the main effect coefficient because it makes the response value move toward the optimal value at the highest speed. In the first-order model of this study, the coefficient value of parameter E is 11.09, which is larger than the coefficients 4.08 of A and 3.41 of D, indicating that parameter E is the main variable of the steepest descent path. The experiment was executed, and the Ti film resistance obtained on this path was measured until it increased progressively.

Figure 9 presents surface plot of the thickness variation for the second-order model of RSM. The p values of RSM are all smaller than 0.05, which confirms the significance in the second-order model experiment.

The first-order items (A, D, and E) and second-order items (A^2, D^2, and E^2) are significant engineering parameters. Simultaneously, Factor A is related to A^2, factor B is related to B^2, and factor C is related to C^2. Therefore, A^2, D^2, and E^2 were adopted as input variables for the neural network. The difference between the Ti film resistance and the specified target value (185 Ω) was taken as the output variable (the smaller is better).

$$\text{Resistance} = 8161 - 6.33\,A - 52.4\,D - 6.75\,E + 0.01029\,A * A + 0.1079D * D + 0.01779E * E. \tag{4}$$

First, 80% of the data were randomly selected from the data set as the training dataset for ANN. The other 20% of the data were used as the training dataset for the network. The learning and momentum rates were set to 0.1 and 0.85, respectively. To determine the number of nodes in the hidden layer, this study performed 1,000 modeling iterations with neural structures, such as different numbers of nodes. Then, the ANN architecture of 3-6-1 is used for modeling as shown in Fig. 10.

To confirm the optimal setting of the engineering parameters, we used a total of five lots in this study, and five wafers were obtained from each lot for confirmation experiments. The experimental measurement data are shown in Table 5. According to the confirmation experiment, average resistance = 185.28 Ω is very close to the

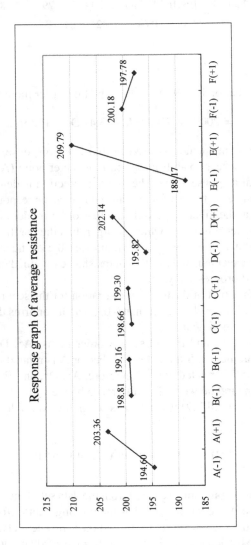

Fig. 8. Response graph of average resistance of Ti film for the fractional factorial design experiment

Table 4. The ANOVA of the resistance of Ti film

Source	DF	SS	MS	F-Value	P-Value
A	1	614.43	614.43	46.61	0
B	1	0.99	0.99	0.07	0.787
C	1	3.23	3.23	0.24	0.625
D	1	319.92	319.92	24.27	0
E	1	3738.96	3738.96	283.64	0
F	1	46.08	46.08	3.5	0.073
Error	25	329.55	13.18		
Total	31	5053.15			
				R-Sq	R-Sq(adj)
				93.48%	91.91%

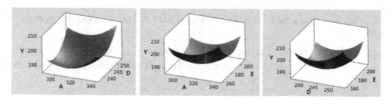

Fig. 9. The surface plot of resistance for the second-order model experiment

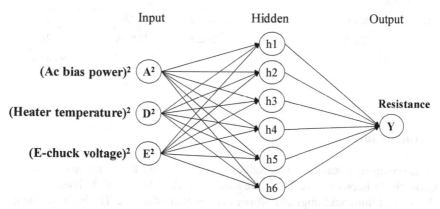

Fig. 10. The neural network structure of the Ti film production process

improvement target 185 Ω. Hence, we confirmed that the global optimal setting of engineering parameters is a feasible combination.

After the DRAM products of the case company were further improved by the artificial neural network and genetic algorithm, we found that the resistance improved significantly. The average resistance of the Ti film improved by 98.88% from 210.33 Ω to 185.28 Ω, as shown in Table 6.

Table 5. Confirmation experiments for the genetic algorithm

EXP	Resistance					Average resistance (Ω)
	Wafer #1	Wafer #2	Wafer #3	Wafer #4	Wafer #5	
Lot #1	184.97	184.80	184.81	186.14	185.52	185.25
Lot #2	185.23	185.09	185.67	184.80	185.94	185.35
Lot #3	185.23	185.92	185.63	185.76	185.09	185.53
Lot #4	185.12	185.75	184.25	185.25	184.99	185.07
Lot #5	185.05	185.20	185.07	184.75	186.05	185.22
						185.28

Table 6. Comparison between the initial data and the proposed approach

Comparison	Ac bias power (W)	Heater temperature (°C)	E-chuck voltage (V)	Average resistance (Ω)	Resistance difference(Ω)
	A	D	E		
Before improvement	450	260	400	210.33	25.33
RSM	307.6	242.8	189.7	187.66	2.66
NN & GA	292.2	240.5	212.8	185.28	0.28
Improvement					98.88%

5 Conclusions

The case company always accrues high experimental costs due to trial and error and has not effectively improved the Ti film resistance of DRAM products. Therefore, in this study, several important engineering parameters that affect the Ti film were identified through fractional factorial experiments. Three important engineering parameters (i.e., AC bias power, heat temperature, and E-chuck voltage) were determined in ANOVA table. A center-point experiment was conducted, and the steepest descent method was used to find the possible experimental region of engineering parameters containing the optimal solution that falls around AC bias power = 313.2 W, hat temperature = 246.9 °C, and E-chuck voltage = 200 V. For the second-order model experiment, the RSM experiment design was implemented according to the above experimental region that may include the optimal value. The RSM experiment obtained the optimal setting of engineering parameters of the second-order model, that is, AC bias power $= 307.6$ W, heat temperature $= 242.8$ °C, and E-chuck voltage $= 189.7$ V. After verifying the optimal factor setting of this second-order model, the average resistance was reduced from 210.33 Ω to 187.66 Ω, with an improvement of 89.5%. In addition, ANOVA of the RSM experiment showed that the second order items of the second-order model (AC bias power)^2, (heat temperature)^2, and (E-chuck voltage)^2 had significant effect on the response values. ANN used the three second order items as the input variables to construct a 3-6-1 neural network. Then, the global optimal setting of engineering parameters found by the genetic algorithm was AC bias power $= 292.2$ W, heat temperature $= 240.5$ °C, and E-chuck voltage $= 212.8$ V. The average resistance improved from 210.33 Ω to 185.28 Ω, with an improvement of 98.88%. To release to the global optimal setting of engineering parameters, the case company will conduct mass production stage to verify the feasibility of the global optimal setting in the future.

Acknowledgement. This work was financially supported by the Center for Open Intelligent Connectivity from The Featured Areas Research Center Program within the framework of the Higher Education Sprout Project by the Ministry of Education (MOE) in Taiwan , R.O.C., and Ministry of Science and Technology Grant 107R491 and 109-2221-E-009-089-MY2.

References

1. Montgomery, D.C.: Design and Analysis of Experiments, 6th edn. John Wiley & Sons, New York (2005)
2. Box, G.E., Hunter, J.S.: The 2^{k-p} fractional factorial designs. Technometrics 3(3), 311–351 (1961)
3. Arévalo, R., Maderuelo, C., Lanao, J.M.: Identification of the critical variables for the development of controlled release matrix tablets: factorial design approach. Farma J. 4(1), 250 (2019)
4. Dias, S.C., Dias, J.A.: Effects of the dealumination methodology on the FER zeolite acidity: a study with fractional factorial design. Mol. Catal. **458**, 139–144 (2018)
5. Harborne, S.P., Wotherspoon, D., Michie, J., McComb, A., Kotila, T., Gilmour, S., Goldman, A.: Revolutionising the design and analysis of protein engineering experiments using fractional factorial design. bioRxiv, 298273 (2018)
6. Box, G.E., Wilson, K.B.: On the experimental attainment of optimum conditions. J. Roy. Stat. Soc.: Ser. B (Methodol.) **13**(1), 1–38 (1951)
7. Myers, R.H., Montgomery, D.C., Anderson-Cook, C.M.: Response Surface Methodology. John Wiley & Sons Inc., New Jersey (2009)
8. Sharifi, H., Zabihzadeh, S.M., Ghorbani, M.: The application of response surface methodology on the synthesis of conductive polyaniline/cellulosic fiber nanocomposites. Carbohyd. Polym. **194**, 384–394 (2018)
9. Tuzen, M., Sarı, A., Saleh, T.A.: Response surface optimization, kinetic and thermodynamic studies for effective removal of rhodamine B by magnetic AC/CeO2 nanocomposite. J. Environ. Manag. **206**, 170–177 (2018)
10. Khuri, A.I.: Response Surface Methodology and Related Topics. World Scientific, London (2006)

11. Su, C.T.: Quality Engineering: Off-Line Methods and Applications. CRC Press/Taylor & Francis Group, Boca Raton (2013)
12. Rosenblatt, F.: Perceptions and the Theory of Brain Mechanisms. Spartan books (1962)
13. Stern, H.S.: Neural networks in applied statistics. Technometrics **38**(3), 205–220 (1996)
14. McClelland, J.L., Rumelhart, D.E.: Explorations in Parallel Distributed Processing: A Handbook of Models, Programs, and Exercises. MIT press, Cambridge (1989)
15. Fausett, L.: Fundamentals of Neural Networks: An Architecture, Algorithms, and Applications. Prentice Hall, Upper Saddle River (1994)
16. Hagan, M.T., Demuth, H.B., Beale, M.: Neural Network Design. PWS, Boston (1995)
17. Wang, W., Osman, M.K., Pei, J., Gan, X., Yin, T.: Artificial neural networks approach for a multi-objective cavitation optimization design in a double-suction centrifugal pump. Processes **7**(5), 246 (2019)
18. Mukherjee, D.S., Rajanikanth, B.S.: Prediction of variation of oxides of nitrogen in plasma-based diesel exhaust treatment using artificial neural network. Int. J. Environ. Sci. Technol. **16**(10), 6315–6328 (2019). https://doi.org/10.1007/s13762-019-02242-5
19. Hu, Q., Liu, Y., Zhang, T., Geng, S., Wang, F.: Modeling the corrosion behavior of Ni-Cr-Mo-V high strength steel in the simulated deep sea environments using design of experiment and artificial neural network. J. Mater. Sci. Technol. **35**(1), 168–175 (2019)
20. Goldberg, D.E.: Genetic Algorithm in Search, Optimization and Machine Learning. Addison-Wesley, New York (1989)
21. Hosseinabadi, A.A.R., Vahidi, J., Saemi, B., Sangaiah, A.K., Elhoseny, M.: Extended genetic algorithm for solving open-shop scheduling problem. Soft. Comput. **23**(13), 5099–5116 (2019)
22. Alipour-Sarabi, R., Nasiri-Gheidari, Z., Tootoonchian, F., Oraee, H.: Improved winding proposal for wound rotor resolver using genetic algorithm and winding function approach. IEEE Trans. Ind. Electron. **66**(2), 1325–1334 (2019)
23. Renders, J.M., Flasse, S.P.: Hybrid methods using genetic algorithms for global optimization. IEEE Trans. Syst. Man Cybern. Part B (Cybern.) **26**(2), 243–258 (1996)

Author Index

Printed in the United States
By Bookmasters